ENVIRONMENTAL PROTECTION

Selected Statutes and Recent Cases 1991

FREDERICK R. ANDERSON
Ann Loeb Bronfman Professor of Law
American University

DANIEL R. MANDELKER
Stamper Professor of Law
Washington University

A. DAN TARLOCK
Professor of Law
IIT Chicago-Kent College of Law

Little, Brown and Company
Boston   Toronto   London

Copyright © 1991 by Frederick R. Anderson, Daniel R. Mandelker, and A. Dan Tarlock

All rights reserved. No part of this book may be reproduced in any form or by any electronic or mechanical means including information storage and retrieval systems without permission in writing from the publisher, except by a reviewer who may quote brief passages in a review.

Library of Congress Catalog Card No. 91-62496

ISBN 0-316-03943-8

ICP

Published simultaneously in Canada
by Little, Brown & Company (Canada) Limited

PRINTED IN THE UNITED STATES OF AMERICA

CONTENTS

Preface ix
Table of Cases xi

PART I. STATUTES 1

Clean Air Act	3
Clean Water Act	91
Endangered Species Act (ESA)	303
Comprehensive Environmental Response, Compensation, and Liability Act of 1980 (CERCLA)	353
Resource Conservation and Recovery Act (RCRA)	479
National Environmental Policy Act of 1969	605

PART II. SUPPLEMENTARY CASES AND NOTES 611

II An Introduction to the Administrative Law of Environment Protection 613

A. Access to the Courts: Standing and Related Preclusion Doctrines 613
  Lujan v. National Wildlife Federation 613

III Protecting the Air Resource 629

C. The Clean Air Act Today 629
  Note on the Clean Air Act Amendments of 1990 629
E. Emissions Standards in the Clean Air Act 630
  1. Motor Vehicle Emissions Standards 630

v

	a. From the Goals of 1970 to Contemporary Realities	630
	Note on the 1990 Amendments to the Mobile Source Emissions Standards	630
	2. Performance Standards for New Stationary Sources	631
F.	State Implementation Plans	631
	Note on the 1990 Amendments to State Implementation Plan and Permit Requirements	631
G.	Non-Attainment: The Special Problems of Dirty Air Areas	632
	2. Non-Attainment Area Plans and Sanctions	632
	Note on Revised Requirements for Non-Attainment Areas in the Clean Air Act Amendments of 1990	632
I.	Special Issues in the Clean Air Act	634
	2. The Acid Rain Controversy	634
	Note on the New Acid Rain Program in the Clean Air Act Amendments of 1990	634
	3. Enforcement	635
	Note on Changes in Enforcement Provisions in the 1990 Amendments to the Clean Air Act	635

IV Protecting the Water Resource — 637

B.	Background of Water Pollution Regulation	637
	2. The Twentieth Century Evolution of Federal Water Pollution Control Policy	637
	c. The Clean Water Act: An Overview	637
C.	Federal Jurisdiction	637
	2. Point and Non-Point Sources	637
D.	Water Quality Standards: Theory and Current Function	638
	Oklahoma v. EPA	638

V Controlling Toxic and Hazardous Substances — 661

D.	Hazardous Substances in the Air and Water	661
	1. Emissions Standards for Hazardous Air Pollutants	661
	Note on the New Program for Air Toxics in the Clean Air Act of 1990	661

Table of Contents

E.	Preventing the Entry of Toxic Substances into the Stream of Commerce	662
	2. Toxic Chemicals and Other Substances	662
	b. Federal Toxic Substances Control Act	662
	Note on the Program for Chlorofluorocarbons in the 1990 Amendments to the Clean Air Act	662
F.	Preventing Harm from Hazardous Wastes	663
	2. Dangerous Existing Sites: Of Deep Pockets, Orphans, and Superfunds	663
	b. Potentially Responsible Parties: Liability, Site Nexus, and Cost Recovery	663
	Louisiana-Pacific Corp. v. Asarco, Inc.	663

VI   The Environment and the Common Law   671

A.	Common Law Damages for Environmental Harm	671
	2. Causation: Multiple Defendants and Alternative, Concert of Action, Enterprise, and Market Share Liability	671
	In re Paoli Railroad Yard PCB Litigation	671

PREFACE

This hybrid case and statutory supplement is intended to provide its student users with a selection of the statutes from the core of modern environmental regulation and to outline for both students and teachers materials on the most important developments that have occurred since the second edition was published. Clearly, the most important statutory development is the passage of the Clean Air Act amendments, which took Congress ten years to enact. We have prepared a special supplementary text section for Chapter III that explains the changes the amendments have made. The amendments are not difficult to teach because the basic structure of the Act is unchanged. New programs are added, such as the acid rain program, that strengthen regulatory requirements. These programs, to be phased in over the next several years, are best taught through textual explanation until EPA regulations and interpretive court decisions are available.

We have also included four 1990 cases that reflect important developments in standing, the Clean Water Act, CERCLA, and toxic torts. A full case and statutory supplement will be published in 1992 and will update the supplementation on the 1990 Clean Air Act amendments.

This supplement is prepared solely for users of this book. To this end, we have not reprinted the complete statutes, omitting sections that have minimal regulatory importance. Significant omissions are generally noted. To conserve space, we have omitted the legislative history of each section. Students and others who are doing research on a particular statute should always consult the latest United States Code version. We hope that the users of the book will find this supplement useful.

Frederick R. Anderson
Daniel R. Mandelker
A. Dan Tarlock

Evanston, Illinois and St. Louis, Missouri
May 1991

TABLE OF CASES

Principal cases are in italics.
All references are to casebook pages.

In re _____ . *See* name of party
Louisiana-Pacific Corp. v. Asarco, Inc., 634
Lujan v. National Wildlife Federation, 107
Natural Resources Defense Council v. Thomas, 210
Oklahoma v. EPA, 407
Paoli Railroad Yard PCB Litig., In re, 738
Union Elec. Co. v. EPA, 235

ENVIRONMENTAL PROTECTION

Selected Statutes and Recent Cases
1991

Part I

STATUTES

Clean Air Act*
42 U.S.C. (with 1990 amendments)
§§101-506

TITLE I — AIR POLLUTION PREVENTION AND CONTROL
Part A — Air Quality and Emission Limitations

- §101. Findings and purposes
- §105. Grants for support of air pollution planning and control programs
- §107. Air quality control regions
- §108. Air quality control criteria and control techniques
- §109. National ambient air quality standards
- §110. Implementation plans
- §111. Standards of performance for new stationary sources
- §112. National emission standards for hazardous air pollutants
- §113. Federal enforcement
- §115. International air pollution
- §116. Retention of state authority
- §118. Control of pollution from federal facilities
- §120. Noncompliance penalty
- §121. Consultation
- §123. Stack heights
- §126. Interstate pollution abatement

Part C — Prevention of Significant Deterioration of Air Quality

Subpart 1

- §160. Purposes
- §161. Plan requirements
- §162. Initial classifications
- §163. Increments and ceilings
- §164. Area redesignation
- §165. Preconstruction requirements
- §166. Other pollutants
- §169. Definitions

Subpart 2

- §169A. Visibility protection for federal class I areas
- §169B. Visibility

---

*This supplement contains the provisions of the Clean Air Act that are necessary to teach the materials on this Act in the casebook. The complex provisions in Title V, dealing with acid rain, and in §182, dealing with requirements for non-attainment plans, are omitted. These provisions are summarized in the text that supplements Chapter III in this supplement. Procedural details in some statutory provisions are also omitted.

Citations in the supplement refer to the section numbers of the Congressional bill. The Clean Air Act is currently codified at 42 U.S.C. §§7401 et seq.

§101   Clean Air Act

PART D — PLAN REQUIREMENTS FOR NONATTAINMENT AREAS

Subpart 1 — Nonattainment Areas in General

§171.   Definitions
§172.   Nonattainment plan provisions in general
§173.   Permit requirements
§174.   Planning procedures
§175.   Environmental Protection Agency grants
§175A. Maintenance plans
§176.   Limitations on certain federal assistance
§176A. Interstate transport commissions
§177.   New motor vehicle emission standards in nonattainment areas
§178.   Guidance Documents
§179.   Sanctions and consequences of failure to attain

Subpart 2 — Additional Provisions for Ozone Nonattainment Areas

§181.   Classification and attainment dates

TITLE II — EMISSION STANDARDS FOR MOVING SOURCES

PART A — MOTOR VEHICLE EMISSION AND FUEL STANDARDS

§202.   Establishment of standards
§211.   Regulations of fuels

TITLE III — GENERAL

§301.   Administration
§302.   Definitions
§304.   Citizen suits
§307.   General provision relating to administrative proceedings and judicial review
§316.   Sewage treatment grants

TITLE V — PERMITS

§501.   Definitions
§502.   Permit programs
§503.   Permit applications
§504.   Permit requirements and conditions
§505.   Notification to administrator and contiguous states
§506.   Other authorities

Title I — Air Pollution Prevention and Control

PART A — AIR QUALITY AND EMISSION LIMITATIONS

Findings and Purposes

Sec. 101. (a) The Congress finds —
    (1) that the predominant part of the Nation's population is located in its rapidly expanding metropolitan and other urban areas, which generally cross

Clean Air Act §107

the boundary lines of local jurisdictions and often extend into two or more States;

(2) that the growth in the amount and complexity of air pollution brought about by urbanization, industrial development, and the increasing use of motor vehicles, has resulted in mounting dangers to the public health and welfare, including injury to agricultural crops and livestock, damage to and the deterioration of property, and hazards to air and ground transportation;

(3) that air pollution prevention (that is, the reduction or elimination, through any measures, of the amount of pollutants produced or created at the source) and air pollution control at its source is the primary responsibility of States and local governments; and

(4) that Federal financial assistance and leadership is essential for the development of cooperative Federal, State, regional, and local programs to prevent and control air pollution.

(b) The purposes of this title are —

(1) to protect and enhance the quality of the Nation's air resources so as to promote the public health and welfare and the productive capacity of its population;

(2) to initiate and accelerate a national research and development program to achieve the prevention and control of air pollution;

(3) to provide technical and financial assistance to State and local governments in connection with the development and execution of their air pollution prevention and control programs; and

(4) to encourage and assist the development and operation of regional air pollution prevention and control programs.

(c) Pollution Prevention. — A primary goal of this Act is to encourage or otherwise promote reasonable Federal, State, and local governmental actions, consistent with the provisions of this Act, for pollution prevention. . . .

Grants for Support of Air Pollution Planning and Control Programs

Sec. 105. (a)(1)(A) The Administrator may make grants to air pollution control agencies, within the meaning of paragraph (1), (2), (3), (4), or (5) of section 302, in an amount up to three-fifths of the cost of implementing programs for the prevention and control of air pollution or implementation of national primary and secondary ambient air quality standards. For the purpose of this section, 'implementing' means any activity related to the planning, developing, establishing, carrying-out, improving, or maintaining of such programs. . . .

Air Quality Control Regions

Sec. 107. (a) Each State shall have the primary responsibility for assuring air quality within the entire geographic area comprising such State by submitting an implementation plan for such State which will specify the manner in which national primary and secondary ambient air quality standards will be achieved and maintained within each air quality control region in such State.

(b) For purposes of developing and carrying out implementation plans under section 110 —

(1) an air quality control region designated under this section before the date of enactment of the Clean Air Amendments of 1970, or a region designated after such date under subsection (c), shall be an air quality control region; and

(2) The portion of such State which is not part of any such designated region shall be an air quality control region, but such portion may be subdivided by the State into two or more air quality control regions with the approval of the Administrator.

(c) The Administrator shall, within 90 days after the date of enactment of the Clean Air Amendments of 1970, after consultation with appropriate State and local authorities, designate as an air quality control region any interstate area or major intrastate area which he deems necessary or appropriate for the attainment and maintenance of ambient air quality standards. The Administrator shall immediately notify the governors of the affected States of any designation made under this subsection.

(d)(1)(A) Submission By Governors Of Initial Designations Following Promulgation Of New Or Revised Standards. — By such date as the Administrator may reasonably require, but not later than 1 year after promulgation of a new or revised national ambient air quality standard for any pollutant under section 109, the Governor of each State shall (and at any other time the Governor of a State deems appropriate the Governor may) submit to the Administrator a list of all areas (or portions thereof) in the State, designating as —

(i) nonattainment, any area that does not meet (or that contributes to ambient air quality in a nearby area that does not meet) the national primary or secondary ambient air quality standard for the pollutant,

(ii) attainment, any area (other than an area identified in clause (i)) that meets the national primary or secondary ambient air quality standard for the pollutant, or

(iii) unclassifiable, any area that cannot be classified on the basis of available information as meeting or not meeting the national primary or secondary ambient air quality standard for the pollutant. . . .

(B) Promulgation By EPA Of Designations. — (i) Upon promulgation or revision of a national ambient air quality standard, the Administrator shall promulgate the designations of all areas (or portions thereof) submitted under subparagraph (A) as expeditiously as practicable, but in no case later than 2 years from the date of promulgation of the new or revised national ambient air quality standard. Such period may be extended for up to one year in the event the Administrator has insufficient information to promulgate the designations. . . .

Air Quality Criteria and Control Techniques

Sec. 108. (a)(1) For the purpose of establishing national primary and secondary ambient air quality standards, the Administrator shall within 30 days after the date of enactment of the Clean Air Amendments of 1970 publish, and shall from time to time thereafter revise, a list which includes each air pollutant —

    (A) emissions of which, in his judgment, cause or contribute to air pollution which may reasonably be anticipated to endanger public health or welfare;

    (B) the presence of which in the ambient air results from numerous or diverse mobile or stationary sources; and

    (C) for which air quality criteria had not been issued before the date of enactment of the Clean Air Amendments of 1970, but for which he plans to issue air quality criteria under this section.

(2) The Administrator shall issue air quality criteria for an air pollutant within 12 months after he has included such pollutant in a list under paragraph (1). Air quality criteria for an air pollutant shall accurately reflect the latest scientific knowledge useful in indicating the kind and extent of all identifiable effects on public health or welfare which may be expected from the presence of such pollutant in the ambient air, in varying quantities. The criteria for an air pollutant, to the extent practicable, shall include information on —

    (A) those variable factors (including atmospheric conditions) which of themselves or in combination with other factors may alter the effects on public health or welfare of such air pollutant;

    (B) the types of air pollutants which, when present in the atmosphere, may interact with such pollutant to produce an adverse effect on public health or welfare; and

    (C) any known or anticipated adverse effects on welfare. . . .

Transportation Planning and Guidelines

(e) The Administrator shall, after consultation with the Secretary of Transportation, and after providing public notice and opportunity for comment, and with State and local officials, within nine months after enactment of the Clean Air Act Amendments of 1989 and periodically thereafter as necessary to maintain a continuous transportation-air quality planning process, update the June 1978 Transportation-Air Quality Planning Guidelines and publish guidance on the development and implementation of transportation and other measures necessary to demonstrate and maintain attainment of national ambient air quality standards. Such guidelines shall include information on —

    (1) methods to identify and evaluate alternative planning and control activities;

    (2) methods of reviewing plans on a regular basis as conditions change or new information is presented;

    (3) identification of funds and other resources necessary to implement the plan, including interagency agreements on providing such funds and resources;

    (4) methods to assure participation by the public in all phases of the planning process; and

(5) such other methods as the Administrator determines necessary to carry out a continuous planning process.

(f)(1) The Administrator shall publish and make available to appropriate Federal, State, and local environmental and transportation agencies not later than one year after enactment of the Clean Air Act Amendments of 1990, and from time to time thereafter —

   (A) information prepared, as appropriate, in consultation with the Secretary of Transportation, and after providing public notice and opportunity for comment, regarding the formulation and emission reduction potential of transportation control measures related to criteria pollutants and their precursors, including, but not limited to —

   (i) programs for improved public transit;

   (ii) restriction of certain roads or lanes to, or construction of such roads or lanes for use by, passenger buses or high occupancy vehicles;

   (iii) employer-based transportation management plans, including incentives;

   (iv) trip-reduction ordinances;

   (v) traffic flow improvement programs that achieve emission reductions;

   (vi) fringe and transportation corridor parking facilities serving multiple occupancy vehicle programs or transit service;

   (vii) programs to limit or restrict vehicle use in downtown areas or other areas of emission concentration particularly during periods of peak use;

   (viii) programs for the provision of all forms of high-occupancy, shared-ride services;

   (ix) programs to limit portions of road surfaces or certain sections of the metropolitan area to the use of non-motorized vehicles or pedestrian use, both as to time and place;

   (x) programs for secure bicycle storage facilities and other facilities, including bicycle lanes, for the convenience and protection of bicyclists, in both public and private areas;

   (xi) programs to control extended idling of vehicles;

   (xii) programs to reduce motor vehicle emissions, consistent with title II, which are caused by extreme cold start conditions;

   (xiii) employer-sponsored programs to permit flexible work schedules;

   (xiv) programs and ordinances to facilitate non-automobile travel, provision and utilization of mass transit, and to generally reduce the need for single-occupant vehicle travel, as part of transportation planning and development efforts of a locality, including programs and ordinances applicable to new shopping centers, special events, and other centers of vehicle activity;

   (xv) programs for new construction and major reconstructions of paths, tracks or areas solely for the use by pedestrian or other non-motorized means of transportation when economically feasible and in the public interest. For purposes of this clause, the Administrator shall also consult with the Secretary of the Interior; and

(xvi) program to encourage the voluntary removal from use and the market-place of pre-1980 model year light duty vehicles and pre-1980 model light duty trucks.

(B) information on additional methods or strategies that will contribute to the reduction of mobile source related pollutants during periods in which any primary ambient air quality standard will be exceeded and during episodes for which an air pollution alert, warning or emergency has been declared;

(C) information on other measures which may be employed to reduce the impact on public health or protect the health of sensitive or susceptible individuals or groups; and

(D) information on the extent to which any process, procedure, or method to reduce or control such air pollutant may cause an increase in the emissions or formation of any other pollutant.

(2) In publishing such information the Administrator shall also include an assessment of —

(A) the relative effectiveness of such processes, procedures, and methods;

(B) the potential effect of such processes, procedures, and methods on transportation systems and the provision of transportation services; and

(C) the environmental, energy, and economic impact of such processes, procedures and methods. . . .

(h) RACT/BACT/LAER Clearinghouse. — The Administrator shall make information regarding emission control technology available to the States and to the general public through a central database. Such information shall include all control technology information received pursuant to State plan provisions requiring permits for sources, including operating permits for existing sources.

National Ambient Air Quality Standards

Sec. 109. (a)(1) The Administrator —

(A) within 30 days after the date of enactment of the Clean Air Amendments of 1970, shall publish proposed regulations prescribing a national primary ambient air quality standard and a national secondary ambient air quality standard for each air pollutant for which air quality criteria have been issued prior to such date of enactment; and

(B) after a reasonable time for interested persons to submit written comments thereon (but no later than 90 days after the initial publication of such proposed standards) shall by regulation promulgate such proposed national primary and secondary ambient air quality standards with such modifications as he deems appropriate.

(2) With respect to any air pollutant for which air quality criteria are issued after the date of enactment of the Clean Air Amendments of 1970, the Administrator shall publish, simultaneously with the issuance of such criteria

and information, proposed national primary and secondary ambient air quality standards for any such pollutant. The procedure provided for in paragraph (1)(B) of this subsection shall apply to the promulgation of such standards.

(b)(1) National primary ambient air quality standards, prescribed under subsection (a) shall be ambient air quality standards the attainment and maintenance of which in the judgment of the Administrator, based on such criteria and allowing an adequate margin of safety, are requisite to protect the public health. Such primary standards may be revised in the same manner as promulgated.

(2) Any national secondary ambient air quality standard prescribed under subsection (a) shall specify a level of air quality the attainment and maintenance of which in the judgment of the Administrator, based on such criteria, is requisite to protect the public welfare from any known or anticipated adverse effects associated with the presence of such air pollutant in the ambient air. Such secondary standards may be revised in the same manner as promulgated.

(c) The Administrator shall, not later than one year after the date of the enactment of the Clean Air Act Amendments of 1977, promulgate a national primary ambient air quality standard for NO_2 concentrations over a period of not more than 3 hours unless, based on the criteria issued under section 108(c), he finds that there is no significant evidence that such a standard for such a period is requisite to protect public health.

(d)(1) Not later than December 31, 1980, and at five year intervals thereafter, the Administrator shall complete a thorough review of the criteria published under section 108 and the national ambient air quality standards promulgated under this section and shall make such revisions in such criteria and standards and promulgate such new standards as may be appropriate in accordance with section 108 and subsection (b) of this section. The Administrator may review and revise criteria or promulgate new standards earlier or more frequently than required under this paragraph.

(2)(A) The Administrator shall appoint an independent scientific review committee composed of seven members including at least one member of the National Academy of Sciences, one physician, and one person, representing State air pollution control agencies.

(B) Not later than January 1, 1980, and at five-year intervals thereafter, the committee referred to in subparagraph (A) shall complete a review of the criteria published under section 108 and the national primary and secondary ambient air quality standards promulgated under this section and shall recommend to the Administrator any new national ambient air quality standards and revisions of existing criteria and standards as may be appropriate under section 108 and subsection (b) of this section. . . .

Implementation Plans

Sec. 110. (a)(1) Each State shall, after reasonable notice and public hearings, adopt and submit to the Administrator, within 3 years (or such shorter

Clean Air Act §110

period as the Administrator may prescribe) after the promulgation of a national primary ambient air quality standard (or any revision thereof) under section 109 for any air pollutant, a plan which provides for implementation, maintenance, and enforcement of such primary standard in each air quality control region (or portion thereof) within such State. In addition, such State shall adopt and submit to the Administrator (either as a part of a plan submitted under the preceding sentence or separately) within 3 years (or such shorter period as the Administrator may prescribe) after the promulgation of a national ambient air quality secondary standard (or revision thereof), a plan which provides for implementation, maintenance, and enforcement of such secondary standard in each air quality control region (or portion thereof) within such State. Unless a separate public hearing is provided, each State shall consider its plan implementing such secondary standard at the hearing required by the first sentence of this paragraph.

(2) Each implementation plan submitted by a State under this Act shall be adopted by the State after reasonable notice and public hearing. Each such plan shall —

(A) include enforceable emission limitations and other control measures, means, or techniques (including economic incentives such as fees, marketable permits, and auctions of emissions rights), as well as schedules and timetables for compliance, as may be necessary or appropriate to meet the applicable requirements of this Act;

(B) provide for establishment and operation of appropriate devices, methods, systems, and procedures necessary to —

(i) monitor, compile, and analyze data on ambient air quality, and

(ii) upon request, make such data available to the Administrator;

(C) include a program to provide for the enforcement of the measures described in subparagraphs (A), and regulation of the modification and construction of any stationary source within the areas covered by the plan as necessary to assure that national ambient air quality standards are achieved, including a permit program as required in parts C and D;

(D) contain adequate provisions —

(i) prohibiting, consistent with the provisions of this title, any source or other type of emissions activity within the State from emitting any air pollutant in amounts which will —

(I) contribute significantly to nonattainment in, or interfere with maintenance by, any other State with respect to any such national primary or secondary ambient air quality standard, or

(II) interfere with measures required to be included in the applicable implementation plan for any other State under part C to prevent significant deterioration of air quality or to protect visibility,

(ii) insuring compliance with the applicable requirements of sections 126 and 115 (relating to interstate and international pollution abatement);

(E) provide (i) necessary assurances that the State (or, except where the Administrator deems inappropriate, the general purpose local govern-

§110   *emergency?*   Clean Air Act

ment or governments, or a regional agency designated by the State or general purpose local governments for such purpose) will have adequate personnel, funding, and authority under State (and, as appropriate, local) law to carry out such implementation plan (and is not prohibited by any provision of Federal or State law from carrying out such implementation plan or portion thereof), (ii) requirements that the State comply with the requirements respecting State boards under section 128, and (iii) necessary assurances that, where the State has relied on a local or regional government, agency, or instrumentality for the implementation of any plan provision, the State has responsibility for ensuring adequate implementation of such plan provision;

(F) require, as may be prescribed by the Administrator —

(i) the installation, maintenance, and replacement of equipment, and the implementation of other necessary steps, by owners or operators of stationary sources to monitor emissions from such sources,

(ii) periodic reports on the nature and amounts of emissions and emissions-related data from such sources, and

(iii) correlation of such reports by the State agency with any emission limitations or standards established pursuant to this Act, which reports shall be available at reasonable times for public inspection;

(G) provide for authority comparable to that in section 303 and adequate contingency plans to implement such authority;

(H) provide for revision of such plan —

(i) from time to time as may be necessary to take account of revisions of such national primary or secondary ambient air quality standard or the availability of improved or more expeditious methods of attaining such standard, and

(ii) except as provided in paragraph (3)(C), whenever the Administrator finds on the basis of information available to the Administrator that the plan is substantially inadequate to attain the national ambient air quality standard which it implements or to otherwise comply with any additional requirements established under this Act;

(I) in the case of a plan or plan revision for an area designated as a nonattainment area, meet the applicable requirements of part D (relating to nonattainment areas);

(J) meet the applicable requirements of section 121 (relating to consultation), section 127 (relating to public notification), and part C (relating to prevention of significant deterioration of air quality and visibility protection);

(K) provide for —

(i) the performance of such air quality modeling as the Administrator may prescribe for the purpose of predicting the effect on ambient air quality of any emissions of any air pollutant for which the Administrator has established a national ambient air quality standard, and

(ii) the submission, upon request, of data related to such air quality modeling to the Administrator;

Clean Air Act   §110

(L) require the owner or operator of each major stationary source to pay to the permitting authority, as a condition of any permit required under this Act, a fee sufficient to cover —

(i) the reasonable costs of reviewing and acting upon any application for such a permit, and

(ii) if the owner or operator receives a permit for such source, the reasonable costs of implementing and enforcing the terms and conditions of any such permit (not including any court costs or other costs associated with any enforcement action),

until such fee requirement is superseded with respect to such sources by the Administrator's approval of a fee program under title V; and

(M) provide for consultation and participation by local political subdivisions affected by the plan. . . .

(k) Environmental Protection Agency Action On Plan Submissions. — (1) Completeness Of Plan Submissions. — (A) Completeness Criteria. — Within 9 months after the date of the enactment of the Clean Air Amendments of 1990, the Administrator shall promulgate minimum criteria that any plan submission must meet before the Administrator is required to act on such submission under this subsection. The criteria shall be limited to the information necessary to enable the Administrator to determine whether the plan submission complies with the provisions of this Act.

(B) Completeness Finding. — Within 60 days of the Administrator's receipt of a plan or plan revision, but no later than 6 months after the date, if any, by which a State is required to submit the plan or revision, the Administrator shall determine whether the minimum criteria established pursuant to subparagraph (A) have been met. Any plan or plan revision that a State submits to the Administrator, and that has not been determined by the Administrator (by the date 6 months after receipt of the submission) to have failed to meet the minimum criteria established pursuant to subparagraph (A), shall on that date be deemed by operation of law to meet such minimum criteria.

(C) Effect of Finding of Incompleteness. — Where the Administrator determines that a plan submission (or part thereof) does not meet the minimum criteria established pursuant to subparagraph (A), the State shall be treated as not having made the submission (or, in the Administrator's discretion, part thereof).

(2) Deadline for Action. — Within 12 months of a determination by the Administrator (or a determination deemed by operation of law) under paragraph (1) that a State has submitted a plan or plan revision (or, in the Administrator's discretion, part thereof) that meets the minimum criteria established pursuant to paragraph (1), if applicable (or, if those criteria are not applicable, within 12 months of submission of the plan or revision), the Administrator shall act on the submission in accordance with paragraph (3).

(3) Full and Partial Approval and Disapproval. — In the case of any submittal on which the Administrator is required to act under paragraph (2), the Administrator shall approve such submittal as a whole if it meets all of

the applicable requirements of this Act. If a portion of the plan revision meets all the applicable requirements of this Act, the Administrator may approve the plan revision in part and disapprove the plan revision in part. The plan revision shall not be treated as meeting the requirements of this Act until the Administrator approves the entire plan revision as complying with the applicable requirements of this Act.

(4) Conditional Approval. — The Administrator may approve a plan revision based on a commitment of the State to adopt specific enforceable measures by a date certain, but not later than 1 year after the date of approval of the plan revision. Any such conditional approval shall be treated as a disapproval if the State fails to comply with such commitment.

(5) Calls For Plan Revisions. — Whenever the Administrator finds that the applicable implementation plan for any area is substantially inadequate to attain or maintain the relevant national ambient air quality standard, to mitigate adequately the interstate pollutant transport described in section 176A or section 184, or to otherwise comply with any requirement of this Act, the Administrator shall require the State to revise the plan as necessary to correct such inadequacies. The Administrator shall notify the State of the inadequacies, and may establish reasonable deadlines (not to exceed 18 months after the date of such notice) for the submission of such plan revisions. Such findings and notice shall be public. Any finding under this paragraph shall, to the extent the Administrator deems appropriate, subject the State to the requirements of this Act to which the State was subject when it developed and submitted the plan for which such finding was made, except that the Administrator may adjust any dates applicable under such requirements as appropriate (except that the Administrator may not adjust any attainment date prescribed under part D, unless such date has elapsed). . . .

(m) Sanctions. — The Administrator may apply any of the sanctions listed in section 179(b) at any time (or at any time after) the Administrator makes a finding, disapproval, or determination under paragraphs (1) through (4), respectively, of section 179(a) in relation to any plan or plan item (as that term is defined by the Administrator) required under this Act, with respect to any portion of the State the Administrator determines reasonable and appropriate, for the purpose of ensuring that the requirements of this Act relating to such plan or plan item are met. The Administrator shall, by rule, establish criteria for exercising his authority under the previous sentence with respect to any deficiency referred to in section 179(a) to ensure that, during the 24-month period following the finding, disapproval, or determination referred to in section 179(a), such sanctions are not applied on a statewide basis where one or more political subdivisions covered by the applicable implementation plan are principally responsible for such deficiency.

(n) Savings Clauses. — . . .

(3) Retention of Construction Moratorium in Certain Areas. — In the case of an area to which, immediately before the date of the enactment of the Clean Air Act Amendments of 1990, the prohibition on construction or mod-

ification of major stationary sources prescribed in subsection (a)(2)(I) (as in effect immediately before the date of the enactment of the Clean Air Act Amendments of 1990) applied by virtue of a finding of the Administrator that the State containing such area had not submitted an implementation plan meeting the requirements of section 172(b)(6) (relating to establishment of a permit program) (as in effect immediately before the date of enactment of the Clean Air Act Amendments of 1990) or 172(a)(1) (to the extent such requirements relate to provision for attainment of the primary national ambient air quality standard for sulfur oxides by December 31, 1982) as in effect immediately before the date of the enactment of the Clean Air Act Amendments of 1990, no major stationary source of the relevant air pollutant or pollutants shall be constructed or modified in such area until the Administrator finds that the plan for such area meets the applicable requirements of section 172(c)(5) (relating to permit programs) or subpart 5 of part D (relating to attainment of the primary national ambient air quality standard for sulfur dioxide), respectively. . . .

Standards of Performance for New Stationary Sources

Sec. 111. (a) For purposes of this section:

(1) The term 'standard of performance' means a standard for emissions of air pollutants which reflects the degree of emission limitation achievable through the application of the best system of emission reduction which (taking into account the cost of achieving such reduction and any nonair quality health and environmental impact and energy requirements) the Administrator determines has been adequately demonstrated.

(2) The term 'new source' means any stationary source, the construction or modification of which is commenced after the publication of regulations (or, if earlier, proposed regulations) prescribing a standard of performance under this section which will be applicable to such source.

(3) The term 'stationary source' means any building, structure, facility, or installation which emits or may emit any air pollutant. . . .

(4) The term 'modification' means any physical change in, or change in the method of operation of, a stationary source which increases the amount of any air pollutant emitted by such source or which results in the emission of any air pollutant not previously emitted.

(5) The term 'owner or operator' means any person who owns, leases, operates, controls, or supervises a stationary source.

(6) The term 'existing source' means any stationary source other than a new source.

(7) The term 'technological system of continuous emission reduction' means —

    (A) a technological process for production or operation by any source which is inherently lowpolluting or nonpolluting, or

    (B) a technological system for continuous reduction of the pollution generated by a source before such pollution is emitted into the ambient air, including precombustion cleaning or treatment of fuels. . . .

(b)(1)(A) The Administrator shall, within 90 days after the date of enactment of the Clean Air Amendments of 1970, publish (and from time to time thereafter shall revise) a list of categories of stationary sources. He shall include a category of sources in such list if in his judgment he determines it causes, or contributes significantly to air pollution which may reasonably be anticipated to endanger public health or welfare.

(B) Within one year after the inclusion of a category of stationary sources in a list under subparagraph (A), the Administrator shall publish proposed regulations, establishing Federal standards of performance for new sources within such category. . . .

(c)(1) Each state may develop and submit to the Administrator a procedure for implementing and enforcing standards of performance for new sources located in such State. If the Administrator finds the State procedure is adequate, he shall delegate to such State any authority he has under this Act to implement and enforce such standards.

(2) Nothing in this subsection shall prohibit the Administrator from enforcing any applicable standard of performance under this section.

(d)(1) The Administrator shall prescribe regulations which shall establish a procedure similar to that provided by section 110 under which each State shall submit to the Administrator a plan which (A) establishes standards of performance for any existing source for any air pollutant (i) for which air quality criteria have not been issued or which is not included on a list published under section 108(a) or emitted from a source category which is regulated under section 112(b) but (ii) to which a standard of performance under this section would apply if such existing source were a new source, and (B) provides for the implementation and enforcement of such standards of performance. Regulations of the Administrator under this paragraph shall permit the State in applying a standard of performance to any particular source under a plan submitted under this paragraph to take into consideration, among other factors, the remaining useful life of the existing source to which such standard applies. . . .

(h)(1) For purposes of this section, if in the judgment of the Administrator, it is not feasible to prescribe or enforce a standard of performance, he may instead promulgate a design, equipment, work practice, or operational standard, or combination thereof, which reflects the best technological system of continuous emission reduction which (taking into consideration the cost of achieving such emission reduction, and any non-air quality health and environmental impact and energy requirements) the Administrator determines has been adequately demonstrated. In the event the Administrator promulgates a design or equipment standard under this subsection, he shall include as part of such standard such requirements as will assure the proper operation and maintenance of any such element of design or equipment.

(2) For the purpose of this subsection, the phrase 'not feasible to prescribe or enforce a standard of performance' means any situation in which

16

Clean Air Act §112

the Administrator determines that (A) a pollutant or pollutants cannot be emitted through a conveyance designed and constructed to emit or capture such pollutant, or that any requirement for, or use of, such conveyance would be inconsistent with any Federal, State, or local law, or (B) the application of measurement methodology to a particular class of sources is not practicable due to technological or economic limitations. . . .

(j)(1)(A) Any person proposing to own or operate a new source may request the Administrator for one or more waivers from the requirements of this section for such source or any portion thereof with respect to any air pollutant to encourage the use of an innovative technological system or systems of continuous emission reduction. The Administrator may, with the consent of the Governor of the State in which the source is to be located, grant a waiver under this paragraph, if the Administrator determines after notice and opportunity for public hearing, that —

    (i) the proposed system or systems have not been adequately demonstrated,

    (ii) the proposed system or systems will operate effectively and there is a substantial likelihood that such system or systems will achieve greater continuous emission reduction than that required to be achieved under the standards of performance which would otherwise apply, or achieve at least an equivalent reduction at lower cost in terms of energy, economic, or nonair quality environmental impact,

    (iii) the owner or operator of the proposed source has demonstrated to the satisfaction of the Administrator that the proposed system will not cause or contribute to an unreasonable risk to public health, welfare, or safety in its operation, function, or malfunction, and

    (iv) the granting of such waiver is consistent with the requirements of subparagraph (C). . . .

National Emission Standards for Hazardous Air Pollutants

Sec. 112. (a) Definitions. — For purposes of this section, except subsection (r) —

(1) Major source. — The term 'major source' means any stationary source or group of stationary sources located within a contiguous area and under common control that emits or has the potential to emit considering controls, in the aggregate, 10 tons per year or more of any hazardous air pollutant or 25 tons per year or more of any combination of hazardous air pollutants. The Administrator may establish a lesser quantity, or in the case of radionuclides different criteria, for a major source than that specified in the previous sentence, on the basis of the potency of the air pollutants, persistence, potential for bioaccumulation, other characteristics of the air pollutant, or other relevant factors.

(2) Area source. — The term 'area source' means any stationary source of hazardous air pollutants that is not a major source. For purposes of this

section, the term 'area source' shall not include motor vehicles or nonroad vehicles subject to regulation under title II.

(3) Stationary source. — The term 'stationary source' shall have the same meaning as such term has under section 111(a).

(4) New source. — The term 'new source' means a stationary source the construction or reconstruction of which is commenced after the Administrator first proposes regulations under this section establishing an emission standard applicable to such source.

(5) Modification. — The term 'modification' means any physical change in, or change in the method of operation of, a major source which increases the actual emissions of any hazardous air pollutant emitted by such source by more than a de minimis amount or which results in the emission of any hazardous air pollutant not previously emitted by more than a de minimis amount.

(6) Hazardous air pollutant. — The term 'hazardous air pollutant' means any air pollutant listed pursuant to subsection (b).

(7) Adverse environmental effect. — The term 'adverse environmental effect' means any significant and widespread adverse effect, which may reasonably be anticipated, to wildlife, aquatic life, or other natural resources, including adverse impacts on populations of endangered or threatened species or significant degradation of environmental quality over broad areas.

(8) Electric utility steam generating unit. — The term 'electric utility steam generating unit' means any fossil fuel fired combustion unit of more than 25 megawatts that serves a generator that produces electricity for sale. A unit that cogenerates steam and electricity and supplies more than one-third of its potential electric output capacity and more than 25 megawatts electrical output to any utility power distribution system for sale shall be considered an electric utility steam generating unit.

(9) Owner or operator. — The term 'owner or operator' means any person who owns, leases, operates, controls, or supervises a stationary source.

(10) Existing source. — The term 'existing source' means any stationary source other than a new source.

(11) Carcinogenic effect. — Unless revised, the term 'carcinogenic effect' shall have the meaning provided by the Administrator under Guidelines for Carcinogenic Risk Assessment as of the date of enactment. Any revisions in the existing Guidelines shall be subject to notice and opportunity for comment.

(b) List of Pollutants. — (1) Initial List. — The Congress establishes for purposes of this section a list of hazardous air pollutants as follows: [The list is omitted. Paragraph (c) requires the administrator to publish a list of major and area sources.]

(d) Emission Standards. — (1) In General. — The Administrator shall promulgate regulations establishing emission standards for each category or subcategory of major sources and area sources of hazardous air listed for regulation pursuant to subsection (c) in accordance with the schedules provided in subsec-

Clean Air Act §112

tions (c) and (e). The Administrator may distinguish among classes, types, and sizes of sources within a category or subcategory in establishing such standards except that, there shall be no delay in the compliance date for any standard applicable to any source under subsection (i) as the result of the authority provided by this sentence.

(2) Standards And Methods. — Emissions standards promulgated under this subsection and applicable to new or existing sources of hazardous air pollutants shall require the maximum degree of reduction in emissions of the hazardous air pollutants subject to this section (including a prohibition on such emissions, where achievable) that the Administrator, taking into consideration the cost of achieving such emission reduction, and any non-air quality health and environmental impacts and energy requirements, determines is achievable for new or existing sources in the category or subcategory to which such emission standard applies, through application of measures, processes, methods, systems or techniques including, but not limited to, measures which —

  (A) reduce the volume of, or eliminate emissions of, such pollutants through process changes, substitution of materials or other modifications,
  (B) enclose systems or processes to eliminate emissions,
  (C) collect, capture or treat such pollutants when released from a process, stack, storage or fugitive emissions point,
  (D) are design, equipment, work practice, or operational standards (including requirements for operator training or certification) as provided in subsection (h), or
  (E) are a combination of the above. . . .

(3) New and Existing Sources. — The maximum degree of reduction in emissions that is deemed achievable for new sources in a category or subcategory shall not be less stringent than the emission control that is achieved in practice by the best controlled similar source, as determined by the Administrator. Emission standards promulgated under this subsection for existing sources in a category or subcategory may be less stringent than standards for new sources in the same category or subcategory but shall not be less stringent, and may be more stringent than —

  (A) the average emission limitation achieved by the best performing 12 percent of the existing sources (for which the Administrator has emissions information), excluding those sources that have, within 18 months before the emission standard is proposed or within 30 months before such standard is promulgated, whichever is later, first achieved a level of emission rate or emission reduction which complies, or would comply if the source is not subject to such standard, with the lowest achievable emission rate (as defined by section 171) applicable to the source category and prevailing at the time, in the category or subcategory for categories and subcategories with 30 or more sources, or
  (B) the average emission limitation achieved by the best performing 5 sources (for which the Administrator has or could reasonably obtain

emissions information) in the category or subcategory for categories or subcategories with fewer than 30 sources.

(4) Health Threshold. — With respect to pollutants for which a health threshold has been established, the Administrator may consider such threshold level, with an ample margin of safety, when establishing emission standards under this subsection.

(5) Alternative Standard for Area Sources. — With respect only to categories and subcategories of area sources listed pursuant to subsection (c), the Administrator may, in lieu of the authorities provided in paragraph (2) and subsection (f), elect to promulgate standards or requirements applicable to sources in such categories or subcategories which provide for the use of generally available control technologies or management practices by such sources to reduce emissions of hazardous air pollutants. . . .

(g) Modifications. — (1) Offsets. — (A) A physical change in, or change in the method of operation of, a major source which results in a greater than de minimis increase in actual emissions of a hazardous air pollutant shall not be considered a modification, if such increase in the quantity of actual emissions of any hazardous air pollutant from such source will be offset by an equal or greater decrease in the quantity of emissions of another hazardous air pollutant (or pollutants) from such source which is deemed more hazardous, pursuant to guidance issued by the Administrator under subparagraph (B). The owner or operator of such source shall submit a showing to the Administrator (or the State) that such increase has been offset under the preceding sentence. . . .

(2) Construction, Reconstruction and Modifications. — (A) After the effective date of a permit program under title V in any State, no person may modify a major source of hazardous air pollutants in such State, unless the Administrator (or the State) determines that the maximum achievable control technology emission limitation under this section for existing sources will be met. Such determination shall be made on a case-by-case basis where no applicable emissions limitations have been established by the Administrator.

(B) After the effective date of a permit program under title V in any State, no person may construct or reconstruct any major source of hazardous air pollutants, unless the Administrator (or the State) determines that the maximum achievable control technology emission limitation under this section for new sources will be met. Such determination shall be made on a case-by-case basis where no applicable emission limitations have been established by the Administrator. . . .

(h) Work Practice Standards And Other Requirements. [Similar to §110(h).]

(4) Numerical Standard Required. — Any standard promulgated under paragraph (1) shall be promulgated in terms of an emission standard whenever it is feasible to promulgate and enforce a standard in such terms.

(i) Schedule for Compliance. — (1) Preconstruction and Operating Requirements. — After the effective date of any emission standard, limitation, or regulation under subsection (d), (f) or (h), no person may construct any new

Clean Air Act §112

major source or reconstruct any existing major source subject to such emission standard, regulation or limitation unless the Administrator (or a State with a permit program approved under title V) determines that such source, if properly constructed, reconstructed and operated, will comply with the standard, regulation or limitation. . . .

(3) Compliance Schedule for Existing Sources. — (A) After the effective date of any emissions standard, limitation or regulation promulgated under this section and applicable to a source, no person may operate such source in violation of such standard, limitation or regulation except, in the case of an existing source, the Administrator shall establish a compliance date or dates for each category or subcategory of existing sources, which shall provide for compliance as expeditiously as practicable, but in no event later than 3 years after the effective date of such standard, except as provided in subparagraph (B) and paragraphs (4) through (8). . . .

(5) Early Reduction. — (A) The Administrator (or a State acting pursuant to a permit program approved under title V) shall issue a permit allowing an existing source, for which the owner or operator demonstrates that the source has achieved a reduction of 90 per centum or more in emissions of hazardous air pollutants (95 per centum in the case of hazardous air pollutants which are particulates) from the source, to meet an alternative emission limitation reflecting such reduction in lieu of an emission limitation promulgated under subsection (d) for a period of 6 years from the compliance date for the otherwise applicable standard, provided that such reduction is achieved before the otherwise applicable standard under subsection (d) is first proposed. Nothing in this paragraph shall preclude a State from requiring reductions in excess of those specified in this subparagraph as a condition of granting the extension authorized by the previous sentence.

(B) An existing source which achieves the reduction referred to in subparagraph (A) after the proposal of an applicable standard but before January 1, 1994, may qualify under subparagraph (A), if the source makes an enforceable commitment to achieve such reduction before the proposal of the standard. Such commitment shall be enforceable to the same extent as a regulation under this section.

(C) The reduction shall be determined with respect to verifiable and actual emissions in a base year not earlier than calendar year 1987, provided that, there is no evidence that emissions in the base year are artificially or substantially greater than emissions in other years prior to implementation of emissions reduction measures. The Administrator may allow a source to use a baseline year of 1985 or 1986 provided that the source can demonstrate to the satisfaction of the Administrator that emissions data for the source reflects verifiable data based on information for such source, received by the Administrator prior to the enactment of the Clean Air Act Amendments of 1990, pursuant to an information request issued under section 114.

(D) For each source granted an alternative emission limitation under this paragraph there shall be established by a permit issued pursuant to title V an enforceable emission limitation for hazardous air pollutants reflecting the reduction which qualifies the source for an alternative emission limitation under this paragraph. An alternative emission limitation under this paragraph shall not be available with respect to standards or requirements promulgated pursuant to subsection (f) and the Administrator shall, for the purpose of determining whether a standard under subsection (f) is necessary, review emissions from sources granted an alternative emission limitation under this paragraph at the same time that other sources in the category or subcategory are reviewed.

(E) With respect to pollutants for which high risks of adverse public health effects may be associated with exposure to small quantities including, but not limited to, chlorinated dioxins and furans, the Administrator shall by regulation limit the use of offsetting reductions in emissions of other hazardous air pollutants from the source as counting toward the 90 per centum reduction in such high-risk pollutants qualifying for an alternative emissions limitation under this paragraph. . . .

(k) Area Source Program. — (1) Findings and Purpose. — The Congress finds that emissions of hazardous air pollutants from area sources may individually, or in the aggregate, present significant risks to public health in urban areas. Considering the large number of persons exposed and the risks of carcinogenic and other adverse health effects from hazardous air pollutants, ambient concentrations characteristic of large urban areas should be reduced to levels substantially below those currently experienced. It is the purpose of this subsection to achieve a substantial reduction in emissions of hazardous air pollutants from area sources and an equivalent reduction in the public health risks associated with such sources including a reduction of not less than 75 per centum in the incidence of cancer attributable to emissions from such sources. . . .

(8) Local Program. — The Administrator may, after notice and opportunity for public comment, approve a program developed and submitted by a local air pollution control agency (after consultation with the State) pursuant to this subsection and any such agency implementing an approved program may take any action authorized to be taken by a State under this section. . . .

(r) Prevention Of Accidental Releases. — (1) Purpose And General Duty. — It shall be the objective of the regulations and programs authorized under this subsection to prevent the accidental release and to minimize the consequences of any such release of any substance listed pursuant to paragraph (3) or any other extremely hazardous substance. The owners and operators of stationary sources producing, processing, handling or storing such substances have a general duty in the same manner and to the same extent as section 654, title 29 of the United States Code, to identify hazards which may result from such releases using appropriate hazard assessment techniques, to design and maintain a safe facility taking such steps as are necessary to prevent releases, and to minimize the consequences of accidental releases which do occur. For purposes of this paragraph, the provisions of section 304 shall not be available to any person

Clean Air Act §112

or otherwise be construed to be applicable to this paragraph. Nothing in this section shall be interpreted, construed, implied or applied to create any liability or basis for suit for compensation for bodily injury or any other injury or property damages to any person which may result from accidental releases of such substances.

(2) Definitions. — (A) The term 'accidental release' means an unanticipated emission of a regulated substance or other extremely hazardous substance into the ambient air from a stationary source.

(B) The term 'regulated substance' means a substance listed under paragraph (3).

(C) The term 'stationary source' means any buildings, structures, equipment, installations or substance emitting stationary activities (i) which belong to the same industrial group, (ii) which are located on one or more contiguous properties, (iii) which are under the control of the same person (or persons under common control), and (iv) from which an accidental release may occur.

(3) List Of Substances. — The Administrator shall promulgate not later than 24 months after enactment of the Clean Air Act Amendments of 1990 an initial list of 100 substances which, in the case of an accidental release, are known to cause or may reasonably be anticipated to cause death, injury, or serious adverse affects to human health or the environment. For purposes of promulgating such list, the Administrator shall use, but is not limited to, the list of extremely hazardous substances published under the Emergency Planning and Community Right-to-Know Act of 1986, with such modifications as the Administrator deems appropriate. . . . No air pollutant for which a national primary ambient air quality standard has been established shall be included on any such list. No substance, practice, process, or activity regulated under title VI shall be subject to regulations under this subsection. . . .

(4) Factors To Be Considered. — In listing substances under paragraph (3), the Administrator shall consider each of the following criteria —

(A) the severity of any acute adverse health effects associated with accidental releases of the substance;

(B) the likelihood of accidental releases of the substance; and

(C) the potential magnitude of human exposure to accidental releases of the substance.

(5) Threshold Quantity. — At the time any substance is listed pursuant to paragraph (3), the Administrator shall establish by rule, a threshold quantity for the substance, taking into account the toxicity, reactivity, volatility, dispersibility, combustibility, or flammability of the substance and the amount of the substance which, as a result of an accidental release, is known to cause or may reasonably be anticipated to cause death, injury or serious adverse effects to human health for which the substance was listed. The Administrator is authorized to establish a greater threshold quantity for, or to exempt entirely, any substance that is a nutrient used in agriculture when held by a farmer. . . .

(7) Accident Prevention. — (A) In order to prevent accidental releases of regulated substances, the Administrator is authorized to promulgate release prevention, detection, and correction requirements which may include monitoring, recordkeeping, reporting, training, vapor recovery, secondary containment, and other design, equipment, work practice, and operational requirements. Regulations promulgated under this paragraph may make distinctions between various types, classes, and kinds of facilities, devices and systems taking into consideration factors including, but not limited to, the size, location, process, process controls, quantity of substances handled, potency of substances, and response capabilities present at any stationary source. Regulations promulgated pursuant to this subparagraph shall have an effective date, as determined by the Administrator, assuring compliance as expeditiously as practicable.

(B)(i) Within 3 years after the date of enactment of the Clean Air Act Amendments of 1990, the Administrator shall promulgate reasonable regulations and appropriate guidance to provide, to the greatest extent practicable, for the prevention and detection of accidental releases of regulated substances and for response to such releases by the owners or operators of the sources of such releases. The Administrator shall utilize the expertise of the Secretaries of Transportation and Labor in promulgating such regulations. As appropriate, such regulations shall cover the use, operation, repair, replacement, and maintenance of equipment to monitor, detect, inspect, and control such releases, including training of persons in the use and maintenance of such equipment and in the conduct of periodic inspections. The regulations shall include procedures and measures for emergency response after an accidental release of a regulated substance in order to protect human health and the environment. The regulations shall cover storage, as well as operations. The regulations shall, as appropriate, recognize differences in size, operations, processes, class and categories of sources and the voluntary actions of such sources to prevent such releases and respond to such releases. The regulations shall be applicable to a stationary source 3 years after the date of promulgation, or 3 years after the date on which a regulated substance present at the source in more than threshold amounts is first listed under paragraph (3), whichever is later.

(iii) The regulations under this subparagraph shall require the owner or operator of stationary sources at which a regulated substance is present in more than a threshold quantity to prepare and implement a risk management plan to detect and prevent or minimize accidental releases of such substances from the stationary source, and to provide a prompt emergency response to any such releases in order to protect human health and the environment. . . .

Federal Enforcement

Sec. 113. (a) In General. — (1) Order to comply with SIP.—Whenever, on the basis of any information available to the Administrator, the Administrator

Clean Air Act §113

finds that any person has violated or is in violation of any requirements or prohibition of an applicable implementation plan or permit, the Administrator shall notify the person and the State in which the plan applies of such finding. At any time after the expiration of 30 days following the date on which such notice of a violation is issued, the Administrator may, without regard to the period of violation (subject to section 2462 of title 28 of the United States Code) —

    (A) Issue an order requiring such person to comply with the requirements or prohibitions of such plan or permit,

    (B) Issue an administrative penalty order in accordance with subsection (d), or

    (C) Bring a civil action in accordance with subsection (b).

(2) Whenever, on the basis of information available to the Administrator, the Administrator finds that violations of an applicable implementation plan or an approved permit program under title V are so widespread that such violations appear to result from a failure of the State in which the plan or permit program applies to enforce the plan or permit program effectively, the Administrator shall so notify the State. In the case of a permit program, the notice shall be made in accordance with title V. If the Administrator finds such failure extends beyond the 30th day after such notice (90 days in the case of such permit program), the Administrator shall give public notice of such finding. During the period beginning with such public notice and ending when such State satisfied the Administrator that it will enforce such plan or permit program (hereafter referred to in this section as 'period of federally assumed enforcement'), the Administrator may enforce any requirement or prohibition of such plan or permit program with respect to any person by —

    (A) issuing an order requiring such person to comply with such requirement or prohibition,

    (B) issuing an administrative penalty order in accordance with subsection (d), or

    (C) bringing a civil action in accordance with subsection (b).

(3) EPA Enforcement Of Other Requirements. [Similar to subsection (1).]

(5) Failure To Comply With New Source Requirements. [Similar to subsection (1).]

(b) Civil Judicial Enforcement. — The Administrator shall, as appropriate, in the case of any person that is the owner or operator of an affected source, a major emitting facility, or a major stationary source, and may, in the case of any other person, commence a civil action for a permanent or temporary injunction, or to assess and recover a civil penalty of not more than $25,000 per day for each violation, or both, in any of the following instances:

(1) Whenever such person has violated, or is in violation of, any requirement or prohibition of an applicable implementation plan or permit. Such an action shall be commenced (A) during any period of federally assumed enforcement, or (B) more than 30 days following the date of the Administrator's notification under subsection (a)(1) that such person has violated, or is in violation of, such requirement or prohibition.

(2) Whenever such person has violated, or is in violation of, any other requirement or prohibition of this title, section 303 of title III, title IV, title V, or title VI, including, but not limited to, a requirement or prohibition of any rule, order, waiver or permit promulgated, issued, or approved under this Act, or for the payment of any fee owed the United States under this Act (other than title II).

(3) Whenever such person attempts to construct or modify a major stationary source in any area with respect to which a finding under subsection (a)(5) has been made. . . .

(c) Criminal Penalties. — (1) Any person who knowingly violates any requirement or prohibition of an applicable implementation plan (during any period of federally assumed enforcement or more than 30 days after having been notified under subsection (a)(1) by the Administrator that such person is violating such requirement or prohibition), any order under subsection (a) of this section, requirement or prohibition of section 111(e) of this title (relating to new source performance standards), section 112 of this title, section 114 of this title (relating to inspections, etc.), section 129 of this title (relating to solid waste combustion), section 165(a) of this title (relating to preconstruction requirements), an order under section 167 of this title (relating to preconstruction requirements), an order under section 303 of title III (relating to emergency orders), section 502(a) or 503(c) of title V (relating to permits), or any requirement or prohibition of title IV (relating to acid deposition control), or title VI (relating to stratospheric ozone control), including a requirement of any rule, order, waiver, or permit promulgated or approved under such sections or titles, and including any requirement for the payment of any fee owed the United States under this Act (other than title II) shall, upon conviction, be punished by a fine pursuant to title 18 of the United States Code, or by imprisonment for not to exceed 5 years, or both. If a conviction of any person under this paragraph is for a violation committed after a first conviction of such person under this paragraph, the maximum punishment shall be doubled with respect to both the fine and imprisonment. . . . [Additional criminal penalties are provided for knowing and negligent releases.]

(d) Administrative Assessment of Civil Penalties. — (1) The Administrator may issue an administrative order against any person assessing a civil administrative penalty of up to $25,000, per day of violation, whenever, on the basis of any available information, the Administrator finds that such person —

(A) has violated or is violating any requirement or prohibition of an applicable implementation plan (such order shall be issued (i) during any period of federally assumed enforcement, or (ii) more than thirty days following the date of the Administrator's notification under subsection (a)(1) of this section of a finding that such person has violated or is violating such requirement or prohibition); or

(B) has violated or is violating any other requirement or prohibition of title I, III, IV, V, or VI, including, but not limited to, a requirement or prohibition of any rule, order, waiver, permit, or plan promulgated, issued, or approved under this Act, or for the payment of any fee owed the United States under this Act (other than title II); or

Clean Air Act §115

(C) attempts to construct or modify a major stationary source in any area with respect to which a finding under subsection (a)(5) of this section has been made. The Administrator's authority under this paragraph shall be limited to matters where the total penalty sought does not exceed $200,000 and the first alleged date of violation occurred no more than 12 months prior to the initiation of the administrative action, except where the Administrator and the Attorney General jointly determine that a matter involving a larger penalty amount or longer period of violation is appropriate for administrative penalty action. Any such determination by the Administrator and the Attorney General shall not be subject to judicial review. . . .

(e) Penalty Assessment Criteria. — (1) In determining the amount of any penalty to be assessed under this section or section 304(a), the Administrator or the court, as appropriate, shall take into consideration (in addition to such other factors as justice may require) the size of the business, the economic impact of the penalty on the business, the violator's full compliance history and good faith efforts to comply, the duration of the violation as established by any credible evidence (including evidence other than the applicable test method), payment by the violator of penalties previously assessed for the same violation, the economic benefit of noncompliance, and the seriousness of the violation. The court shall not assess penalties for noncompliance with administrative subpoenas under section 307(a), or actions under section 114 of this Act, where the violator had sufficient cause to violate or fail or refuse to comply with such subpoena or action.

(2) A penalty may be assessed for each day of violation. For purposes of determining the number of days of violation for which a penalty may be assessed under subsection (b) or (d)(1) of this section, or section 304(a), or an assessment may be made under section 120, where the Administrator or an air pollution control agency has notified the source of the violation, and the plaintiff makes a prima facie showing that the conduct or events giving rise to the violation are likely to have continued or recurred past the date of notice, the days of violation shall be presumed to include the date of such notice and each and every day thereafter until the violator establishes that continuous compliance has been achieved, except to the extent that the violator can prove by a preponderance of the evidence that there were intervening days during which no violation occurred or that the violation was not continuing in nature. . . .

International Air Pollution

Sec. 115. (a) Whenever the Administrator, upon receipt of reports, surveys or studies from any duly constituted international agency has reason to believe that any air pollutant or pollutants emitted in the United States cause or contribute to air pollution which may reasonably be anticipated to endanger public health or welfare in a foreign country or whenever the Secretary of State requests him to do so with respect to such pollution which the Secretary of State alleges is of such a nature the Administrator shall give formal notification thereof to the Governor of the State in which such emissions originate.

(b) The notice of the Administrator shall be deemed to be a finding under section 110.(a)(2)(H)(ii) which requires a plan revision with respect to so much of the applicable implementation plan as is inadequate to prevent or eliminate the endangerment referred to in subsection (a). Any foreign country so affected by such emission of pollutant or pollutants shall be invited to appear at any public hearing associated with any revision of the appropriate portion of the applicable implementation plan.

(c) This section shall apply only to a foreign country which the Administrator determines has given the United States essentially the same rights with respect to the prevention or control of air pollution occurring in that country as is given that country by this section.

(d) Recommendations issued following any abatement conference conducted prior to the enactment of the Clean Air Act Amendments of 1977 shall remain in effect with respect to any pollutant for which no national ambient air quality standard has been established under section 109 of this Act unless the Administrator, after consultation with all agencies which were party to the conference, rescinds any such recommendation on grounds of obsolescence.

Retention of State Authority

Sec. 116. Except as otherwise provided in sections 119.(c), (e) and (f) (as in effect before the date of the enactment of the Clean Air Act Amendments of 1977), 209.211.(c)(4), and 233 (preempting certain State regulation of moving sources) nothing in this Act shall preclude or deny the right of any State or political subdivision thereof to adopt or enforce (1) any standard or limitation respecting emissions of air pollutants or (2) any requirement respecting control or abatement of air pollution; except that if an emission standard or limitation is in effect under an applicable implementation plan or under section 111 or 112, such State or political subdivision may not adopt or enforce any emission standard or limitation which is less stringent than the standard or limitation under such plan or section.

Control of Pollution from Federal Facilities

Sec. 118. (a) Each department, agency, and instrumentality of the executive, legislative, and judicial branches of the Federal Government (1) having jurisdiction over any property or facility, or (2) engaged in any activity resulting, or which may result, in the discharge of air pollutants, and each officer, agent, or employee, thereof, shall be subject to, and comply with, all Federal, State, interstate, and local requirements, administrative authority, and process and sanctions respecting the control and abatement of air pollution in the same manner, and to the same extent as any non-governmental entity. The preceding sentence shall apply (A) to any requirement whether substantive or procedural

Clean Air Act §120

(including any recordkeeping or reporting requirement, any requirement respecting permits and any other requirement whatsoever), (B) to any requirement to pay a fee or charge imposed by any State or local agency to defray the costs of its air pollution regulatory program, (C) to the exercise of any Federal, State, or local administrative authority, and (D) to any process and sanction, whether enforced in Federal, State, or local courts, or in any other manner.

(b) The President may exempt any emission source of any department, agency, or instrumentality in the executive branch from compliance with such a requirement if he determines it to be in the paramount interest of the United States to do so, except that no exemption may be granted from section 111, and an exemption from section 112 may be granted only in accordance with section 112(i)(4). No such exemption shall be granted due to lack of appropriation unless the President shall have specifically requested such appropriation as a part of the budgetary process and the Congress shall have failed to make available such requested appropriation. Any exemption shall be for a period not in excess of one year, but additional exemptions may be granted for periods of not to exceed one year upon the President's making a new determination. In addition to any such exemption of a particular emission source, the President may, if he determines it to be in the paramount interest of the United States to do so, issue regulations exempting from compliance with the requirements of this section any weaponry, equipment, aircraft, vehicles, or other classes or categories of property which are owned or operated by the Armed Forces of the United States (including the Coast Guard) or by the National Guard of any State and which are uniquely military in nature. The President shall reconsider the need for such regulations at three-year intervals. The President shall report each January to the Congress all exemptions from the requirements of this section granted during the preceding calendar year, together with his reason for granting each such exemption. . . .

Noncompliance Penalty

Section 120. (a)(1)(A) Not later than 6 months after the date of enactment of this section, and after notice and opportunity for a public hearing, the Administrator shall promulgate regulations requiring the assessment and collection of a noncompliance penalty against persons referred to in paragraph (2)(A).

(B)(i) Each State may develop and submit to the Administrator a plan for carrying out this section in such State. If the Administrator finds that the State plan meets the requirements of this section, he may delegate to such State any authority he has to carry out this section.

(ii) Notwithstanding a delegation to a State under clause (i), the Administrator may carry out this section in such State under the circumstances described in subsection (b)(2)(B).

(2)(A) Except as provided in subparagraph (B) or (C) of this paragraph, the State or the Administrator shall assess and collect a noncompliance penalty against every person who owns or operates —

(i) a major stationary source (other than a primary nonferrous smelter which has received a primary nonferrous smelter order under section 119) which is not in compliance with any emission limitation, emission standard or compliance schedule under any applicable implementation plan (whether or not such source is subject to a Federal or State consent decree), or

(ii) a stationary source which is not in compliance with an emission limitation, emission standard, standard of performance, or other requirement established under section 111, 167, 303, or 112 of this Act, or

(iii) a stationary source which is not in compliance with any requirement of title IV, V, or VI of this Act, or

(iv) any source referred to in clause (i), (ii), or (iii) (for which an extension, order, or suspension referred to in subparagraph (B), or Federal or State consent decree is in effect), or a primary nonferrous smelter which has received a primary non-ferrous smelter order under section 119 which is not in compliance with any interim emission control requirement or schedule of compliance under such extension, order, suspension, or consent decree.

For purposes of subsection (d)(2), in the case of a penalty assessed with respect to a source referred to in clause (iii) of this subparagraph, the costs referred to in such subsection (d)(2) shall be the economic value of noncompliance with the interim emission control requirement or the remaining steps in the schedule of compliance referred to in such clause. . . .

(d)(1) All penalties assessed by the Administrator under this section shall be paid to the United States Treasury. All penalties assessed by the State under this section shall be paid to such State.

(2) The amount of the penalty which shall be assessed and collected with respect to any source under this section shall be equal to —

(A) the amount determined in accordance with regulations promulgated by the Administrator under subsection (a), which is no less than the economic value which a delay in compliance beyond July 1, 1979, may have for the owner of such source, including the quarterly equivalent of the capital costs of compliance and debt service over a normal amortization period, not to exceed ten years, operation and maintenance costs foregone as a result of noncompliance, and any additional economic value which such a delay may have for the owner or operator of such source, minus

(B) the amount of any expenditure made by the owner or operator of that source during any such quarter for the purpose of bringing that source into, and maintaining compliance with, such requirement to the extent that such expenditures have not been taken into account in the calculation of the penalty under subparagraph (A).

To the extent that any expenditure under subparagraph (B) made during any quarter is not subtracted for such quarter from the costs under subparagraph

(A), such expenditure may be subtracted for any subsequent quarter from such costs, except that in no event shall the amount paid be less than the quarterly payment minus the amount attributed to actual cost of construction. . . .

Consultation

Sec. 121. In carrying out the requirements of this Act requiring applicable implementation plans to contain —
  (1) any transportation controls, air quality maintenance plan requirements or preconstruction review of direct sources of air pollution, or
  (2) any measure referred to —
    (A) in part D (pertaining to nonattainment requirements), or
    (B) in part C (pertaining to prevention of significant deterioration),
and in carrying out the requirements of Section 113(d) (relating to certain enforcement orders), the State shall provide a satisfactory process of consultation with general purpose local governments, designated organizations of elected officials of local governments and any Federal land manager having authority over Federal land to which the State plan applies, effective with respect to any such requirement which is adopted more than one year after the date of enactment of the Clean Air Act amendments of 1977 as part of such plan. Such process shall be in accordance with regulations promulgated by the Administrator to assure adequate consultation. . . .

Stack Heights

Sec. 123. (a) The degree of emission limitation required for control of any air pollutant under an applicable implementation plan under this title shall not be affected in any manner by —
  (1) so much of the stack height of any source as exceeds good engineering practice (as determined under regulations promulgated by the Administrator), or
  (2) any other dispersion technique.
The preceding sentence shall not apply with respect to stack heights in existence before the date of enactment of the Clean Air Amendments of 1970 or dispersion techniques implemented before such date. In establishing an emission limitation for coal-fired steam electric generating units which are subject to the provisions of section 118 and which commenced operation before July 1, 1957, the effect of the entire stack height of stacks for which a construction contract was awarded before February 8, 1974, may be taken into account.
  (b) For the purpose of this section, the term 'dispersion technique' includes any intermittent of supplemental control of air pollutants varying with atmospheric conditions.
  (c) No later than six months after the date of enactment of this section, the Administrator, shall after notice and opportunity for public hearing, promulgate regulations to carry out this section. For purposes of this section, good engi-

neering practice means, with respect to stack heights, the height necessary to insure that emissions from the stack do not result in excessive concentrations of any air pollutant in the immediate vicinity of the source as a result of atmospheric downwash, eddies and wakes which may be created by the source itself, nearby structures or nearby terrain obstacles (as determined by the Administrator). For purposes of this section such height shall not exceed two and a half times the height of such source unless the owner or operator of the source demonstrates, after notice and opportunity for public hearing, to the satisfaction of the Administrator, that a greater height is necessary as provided under the preceding sentence. In no event may the administrator prohibit any increase in any stack height or restrict in any manner the stack height of any source. . . .

Interstate Pollution Abatement

Sec. 126. (a) Each applicable implementation plan shall —
 (1) require each major proposed new (or modified source —
  (A) subject to part C (relating to significant deterioration of air quality) or
  (B) which may significantly contribute to levels of air pollution in excess of the national ambient air quality standards in any air quality control region outside the State in which such source intends to locate (or make such modification),
 to provide written notice to all nearby States the air pollution levels of which may be affected by such source at least sixty days prior to the date on which commencement of construction is to be permitted by the State providing notice, and
 (2) identify all major existing stationary sources which may have the impact described in paragraph (1) with respect to new or modified sources and provide notice to all nearby States of the identity of such sources not later than three months after the date of enactment of the Clean Air Act Amendments of 1977.

(b) Any State or political subdivision may petition the Administrator for a finding that any major source or group of stationary sources emits or would emit any air pollutant in violation of the prohibition of section 110(a)(2)(D)(ii). Within 60 days after receipt of any petition under this subsection and after public hearing, the Administrator shall make such a finding or deny the petition.

(c) Notwithstanding any permit which may have been granted by the State in which the source is located (or intends to locate), it shall be a violation of this section and the applicable implementation plan in such State —
 (1) for any major proposed new (or modified) source with respect to which a finding has been made under subsection (b) to be constructed or to operate in violation of the prohibition of section 110(a)(2)(D)(ii), or
 (2) for any major existing source to operate more than three months after such finding has been made with respect to it. The Administrator may permit the continued operation of a source referred to in paragraph (2) beyond

Clean Air Act §161

the expiration of such three-month period if such source complies with such emission limitations and compliance schedules (containing increments of progress) as may be provided by the Administrator to bring about compliance with the requirement contained in section 110(a)(2)(D)(ii) as expeditiously as practicable, but in no case later than three years after the date of such finding. Nothing in the preceding sentence shall be construed to preclude any such source from being eligible for an enforcement order under section 113(d) after the expiration of such period during which the Administrator has permitted continuous operation. . . .

PART C — PREVENTION OF SIGNIFICANT DETERIORATION OF AIR QUALITY

SUBPART 1.

Purposes

Sec. 160. The purposes of this part are as follows:

(1) to protect public health and welfare from any actual or potential adverse effect which in the Administrator's judgment may reasonably be anticipated to occur from air pollution (or from exposures to pollutants in other media, which pollutants originate as emissions to the ambient air), notwithstanding attainment and maintenance of all national ambient air quality standards;

(2) to preserve, protect, and enhance the air quality in national parks, national wilderness areas, national monuments, national seashores, and other areas of special national or regional natural recreational, scenic, or historic value;

(3) to insure that economic growth will occur in a manner consistent with the preservation of existing clean air resources;

(4) to assure that emissions from any source in any State will not interfere with any portion of the applicable implementation plan to prevent significant deterioration of air quality for any other State; and

(5) to assure that any decision to permit increased air pollution in any area to which this section applies is made only after careful evaluation of all the consequences of such a decision and after adequate procedural opportunities for informed public participation for the decisionmaking process.

Plan Requirements

Sec. 161. In accordance with the policy of section 101(b)(1), each applicable implementation plan shall contain emission limitations and such other measures as may be necessary, as determined under regulations promulgated under this part, to prevent significant deterioration of air quality in each region (or portion thereof) designated pursuant to section 107 as attainment or unclassifiable.

§162 Clean Air Act

Initial Classifications

Sec. 162. (a) Upon the enactment of this part, all —
  (1) international parks,
  (2) national wilderness areas which exceed 5,000 acres in size,
  (3) national memorial parks which exceed 5,000 acres in size, and
  (4) national parks which exceed six thousand acres in size, and which are in existence on the date of enactment of the Clean Air Act Amendments of 1977 shall be class I areas and may not be redesignated. All areas which were redesignated as class I under regulations promulgated before such date of enactment shall be class I areas which may be redesignated as provided in this part.
The extent of the areas designated as Class I under this section shall conform to any changes in the boundaries of such areas which have occurred subsequent to the date of the enactment of the Clean Air Act Amendments of 1977, or which may occur subsequent to the date of the enactment of the Clean Air Act Amendments of 1990.

  (b) All areas in such State designated pursuant to section 107(d) as attainment or unclassifiable which are not established as class I under subsection (a) shall be class II areas unless redesignated under section 164.

Increments and Ceilings

Sec. 163. (a) In the case of sulfur oxides and particulates, each applicable implementation plan shall contain measures assuring that maximum allowable increases over baseline concentrations of, and maximum allowable concentrations of, such pollutant shall not be exceeded. In the case of any maximum allowable increase (except an allowable increase specified under 165(d)(2)(C)(iv)) for a pollutant based on concentrations permitted under national ambient air quality standards for any period other than an annual period, such regulations shall permit such maximum allowable increase to be exceeded during one such period per year.

  (b)(1) For any class I area, the maximum allowable increase in concentrations of sulfur dioxide and particulate matter over the baseline concentration of such pollutants shall not exceed the following amounts:

Pollutants	Maximum allowable increase (in micrograms per cubic meter)
Particulate matter:	
Annual geometric mean	5
Twenty-four-hour maximum	10
Sulfur dioxide:	
Annual arithmetic mean	2
Twenty-four-hour maximum	5
Three-hour maximum	25

Clean Air Act §163

(2) For any class II area, the maximum allowable increase in concentrations of sulfur dioxide and particulate matter over the baseline concentration of such pollutants shall not exceed the following amounts:

Pollutants	Maximum allowable increase (in micrograms per cubic meter)
Particulate matter:	
Annual geometric mean	19
Twenty-four-hour maximum	37
Sulfur dioxide:	
Annual arithmetic mean	20
Twenty-four-hour maximum	91
Three-hour maximum	512

(3) For each class III area, the maximum allowable increase in concentrations of sulfur dioxide and particulate matter over the baseline concentration of such pollutants shall not exceed the following amounts:

Pollutants	Maximum allowable increase (in micrograms per cubic meter)
Particulate matter:	
Annual geometric mean	37
Twenty-four-hour maximum	75
Sulfur dioxide:	
Annual arithmetic mean	40
Twenty-four-hour maximum	182
Three-hour maximum	700

(4) The maximum allowable concentrations of any air pollutant in any area to which this part applies shall not exceed a concentration for such pollutant for each period of exposure equal to —

(A) the concentration permitted under the national secondary ambient air quality standards, or

(B) the concentration permitted under the national primary ambient air quality standard,

whichever concentration is lowest for such pollutant for such period of exposure.

(c)(1) In the case of any State which has a plan approved by the Administrator for purposes of carrying out this part, the Governor of such State may, after notice and opportunity for public hearing, issue orders or promulgate rules providing that for purposes of determining compliance with the maximum allowable increases in ambient concentrations of an air pollutant, the following concentrations of such pollutant shall not be taken into account:

(A) concentrations of such pollutant attributable to the increase in emissions from stationary sources which have converted from the use of petroleum products, or natural gas, or both, by reason of an order which is in effect under the provisions of section 2(a) and (b) of the Energy Supply and Environmental Coordination Act of 1974 (or any subsequent legislation which supersedes such provisions) over the emissions from such sources before the effective date of such order.

(B) the concentrations of such pollutant attributable to the increase in emissions from stationary sources which have converted from using natural gas by reason of a natural gas curtailment pursuant to a natural gas curtailment plan in effect pursuant to the Federal Power Act over the emissions from such sources before the effective date of such plan,

(C) concentrations of particulate matter attributable to the increase in emissions from construction or other temporary emission-related activities, and

(D) the increase in concentrations attributable to new sources outside the United States over the concentrations attributable to existing sources which are included in the baseline concentration determined in accordance with section 169(4).

(2) No action taken with respect to a source under paragraph (1)(A) or (1)(B) shall apply more than five years after the effective date of the order referred to in paragraphs (1)(A) or the plan referred to in paragraph (1)(B), whichever is applicable. If both such order and plan are applicable, no such action shall apply more than five years after the later of such effective dates.

(3) No action under this subsection shall take effect unless the Governor submits the order or rule providing for such exclusion to the Administrator and the Administrator determines that such order or rule is in compliance with the provisions of this subsection.

Area Redesignation

Sec. 164. (a) Except as otherwise provided under subsection (c), a State may redesignate such areas as it deems appropriate as class I areas. The following areas may be redesignated only as class I or II:

(1) an area which exceeds ten thousand acres in size and is a national monument, a national primitive area, a national preserve, a national recreation area, a national wild and scenic river, national wildlife refuge, a national lakeshore or seashore, and

(2) a national park or national wilderness area established after the date of enactment of this Act which exceeds ten thousand acres in size.

The extent of the areas referred to in paragraph (1) and (2) shall conform to any changes in the boundaries of such areas which have occurred subsequent to the date of the enactment of the Clean Air Act Amendments of 1977, or which may occur subsequent to the date of the enactment of the Clean Air Act Amendments of 1990. Any area (other than an area referred to in paragraph (1) or (2) or an area established as class I under section 162(a)) may be redesignated by the State as class III if —

Clean Air Act §164

(A) such redesignation has been specifically approved by the Governor of the State, after consultation with the appropriate Committees of the legislature if it is in session or with the leadership of the legislature if it is not in session (unless State law provides that such redesignation must be specifically approved by State legislation) and if general purpose units of local government representing a majority of the residents of the area so redesignated enact legislation (including for such units of local government resolutions where appropriate) concurring in the State's redesignation;

(B) such redesignation will not cause, or contribute to, concentrations of any air pollutant which exceed any maximum allowable increase or maximum allowable concentration permitted under the classification of any other area; and

(C) such redesignation otherwise meets the requirements of this part.

Subparagraph (A) of this paragraph shall not apply to area redesignation by Indian tribes.

(b)(1)(A) Prior to redesignation of any area under this part, notice shall be afforded and public hearings shall be conducted in areas proposed to be redesignated and in areas which may be affected by the proposed redesignation. Prior to any such public hearing a satisfactory description and analysis of the health, environmental, economic, social, and energy effects of the proposed redesignation shall be prepared and made available for public inspection and prior to any such redesignation, the description and analysis of such effects shall be reviewed and examined by the redesignating authorities.

(B) Prior to the issuance of notice under subparagraph (A) respecting the redesignation of any area under this subsection, if such area includes any Federal lands, the State shall provide written notice to the appropriate Federal land manager and afford adequate opportunity (but not in excess of 60 days) to confer with the State respecting the intended notice of redesignation and to submit written comments and recommendations with respect to such intended notice of redesignation. In redesignating any area under this section with respect to which any Federal land manager has submitted written comments and recommendations, the State shall publish a list of any inconsistency between such recommendations and an explanation of such inconsistency (together with the reasons for making such redesignation against the recommendation of the Federal land manager).

(C) The Administrator shall promulgate regulations not later than six months after date of enactment of this part, to assure, insofar as practicable, that prior to any public hearing on redesignation of any area, there shall be available for public inspection any specific plans for any new or modified major emitting facility which may be permitted to be constructed and operated only if the area in question is designated or redesignated as class III.

(2) The Administrator may disapprove the redesignation of any area only if he finds, after notice and opportunity for public hearing, that such redesignation does not meet the procedural requirements of this section or is

inconsistent with the requirements of section 162(a) or of subsection (a) of this section. If any such disapproval occurs, the classification of the area shall be that which was in effect prior to the redesignation which was disapproved. . . .

(d) The Federal Land Manager shall review all national monuments, primitive areas, and national preserves, and shall recommend any appropriate areas for redesignation as class I where air quality related values are important attributes of the area. The Federal Land Manager shall report such recommendations, with supporting analysis, to the Congress and the affected States within one year after enactment of this section. The Federal Land Manager shall consult with the appropriate States before making such recommendations. . . .

Preconstruction Requirements

Sec. 165. (a) No major emitting facility on which construction is commenced after the date of the enactment of this part may be constructed in any area to which this part applies unless —

(1) a permit has been issued for such proposed facility in accordance with this part setting forth emission limitations for such facility which conform to the requirements of this part;

(2) the proposed permit has been subject to a review in accordance with this section, the required analysis has been conducted in accordance with regulations promulgated by the Administrator, and a public hearing has been held with opportunity for interested persons including representatives of the Administrator to appear and submit written or oral presentations on the air quality impact of such source, alternatives thereto, control technology requirements, and other appropriate considerations;

(3) the owner or operator of such facility demonstrates, as required pursuant to section 110(j), that emissions from construction or operation of such facility will not cause, or contribute to, air pollution in excess of any (A) maximum allowable increase or maximum allowable concentration for any pollutant in any area to which this part applies more than one time per year, (B) national ambient air quality standard in any air quality control region, or (C) any other applicable emission standard or standard of performance under this Act;

(4) the proposed facility is subject to the best available control technology for each pollutant subject to regulation under this Act emitted from, or which results from, such facility;

(5) the provisions of subsection (d) with respect to protection of class I areas have been complied with for such facility;

(6) there has been an analysis of any air quality impacts projected for the area as a result of growth associated with such facility;

(7) the person who owns or operates, or proposes to own or operate, a major emitting facility for which a permit is required under this part agrees to conduct such monitoring as may be necessary to determine the effect which

Clean Air Act §165

emissions from any such facility may have, or is having, on air quality in any area which may be affected by emissions from such source; . . .

(d)(1) Each State shall transmit to the Administrator a copy of each permit application relating to a major emitting facility received by such State and provided notice to the Administrator of every action related to the consideration of such permit.

(2)(A) The Administrator shall provide notice of the permit application to the Federal Land Manager and the Federal official charged with direct responsibility for management of any lands within a class I area which may be affected by emissions from the proposed facility.

(B) The Federal Land Manager and the Federal official charged with direct responsibility for management of such lands shall have an affirmative responsibility to protect the air quality related values (including visibility) of such lands within a class I area and to consider, in consultation with the Administrator, whether a proposed major emitting facility will have an adverse impact on such values.

(C)(i) In any case where the Federal official charged with direct responsibility for management of any lands within a class I area or the Federal Land Manager of such lands, or the Administrator, or the Governor of an adjacent State containing such a class I area files a notice alleging that emissions from a proposed major emitting facility may cause or contribute to a change in the air quality in such area and identifying the potential adverse impact of such change, a permit shall not be issued unless the owner or operator of such facility demonstrates that emissions of particulate matter and sulfur dioxide will not cause or contribute to concentrations which exceed maximum allowable increases for a class I area.

(ii) In any case where the Federal Land Manager demonstrates to the satisfaction of the State that the emissions from such facility will have an adverse impact on the air quality-related values (including visibility) of such lands, notwithstanding the fact that the change in air quality resulting from emissions from such facility will not cause or contribute to concentrations which exceed the maximum allowable increases for a class I area, a permit shall not be issued.

(iii) In any case where the owner or operator of such facility demonstrates to the satisfaction of the Federal Land Managers, and the Federal Land Manager so certifies, that the emissions from such facility will have no adverse impact on the air quality related values of such lands (including visibility), notwithstanding the fact that the change in air quality resulting from emissions from such facility will cause or contribute to concentrations which exceed the maximum allowable increases for class I areas, the State may issue a permit.

(iv) In the case of a permit issued pursuant to clause (iii), such facility shall comply with such emission limitations under such permit as may be necessary to assure that emissions of sulfur oxides and particulates from such facility, will not cause or contribute to concentrations of such pollutant which exceed the following maximum allowable increases over the baseline concentration for such pollutants.

Pollutants	Maximum allowable increase (in micrograms per cubic meter)
Particulate matter:	
Annual geometric mean	19
Twenty-four-hour maximum	37
Sulfur dioxide:	
Annual arithmetic mean	20
Twenty-four-hour maximum	91
Three-hour maximum	325

(D)(i) In any case where the owner or operator of a proposed major emitting facility who has been denied a certification under subparagraph (C)(iii) demonstrates to the satisfaction of the Governor, after notice and public hearing, and the Governor finds, that the facility cannot be constructed by reason of any maximum allowable increase for sulfur dioxide for periods of 24 hours or less applicable to any class I area and, in the case of Federal mandatory class I areas, that a variance under this clause will not adversely affect the air quality related values of the area (including visibility), the Governor, after consideration of the federal land manager's recommendation (if any) and subject to his concurrence, may grant a variance from such maximum allowable increase. If such variance is granted, a permit may be issued to such source pursuant to the requirements of this subparagraph.

(ii) In any case in which the Governor recommends a variance under this subparagraph in which the Federal land manager does not concur, the recommendations of the Governor and the Federal land manager shall be transmitted to the President. The President may approve the Governor's recommendation if he finds that such variance is in the national interest. No Presidential finding shall be reviewable in any court. The variance shall take effect if the President approves the Governor's recommendations. The President shall approve or disapprove such recommendation within 90 days after his receipt of the recommendations of the Governor and the Federal land manager.

(iii) In the case of a permit issued pursuant to this subparagraph, such facility shall comply with such emission limitations under such permit as may be necessary to assure that emissions of sulfur oxides from such facility will not (during any day on which the otherwise applicable maximum allowable increases are exceeded) cause or contribute to concentrations which exceed the following maximum allowable increases for such areas over the baseline concentration for such pollutant and to assure that such emissions will not cause or contribute to concentrations

Clean Air Act §165

which exceed the otherwise applicable maximum allowable increases for periods of exposure of 24 hours or less on more than 18 days during any annual period:

Maximum Allowable Increase
[In micrograms per cubic meter]

Period of exposure	Low terrain areas	High terrain areas
24-hr maximum	36	62
3-hr maximum	130	221

(iv) For purposes of clause (iii), the term 'high terrain area' means with respect to any facility, any area having an elevation of 900 feet or more above the base of the stack of such facility, and the term 'low terrain area' means any area other than a high terrain area.

(e)(1) The review provided for in subsection (a) shall be preceded by an analysis in accordance with regulations of the Administrator, promulgated under this subsection, which may be conducted by the State (or any general purpose unit of local government) or by the major emitting facility applying for such permit, of the ambient air quality at the proposed site and in areas which may be affected by emissions from such facility for each pollutant subject to regulation under this Act which will be emitted from such facility.

(2) Effective one year after date of enactment of this part, the analysis required by this subsection shall include continuous air quality monitoring data gathered for purposes of determining whether emissions from such facility will exceed the maximum allowable increases or the maximum allowable concentration permitted under this part. Such data shall be gathered over a period of one calendar year preceding the date of application for a permit under this part unless the State, in accordance with regulations promulgated by the Administrator, determines that a complete and adequate analysis for such purposes may be accomplished in a shorter period. The results of such analysis shall be available at the time of the public hearing on the application for such permit.

(3) The Administrator shall within six months after the date of enactment of this part promulgate regulations respecting the analysis required under this subsection which regulations —

(A) shall not require the use of any automatic or uniform buffer zone or zones,

(B) shall require an analysis of the ambient air quality, climate and meteorology, terrain, soils and vegetation, and visibility at the site of the proposed major emitting facility and in the area potentially affected by the emissions from such facility for each pollutant regulated under this Act which will be emitted from, or which results from the construction or operation of, such facility, the size and nature of the proposed facility, the degree of continuous emission reduction which could be achieved by such facility, and such other factors as may be relevant in determining the effect of emissions from a proposed facility on any air quality control region.

(C) shall require the results of such analysis shall be available at the time of the public hearing on the application for such permit, and

(D) shall specify with reasonable particularity each air quality model or models to be used under specified sets of conditions for purposes of this part.

Any model or models designated under such regulations may be adjusted upon a determination, after notice and opportunity for public hearing, by the Administrator that such adjustment is necessary to take into account unique terrain or meteorological characteristics of an area potentially affected by emissions from a source applying for a permit required under this part.

Other Pollutants

Sec. 166. (a) In the case of the pollutants hydrocarbons, carbon monoxide, photochemical oxidants, and nitrogen oxides, the Administrator shall conduct a study and not later than two years after the date of enactment of this part, promulgate regulations to prevent the significant deterioration of air quality which would result from the emissions of such pollutants. In the case of pollutants for which national ambient air quality standards are promulgated after the date of the enactment of this part, he shall promulgate such regulations not more than 2 years after the date of promulgation of such standards.

(b) Regulations referred to in subsection (a) shall become effective one year after the date of promulgation. Within 21 months after such date of promulgation such plan revision shall be submitted to the Administrator who shall approve or disapprove the plan within 25 months after such date or promulgation in the same manner as required under section 110.

(c) Such regulations shall provide specific numerical measures against which permit applications may be evaluated, a framework for stimulating improved control technology, protection of air quality values, and fulfill the goals and purposes set forth in section 101 and section 160.

(d) The regulation of the Administrator under subsection (a) shall provide specific measures at least as effective as the increments established in section 163 to fulfill such goals and purposes, and may contain air quality increments, emission density requirements, or other measures. . . .

(f) PM-10 Increments. — The Administrator is authorized to substitute, for the maximum allowable increases in particulate matter specified in section 163(b) and section 165(d)(2)(C)(iv), maximum allowable increases in particulate matter with an aerodynamic diameter smaller than or equal to 10 micrometers. Such substituted maximum allowable increases shall be of equal stringency in effect as those specified in the provisions for which they are substituted. Until the Administrator promulgates regulations under the authority of this subsection, the current maximum allowable increases in concentrations of particulate matter shall remain in effect. . . .

Definitions

Sec. 169. For purposes of this part —

(1) The term 'major emitting facility' means any of the following stationary sources of air pollutants which emit, or have the potential to emit, one hundred tons per year or more of any air pollutant from the following types of stationary sources; fossil-fuel fired steam electric plants of more than two hundred and fifty million British thermal units per hour heat input, coal cleaning plants (thermal dryers), kraft pulp mills, Portland Cement plants, primary zinc smelters, iron and steel mill plants, primary aluminum ore reduction plants, primary copper smelters, municipal incinerators capable of charging more than fifty tons of refuse per day, hydrofluoric, sulfuric, and nitric acid plants, petroleum refineries, lime plants, phosphate rock processing plants, coke oven batteries, sulfur recovery plants, carbon black plants (furnace process), primary lead smelters, fuel conversion plants, sintering plants, secondary metal production facilities, chemical process plants, fossil-fuel boilers of more than two hundred and fifty million British thermal units per hour heat input, petroleum storage and transfer facilities with a capacity exceeding three hundred thousand barrels, taconite ore processing facilities, glass fiber processing plants, charcoal production facilities. Such term also includes any other source with the potential to emit two hundred and fifty tons per year or more of any air pollutant. This term shall not include new or modified facilities which are nonprofit health or education institutions which have been exempted by the State.

(2)(A) The term 'commenced' as applied to construction of a major emitting facility means that the owner or operator has obtained all necessary preconstruction approvals or permits required by Federal, State, or local air pollution emissions and air quality laws or regulations and either has (i) begun, or caused to begin, a continuous program of physical on-site construction of the facility or (ii) entered into binding agreements or contractual obligations, which cannot be canceled or modified without substantial loss to the owner or operator, to undertake a program of construction of the facility to be completed within a reasonable time.

(B) The term 'necessary preconstruction approvals or permits' means those permits or approvals, required by the permitting authority as a precondition to undertaking any activity under clauses (i) or (ii) of subparagraph (A) of this paragraph.

(C) the term 'construction' when used in connection with any source or facility, includes the modification (as defined in section 111(a)) of any source or facility.

(3) The term 'best available control technology' means an emission limitation based on the maximum degree of reduction of each pollutant subject to regulation under this Act emitted from or which results from any major emitting facility, which the permitting authority, on a case-by-case basis, taking into account energy, environmental, and economic impacts and other costs, determines is achievable for such facility through application of pro-

duction, processes and available methods, systems, and techniques, including fuel cleaning, clean fuels, or treatment or innovative fuel combustion techniques for control of each such pollutant. In no event shall application of 'best available control technology' result in emissions of any pollutants which will exceed the emissions allowed by any applicable standard established pursuant to section 111 or 112 of this Act. Emissions from any source utilizing clean fuels, or any other means, to comply with this paragraph shall not be allowed to increase above levels that would have been required under this paragraph as it existed prior to enactment of the Clean Air Act Amendments of 1990.

(4) The term 'baseline concentration' means, with respect to a pollutant, the ambient concentration levels which exist at the time of the first application for a permit in an area subject to this part, based on air quality data available in the Environmental Protection Agency or a State air pollution control agency and on such monitoring data as the permit applicant is required to submit. Such ambient concentration levels shall take into account all projected emissions in, or which may affect, such area from any major emitting facility on which construction commenced prior to January 6, 1975, but which has not begun operation by the date of the baseline air quality concentration determination. Emissions of sulfur oxides and particulate matter from any major emitting facility on which construction commenced after January 6, 1975, shall not be included in the baseline and shall be counted against the maximum allowable increases in pollutant concentrations established under this part.

SUBPART 2

Visibility Protection for Federal Class I Areas

Sec. 169A. (a)(1) Congress hereby declares as a national goal the prevention of any future, and the remedying of any existing, impairment of visibility in mandatory class I Federal areas which impairment results from manmade air pollution.

(2) Not later than six months after the date of the enactment of this section, the Secretary of the Interior in consultation with other Federal land managers shall review all mandatory class I Federal areas and identify those where visibility is an important value of the area. From time to time the Secretary of the Interior may revise such identification. Not later than one year after such date of enactment, the Administrator shall, after consultation with the Secretary of the Interior, promulgate a list of mandatory class I Federal areas in which he determines visibility is an important value.

(3) Not later than eighteen months after the date of enactment of this section, the Administrator shall complete a study and report to Congress on available methods for implementing the national goal set forth in paragraph (1). Such report shall include recommendations for —

(A) methods for identifying, characterizing, determining, quantifying, and measuring visibility impairment in Federal areas referred to in paragraph (1), and

(B) modeling techniques (or other methods) for determining the extent to which manmade air pollution may reasonably be anticipated to cause or contribute to such impairment, and

(C) methods for preventing and remedying such manmade air pollution and resulting visibility impairment.

Such report shall also identify the classes or categories of sources and the types of air pollutants which, alone or in conjunction with other sources or pollutants, may reasonably be anticipated to cause or contribute significantly to impairment of visibility.

(4) Not later than twenty-four months after the date of enactment of this section, and after notice and public hearing, the Administrator shall promulgate regulations to assure (A) reasonable progress toward meeting the national goal specified in paragraph (1), and (B) compliance with the requirements of this section.

(b) Regulations under subsection (a)(4) shall —

(1) provide guidelines to the States, taking into account the recommendations under subsection (a)(3) on appropriate techniques and methods for implementing this section (as provided in subparagraphs (A) through (C) of such subsection (a)(3)), and

(2) require each applicable implementation plan for a State in which any area listed by the Administrator under subsection (a)(2) is located (or for a State the emissions from which may reasonably be anticipated to cause or contribute to any impairment of visibility in any such area) to contain such emission limits, schedules of compliance and other measures as may be necessary to make reasonable progress toward meeting the national goal specified in subsection (a), including —

(A) except as otherwise provided pursuant to subsection (c), a requirement that each major stationary source which is in existence on the date of enactment of this section, but which has not been in operation for more than fifteen years as of such date, and which, as determined by the State (or the Administrator in the case of a plan promulgated under section 110(c)) emits any air pollutant which may reasonably be anticipated to cause or contribute to any impairment of visibility in any such area, shall procure, install, and operate, as expeditiously as practicable (and maintain thereafter) the best available retrofit technology, as determined by the State (or the Administrator in the case of a plan promulgated under section 110(c)) for controlling emissions from such source for the purpose of eliminating or reducing any such impairment, and

(B) a long-term (ten to fifteen years) strategy for making reasonable progress toward meeting the national goal specified in subsection (a).

In the case of a fossil-fuel fired generating powerplant having a total generating capacity in excess of 750 megawatts, the emission limitations required under this paragraph shall be determined pursuant to guidelines, promulgated by the Administrator under paragraph (1).

(c)(1) The Administrator may, by rule, after notice and opportunity for public hearing, exempt any major stationary source from the requirement of subsection (b)(2)(A), upon his determination that such source does not or will not, by itself or in combination with other sources, emit any air pollutant which may reasonably be anticipated to cause or contribute to a significant impairment of visibility in any mandatory class I Federal area.

(2) Paragraph (1) of this subsection shall not be applicable to any fossil-fuel fired powerplant with total design capacity of 750 megawatts or more, unless the owner or operator of any such plant demonstrates to the satisfaction of the Administrator that such power-plant is located at such distance from all areas listed by the Administrator under subsection (a)(2) that such power-plant does not or will not, by itself or in combination with other sources, emit any air pollutant which may reasonably be anticipated to cause or contribute to significant impairment of visibility in any such area.

(3) An exemption under this subsection shall be effective only upon concurrence by the appropriate Federal land manager or managers with the Administrator's determination under this subsection.

(d) Before holding the public hearing on the proposed revision of an applicable implementation plan to meet the requirements of this section, the State (or the Administrator, in the case of a plan promulgated under section 110(c)) shall consult in person with the appropriate Federal land manager or managers and shall include a summary of the conclusions and recommendations of the Federal land managers in the notice to the public.

(e) In promulgating regulations under this section, the Administrator shall not require the use of any automatic or uniform buffer zone or zones.

(f) For purposes of section 304(a)(2), the meeting of the national goal specified in subsection (a)(1) by any specific date or dates shall not be considered a 'nondiscretionary duty' of the Administrator.

(g) For the purpose of this section —

(1) in determining reasonable progress there shall be taken into consideration the costs of compliance, the time necessary for compliance, and the energy and non-air quality environmental impacts of compliance, and the remaining useful life of any existing source subject to such requirements;

(2) in determining best available retrofit technology the State (or the Administrator in determining emission limitations which reflect such technology) shall take into consideration the costs of compliance, the energy and non-air quality environmental impacts of compliance, any existing pollution control technology in use at the source, the remaining useful life of the source, and the degree of improvement in visibility which may reasonably be anticipated to result from the use of such technology;

(3) the term 'manmade air pollution' means air pollution which results directly or indirectly from human activities;

(4) the term 'as expeditiously as practicable' means as expeditiously as practicable but in no event later than five years after the date of approval of a plan revision under this section (or the date of promulgation of such a plan

Clean Air Act §169B

revision in the case of action by the Administrator under section 110(c) for purposes of this section);

(5) the term 'mandatory class I Federal areas' means Federal areas which may not be designated as other than class I under this part.

(6) the terms 'visibility impairment' and 'impairment of visibility' shall include reduction in visual range and atmospheric discoloration; and

(7) the term 'major stationary source' means the following types of stationary sources with the potential to emit 250 tons or more of any pollutant; fossil-fuel fired steam electric plants of more than 250 million British thermal units per hour heat input, coal cleaning plants (thermal dryers), kraft pulp mills, Portland Cement plants, primary zinc smelters, iron and steel mill plants, primary aluminum ore reduction plants, primary coppers smelters, municipal incinerators capable of charging more than 250 tons of refuse per day, hydrofluoric, sulfuric, and nitric acid plants, petroleum refineries, lime plants, phosphate rock processing plants, coke oven batteries, sulfur recovery plants, carbon black plants (furnace process), primary lead smelters, fuel conversion plants, sintering plants, secondary metal production facilities, chemical process plants, fossil-fuel boilers of more than 250 million British thermal units per hour heat input, petroleum storage and transfer facilities with a capacity exceeding 300,000 barrels, taconite ore processing facilities, glass fiber processing plants, charcoal production facilities.

Visibility

Sec. 169B. (a) Studies. — (1) The Administrator, in conjunction with the National Park Service and other appropriate Federal agencies, shall conduct research to identify and evaluate sources and source regions of both visibility impairment and regions that provide predominantly clean air in class I areas. A total of $8,000,000 per year for 5 years is authorized to be appropriated for the Environmental Protection Agency and the other Federal agencies to conduct this research. . . .

(b) Impacts of Other Provisions. — Within 24 months after enactment of the Clean Air Act Amendments of 1990, the Administrator shall conduct an assessment of the progress and improvements in visibility in class I areas that are likely to result from the implementation of the provisions of the Clean Air Act Amendments of 1990 other than the provisions of this section. Every 5 years thereafter the Administrator shall conduct an assessment of actual progress and improvement in visibility in class I areas. The Administrator shall prepare a written report on each assessment and transmit copies of these reports to the appropriate committees of Congress.

(c) Establishment of Visibility Transport Regions and Commissions. — (1) Authority to establish visibility transport regions. — Whenever, upon the Administrator's motion or by petition from the Governors of at least two affected States, the Administrator has reason to believe that the current or projected interstate transport of air pollutants from one or more States contributes significantly to visibility impairment in class I areas located in the affected States, the Administrator may establish a transport region for such pollutants that includes such States. . . .

(d) Duties of Visibility Transport Commissions. — A Visibility Transport Commission — (1) shall assess the scientific and technical data, studies, and other currently available information, including studies conducted pursuant to subsection (a)(1), pertaining to adverse impacts on visibility from potential or projected growth in emissions from sources located in the Visibility Transport Region; and

(2) shall, within 4 years of establishment, issue a report to the Administrator recommending what measures, if any, should be taken under the Clean Air Act to remedy such adverse impacts. The report required by this subsection shall address at least the following measures:

(A) the establishment of clean air corridors, in which additional restrictions on increases in emissions may be appropriate to protect visibility in affected class I areas;

(B) the imposition of the requirements of part D of this title affecting the construction of new major stationary sources or major modifications to existing sources in such clean air corridors specifically including the alternative siting analysis provisions of section 173(a)(5); and

(C) the promulgation of regulations under section 169A to address long range strategies for addressing regional haze which impairs visibility in affected class I areas.

(e) Duties of the Administrator. — (1) The Administrator shall, taking into account the studies pursuant to subsection (a)(1) and the reports pursuant to subsection (d)(2) and any other relevant information, within eighteen months of receipt of the report referred to in subsection (d)(2) of this section, carry out the Administrator's regulatory responsibilities under section 169A, including criteria for measuring 'reasonable progress' toward the national goal.

(2) Any regulations promulgated under section 169A of this title pursuant to this subsection shall require affected States to revise within 12 months their implementation plans under section 110 of this title to contain such emission limits, schedules of compliance, and other measures as may be necessary to carry out regulations promulgated pursuant to this subsection. . . .

PART D — PLAN REQUIREMENTS FOR NONATTAINMENT AREAS

SUBPART 1 — NONATTAINMENT AREAS IN GENERAL

Definitions

Sec. 171. For the purpose of this part

(1) Reasonable Further Progress. — The term 'reasonable further progress' means such annual incremental reductions in emissions of the relevant air pollutant as are required by this part or may reasonably be required by the Administrator for the purpose of ensuring attainment of the applicable national ambient air quality standard by the applicable date.

(2) Nonattainment Area. — The term 'nonattainment area' means, for any air pollutant, an area which is designated 'nonattainment' with respect to that pollutant within the meaning of section 107(d).

(3) The term 'lowest achievable emission rate' means for any source that rate of emissions which reflects —

    (A) the most stringent emission limitation which is contained in the implementation plan of any State for such class or category of source, unless the owner or operator of the proposed source demonstrates that such limitations are not achievable, or

    (B) the most stringent emission limitation which is achieved in practice by such class or category of source, whichever is more stringent.

In no event shall the application of this term permit a proposed new or modified source to emit any pollutant in excess of the amount allowable under applicable new source standards of performance.

(4) The terms 'modification' and 'modified' mean the same as the term 'modification' as used in section 111(a)(4) of this Act.

Nonattainment Plan Provisions in General

Sect. 172. (a) Classifications And Attainment Dates. — (1) Classifications. — (A) On or after the date the Administrator promulgates the designation of an area as a nonattainment area pursuant to section 107(d) with respect to any national ambient air quality standard (or any revised standard, including a revision of any standard in effect on the date of the enactment of the Clean Air Act Amendments of 1990), the Administrator may classify the area for the purpose of applying an attainment date pursuant to paragraph (2), and for other purposes. In determining the appropriate classification, if any, for a nonattainment area, the Administrator may consider such factors as the severity of nonattainment in such area and the availability and feasibility of the pollution control measures that the Administrator believes may be necessary to provide for attainment of such standard in such area.

(B) The Administrator shall publish a notice in the Federal Register announcing each classification under subparagraph (A), except the Administrator shall provide an opportunity for at least 30 days for written comment. Such classification shall not be subject to the provisions of sections 553 through 557 of title 5 of the United States Code (concerning notice and comment) and shall not be subject to judicial review until the Administrator takes final action under subsection (k) or (l) of section 110 (concerning action on plan submissions) or section 179 (concerning sanctions) with respect to any plan submissions required by virtue of such classification.

(C) This paragraph shall not apply with respect to nonattainment areas for which classifications are specifically provided under other provisions of this part.

(2) Attainment Dates for Nonattainment Areas. — (A) The attainment date for an area designated nonattainment with respect to a national primary

ambient air quality standard shall be the date by which attainment can be achieved as expeditiously as practicable, but no later than 5 years from the date such area was designated nonattainment under section 107(d), except that the Administrator may extend the attainment date to the extent the Administrator determines appropriate, for a period no greater than 10 years from the date of designation as nonattainment, considering the severity of nonattainment and the availability, and feasibility of pollution control measures.

(B) The attainment date for an area designated nonattainment with respect to a secondary national ambient air quality standard shall be the date by which attainment can be achieved as expeditiously as practicable after the date such area was designated nonattainment under section 107(d).

(C) Upon application by any State, the Administrator may extend for 1 additional year (hereinafter referred to as the 'Extension year') the attainment date determined by the Administrator under subparagraph (A) or (B) if —

(i) the State has complied with all requirements and commitments pertaining to the area in the applicable implementation plan, and

(ii) in accordance with guidance published by the Administrator, no more than a minimal number of exceedances of the relevant national ambient air quality standard has occurred in the area in the year preceding the Extension Year.

No more than 2 one-year extensions may be issued under this subparagraph for a single nonattainment area.

(D) This paragraph shall not apply with respect to nonattainment areas for which attainment dates are specifically provided under other provisions of this part.

(b) Schedule for Plan Submissions. — At the time the Administrator promulgates the designation of an area as nonattainment with respect to a national ambient air quality standard under section 107(d), the Administrator shall establish a schedule according to which the State containing such area shall submit a plan or plan revision (including the plan items) meeting the applicable requirements of subsection (c) and section 110(a)(2). Such schedule shall at a minimum, include a date or dates, extending no later than 3 years from the date of the nonattainment designation, for the submission of a plan or plan revision (including the plan items) meeting the applicable requirements of subsection (c) and section 110(a)(2).

(c) Nonattainment Plan Provisions. — The plan provisions (including plan items) required to be submitted under this part shall comply with each of the following:

(1) In General. — Such plan provisions shall provide for the implementation of all reasonably available control measures as expeditiously as practicable (including such reduction in emissions from existing sources in the area as may be obtained through the adoption, at a minimum, of reason-

Clean Air Act §172

ably available control technology) and shall provide for attainment of the national primary ambient air quality standards.

(2) RFP. — Such plan provisions shall require reasonable further progress.

(3) Inventory. — Such plan provisions shall include a comprehensive, accurate, current inventory of actual emissions from all sources of the relevant pollutant or pollutants in such area, including such periodic revisions as the Administrator may determine necessary to assure that the requirements of this part are met.

(4) Identification and Quantification. — Such plan provisions shall expressly identify and quantify the emissions, if any, of any such pollutant or pollutants which will be allowed, in accordance with section 173(a)(1)(B), from the construction and operation of major new or modified stationary sources in each such area. The plan shall demonstrate to the satisfaction of the Administrator that the emissions quantified for this purpose will be consistent with the achievement of reasonable further progress and will not interfere with attainment of the applicable national ambient air quality standard by the applicable attainment date.

(5) Permits for New and Modified Major Stationary Sources. — Such plan provisions shall require permits for the construction and operation of new or modified major stationary sources anywhere in the nonattainment area, in accordance with section 173.

(6) Other Measures. — Such plan provisions shall include enforceable emission limitations, and such other control measures, means or techniques (including economic incentives such as fees, marketable permits, and auctions of emission rights), as well as schedules and timetables for compliance, as may be necessary or appropriate to provide for attainment of such standard in such area by the applicable attainment date specified in this part.

(7) Compliance With Section 110(a)(2). — Such plan provisions shall also meet the applicable provisions of section 110(a)(2).

(8) Equivalent Techniques. — Upon application by any State, the Administrator may allow the use of equivalent modeling, emission inventory, and planning procedures, unless the Administrator determines that the proposed techniques are, in the aggregate, less effective than the methods specified by the Administrator.

(9) Contingency Measures. — Such plan shall provide for the implementation of specific measures to be undertaken if the area fails to make reasonable further progress, or to attain the national primary ambient air quality standard by the attainment date applicable under this part. Such measures shall be included in the plan revision as contingency measures to take effect in any such case without further action by the State or the Administrator.

(d) Plan Revisions Required in Response to Finding of Plan Inadequacy. — Any plan revision for a nonattainment area which is required to be submitted in response to a finding by the Administrator pursuant to section 110(k)(5) (relating to calls for plan revisions) must correct the plan deficiency (or deficiencies) specified by the Administrator and meet all other applicable plan requirements of section 110 and this part. The Administrator may reasonably adjust the dates otherwise applicable under such requirements to such revision (except for attainment dates that have not yet elapsed), to the extent necessary to achieve a consistent application of such requirements. In order to facilitate submittal by the States of adequate and approvable plans consistent with the applicable requirements of this Act, the Administrator shall, as appropriate and from time to time, issue written guidelines, interpretations, and information to the States which shall be available to the public, taking into consideration any such guidelines, interpretations, or information provided before the date of the enactment of the Clean Air Act Amendments of 1990.

(e) Future Modification of Standard. — If the Administrator relaxes a national primary ambient air quality standard after the date of the enactment of the Clean Air Act Amendments of 1990, the Administrator shall, within 12 months after the relaxation, promulgate requirements applicable to all areas which have not attained that standard as the date of such relaxation. Such requirements shall provide for controls which are not less stringent than the controls applicable to areas designated nonattainment before such relaxation.

Permit Requirements

Sec. 173. (a) In General — The permit program required by section 172(b)(6) shall provide that permits to construct and operate may be issued if —

(1) In accordance with regulations issued by the Administrator for the determination of baseline emissions in a manner consistent with the assumptions underlying the applicable implementation plan approved under section 110 and this part, the permitting agency determines that —

(A) by the time the source is to commence operation, sufficient offsetting emissions reductions have been obtained, such that total allowable emissions from existing sources in the region, from new or modified sources which are not major emitting facilities, and from the proposed source will be sufficiently less than total emissions from existing sources (as determined in accordance with the regulations under this paragraph) prior to the application for such permit to construct or modify so as to represent (when considered together with the plan provisions required under section 172) reasonable further progress (as defined in section 171); or

(B) in the case of a new or modified major stationary source which is located in a zone (within the nonattainment area) identified by the Administrator, in consultation with the Secretary of Housing and Urban Development, as a zone to which economic development should be targeted, that emissions of such pollutant resulting from the proposed new or modified major stationary source will not cause or contribute to emissions levels which exceed the allowance permitted for such pollutant for such area from new or modified major stationary sources under section 172(c);

(2) the proposed source is required to comply with the lowest achievable emission rate;

(3) the owner or operator of the proposed new or modified source has demonstrated that all major stationary sources owned or operated by such person (or by any entity controlling, controlled by, or under common control with such person) in such State are subject to emission limitations and are in compliance, or on a schedule for compliance, with all applicable emission limitations and standards under this Act; and

(4) the Administrator has not determined that the applicable implementation plan is not being adequately implemented for the nonattainment area in which the proposed source is to be constructed or modified in accordance with the requirements of this part; and

(5) an analysis of alternative sites, sizes, production processes, and environmental control techniques for such proposed source demonstrates that benefits of the proposed source significantly outweigh the environmental and social costs imposed as a result of its location, construction, or modification.

(a)[1] Any emission reductions required as a precondition of the issuance of a permit under paragraph (1) shall be federally enforceable before such permit may be issued.

(b) Prohibition on Use of Old Growth Allowances. — Any growth allowance included in an applicable implementation plan to meet the requirements of section 172(b)(5) (as in effect immediately before the date of the enactment of the Clean Air Act Amendments of 1990) shall not be valid for use in any area that received or receives a notice under section 110(a)(2)(H)(ii) (as in effect immediately before the date of the enactment of the Clean Air Act Amendments of 1990) or under section 110(k)(1) that its applicable implementation plan containing such allowance is substantially inadequate.

(c) Offsets. — (1) The owner or operator of a new or modified major stationary source may comply with any offset requirement in effect under this part for increased emissions of any air pollutant only by obtaining emission reductions of such air pollutant from the same source or other sources in the same nonattainment area, except that the State may allow the owner or operator of a source to obtain such emission reductions in another nonattainment area if (A) the other area has an equal or higher nonattainment classification than the area in which the source is located and (B) emissions from such other area contribute to a violation of the national ambient air quality standard in the nonattainment area in which the source is located. Such emission reductions shall be, by the time a new or modified source commences operation, in effect and enforceable and shall assure that the total tonnage of increased emissions of the air pollutant from the new or modified source shall be offset by an equal or greater reduction, as applicable in the actual emissions of such air pollutant from the same or other sources in the area.

(2) Emission reductions otherwise required by this Act shall not be creditable as emissions reductions for purposes of any such offset requirement. Incidental emission reductions which are not otherwise required by this Act

---

1. As in original — Ed.

shall be creditable as emission reductions for such purposes if such emission reductions meet the requirements of paragraph (1).

(d) Control Technology Information. — The State shall provide that control technology information from permits issued under this section will be promptly submitted to the Administrator for purposes of making such information available through the RACT/BACT/LAER clearinghouse to other States and to the general public. . . .

Planning Procedures

Sec. 174. (a) In General. — For any ozone, carbon monoxide, or PM-10 nonattainment area, the State containing such area and elected officials of affected local governments shall, before the date required for submittal of the inventory described under sections 182(a)(1) and 187(a)(1), jointly review and update as necessary the planning procedures adopted pursuant to this subsection as in effect immediately before the date of the enactment of the Clean Air Act Amendments of 1990, or develop new planning procedures pursuant to this subsection, as appropriate. In preparing such procedures the State and local elected officials shall determine which elements of a revised implementation plan will be developed, adopted, and implemented (through means including enforcement) by the State and which by local governments or regional agencies, or any combination of local governments, regional agencies, or the State. The implementation plan required by this part shall be prepared by an organization certified by the State, in consultation with elected officials of local governments and in accordance with the determination under the second sentence of this subsection. Such organization shall include elected officials of local governments in the affected area, and representatives of the State air quality planning agency, the State transportation planning agency, the metropolitan planning organization designated to conduct the continuing, cooperative and comprehensive transportation planning process for the area under section 134 of title 23, United States Code, the organization responsible for the air quality maintenance planning process under regulations implementing this Act, and any other organization with responsibilities for developing, submitting, or implementing the plan required by this part. Such organization may be one that carried out these functions before the date of the enactment of the Clean Air Act Amendments of 1990.

(b) Coordination. — The preparation of implementation plan provisions and subsequent plan revisions under the continuing transportation-air quality planning process described in section 108(e) shall be coordinated with the continuing, cooperative and comprehensive transportation planning process required under section 134 of title 23, United States Code, and such planning processes shall take into account the requirements of this part.

(c) Joint Planning. — In the case of a nonattainment area that is included within more than one State, the affected States may jointly, through interstate

Clean Air Act §175A

compact or otherwise, undertake and implement all or part of the planning procedures described in this section.

Environmental Protection Agency Grants

Sec. 175. (a) The Administrator shall make grants to any organization of local elected officials with transportation or air quality maintenance planning responsibilities recognized by the State under section 174(a) for payment of the reasonable costs of developing a plan revision under this part.

(b) The amount granted to any organization under subsection (a) shall be 100 percent of any additional costs of developing a plan revision under this part for the first two fiscal years following receipt of the grant under this paragraph, and shall supplement any funds available under Federal law to such organization for transportation or air quality maintenance planning. Grants under this section shall not be used for construction.

Maintenance Plans

Sec. 175A. (a) Plan Revision. — Each State which submits a request under section 107(d) for redesignation of a nonattainment area for any air pollutant as an area which has attained the national primary ambient air quality standard for that air pollutant shall also submit a revision of the applicable State implementation plan to provide for the maintenance of the national primary ambient air quality standard for such air pollutant in the area concerned for at least 10 years after the redesignation. The plan shall contain such additional measures, if any, as may be necessary to ensure such maintenance.

(b) Subsequent Plan Revisions. — 8 years after redesignation of any area as an attainment area under section 107(d), the State shall submit to the Administrator an additional revision of the applicable State implementation plan for maintaining the national primary ambient air quality standard for 10 years after the expiration of the 10-year period referred to in subsection (a).

(c) Nonattainment Requirements Applicable Pending Plan Approval. — Until such plan revision is approved and an area is redesignated as attainment for any area designated as a nonattainment area, the requirements of this part shall continue in force and effect with respect to such area.

(d) Contingency Provisions. — Each plan revision submitted under this section shall contain such contingency provisions as the Administrator deems necessary to assure that the State will promptly correct any violation of the standard which occurs after the redesignation of the area as an attainment area. Such provisions shall include a requirement that the State will implement all measures with respect to the control of the air pollutant concerned which were contained in the State implementation plan for the area before redesignation of the area as an attainment area. The failure of any area redesignated as an attainment area

§175A   Clean Air Act

to maintain the national ambient air quality standard concerned shall not result in a requirement that the State revise its State implementation plan unless the Administrator, in the Administrator's discretion, requires the State to submit a revised State implementation plan.

Limitations on Certain Federal Assistance

Sec. 176. (c)(1) No department, agency, or instrumentality of the Federal Government shall engage in, support in any way or provide financial assistance for, license or permit, or approve, any activity which does not conform to an implementation plan after it has been approved or promulgated under section 110. No metropolitan planning organization designated under section 134 of title 23, United States Code, shall give its approval to any project, program, or plan which does not conform to an implementation plan approved or promulgated under section 110. The assurance of conformity to such an implementation plan shall be an affirmative responsibility of the head of such department, agency, or instrumentality. Conformity to an implementation plan means —

    (A) conformity to an implementation plan's purpose of eliminating or reducing the severity and number of violations of the national ambient air quality standards and achieving expeditious attainment of such standards; and

    (B) that such activities will not —

        (i) cause or contribute to any new violation of any standard in any area;

        (ii) increase the frequency or severity of any existing violation of any standard in any area; or

        (iii) delay timely attainment of any standard or any required interim emission reductions or other milestones in any area. The determination of conformity shall be based on the most recent estimates of emissions, and such estimates shall be determined from the most recent population, employment, travel and congestion estimates as determined by the metropolitan planning organization or other agency authorized to make such estimates.

    (2) Any transportation plan or program developed pursuant to title 23, United States Code, or the Urban Mass Transportation Act shall implement the transportation provisions of any applicable implementation plan approved under this Act applicable to all or part of the area covered by such transportation plan or program. No Federal agency may approve, accept or fund any transportation plan, program or project unless such plan, program or project has been found to conform to any applicable implementation plan in effect under this Act. In particular —

    (A) no transportation plan or transportation improvement program may be adopted by a metropolitan planning organization designated under title 23, United States Code, or the Urban Mass Transportation Act, or be found to be in conformity by a metropolitan planning organization until a final determination has been made that emissions expected from implementation of such plans and programs are consistent with estimates of emissions from motor vehicles and necessary emissions reductions contained in the applicable implementation plan, and that the plan or program will conform to the requirements of paragraph (1)(B);

(B) no metropolitan planning organization or other recipient of funds under title 23, United States Code, or the Urban Mass Transportation Act shall adopt or approve a transportation improvement program of projects until it determines that such program provides for timely implementation of transportation control measures consistent with schedules included in the applicable implementation plan;

(C) a transportation project may be adopted or approved by a metropolitan planning organization or any recipient of funds designated under title 23, United States Code, or the Urban Mass Transportation Act, or found in conformity by a metropolitan planning organization or approved, accepted, or funded by the Department of Transportation only if it meets either the requirements of subparagraph (D) or the following requirements —

(i) such a project comes from a conforming plan and program;

(ii) the design concept and scope of such project have not changed significantly since the conformity finding regarding the plan and program from which the project derived; and

(iii) the design concept and scope of such project at the time of the conformity determination for the program was adequate to determine emissions.

(D) Any project not referred to in subparagraph (C) shall be treated as conforming to the applicable implementation plan only if it is demonstrated that the projected emissions from such project, when considered together with emissions projected for the conforming transportation plans and programs within the nonattainment area, do not cause such plans and programs to exceed the emission reduction projections and schedules assigned to such plans and programs in the applicable implementation plan.

(3) Until such time as the implementation plan revision referred to in paragraph (4)(C) is approved, conformity of such plans, programs, and projects will be demonstrated if —

(A) the transportation plans and programs —

(i) are consistent with the most recent estimates of mobile source emissions;

(ii) provide for the expeditious implementation of transportation control measures in the applicable implementation plan; and

(iii) with respect to ozone and carbon monoxide nonattainment areas, contribute to annual emissions reductions consistent with sections 182(b)(1) and 187(a)(7); and

(B) the transportation projects —

§176   Clean Air Act

          (i) come from a conforming transportation plan and program as defined in subparagraph (A) or for 12 months after the date of the enactment of the Clean Air Act Amendments of 1990, from a transportation program found to conform within 3 years prior to such date of enactment; and

          (ii) in carbon monoxide nonattainment areas, eliminate or reduce the severity and number of violations of the carbon monoxide standards in the area substantially affected by the project.

With regard to subparagraph (B)(ii), such determination may be made as part of either the conformity determination for the transportation program or for the individual project taken as a whole during the environmental review phase of project development.

    (4)(A) No later than one year after the date of enactment of the Clean Air Act Amendments of 1990, the Administrator shall promulgate criteria and procedures for determining conformity (except in the case of transportation plans, programs, and projects) of, and for keeping the Administrator informed about, the activities referred to in paragraph (1). No later than one year after such date of enactment, the Administrator, with the concurrence of the Secretary of Transportation, shall promulgate criteria and procedures for demonstrating and assuring conformity in the case of transportation plans, programs, and projects. A suit may be brought against the Administrator and the Secretary of Transportation under section 304 to compel promulgation of such criteria and procedures and the Federal district court shall have jurisdiction to order such promulgation.

    (B) The procedures and criteria shall, at a minimum —

          (i) address the consultation procedures to be undertaken by metropolitan planning organizations and the Secretary of Transportation with State and local air quality agencies and State departments of transportation before such organizations and the Secretary make conformity determinations;

          (ii) address the appropriate frequency for making conformity determinations, but in no case shall such determinations for transportation plans and programs be less frequent than every three years; and

          (iii) address how conformity determinations will be made with respect to maintenance plans.

    (C) Such procedures shall also include a requirement that each State shall submit to the Administrator and the Secretary of Transportation within 24 months of such date of enactment, a revision to its implementation plan that includes criteria and procedures for assessing the conformity of any plan, program, or project subject to the conformity requirements of this subsection.

    (d) Each department, agency, or instrumentality of the Federal Government having authority to conduct or support any program with air-quality related transportation consequences shall give priority in the exercise of such authority, consistent with statutory requirements for allocation among States or other jurisdictions, to the implementation of those portions of plans prepared under this

Clean Air Act

section to achieve and maintain the national primary ambient air quality standards. This paragraph extends to, but is not limited to, authority exercised under the Urban Mass Transportation Act, title 23 of the United States Code, and the Housing and Urban Development Act.

Interstate Transport Commissions

Sec. 176A. (a) Authority to Establish Interstate Transport Regions. — Whenever, on the Administrator's own motion or by petition from the Governor of any State, the Administrator has reason to believe that the interstate transport of air pollutants from one or more States contributed significantly to a violation of a national ambient air quality standard in one or more other States, the Administrator may establish, by rule, a transport region for such pollutant that includes such States. . . .

(2) Recommendations. — The transport commission shall assess the degree of interstate transport of the pollutant or precursors to the pollutant throughout the transport region, assess strategies for mitigating the interstate pollution, and recommend to the Administrator such measures as the Commission determines to be necessary to ensure that the plans for the relevant States meet the requirements of section 110(a)(2)(D). . . .

(c) Commission Requests. — A transport commission established under subsection (b) may request the Administrator to issue a finding under section 110(k)(5) that the implementation plan for one or more of the States in the transport region is substantially inadequate to meet the requirements of section 110(a)(2)(D). The Administrator shall approve, disapprove, or partially approve and partially disapprove such a request within 18 months of its receipt and, to the extent the Administrator approves such request, issue the finding under section 110(k)(5) at the time of such approval. In acting on such request, the Administrator shall provide an opportunity for public participation and shall address each specific recommendation made by the commission. Approval or disapproval of such a request shall constitute final agency action within the meaning of section 307(b).

New Motor Vehicle Emission Standards in Nonattainment Areas

Sec. 177. Notwithstanding section 209(a), any State which has plan provisions approved under this part may adopt and enforce for any model year standards relating to control of emissions from new motor vehicles or new motor vehicle engines and take such other actions as are referred to in section 209(a) respecting such vehicles if —

(1) such standards are identical to the California standards for which a waiver has been granted for such model year, and

(2) California and such State adopt such standards at least two years before commencement of such model year (as determined by regulations of the Administrator).

Nothing in this section or in title II of this Act shall be construed as authorizing any such State to prohibit or limit, directly or indirectly, the manufacture or sale of a new motor vehicle or motor vehicle engine that is certified in California as meeting California standards, or to take any action of any kind to create, or have the effect of creating, a motor vehicle or motor vehicle engine different than a motor vehicle or engine certified in California under California standards (a 'third vehicle') or otherwise create such a 'third vehicle.'

Guidance Documents

Sec. 178. The Administrator shall issue guidance documents under section 108 for purposes of assisting States in implementing requirements of this part respecting the lowest achievable emission rate. Such a document shall be published not later than nine months after the date of enactment of this part and shall be revised at least every two years thereafter.

Sanctions and Consequences of Failure to Attain

Sec. 179. (a) State Failure. — For any implementation plan or plan revision required under this part (or required in response to a finding of substantial inadequacy as described in section 110(k)(5)), if the Administrator —

(1) finds that a State has failed, for an area designated nonattainment under section 107(d), to submit a plan, or to submit 1 or more of the elements (as determined by the Administrator) required by the provisions of this Act applicable to such an area, or has failed to make a submission for such an area that satisfies the minimum criteria established in relation to any such element under section 110(k).

(2) disapproves a submission under section 110(k), for an area designated nonattainment under section 107, based on the submission's failure to meet one or more of the elements required by the provisions of this Act applicable to such an area.

(3)(A) determines that a State has failed to make any submission as may be required under this Act, other than one described under paragraph (1) or (2), including an adequate maintenance plan, or has failed to make any submission, as may be required under this Act, other than one described under paragraph (1) or (2), that satisfies the minimum criteria established in relation to such submission under section 110(k)(1)(A), or

(B) disapproves in whole or in part a submission described under subparagraph (A), or

(4) finds that any requirement of an approved plan (or approved part of a plan) is not being implemented, unless such deficiency has been corrected within 18 months after the finding, disapproval, or determination referred to in paragraphs (1), (2), (3), and (4), one of the sanctions referred to in subsection (b) shall apply, as selected by the Administrator, until the Administrator determines that the State has come into compliance, except that if the Administrator finds a lack of good faith, sanctions under both paragraph (1) and

paragraph (2) or subsection (b) shall apply until the Administrator determines that the State has come into compliance. If the Administrator has selected one of such sanctions and the deficiency has not been corrected within 6 months thereafter, sanctions under both paragraph (1) and paragraph (2) of subsection (b) shall apply until the Administrator determines that the State has come into compliance. In addition to any other sanction applicable as provided in this section, the Administrator may withhold all or part of the grants for support of air pollution planning and control programs that the Administrator may award under section 105.

(b) Sanctions. — The sanctions available to the Administrator as provided in subsection (a) are as follows:

(1) Highway Sanctions. — (A) The Administrator may impose a prohibition, applicable to a nonattainment area, on the approval by the Secretary of Transportation of any projects or the awarding by the Secretary of any grants, under title 23, United States Code, other than projects or grants for safety where the Secretary determines, based on accident or other appropriate data submitted by the State, that the principal purpose of the project is an improvement in safety to resolve a demonstrated safety problem and likely will result in a significant reduction in, or avoidance of, accidents. Such prohibition shall become effective upon the selection by the Administrator of this sanction.

(B) In addition to safety, projects or grants that may be approved by the Secretary, notwithstanding the prohibition in subparagraph (A), are the following —

(i) capital programs for public transit;

(ii) construction or restriction of certain roads or lanes solely for the use of passenger buses or high occupancy vehicles;

(iii) planning for requirements for employers to reduce employee work-trip-related vehicle emissions;

(iv) highway ramp metering, traffic signalization, and related programs that improve traffic flow and achieve a net emission reduction;

(v) fringe and transportation corridor parking facilities serving multiple occupancy vehicle program or transit operations;

(vi) programs to limit or restrict vehicle use in downtown areas or other areas of emission concentration particularly during periods of peak use, through road use charges, tolls, parking surcharges, or other pricing mechanisms, vehicle restricted zones or periods, or vehicle registration programs;

(vii) programs for breakdown and accident scene management, nonrecurring congestion, and vehicle information systems, to reduce congestion and emissions; and

(viii) such other transportation-related programs as the Administrator, in consultation with the Secretary of Transportation, finds would improve air quality and would not encourage single occupancy vehicle capacity.

In considering such measures, the State should seek to ensure adequate access to downtown, other commercial, and residential areas, and avoid increasing or relocating emissions and congestion rather than reducing them.

(2) Offsets. — In applying the emissions offset requirements of section 173 to new or modified sources or emissions units for which a permit is required under part D, the ratio of emission reductions to increased emissions shall be at least 2 to 1.

(c) Notice of Failure to Attain. — (1) As expeditiously as practicable after the applicable attainment date for any nonattainment area, but not later than 6 months after such date, the Administrator shall determine, based on the area's air quality as of the attainment date, whether the area attained the standard by that date.

(2) Upon making the determination under paragraph (1), the Administrator shall publish a notice in the Federal Register containing such determination and identifying each area that the Administrator has determined to have failed to attain. The Administrator may revise or supplement such determination at any time based on more complete information or analysis concerning the area's air quality as of the attainment date.

(d) Consequences for Failure to Attain. — (1) Within 1 year after the Administrator publishes the notice under subsection (c)(2) (relating to notice of failure to attain), each State containing a nonattainment area shall submit a revision to the applicable implementation plan meeting the requirements of paragraph (2) of this subsection.

(2) The revision required under paragraph (1) shall meet the requirements of section 110 and section 172. In addition, the revision shall include such additional measures as the Administrator may reasonably prescribe, including all measures that can be feasibly implemented in the area in light of technological achievability, costs, and any nonair quality and other air quality-related health and environmental impacts.

SUBPART 2 — ADDITIONAL PROVISIONS FOR OZONE NONATTAINMENT AREAS.

Classification and Attainment Dates

Sec. 181. (a) Classification and Attainment Dates for 1989 Nonattainment Areas. — (1) Each area designated nonattainment for ozone pursuant to section 107(d) shall be classified at the time of such designation under table 1, by operation of law, as a Marginal Area, a Moderate Area, a Serious Area, a Severe Area, or an Extreme Area based on the design value for the area. The design value shall be calculated according to the interpretation methodology issued by the Administrator most recently before the date of the enactment of the Clean Air Act Amendments of 1990. For each area classified under this subsection, the primary standard attainment date for ozone shall be as expeditiously as practicable but not later than the date provided in table 1. . . .

TABLE 1

Area class	Design value*	Primary standard attainment date**
Marginal	0.121 up to 0.138	3 years after enactment
Moderate	0.138 up to 0.160	6 years after enactment
Serious	0.160 up to 0.180	9 years after enactment
Severe	0.180 up to 0.280	15 years after enactment
Extreme	0.280 and above	20 years after enactment

*The design value is measured in parts per million (ppm).
**The primary standard attainment date is measured from the date of the enactment of the Clean Air Amendments of 1990.

[The requirements for non-attainment plans contained in §§182-192 are omitted.]

Title II — Emission Standards for Moving Sources

Short Title

Sec. 201. This part may be cited as the 'National Emission Standards Act.'

PART A — MOTOR VEHICLE EMISSION AND FUEL STANDARDS

Establishment of Standards

Sec. 202. (a) Except as otherwise provided in subsection (b) —
(1) The Administration shall by regulation prescribe (and from time to time revise) in accordance with the provisions of this section, standards applicable to the emission of any air pollution from any class or classes of new motor vehicles or new motor vehicle engines, which in his judgment cause or contribute to, air pollution which may reasonably be anticipated to endanger public health or welfare. Such standards shall be applicable to such vehicles and engines for their useful life (as determined under subsection (d), relating to useful life of vehicles for purposes of certification), whether such vehicles and engines are designed as complete systems or incorporate devices to prevent or control such pollution.

(2) Any regulation prescribed under paragraph (1) of this subsection (and any revision thereof) shall take effect after such period as the Administrator finds necessary to permit the development and application of the requisite technology, giving appropriate consideration to the cost of compliance within such period.

Emission Standards for Heavy Duty Vehicles or Engines and Certain Other Vehicles or Engines

(3)(A) In General. — (i) Unless the standard is changed as provided in subparagraph (B), regulations under paragraph (1) of this subsection applicable to emissions of hydrocarbons, carbon monoxide, oxides of nitrogen, and particulate matter from classes or categories of heavy-duty vehicles or engines manufactured during or after model year 1983 shall contain standards which reflect the greatest degree of emission reduction achievable through the application of technology which the Administrator determines will be available for the model year to which such standards apply, giving appropriate consideration to cost, energy, and safety factors associated with the application of such technology.

>(ii) In establishing classes or categories of vehicles or engines for purposes of regulations under this paragraph, the Administrator may base such classes or categories on gross vehicle weight, horsepower, type of fuel used, or other appropriate factors.

(B) Revised Standards for Heavy Duty Trucks. — (i) On the basis of information available to the Administrator concerning the effects of air pollutants emitted from heavy-duty vehicles or engines and from other sources of mobile source related pollutants on the public health and welfare, and taking costs into account, the Administrator may promulgate regulations under paragraph (1) of this subsection revising any standard promulgated under, or before the date of, the enactment of the Clean Air Act Amendments of 1990 (or previously revised under this subparagraph) and applicable to classes or categories of heavy-duty vehicles or engines.

(ii) Effective for the model year 1998 and thereafter, the regulations under paragraph (1) of this subsection applicable to emissions of oxides of nitrogen (NO_x) from gasoline and diesel-fueled heavy duty trucks shall contain standards which provide that such emissions may not exceed 4.0 grams per brake horsepower hour (gbh).

(C) Lead Time and Stability. — Any standard promulgated or revised under this paragraph and applicable to classes or categories of heavy-duty vehicles or engines shall apply for a period of no less than 3 model years beginning no earlier than the model year commencing 4 years after such revised standard is promulgated. . . .

Onboard Hydrocarbon Technology

(6) Onboard Vapor Recovery. — Within 1 year after the date of the enactment of the Clean Air Act Amendments of 1990, the Administrator shall, after consultation with the Secretary of Transportation regarding the safety of vehicle-based ('on-board') systems for the control of vehicle refueling emissions, promulgate standards under this section requiring that new light-duty vehicles manufactured beginning in the fourth model year after the model year in which the standards are promulgated and thereafter shall be equipped with such systems. The standards required under this paragraph shall apply to a percentage of each manufacturer's fleet of new light-duty vehicles beginning with the fourth model year after the model year in which the standards are promulgated. The percentage shall be as specified in the following table: . . .

Clean Air Act §202

Implementation Schedule for Onboard Vapor Recovery Requirements

Model year commencing after standards promulgated	Percentage*
Fourth	40
Fifth	80
After Fifth	100

*Percentages in the table refer to a percentage of the manufacturer's sales volume.

Emission Standards for Conventional Motor Vehicles

(g) Light-Duty Trucks up to 6,000 lbs. GVWR and Light-Duty Vehicles; Standards for Model Years After 1993. —

(1) NMHC, CO, and NO_x. — Effective with respect to the model year 1994 and thereafter, the regulations under subsection (a) applicable to emissions of nonmethane hydrocarbons (NMHC), carbon monoxide (CO), and oxides of nitrogen (NO_x) from light-duty trucks (LDTs) of up to 6,000 lbs. gross vehicle weight rating (GVWR) and light-duty vehicles (LDVs) shall contain standards which provide that emissions from a percentage of each manufacturer's sales volume of such vehicles and trucks shall comply with the levels specified in table G. The percentage shall be as specified in the implementation schedule below:

TABLE G

Emission Standards for NMHC, CO, and NO_x from Light-Duty Trucks of Up to 6,000 Lbs. GVWR and Light-Duty Vehicles

Vehicle type	Column A (5 yrs/50,000 mi) NMHC	CO	NO_x	Column B (10 yrs/100,000 mi) NMHC	CO	NO_x
LDTs (0-3,750 lbs. LVW) and light-duty vehicles	0.25	3.4	0.4*	0.31	4.2	0.6*
LDTs (3,751-5,750 lbs. LVW)	0.32	4.4	0.7**	0.40	5.5	0.97

Standards are expressed in grams per mile (gpm).
For standards under column A, for purposes of certification under section 206, the applicable useful life shall be 5 years or 50,000 miles (or the equivalent), whichever first occurs.
For standards under column B, for purposes of certification under section 206, the applicable useful life shall be 10 years or 100,000 miles (or the equivalent), whichever first occurs.
*In the case of diesel-fueled LDTs (0-3,750 lvw) and light-duty vehicles, before the model year 2004, in lieu of the 0.4 and 0.6 standards for NO_x, the applicable standards for NO_x shall be 1.0 gpm for a useful life of 5 years or 50,000 miles (or the equivalent), whichever first occurs, and 1.25 gpm for a useful life of 10 years or 100,000 miles (or the equivalent) whichever first occurs.
**This standard does not apply to diesel-fueled LDTs (3,751-5,750 lbs. LVW).

Implementation Schedule for Table G Standards

Model year	Percentage*
1994	40
1995	80
after 1995	100

*Percentages in the table refer to a percentage of each manufacturer's sales volume.

(2) PM Standard. — Effective with respect to model year 1994 and thereafter in the case of light-duty vehicles and effective with respect to the model year 1993 and thereafter in the case of light-duty trucks (LDTs) of up to 6,000 lbs. gross vehicle weight rating (GVWR), the regulations under subsection (a) applicable to emissions of particulate matter (PM) from such vehicles and trucks shall contain standards which provide that such emissions from a percentage of each manufacturer's sales volume of such vehicles and trucks shall not exceed the levels specified in the table below. The percentage shall be as specified in the Implementation Schedule below. . . .

PM Standard for LDTs of up to 6,000 Lbs. GVWR

Useful life period	Standard
5/50,000	0.08 gpm
10/100,000	0.10 gpm

The applicable useful life, for purposes of certification under section 206 and for purposes of in-use compliance under section 207, shall be 5 years or 50,000 miles (or the equivalent), whichever first occurs, in the case of the 5/50,000 standard.

The applicable useful life, for purposes of certification under section 206 and for purposes of in-use compliance under section 207, shall be 10 years or 100,000 miles (or the equivalent), whichever first occurs in the case of the 10/100,000 standard.

Implementation Schedule for PM Standards

Model year	Light-duty vehicles	LDTs
1994	40%*	—
1995	80%*	40%*
1996	100%*	80%*
after 1996	100%*	100%*

*Percentages in the table refer to a percentage of each manufacturer's sales volume.

(i) Phase II Study for Certain Light-Duty Vehicles and Light-Duty Trucks. — (1) The Administrator, with the participation of the Office of Technology Assessment, shall study whether or not further reductions in emissions from light-duty vehicles and light-duty trucks should be required pursuant to this title. The study shall consider whether to establish with respect to model years commencing after January 1, 2003, the standards and useful life period for gasoline and diesel-fueled light-duty vehicles and light-duty trucks with a loaded vehicle weight (LVW) of 3,750 lbs. or less specified in the following table:

TABLE 3
Pending Emission Standards for Gasoline and Diesel Fueled Light-Duty Vehicles and Light-Duty Trucks 3,750 Lbs. LVW or Less

Pollutant	*Emission level**
NMHC	0.125 GPM
NO_x	0.2 GPM
CO	1.7 GPM

*Emission levels are expressed in grams per mile (GPM). For vehicles and engines subject to this subsection for purposes of section 202(d) and any reference thereto, the useful life of such vehicles and engines shall be a period of 10 years or 100,000 miles (or the equivalent), whichever first occurs.

Such study shall also consider other standards and useful life periods which are more stringent or less stringent than those set forth in table 3 (but more stringent than those referred to in subsections (g) and (h)).

(2)(A) As part of the study under paragraph (1), the Administrator shall examine the need for further reductions in emissions in order to attain or maintain the national ambient air quality standards, taking into consideration the waiver provisions of section 209(b). As part of such study, the Administrator shall also examine —

(i) the availability of technology (including the costs thereof), in the case of light-duty vehicles and light-duty trucks with a loaded vehicle weight (LVW) of 3,750 lbs. or less, for meeting more stringent emission standards than those provided in subsections (g) and (h) for model years commencing not earlier than after January 1, 2003, and not later than model year 2006, including the lead time and safety and energy impacts of meeting more stringent emission standards; and

(ii) the need for, and cost effectiveness of, obtaining further reductions in emissions from such light-duty vehicles and light-duty trucks, taking into consideration alternative means of attaining or maintaining the national primary ambient air quality standards pursuant to State implementation plans and other requirements of this Act, including their feasibility and cost effectiveness.

(B) The Administrator shall submit a report to Congress no later than June 1, 1997, containing the results of the study under this subsection, including the results of the examination conducted under subparagraph (A). Before submittal of such report the Administrator shall provide a reasonable opportunity for public comment and shall include a summary of such comments in the report to Congress.

(3)(A) Based on the study under paragraph (1) the Administrator shall determine, by rule, within 3 calendar years after the report is submitted to Congress, but not later than December 31, 1999, whether —

(i) there is a need for further reductions in emissions as provided in paragraph (2)(A);

(ii) the technology for meeting more stringent emission standards will be available, as provided in paragraph (2)(A)(i), in the case of light-duty vehicles and light-duty trucks with a loaded vehicle weight (LVW) of 3,750 lbs. or less, for model years commencing not earlier than January 1, 2003, and not later than model year 2006, considering the factors listed in paragraph (2)(A)(i); and

(iii) obtaining further reductions in emissions from such vehicles will be needed and cost effective, taking into consideration alternatives as provided in paragraph (2)(A)(ii).

The rulemaking under this paragraph shall commence within 3 months after submission of the report to Congress under paragraph (2)(B).

(B) If the Administrator determines under subparagraph (A) that —

(i) there is no need for further reductions in emissions as provided in paragraph (2)(A);

(ii) the technology for meeting more stringent emission standards will not be available as provided in paragraph (2)(A)(i), in the case of light-duty vehicles and light-duty trucks with a loaded vehicle weight (LVW) of 3,750 lbs. or less, for model years commencing not earlier than January 1, 2003, and not later than model year 2006, considering the factors listed in paragraph (2)(A)(i); or

(iii) obtaining further reductions in emissions from such vehicles will not be needed or cost effective, taking into consideration alternatives as provided in paragraph (2)(A)(ii),

the Administrator shall not promulgate more stringent standards than those in effect pursuant to subsections (g) and (h). Nothing in this paragraph shall prohibit the Administrator from exercising the Administrator's authority under subsection (a) to promulgate more stringent standards for light-duty vehicles and light-duty trucks with a loaded vehicle weight (LVW) of 3,750 lbs. or less at any other time thereafter in accordance with subsection (a).

(C) If the Administrator determines under subparagraph (A) that —

(i) there is need for further reductions in emissions as provided in paragraph (2)(A);

(ii) the technology for meeting more stringent emission standards will be available, as provided in paragraph (2)(A)(i), in the case of light-duty vehicles and light-duty trucks with a loaded vehicle weight (LVW) of 3,750 lbs. or less, for model years commencing not earlier than January 1, 2003, and not later than model year 2006, considering the factors listed in paragraph (2)(A)(i); and

(iii) obtaining further reductions in emissions from such vehicles will be needed and cost effective, taking into consideration alternatives as provided in paragraph (2)(A)(ii), the Administrator shall either promulgate the standards (and useful life periods) set forth in Table 3 in paragraph (1) or promulgate alternative standards (and useful life periods) which are more stringent than those referred to in subsections (g) and (h). Any such standards (or useful life periods) promulgated by the Administrator shall take effect with respect to any such vehicles or engines no earlier than the model year 2003 but not later than model year 2006, as determined by the Administrator in the rule.

(D) Nothing in this paragraph shall be construed by the Administrator or by a court as a presumption that any standards (or useful life period) set forth in Table 3 shall be promulgated in the rule-making required under this paragraph. The action required of the Administrator in accordance with this paragraph shall be treated as a nondiscretionary duty for purposes of section 304(a)(2) (relating to citizen suits).

(E) Unless the Administrator determines not to promulgate more stringent standards as provided in subparagraph (B) or to postpone the effective date of standards referred to in Table 3 in paragraph (1) or to establish alternative standards as provided in subparagraph (C), effective with respect to model years commencing after January 1, 2003, the regulations under subsection (a) applicable to emissions of nonmethane hydrocarbons (NMHC), oxides of nitrogen (NO_x), and carbon monoxide (CO) from motor vehicles and motor vehicle engines in the classes specified in Table 3 in paragraph (1) above shall contain standards which provide that emissions may not exceed the pending emission level specified in Table 3 in paragraph (1). . . .

Regulations of Fuels

Sec. 211. . . .
(A) to conduct tests to determine potential public health effects of such fuel or additive (including, but not limited to, carcinogenic, teratogenic, or mutagenic effects), and

(B) to furnish the description of any analytical technique that can be used to detect and measure any additive in such fuel, the recommended range of concentration of such additive, and the recommended purpose-in-use of such additive, and such other information as is reasonable and necessary to determine the emissions resulting from the use of the fuel or additive contained in such fuel, the effect of such fuel or additive on the emission control performance of any vehicle, vehicle engine, nonroad engine or nonroad vehicle, or the extent to which such emissions affect the public health or welfare.

Tests under subparagraph (A) shall be conducted in conformity with test procedures and protocols established by the Administrator. The result of such tests shall not be considered confidential.

(3) Upon compliance with the provision of this subsection, including

assurances that the Administrator will receive changes in the information required, the Administrator shall register such fuel or fuel additive.

(c)(1) The Administrator may, from time to time on the basis of information obtained under subsection (b) of this section or other information available to him, by regulation, control or prohibit the manufacture, introduction into commerce, offering for sale, or sale of any fuel additive for use in a motor vehicle, motor vehicle engine, or nonroad engine or nonroad vehicle (A) if in the judgment of the Administrator any emission product of such fuel or fuel additives causes, or contributes to, air pollution which may reasonably be anticipated to endanger the public health or welfare, or (B) if emission products of such fuel or fuel additive will impair to a significant degree the performance of any emission control device or system which is in general use, or which the Administrator finds has been developed to a point where in a reasonable time it would be in general use were such regulation to be promulgated.

(2)(A) No fuel, class of fuels, or fuel additive may be controlled or prohibited by the Administrator pursuant to clause (A) of paragraph (1) except after consideration of all relevant medical and scientific evidence available to him, including consideration of other technologically or economically feasible means of achieving emission standards under section 202.

(B) No fuel or fuel additive may be controlled or prohibited by the Administrator pursuant to clause (B) of paragraph (1) except after consideration of available scientific and economic data, including a cost benefit analysis comparing emission control devices or systems which are or will be in general use and require the proposed control or prohibition with emission control devices or systems which are or will be in general use and do not require the proposed control or prohibition. On request of a manufacturer of motor vehicles, motor vehicle engines, fuels, or fuel additives submitted within 10 days of notice of proposed rulemaking, the Administrator shall hold a public hearing and publish his findings with respect to any matter he is required to consider under this subparagraph. Such findings shall be published at the time of promulgation of final regulations.

(C) No fuel or fuel additive may be prohibited by the Administrator under paragraph (1) unless he finds, and publishes such findings, that in his judgment such prohibition will not cause the use of any other fuel or fuel additive which will produce emissions which will endanger the public health or welfare to the same or greater degree than the use of the fuel or fuel additive proposed to be prohibited. . . .

Title III — General

Administration

Sec. 301. (a)(1) The Administrator is authorized to prescribe such regulations as are necessary to carry out his functions under this Act. The Administra-

Clean Air Act §302

tor may delegate to any officer or employee of the Environmental Protection Agency such of his powers and duties under this Act, except the making of regulations subject to section 307(d), as he may deem necessary or expedient.

Definitions

Sec. 302. When used in this Act —

(a) The term 'Administrator' means the Administrator of the Environmental Protection Agency. . . .

(g) The term 'air pollutant' means any air pollution agent or combination of such agents, including any physical, chemical, biological, radioactive (including source material, special nuclear material, and by-product material) substance or matter which is emitted into or otherwise enters the ambient air. Such term includes any precursors to the formation of any air pollutant, to the extent the Administrator has identified such precursor or precursors for the particular purpose for which the term 'air pollutant' is used.

(h) All language referring to effects on welfare includes, but is not limited to, effects on soils, water, crops, vegetation, manmade materials, animals, wildlife, weather, visibility, and climate, damage to and deterioration of property, and hazards to transportation, as well as effects on economic values and on personal comfort and well-being, whether caused by transformation, conversion, or combination with other air pollutants.

(i) The term 'Federal land manager' means with respect to any lands in the United States the Secretary of the department with authority over such lands.

(j) Except as otherwise expressly provided, the terms 'major stationary source' and 'major emitting facility' mean any stationary facility or source of air pollutants which directly emits, or has the potential to emit, one hundred tons per year or more of any air pollutant (including any major emitting facility or source of fugitive emissions of any such pollutant, as determined by rule by the Administrator).

(k) The terms 'emission limitation' and 'emission standard' mean a requirement established by the State or the Administrator which limits the quantity, rate, or concentration of emissions of air pollutants on a continuous basis including any requirement relating to the operation or maintenance of a source to assure continuous emission reduction, and any design, equipment, work practice or operational standard promulgated under this Act.

(l) The term 'standard of performance' means a requirement of continuous emission reduction, including any requirement relating to the operation or maintenance of a source to assure continuous emission reduction.

(m) The term 'means of emission limitation' means a system of continuous emission reduction (including the use of specific technology or fuels with specified pollution characteristics).

(n) The term 'primary standard attainment date' means the date specified in the applicable implementation plan for the attainment of a national primary ambient air quality standard for any air pollutant.

(o) The term 'delayed compliance order' means an order issued by the State

§302 Clean Air Act

or by the Administrator to an existing stationary source, postponing the date required under an applicable implementation plan for compliance by such source with any requirement of such plan.

(p) The term 'schedule and timetable of compliance' means a schedule of remedial measures including an enforceable sequence of actions or operations leading to compliance with an emission limitation, other limitation, prohibition, or standard.

(q) For purposes of this Act, the term 'applicable implementation plan' means the portion (or portions) of the implementation plan, or most recent revision thereof, which has been approved under section 110, or promulgated under section 110(c), or promulgated or approved pursuant to regulations promulgated under section 301(d) and which implements the relevant requirements of this Act. . . .

(s) VOC. — The term 'VOC' means volatile organic compound, as defined by the Administrator.

(t) PM-10. — The term 'PM-10' means particulate matter with an aerodynamic diameter less than or equal to a nominal ten micrometers, as measured by such method as the Administrator may determine.

(u) NAAQS And CTG. — The term 'NAAQS' means national ambient air quality standard. The term 'CTG' means a Control Technique Guideline published by the Administrator under section 108.

(v) NO_x. — The term 'NO_x' means oxides of nitrogen.

(w) CO. — The term 'CO' means carbon monoxide.

(x) Small Source. — The term 'small source' means a source that emits less than 100 tons of regulated pollutants per year, or any class of persons that the Administrator determines, through regulation, generally lack technical ability or knowledge regarding control of air pollution.

(y) Federal Implementation Plan. — The term 'Federal implementation plan' means a plan (or portion thereof) promulgated by the Administrator to fill all or a portion of a gap or otherwise correct all or a portion of an inadequacy in a State implementation plan, and which includes enforceable emission limitations or other control measures, means or techniques (including economic incentives, such as marketable permits or auctions of emissions allowances), and provides for attainment of the relevant national ambient air quality standard.

(z) Stationary Source. — The term 'stationary source' means generally any source of an air pollutant except those emissions resulting directly from an internal combustion engine for transportation purposes or from a nonroad engine or nonroad vehicle as defined in section 216. . . .

Citizen Suits

Sec. 304. (a) Except as provided in subsection (b), any person may commence a civil action on his own behalf —

(1) against any person (including (i) the United States, and (ii) any other governmental instrumentality or agency to the extent permitted by the Elev-

enth Amendment to the Constitution) who is alleged to have violated (if there is evidence that the alleged violation has been repeated) or to be in violation of (A) an emission standard or limitation under this Act or (B) an order issued by the Administrator or a State with respect to such a standard or limitation.

(2) against the Administrator where there is alleged a failure of the administrator to perform any act or duty under this Act which is not discretionary with the Administrator, or

(3) against any person who proposes to construct or constructs any new or modified major emitting facility without a permit required under part C of title I (relating to significant deterioration of air quality) or part D of title I (relating to nonattainment) or who is alleged to have violated (if there is evidence that the alleged violation has been repeated) or to be in violation of any condition of such permit.

The district courts shall have jurisdiction, without regard to the amount in controversy or the citizenship of the parties, to enforce such an emission standard or limitation, or such an order, or to order the Administrator to perform such act or duty, as the case may be, and to apply any appropriate civil penalties (except for actions under paragraph (2)). The district courts of the United States shall have jurisdiction to compel (consistent with paragraph (2) of this subsection) agency action unreasonably delayed, except that an action to compel agency action referred to in section 307(b) which is unreasonably delayed may only be filed in a United States District Court within the circuit in which such action would be reviewable under section 307(b). In any such action for unreasonable delay; notice to the entities referred to in subsection (b)(1)(A) shall be provided 180 days before commencing such action.

(b) No action may be commenced —

(1) under subsection (a)(1) —

(A) prior to 60 days after the plaintiff has given notice of the violation (i) to the Administrator, (ii) to the State in which the violation occurs, and (iii) to any alleged violator of the standard, limitation, or order, or

(B) if the Administrator or State has commenced and is diligently prosecuting a civil action in a court of the United States or a State to require compliance with the standard, limitation, or order, but in any such action in a court of the United States any person may intervene as a matter of right.

(2) under subsection (a)(2) prior to 60 days after the plaintiff has given notice of such action to the Administrator, except that such action may be brought immediately after such notification in the case of an action under this section respecting a violation of section 112(i)(3)(A) or (f)(4) or an order issued by the Administrator pursuant to section 113(a). Notice under this subsection shall be given in such manner as the Administrator shall prescribe by regulation.

(c)(1) Any action respecting a violation by a stationary source of an emission standard or limitation or an order respecting such standard or limitation may be brought only in the judicial district in which such source is located.

(2) In any action under this section, the Administrator, if not a party, may intervene as a matter of right at any time in the proceeding. A judgment in an action under this section to which the United States is not a party shall not, however, have any binding effect upon the United States.

(3) Whenever any action is brought under this section the plaintiff shall serve a copy of the complaint on the Attorney General of the United States and on the Administrator. No consent judgment shall be entered in an action brought under this section in which the United States is not a party prior to 45 days following the receipt of a copy of the proposed consent judgment by the Attorney General and the Administrator during which time the Government may submit its comments on the proposed consent judgment to the court and parties or may intervene as a matter of right.

(d) The court, in issuing any final order in any action brought pursuant to subsection (a) of this section, may award costs of litigation (including reasonable attorney and expert witness fees) to any party, whenever the court determines such award is appropriate. The court may, if a temporary restraining order or preliminary injunction is sought, require the filing of a bond or equivalent security in accordance with the Federal Rules of Civil Procedure.

(e) Nothing in this section shall restrict any right which any person (or class of persons) may have under any statute or common law to seek enforcement of any emission standard or limitation or to seek any other relief (including relief against the Administrator or a State agency). Nothing in this section or in any other law of the United States shall be construed to prohibit, exclude, or restrict any State, local, or interstate authority from —

(1) bringing any enforcement action or obtaining any judicial remedy or sanction in any State or local court, or

(2) bringing any administrative enforcement action or obtaining any administrative remedy or sanction in any State or local administrative agency, department or instrumentality, against the United States, any department, agency, or instrumentality therefore, or any officer, agent, or employee thereof under State or local law respecting control and abatement of air pollution. For provisions requiring compliance by the United States, departments, agencies, instrumentalities, officers, agents, and employees in the same manner as non-governmental entities, see section 118.

(f) For purposes of this section, the term 'emission standard or limitation under this Act' means —

(1) a schedule or timetable of compliance, emission limitation, standard or performance or emission standard,

(2) a control or prohibition respecting a motor vehicle fuel or fuel additive, which is in effect under this Act (including a requirement applicable by reason of section 118) or under an applicable implementation plan, or

(3) any condition or requirement of a permit under part C of title I (relating to significant deterioration of air quality) or part D of title I (relating to nonattainment), 119 (relating to primary nonferrous smelter orders), any condition or requirement under an applicable implementation plan relating

Clean Air Act §307

to transportation control measures, air quality maintenance plans, vehicle inspection and maintenance programs, or vapor recovery requirements, section 211(e) and (f) (relating to fuels and fuel additives), section 169A (relating to visibility protection), any condition or requirement under title VI (relating to ozone protection), or any requirement under section 111 or 112 without regard to whether such requirement is expressed as an emission standard or otherwise; or

(4) any other standard, limitation, or schedule established under any permit issued pursuant to title V or under any applicable State implementation plan approved by the Administrator, any permit term or condition, and any requirement to obtain a permit as a condition of operations.

(g) Penalty Fund. — (1) Penalties received under subsection (a) shall be deposited in a special fund in the United States Treasury for licensing and other services. Amounts in such fund are authorized to be appropriated and shall remain available until expended, for use by the Administrator to finance air compliance and enforcement activities. The Administrator shall annually report to the Congress about the sums deposited into the fund, the sources thereof, and the actual and proposed uses thereof.

(2) Notwithstanding paragraph (1) the court in any action under this subsection to apply civil penalties shall have discretion to order that such civil penalties, in lieu of being deposited in the fund referred to in paragraph (1), be used in beneficial mitigation projects which are consistent with this Act and enhance the public health or the environment. The court shall obtain the view of the Administrator in exercising such discretion and selecting any such projects. The amount of any such payment in any such action shall not exceed $100,000. . . .

General Provision Relating to Administrative Proceedings and Judicial Review

Sec. 307. . . .

(b)(1) A petition for review of action of the Administrator in promulgating any national primary or secondary ambient air quality standard, any emission standard or requirement under section 112, any standard of performance or requirement under 111; any standard under section 202 (other than a standard required to be prescribed under section 202(b)(1)), any determination under section 202(b)(5), any control or prohibition under section 211, any standard under section 231 or any rule issued under section 113, 119, or under section 120 or any other nationally applicable regulations promulgated, or final action taken, by the Administrator under this Act may be filed only in the United States Court of Appeals for the District of Columbia. A petition for review of the Administrator's action in approving or promulgating any implementation plan under section 110 or section 111(d), any order under section 111(j), under section 112, under section 119, or under section 120, or his action under section 119(c)(2)(A), (B), or (C) (as in effect before the enactment of the Clean Air Act Amendments of

1977) or under regulations thereunder, or revising regulations for enhanced monitoring and compliance certification programs under section 114(a)(3) of this Act, or any other final action of the Administrator under this (including any denial or disapproval by the Administrator under Title I) Act which is locally or regionally applicable may be filed only in the United States Court of Appeals for the appropriate circuit. Any petition for review under this subsection shall be filed within sixty days from the date notice of such promulgation, approval, or action appears in the Federal Register, except that if such petition is based solely on grounds arising after such sixtieth day, then any petition for review under this subsection shall be filed within sixty days after such grounds arise. Notwithstanding the preceding sentence a petition for review of any action referred to in such sentence may be filed only in the United States Court of Appeals for the District of Columbia if such action is based on a determination of nationwide scope or effect and if in taking such action the Administrator finds and publishes that such action is based on such a determination. The filing of a petition for reconsideration by the Administrator of any otherwise final rule or action shall not affect the finality of such rule or action for purposes of judicial review nor extend the time within which a petition for judicial review of such rule or action under this section may be filed, and shall not postpone the effectiveness of such rule or action; and

    (2) Action of the Administrator with respect to which review could have been obtained under paragraph (1) shall not be subject to judicial review in civil or criminal proceedings for enforcement. Where a final decision by the Administrator defers performance of any non-discretionary statutory action to a later time, any person may challenge the deferral pursuant to paragraph (1).

  (c) In any judicial proceeding in which review is sought of a determination under this Act required to be made on the record after notice and opportunity for hearing, if any part applies to the court for leave to adduce additional evidence, and shows to the satisfaction of the court that such additional evidence is material and that there were reasonable grounds for the failure to adduce such evidence in the proceeding before the Administrator the court may order such additional evidence (and evidence in rebuttal thereof) to be taken before the Administrator, in such manner and upon such terms and conditions as to the court may deem proper. The Administrator may modify his findings as to the facts, or make new findings, by reason of the additional evidence so taken and he shall file such modified or new findings, and his recommendation, if any, for the modification or setting aside of his original determination, with the return of such additional evidence.

  (d)(1) This subsection applies to —

    (A) the promulgation or revision of any national ambient air quality standard under section 109,

    (B) the promulgation or revision of an implementation plan by the Administrator under section 110(c),

    (C) the promulgation or revision of any standard of performance under section 111, or emission standard or limitation under section 112(d), any standard under section 112(f), or any regulation under section 112(g)(1)(D) and (F), or any regulation under section 112(m) or (n),

(D) The promulgation of any requirement for solid waste combustion under section 129,

(E) the promulgation or revision of any regulation pertaining to any fuel or fuel additive under section 211.

(F) the promulgation or revision of any aircraft emission standard under section 231.

(G) the promulgation or revision of any regulation under title IV (relating to control of acid deposition),

(H) promulgation or revision of regulation pertaining to primary nonferrous smelter orders under section 119 (but not including the granting or denying of any such order),

(I) promulgation or revision of regulations under title VI (relating to stratosphere and ozone protection),

(J) promulgation or revision of regulations under subtitle C of title I (relating to prevention of significant deterioration of air quality and protection of visibility),

(K) promulgation or revision of regulations under section 202 and test procedures for new motor vehicles or engines under section 206, and the revision of a standard, under section 202(a)(3),

(L) promulgation or revision of regulations for noncompliance penalties under section 120,

(M) promulgation or revision of any regulations promulgated under section 207 (relating to warranties and compliance by vehicles in actual use),

(N) action of the Administrator under section 126 (relating to interstate pollution abatement),

(O) the promulgation or revision of any regulation pertaining to consumer and commercial products under section 183(e),

(P) the promulgation or revision of any regulation pertaining to field citations under section 113(d)(3),

(Q) the promulgation or revision of any regulation pertaining to urban buses or the clean-fuel vehicle, clean-fuel fleet, and clean fuel programs under part C of title II,

(R) the promulgation or revision of any regulation pertaining to nonroad engines or nonroad vehicles under section 213,

(S) the promulgation or revision of any regulation relating to motor vehicle compliance program fees under section 217,

(T) the promulgation or revision of any regulation under title IV (relating to acid deposition),

(U) the promulgation or revision of any regulation under section 183(f) pertaining to marine vessels, and

(V) Such other actions as the Administrator may determine. The provisions of section 553 through 557 and section 706 of title 5 of the

United States Code shall not, except as expressly provided in this subsection, apply to actions to which this subsection applies. This subsection shall not apply in the case of any rule or circumstance referred to in subparagraphs (A) or (B) of subsection 553(b) of title 5 of the United States Code;

(2) Not later than the date of proposal of any action to which this subsection applies, the Administrator shall establish a rulemaking docket for such action (hereinafter in this subsection referred to as a 'rule'). Whenever a rule applies only within a particular State, a second (identical) docket shall be simultaneously established in the appropriate regional office of the Environmental Protection Agency.

(3) In the case of any rule to which this subsection applies, notice of proposed rulemaking shall be published in the Federal Register, as provided under section 553(b) of title 5, United States Code, shall be accompanied by a statement of its basis and purpose and shall specify the period available for public comment (hereinafter referred to as the 'comment period'). The notice of proposed rulemaking shall also state the docket number, the location or locations of the docket, and the times it will be open to public inspection. The statement of basis and purpose shall include a summary of —

(A) the factual data on which the proposed rule is based;

(B) the methodology used in obtaining the data and in analyzing the data; and

(C) the major legal interpretations and policy considerations underlying the proposed rule.

The statement shall also set forth or summarize and provide a reference to any pertinent findings, recommendations, and comments by the Scientific Review Committee established under section 109(d) and the National Academy of Sciences, and, if the proposed differs in any important respect from any of these recommendations, an explanation of the reasons for such differences. All data, information, and documents referred to in this paragraph on which the proposed rule relies shall be included in the docket on the date of publication of the proposed rule.

(4)(A) The rulemaking docket required under paragraph (2) shall be open for inspection by the public at reasonable times specified in the notice of proposed rulemaking. Any person may copy documents contained in the docket. The Administrator shall provide copying facilities which may be used at the expense of the person seeking copies, but the Administrator may waive or reduce such expenses in such instances as the public interest requires. Any person may request copies by mail if the person pays the expenses, including personnel costs to do the copying.

(B)(i) Promptly upon receipt by the agency, all written comments and documentary information on the proposed rule received from any person for inclusion in the docket during the comment period shall be placed in the docket. The transcript of public hearings, if any, on the proposed rule shall also be included in the docket promptly upon receipt from the person

Clean Air Act §307

who transcribed such hearings. All documents which become available after the proposed rule has been published and which the Administrator determines are of central relevance to the rulemaking shall be placed in the docket as soon as possible after their availability.

(ii) The drafts of proposed rules submitted by the Administrator to the Office of Management and Budget for any inter-agency review process prior to proposal of any such rule, all documents accompanying such drafts, and all written comments thereon by other agencies and all written responses to such written comments by the Administrator shall be placed in the docket no later than the date of proposal of the rule. The drafts of the final rule submitted for such review process prior to promulgation and all such written comments thereon, all documents accompanying such drafts, and written responses thereto shall be placed in the docket no later than the date of promulgation.

(5)(A) In promulgating a rule to which this subsection applies (i) the Administrator shall allow any person to submit written comments, data, or documentary information; (ii) the Administrator shall give interested persons an opportunity for the oral presentation of data, views, or arguments, in addition to an opportunity to make written submissions; (iii) a transcript shall be kept of any oral presentation; and (iv) the Administrator shall keep the record of such proceeding open for thirty days after completion of the proceeding to provide an opportunity for submission of rebuttal and supplementary information.

(6)(A) The promulgated rule shall be accompanied by (i) a statement of basis and purpose like that referred to in paragraph (3) with respect to a proposed rule and (ii) an explanation of the reasons for any major changes in the promulgated rule from the proposed rule.

(B) The promulgated rule shall also be accompanied by a response to each of the significant comments, criticisms, and new data submitted, in written or oral presentations during the comment period.

(C) The promulgated rule may not be based (in part or whole) on any information or data which has not been placed in the docket as of the date of such promulgation.

(7)(A) The record for judicial review shall consist exclusively of the material referred to in paragraph (3), clause (i) of paragraph (4)(B), and subparagraphs (A) and (B) of paragraph (6).

(B) Only an objection to a rule or procedure which was raised with reasonable specificity during the period for public comment (including any public hearing) may be raised during judicial review. If the person raising an objection can demonstrate to the Administrator that it was impracticable to raise such objection within such time or if the grounds for such objection arose after the period for public comment (but within the time specified for judicial review) and if such objection is of central relevance to the outcome of the rule, the Administrator shall convene a proceeding for reconsideration of the rule and provide the same procedural rights as would have been afforded had the information been available at the time the rule was proposed. If the Administrator refuses to convene such a proceeding, such person may seek review of such refusal in the United States court of appeals for the appropriate circuit (as provided in subsection (b)). Such reconsideration shall not postpone the effectiveness of the rule. The effectiveness of the rule may be stayed during such reconsideration, however, by the Administrator or the court for a period not to exceed three months.

(8) The sole forum for challenging procedural determinations made by the Administrator under this subsection shall be in the United States court of appeals for the appropriate circuit (as provided in subsection (b)) at the time of the substantive review of the rule. No interlocutory appeals shall be permitted with respect to such procedural determinations. In reviewing alleged procedural errors, the court may invalidate the rule only if the errors were so serious and related to matters of such central relevance to the rule that there is a substantial likelihood that the rule would have been significantly changed if such errors had not been made.

(9) In the case of review of any action of the Administrator to which this subsection applies, the court may reverse any such action found to be —

(A) arbitrary, capricious, an abuse of discretion, or otherwise not in accordance with law;

(B) contrary to constitutional right, power, privilege, or immunity;

(C) in excess of statutory jurisdiction, authority, or limitations, or short of statutory right; or

(D) without observance of procedure required by law if (i) such failure to observance such procedure is arbitrary or capricious, (ii) the requirement of paragraph (7)(B) has been met, and (iii) the condition of the last sentence of paragraph (8) is met.

(10) Each statutory deadline for promulgation of rules to which this subsection applies which requires promulgation less than six months after date of proposal may be extended to not more than six months after date of proposal by the Administrator upon a determination that such extension is necessary to afford the public, and the agency, adequate opportunity to carry out the purposes of this subsection. . . .

(e) Nothing in this Act shall be construed to authorize judicial review of regulations or orders of the Administrator under this Act, except as provided in this section.

(f) In any judicial proceeding under this section, the court may award costs of litigation (including reasonable attorney and expert witness fees) whenever it determines that such award is appropriate.

(g) In any action respecting the promulgation of regulations under section 120 or the administration or enforcement of section 120 no court shall grant any stay, injunctive, or similar relief before final judgment by such court in such action.

(h) Public Participation. — It is the intent of Congress that, consistent

Clean Air Act §316

with the policy of the Administrative Procedures Act, the Administrator in promulgating any regulation under this Act, including a regulation subject to a deadline, shall ensure a reasonable period for public participation of at least 30 days, except as otherwise expressly provided in section 107(d), 172(a), 181(a) and (b), and 186(a) and (b). . . .

Sewage Treatment Grants

Sec. 316. (a) No grant which the Administrator is authorized to make to any applicant for construction of sewage treatment works in any area in any State may be withheld, conditioned, or restricted by the Administrator on the basis of any requirement of this Act except as provided in subsection (b).

(b) The Administrator may withhold, condition, or restrict the making of any grant for construction referred to in subsection (a) only if he determines that —

(1) such treatment works will not comply with applicable standards under section 111 or 112,

(2) the State does not have in effect, or is not carrying out, a State implementation plan approved by the Administrator which expressly quantifies and provides for the increase in emissions of each air pollutant (from stationary and mobile sources in any area to which either part C or Part D of title I applies for such pollutant) which increase may reasonably be anticipated to result directly or indirectly from the new sewage treatment capacity which would be created by such construction,

(3) the construction of such treatment works would create a new sewage treatment capacity which —

(A) may reasonably be anticipated to cause or contribute to, directly or indirectly, an increase in emissions of any air pollutant in excess of the increase provided for under the provisions referred to in paragraph (2) for any such area, or

(B) would otherwise not be in conformity with the applicable implementation plan, or

(4) such increase in emissions would interfere with, or be inconsistent with, the applicable implementation plan for any other State.

In the case of construction of a treatment works which would result, directly or indirectly, in an increase in emissions of any air pollutant from stationary and mobile sources in an area to which part D of title I applies, the quantification of emissions referred to in paragraph (2) shall include the emissions of any such pollutant resulting directly or indirectly from areawide and nonmajor stationary source growth (mobile and stationary) for each such area.

(c) Nothing in this section shall be construed to amend or alter any provision of the National Environmental Policy Act or to affect any determination as to whether or not the requirements of such Act have been met in the case of the construction of any sewage treatment works. . . .

[Title IV, which enacts the program for the control of acid rain, is omitted.]

Title V — Permits

Definitions

Sec. 501. As used in this title —

(1) Affected Sources. — The term 'affected source' shall have the meaning given such term in title IV.

(2) Major Source. — The term 'major source' means any stationary source (or any group of stationary sources located within a contiguous area and under common control) that is either of the following:

(A) A major source as defined in section 112.

(B) A major stationary source and defined in section 302 or part D of title I.

(3) Schedule of Compliance. — The term 'schedule of compliance' means a schedule of remedial measures, including an enforceable sequence of actions or operations, leading to compliance with an applicable implementation plan, emission standard, emission limitation, or emission prohibition.

(4) Permitting Authority. — The term 'permitting authority' means the Administrator or the air pollution control agency authorized by the Administrator to carry out a permit program under this title.

Permit Programs

Sec. 502. (a) Violations. — After the effective date of any permit program approved or promulgated under this title, it shall be unlawful for any person to violate any requirement of a permit issued under this title, or to operate an affected source (as provided in title IV), a major source, any other source (including an area source) subject to standards or regulations under section 111 or 112, any other source required to have a permit under parts C or D of title I, or any other stationary source in a category designated (in whole or in part) by regulations promulgated by the Administrator (after notice and public comment) which shall include a finding setting forth the basis of such designation, except in compliance with a permit issued by a permitting authority under this title. (Nothing in this subsection shall be construed to alter the applicable requirements of this Act that a permit be obtained before construction or modification.) The Administrator may, in the Administrator's discretion and consistent with the applicable provisions of this Act, promulgate regulations to exempt one or more source categories (in whole or in part) from the requirements of this subsection if the Administrator finds that compliance with such requirements is impracticable, infeasible, or unnecessarily burdensome on such categories, except that the Administrator may not exempt any major source from such requirements.

(b) Regulations. — The Administrator shall promulgate within 12 months after the date of the enactment of the Clean Air Act Amendments of 1990 regulations establishing the minimum elements of a permit program to be administered by any air pollution control agency. These elements shall include each of the following:

Clean Air Act §502

(1) Requirements for permit applications, including a standard application form and criteria for determining in a timely fashion the completeness of applications.

(2) Monitoring and reporting requirements.

(3)(A) A requirement under State or local law or interstate compact that the owner or operator of all sources subject to the requirement to obtain a permit under this title pay an annual fee, or the equivalent over some other period, sufficient to cover all reasonable (direct and indirect) costs required to develop and administer the permit program requirements of this title, including section 507, including the reasonable costs of —

    (i) reviewing and acting upon any application for such a permit,

    (ii) if the owner or operator receives a permit for such source, whether before of after the date of the enactment of the Clean Air Act Amendments of 1990, implementing and enforcing the terms and conditions of any such permit (not including any court costs or other costs associated with any enforcement action),

    (iii) emissions and ambient monitoring,

    (iv) preparing generally applicable regulations, or guidance,

    (v) modeling, analyses, and demonstrations, and

    (vi) preparing inventories and tracking emissions. . . .

(4) Requirements for adequate personnel and funding to administer the program.

(5) A requirement that the permitting authority have adequate authority to:

    (A) issue permits and assure compliance by all sources required to have a permit under this title with each applicable standard, regulation or requirement under this Act;

    (B) issue permits for a fixed term, not to exceed 5 years;

    (C) assure that upon issuance or renewal permits incorporate emission limitations and other requirements in an applicable implementation plan;

    (D) terminate, modify, or revoke and reissue permits for cause;

    (E) enforce permits, permit fee requirements, and the requirement to obtain a permit, including authority to recover civil penalties in a maximum amount of not less than $10,000 per day for each violation, and provide appropriate criminal penalties; and

    (F) assure that no permit will be issued if the Administrator objects to its issuance in a timely manner under this title.

(6) Adequate, streamlined, and reasonable procedures for expeditiously determining when applications are complete, for processing such applications, for public notice, including offering an opportunity for public comment and a hearing, and for expeditious review of permit actions, including applications, renewals, or revisions, and including an opportunity for judicial review in State court of the final permit action by the applicant, any person who participated in the public comment process, and any other person who could obtain judicial review of that action under applicable law.

(7) To ensure against unreasonable delay by the permitting authority, adequate authority and procedures to provide that a failure of such permitting authority to act on a permit application or permit renewal application (in accordance with the time periods specified in section 503 or, as appropriate, title IV) shall be treated as a final permit action solely for purposes of obtaining judicial review in State court of an action brought by any person referred to in paragraph (6) to require that action be taken by the permitting authority on such application without additional delay.

(8) Authority, and reasonable procedures consistent with the need for expeditious action by the permitting authority on permit applications and related matters, to make available to the public any permit application, compliance plan, permit, and monitoring or compliance report under section 503(e), subject to the provisions of section 114(c) of this Act.

(9) A requirement that the permitting authority, in the case of permits with a term of 3 or more years for major sources, shall require revisions to the permit to incorporate applicable standards and regulations promulgated under this Act after the issuance of such permit. Such revisions shall occur as expeditiously as practicable and consistent with the procedures established under paragraph (6) but not later than 18 months after the promulgation of such standards and regulations. No such revision shall be required if the effective date of the standards or regulations is a date after the expiration of the permit term. Such permit revision shall be treated as a permit renewal if it complies with the requirements of this title regarding renewals.

(10) Provisions to allow changes within a permitted facility (or one operating pursuant to section 503(d)) without requiring a permit revision, if the changes are not modifications under any provision of title I and the changes do not exceed the emissions allowable under the permit (whether expressed therein as a rate of emissions or in terms of total emissions): *Provided,* That the facility provides the Administrator and the permitting authority with written notification in advance of the proposed changes which shall be a minimum of 7 days, unless the permitting authority provides in its regulations a different time-frame for emergencies.

(c) Single Permit. — A single permit may be issued for a facility with multiple sources.

(d) Submission and Approval. — (1) Not later than 3 years after the date of the enactment of the Clean Air Act Amendments of 1990, the Governor of each State shall develop and submit to the Administrator a permit program under State or local law or under an interstate compact meeting the requirements of this title. In addition, the Governor shall submit a legal opinion from the attorney general (or the attorney for those State air pollution control agencies that have independent legal counsel), or from the chief legal officer of an interstate agency, that the laws of the State, locality, or the interstate compact provide adequate authority to carry out the program. Not later than 1 year after receiving a program, and after notice and opportunity for public comment, the Administrator shall approve or disapprove such program, in whole or in part. The Ad-

Clean Air Act §502

ministrator may approve a program to the extent that the program meets the requirements of this Act, including the regulations issued under subsection (b). If the program is disapproved, in whole or in part, the Administrator shall notify the Governor of any revisions or modifications necessary to obtain approval. The Governor shall revise and resubmit the program for review under this section within 180 days after receiving notification.

(2)(A) If the Governor does not submit a program as required under paragraph (1) or if the Administrator disapproves a program submitted by the Governor under paragraph (1), in whole or in part, the Administrator may, prior to the expiration of the 18-month period referred to in subparagraph (B), in the Administrator's discretion, apply any of the sanctions specified in section 179(b).

(B) If the Governor does not submit a program as required under paragraph (1), or if the Administrator disapproves any such program submitted by the Governor under paragraph (1), in whole or in part, 18 months after the date required for such submittal or the date of such disapproval, as the case may be, the Administrator shall apply sanctions under section 179(b) in the same manner and subject to the same deadlines and other conditions as are applicable in the case of a determination, disapproval, or finding under section 179(a).

(C) The sanctions under section 179(b)(2) shall not apply pursuant to this paragraph in any area unless the failure to submit or the disapproval referred to in subparagraph (A) or (B) relates to an air pollutant for which such area has been designated a nonattainment area (as defined in part D of title I).

(3) If a program meeting the requirements of this title has not been approved in whole for any State, the Administrator shall, 2 years after the date required for submission of such a program under paragraph (1), promulgate, administer, and enforce a program under this title for that State.

(e) Suspension. — The Administrator shall suspend the issuance of permits promptly upon publication of notice of approval of a permit program under this section, but may, in such notice, retain jurisdiction over permits that have been federally issued, but for which the administrative or judicial review process is not complete. The Administrator shall continue to administer and enforce federally issued permits under this title until they are replaced by a permit issued by a permitting program. Nothing in this subsection should be construed to limit the Administrator's ability to enforce permits issued by a State. . . .

(i) Administration and Enforcement. —
(1) Whenever the Administrator makes a determination that a permitting authority is not adequately administering and enforcing a program, or portion thereof, in accordance with the requirements of this title, the Administrator shall provide notice to the State and may, prior to the expiration of the 18-month period referred to in paragraph (2), in the Administrator's discretion, apply any of the sanctions specified in section 179(b).

(2) Whenever the Administrator makes a determination that a permit-

ting authority is not adequately administering and enforcing a program, or portion thereof, in accordance with the requirements of this title, 18 months after the date of the notice under paragraph (1), the Administrator shall apply the sanctions under section 179(b) in the same manner and subject to the same deadline and other conditions as are applicable in the case of a determination, disapproval, or finding under section 179(a).

(3) The sanctions under section 179(b)(2) shall not apply pursuant to this subsection in any area unless the failure to adequately enforce and administer the program relates to an air pollutant for which such area has been designated a nonattainment area.

(4) Whenever the Administrator has made a finding under paragraph (1) with respect to any State, unless the State has corrected such deficiency within 18 months after the date of such finding, the Administrator shall, 2 years after the date of such finding, promulgate, administer, and enforce a program under this title for that State. Nothing in this paragraph shall be construed to affect the validity of a program which has been approved under this title or the authority of any permitting authority acting under such program until such time as such program is promulgated by the Administrator under this paragraph.

Permit Applications

Sec. 503. (a) Applicable Date. — Any source specified in section 502(a) shall become subject to a permit program, and required to have a permit, on the later of the following dates —

(1) the effective date of a permit program or partial or interim permit program applicable to the source; or

(2) the date such source becomes subject to section 502(a).

(b) Compliance Plan. — (1) The regulations required by section 502(b) shall include a requirement that the applicant submit with the permit application a compliance plan describing how the source will comply with all applicable requirements under this Act. The compliance plan shall include a schedule of compliance, and a schedule under which the permittee will submit progress reports to the permitting authority no less frequently than every 6 months.

(2) The regulations shall further require the permittee to periodically (but no less frequently than annually) certify that the facility is in compliance with any applicable requirements of the permit, and to promptly report any deviations from permit requirements to the permitting authority.

(c) Deadline. — Any person required to have a permit shall, not later than 12 months after the date on which the source becomes subject to a permit program approved or promulgated under this title, or such earlier date as the permitting authority may establish, submit to the permitting authority a compliance plan and an application for a permit signed by a responsible official, who shall certify the accuracy of the information submitted. The permitting authority shall approve or disapprove a completed application (consistent with the procedures established under this title for consideration of such applications), and shall issue or deny the permit, within 18 months after the date of receipt thereof, except that the permitting authority shall establish a phased schedule for acting on permit applications submitted within the first full year after the effective date of a permit program (or a partial or interim program). Any such schedule shall assure that at least one-third of such permits will be acted on by such authority annually over a period of not to exceed 3 years after such effective date. Such authority shall establish reasonable procedures to prioritize such approval or disapproval actions in the case of applications for construction or modification under the applicable requirements of this Act. . . .

Permit Requirements and Conditions

Sec. 504. (a) Conditions. — Each permit issued under this title shall include enforceable emission limitations and standards, a schedule of compliance, a requirement that the permittee submit to the permitting authority, no less often than every 6 months, the results of any required monitoring, and such other conditions as are necessary to assure compliance with applicable requirements of this Act, including the requirements of the applicable implementation plan.

(b) Monitoring and Analysis. — The Administrator may by rule prescribe procedures and methods for determining compliance and for monitoring and analysis of pollutants regulated under this Act, but continuous emissions monitoring need not be required if alternative methods are available that provide sufficiently reliable and timely information for determining compliance. Nothing in this subsection shall be construed to affect any continuous emissions monitoring requirement of title IV, or where required elsewhere in this Act.

(c) Inspection, Entry, Monitoring, Certification, and Reporting. — Each permit issued under this title shall set forth inspection, entry, monitoring, compliance certification, and reporting requirements to assure compliance with the permit terms and conditions. Such monitoring and reporting requirements shall conform to any applicable regulation under subsection (b). Any report required to be submitted by a permit issued to a corporation under this title shall be signed by a responsible corporate official, who shall certify its accuracy.

(d) General Permits. — The permitting authority may, after notice and opportunity for public hearing, issue a general permit covering numerous similar sources. Any general permit shall comply with all requirements applicable to permits under this title. No source covered by a general permit shall thereby be relieved from the obligation to file an application under section 503. . . .

(f) Permit Shield. — Compliance with a permit issued in accordance with this title shall be deemed compliance with section 502. Except as otherwise provided by the Administrator by rule, the permit may also provide that compliance with the permit shall be deemed compliance with other applicable provisions of this Act that relate to the permittee if —

(1) the permit includes the applicable requirements of such provisions, or

(2) the permitting authority in acting on the permit application makes a determination relating to the permittee that such other provisions (which

§504   Clean Air Act

shall be referred to in such determination) are not applicable and the permit includes the determination or a concise summary thereof.

Nothing in the preceding sentence shall alter or affect the provisions of section 303, including the authority of the Administrator under that section.

Notification to Administrator and Contiguous States

Sec. 505. (a) *Transmission and Notice.* — (1) Each permitting authority —

    (A) shall transmit to the Administrator a copy of each permit application (and any application for a permit modification or renewal) or such portion thereof, including any compliance plan, as the Administrator may require to effectively review the application and otherwise to carry out the Administrator's responsibilities under this Act, and

    (B) shall provide to the Administrator a copy of each permit proposed to be issued and issued as a final permit.

(2) The permitting authority shall notify all States —

    (A) whose air quality may be affected and that are contiguous to the State in which the emission originates, or

    (B) that are within 50 miles of the source,

of each permit application or proposed permit forwarded to the Administrator under this section, and shall provide an opportunity for such States to submit written recommendations respecting the issuance of the permit and its terms and conditions. If any part of those recommendations are not accepted by the permitting authority, such authority shall notify the State submitting the recommendations and the Administrator in writing of its failure to accept those recommendations and the reasons therefor.

(b) *Objection by EPA.* — (1) If any permit contains provisions that are determined by the Administrator as not in compliance with the applicable requirements of this Act, including the requirements of an applicable implementation plan, the Administrator shall, in accordance with this subsection, object to its issuance. The permitting authority shall respond in writing if the Administrator (A) within 45 days after receiving a copy of the proposed permit under subsection (a)(1), or (B) within 45 days after receiving notification under subsection (a)(2), objects in writing to its issuance as not in compliance with such requirements. With the objection, the Administrator shall provide a statement of the reasons for the objection. A copy of the objection and statement shall be provided to the applicant.

(2) If the Administrator does not object in writing to the issuance of a permit pursuant to paragraph (1), any person may petition the Administrator within 60 days after the expiration of the 45-day review period specified in paragraph (1) to take such action. A copy of such petition shall be provided to the permitting authority and the applicant by the petitioner. The petition shall be based only on objections to the permit that were raised with reasonable specificity during the public comment period provided by the permitting agency (unless the petitioner demonstrates in the petition to the Administrator

Clean Air Act §505

that it was impracticable to raise such objections within such period or unless the grounds for such objection arose after such period.) The petition shall identify all such objections. If the permit has been issued by the permitting agency, such petition shall not postpone the effectiveness of the permit. The Administrator shall grant or deny such petition within 60 days after the petition is filed. The Administrator shall issue an objection within such period if the petitioner demonstrates to the Administrator that the permit is not in compliance with the requirements of this Act, including the requirements of the applicable implementation plan. Any denial of such petition shall be subject to judicial review under section 307. The Administrator shall include in regulations under this title provisions to implement this paragraph. The Administrator may not delegate the requirements of this paragraph.

(3) Upon receipt of an objection by the Administrator under this subsection, the permitting authority may not issue the permit unless it is revised and issued in accordance with subsection (c). If the permitting authority has issued a permit prior to receipt of an objection by the Administrator under paragraph (2) of this subsection, the Administrator shall modify, terminate, or revoke such permit and the permitting authority may thereafter only issue a revised permit in accordance with subsection (c).

(c) Issuance or Denial. — If the permitting authority fails, within 90 days after the date of an objection under subsection (b), to submit a permit revised to meet the objection, the Administrator shall issue or deny the permit in accordance with the requirements of this title. No objection shall be subject to judicial review until the Administrator takes final action to issue or deny a permit under this subsection.

(d) Waiver Of Notification Requirements. — (1) The Administrator may waive the requirements of subsections (a) and (b) at the time of approval of a permit program under this title for any category (including any class, type, or size within such category) of sources covered by the program other than major sources.

(2) The Administrator may, by regulation, established categories of sources (including any class, type, or size within such category) to which the requirements of subsections (a) and (b) shall not apply. The preceding sentence shall not apply to major sources.

(3) The Administrator may exclude from any waiver under this subsection notification under subsection (a)(2). Any waiver granted under this subsection may be revoked or modified by the Administrator by rule.

(e) Refusal of Permitting Authority To Terminate, Modify, or Revoke and Reissue. — If the Administrator finds that cause exists to terminate, modify, or revoke and reissue a permit under this title, the Administrator shall notify the permitting authority and the source of the Administrator's finding. The permitting authority shall, within 90 days after receipt of such notification, forward to the Administrator under this section a proposed determination of termination, modification, or revocation and reissuance, as appropriate. The Administrator may extend such 90 day period for an additional 90 days if the Administrator finds that a new or revised permit application is necessary, or that the permitting authority must require the permittee to submit additional information. The Administrator may review such proposed determination under the provisions of subsections (a) and (b). If the permitting authority fails to submit the required proposed determination, or if the Administrator objects and the permitting authority fails to resolve the objection within 90 days, the Administrator may, after notice and in accordance with fair and reasonable procedures, terminate, modify, or revoke and reissue the permit.

Other Authorities

Sec. 506. (a) In General. — Nothing in this title shall prevent a State, or interstate permitting authority, from establishing additional permitting requirements not inconsistent with this Act.

(b) Permits Implementing Acid Rain Provisions. — The provisions of this title, including provisions regarding schedules for submission and approval or disapproval of permit applications, shall apply to permits implementing the requirements of title IV except as modified by that title.

Clean Water Act
33 U.S.C. §§1251-1386

CHAPTER 26 — WATER POLLUTION PREVENTION AND CONTROL
Subchapter I — Research and Related Programs

Sec.
1251. Congressional declaration of goals and policy.
  (a) Restoration and maintenance of chemical, physical and biological integrity of Nation's waters; national goals for achievement of objective.
  (b) Congressional recognition, preservation, and protection of primary responsibilities and rights of States.
  (c) Congressional policy toward Presidential activities with foreign countries.
  (d) Administrator of Environmental Protection Agency to administer chapter.
  (e) Public participation in development, revision, and enforcement of any regulation, etc.
  (f) Procedures utilized for implementing chapter.
  (g) Authority of States over water.
1252. Comprehensive programs for water pollution control
  (a) Preparation and development.
  (b) Planning for reservoirs; storage for regulation of streamflow.
  (c) Basins; grants to State agencies.
  (d) Report to Congress.
1252a. Reservoir projects, water storage; modification; storage for other than for water quality, opinion of Federal agency, committee resolutions of approval; provisions inapplicable to projects with certain prescribed water quality benefits in relation to total project benefits.
1253. Interstate cooperation and uniform laws.
1254. Research, investigations, training, and information.
  (a) Establishment of national programs; cooperation; investigations; water quality surveillance system; reports.
  (b) Authorized activities of Administrator.
  (c) Research and studies on harmful effects of pollutants; cooperation with Secretary of Health and Human Services.
  (d) Sewage treatment; identification and measurement of effects of pollutants; augmented streamflow.
  (e) Field laboratory and research facilities.
1254a. Research on effects of pollutants.
1255. Grants for research and development.
  (a) Demonstration projects covering storm waters, advanced waste treatment and water purification methods, and joint treatment systems for municipal and industrial wastes.
  (b) Demonstration projects for advanced treatment and environmental enhancement techniques to control pollution in river basins.

Clean Water Act

(c) Research and demonstration projects for prevention of water pollution by industry.
(d) Accelerated and priority development of waste management and waste treatment methods and identification and measurement methods.
(e) Research and demonstration projects covering agricultural pollution and pollution from sewage in rural areas; dissemination of information.
(f) Limitations.
(g) Maximum grants.
(h) Authorization of appropriations.
(i) Assistance for research and demonstration projects.
(j) Assistance for recycle, reuse, and land treatment projects.

1267. Chesapeake Bay.
(a) Office.
(b) Interstate development plan grants.
(c) Reports.
(d) Authorization of appropriations.

1268. Great Lakes.
(a) Findings, purpose, and definitions.
(b) Great Lakes National Program Office.
(c) Great Lakes management.
(d) Great Lakes research.
(e) Research and management coordination.
(f) Interagency cooperation.
(g) Relationship to existing Federal and State laws and international treaties.
(h) Authorizations of Great Lakes appropriations.

SUBCHAPTER II — GRANTS FOR CONSTRUCTION OF TREATMENT WORKS

1281. Congressional declaration of purpose.
(a) Development and implementation of waste treatment management plans and practices.
(b) Application of technology: confined disposal of pollutants; consideration of advanced techniques.
(c) Waste treatment management area and scope.
(d) Waste treatment management construction of revenue producing facilities.
(e) Waste treatment management integration of facilities.
(f) Waste treatment management "open space" and recreational considerations.
(g) Grants to construct publicly owned treatment works.
(h) Grants to construct privately owned treatment works.
(i) Waste treatment management methods, processes, and techniques to reduce energy requirements.
(j) Grants for treatment works utilizing processes and techniques of guidelines under section 1314(d)(3) of this title.
(k) Limitation on use of grants for publicly owned treatment works.
(l) Grants for facility plans, or plans, specifications, and estimates for proposed project for construction of treatment works; limitations, allotments, advances, etc.
(m) Grants for State of California projects.

Clean Water Act

- (n) Water quality problems; funds, scope, etc.
- (o) Capital financing plan.
- (p) Time limit on resolving certain disputes.

1281a. Total treatment system funding.

1282. Federal share.
- (a) Amount of grants for treatment works.
- (b) Amount of grants for construction of treatment works not commenced prior to July 1, 1971.
- (c) Availability of sums allotted to Puerto Rico.

1283. Plans, specifications, estimates, and payments.
- (a) Submission; contractual nature of approval by Administrator; agreement on eligible costs; single grant.
- (b) Periodic payments.
- (c) Final payments.
- (d) Projects eligible.
- (e) Technical and legal assistance in administration and enforcement of contracts; intervention in civil actions.
- (f) Design/build projects.

1284. Limitations and conditions.
- (a) Determinations by Administrator.
- (b) Additional determinations; issuance of guidelines; approval by Administrator; system of charges.
- (c) Applicability of reserve capacity restrictions to primary, secondary, or advanced waste treatment facilities or related interceptors.
- (d) Engineering requirements; certification by owner and operator; contractual assurances, etc.

1285. Allotment of grant funds.
- (a) Funds for fiscal years during period June 30, 1972, and September 30, 1977; determination of amount.
- (b) Availability and use of funds allotted for fiscal years during period June 30, 1972, and September 30, 1977; reallotment.
- (c) Funds for fiscal years during period October 1, 1977, and September 30, 1981; funds for fiscal years 1982 to 1990; determination of amount.
- (d) Availability and use of funds; reallotment.
- (e) Minimum allotment; additional appropriations; ratio of amount available.
- (f) Omitted.
- (g) Reservation of funds; State management assistance.
- (h) Alternate systems for small communities.
- (i) Set-aside for innovative and alternative projects.
- (j) Water quality management plan; reservation of funds for nonpoint source management.
- (k) New York City Convention Center.
- (l) Marine estuary reservation.
- (m) Discretionary deposits into State water pollution control revolving funds.

1286. Reimbursement and advanced construction.
- (a) Publicly owned treatment works construction initiated after June 30, 1966, but before July 1, 1973; reimbursement formula.
- (b) Publicly owned treatment works construction initiated between June 30, 1956, and June 30, 1966; reimbursement formula.

Clean Water Act

      (c) Application for reimbursement.
      (d) Allocation of funds.
      (e) Authorization of appropriations.
      (f) Additional funds.
1288. Areawide waste treatment management.
      (a) Identification and designation of areas having substantial water quality control problems.
      (b) Planning process.
      (c) Regional operating agencies.
      (d) Conformity of works with area plan.
      (e) Permits not to conflict with approved plans.
      (f) Grants.
      (g) Technical assistance by Administrator.
      (h) Technical assistance by Secretary of the Army.
1292. Definitions.
1293. Loan guarantees.
      (a) State or local obligations issued exclusively to Federal Financing Bank for publicly owned treatment works; determination of eligibility of project by Administrator.
      (b) Conditions for issuance.
      (c) Fees for application investigation and issuance of commitment guarantee.
      (d) Commitment for repayment.
1293a. Contained spoil disposal facilities.
      (a) Construction, operation, and maintenance; period; conditions; requirements.
      (b) Time for establishment; consideration of area needs; requirements.
      (c) Written agreement requirement; terms of agreement.
      (d) Waiver of construction costs contribution from non-Federal interests; findings of participation in waste treatment facilities for general geographical area and compliance with water quality standards; waiver of payments in event of written agreement before occurrence of findings.
      (e) Federal payment of costs for disposal of dredged spoil from project.
      (f) Title to lands, easements, and rights-of-way; retention by non-Federal interests; conveyance of facilities; agreement of transferee.
      (g) Federal licenses or permits; charges; remission of charge.
      (h) Provisions applicable to Great Lakes and their connecting channels.
      (i) Research, study, and experimentation program relating to dredged spoil extended to navigable waters, etc.; cooperative program; scope of program; utilization of facilities and personnel of Federal agency.
      (j) Period of depositing dredged materials.
      (k) Study and monitoring program.
1294. Public information and education on recycling and reuse of wastewater, use of land treatment, and reduction of wastewater volume.
1295. Requirements for American materials.
1296. Determination of priority of projects.
1298. Cost effectiveness.
      (a) Congressional statement of policy.
      (b) Determination by Administrator as prerequisite to approval of grant.

Clean Water Act

- (c) Value engineering review.
- (d) Projects affected.
1299. State certification of projects.

Subchapter III — Standards and Enforcement

wetlands?

1311. Effluent limitations.
   - (a) Illegality of pollutant discharges except in compliance with law.
   - (b) Timetable for achievement of objectives.
   - (c) Modification of timetable.
   - (d) Review and revision of effluent limitations.
   - (e) All point discharge source application of effluent limitations.
   - (f) Illegality of discharge of radiological, chemical, or biological warfare agents, high-level radioactive waste, or medical waste.
   - (g) Modifications for certain nonconventional pollutants.
   - (h) Modification of secondary treatment requirements.
   - (i) Municipal time extensions.
   - (j) Modification procedures.
   - (k) Innovative technology.
   - (l) Toxic pollutants.
   - (m) Modification of effluent limitation requirements for point sources.
   - (n) Fundamentally different factors.
   - (o) Application fees.
   - (p) Modified permit for coal remining operations.
1312. Water quality related effluent limitations.
   - (a) Establishment.
   - (b) Modifications of effluent limitations.
   - (c) Delay in application of other limitations.
1313. Water quality standards and implementation plans.
   - (a) Existing water quality standards.
   - (b) Proposed regulations.
   - (c) Review; revised standards; publication.
   - (d) Identification of areas with insufficient controls; maximum daily load; certain effluent limitations revision.
   - (e) Continuing planning process.
   - (f) Earlier compliance.
   - (g) Heat standards.
   - (h) Thermal water quality standards.
1313a. Revised water quality standards.
1314. Information and guidelines
   - (a) Criteria development and publication.
   - (b) Effluent limitation guidelines.
   - (c) Pollution discharge elimination procedures.
   - (d) Secondary treatment information; alternative waste treatment management techniques; innovative and alternative wastewater treatment processes; facilities deemed equivalent of secondary treatment.
   - (e) Best management practices for industry.
   - (f) Identification and evaluation of nonpoint sources of pollution; processes, procedures, and methods to control pollution.

Clean Water Act

      (g) Guidelines for pretreatment of pollutants.
      (h) Test procedures guidelines.
      (i) Guidelines for monitoring, reporting, enforcement, funding, personnel, and manpower.
      (j) Lake restoration guidance manual.
      (k) Agreements with Secretaries of Agriculture, Army, and Interior to provide maximum utilization of programs to achieve and maintain water quality; transfer of funds; authorization of appropriations.
      (l) Individual control strategies for toxic pollutants.
      (m) Schedule for review of guidelines.

1315. State reports on water quality; transmittal to Congress.
1316. National standards of performance.
      (a) Definitions.
      (b) Categories of sources; Federal standards of performance for new sources.
      (c) State enforcement of standards of performance.
      (d) Protection from more stringent standards.
      (e) Illegality of operation of new sources in violation of applicable standards of performance.

1317. Toxic and pretreatment effluent standards.
      (a) Toxic pollutant list; revision; hearing; promulgation of standards; effective date; consultation.
      (b) Pretreatment standards; hearing; promulgation; compliance period; revision; application to State and local laws.
      (c) New sources of pollutants into publicly owned treatment works.
      (d) Operation in violation of standards unlawful.
      (e) Compliance date extension for innovative pretreatment systems.

1318. Records and reports; inspections.
      (a) Maintenance; monitoring equipment; entry; access to information.
      (b) Availability to public; trade secrets exception; penalty for disclosure of confidential information.
      (c) Application of State law.
      (d) Access by Congress.

1319. Enforcement.
      (a) State enforcement; compliance orders.
      (b) Civil actions.
      (c) Criminal penalties.
      (d) Civil penalties; factors considered in determining amount.
      (e) State liability for judgments and expenses.
      (f) Wrongful introduction of pollutant into treatment works.
      (g) Administrative penalties.

1320. International pollution abatement.
      (a) Hearing; participation by foreign nations.
      (b) Functions and responsibilities of Administrator not affected.
      (c) Hearing board; composition; findings of fact; recommendations; implementation of board's decision.
      (d) Report by alleged pollutor.
      (e) Compensation of board members.
      (f) Enforcement proceedings.

1321. Oil and hazardous substance liability.
      (a) Definitions.

Clean Water Act

- (b) Congressional declaration of policy against discharges of oil or hazardous substances; designation of hazardous substances; study of higher standard of care incentives and report to Congress; liability; penalties; civil actions: penalty limitations, separate offenses, jurisdiction, mitigation of damages and costs, recovery of removal costs and alternative remedies.
- (c) Removal of discharged oil or hazardous substances; National Contingency Plan.
- (d) Maritime disaster discharges.
- (e) Judicial relief.
- (f) Liability for actual costs of removal.
- (g) Third party liability.
- (h) Rights against third parties who caused or contributed to discharge.
- (i) Recovery of removal costs.
- (j) Regulations; penalty.
- (k) Authorization of appropriations; supplemental appropriations.
- (l) Administration.
- (m) Boarding and inspection of vessels; arrest; execution of warrants or other process.
- (n) Jurisdiction.
- (o) Obligation for damages unaffected; local authority not preempted; existing Federal authority not modified or affected.
- (p) Financial responsibility.
- (q) Establishment of maximum limit of liability with respect to onshore or offshore facilities.
- (r) Liability limitations not to limit liability under other legislation.

1322. Marine sanitation devices.
- (a) Definitions.
- (b) Federal standards of performance.
- (c) Initial standards; effective dates; revision; waiver.
- (d) Vessels owned and operated by the United States.
- (e) Pre-promulgation consultation.
- (f) Regulation by States or political subdivisions thereof; complete prohibition upon discharge of sewage.
- (g) Sales limited to certified devices; certification of test device; recordkeeping; reports.
- (h) Sale and resale of properly equipped vessels; operability of certified marine sanitation devices.
- (i) Jurisdiction to restrain violations; contempts.
- (j) Penalties.
- (k) Enforcement authority.
- (l) Boarding and inspection of vessels; execution of warrants and other process.
- (m) Enforcement in United States possessions.

1323. Federal facilities pollution control.

1324. Clean lakes.
- (a) Establishment and scope of program.
- (b) Financial assistance to States.
- (c) Maximum amount of grant; authorization of appropriations.
- (d) Demonstration program.

1325. National Study Commission.

Clean Water Act

       (a) Establishment.
       (b) Membership; chairman.
       (c) Contract authority.
       (d) Cooperation of departments, agencies, and instrumentalities of executive branch.
       (e) Report to Congress.
       (f) Compensation and allowances.
       (g) Appointment of personnel.
       (h) Authorization of appropriation.

1326. Thermal discharges.
       (a) Effluent limitations that will assure protection and propagation of balanced, indigenous population of shellfish, fish, and wildlife.
       (b) Cooling water intake structures.
       (c) Period of protection from more stringent effluent limitations following discharge point source modification commenced after October 18, 1972.

1329. Nonpoint source management programs.
       (a) State assessment reports.
       (b) State management programs.
       (c) Administrative provisions.
       (d) Approval or disapproval of reports and management programs.
       (e) Local management programs; technical assistance.
       (f) Technical assistance for States.
       (g) Interstate management conference.
       (h) Grant program.
       (i) Grants for protecting groundwater quality.
       (j) Authorization of appropriations.
       (k) Consistency of other programs and projects with management programs.
       (l) Collection of information.
       (m) Reports of Administrator.
       (n) Set aside for administrative personnel.

1330. National estuary program.
       (a) Management conference.
       (b) Purposes of conference.
       (c) Members of conference.
       (d) Utilization of existing data.
       (e) Period of conference.
       (f) Approval and implementation of plans.
       (g) Grants.
       (h) Grant reporting.
       (i) Authorization of appropriations.
       (j) Research.
       (k) Definitions.

SUBCHAPTER IV — PERMITS AND LICENSES

1341. Certification.
       (a) Compliance with applicable requirements; application; procedures; license suspension.
       (b) Compliance with other provisions of law setting applicable water quality requirements.

Clean Water Act

- (c) Authority of Secretary of the Army to permit use of spoil disposal areas by Federal licensees or permittees.
- (d) Limitations and monitoring requirements of certification.

1342. National pollutant discharge elimination system.
- (a) Permits for discharge of pollutants.
- (b) State permit programs.
- (c) Suspension of Federal program upon submission of State program; withdrawal of approval of State program; return of State program to Administrator.
- (d) Notification of Administrator.
- (e) Waiver of notification requirement.
- (f) Point source categories.
- (g) Other regulations for safe transportation, handling, carriage, storage, and stowage of pollutants.
- (h) Violation of permit conditions; restriction or prohibition upon introduction of pollutant by source not previously utilizing treatment works.
- (i) Federal enforcement not limited.
- (j) Public information.
- (k) Compliance with permits.
- (l) Limitation on permit requirement.
- (m) Additional pretreatment of conventional pollutants not required.
- (n) Partial permit program.
- (o) Anti-backsliding.
- (p) Municipal and industrial stormwater discharges.

1343. Ocean discharge criteria.
- (a) Issuance of permits.
- (b) Waiver.
- (c) Guidelines for determining degradation of waters.

1344. Permits for dredged or fill material.
- (a) Discharge into navigable waters at specified disposal sites.
- (b) Specification for disposal sites.
- (c) Denial or restriction of use of defined areas as disposal sites.
- (d) "Secretary" defined.
- (e) General permits on State, regional, or nationwide basis.
- (f) Non-prohibited discharge of dredged or fill material.
- (g) State administration.
- (h) Determination of State's authority to issue permits under State program; approval; notification; transfers to State program.
- (i) Withdrawal of approval.
- (j) Copies of applications for State permits and proposed general permits to be transmitted to Administrator.
- (k) Waiver.
- (l) Categories of discharges not subject to requirements.
- (m) Comments on permit applications or proposed general permits by Secretary of the Interior acting through Director of United States Fish and Wildlife Service.
- (n) Enforcement authority not limited.
- (o) Public availability of permits and permit applications.
- (p) Compliance.

Clean Water Act

(q) Minimization of duplication, needless paperwork, and delays in issuance; agreements.
(r) Federal projects specifically authorized by Congress.
(s) Violation of permits.
(t) Navigable waters within State jurisdiction.

1345. Disposal or use of sewage sludge.
(a) Permit.
(b) Issuance of permit; regulations.
(c) State permit program.
(d) Regulations.
(e) Manner of sludge disposal.
(f) Implementation of regulations.
(g) Studies and projects.

SUBCHAPTER V — GENERAL PROVISIONS

1361. Administration.
(a) Authority of Administrator to prescribe regulations.
(b) Utilization of other agency officers and employees.
(c) Recordkeeping.
(d) Audit.
(e) Awards for outstanding technological achievement or innovative processes, methods, or devices in waste treatment and pollution abatement programs.
(f) Detail of Environmental Protection Agency personnel to State water pollution control agencies.

1362. Definitions.

1363. Water Pollution Control Advisory Board.
(a) Establishment; composition; terms of office.
(b) Functions.
(c) Clerical and technical assistance.

1364. Emergency powers.
(a) Emergency powers.

1365. Citizen suits.
(a) Authorization; jurisdiction.
(b) Notice.
(c) Venue; intervention by Administrator; United States interests protected.
(d) Litigation costs.
(e) Statutory or common law rights not restricted.
(f) Effluent standard or limitation.
(g) "Citizen" defined.
(h) Civil action by State Governors.

1366. Appearance.

1367. Employee protection.
(a) Discrimination against persons filing, instituting, or testifying in proceedings under this chapter prohibited.
(b) Application for review; investigation; hearing; review.
(c) Costs and expenses.
(d) Deliberate violations by employee acting without direction from his employer or his agent.
(e) Investigations of employment reductions.

Clean Water Act

1368. Federal procurement.
    (a) Contracts with violators prohibited.
    (b) Notification of agencies.
    (c) Omitted.
    (d) Exemptions.
    (e) Annual report to Congress.
1369. Administrative procedure and judicial review.
    (a) Subpenas.
    (b) Review of Administrator's actions; selection of court; fees.
    (c) Additional evidence.
1370. State authority.
1371. Authority under other laws and regulations.
    (a) Impairment of authority or functions of officials and agencies; treaty provisions.
    (b) Discharges of pollutants into navigable waters.
    (c) Action of the Administrator deemed major Federal action; construction of the National Environmental Policy Act of 1969.
    (d) Consideration of international water pollution control agreements.
1372. Labor standards.
1373. Public health agency coordination.
1377. Indian tribes.
    (a) Policy.
    (b) Assessment of sewage treatment needs; report.
    (c) Reservation of funds.
    (d) Cooperative agreements.
    (e) Treatment as States.
    (f) Grants for nonpoint source programs.
    (g) Alaska native organizations.
    (h) Definitions.

SUBCHAPTER VI — STATE WATER POLLUTION CONTROL REVOLVING FUNDS

1381. Grants to States for establishment of revolving funds.
    (a) General authority.
    (b) Schedule of grant payments.
1382. Capitalization grant agreements.
    (a) General rule.
    (b) Specific requirements.
1383. Water pollution control revolving loan funds.
    (a) Requirements for obligation of grant funds.
    (b) Administration.
    (c) Projects eligible for assistance.
    (d) Types of assistance.
    (e) Limitation to prevent double benefits.
    (f) Consistency with planning requirements.
    (g) Priority list requirement.
    (h) Eligibility of non-Federal share of construction grant projects.
1384. Allotment of funds.
    (a) Formula.
    (b) Reservation of funds for planning.
    (c) Allotment period.

1385. Corrective action.
(a) Notification of noncompliance.
(b) Withholding of payments.
(c) Reallotment of withheld payments.
1386. Audits, reports, and fiscal controls; intended use plan.
(a) Fiscal control and auditing procedures.
(b) Annual Federal audits.
(c) Intended use plan.
(d) Annual report.
(e) Annual Federal oversight review.
(f) Applicability of subchapter II provisions.

Chapter 26 — Water Pollution Prevention and Control

SUBCHAPTER I — RESEARCH AND RELATED PROGRAMS

§1251. CONGRESSIONAL DECLARATION OF GOALS AND POLICY

(a) **RESTORATION AND MAINTENANCE OF CHEMICAL, PHYSICAL AND BIOLOGICAL INTEGRITY OF NATION'S WATERS; NATIONAL GOALS FOR ACHIEVEMENT OF OBJECTIVE**

The objective of this chapter is to restore and maintain the chemical, physical, and biological integrity of the Nation's waters. In order to achieve this objective it is hereby declared that, consistent with the provisions of this chapter —

(1) it is the national goal that the discharge of pollutants into the navigable waters be eliminated by 1985;

(2) it is the national goal that wherever attainable, an interim goal of water quality which provides for the protection and propagation of fish, shellfish, and wildlife and provides for recreation in and on the water be achieved by July 1, 1983;

(3) it is the national policy that the discharge of toxic pollutants in toxic amounts be prohibited;

(4) it is the national policy that Federal financial assistance be provided to construct publicly owned waste treatment works;

(5) it is the national policy that areawide waste treatment management planning processes be developed and implemented to assure adequate control of sources of pollutants in each State;

(6) it is the national policy that a major research and demonstration effort be made to develop technology necessary to eliminate the discharge of pollutants into the navigable waters, waters of the contiguous zone, and the oceans; and

(7) it is the national policy that programs for the control of nonpoint sources of pollution be developed and implemented in an expeditious manner so as to enable the goals of this chapter to be met through the control of both point and nonpoint sources of pollution.

Clean Water Act §1251

(b) CONGRESSIONAL RECOGNITION, PRESERVATION, AND PROTECTION OF PRIMARY RESPONSIBILITIES AND RIGHTS OF STATES

It is the policy of the Congress to recognize, preserve, and protect the primary responsibilities and rights of States to prevent, reduce, and eliminate pollution, to plan the development and use (including restoration, preservation, and enhancement) of land and water resources, and to consult with the Administrator in the exercise of his authority under this chapter. It is the policy of Congress that the States manage the construction grant program under this chapter and implement the permit programs under sections 1342 and 1344 of this title. It is further the policy of the Congress to support and aid research relating to the prevention, reduction, and elimination of pollutions and to provide Federal technical services and financial aid to State and interstate agencies and municipalities in connection with the prevention, reduction, and elimination of pollution.

(c) CONGRESSIONAL POLICY TOWARD PRESIDENTIAL ACTIVITIES WITH FOREIGN COUNTRIES

It is further the policy of Congress that the President, acting through the Secretary of State and such national and international organizations as he determines appropriate, shall take such action as may be necessary to insure that to the fullest extent possible all foreign countries shall take meaningful action for the prevention, reduction, and elimination of pollution in their waters and in international waters and for the achievement of goals regarding the elimination of discharge of pollutants and the improvement of water quality to at least the same extent as the United States does under its laws.

(d) ADMINISTRATOR OF ENVIRONMENTAL PROTECTION AGENCY TO ADMINISTER CHAPTER

Except as otherwise expressly provided in this chapter, the Administrator of the Environmental Protection Agency (hereinafter in this chapter called "Administrator") shall administer this chapter.

(e) PUBLIC PARTICIPATION IN DEVELOPMENT, REVISION, AND ENFORCEMENT OF ANY REGULATION, ETC.

Public participation in the development, revision, and enforcement of any regulation, standard, effluent limitation, plan, or program established by the Administrator or any State under this chapter shall be provided for, encouraged, and assisted by the Administrator and the States. The Administrator, in cooperation with the States, shall develop and publish regulations specifying minimum guidelines for public participation in such processes.

(f) PROCEDURES UTILIZED FOR IMPLEMENTING CHAPTER

It is the national policy that to the maximum extent possible the procedures utilized for implementing this chapter shall encourage the drastic minimization of paperwork and interagency decision procedures, and the best use of

§1251

available manpower and funds, so as to prevent needless duplication and unnecessary delays at all levels of government.

(g) AUTHORITY OF STATES OVER WATER

It is the policy of Congress that the authority of each State to allocate quantities of water within its jurisdiction shall not be superseded, abrogated or otherwise impaired by this chapter. It is the further policy of Congress that nothing in this chapter shall be construed to supersede or abrogate rights to quantities of water which have been established by any State. Federal agencies shall cooperate with State and local agencies to develop comprehensive solutions to prevent, reduce and eliminate pollution in concert with programs for managing water resources.

§1252. COMPREHENSIVE PROGRAMS FOR WATER POLLUTION CONTROL

(a) PREPARATION AND DEVELOPMENT

The Administrator shall, after careful investigation, and in cooperation with other Federal agencies, State water pollution control agencies, interstate agencies, and the municipalities and industries involved, prepare or develop comprehensive programs for preventing, reducing, or eliminating the pollution of the navigable waters and ground waters and improving the sanitary condition of surface and underground waters. In the development of such comprehensive programs due regard shall be given to the improvements which are necessary to conserve such waters for the protection and propagation of fish and aquatic life and wildlife, recreational purposes, and the withdrawal of such waters for public water supply, agricultural, industrial, and other purposes. For the purpose of this section, the Administrator is authorized to make joint investigations with any such agencies of the condition of any waters in any State or States, and of the discharges of any sewage, industrial wastes, or substance which may adversely affect such waters.

(b) PLANNING FOR RESERVOIRS; STORAGE FOR REGULATION OF STREAMFLOW

(1) In the survey or planning of any reservoir by the Corps of Engineers, Bureau of Reclamation, or other Federal agency, consideration shall be given to inclusion of storage for regulation of streamflow, except that any such storage and water releases shall not be provided as a substitute for adequate treatment or other methods of controlling waste at the source.

(2) The need for and the value of storage for regulation of streamflow (other than for water quality) including but not limited to navigation, salt water intrusion, recreation, esthetics, and fish and wildlife, shall be determined by the Corps of Engineers, Bureau of Reclamation, or other Federal agencies.

(3) The need for, the value of, and the impact of, storage for water quality control shall be determined by the Administrator, and his views on these matters

Clean Water Act §1252

shall be set forth in any report or presentation to Congress proposing authorization or construction of any reservoir including such storage.

(4) The value of such storage shall be taken into account in determining the economic value of the entire project of which it is a part, and costs shall be allocated to the purpose of regulation of streamflow in a manner which will insure that all project purposes, share equitably in the benefit of multiple-purpose construction.

(5) Costs of regulation of streamflow features incorporated in any Federal reservoir or other impoundment under the provisions of this chapter shall be determined and the beneficiaries identified and if the benefits are widespread or national in scope, the costs of such features shall be nonreimbursable.

(6) No license granted by the Federal Energy Regulatory for a hydroelectric power project shall include storage for regulation of streamflow for the purpose of water quality control unless the Administrator shall recommend its inclusion and such reservoir storage capacity shall not exceed such proportion of the total storage required for the water quality control plan as the drainage area of such reservoir bears to the drainage area of the river basin or basins involved in such water quality control plan.

(c) BASINS; GRANTS TO STATE AGENCIES

(1) The Administrator shall, at the request of the Governor of a State, or a majority of the Governors when more than one State is involved, make a grant to pay not to exceed 50 per centum of the administrative expenses of a planning agency for a period not to exceed three years, which period shall begin after October 18, 1972, if such agency provides for adequate representation of appropriate State, interstate, local, or (when appropriate) international interests in the basin or portion thereof involved and is capable of developing an effective, comprehensive water quality control plan for a basin or portion thereof.

(2) Each planning agency receiving a grant under this subsection shall develop a comprehensive pollution control plan for the basin or portion thereof which —

(A) is consistent with any applicable water quality standards effluent and other limitations, and thermal discharge regulations established pursuant to current law within the basin;

(B) recommends such treatment works as will provide the most effective and economical means of collection, storage, treatment, and elimination of pollutants and recommends means to encourage both municipal and industrial use of such works;

(C) recommends maintenance and improvement of water quality within the basin or portion thereof and recommends methods of adequately financing those facilities as may be necessary to implement the plan; and

(D) as appropriate, is developed in cooperation with, and is consistent with any comprehensive plan prepared by the Water Resources Council, any areawide waste management plans developed pursuant to section 1288 of

§1252

this title, and any State plan developed pursuant to section 1313(e) of this title.

(3) For the purposes of this subsection the term "basin" includes, but is not limited to, rivers and their tributaries, streams, coastal waters, sounds, estuaries, bays, lakes, and portions thereof as well as the lands drained thereby.

(d) **REPORT TO CONGRESS**

The Administrator, after consultation with the States, and River Basin Commissions established under the Water Resources Planning Act [42 U.S.C. 1962 et seq.], shall submit a report to Congress on or before July 1, 1978, which analyzes the relationship between programs under this chapter, and the programs by which State and Federal agencies allocate quantities of water. Such report shall include recommendations concerning the policy in section 1251(g) of this title to improve coordination of efforts to reduce and eliminate pollution in concert with programs for managing water resources.

§1252a. RESERVOIR PROJECTS, WATER STORAGE; MODIFICATION; STORAGE FOR OTHER THAN FOR WATER QUALITY, OPINION OF FEDERAL AGENCY, COMMITTEE RESOLUTIONS OF APPROVAL; PROVISIONS INAPPLICABLE TO PROJECTS WITH CERTAIN PRESCRIBED WATER QUALITY BENEFITS IN RELATION TO TOTAL PROJECT BENEFITS

In the case of any reservoir project authorized for construction by the Corps of Engineers, Bureau of Reclamation, or other Federal agency when the Administrator of the Environmental Protection Agency determines pursuant to section 1252(b) of this title that any storage in such project for regulation of streamflow for water quality is not needed, or is needed in a different amount, such project may be modified accordingly by the head of the appropriate agency, and any storage no longer required for water quality may be utilized for other authorized purposes of the project when, in the opinion of the head of such agency, such use is justified. Any such modification of a project where the benefits attributable to water quality are 15 per centum or more but not greater than 25 per centum of the total project benefits shall take effect only upon the adoption of resolutions approving such modification by the appropriate committees of the Senate and House of Representatives. The provisions of the section shall not apply to any project where the benefits attributable to water quality exceed 25 per centum of the total project benefits.

§1253. INTERSTATE COOPERATION AND UNIFORM LAWS

(a) The Administrator shall encourage cooperative activities by the States for the prevention, reduction, and elimination of pollution, encourage the enactment of improved and, so far as practicable, uniform State laws relating to the prevention, reduction, and elimination of pollution; and encourage compacts between States for the prevention and control of pollution.

(b) The consent of the Congress is hereby given to two or more States to negotiate and enter into agreements or compacts, not in conflict with any law or treaty of the United States, for (1) cooperative effort and mutual assistance for the prevention and control of pollution and the enforcement of their respective laws relating thereto, and (2) the establishment of such agencies, joint or otherwise, as they may deem desirable for making effective such agreements and compacts. No such agreement or compact shall be binding or obligatory upon any State a party thereto unless and until it has been approved by the Congress.

§1254. RESEARCH, INVESTIGATIONS, TRAINING, AND INFORMATION

(a) ESTABLISHMENT OF NATIONAL PROGRAMS; COOPERATION; INVESTIGATIONS; WATER QUALITY SURVEILLANCE SYSTEM; REPORTS

The Administrator shall establish national programs for the prevention, reduction, and elimination of pollution and as part of such programs shall —

(1) in cooperation with other Federal, State, and local agencies, conduct and promote the coordination and acceleration of, research, investigations, experiments, training, demonstrations, surveys, and studies relating to the causes, effects, extent, prevention, reduction, and elimination of pollution;

(2) encourage, cooperate with, and render technical services to pollution control agencies and other appropriate public or private agencies, institutions, and organizations, and individuals, including the general public, in the conduct of activities referred to in paragraph (1) of this subsection;

(3) conduct, in cooperation with State water pollution control agencies and other interested agencies, organizations and persons, public investigations concerning the pollution of any navigable waters, and report on the results of such investigations;

(4) establish advisory committees composed of recognized experts in various aspects of pollution and representatives of the public to assist in the examination and evaluation of research progress and proposals and to avoid duplication of research;

(5) in cooperation with the States, and their political subdivisions, and other Federal agencies establish, equip, and maintain a water quality surveillance system for the purpose of monitoring the quality of the navigable waters and ground waters and the contiguous zone and the oceans and the Administrator shall, to the extent practicable, conduct such surveillance by utilizing the resources of the National Aeronautics and Space Administration, the National Oceanic and Atmospheric Administration, the Geological Survey, and the Coast Guard, and shall report on such quality in the report required under subsection (a) of section 1375 of this title; and

(6) initiate and promote the coordination and acceleration of research designed to develop the most effective practicable tools and techniques for measuring the social and economic costs and benefits of activities which are

subject to regulation under this chapter, and shall transmit a report on the results of such research to the Congress not later than January 1, 1974.

(b) AUTHORIZED ACTIVITIES OF ADMINISTRATOR

In carrying out the provisions of subsection (a) of this section the Administrator is authorized to —

(1) collect and make available, through publications and other appropriate means, the results of and other information, including appropriate recommendations by him in connection therewith, pertaining to such research and other activities referred to in paragraph (1) of subsection (a) of this section;

(2) cooperate with other Federal departments and agencies, State water pollution control agencies, interstate agencies, other public and private agencies, institutions, organizations, industries involved, and individuals, in the preparation and conduct of such research and other activities referred to in paragraph (1) of subsection (a) of this section;

(3) make grants to State water pollution control agencies, interstate agencies, other public or nonprofit private agencies, institutions, organizations, and individuals, for purposes stated in paragraph (1) of subsection (a) of this section;

(4) contract with public or private agencies, institutions, organizations, and individuals, without regard to section 3324(a) and (b) of title 31 and section 5 of title 41, referred to in paragraph (1) of subsection (a) of this section;

(5) establish and maintain research fellowships at public or nonprofit private educational institutions or research organizations;

(6) collect and disseminate, in cooperation with other Federal departments and agencies, and with other public or private agencies, institutions, and organizations having related responsibilities, basic data on chemical, physical, and biological effects of varying water quality and other information pertaining to pollution and the prevention, reduction, and elimination thereof; and

(7) develop effective and practical processes, methods, and prototype devices for the prevention, reduction, and elimination of pollution.

(c) RESEARCH AND STUDIES ON HARMFUL EFFECTS OF POLLUTANTS; COOPERATION WITH SECRETARY OF HEALTH AND HUMAN SERVICES

In carrying out the provisions of subsection (a) of this section the Administrator shall conduct research on, and survey the results of other scientific studies on, the harmful effects on the health or welfare of persons caused by pollutants. In order to avoid duplication of effort, the Administrator shall, to the extent practicable, conduct such research in cooperation with and through the facilities of the Secretary of Health and Human Services.

Clean Water Act

(d) SEWAGE TREATMENT; IDENTIFICATION AND MEASUREMENT OF EFFECTS OF POLLUTANTS; AUGMENTED STREAMFLOW

In carrying out the provisions of this section the Administrator shall develop and demonstrate under varied conditions (including conducting such basic and applied research, studies, and experiments as may be necessary):

(1) Practicable means of treating municipal sewage, and other waterborne wastes to implement the requirements of section 1281 of this title;

(2) Improved methods and procedures to identify and measure the effects of pollutants, including those pollutants created by new technological developments; and

(3) Methods and procedures for evaluating the effects on water quality of augmented streamflows to control pollution not susceptible to other means of prevention, reduction, or elimination.

(e) FIELD LABORATORY AND RESEARCH FACILITIES

The Administrator shall establish, equip, and maintain field laboratory and research facilities, including, but not limited to, one to be located in the northeastern area of the United States, one in the Middle Atlantic area, one in the southeastern area, one in the midwestern area, one in the southwestern area, one in the Pacific Northwest, and one in the State of Alaska, for the conduct of research, investigations, experiments, field demonstrations and studies, and training relating to the prevention, reduction and elimination of pollution. Insofar as practicable, each such facility shall be located near institutions of higher learning in which graduate training in such research might be carried out. In conjunction with the development of criteria under section 1343 of this title, the Administrator shall construct the facilities authorized for the National Marine Water Quality Laboratory established under this subsection.

[Various sections that authorize specific research projects are omitted.]

§1254a. RESEARCH ON EFFECTS OF POLLUTANTS

In carrying out the provisions of section 1254(a) of this title, the Administrator shall conduct research on the harmful effects on the health and welfare of persons caused by pollutants in water, in conjunction with the United States Fish and Wildlife Service, the National Oceanic and Atmospheric Administration, and other Federal, State, and interstate agencies carrying on such research. Such research shall include, and shall place special emphasis on, the effect that bioaccumulation of these pollutants in aquatic species has upon reducing the value of aquatic commercial and sport industries. Such research shall further study methods to reduce and remove these pollutants from the relevant affected aquatic species so as to restore and enhance these valuable resources.

§1255. GRANTS FOR RESEARCH AND DEVELOPMENT

(a) DEMONSTRATION PROJECTS COVERING STORM WATERS, ADVANCED WASTE TREATMENT AND WATER PURIFICATION METHODS, AND JOINT TREATMENT SYSTEMS FOR MUNICIPAL AND INDUSTRIAL WASTES

The Administrator is authorized to conduct in the Environmental Protection Agency, and to make grants to any State, municipality, or intermunicipal or interstate agency for the purpose of assisting in the development of —

(1) any project which will demonstrate a new or improved method of preventing, reducing, and eliminating the discharge into any waters of pollutants from sewers which carry storm water or both storm water and pollutants; or

(2) any project which will demonstrate advanced waste treatment and water purification methods (including the temporary use of new or improved chemical additives which provide substantial immediate improvements to existing treatment processes), or new or improved methods of joint treatment systems for municipal and industrial wastes;

and to include in such grants such amounts as are necessary for the purpose of reports, plans, and specifications in connection therewith.

(b) DEMONSTRATION PROJECTS FOR ADVANCED TREATMENT AND ENVIRONMENTAL ENHANCEMENT TECHNIQUES TO CONTROL POLLUTION IN RIVER BASINS

The Administrator is authorized to make grants to any State or States or interstate agency to demonstrate, in river basins or portions thereof, advanced treatment and environmental enhancement techniques to control pollution from all sources, within such basins or portions thereof, including nonpoint sources, together with in stream[1] water quality improvement techniques.

(c) RESEARCH AND DEMONSTRATION PROJECTS FOR PREVENTION OF WATER POLLUTION BY INDUSTRY

In order to carry out the purposes of section 1311 of this title, the Administrator is authorized to (1) conduct in the Environmental Protection Agency, (2) make grants to persons, and (3) enter into contracts with persons, for research and demonstration projects for prevention of pollution of any waters by industry including, but not limited to, the prevention, reduction, and elimination of the discharge of pollutants. No grant shall be made for any project under this subsection unless the Administrator determines that such project will develop or demonstrate a new or improved method of treating industrial wastes or otherwise prevent pollution by industry, which method shall have industrywide application.

---

1. So in original.

(d) ACCELERATED AND PRIORITY DEVELOPMENT OF WASTE MANAGEMENT AND WASTE TREATMENT METHODS AND IDENTIFICATION AND MEASUREMENT METHODS

In carrying out the provisions of this section, the Administrator shall conduct, on a priority basis, an accelerated effort to develop, refine, and achieve practical application of:

(1) waste management methods applicable to point and nonpoint sources of pollutants to eliminate the discharge of pollutants, including, but not limited to, elimination of runoff of pollutants and the effects of pollutants from inplace or accumulated sources;

(2) advanced waste treatment methods applicable to point and nonpoint sources, including inplace or accumulated sources of pollutants, and methods for reclaiming and recycling water and confining pollutants so they will not migrate to cause water or other environmental pollution; and

(3) improved methods and procedures to identify and measure the effects of pollutants on the chemical, physical, and biological integrity of water, including those pollutants created by new technological developments.

(e) RESEARCH AND DEMONSTRATION PROJECTS COVERING AGRICULTURAL POLLUTION AND POLLUTION FROM SEWAGE IN RURAL AREAS; DISSEMINATION OF INFORMATION

(1) The Administrator is authorized to (A) make, in consultation with the Secretary of Agriculture, grants to persons for research and demonstration projects with respect to new and improved methods of preventing, reducing, and eliminating pollution from agriculture, and (B) disseminate, in cooperation with the Secretary of Agriculture, such information obtained under this subsection, section 1254(p) of this title, and section 1314 of this title as will encourage and enable the adoption of such methods in the agricultural industry.

(2) The Administrator is authorized, (A) in consultation with other interested Federal agencies, to make grants for demonstration projects with respect to new and improved methods of preventing, reducing, storing, collecting, treating, or otherwise eliminating pollution from sewage in rural and other areas where collection of sewage in conventional, community-wide sewage collection systems is impractical, uneconomical, or otherwise infeasible, or where soil conditions or other factors preclude the use of septic tank and drainage field systems, and (B) in cooperation with other interested Federal and State agencies, to disseminate such information obtained under this subsection as will encourage and enable the adoption of new and improved methods developed pursuant to this subsection.

(f) LIMITATIONS

Federal grants under subsection (a) of this section shall be subject to the following limitations:

(1) No grant shall be made for any project unless such project shall have

§1255   Clean Water Act

been approved by the appropriate State water pollution control agency or agencies and by the Administrator;

(2) No grant shall be made for any project in an amount exceeding 75 per centum of cost thereof as determined by the Administrator; and

(3) No grant shall be made for any project unless the Administrator determines that such project will serve as a useful demonstration for the purpose set forth in clause (1) or (2) of subsection (a) of this section.

(g)   MAXIMUM GRANTS

Federal grants under subsections (c) and (d) of this section shall not exceed 75 per centum of the cost of the project.

(h)   AUTHORIZATION OF APPROPRIATIONS

For the purpose of this section there is authorized to be appropriated $75,000,000 per fiscal year for the fiscal year ending June 30, 1973, the fiscal year ending June 30, 1974, and the fiscal year ending June 30, 1975, and from such appropriations at least 10 per centum of the funds actually appropriated in each fiscal year shall be available only for the purposes of subsection (e) of this section.

(i)   ASSISTANCE FOR RESEARCH AND DEMONSTRATION PROJECTS

The Administrator is authorized to make grants to a municipality to assist in the costs of operating and maintaining a project which received a grant under this section, section 1254 of this title, or section 1263 of this title prior to December 27, 1977, so as to reduce the operation and maintenance costs borne by the recipients of services from such project to costs comparable to those for projects assisted under subchapter II of this chapter.

(j)   ASSISTANCE FOR RECYCLE, REUSE, AND LAND TREATMENT PROJECTS

The Administrator is authorized to make a grant to any grantee who received an increased grant pursuant to section 1282(a)(2) of this title. Such grant may pay up to 100 per centum of the costs of technical evaluation of the operation of the treatment works, costs of training of persons (other than employees of the grantee), and costs of disseminating technical information on the operation of the treatment works. . . .

§1267.   CHESAPEAKE BAY

(a)   OFFICE

The Administrator shall continue the Chesapeake Bay Program and shall establish and maintain in the Environmental Protection Agency an office, division, or branch of Chesapeake Bay Programs to —

(1) collect and make available, through publications and other appro-

priate means, information pertaining to the environmental quality of the Chesapeake Bay (hereinafter in this subsection referred to as the "Bay");

(2) coordinate Federal and State efforts to improve the water quality of the Bay;

(3) determine the impact of sediment deposition in the Bay and identify the sources, rates, routes, and distribution patterns of such sediment deposition; and

(4) determine the impact of natural and man-induced environmental changes on the living resources of the Bay and the relationships among such changes, with particular emphasis placed on the impact of pollutant loadings of nutrients, chlorine; acid precipitation, dissolved oxygen, and toxic pollutants, including organic chemicals and heavy metals, and with special attention given to the impact of such changes on striped bass.

(b) INTERSTATE DEVELOPMENT PLAN GRANTS

(1) AUTHORITY

The Administrator shall, at the request of the Governor of a State affected by the interstate management plan developed pursuant to the Chesapeake Bay Program (hereinafter in this section referred to as the "plan"), make a grant for the purpose of implementing the management mechanisms contained in the plan if such State has, within 1 year after February 4, 1987, approved and committed to implement all or substantially all aspects of the plan. Such grants shall be made subject to such terms and conditions as the Administrator considers appropriate.

(2) SUBMISSION OF PROPOSAL

A State or combination of States may elect to avail itself of the benefits of this subsection by submitting to the Administrator a comprehensive proposal to implement management mechanisms contained in the plan which shall include (A) a description of proposed abatement actions which the State or combination of States commits to take within a specified time period to reduce pollution in the Bay and to meet applicable water quality standards, and (B) the estimated cost of the abatement actions proposed to be taken during the next fiscal year. If the Administrator finds that such proposal is consistent with the national policies set forth in section 1251(a) of this title and will contribute to the achievement of the national goals set forth in such section, the Administrator shall approve such proposal and shall finance the costs of implementing segments of such proposal.

(3) FEDERAL SHARE

Grants under this subsection shall not exceed 50 percent of the costs of implementing the management mechanisms contained in the plan in any fiscal year and shall be made on condition that non-Federal sources provide the remainder of the cost of implementing the management mechanisms contained in the plan during such fiscal year.

(4) ADMINISTRATIVE COSTS

Administrative costs in the form of salaries, overhead, or indirect costs for services provided and charged against programs or projects supported by funds made available under this subsection shall not exceed in any one fiscal year 10 percent of the annual Federal grant made to a State under this subsection.

(c) REPORTS

Any State or combination of States that receives a grant under subsection (b) of this section shall, within 18 months after the date of receipt of such grant and biennially thereafter, report to the Administrator on the progress made in implementing the interstate management plan developed pursuant to the Chesapeake Bay Program. The Administrator shall transmit each such report along with the comments of the Administrator on such report to Congress.

(d) AUTHORIZATION OF APPROPRIATIONS

There are hereby authorized to be appropriated the following sums, to remain available until expended, to carry out the purposes of this section:

(1) $3,000,000 per fiscal year for each of the fiscal years 1987, 1988, 1989, and 1990, to carry out subsection (a) of this section; and

(2) $10,000,000 per fiscal year for each of the fiscal years 1987, 1988, 1989, and 1990, for grants to States under subsection (b) of this section.

§1268. GREAT LAKES

(a) FINDINGS, PURPOSE, AND DEFINITIONS

(1) FINDINGS

The Congress finds that —

(A) the Great Lakes are a valuable national resource, continuously serving the people of the United States and other nations as an important source of food, fresh water, recreation, beauty, and enjoyment;

(B) the United States should seek to attain the goals embodied in the Great Lakes Water Quality Agreement of 1978, as amended by the Water Quality Agreement of 1987 and any other agreements and amendments, with particular emphasis on goals related to toxic pollutants; and

(C) the Environmental Protection Agency should take the lead in the effort to meet those goals, working with other Federal agencies and State and local authorities.

Clean Water Act §1268

(2) PURPOSE

It is the purpose of this section to achieve the goals embodied in the Great Lakes Water Quality Agreement of 1978, as amended by the Water Quality Agreement of 1987 and any other agreements and amendments, through improved organization and definition of mission on the part of the Agency, funding of State grants for pollution control in the Great Lakes area, and improved accountability for implementation of such agreement.

(3) DEFINITIONS

For purposes of this section, the term —
 (A) "Agency" means the Environmental Protection Agency;
 (B) "Great Lakes" means Lake Ontario, Lake Erie, Lake Huron (including Lake St. Clair), Lake Michigan, and Lake Superior, and the connecting channels (Saint Mary's River, Saint Clair River, Detroit River, Niagara River, and Saint Lawrence River to the Canadian Border);
 (C) "Great Lakes System" means all the streams, rivers, lakes, and other bodies of water within the drainage basin of the Great Lakes;
 (D) "Program Office" means the Great Lakes National Program Office established by this section; and
 (E) "Research Office" means the Great Lakes Research Office established by subsection (d) of this section.

(b) GREAT LAKES NATIONAL PROGRAM OFFICE

The Great Lakes National Program Office (previously established by the Administrator) is hereby established within the Agency. The Program Office shall be headed by a Director who, by reason of management experience and technical expertise relating to the Great Lakes, is highly qualified to direct the development of programs and plans on a variety of Great Lakes issues. The Great Lakes National Program Office shall be located in the Great Lakes State.

(c) GREAT LAKES MANAGEMENT

(1) FUNCTIONS

The Program Office shall —
 (A) in cooperation with appropriate Federal, State, tribal, and international agencies, and in accordance with section 1251(e) of this title, develop and implement specific action plans to carry out the responsibilities of the United States under the Great Lakes Water Quality Agreement of 1978, as amended by the Water Quality Agreement of 1987 and any other agreements and amendments,;[2]
 (B) establish a Great Lakes system-wide surveillance network to mon-

---

2. So in original.

itor the water quality of the Great Lakes, with specific emphasis on the monitoring of toxic pollutants;

(C) serve as the liaison with, and provide information to, the Canadian members of the International Joint Commission and the Canadian counterpart to the Agency;

(D) coordinate actions of the Agency (including actions by headquarters and regional offices thereof) aimed at improving Great Lakes water quality; and

(E) coordinate actions of the Agency with the actions of other Federal agencies and State and local authorities, so as to ensure the input of those agencies and authorities in developing water quality strategies and obtain the support of those agencies and authorities in achieving the objectives of such agreement.

(2) 5-YEAR PLAN AND PROGRAM

The Program Office shall develop, in consultation with the States, a five-year plan and program for reducing the amount of nutrients introduced into the Great Lakes. Such program shall incorporate any management program for reducing nutrient runoff from nonpoint sources established under section 1329 of this title and shall include a program for monitoring nutrient runoff into, and ambient levels in, the Great Lakes.

(3) 5-YEAR STUDY AND DEMONSTRATION PROJECTS

The Program Office shall carry out a five-year study and demonstration projects relating to the control and removal of toxic pollutants in the Great Lakes, with emphasis on the removal of toxic pollutants from bottom sediments. In selecting locations for conducting demonstration projects under this paragraph, priority consideration shall be given to projects at the following locations: Saginaw Bay, Michigan; Sheboygan Harbor, Wisconsin; Grand Calumet River, Indiana; Ashtabula River, Ohio; and Buffalo River, New York.

(4) ADMINISTRATOR'S RESPONSIBILITY

The Administrator shall ensure that the Program Office enters into agreements with the various organizational elements of the Agency involved in Great Lakes activities and the appropriate State agencies specifically delineating —

(A) the duties and responsibilities of each such element in the Agency with respect to the Great Lakes;

(B) the time periods for carrying out such duties and responsibilities; and

(C) the resources to be committed to such duties and responsibilities.

Clean Water Act §1268

(5) BUDGET ITEM

The Administrator shall, in the Agency's annual budget submission to Congress, include a funding request for the Program Office as a separate budget line item.

(6) COMPREHENSIVE REPORT

Within 90 days after the end of each fiscal year, the Administrator shall submit to Congress a comprehensive report which —

(A) describes the achievements in the preceding fiscal year in implementing the Great Lakes Water Quality Agreement of 1978, as amended by the Water Quality Agreement of 1987 and any other agreements and amendments, and shows by categories (including judicial enforcement, research, State cooperative efforts, and general administration) the amounts expended on Great Lakes water quality initiatives in such preceding fiscal year;

(B) describes the progress made in such preceding fiscal year in implementing the system of surveillance of the water quality in the Great Lakes System, including the monitoring of groundwater and sediment with particular reference to toxic pollutants;

(C) describes the long-term prospects for improving the condition of the Great Lakes, and

(D) provides a comprehensive assessment of the planned efforts to be pursued in the succeeding fiscal year for implementing the Great Lakes Water Quality Agreement of 1978, as amended by the Water Quality Agreement of 1987 and any other agreements and amendments,,[2] which assessment shall —

(i) show by categories (including judicial enforcement, research, State cooperative efforts, and general administration), the amount anticipated to be expended on Great Lakes water quality initiatives in the fiscal year to which the assessment relates; and

(ii) include a report of current programs administered by other Federal agencies which make available resources to the Great Lakes water quality management efforts.

(d) GREAT LAKES RESEARCH

(1) ESTABLISHMENT OF RESEARCH OFFICE

There is established within the National Oceanic and Atmospheric Administration the Great Lakes Research Office.

(2) IDENTIFICATION OF ISSUES

The Research Office shall identify issues relating to the Great Lakes resources on which research is needed. The Research Office shall submit a

---

[2]So in original.

report to Congress on such issues before the end of each fiscal year which shall identify any changes in the Great Lakes system[3] with respect to such issues.

(3) INVENTORY

The Research Office shall identify and inventory Federal, State, university, and tribal environmental research programs (and, to the extent feasible, those of private organizations and other nations) relating to the Great Lakes system,[3] and shall update that inventory every four years.

(4) RESEARCH EXCHANGE

The Research Office shall establish a Great Lakes research exchange for the purpose of facilitating the rapid identification, acquisition, retrieval, dissemination, and use of information concerning research projects which are ongoing or completed and which affect the Great Lakes System.

(5) RESEARCH PROGRAM

The Research Office shall develop, in cooperation with the Coordination Office, a comprehensive environmental research program and data base for the Great Lakes system.[3] The data base shall include, but not be limited to, data relating to water quality, fisheries, and biota.

(6) MONITORING

The Research Office shall conduct, through the Great Lakes Environmental Research Laboratory, the National Sea Grant College program, other Federal laboratories, and the private sector, appropriate research and monitoring activities which address priority issues and current needs relating to the Great Lakes.

(7) LOCATION

The Research Office shall be located in a Great Lakes State.

(e) RESEARCH AND MANAGEMENT COORDINATION

(1) JOINT PLAN

Before October 1 of each year, the Program Office and the Research Office shall prepare a joint research plan for the fiscal year which begins in the following calendar year.

(2) CONTENTS OF PLAN

Each plan prepared under paragraph (1) shall —
   (A) identify all proposed research dedicated to activities conducted under the Great Lakes Water Quality Agreement of 1978, as amended by

---

3. So in original. Probably should be capitalized.

Clean Water Act §1268

the Water Quality Agreement of 1987 and any other agreements and amendments,;[4]

(B) include the Agency's assessment of priorities for research needed to fulfill the terms of such Agreement; and

(C) identify all proposed research that may be used to develop a comprehensive environmental data base for the Great Lakes System and establish priorities for development of such data base.

(f) INTERAGENCY COOPERATION

The head of each department, agency, or other instrumentality of the Federal Government which is engaged in, is concerned with, or has authority over programs relating to research, monitoring, and planning to maintain, enhance, preserve, or rehabilitate the environmental quality and natural resources of the Great Lakes, including the Chief of Engineers of the Army, the Chief of the Soil Conservation Service, the Commandant of the Coast Guard, the Director of the Fish and Wildlife Service, and the Administrator of the National Oceanic and Atmospheric Administration, shall submit an annual report to the Administrator with respect to the activities of that agency or office affecting compliance with the Great Lakes Water Quality Agreement of 1978, as amended by the Water Quality Agreement of 1987 and any other agreements and amendments,.[4]

(g) RELATIONSHIP TO EXISTING FEDERAL AND STATE LAWS AND INTERNATIONAL TREATIES

Nothing in this section shall be construed to affect the jurisdiction, powers, or prerogatives of any department, agency, or officer of the Federal Government or of any State government, or of any tribe, nor any powers, jurisdiction, or prerogatives of any international body created by treaty with authority relating to the Great Lakes.

(h) AUTHORIZATION OF GREAT LAKES APPROPRIATIONS

There are authorized to be appropriated to the Administrator to carry out this section not to exceed $11,000,000 per fiscal year for the fiscal years 1987, 1988, 1989, 1990, and 1991. Of the amounts appropriated each fiscal year —

(1) 40 percent shall be used by the Great Lakes National Program Office on demonstration projects on the feasibility of controlling and removing toxic pollutants;

(2) 7 percent shall be used by the Great Lakes National Program Office for the program of nutrient monitoring; and

(3) 30 percent shall be transferred to the National Oceanic and Atmospheric Administration for use by the Great Lakes Research Office.

---

4. So in original.

SUBCHAPTER II — GRANTS FOR CONSTRUCTION OF TREATMENT WORKS

§1281. CONGRESSIONAL DECLARATION OF PURPOSE

(a) **DEVELOPMENT AND IMPLEMENTATION OF WASTE TREATMENT MANAGEMENT PLANS AND PRACTICES**

It is the purpose of this subchapter to require and to assist the development and implementation of waste treatment management plans and practices which will achieve the goals of this chapter.

(b) **APPLICATION OF TECHNOLOGY: CONFINED DISPOSAL OF POLLUTANTS; CONSIDERATION OF ADVANCED TECHNIQUES**

Waste treatment management plans and practices shall provide for the application of the best practicable waste treatment technology before any discharge into receiving waters, including reclaiming and recycling of water, and confined disposal of pollutants so they will not migrate to cause water or other environmental pollution and shall provide for consideration of advanced waste treatment techniques.

(c) **WASTE TREATMENT MANAGEMENT AREA AND SCOPE**

To the extent practicable, waste treatment management shall be on an areawide basis and provide control or treatment of all point and nonpoint sources of pollution, including in place or accumulated pollution sources.

(d) **WASTE TREATMENT MANAGEMENT CONSTRUCTION OF REVENUE PRODUCING FACILITIES**

The Administrator shall encourage waste treatment management which results in the construction of revenue producing facilities providing for —

(1) the recycling of potential sewage pollutants through the production of agriculture, silviculture, or aquaculture products, or any combination thereof;

(2) the confined and contained disposal of pollutants not recycled;

(3) the reclamation of wastewater; and

(4) the ultimate disposal of sludge in a manner that will not result in environmental hazards.

(e) **WASTE TREATMENT MANAGEMENT INTEGRATION OF FACILITIES**

The Administrator shall encourage waste treatment management which results in integrating facilities for sewage treatment and recycling with facilities to treat, dispose of, or utilize other industrial and municipal wastes, including but not limited to solid waste and waste heat and thermal discharges. Such integrated facilities shall be designed and operated to produce revenues in excess of capital and operation and maintenance costs and such revenues shall be used by the designated regional management agency to aid in financing other environmental improvement programs.

Clean Water Act §1281

(f) WASTE TREATMENT MANAGEMENT "OPEN SPACE" AND RECREATIONAL CONSIDERATIONS

The Administrator shall encourage waste treatment management which combines "open space" and recreational considerations with such management.

(g) GRANTS TO CONSTRUCT PUBLICLY OWNED TREATMENT WORKS

(1) The Administrator is authorized to make grants to any State, municipality, or intermunicipal or interstate agency for the construction of publicly owned treatment works. On and after October 1, 1984, grants under this subchapter shall be made only for projects for secondary treatment or more stringent treatment, or any cost effective alternative thereto, new interceptors and appurtenances, and infiltration-in-flow correction. Notwithstanding the preceding sentences, the Administrator may make grants on and after October 1, 1984, for (A) any project within the definition set forth in section 1292(2) of this title, other than for a project referred to in the preceding sentence and (B) any purpose for which a grant may be made under sections[1] 1329(h) and (i) of this title (including any innovative and alternative approaches for the control of nonpoint sources of pollution), except that not more than 20 per centum (as determined by the Governor of the State) of the amount allotted to a State under section 1285 of this title for any fiscal year shall be obligated in such State under authority of this sentence.

(2) The Administrator shall not make grants from funds authorized for any fiscal year beginning after June 30, 1974, to any State, municipality, or intermunicipal or interstate agency for the erection, building, acquisition, alteration, remodeling, improvement, or extension of treatment works unless the grant applicant has satisfactorily demonstrated to the Administrator that —

    (A) alternative waste management techniques have been studied and evaluated and the works proposed for grant assistance will provide for the application of the best practicable waste treatment technology over the life of the works consistent with the purposes of this subchapter; and

    (B) as appropriate, the works proposed for grant assistance will take into account and allow to the extent practicable the application of technology at a later date which will provide for the reclaiming or recycling of water or otherwise eliminate the discharge of pollutants.

(3) The Administrator shall not approve any grant after July 1, 1973, for treatment areas under this section unless the applicant shows to the satisfaction of the Administrator that each sewer collection system discharging into such treatment works is not subject to excessive infiltration.

(4) The Administrator is authorized to make grants to applicants for treatment works grants under this section for such sewer system evaluation studies as may be necessary to carry out the requirements of paragraph (3) of this subsection. Such grants shall be made in accordance with rules and

---

1. So in original. Probably should be "section."

§1281

regulations promulgated by the Administrator. Initial rules and regulations shall be promulgated under this paragraph not later than 120 days after October 18, 1972.

(5) The Administrator shall not make grants from funds authorized for any fiscal year beginning after September 30, 1978, to any State, municipality, or intermunicipal or interstate agency for the erection, building, acquisition, alteration, remodeling, improvement, or extension of treatment works unless the grant applicant has satisfactorily demonstrated to the Administrator that innovative and alternative wastewater treatment processes and techniques which provide for the reclaiming and reuse of water, otherwise eliminate the discharge of pollutants, and utilize recycling techniques, land treatment, new or improved methods of waste treatment management for municipal and industrial waste (discharged into municipal systems) and the confined disposal of pollutants, so that pollutants will not migrate to cause water or other environmental pollution, have been fully studied and evaluated by the applicant taking into account subsection (d) of this section and taking into account and allowing to the extent practicable the more efficient use of energy and resources.

(6) The Administrator shall not make grants from funds authorized for any fiscal year beginning after September 30, 1978, to any State, municipality, or intermunicipal or interstate agency for the erection, building, acquisition, alteration, remodeling, improvement, or extension of treatment works unless the grant applicant has satisfactorily demonstrated to the Administrator that the applicant has analyzed the potential recreation and open space opportunities in the planning of the proposed treatment works.

(h) GRANTS TO CONSTRUCT PRIVATELY OWNED TREATMENT WORKS

A grant may be made under this section to construct a privately owned treatment works serving one or more principal residences or small commercial establishments constructed prior to, and inhabited on, December 27, 1977, where the Administrator finds that —

(1) a public body otherwise eligible for a grant under subsection (g) of this section has applied on behalf of a number of such units and certified that public ownership of such works is not feasible;

(2) such public body has entered into an agreement with the Administrator which guarantees that such treatment works will be properly operated and maintained and will comply with all other requirements of section 1284 of this title and includes a system of charges to assure that each recipient of waste treatment services under such a grant will pay its proportionate share of the cost of operation and maintenance (including replacement); and

(3) the total cost and environmental impact of providing waste treatment services to such residences or commercial establishments will be less than the cost of providing a system of collection and central treatment of such wastes.

Clean Water Act § 1281

(i) WASTE TREATMENT MANAGEMENT METHODS, PROCESSES, AND TECHNIQUES TO REDUCE ENERGY REQUIREMENTS

The Administrator shall encourage waste treatment management methods, processes, and techniques which will reduce total energy requirements.

(j) GRANTS FOR TREATMENT WORKS UTILIZING PROCESSES AND TECHNIQUES OF GUIDELINES UNDER SECTION 1314(d)(3) OF THIS TITLE

The Administrator is authorized to make a grant for any treatment works utilizing processes and techniques meeting the guidelines promulgated under section 1314(d)(3) of this title, if the Administrator determines it is in the public interest and if in the cost effectiveness study made of the construction grant application for the purpose of evaluating alternative treatment works, the life cycle cost of the treatment works for which the grant is to be made does not exceed the life cycle cost of the most cost effective alternative by more than 15 per centum.

(k) LIMITATION ON USE OF GRANTS FOR PUBLICLY OWNED TREATMENT WORKS

No grant made after November 15, 1981, for a publicly owned treatment works, other than for facility planning and the preparation of construction plans and specifications, shall be used to treat, store, or convey the flow of any industrial user into such treatment works in excess of a flow per day equivalent to fifty thousand gallons per day of sanitary waste. The subsection shall not apply to any project proposed by a grantee which is carrying out an approved project to prepare construction plans and specifications for a facility to treat wastewater, which received its grant approval before May 15, 1980. This subsection shall not be in effect after November 15, 1981.

(*l*) GRANTS FOR FACILITY PLANS, OR PLANS, SPECIFICATIONS, AND ESTIMATES FOR PROPOSED PROJECT FOR CONSTRUCTION OF TREATMENT WORKS; LIMITATIONS, ALLOTMENTS, ADVANCES, ETC.

(1) After December 29, 1981, Federal grants shall not be made for the purpose of providing assistance solely for facility plans, or plans, specifications, and estimates for any proposed project for the construction of treatment works. In the event that the proposed project receives a grant under this section for construction, the Administrator shall make an allowance in such grant for non-Federal funds expended during the facility planning and advanced engineering and design phase at the prevailing Federal share under section 1282(a) of this title, based on the percentage of total project costs which the Administrator determines is the general experience for such projects.

(2)(A) Each State shall use a portion of the funds allotted to such State each fiscal year, but not to exceed 10 per centum of such funds, to advance to potential grant applicants under this subchapter the costs of facility planning or the preparation of plans, specifications, and estimates.

(B) Such an advance shall be limited to the allowance for such costs which the Administrator establishes under paragraph (1) of this subsection, and shall be provided only to a potential grant applicant which is a small community and which in the judgment of the State would otherwise be unable to prepare a request for a grant for construction costs under this section.

(C) In the event a grant for construction costs is made under this section for a project for which an advance has been made under this paragraph, the Administrator shall reduce the amount of such grant by the allowance established under paragraph (1) of this subsection. In the event no such grant is made, the State is authorized to seek repayment of such advance on such terms and conditions as it may determine.

(m) GRANTS FOR STATE OF CALIFORNIA PROJECTS

(1) Notwithstanding any other provisions of this subchapter, the Administrator is authorized to make a grant from any funds otherwise allotted to the State of California under section 1285 of this title to the project (and in the amount) specified in Order WQG 81-1 of the California State Water Resources Control Board.

(2) Notwithstanding any other provision of this chapter, the Administrator shall make a grant from any funds otherwise allotted to the State of California to the city of Eureka, California, in connection with project numbered C-06-2772, for the purchase of one hundred and thirty-nine acres of property as environmental mitigation for siting of the proposed treatment plant.

(3) Notwithstanding any other provision of this chapter, the Administrator shall make a grant from any funds otherwise allotted to the State of California to the city of San Diego, California, in connection with that city's aquaculture sewage process (total resources recovery system) as an innovative and alternative waste treatment process.

(n) WATER QUALITY PROBLEMS; FUNDS, SCOPE, ETC.

(1) On and after October 1, 1984, upon the request of the Governor of an affected State, the Administrator is authorized to use funds available to such State under section 1285 of this title to address water quality problems due to the impacts of discharges from combined storm water and sanitary sewer overflows, which are not otherwise eligible under this subsection, where correction of such discharges is a major priority for such State.

(2) Beginning fiscal year 1983, the Administrator shall have available $200,000,000 per fiscal year in addition to those funds authorized in section 1287 of this title to be utilized to address water quality problems of marine bays and estuaries subject to lower levels of water quality due to the impacts of discharges from combined storm water and sanitary sewer overflows from adjacent urban complexes, not otherwise eligible under this subsection. Such sums may be used as deemed appropriate by the Administrator as provided in paragraphs (1) and (2) of this subsection, upon the request of and demonstration of water quality benefits by the Governor of an affected State.

Clean Water Act §1282

(o) CAPITAL FINANCING PLAN

The Administrator shall encourage and assist applicants for grant assistance under this subchapter to develop and file with the Administrator a capital financing plan which, at a minimum —

(1) projects the future requirements for waste treatment services within the applicant's jurisdiction for a period of no less than ten years;

(2) projects the nature, extent, timing, and costs of future expansion and reconstruction of treatment works which will be necessary to satisfy the applicant's projected future requirements for waste treatment services; and

(3) sets forth with specificity the manner in which the applicant intends to finance such future expansion and reconstruction.

(p) TIME LIMIT ON RESOLVING CERTAIN DISPUTES

In any case in which a dispute arises with respect to the awarding of a contract for construction of treatment works by a grantee of funds under this subchapter and a party to such dispute files an appeal with the Administrator under this subchapter for resolution of such dispute, the Administrator shall make a final decision on such appeal within 90 days of the filing of such appeal.

§1281a. TOTAL TREATMENT SYSTEM FUNDING

Notwithstanding any other provision of law, in any case where the Administrator of the Environmental Protection Agency finds that the total of all grants made under section 1281 of this title for the same treatment works exceeds the actual construction costs for such treatment works (as defined in this chapter) such excess amount shall be a grant of the Federal share (as defined in this chapter) of the cost of construction of a sewage collection system if —

(1) such sewage collection system was constructed as part of the same total treatment system as the treatment works for which such grants under section 1281 of this title were approved, and

(2) an application for assistance for the construction of such sewage collection system was filed in accordance with section 3102 of title 42 before all such grants under section 1281 of this title were made and such grant under section 3102 of title 42 could not be approved due to lack of funding under such section 3102 of title 42.

The total of all grants for sewage collection systems made under this section shall not exceed $2,800,000. . . .

§1282. FEDERAL SHARE

(a) AMOUNT OF GRANTS FOR TREATMENT WORKS

(1) The amount of any grant for treatment works made under this chapter from funds authorized for any fiscal year beginning after June 30, 1971, and ending before October 1, 1984, shall be 75 per centum of the cost of construc-

tion thereof (as approved by the Administrator), and for any fiscal year beginning on or after October 1, 1984, shall be 55 per centum of the cost of construction thereof (as approved by the Administrator), unless modified to a lower percentage rate uniform throughout a State by the Governor of that State with the concurrence of the Administrator. Within ninety days after October 21, 1980, the Administrator shall issue guidelines for concurrence in any such modification, which shall provide for the consideration of the unobligated balance of sums allocated to the State under section 1285 of this title, the need for assistance under this subchapter in such State, and the availability of State grant assistance to replace the Federal share reduced by such modification. The payment of any such reduced Federal share shall not constitute an obligation on the part of the United States or a claim on the part of any State or grantee to reimbursement for the portion of the Federal share reduced in any such State. Any grant (other than for reimbursement) made prior to October 18, 1972, from any funds authorized for any fiscal year beginning after June 30, 1971, shall, upon the request of the applicant, be increased to the applicable percentage under this section. Notwithstanding the first sentence of this paragraph, in any case where a primary, secondary, or advanced waste treatment facility or its related interceptors or a project for infiltration-in-flow correction has received a grant for erection, building, acquisition, alteration, remodeling, improvement, extension, or correction before October 1, 1984, all segments and phases of such facility, interceptors, and project for infiltration-in-flow correction shall be eligible for grants at 75 per centum of the cost of construction thereof for any grant made pursuant to a State obligation which obligation occurred before October 1, 1990. Notwithstanding the first sentence of this paragraph, in the case of a project for which an application for a grant under this subchapter has been made to the Administrator before October 1, 1984, and which project is under judicial injunction on such date prohibiting its construction, such project shall be eligible for grants at 75 percent of the cost of construction thereof. Notwithstanding the first sentence of this paragraph, in the case of the Wyoming Valley Sanitary Authority project mandated by judicial order under a proceeding begun prior to October 1, 1984, and a project for wastewater treatment for Altoona, Pennsylvania, such projects shall be eligible for grants at 75 percent of the cost of construction thereof.

(2) The amount of any grant made after September 30, 1978, and before October 1, 1981, for any eligible treatment works or significant portion thereof utilizing innovative or alternative wastewater treatment processes and techniques referred to in section 1281(g)(5) of this title shall be 85 per centum of the cost of construction thereof, unless modified by the Governor of the State with the concurrence of the Administrator to a percentage rate no less than 15 per centum greater than the modified uniform percentage rate in which the Administrator has concurred pursuant to paragraph (1) of this subsection. The amount of any grant made after September 30, 1981, for any eligible treatment works or unit processes and techniques thereof utilizing innovative or alternative wastewater treatment processes and techniques referred to in section 1281(g)(5) of this title

shall be a percentage of the cost of construction thereof equal to 20 per centum greater than the percentage in effect under paragraph (1) of this subsection for such works or unit processes and techniques, but in no event greater than 85 per centum of the cost of construction thereof. No grant shall be made under this paragraph for construction of a treatment works in any State unless the proportion of the State contribution to the non-Federal share of construction costs for all treatment works in such State receiving a grant under this paragraph is the same as or greater than the proportion of the State contribution (if any) to the non-Federal share of construction costs for all treatment works receiving grants in such State under paragraph (1) of this subsection.

(3) In addition to any grant made pursuant to paragraph (2) of this subsection, the Administrator is authorized to make a grant to fund all of the costs of the modification or replacement of any facilities constructed with a grant made pursuant to paragraph (2) if the Administrator finds that such facilities have not met design performance specifications unless such failure is attributable to negligence on the part of any person and if such failure has significantly increased capital or operating and maintenance expenditures. In addition, the Administrator is authorized to make a grant to fund all of the costs of the modification or replacement of biodisc equipment (rotating biological contactors) in any publicly owned treatment works if the Administrator finds that such equipment has failed to meet design performance specifications, unless such failure is attributable to negligence on the part of any person, and if such failure has significantly increased capital or operating and maintenance expenditures.

(4) For the purposes of this section, the term "eligible treatment works" means those treatment works in each State which meet the requirements of section 1281(g)(5) of this title and which can be fully funded from funds available for such purpose in such State.

(b) AMOUNT OF GRANTS FOR CONSTRUCTION OF TREATMENT WORKS NOT COMMENCED PRIOR TO JULY 1, 1971

The amount of the grant for any project approved by the Administrator after January 1, 1971, and before July 1, 1971, for the construction of treatment works, the actual erection, building or acquisition of which was not commenced prior to July 1, 1971, shall, upon the request of the applicant, be increased to the applicable percentage under subsection (a) of this section for grants for treatment works from funds for fiscal years beginning after June 30, 1971, with respect to the cost of such actual erection, building, or acquisition. Such increased amount shall be paid from any funds allocated to the State in which the treatment works is located without regard to the fiscal year for which such funds were authorized. Such increased amount shall be paid for such project only if —

(1) a sewage collection system that is a part of the same total waste treatment system as the treatment works for which such grant was approved is under construction or is to be constructed for use in conjunction with such treatment works, and if the cost of such sewage collection system exceeds the cost of such treatment works, and

(2) the State water pollution control agency or other appropriate State authority certifies that the quantity of available ground water will be insufficient, inadequate, or unsuitable for public use, including the ecological preservation and recreational use of surface water bodies, unless effluents from publicly-owned treatment works after adequate treatment are returned to the ground water consistent with acceptable technological standards.

(c) **AVAILABILITY OF SUMS ALLOTTED TO PUERTO RICO**

Notwithstanding any other provision of law, sums allotted to the Commonwealth of Puerto Rico under section 1285 of this title for fiscal year 1981 shall remain available for obligation for the fiscal year for which authorized and for the period of the next succeeding twenty-four months. Such sums and any unobligated funds available to Puerto Rico from allotments for fiscal years ending prior to October 1, 1981, shall be available for obligation by the Administrator of the Environmental Protection Agency only to fund the following systems: Aguadilla, Arecibo, Mayaguez, Carolina, and Camuy Hatillo. These funds may be used by the commonwealth of Puerto Rico to fund the non-Federal share of the costs of such projects. To the extent that these funds are used to pay the non-Federal share, the Commonwealth of Puerto Rico shall repay to the Environmental Protection Agency such amounts on terms and conditions developed and approved by the Administrator in consultation with the Governor of the Commonwealth of Puerto Rico. Agreement on such terms and conditions, including the payment of interest to be determined by the Secretary of the Treasury, shall be reached prior to the use of these funds for the Commonwealth's non-Federal share. No Federal funds awarded under this provision shall be used to replace local governments funds previously expended on these projects.

§1283. PLANS, SPECIFICATIONS, ESTIMATES, AND PAYMENTS

(a) **SUBMISSION; CONTRACTUAL NATURE OF APPROVAL BY ADMINISTRATOR; AGREEMENT ON ELIGIBLE COSTS; SINGLE GRANT**

(1) Each applicant for a grant shall submit to the Administrator for his approval, plans, specifications, and estimates for each proposed project for the construction of treatment works for which a grant is applied for under section 1281(g)(1) of this title from funds allotted to the State under section 1285 of this title and which otherwise meets the requirements of this chapter. The Administrator shall act upon such plans, specifications, and estimates as soon as practicable after the same have been submitted, and his approval of any such plans, specifications, and estimates shall be deemed a contractual obligation of the United States for the payment of its proportional contribution to such project.

Clean Water Act §1283

(2) **AGREEMENT ON ELIGIBLE COSTS**

(A) **LIMITATION ON MODIFICATIONS**

Before taking final action on any plans, specifications, and estimates submitted under this subsection after the 60th day following February 4, 1987, the Administrator shall enter into a written agreement with the applicant which establishes and specifies which items of the proposed project are eligible for Federal payments under this section. The Administrator may not later modify such eligibility determinations unless they are found to have been made in violation of applicable Federal statutes and regulations.

(B) **LIMITATION ON EFFECT**

Eligibility determinations under this paragraph shall not preclude the Administrator from auditing a project pursuant to section 1361 of this title, or other authority, or from withholding or recovering Federal funds for costs which are found to be unreasonable, unsupported by adequate documentation, or otherwise unallowable under applicable Federal cost principles, or which are incurred on a project which fails to meet the design specifications or effluent limitations contained in the grant agreement and permit pursuant to section 1342 of this title for such project.

(3) In the case of a treatment works that has an estimated total cost of $8,000,000 or less (as determined by the Administrator), and the population of the applicant municipality is twenty-five thousand or less (according to the most recent United States census), upon completion of an approved facility plan, a single grant may be awarded for the combined Federal share of the cost of preparing construction plans and specifications, and the building and erection of the treatment works.

(b) **PERIODIC PAYMENTS**

The Administrator shall, from time to time as the work progresses, make payments to the recipient of a grant for costs of construction incurred on a project. These payments shall at no time exceed the Federal share of the cost of construction incurred to the date of the voucher covering such payment plus the Federal share of the value of the materials which have been stockpiled in the vicinity of such construction in conformity to plans and specifications for the project.

(c) **FINAL PAYMENTS**

After completion of a project and approval of the final voucher by the Administrator, he shall pay out of the appropriate sums the unpaid balance of the Federal share payable on account of such project.

(d) **PROJECTS ELIGIBLE**

Nothing in this chapter shall be construed to require, or to authorize the Administrator to require, that grants under this chapter for construction of treatment works be made only for projects which are operable units usable for sewage collection, transportation, storage, waste treatment, or for similar purposes without additional construction.

(e) TECHNICAL AND LEGAL ASSISTANCE IN ADMINISTRATION AND ENFORCEMENT OF CONTRACTS; INTERVENTION IN CIVIL ACTIONS

At the request of a grantee under this subchapter, the Administrator is authorized to provide technical and legal assistance in the administration and enforcement of any contract in connection with treatment works assisted under this subchapter, and to intervene in any civil action involving the enforcement of such a contract.

(f) DESIGN/BUILD PROJECTS

(1) AGREEMENT

Consistent with State law, an applicant who proposes to construct waste water treatment works may enter into an agreement with the Administrator under this subsection providing for the preparation of construction plans and specifications and the erection of such treatment works, in lieu of proceeding under the other provisions of this section.

(2) LIMITATION ON PROJECTS

Agreements under this subsection shall be limited to projects under an approved facility plan which projects are —

(A) treatment works that have an estimated total cost of $8,000,000 or less; and

(B) any of the following types of waste water treatment systems: aerated lagoons, trickling filters, stabilization ponds, land application systems, sand filters, and subsurface disposal systems.

(3) REQUIRED TERMS

An agreement entered into under this subsection shall —

(A) set forth an amount agreed to as the maximum Federal contribution to the project, based upon a competitively bid document of basic design data and applicable standard construction specifications and a determination of the federally eligible costs of the project at the applicable Federal share under section 1282 of this title;

(B) set forth dates for the start and completion of construction of the treatment works by the applicant and a schedule of payments of the Federal contribution to the project;

(C) contain assurances by the applicant that (i) engineering and management assistance will be provided to manage the project; (ii) the proposed treatment works will be an operable unit and will meet all the requirements of this subchapter; and (iii) not later than 1 year after the date specified as the date of completion of construction of the treatment works, the treatment works will be operating so as to meet the requirements of any applicable permit for such treatment works under section 1342 of this title;

(D) require the applicant to obtain a bond from the contractor in an amount determined necessary by the Administrator to protect the Federal interest in the project; and

(E) contain such other terms and conditions as are necessary to assure compliance with this subchapter (except as provided in paragraph (4) of this subsection).

(4) LIMITATION ON APPLICATION

Subsections (a), (b), and (c) of this section shall not apply to grants made pursuant to this subsection.

(5) RESERVATION TO ASSURE COMPLIANCE

The Administrator shall reserve a portion of the grant to assure contract compliance until final project approval as defined by the Administrator. If the amount agreed to under paragraph (3)(A) exceeds the cost of designing and constructing the treatment works, the Administrator shall reallot the amount of the excess to the State in which such treatment works are located for the fiscal year in which such audit is completed.

(6) LIMITATION ON OBLIGATIONS

The Administrator shall not obligate more than 20 percent of the amount allotted to a State for a fiscal year under section 1285 of this title for grants pursuant to this subsection.

(7) ALLOWANCE

The Administrator shall determine an allowance for facilities planning for projects constructed under this subsection in accordance with section 1281(l) of this title.

(8) LIMITATION ON FEDERAL CONTRIBUTIONS

In no event shall the Federal contribution for the cost of preparing construction plans and specifications and the building and erection of treatment works pursuant to this subsection exceed the amount agreed upon under paragraph (3).

(9) RECOVERY ACTION

In any case in which the recipient of a grant made pursuant to this subsection does not comply with the terms of the agreement entered into under paragraph (3), the Administrator is authorized to take such action as may be necessary to recover the amount of the Federal contribution to the project.

(10) **PREVENTION OF DOUBLE BENEFITS**

A recipient of a grant made pursuant to this subsection shall not be eligible for any other grants under this subchapter for the same project.

§1284. LIMITATIONS AND CONDITIONS

(a) **DETERMINATIONS BY ADMINISTRATOR**

Before approving grants for any project for any treatment works under section 1281(g)(1) of this title the Administrator shall determine —

(1) that any required areawide waste treatment management plan under section 1288 of this title (A) is being implemented for such area and the proposed treatment works are included in such plan, or (B) is being developed for such area and reasonable progress is being made toward its implementation and the proposed treatment works will be included in such plan;

(2) that (A) the State in which the project is to be located (i) is implementing any required plan under section 1313(e) of this title and the proposed treatment works are in conformity with such plan, or (ii) is developing such a plan and the proposed treatment works will be in conformity with such plan, and (B) such State is in compliance with section 1315(b) of this title;

(3) that such works have been certified by the appropriate State water pollution control agency as entitled to priority over such other works in the State in accordance with any applicable State plan under section 1313(e) of this title, except that any priority list developed pursuant to section 1313(e)(3)(H) of this title may be modified by such State in accordance with regulations promulgated by the Administrator to give higher priority for grants for the Federal share of the cost of preparing construction drawings and specifications for any treatment works utilizing processes and techniques meeting the guidelines promulgated under section 1314(d)(3) of this title and for grants for the combined Federal share of the cost of preparing construction drawings and specifications and the building and erection of any treatment works meeting the requirements of the next to the last sentence of section 1283(a) of this title which utilizes processes and techniques meeting the guidelines promulgated under section 1314(d)(3) of this title.[2]

(4) that the applicant proposing to construct such works agrees to pay the non-Federal costs of such works and has made adequate provisions satisfactory to the Administrator for assuring proper and efficient operation, including the employment of trained management and operations personnel, and the maintenance of such works in accordance with a plan of operation approved by the State water pollution control agency or, as appropriate, the interstate agency, after construction thereof;

(5) that the size and capacity of such works relate directly to the needs to be served by such works, including sufficient reserve capacity. The amount

---

2. So in original. The period probably should be a semicolon.

of reserve capacity provided shall be approved by the Administrator on the basis of a comparison of the cost of constructing such reserves as a part of the works to be funded and the anticipated cost of providing expanded capacity at a date when such capacity will be required, after taking into account, in accordance with regulations promulgated by the Administrator, efforts to reduce total flow of sewage and unnecessary water consumption. The amount of reserve capacity eligible for a grant under this subchapter shall be determined by the Administrator taking into account the projected population and associated commercial and industrial establishments within the jurisdiction of the applicant to be served by such treatment works as identified in an approved facilities plan, an areawide plan under section 1288 of this title, or an applicable municipal master plan of development. For the purpose of this paragraph, section 1288 of this title, and any such plan, projected population shall be determined on the basis of the latest information available from the United States Department of Commerce or from the States as the Administrator, by regulation, determines appropriate. Beginning October 1, 1984, no grant shall be made under this subchapter to construct that portion of any treatment works providing reserve capacity in excess of existing needs (including existing needs of residential, commercial, industrial, and other users) on the date of approval of a grant for the erection, building, acquisition, alteration, remodeling, improvement, or extension of a project for secondary treatment or more stringent treatment or new interceptors and appurtenances, except that in no event shall reserve capacity of a facility and its related interceptors to which this subsection applies be in excess of existing needs on October 1, 1990. In any case in which an applicant proposes to provide reserve capacity greater than that eligible for Federal financial assistance under this subchapter, the incremental costs of the additional reserve capacity shall be paid by the applicant;

(6) that no specification for bids in connection with such works shall be written in such a manner as to contain proprietary, exclusionary, or discriminatory requirements other than those based upon performance, unless such requirements are necessary to test or demonstrate a specific thing or to provide for necessary interchangeability of parts and equipment. When in the judgment of the grantee, it is impractical or uneconomical to make a clear and accurate description of the technical requirements, a "brand name or equal" description may be used as a means to define the performance or other salient requirements of a procurement, and in doing so the grantee need not establish the existence of any source other than the brand or source so named.

(b) ADDITIONAL DETERMINATIONS; ISSUANCE OF GUIDELINES; APPROVAL BY ADMINISTRATOR; SYSTEM OF CHARGES

(1) Notwithstanding any other provision of this subchapter, the Administrator shall not approve any grant for any treatment works under section 1281(g)(1) of this title after March 1, 1973, unless he shall first have determined that the applicant (A) has adopted or will adopt a system of charges to assure that

§1284 Clean Water Act

each recipient of waste treatment services within the applicant's jurisdiction, as determined by the Administrator, will pay its proportionate share (except as otherwise provided in this paragraph) of the costs of operation and maintenance (including replacement) of any waste treatment services provided by the applicant; and (B) has legal, institutional, managerial, and financial capability to insure adequate construction, operation, and maintenance of treatment works throughout the applicant's jurisdiction, as determined by the Administrator. In any case where an applicant which, as of December 27, 1977, uses a system of dedicated ad valorem taxes and the Administrator determines that the applicant has a system of charges which results in the distribution of operation and maintenance costs for treatment works within the applicant's jurisdiction, to each user class, in proportion to the contribution to the total cost of operation and maintenance of such works by each user class (taking into account total waste water loading of such works, the constituent elements of the wastes, and other appropriate factors), and such applicant is otherwise in compliance with clause (A) of this paragraph with respect to each industrial user, then such dedicated ad valorem tax system shall be deemed to be the user charge system meeting the requirements of clause (A) of this paragraph for the residential user class and such small non-residential user classes as defined by the Administrator. In defining small non-residential users, the Administrator shall consider the volume of wastes discharged into the treatment works by such users and the constituent elements of such wastes as well as such other factors as he deems appropriate. A system of user charges which imposes a lower charge for low-income residential users (as defined by the Administrator) shall be deemed to be a user charge system meeting the requirements of clause (A) of this paragraph if the Administrator determines that such system was adopted after public notice and hearing.

(2) The Administrator shall, within one hundred and eighty days after October 18, 1972, and after consultation with appropriate State, interstate, municipal, and intermunicipal agencies, issue guidelines applicable to payment of waste treatment costs by industrial and nonindustrial recipients of waste treatment services which shall establish (A) classes of users of such services, including categories of industrial users; (B) criteria against which to determine the adequacy of charges imposed on classes and categories of users reflecting all factors that influence the cost of waste treatment, including strength, volume, and delivery flow rate characteristics of waste; and (C) model systems and rates of user charges typical of various treatment works serving municipal-industrial communities.

(3) Approval by the Administrator of a grant to an interstate agency established by interstate compact for any treatment works shall satisfy any other requirement that such works be authorized by Act of Congress.

(4) A system of charges which meets the requirement of clause (A) of paragraph (1) of this subsection may be based on something other than metering the sewage or water supply flow of residential recipients of waste treatment services, including ad valorem taxes. If the system of charges is based on something other than metering the Administrator shall require (A) the applicant to establish a

system by which the necessary funds will be available for the proper operation and maintenance of the treatment works; and (B) the applicant to establish a procedure under which the residential user will be notified as to that portion of his total payment which will be allocated to the cost of the waste treatment services.

(c) APPLICABILITY OF RESERVE CAPACITY RESTRICTIONS TO PRIMARY, SECONDARY, OR ADVANCED WASTE TREATMENT FACILITIES OR RELATED INTERCEPTORS

The next to the last sentence of paragraph (5) of subsection (a) of this section shall not apply in any case where a primary, secondary, or advanced waste treatment facility or its related interceptors has received a grant for erection, building, acquisition, alteration, remodeling, improvement, or extension before October 1, 1984, and all segments and phases of such facility and interceptors shall be funded based on a 20-year reserve capacity in the case of such facility and a 20-year reserve capacity in the case of such interceptors, except that, if a grant for such interceptors has been approved prior to December 29, 1981, such interceptors shall be funded based on the approved reserve capacity not to exceed 40 years.

(d) ENGINEERING REQUIREMENTS; CERTIFICATION BY OWNER AND OPERATOR; CONTRACTUAL ASSURANCES, ETC.

(1) A grant for the construction of treatment works under this subchapter shall provide that the engineer or engineering firm supervising construction or providing architect engineering services during construction shall continue its relationship to the grant applicant for a period of one year after the completion of construction and initial operation of such treatment works. During such period such engineer or engineering firm shall supervise operation of the treatment works, train operating personnel, and prepare curricula and training material for operating personnel. Costs associated with the implementation of this paragraph shall be eligible for Federal assistance in accordance with this subchapter.

(2) On the date one year after the completion of construction and initial operation of such treatment works, the owner and operator of such treatment works shall certify to the Administrator whether or not such treatment works meet the design specifications and effluent limitations contained in the grant agreement and permit pursuant to section 1342 of this title for such works. If the owner and operator of such treatment works cannot certify that such treatment works meet such design specifications and effluent limitations, any failure to meet such design specifications and effluent limitations shall be corrected in a timely manner, to allow such affirmative certification, at other than Federal expense.

(3) Nothing in this section shall be construed to prohibit a grantee under this subchapter from requiring more assurances, guarantees, or indemnity or other contractual requirements from any party to a contract pertaining to a project assisted under this subchapter, than those provided under this subsection.

§1285. ALLOTMENT OF GRANT FUNDS

(a) FUNDS FOR FISCAL YEARS DURING PERIOD JUNE 30, 1972, AND SEPTEMBER 30, 1977; DETERMINATION OF AMOUNT

Sums authorized to be appropriated pursuant to section 1287 of this title for each fiscal year beginning after June 30, 1972, and before September 30, 1977, shall be allotted by the Administrator not later than the January 1st immediately preceding the beginning of the fiscal year for which authorized, except that the allotment for fiscal year 1973 shall be made not later than 30 days after October 18, 1972. Such sums shall be allotted among the States by the Administrator in accordance with regulations promulgated by him, in the ratio that the estimated cost of constructing all needed publicly owned treatment works in each State bears to the estimated cost of construction of all needed publicly owned treatment works in all of the States. For the fiscal years ending June 30, 1973, and June 30, 1974, such ratio shall be determined on the basis of table III of House Public Works Committee Print No. 92-50. For the fiscal year ending June 30, 1975, such ratio shall be determined one-half on the basis of table I of House Public Works Committee Print Numbered 93-28 and one-half on the basis of table II of such print, except that no State shall receive an allotment less than that which it received for the fiscal year ending June 30, 1972, as set forth in table III of such print. Allotments for fiscal years which begin after the fiscal year ending June 30, 1975, shall be made only in accordance with a revised cost estimate made and submitted to Congress in accordance with section 1375(b) of this title and only after such revised cost estimate shall have been approved by law specifically enacted after October 18, 1972.

(b) AVAILABILITY AND USE OF FUNDS ALLOTTED FOR FISCAL YEARS DURING PERIOD JUNE 30, 1972, AND SEPTEMBER 30, 1977; REALLOTMENT

(1) Any sums allotted to a State under subsection (a) of this section shall be available for obligation under section 1283 of this title on and after the date of such allotment. Such sums shall continue available for obligation in such State for a period of one year after the close of the fiscal year for which such sums are authorized. Any amounts so allotted which are not obligated by the end of such one-year period shall be immediately reallotted by the Administrator, in accordance with regulations promulgated by him, generally on the basis of the ratio used in making the last allotment of sums under this section. Such reallotted sums shall be added to the last allotments made to the States. Any sum made available to a State by reallotment under this subsection shall be in addition to any funds otherwise allotted to such State for grants under this subchapter during any fiscal year.

(2) Any sums which have been obligated under section 1283 of this title and which are released by the payment of the final voucher for the project shall be immediately credited to the State to which such sums were last allotted. Such released sums shall be added to the amounts last allotted to such State and shall be immediately available for obligation in the same manner and to the same extent as such last allotment.

Clean Water Act §1285

(c) **FUNDS FOR FISCAL YEARS DURING PERIOD OCTOBER 1, 1977, AND SEPTEMBER 30, 1981; FUNDS FOR FISCAL YEARS 1982 TO 1990; DETERMINATION OF AMOUNT**

(1) Sums authorized to be appropriated pursuant to section 1287 of this title for the fiscal years during the period beginning October 1, 1977, and ending September 30, 1981, shall be allotted for each such year by the Administrator not later than the tenth day which begins after December 27, 1977. Notwithstanding any other provision of law, sums authorized for the fiscal years ending September 30, 1978, September 30, 1979, September 30, 1980, and September 30, 1981, shall be allotted in accordance with table 3 of Committee Print Numbered 95-30 of the Committee on Public Works and Transportation of the House of Representatives.

(2) Sums authorized to be appropriated pursuant to section 1287 of this title for the fiscal years 1982, 1983, 1984, and 1985 shall be allotted for each such year by the Administrator not later than the tenth day which begins after December 29, 1981. Notwithstanding any other provision of law, sums authorized for the fiscal year ending September 30, 1982, shall be allotted in accordance with table 3 of Committee Print Numbered 95-30 of the Committee on Public Works and Transportation of the House of Representatives. Sums authorized for the fiscal years ending September 30, 1983, September 30, 1984, September 30, 1985, and September 30, 1986, shall be allotted in accordance with the following table:

States	Fiscal years 1983 through 1985[3]
Alabama	.011398
Alaska	.006101
Arizona	.006885
Arkansas	.006668
California	.072901
Colorado	.008154
Connecticut	.012487
Delaware	.004965
District of Columbia	.004965
Florida	.034407
Georgia	.017234
Hawaii	.007895
Idaho	.004965
Illinois	.046101
Indiana	.024566

---

[3] So in original. Probably should be "1986."

States	Fiscal years 1983 through 1985[3]
Iowa	.013796
Kansas	.009201
Kentucky	.012973
Louisiana	.011205
Maine	.007788
Maryland	.024653
Massachusetts	.034608
Michigan	.043829
Minnesota	.018735
Mississippi	.009184
Missouri	.028257
Montana	.004965
Nebraska	.005214
Nevada	.004965
New Hampshire	.010186
New Jersey	.041654
New Mexico	.004965
New York	.113097
North Carolina	.018396
North Dakota	.004965
Ohio	.057383
Oklahoma	.008235
Oregon	.011515
Pennsylvania	.040377
Rhode Island	.006750
South Carolina	.010442
South Dakota	.004965
Tennessee	.014807
Texas	.038726
Utah	.005371
Vermont	.004965
Virginia	.020861
Washington	.017726
West Virginia	.015890
Wisconsin	.027557
Wyoming	.004965
Samoa	.000915
Guam	.000662
Northern Marianas	.000425
Puerto Rico	.013295
Pacific Trust Territories	.001305
Virgin Islands	.000531
United States totals	.999996

Clean Water Act §1285

(3) **FISCAL YEARS 1987-1990**

Sums authorized to be appropriated pursuant to section 1287 of this title for the fiscal years 1987, 1988, 1989, and 1990 shall be allotted for each such year by the Administrator not later than the 10th day which begins after February 4, 1987. Sums authorized for such fiscal years shall be allotted in accordance with the following table:

States	Fiscal years 1987 through 1990
Alabama	.011309
Alaska	.006053
Arizona	.006831
Arkansas	.006616
California	.072333
Colorado	.008090
Connecticut	.012390
Delaware	.004965
District of Columbia	.004965
Florida	.034139
Georgia	.017100
Hawaii	.007833
Idaho	.004965
Illinois	.045741
Indiana	.024374
Iowa	.013688
Kansas	.009129
Kentucky	.012872
Louisiana	.011118
Maine	.007829
Maryland	.024461
Massachusetts	.034338
Michigan	.043487
Minnesota	.018589
Mississippi	.009112
Missouri	.028037
Montana	.004965
Nebraska	.005173
Nevada	.004965
New Hampshire	.010107
New Jersey	.041329
New Mexico	.004965
New York	.111632
North Carolina	.018253
North Dakota	.004965
Ohio	.056936

States	Fiscal years 1987 through 1990
Oklahoma	.008171
Oregon	.011425
Pennsylvania	.040062
Rhode Island	.006791
South Carolina	.010361
South Dakota	.004965
Tennessee	.014692
Texas	.046226
Utah	.005329
Vermont	.004965
Virginia	.020698
Washington	.017588
West Virginia	.015766
Wisconsin	.027342
Wyoming	.004965
American Samoa	.000908
Guam	.000657
Northern Marianas	.000422
Puerto Rico	.013191
Pacific Trust Territories	.001295
Virgin Islands	.000527

(d) AVAILABILITY AND USE OF FUNDS; REALLOTMENT

Sums allotted to the States for a fiscal year shall remain available for obligation for the fiscal year for which authorized and for the period of the next succeeding twelve months. The amount of any allotment not obligated by the end of such twenty-four-month period shall be immediately reallotted by the Administrator on the basis of the same ratio as applicable to sums allotted for the then current fiscal year, except that none of the funds reallotted by the Administrator for fiscal year 1978 and for fiscal years thereafter shall be allotted to any State which failed to obligate any of the funds being reallotted. Any sum made available to a State by reallotment under this subsection shall be in addition to any funds otherwise allotted to such State for grants under this subchapter during any fiscal year.

(e) MINIMUM ALLOTMENT; ADDITIONAL APPROPRIATIONS; RATIO OF AMOUNT AVAILABLE

For the fiscal years 1978, 1979, 1980, 1981, 1982, 1983, 1984, 1985, 1986, 1987, 1988, 1989, and 1990, no State shall receive less than one-half of 1 per centum of the total allotment under subsection (c) of this section, except that in the case of Guam, Virgin Islands, American Samoa, and the Trust Territories not more than thirty-three one-hundredths of 1 per centum in the aggregate shall be allotted to all four of these jurisdictions. For the purpose of carrying out this subsection there are authorized to be appropriated, subject to such

Clean Water Act §1285

amounts as are provided in appropriation Acts, not to exceed $75,000,000 for each of fiscal years 1978, 1979, 1980, 1981, 1982, 1983, 1984, 1985, 1986, 1987, 1988, 1989, and 1990. If for any fiscal year the amount appropriated under authority of this subsection is less than the amount necessary to carry it out this subsection, the amount each State receives under this subsection for such year shall bear the same ratio to the amount such State would have received under this subsection in such year if the amount necessary to carry it out had been appropriated as the amount appropriated for such year bears to the amount necessary to carry out this subsection for such year.

(f) OMITTED

(g) RESERVATION OF FUNDS; STATE MANAGEMENT ASSISTANCE

(1) The Administrator is authorized to reserve each fiscal year not to exceed 2 per centum of the amount authorized under section 1287 of this title for purposes of the allotment made to each State under this section on or after October 1, 1977, except in the case of any fiscal year beginning on or after October 1, 1981, and ending before October 1, 1994, in which case the percentage authorized to be reserved shall not exceed 4 per centum.[4] or $400,000 whichever amount is the greater. Sums so reserved shall be available for making grants to such State under paragraph (2) of this subsection for the same period as sums are available from such allotment under subsection (d) of this section, and any such grant shall be available for obligation only during such period. Any grant made from sums reserved under this subsection which has not been obligated by the end of the period for which available shall be added to the amount last allotted to such State under this section and shall be immediately available for obligation in the same manner and to the same extent as such last allotment. Sums authorized to be reserved by this paragraph shall be in addition to and not in lieu of any other funds which may be authorized to carry out this subsection.

(2) The Administrator is authorized to grant to any State from amounts reserved to such State under this subsection, the reasonable costs of administering any aspects of sections 1281, 1283, 1284, and 1292 of this title the responsibility for administration of which the Administrator has delegated to such State. The Administrator may increase such grant to take into account the reasonable costs of administering an approved program under section 1342 or 1344 of this title, administering a state-wide waste treatment management planning program under section 1288(b)(4) of this title, and managing waste treatment construction grants for small communities.

(h) ALTERNATE SYSTEMS FOR SMALL COMMUNITIES

The Administrator shall set aside from funds authorized for each fiscal year beginning on or after October 1, 1978, a total (as determined by the Governor of the State) of not less than 4 percent nor more than 7½ percent of the sums allotted to any State with a rural population of 25 per centum or more of the

---

4. So in original. The period probably should be a comma.

total population of such State, as determined by the Bureau of the Census. The Administrator may set aside no more than 7½ percent of the sums allotted to any other State for which the Governor requests such action. Such sums shall be available only for alternatives to conventional sewage treatment works for municipalities having a population of three thousand five hundred or less, or for the highly dispersed sections of larger municipalities, as defined by the Administrator.

(i) SET-ASIDE FOR INNOVATIVE AND ALTERNATIVE PROJECTS

Not less than ½ of 1 percent of funds allotted to a State for each of the fiscal years ending September 30, 1979, through September 30, 1990, under subsection (c) of this section shall be expended only for increasing the Federal share of grants for construction of treatment works utilizing innovative processes and techniques pursuant to section 1282(a)(2) of this title. Including the expenditures authorized by the preceding sentence, a total of 2 percent of the funds allotted to a State for each of the fiscal years ending September 30, 1979, and September 30, 1980, and 3 percent of the funds allotted to a State for the fiscal year ending September 30, 1981, under subsection (c) of this section shall be expended only for increasing grants for construction of treatment works pursuant to section 1282(a)(2) of this title. Including the expenditures authorized by the first sentence of this subsection, a total (as determined by the Governor of the State) of not less than 4 percent nor more than 7½ percent of the funds allotted to such State under subsection (c) of this section for each of the fiscal years ending September 30, 1982, through September 30, 1990, shall be expended only for increasing the Federal share of grants for construction of treatment works pursuant to section 1282(a)(2) of this title.

(j) WATER QUALITY MANAGEMENT PLAN; RESERVATION OF FUNDS FOR NONPOINT SOURCE MANAGEMENT

(1) The Administrator shall reserve each fiscal year not to exceed 1 per centum of the sums allotted and available for obligation to each State under this section for each fiscal year beginning on or after October 1, 1981, or $100,000, whichever amount is the greater.

(2) Such sums shall be used by the Administrator to make grants to the States to carry out water quality management planning, including, but not limited to —

(A) identifying most cost effective and locally acceptable facility and non-point measures to meet and maintain water quality standards;

(B) developing an implementation plan to obtain State and local financial and regulatory commitments to implement measures developed under subparagraph (A);

(C) determining the nature, extent, and causes of water quality problems in various areas of the State and interstate region, and reporting on these annually; and

(D) determining those publicly owned treatment works which should be constructed with assistance under this subchapter, in which areas and in what sequence, taking into account the relative degree of effluent reduction attained, the relative contributions to water quality of other point or nonpoint sources, and the consideration of alternatives to such construction, and implementing section 1313(e) of this title.

(3) In carrying out planning with grants made under paragraph (2) of this subsection, a State shall develop jointly with local, regional, and interstate entities, a plan for carrying out the program and give funding priority to such entities and designated or undesignated public comprehensive planning organizations to carry out the purposes of this subsection. In giving such priority, the State shall allocate at least 40 percent of the amount granted to such State for a fiscal year under paragraph (2) of this subsection to regional public comprehensive planning organizations in such state and appropriate interstate organizations for the development and implementation of the plan described in this paragraph. In any fiscal year for which the Governor, in consultation with such organizations and with the approval of the Administrator, determines that allocation of at least 40 percent of such amount to such organizations will not result in significant participation by such organizations in water quality management planning and not significantly assist in development and implementation of the plan described in this paragraph and achieving the goals of this chapter, the allocation to such organization may be less than 40 percent of such amount.

(4) All activities undertaken under this subsection shall be in coordination with other related provisions of this chapter.

(5) Nonpoint source reservation. — In addition to the sums reserved under paragraph (1), the Administrator shall reserve each fiscal year for each State 1 percent of the sums allotted and available for obligation to such State under this section for each fiscal year beginning on or after October 1, 1986, or $100,000, whichever is greater, for the purpose of carrying out section 1329 of this title. Sums so reserved in a State in any fiscal year for which such State does not request the use of such sums, to the extent such sums exceed $100,000, may be used by such State for other purposes under this subchapter.

(k) NEW YORK CITY CONVENTION CENTER

The Administrator shall allot to the State of New York from sums authorized to be appropriated for the fiscal year ending September 30, 1982, an amount necessary to pay the entire cost of conveying sewage from the Convention Center of the city of New York to the Newtown sewage treatment plant, Brooklyn-Queens area, New York. The amount allotted under this subsection shall be in addition to and not in lieu of any other amounts authorized to be allotted to such State under this chapter.

(l) MARINE ESTUARY RESERVATION

(1) RESERVATION OF FUNDS

(A) GENERAL RULE

Prior to making allotments among the States under subsection (c) of this section, the Administrator shall reserve funds from sums appropriated pursuant to section 1287 of this title for each fiscal year beginning after September 30, 1986.

(B) FISCAL YEARS 1987 AND 1988

For each of fiscal years 1987 and 1988 the reservation shall be 1 percent of the sums appropriated pursuant to section 1287 of this title for such fiscal year.

(C) FISCAL YEARS 1989 AND 1990

For each of fiscal years 1989 and 1990 the reservation shall be 1½ percent of the funds appropriated pursuant to section 1287 of this title for such fiscal year.

(2) USE OF FUNDS

Of the sums reserved under this subsection, two-thirds shall be available to address water quality problems of marine bays and estuaries subject to lower levels of water quality due to the impacts of discharges from combined storm water and sanitary sewer overflows from adjacent urban complexes, and one-third shall be available for the implementation of section 1330 of this title, relating to the national estuary program.

(3) PERIOD OF AVAILABILITY

Sums reserved under this subsection shall be subject to the period of availability for obligation established by subsection (d) of this section.

(4) TREATMENT OF CERTAIN BODY OF WATER

For purposes of this section and section 1281(n) of this title, Newark Bay, New Jersey, and the portion of the Passaic River up to Little Falls, in the vicinity of Beatties Dam, shall be treated as a marine bay and estuary.

(m) DISCRETIONARY DEPOSITS INTO STATE WATER POLLUTION CONTROL REVOLVING FUNDS

(1) FROM CONSTRUCTION GRANT ALLOTMENTS

In addition to any amounts deposited in a water pollution control revolving fund established by a State under subchapter VI of this chapter, upon request of the Governor of such State, the Administrator shall make available to the State for deposit, as capitalization grants, in such fund in any fiscal year beginning after September 30, 1986, such portion of the amounts allotted to such State under this section for such fiscal year as the Governor considers appropriate; except that (A) in fiscal year 1987, such deposit may not exceed 50 percent of the amounts allotted to such State under this section for such fiscal year, and (B) in fiscal year 1988, such deposit may not exceed 75 percent of the amounts allotted to such State under this section for this fiscal year.

(2) NOTICE REQUIREMENT

The Governor of a State may make a request under paragraph (1) for a deposit into the water pollution control revolving fund of such State —

(A) in fiscal year 1987 only if no later than 90 days after February 4, 1987, and

(B) in each fiscal year thereafter only if 90 days before the first day of such fiscal year,

the State provides notice of its intent to make such deposit.

(3) EXCEPTION

Sums reserved under section 1285(j) of this title shall not be available for obligation under this subsection.

§1286. REIMBURSEMENT AND ADVANCED CONSTRUCTION

(a) PUBLICLY OWNED TREATMENT WORKS CONSTRUCTION INITIATED AFTER JUNE 30, 1966, BUT BEFORE JULY 1, 1973; REIMBURSEMENT FORMULA

Any publicly owned treatment works in a State on which construction was initiated after June 30, 1966, but before July 1, 1973, which was approved by the appropriate State water pollution control agency and which the Administrator finds meets the requirements of section 1158 of this title in effect at the time of the initiation of construction shall be reimbursed a total amount equal to the difference between the amount of Federal financial assistance, if any, received under such section 1158 of this title for such project and 50 per centum of the cost of such project, or 55 per centum of the project cost where the Administrator also determines that such treatment works was constructed in conformity with a comprehensive metropolitan treatment plan as described in section 1158(f) of this title as in effect immediately prior to October 18, 1972. Nothing in this subsection shall result in any such works receiving Federal grants from all sources in excess of 80 per centum of the cost of such project.

(b) PUBLICLY OWNED TREATMENT WORKS CONSTRUCTION INITIATED BETWEEN JUNE 30, 1956, AND JUNE 30, 1966; REIMBURSEMENT FORMULA

Any publicly owned treatment works constructed with or eligible for Federal financial assistance under this Act in a State between June 30, 1956, and June 30, 1966, which was approved by the State water pollution control agency and which the Administrator finds meets the requirements of section 1158 of this title prior to October 18, 1972 but which was constructed without assistance under such section 1158 of this title or which received such assistance in an amount less than 30 per centum of the cost of such project shall qualify for payments and reimbursement of State or local funds used for such project from sums allocated to such State under this section in an amount which shall not exceed the difference between the amount of such assistance, if any, received for such project and 30 per centum of the cost of such project.

(c) APPLICATION FOR REIMBURSEMENT

No publicly owned treatment works shall receive any payment or reimbursement under subsection (a) or (b) of this section unless an application for such assistance is filed with the Administrator within the one year period which begins on October 18, 1972. Any application filed within such one year period may be revised from time to time, as may be necessary.

(d) ALLOCATION OF FUNDS

The Administrator shall allocate to each qualified project under subsection (a) of this section each fiscal year for which funds are appropriated under subsection (e) of this section an amount which bears the same ratio to the unpaid balance of the reimbursement due such project as the total of such funds for such year bears to the total unpaid balance of reimbursement due all such approved projects on the date of enactment of such appropriation. The Administrator shall allocate to each qualified project under subsection (b) of this section each fiscal year for which funds are appropriated under subsection (e) of this section an amount which bears the same ratio to the unpaid balance of the reimbursement due such project as the total of such funds for such year bears to the total unpaid balance of reimbursement due all such approved projects on the date of enactment of such appropriation.

(e) AUTHORIZATION OF APPROPRIATIONS

There is authorized to be appropriated to carry out subsection (a) of this section not to exceed $2,600,000,000 and, to carry out subsection (b) of this section, not to exceed $750,000,000. The authorizations contained in this subsection shall be the sole source of funds for reimbursements authorized by this section.

(f) ADDITIONAL FUNDS

(1) In any case where a substantial portion of the funds allotted to a State for the current fiscal year under this subchapter have been obligated under section 1281(g) of this title, or will be so obligated in a timely manner (as determined by the Administrator), and there is construction of any treatment works project without the aid of Federal funds and in accordance with all procedures and all requirements applicable to treatment works projects, except those procedures and requirements which limit construction of projects to those constructed with the aid of previously allotted Federal funds, the Administrator, upon his approval of an application made under this subsection therefor, is authorized to pay the Federal share of the cost of construction of such project when additional funds are allotted to the State under this subchapter if prior to the construction of the project the Administrator approves plans, specifications, and estimates therefor in the same manner as other treatment works projects. The Administrator may not approve an application under this subsection unless an authorization is in effect for the first fiscal year in the period for which the application requests payment and such requested payment for that fiscal year does not exceed the State's expected allotment from such authorization. The Administrator shall not be required to make such requested payment for any fiscal year —

(A) to the extent that such payment would exceed such State's allotment of the amount appropriated for such fiscal year; and

(B) unless such payment is for a project which, on the basis of an approved funding priority list of such State, is eligible to receive such payment based on the allotment and appropriation for such fiscal year.

To the extent that sufficient funds are not appropriated to pay the full Federal share with respect to a project for which obligations under the provisions of this subsection have been made, the Administrator shall reduce the Federal share to such amount less than 75 per centum as such appropriations do provide.

(2) In determining the allotment for any fiscal year under this subchapter, any treatment works project constructed in accordance with this section and without the aid of Federal funds shall not be considered completed until an application under the provisions of this subsection with respect to such project has been approved by the Administrator, or the availability of funds from which this project is eligible for reimbursement has expired, whichever first occurs.

§1288. AREAWIDE WASTE TREATMENT MANAGEMENT

(a) IDENTIFICATION AND DESIGNATION OF AREAS HAVING SUBSTANTIAL WATER QUALITY CONTROL PROBLEMS

For the purpose of encouraging and facilitating the development and implementation of areawide waste treatment management plans —

(1) The Administrator, within ninety days after October 18, 1972, and after consultation with appropriate Federal, State, and local authorities, shall by regulation publish guidelines for the identification of those areas which, as a result of urban-industrial concentrations or other factors, have substantial water quality control problems.

(2) The Governor of each State, within sixty days after publication of the guidelines issued pursuant to paragraph (1) of this subsection, shall identify each area within the State which, as a result of urban-industrial concentrations or other factors, has substantial water quality control problems. Not later than one hundred and twenty days following such identification and after consultation with appropriate elected and other officials of local governments having jurisdiction in such areas, the Governor shall designate (A) the boundaries of each such area, and (B) a single representative organization, including elected officials from local governments or their designees, capable of developing effective areawide waste treatment management plans for such area. The Governor may in the same manner at any later time identify any additional area (or modify an existing area) for which he determines areawide waste treatment management to be appropriate, designate the boundaries of such area, and designate an organization capable of developing effective areawide waste treatment management plans for such area.

(3) With respect to any area which, pursuant to the guidelines published under paragraph (1) of this subsection, is located in two or more States, the Governors of the respective States shall consult and cooperate in carrying out the provisions of paragraph (2), with a view toward designating the boundaries

of the interstate area having common water quality control problems and for which areawide waste treatment management plans would be most effective, and toward designating, within one hundred and eighty days after publication of guidelines issued pursuant to paragraph (1) of this subsection, of a single representative organization capable of developing effective areawide waste treatment management plans for such area.

(4) If a Governor does not act, either by designating or determining not to make a designation under paragraph (2) of this subsection, within the time required by such paragraph, or if, in the case of an interstate area, the Governors of the States involved do not designate a planning organization within the time required by paragraph (3) of this subsection, the chief elected officials of local governments within an area may by agreement designate (A) the boundaries for such an area, and (B) a single representative organization including elected officials from such local governments, or their designees, capable of developing an areawide waste treatment management plan for such area.

(5) Existing regional agencies may be designated under paragraphs (2), (3), and (4) of this subsection.

(6) The State shall act as a planning agency for all portions of such State which are not designated under paragraphs (2), (3), or (4) of this subsection.

(7) Designations under this subsection shall be subject to the approval of the Administrator.

(b) **PLANNING PROCESS**

(1)(A) Not later than one year after the date of designation of any organization under subsection (a) of this section such organization shall have in operation a continuing areawide waste treatment management planning process consistent with section 1281 of this title. Plans prepared in accordance with this process shall contain alternatives for waste treatment management, and be applicable to all wastes generated within the area involved. The initial plan prepared in accordance with such process shall be certified by the Governor and submitted to the Administrator not later than two years after the planning process is in operation.

(B) For any agency designated after 1975 under subsection (a) of this section and for all portions of a State for which the State is required to act as the planning agency in accordance with subsection (a)(6) of this section, the initial plan prepared in accordance with such process shall be certified by the Governor and submitted to the Administrator not later than three years after the receipt of the initial grant award authorized under subsection (f) of this section.

(2) Any plan prepared under such process shall include, but not be limited to —

(A) the identification of treatment works necessary to meet the anticipated municipal and industrial waste treatment needs of the area over a twenty-year period, annually updated (including an analysis of alternative waste treatment systems), including any requirements for the acquisition of land for treatment purposes; the necessary waste water collection and urban storm water runoff systems; and a program to provide the necessary financial arrangements for the development of such treatment works, and an identification of open space and recreation opportunities that can be expected to result from improved water quality, including consideration of potential use of lands associated with treatment works and increased access to water-based recreation;

(B) the establishment of construction priorities for such treatment works and time schedules for the initiation and completion of all treatment works;

(C) the establishment of a regulatory program to —

(i) implement the waste treatment management requirements of section 1281(c) of this title,

(ii) regulate the location, modification, and construction of any facilities within such area which may result in any discharge in such area, and

(iii) assure that any industrial or commercial wastes discharged into any treatment works in such area meet applicable pretreatment requirements;

(D) the identification of those agencies necessary to construct, operate, and maintain all facilities required by the plan and otherwise to carry out the plan;

(E) the identification of the measures necessary to carry out the plan (including financing), the period of time necessary to carry out the plan, the costs of carrying out the plan within such time, and the economic, social, and environmental impact of carrying out the plan within such time;

(F) a process to (i) identify, if appropriate, agriculturally and silviculturally related non-point sources of pollution, including return flows from irrigated agriculture, and their cumulative effects, runoff from manure disposal areas, and from land used for livestock and crop production, and (ii) set forth procedures and methods (including land use requirements) to control to the extent feasible such sources;

(G) a process to (i) identify, if appropriate, mine-related sources of pollution including new, current, and abandoned surface and underground mine runoff, and (ii) set forth procedures and methods (including land use requirements) to control to the extent feasible such sources;

(H) a process to (i) identify construction activity related sources of pollution, and (ii) set forth procedures and methods (including land use requirements) to control to the extent feasible such sources;

(I) a process to (i) identify, if appropriate, salt water intrusion into rivers, lakes, and estuaries resulting from reduction of fresh water flow from any cause, including irrigation, obstruction, ground water extraction, and diversion, and (ii) set forth procedures and methods to control such intrusion to the extent feasible where such procedures and methods are otherwise a part of the waste treatment management plan;

(J) a process to control the disposition of all residual waste generated in such area which could affect water quality; and

(K) a process to control the disposal of pollutants on land or in subsurface excavations within such area to protect ground and surface water quality.

(3) Areawide waste treatment management plans shall be certified annually by the Governor or his designee (or Governors or their designees, where more than one State is involved) as being consistent with applicable basin plans and such areawide waste treatment management plans shall be submitted to the Administrator for his approval.

(4)(A) Whenever the Governor of any State determines (and notifies the Administrator) that consistency with a statewide regulatory program under section 1313 of this title so requires, the requirements of clauses (F) through (K) of paragraph (2) of this subsection shall be developed and submitted by the Governor to the Administrator for approval for application to a class or category of activity throughout such State.

(B) Any program submitted under subparagraph (A) of this paragraph which, in whole or in part, is to control the discharge or other placement of dredged or fill material into the navigable waters shall include the following:

(i) A consultation process which includes the State agency with primary jurisdiction over fish and wildlife resources.

(ii) A process to identify and manage the discharge or other placement of dredged or fill material which adversely affects navigable waters, which shall complement and be coordinated with a State program under section 1344 of this title conducted pursuant to this chapter.

(iii) A process to assure that any activity conducted pursuant to a best management practice will comply with the guidelines established under section 1344(b)(1) of this title, and sections 1317 and 1343 of this title.

(iv) A process to assure that any activity conducted pursuant to a best management practice can be terminated or modified for cause including, but not limited to, the following:

(I) violation of any condition of the best management practice;

(II) change in any activity that requires either a temporary or permanent reduction or elimination of the discharge pursuant to the best management practice.

(v) A process to assure continued coordination with Federal and Federal-State water-related planning and reviewing processes, including the National Wetlands Inventory.

(C) If the Governor of a State obtains approval from the Administrator of a statewide regulatory program which meets the requirements of subparagraph (B) of this paragraph and if such State is administering a permit program under section 1344 of this title, no person shall be required to obtain an individual permit pursuant to such section, or to comply with a general permit issued pursuant to such section, with respect to any appropriate activity within such State for which a best management practice has been approved by the Administrator under the program approved by the Administrator pursuant to this paragraph.

(D)(i) Whenever the Administrator determines after public hearing that a State is not administering a program approved under this section in accordance with the requirements of this section, the Administrator shall so notify the State, and if appropriate corrective action is not taken within a reasonable time, not to exceed ninety days, the Administrator shall withdraw approval of such program. The Administrator shall not withdraw approval of any such program unless he shall first have notified the State, and made public, in writing, the reasons for such withdrawal.

(ii) In the case of a State with a program submitted and approved under this paragraph, the Administrator shall withdraw approval of such program under this subparagraph only for a substantial failure of the State to administer its program in accordance with the requirements of this paragraph.

(c) **REGIONAL OPERATING AGENCIES**

(1) The Governor of each State, in consultation with the planning agency designated under subsection (a) of this section, at the time a plan is submitted to the Administrator, shall designate one or more waste treatment management agencies (which may be an existing or newly created local, regional, or State agency or political subdivision) for each area designated under subsection (a) of this section and submit such designations to the Administrator.

(2) The Administrator shall accept any such designation, unless, within 120 days of such designation, he finds that the designated management agency (or agencies) does not have adequate authority —

(A) to carry out appropriate portions of an areawide waste treatment management plan developed under subsection (b) of this section;

(B) to manage effectively waste treatment works and related facilities serving such area in conformance with any plan required by subsection (b) of this section;

(C) directly or by contract, to design and construct new works, and to operate and maintain new and existing works as required by any plan developed pursuant to subsection (b) of this section;

(D) to accept and utilize grants, or other funds from any source, for waste treatment management purposes;

(E) to raise revenues, including the assessment of waste treatment charges;

(F) to incur short- and long-term indebtedness;

(G) to assure in implementation of an areawide waste treatment management plan that each participating community pays its proportionate share of treatment costs;

(H) to refuse to receive any wastes from any municipality or subdivision thereof, which does not comply with any provisions of an approved plan under this section applicable to such area; and

(I) to accept for treatment industrial wastes.

(d) **CONFORMITY OF WORKS WITH AREA PLAN**

After a waste treatment management agency having the authority required by subsection (c) of this section has been designated under such subsection for an area and a plan for such area has been approved under subsection (b) of this section, the Administrator shall not make any grant for construction of a publicly owned treatment works under section 1281(g)(1) of this title within such area except to such designated agency and for works in conformity with such plan.

(e) **PERMITS NOT TO CONFLICT WITH APPROVED PLANS**

No permit under section 1342 of this title shall be issued for any point source which is in conflict with a plan approved pursuant to subsection (b) of this section.

(f) **GRANTS**

(1) The Administrator shall make grants to any agency designated under subsection (a) of this section for payment of the reasonable costs of developing and operating a continuing areawide waste treatment management planning process under subsection (b) of this section.

(2) For the two-year period beginning on the date the first grant is made under paragraph (1) of this subsection to an agency, if such first grant is made before October 1, 1977, the amount of each such grant to such agency shall be 100 per centum of the costs of developing and operating a continuing areawide waste treatment management planning process under subsection (b) of this section, and thereafter the amount granted to such agency shall not exceed 75 per centum of such costs in each succeeding one-year period. In the case of any other grant made to an agency under such paragraph (1) of this subsection, the amount of such grant shall not exceed 75 per centum of the costs of developing and operating a continuing areawide waste treatment management planning process in any year.

(3) Each applicant for a grant under this subsection shall submit to the Administrator for his approval each proposal for which a grant is applied for under this subsection. The Administrator shall act upon such proposal as soon as practicable after it has been submitted, and his approval of that proposal shall be deemed a contractual obligation of the United States for the payment of its contribution to such proposal, subject to such amounts as are provided in appropriation Acts. There is authorized to be appropriated to carry out this subsection not to exceed $50,000,000 for the fiscal year ending June 30, 1973, not to exceed $100,000,000 for the fiscal year ending June 30, 1974, not to exceed $150,000,000 per fiscal year for the fiscal years ending June 30, 1975, September 30, 1977, September 30, 1978, September 30, 1979, and September 30, 1980, not to exceed $100,000,000 per fiscal year for the fiscal years ending Sep-

Clean Water Act §1288

tember 30, 1981, and September 30, 1982, and such sums as may be necessary for fiscal years 1983 through 1990.

(g) TECHNICAL ASSISTANCE BY ADMINISTRATOR

The Administrator is authorized, upon request for the Governor or the designated planning agency, and without reimbursement, to consult with, and provide technical assistance to, any agency designated under subsection (a) of this section in the development of areawide waste treatment management plans under subsection (b) of this section.

(h) TECHNICAL ASSISTANCE BY SECRETARY OF THE ARMY

(1) The Secretary of the Army, acting through the Chief of Engineers, in cooperation with the Administrator is authorized and directed, upon request of the Governor or the designated planning organization, to consult with, and provide technical assistance to any agency designed[5] under subsection (a) of this section in developing and operating a continuing areawide waste treatment management planning process under subsection (b) of this section.

(2) There is authorized to be appropriated to the Secretary of the Army, to carry out this subsection, not to exceed $50,000,000 per fiscal year for the fiscal years ending June 30, 1973, and June 30, 1974.

(i) STATE BEST MANAGEMENT PRACTICES PROGRAM

(1) The Secretary of the Interior, acting through the Director of the United States Fish and Wildlife Service, shall, upon request of the Governor of a State, and without reimbursement, provide technical assistance to such State in developing a statewide program for submission to the Administrator under subsection (b)(4)(B) of this section and in implementing such program after its approval.

(2) There is authorized to be appropriated to the Secretary of the Interior $6,000,000 to complete the National Wetlands Inventory of the United States, by December 31, 1981, and to provide information from such Inventory to States as it becomes available to assist such States in the development and operation of programs under this chapter.

(j) AGRICULTURAL COST SHARING

(1) The Secretary of Agriculture, with the concurrence of the Administrator, and acting through the Soil Conservation Service and such other agencies of the Department of Agriculture as the Secretary may designate, is authorized and directed to establish and administer a program to enter into contracts, subject to such amounts as are provided in advance by appropriation acts, of not less than five years nor more than ten years with owners and operators having control of rural land for the purpose of installing and maintaining measures incorporating best management practices to control nonpoint source pollution for improved water quality in those States or areas for which the Administrator has approved a plan under subsection (b) of this section where the practices to

---

5. So in original. Probably should be "designated."

which the contracts apply are certified by the management agency designated under subsection (c)(1) of this section to be consistent with such plans and will result in improved water quality. Such contracts may be entered into during the period ending not later than September 31, 1988. Under such contracts the land owner or operator shall agree —

(i) to effectuate a plan approved by a soil conservation district, where one exists, under this section for his farm, ranch, or other land substantially in accordance with the schedule outlined therein unless any requirement thereof is waived or modified by the Secretary;

(ii) to forfeit all rights to further payments or grants under the contract and refund to the United States all payments and grants received thereunder, with interest, upon his violation of the contract at any stage during the time he has control of the land if the Secretary, after considering the recommendations of the soil conservation district, where one exists, and the Administrator, determines that such violation is of such a nature as to warrant termination of the contract, or to make refunds or accept such payment adjustments as the Secretary may deem appropriate if he determines that the violation by the owner or operator does not warrant termination of the contract;

(iii) upon transfer of his right and interest in the farm, ranch, or other land during the contract period to forfeit all rights to further payments or grants under the contract and refund to the United States all payments or grants received thereunder, with interest, unless the transferee of any such land agrees with the Secretary to assume all obligations of the contract;

(iv) not to adopt any practice specified by the Secretary on the advice of the Administrator in the contract as a practice which would tend to defeat the purposes of the contract;

(v) to such additional provisions as the Secretary determines are desirable and includes in the contract to effectuate the purposes of the program or to facilitate the practical administration of the program.

(2) In return for such agreement by the landowner or operator the Secretary shall agree to provide technical assistance and share the cost of carrying out those conservation practices and measures set forth in the contract for which he determines that cost sharing is appropriate and in the public interest and which are approved for cost sharing by the agency designated to implement the plan developed under subsection (b) of this section. The portion of such cost (including labor) to be shared shall be that part which the Secretary determines is necessary and appropriate to effectuate the installation of the water quality management practices and measures under the contract, but not to exceed 50 per centum of the total cost of the measures set forth in the contract; except the Secretary may increase the matching cost share where he determines that (1) the main benefits to be derived from the measures are related to improving offsite water quality, and (2) the matching share requirement would place a burden on the landowner which would probably prevent him from participating in the program.

(3) The Secretary may terminate any contract with a landowner or operator by mutual agreement with the owner or operator if the Secretary determines that

such termination would be in the public interest, and may agree to such modification of contracts previously entered into as he may determine to be desirable to carry out the purposes of the program or facilitate the practical administration thereof or to accomplish equitable treatment with respect to other conservation, land use, or water quality programs.

(4) In providing assistance under this subsection the Secretary will give priority to those areas and sources that have the most significant effect upon water quality. Additional investigations or plans may be made, where necessary, to supplement approved water quality management plans, in order to determine priorities.

(5) The Secretary shall, where practicable, enter into agreements with soil conservation districts, State soil and water conservation agencies, or State water quality agencies to administer all or part of the program established in this subsection under regulations developed by the Secretary. Such agreements shall provide for the submission of such reports as the Secretary deems necessary, and for payment by the United States of such portion of the costs incurred in the administration of the program as the Secretary may deem appropriate.

(6) The contracts under this subsection shall be entered into only in areas where the management agency designated under subsection (c)(1) of this section assures an adequate level of participation by owners and operators having control of rural land in such areas. Within such areas the local soil conservation district, where one exists, together with the Secretary of Agriculture, will determine the priority of assistance among individual land owners and operators to assure that the most critical water quality problems are addressed.

(7) The Secretary, in consultation with the Administrator and subject to section 1314(k) of this title, shall, not later than September 30, 1978, promulgate regulations for carrying out this subsection and for support and cooperation with other Federal and non-Federal agencies for implementation of this subsection.

(8) This program shall not be used to authorize or finance projects that would otherwise be eligible for assistance under the terms of Public Law 83-566 [16 U.S.C. 1001 et seq.].

(9) There are hereby authorized to be appropriated to the Secretary of Agriculture $200,000,000 for fiscal year 1979, $400,000,000 for fiscal year 1980, $100,000,000 for fiscal year 1981, $100,000,000 for fiscal year 1982, and such sums as may be necessary for fiscal years 1983 through 1990, to carry out this subsection. The program authorized under this subsection shall be in addition to, and not in substitution of, other programs in such area authorized by this or any other public law. . . .

§1292. DEFINITIONS

As used in this subchapter —

(1) The term "construction" means any one or more of the following: preliminary planning to determine the feasibility of treatment works, engineering, agricultural, legal, fiscal, or economic investigations or studies, surveys, designs, plans, working drawings, specifications, procedures, field

testing of innovative or alternative waste water treatment processes and techniques meeting guidelines promulgated under section 1314(d)(3) of this title, or other necessary actions, erection, building, acquisition, alteration, remodeling, improvement, or extension of treatment works, or the inspection or supervision of any of the foregoing items.

(2)(A) The term "treatment works" means any devices and systems used in the storage, treatment, recycling, and reclamation of municipal sewage or industrial wastes of a liquid nature to implement section 1281 of this title, or necessary to recycle or reuse water at the most economical cost over the estimated life of the works, including intercepting sewers, outfall sewers, sewage collection systems, pumping, power, and other equipment, and their appurtenances; extensions, improvements, remodeling, additions, and alterations thereof; elements essential to provide a reliable recycled supply such as standby treatment units and clear well facilities; and any works, including site acquisition of the land that will be an integral part of the treatment process (including land used for the storage of treated wastewater in land treatment systems prior to land application) or is used for ultimate disposal of residues resulting from such treatment.

(B) In addition to the definition contained in subparagraph (A) of this paragraph, "treatment works" means any other method or system for preventing, abating, reducing, storing, treating, separating, or disposing of municipal waste, including storm water runoff, or industrial waste, including waste in combined storm water and sanitary sewer systems. Any application for construction grants which includes wholly or in part such methods or systems shall, in accordance with guidelines published by the Administrator pursuant to subparagraph (C) of this paragraph, contain adequate data and analysis demonstrating such proposal to be, over the life of such works, the most cost efficient alternative to comply with sections 1311 or 1312 of this title, or the requirements of section 1281 of this title.

(C) For the purposes of subparagraph (B) of this paragraph, the Administrator shall, within one hundred and eighty days after October 18, 1972, publish and thereafter revise no less often than annually, guidelines for the evaluation of methods, including cost-effective analysis, described in subparagraph (B) of this paragraph.

(3) The term "replacement" as used in this subchapter means those expenditures for obtaining and installing equipment, accessories, or appurtenances during the useful life of the treatment works necessary to maintain the capacity and performance for which such works are designed and constructed.

§1293. LOAN GUARANTEES

(a) STATE OR LOCAL OBLIGATIONS ISSUED EXCLUSIVELY TO FEDERAL FINANCING BANK FOR PUBLICLY OWNED TREATMENT WORKS; DETERMINATION OF ELIGIBILITY OF PROJECT BY ADMINISTRATOR

Subject to the conditions of this section and to such terms and conditions as the Administrator determines to be necessary to carry out the purposes of this subchapter, the Administrator is authorized to guarantee, and to make commitments to guarantee, the principal and interest (including interest accruing between the date of default and the date of the payment in full of the guarantee) of any loan, obligation, or participation therein of any State, municipality, or intermunicipal or interstate agency issued directly and exclusively to the Federal Financing Bank to finance that part of the cost of any grant-eligible project for the construction of publicly owned treatment works not paid for with Federal financial assistance under this subchapter (other than this section), which project the Administrator has determined to be eligible for such financial assistance under this subchapter, including, but not limited to, projects eligible for reimbursement under section 1286 of this title.

(b) CONDITIONS FOR ISSUANCE

No guarantee, or commitment to make a guarantee, may be made pursuant to this section —

(1) unless the Administrator certifies that the issuing body is unable to obtain on reasonable terms sufficient credit to finance its actual needs without such guarantee; and

(2) unless the Administrator determines that there is a reasonable assurance of repayment of the loan, obligation, or participation therein.

A determination of whether financing is available at reasonable rates shall be made by the Secretary of the Treasury with relationship to the current average yield on outstanding marketable obligations of municipalities of comparable maturity.

(c) FEES FOR APPLICATION INVESTIGATION AND ISSUANCE OF COMMITMENT GUARANTEE

The Administrator is authorized to charge reasonable fees for the investigation of an application for a guarantee and for the issuance of a commitment to make a guarantee.

(d) COMMITMENT FOR REPAYMENT

The Administrator, in determining whether there is a reasonable assurance of repayment, may require a commitment which would apply to such repayment. Such commitment may include, but not be limited to, any funds received by such grantee from the amounts appropriated under section 1286 of this title.

§1293a. CONTAINED SPOIL DISPOSAL FACILITIES

(a) CONSTRUCTION, OPERATION, AND MAINTENANCE; PERIOD; CONDITIONS; REQUIREMENTS

The Secretary of the Army, acting through the Chief of Engineers, is authorized to construct, operate, and maintain, subject to the provisions of subsection (c) of this section, contained spoil disposal facilities of sufficient capacity for a period not to exceed ten years, to meet the requirements of this section. Before establishing each such facility, the Secretary of the Army shall obtain the concurrence of appropriate local governments and shall consider the views and recommendations of the Administrator of the Environmental Protection Agency and shall comply with requirements of section 1171 of this title, and of the National Environmental Policy Act of 1969 [42 U.S.C. 4321 et seq.]. Section 401 of this title shall not apply to any facility authorized by this section.

(b) TIME FOR ESTABLISHMENT; CONSIDERATION OF AREA NEEDS; REQUIREMENTS

The Secretary of the Army, acting through the Chief of Engineers, shall establish the contained spoil disposal facilities authorized in subsection (a) of this section at the earliest practicable date, taking into consideration the views and recommendations of the Administrator of the Environmental Protection Agency as to those areas which, in the Administrator's judgment, are most urgently in need of such facilities and pursuant to the requirements of the National Environmental Policy Act of 1969 [42 U.S.C. 4321 et seq.] and the Federal Water Pollution Control Act [33 U.S.C. 1251 et seq.].

(c) WRITTEN AGREEMENT REQUIREMENT; TERMS OF AGREEMENT

Prior to construction of any such facility, the appropriate State or States, interstate agency, municipality, or other appropriate political subdivision of the State shall agree in writing to (1) furnish all lands, easements, and rights-of-way necessary for the construction, operation, and maintenance of the facility; (2) contribute to the United States 25 per centum of the construction costs, such amount to be payable either in cash prior to construction, in installments during construction, or in installments, with interest at a rate to be determined by the Secretary of the Treasury, as of the beginning of the fiscal year in which construction is initiated, on the basis of the computed average interest rate payable by the Treasury upon its outstanding marketable public obligations, which are neither due or callable for redemption for fifteen years from date of issue; (3) hold and save the United States free from damages due to construction, operation, and maintenance of the facility; and (4) except as provided in subsection (f) of this section, maintain the facility after completion of its use for disposal purposes in a manner satisfactory to the Secretary of the Army.

(d) WAIVER OF CONSTRUCTION COSTS CONTRIBUTION FROM NON-FEDERAL INTERESTS; FINDINGS OF PARTICIPATION IN WASTE TREATMENT FACILITIES FOR GENERAL GEOGRAPHICAL AREA AND COMPLIANCE WITH WATER QUALITY STANDARDS; WAIVER OF PAYMENTS IN EVENT OF WRITTEN AGREEMENT BEFORE OCCURRENCE OF FINDINGS

The requirement for appropriate non-Federal interest or interests to furnish an agreement to contribute 25 per centum of the construction costs as set forth in subsection (c) of this section shall be waived by the Secretary of the Army upon a finding by the Administrator of the Environmental Protection Agency that for the area to which such construction applies, the State or States involved, interstate agency, municipality, and other appropriate political subdivision of the State and industrial concerns are participating in and in compliance with an approved plan for the general geographical area of the dredging activity for construction, modification, expansion, or rehabilitation of waste treatment facilities and the Administrator has found that applicable water quality standards are not being violated. In the event such findings occur after the appropriate non-Federal interest or interests have entered into the agreement required by subsection (c) of this section, any payments due after the date of such findings as part of the required local contribution of 25 per centum of the construction costs shall be waived by the Secretary of the Army.

(e) **FEDERAL PAYMENT OF COSTS FOR DISPOSAL OF DREDGED SPOIL FROM PROJECT**

Notwithstanding any other provision of law, all costs of disposal of dredged spoil from the project for the Great Lakes connecting channels, Michigan, shall be borne by the United States.

(f) **TITLE TO LANDS; EASEMENTS, AND RIGHTS-OF-WAY; RETENTION BY NON-FEDERAL INTERESTS; CONVEYANCE OF FACILITIES; AGREEMENTS OF TRANSFEREE**

The participating non-Federal interest or interests shall retain title to all lands, easements, and rights-of-way furnished by it pursuant to subsection (c) of this section. A spoil disposal facility owned by a non-Federal interest or interests may be conveyed to another party only after completion of the facility's use for disposal purposes and after the transferee agrees in writing to use or maintain the facility in a manner which the Secretary of the Army determines to be satisfactory.

(g) **FEDERAL LICENSES OR PERMITS; CHARGES; REMISSION OF CHARGE**

Any spoil disposal facilities constructed under the provisions of this section shall be made available to Federal licensees or permittees upon payment of an appropriate charge for such use. Twenty-five per centum of such charge shall be remitted to the participating non-Federal interest or interests except for those excused from contributing to the construction costs under subsections (d) and (e) of this section.

(h) **PROVISIONS APPLICABLE TO GREAT LAKES AND THEIR CONNECTING CHANNELS**

This section, other than subsection (i), shall be applicable only to the Great Lakes and their connecting channels.

(i) **RESEARCH, STUDY, AND EXPERIMENTATION PROGRAM RELATING TO DREDGED SPOIL EXTENDED TO NAVIGABLE WATERS, ETC.; COOPERATIVE PROGRAM; SCOPE OF PROGRAM; UTILIZATION OF FACILITIES AND PERSONNEL OF FEDERAL AGENCY**

The Chief of Engineers, under the direction of the Secretary of the Army, is hereby authorized to extend to all navigable waters, connecting channels, tributary streams, other waters of the United States and waters contiguous to the

United States, a comprehensive program of research, study, and experimentation relating to dredged spoil. This program shall be carried out in cooperation with other Federal and State agencies, and shall include, but not be limited to, investigations on the characteristics of dredged spoil, and alternative methods of its disposal. To the extent that such study shall include the effects of such dredge spoil on water quality, the facilities and personnel of the Environmental Protection Agency shall be utilized.

(j) PERIOD FOR DEPOSITING DREDGED MATERIALS

The Secretary of the Army, acting through the Chief of Engineers, is authorized to continue to deposit dredged materials into a contained spoil disposal facility constructed under this section until the Secretary determines that such facility is no longer needed for such purpose or that such facility is completely full.

(k) STUDY AND MONITORING PROGRAM

(1) STUDY

The Secretary of the Army, acting through the Chief of Engineers, shall conduct a study of the materials disposed of in contained spoil disposal facilities constructed under this section for the purpose of determining whether or not toxic pollutants are present in such facilities and for the purpose of determining the concentration levels of each of such pollutants in such facilities.

(2) REPORT

Not later than 1 year after November 17, 1988, the Secretary shall transmit to Congress a report on the results of the study conducted under paragraph (1).

(3) INSPECTION AND MONITORING PROGRAM

The Secretary shall conduct a program to inspect and monitor contained spoil disposal facilities constructed under this section for the purpose of determining whether or not toxic pollutants are leaking from such facilities.

(4) TOXIC POLLUTANT DEFINED

For purposes of this subsection, the term "toxic pollutant" means those toxic pollutants referred to in section 1311(b)(2)(C) and 1311(b)(2)(D) of this title and such other pollutants as the Secretary, in consultation with the Administrator of the Environmental Protection Agency, determines are appropriate based on their effects on human health and the environment.

§1294. PUBLIC INFORMATION AND EDUCATION ON RECYCLING AND REUSE OF WASTEWATER, USE OF LAND TREATMENT, AND REDUCTION OF WASTEWATER VOLUME

The Administrator shall develop and operate within one year of December 27, 1977, a continuing program of public information and education on recycling and reuse of wastewater (including sludge), the use of land treatment, and methods for the reduction of wastewater volume.

§1295. REQUIREMENTS FOR AMERICAN MATERIALS

Notwithstanding any other provision of law, no grant for which application is made after February 1, 1978, shall be made under this subchapter for any treatment works unless only such unmanufactured articles, materials, and supplies as have been mined or produced in the United States, and only such manufactured articles, materials, and supplies as have been manufactured in the United States, substantially all from articles, materials, or supplies mined, produced, or manufactured, as the case may be, in the United States will be used in such treatment works. This section shall not apply in any case where the Administrator determines, based upon those factors the Administrator deems relevant, including the available resources of the agency, it to be inconsistent with the public interest (including multilateral government procurement agreements) or the cost to be unreasonable, or if articles, materials, or supplies of the class or kind to be used or the articles, materials, or supplies from which they are manufactured are not mined, produced, or manufactured, as the case may be, in the United States in sufficient and reasonably available commercial quantities and of a satisfactory quality.

§1296. DETERMINATION OF PRIORITY OF PROJECTS

Notwithstanding any other provision of this chapter, the determination of the priority to be given each category of projects for construction of publicly owned treatment works within each State shall be made solely by that State, except that if the Administrator, after a public hearing, determines that a specific project will not result in compliance with the enforceable requirements of this chapter, such project shall be removed from the State's priority list and such State shall submit a revised priority list. These categories shall include, but not be limited to (A) secondary treatment, (B) more stringent treatment, (C) infiltration-in-flow correction, (D) major sewer system rehabilitation, (E) new collector sewers and appurtenances, (F) new interceptors and appurtenances, and (G) correction of combined sewer overflows. Not less than 25 per centum of funds allocated to a State in any fiscal year under this subchapter for construction of publicly owned treatment works in such State shall be obligated for those types of projects referred to in clauses (D), (E), (F), and (G) of this section, if such projects are on such State's priority list for that year and are otherwise eligible for funding in that fiscal year. It is the policy of Congress that projects for wastewater treatment and management undertaken with Federal financial assistance under this chapter by any State, municipality, or intermunicipal or interstate agency shall be projects which, in the estimation of the State, are designed to achieve optimum water quality management, consistent with the public health and water quality goals and requirements of this chapter. . . .

§1298. COST EFFECTIVENESS

(a) CONGRESSIONAL STATEMENT OF POLICY

It is the policy of Congress that a project for waste treatment and management undertaken with Federal financial assistance under this chapter by any State, municipality, or intermunicipal or interstate agency shall be considered as an overall waste treatment system for waste treatment and management, and shall be that system which constitutes the most economical and cost-effective combination of devices and systems used in the storage, treatment, recycling, and reclamation of municipal sewage or industrial wastes of a liquid nature to implement section 1281 of this title, or necessary to recycle or reuse water at the most economical cost over the estimated life of the works, including intercepting sewers, outfall sewers, sewage collection systems, pumping power, and other equipment, and their appurtenances; extension, improvements, remodeling, additions, and alterations thereof; elements essential to provide a reliable recycled supply such as standby treatment units and clear well facilities; and any works, including site acquisition of the land that will be an integral part of the treatment process (including land use for the storage of treated wastewater in land treatment systems prior to land application) or which is used for ultimate disposal of residues resulting from such treatment; water efficiency measures and devices; and any other method or system for preventing, abating, reducing, storing, treating, separating, or disposing of municipal waste, including storm water runoff, or industrial waste, including waste in combined storm water and sanitary sewer systems; to meet the requirements of this chapter.

(b) DETERMINATION BY ADMINISTRATOR AS PREREQUISITE TO APPROVAL OF GRANT

In accordance with the policy set forth in subsection (a) of this section, before the Administrator approves any grant to any State, municipality, or intermunicipal or interstate agency for the erection, building, acquisition, alteration, remodeling, improvement, or extension of any treatment works the Administrator shall determine that the facilities plan of which such treatment works are a part constitutes the most economical and cost-effective combination of treatment works over the life of the project to meet the requirements of this chapter, including, but not limited to, consideration of construction costs, operation, maintenance, and replacement costs.

(c) VALUE ENGINEERING REVIEW

In furtherance of the policy set forth in subsection (a) of this section, the Administrator shall require value engineering review in connection with any treatment works, prior to approval of any grant for the erection, building, acquisition, alteration, remodeling, improvement, or extension of such treatment works, in any case in which the cost of such erection, building, acquisition, alteration, remodeling, improvement, or extension is projected to be in excess of $10,000,000. For purposes of this subsection, the term "value engineering review" means a specialized cost control technique which uses a systematic and

Clean Water Act §1311

creative approach to identify and to focus on unnecessarily high cost in a project in order to arrive at a cost saving without sacrificing the reliability or efficiency of the project.

(d) **PROJECTS AFFECTED**

This section applies to projects for waste treatment and management for which no treatment works including a facilities plan for such project have received Federal financial assistance for the preparation of construction plans and specifications under this chapter before December 29, 1981.

§1299. STATE CERTIFICATION OF PROJECTS

Whenever the Governor of a State which has been delegated sufficient authority to administer the construction grant program under this subchapter in that State certifies to the Administrator that a grant application meets applicable requirements of Federal and State law for assistance under this subchapter, the Administrator shall approve or disapprove such application within 45 days of the date of receipt of such application. If the Administrator does not approve or disapprove such application within 45 days of receipt, the application shall be deemed approved. If the Administrator disapproves such application the Administrator shall state in writing the reasons for such disapproval. Any grant approved or deemed approved under this section shall be subject to amounts provided in appropriation Acts.

SUBCHAPTER III — STANDARDS AND ENFORCEMENT

§1311. EFFLUENT LIMITATIONS

(a) **ILLEGALITY OF POLLUTANT DISCHARGES EXCEPT IN COMPLIANCE WITH LAW**

Except as in compliance with this section and sections 1312, 1316, 1317, 1328, 1342, and 1344 of this title, the discharge of any pollutant by any person shall be unlawful.

(b) **TIMETABLE FOR ACHIEVEMENT OF OBJECTIVES**

In order to carry out the objective of this chapter there shall be achieved —
  (1)(A) not later than July 1, 1977, effluent limitations for point sources, other than publicly owned treatment works, (i) which shall require the application of the best practicable control technology currently available as defined by the Administrator pursuant to section 1314(b) of this title, or (ii) in the case of a discharge into a publicly owned treatment works which meets the requirements of subparagraph (B) of this paragraph, which shall require compliance with any applicable pretreatment requirements and any requirements under section 1317 of this title; and
    (B) for publicly owned treatment works in existence on July 1, 1977, or approved pursuant to section 1283 of this title prior to June 30, 1974

§1311

(for which construction must be completed within four years of approval), effluent limitations based upon secondary treatment as defined by the Administrator pursuant to section 1314(d)(1) of this title; or,

(C) not later than July 1, 1977, any more stringent limitation, including those necessary to meet water quality standards, treatment standards, or schedules of compliance, established pursuant to any State law or regulations (under authority preserved by section 1370 of this title) or any other Federal law or regulation, or required to implement any applicable water quality standard established pursuant to this chapter.

(2)(A) for pollutants identified in subparagraphs (C), (D), and (F) of this paragraph, effluent limitations for categories and classes of point sources, other than publicly owned treatment works, which (i) shall require application of the best available technology economically achievable for such category or class, which will result in reasonable further progress toward the national goal of eliminating the discharge of all pollutants, as determined in accordance with regulations issued by the Administrator pursuant to section 1314(b)(2) of this title, which such effluent limitations shall require the elimination of discharges of all pollutants if the Administrator finds, on the basis of information available to him (including information developed pursuant to section 1325 of this title), that such elimination is technologically and economically achievable for a category or class of point sources as determined in accordance with regulations issued by the Administrator pursuant to section 1314(b)(2) of this title, or (ii) in the case of the introduction of a pollutant into a publicly owned treatment works which meets the requirements of subparagraph (B) of this paragraph, shall require compliance with any applicable pretreatment requirements and any other requirement under section 1317 of this title;

(B) Repealed. Pub. L. 97-117, §21(b), Dec. 29, 1981, 95 Stat. 1632.

(C) with respect to all toxic pollutants referred to in table 1 of Committee Print Numbered 95-30 of the Committee on Public Works and Transportation of the House of Representatives compliance with effluent limitations in accordance with subparagraph (A) of this paragraph as expeditiously as practicable but in no case later than three years after the date such limitations are promulgated under section 1314(b) of this title, and in no case later than March 31, 1989;

(D) for all toxic pollutants listed under paragraph (1) of subsection (a) of section 1317 of this title which are not referred to in subparagraph (C) of this paragraph compliance with effluent limitations in accordance with subparagraph (A) of this paragraph as expeditiously as practicable, but in no case later than three years after the date such limitations are promulgated under section 1314(b) of this title, and in no case later than March 31, 1989;

(E) as expeditiously as practicable but in no case later than three years after the date such limitations are promulgated under section 1314(b) of this title, and in no case later than March 31, 1989, compliance with effluent limitations for categories and classes of point sources, other than publicly owned treatment works, which in the case of pollutants identified pursuant to section 1314(a)(4) of this title shall require application of the best conventional pollutant control technology as determined in accordance with regulations issued by the Administrator pursuant to section 1314(b)(4) of this title; and

(F) for all pollutants (other than those subject to subparagraphs (C), (D), or (E) of this paragraph) compliance with effluent limitations in accordance with subparagraph (A) of this paragraph as expeditiously as practicable but in no case later than 3 years after the date such limitations are established, and in no case later than March 31, 1989.

(3)(A) for effluent limitations under paragraph (1)(A)(i) of this subsection promulgated after January 1, 1982, and requiring a level of control substantially greater or based on fundamentally different control technology than under permits for an industrial category issued before such date, compliance as expeditiously as practicable but in no case later than three years after the date such limitations are promulgated under section 1314(b) of this title, and in no case later than March 31, 1989; and

(B) for any effluent limitation in accordance with paragraph (1)(A)(i), (2)(A)(i), or (2)(E) of this subsection established only on the basis of section 1342(a)(1) of this title in a permit issued after February 4, 1987, compliance as expeditiously as practicable but in no case later than three years after the date such limitations are established, and in no case later than March 31, 1989.

(c) **MODIFICATION OF TIMETABLE**

The Administrator may modify the requirements of subsection (b)(2)(A) of this section with respect to any point source for which a permit application is filed after July 1, 1977, upon a showing by the owner or operator of such point source satisfactory to the Administrator that such modified requirements (1) will represent the maximum use of technology within the economic capability of the owner or operator; and (2) will result in reasonable further progress toward the elimination of the discharge of pollutants.

(d) **REVIEW AND REVISION OF EFFLUENT LIMITATIONS**

Any effluent limitation required by paragraph (2) of subsection (b) of this section shall be reviewed at least every five years and, if appropriate, revised pursuant to the procedure established under such paragraph.

(e) **ALL POINT DISCHARGE SOURCE APPLICATION OF EFFLUENT LIMITATIONS**

Effluent limitations established pursuant to this section or section 1312 of this title shall be applied to all point sources of discharge of pollutants in accordance with the provisions of this chapter.

§1311

(f) ILLEGALITY OF DISCHARGE OF RADIOLOGICAL, CHEMICAL, OR BIOLOGICAL WARFARE AGENTS, HIGH-LEVEL RADIOACTIVE WASTE, OR MEDICAL WASTE

Notwithstanding any other provisions of this chapter it shall be unlawful to discharge any radiological, chemical, or biological warfare agent, any high-level radioactive waste, or any medical waste, into the navigable waters.

(g) MODIFICATIONS FOR CERTAIN NONCONVENTIONAL POLLUTANTS

(1) GENERAL AUTHORITY

The Administrator, with the concurrence of the State, may modify the requirements of subsection (b)(2)(A) of this section with respect to the discharge from any point source of ammonia, chlorine, color, iron, and total phenols (4AAP) (when determined by the Administrator to be a pollutant covered by subsection (b)(2)(F) of this section) and any other pollutant which the Administrator lists under paragraph (4) of this subsection.

(2) REQUIREMENTS FOR GRANTING MODIFICATIONS

A modification under this subsection shall be granted only upon a showing by the owner or operator of a point source satisfactory to the Administrator that —

(A) such modified requirements will result at a minimum in compliance with the requirements of subsection (b)(1)(A) or (C) of this section, whichever is applicable;

(B) such modified requirements will not result in any additional requirements on any other point or nonpoint source; and

(C) such modification will not interfere with the attainment or maintenance of that water quality which shall assure protection of public water supplies, and the protection and propagation of a balanced population of shellfish, fish, and wildlife, and allow recreational activities, in and on the water and such modification will not result in the discharge of pollutants in quantities which may reasonably be anticipated to pose an unacceptable risk to human health or the environment because of bioaccumulation, persistency in the environment, acute toxicity, chronic toxicity (including carcinogenicity, mutagenicity, or teratogenicity), or synergistic propensities.

(3) LIMITATION ON AUTHORITY TO APPLY FOR SUBSECTION (C) MODIFICATION

If an owner or operator of a point source applies for a modification under this subsection with respect to the discharge of any pollutant, such owner or operator shall be eligible to apply for modification under subsection (c) of this section with respect to such pollutant only during the same time period as he is eligible to apply for a modification under this subsection.

(4) PROCEDURES FOR LISTING ADDITIONAL POLLUTANTS

(A) GENERAL AUTHORITY

Upon petition of any person, the Administrator may add any pollutant to the list of pollutants for which modification under this section is authorized (except for pollutants identified pursuant to section 1314(a)(4) of this title, toxic pollutants subject to section 1317(a) of this title, and the thermal component of discharges) in accordance with the provisions of this paragraph.

(B) REQUIREMENTS FOR LISTING

(i) SUFFICIENT INFORMATION

The person petitioning for listing of an additional pollutant under this subsection shall submit to the Administrator sufficient information to make the determinations required by this subparagraph.

(ii) TOXIC CRITERIA DETERMINATION

The Administrator shall determine whether or not the pollutant meets the criteria for listing as a toxic pollutant under section 1317(a) of this title.

(iii) LISTING AS TOXIC POLLUTANT

If the Administrator determines that the pollutant meets the criteria for listing as a toxic pollutant under section 1317(a) of this title, the Administrator shall list the pollutant as a toxic pollutant under section 1317(a) of this title.

(iv) NONCONVENTIONAL CRITERIA DETERMINATION

If the Administrator determines that the pollutant does not meet the criteria for listing as a toxic pollutant under such section and determines that adequate test methods and sufficient data are available to make the determinations required by paragraph (2) of this subsection with respect to the pollutant, the Administrator shall add the pollutant to the list of pollutants specified in paragraph (1) of this subsection for which modifications are authorized under this subsection.

(C) REQUIREMENTS FOR FILING OF PETITIONS

A petition for listing of a pollutant under this paragraph —
(i) must be filed not later than 270 days after the date of promulgation of an applicable effluent guideline under section 1314 of this title;
(ii) may be filed before promulgation of such guideline; and
(iii) may be filed with an application for a modification under paragraph (1) with respect to the discharge of such pollutant.

(D) DEADLINE FOR APPROVAL OF PETITION

A decision to add a pollutant to the list of pollutants for which modifications under this subsection are authorized must be made within 270 days after the date of promulgation of an applicable effluent guideline under section 1314 of this title.

(E) BURDEN OF PROOF

The burden of proof for making the determinations under subparagraph (B) shall be on the petitioner.

(5) REMOVAL OF POLLUTANTS

The Administrator may remove any pollutant from the list of pollutants for which modifications are authorized under this subsection if the Administrator determines that adequate test methods and sufficient data are no longer available for determining whether or not modifications may be granted with respect to such pollutant under paragraph (2) of this subsection.

(h) MODIFICATION OF SECONDARY TREATMENT REQUIREMENTS

The Administrator, with the concurrence of the State, may issue a permit under section 1342 of this title which modifies the requirements of subsection (b)(1)(B) of this section with respect to the discharge of any pollutant from a publicly owned treatment works into marine waters, if the applicant demonstrates to the satisfaction of the Administrator that —

(1) there is an applicable water quality standard specific to the pollutant for which the modification is requested, which has been identified under section 1314(a)(6) of this title;

(2) the discharge of pollutants in accordance with such modified requirements will not interfere, alone or in combination with pollutants from other sources, with the attainment or maintenance of that water quality which assures protection of public water supplies and the protection and propagation of a balanced, indigenous population of shellfish, fish, and wildlife, and allows recreational activities, in and on the water;

(3) the applicant has established a system for monitoring the impact of such discharge on a representative sample of aquatic biota, to the extent practicable, and the scope of such monitoring is limited to include only those scientific investigations which are necessary to study the effects of the proposed discharge;

(4) such modified requirements will not result in any additional requirements on any other point or nonpoint source;

(5) all applicable pretreatment requirements for sources introducing waste into such treatment works will be enforced;

(6) in the case of any treatment works serving a population of 50,000 or more, with respect to any toxic pollutant introduced into such works by an industrial discharger for which pollutant there is no applicable pretreatment

Clean Water Act §1311

requirement in effect, sources introducing waste into such works are in compliance with all applicable pretreatment requirements, the applicant will enforce such requirements, and the applicant has in effect a pretreatment program which, in combination with the treatment of discharges from such works, removes the same amount of such pollutant as would be removed if such works were to apply secondary treatment to discharges and if such works had no pretreatment program with respect to such pollutant.

(7) to the extent practicable, the applicant has established a schedule of activities designed to eliminate the entrance of toxic pollutants from nonindustrial sources into such treatment works;

(8) there will be no new or substantially increased discharges from the point source of the pollutant to which the modification applies above that volume of discharge specified in the permit;

(9) the applicant at the time such modification becomes effective will be discharging effluent which has received at least primary or equivalent treatment and which meets the criteria established under section 1314(a)(1) of this title after initial mixing in the waters surrounding or adjacent to the point at which such effluent is discharged.

For the purposes of this subsection the phrase "the discharge of any pollutant into marine waters" refers to a discharge into deep waters of the territorial sea or the waters of the contiguous zone, or into saline estuarine waters where there is strong tidal movement and other hydrological and geological characteristics which the Administrator determines necessary to allow compliance with paragraph (2) of this subsection, and section 1251(a)(2) of this title. For the purposes of paragraph (9), "primary or equivalent treatment" means treatment by screening, sedimentation, and skimming adequate to remove at least 30 percent of the biological oxygen demanding material and of the suspended solids in the treatment works influent, and disinfection, where appropriate. A municipality which applies secondary treatment shall be eligible to receive a permit pursuant to this subsection which modifies the requirements of subsection (b)(1)(B) of this section with respect to the discharge of any pollutant from any treatment works owned by such municipality into marine waters. No permit issued under this subsection shall authorize the discharge of sewage sludge into marine waters. In order for a permit to be issued under this subsection for the discharge of a pollutant into marine waters, such marine waters must exhibit characteristics assuring that water providing dilution does not contain significant amounts of previously discharged effluent from such treatment works. No permit issued under this subsection shall authorize the discharge of any pollutant into saline estuarine waters which at the time of application do not support a balanced indigenous population of shellfish, fish and wildlife, or allow recreation in and on the waters or which exhibit ambient water quality below applicable water quality standards adopted for the protection of public water supplies, shellfish, fish and wildlife or recreational activities or such other standards necessary to assure support and protection of such uses. The prohibition contained in the preceding sentence shall apply without regard to the presence or absence of a causal relationship

§1311

between such characteristics and the applicant's current or proposed discharge. Notwithstanding any other provisions of this subsection, no permit may be issued under this subsection for discharge of a pollutant into the New York Bight Apex consisting of the ocean waters of the Atlantic Ocean westward of 73 degrees 30 minutes west longitude and northward of 40 degrees 10 minutes north latitude.

(i) MUNICIPAL TIME EXTENSIONS

(1) Where construction is required in order for a planned or existing publicly owned treatment works to achieve limitations under subsection (b)(1)(B) or (b)(1)(C) of this section, but (A) construction cannot be completed within the time required in such subsection, or (B) the United States has failed to make financial assistance under this chapter available in time to achieve such limitations by the time specified in such subsection, the owner or operator of such treatment works may request the Administrator (or if appropriate the State) to issue a permit pursuant to section 1342 of this title or to modify a permit issued pursuant to that section to extend such time for compliance. Any such request shall be filed with the Administrator (or if appropriate the State) within 180 days after February 4, 1987. The Administrator (or if appropriate the State) may grant such request and issue or modify such a permit, which shall contain a schedule of compliance for the publicly owned treatment works based on the earliest date by which such financial assistance will be available from the United States and construction can be completed, but in no event later than July 1, 1988, and shall contain such other terms and conditions, including those necessary to carry out subsections (b) through (g) of section 1281 of this title, section 1317 of this title, and such interim effluent limitations applicable to that treatment works as the Administrator determines are necessary to carry out the provisions of this chapter.

(2)(A) Where a point source (other than a publicly owned treatment works) will not achieve the requirements of subsections (b)(1)(A) and (b)(1)(C) of this section and —

(i) if a permit issued prior to July 1, 1977, to such point source is based upon a discharge into a publicly owned treatment works; or

(ii) if such point source (other than a publicly owned treatment works) had before July 1, 1977, a contract (enforceable against such point source) to discharge into a publicly owned treatment works; or

(iii) if either an application made before July 1, 1977, for a construction grant under this chapter for a publicly owned treatment works, or engineering or architectural plans or working drawings made before July 1, 1977, for a publicly owned treatment works, show that such point source was to discharge into such publicly owned treatment works,

and such publicly owned treatment works is presently unable to accept such discharge without construction, and in the case of a discharge to an existing publicly owned treatment works, such treatment works has an extension pursuant to paragraph (1) of this subsection, the owner or operator of such point source may request the Administrator (or if appropriate the State) to issue or modify such a permit pursuant to such section 1342 of this title to extend such time for compliance. Any such request shall be filed with the Administrator (or if appropriate the State) within 180 days after December 27, 1977, or the filing of a request by the appropriate publicly owned treatment works under paragraph (1) of this subsection, whichever is later. If the Administrator (or if appropriate the State) finds that the owner or operator of such point source has acted in good faith, he may grant such request and issue or modify such a permit, which shall contain a schedule of compliance for the point source to achieve the requirements of subsections (b)(1)(A) and (C) of this section and shall contain such other terms and conditions, including pretreatment and interim effluent limitations and water conservation requirements applicable to that point source, as the Administrator determines are necessary to carry out the provisions of this chapter.

(B) No time modification granted by the Administrator (or if appropriate the State) pursuant to paragraph (2)(A) of this subsection shall extend beyond the earliest date practicable for compliance or beyond the date of any extension granted to the appropriate publicly owned treatment works pursuant to paragraph (1) of this subsection, but in no event shall it extend beyond July 1, 1988; and no such time modification shall be granted unless (i) the publicly owned treatment works will be in operation and available to the point source before July 1, 1988, and will meet the requirements of subsections (b)(1)(B) and (C) of this section after receiving the discharge from that point source; and (ii) the point source and the publicly owned treatment works have entered into an enforceable contract requiring the point source to discharge into the publicly owned treatment works, the owner or operator of such point source to pay the costs required under section 1284 of this title, and the publicly owned treatment works to accept the discharge from the point source; and (iii) the permit for such point source requires that point source to meet all requirements under section 1317(a) and (b) of this title during the period of such time modification.

(j) MODIFICATION PROCEDURES

(1) Any application filed under this section for a modification of the provisions of —

(A) subsection (b)(1)(B) of this section under subsection (h) of this section shall be filed not later that[1] the 365th day which begins after December 29, 1981, except that a publicly owned treatment works which prior to December 31, 1982, had a contractual arrangement to use a portion of the capacity of an ocean outfall operated by another publicly owned treatment works which has applied for or received modification under subsection (h) of this section, may apply for a modification of subsection (h) of this section in its own right not later than 30 days after February 4, 1987;

(B) subsection (b)(2)(A) of this section as it applies to pollutants identified in subsection (b)(2)(F) of this section shall be filed not later than 270 days after the date of promulgation of an applicable effluent guideline under sec-

---

1. So in original. Probably should be "than."

tion 1314 of this title or not later than 270 days after December 27, 1977, whichever is later.

(2) Subject to paragraph (3) of this section, any application for a modification filed under subsection (g) of this section shall not operate to stay any requirement under this chapter, unless in the judgment of the Administrator such a stay or the modification sought will not result in the discharge of pollutants in quantities which may reasonably be anticipated to pose an unacceptable risk to human health or the environment because of bioaccumulation, persistency in the environment, acute toxicity, chronic toxicity (including carcinogenicity, mutagenicity, or teratogenicity), or synergistic propensities, and that there is a substantial likelihood that the applicant will succeed on the merits of such application. In the case of an application filed under subsection (g) of this section, the Administrator may condition any stay granted under this paragraph on requiring the filing of a bond or other appropriate security to assure timely compliance with the requirements from which a modification is sought.

(3) Compliance requirements under subsection (g). —

(A) Effect of filing. — An application for a modification under subsection (g) of this section and a petition for listing of a pollutant as a pollutant for which modifications are authorized under such subsection shall not stay the requirement that the person seeking such modification or listing comply with effluent limitations under this chapter for all pollutants not the subject of such application or petition.

(B) Effect of disapproval. — Disapproval of an application for a modification under subsection (g) of this section shall not stay the requirement that the person seeking such modification comply with all applicable effluent limitations under this chapter.

(4) Deadline for subsection (g) decision. — An application for a modification with respect to a pollutant filed under subsection (g) of this section must be approved or disapproved not later than 365 days after the date of such filing; except that in any case in which a petition for listing such pollutant as a pollutant for which modifications are authorized under such subsection is approved, such application must be approved or disapproved not later than 365 days after the date of approval of such petition.

(k) INNOVATIVE TECHNOLOGY

In the case of any facility subject to a permit under section 1342 of this title which proposes to comply with the requirements of subsection (b)(2)(A) or (b)(2)(E) of this section by replacing existing production capacity with an innovative production process which will result in an effluent reduction significantly greater than that required by the limitation otherwise applicable to such facility and moves toward the national goal of eliminating the discharge of all pollutants, or with the installation of an innovative control technique that has a substantial likelihood for enabling the facility to comply with the applicable effluent limitation by achieving a significantly greater effluent reduction than that required by the applicable effluent limitation and moves toward the national goal of elim-

Clean Water Act §1311

inating the discharge of all pollutants, or by achieving the required reduction with an innovative system that has the potential for significantly lower costs than the systems which have been determined by the Administrator to be economically achievable, the Administrator (or the State with an approved program under section 1342 of this title, in consultation with the Administrator) may establish a date for compliance under subsection (b)(2)(A) or (b)(2)(E) of this section no later than two years after the date for compliance with such effluent limitation which would otherwise be applicable under such subsection, if it is also determined that such innovative system has the potential for industrywide application.

(*l*) TOXIC POLLUTANTS

Other than as provided in subsection (n) of this section, the Administrator may not modify any requirement of this section as it applies to any specific pollutant which is on the toxic pollutant list under section 1317(a)(1) of this title.

(m) MODIFICATION OF EFFLUENT LIMITATION REQUIREMENTS FOR POINT SOURCES

(1) The Administrator, with the concurrence of the State, may issue a permit under section 1342 of this title which modifies the requirements of subsections (b)(1)(A) and (b)(2)(E) of this section, and of section 1343 of this title, with respect to effluent limitations to the extent such limitations relate to biochemical oxygen demand and pH from discharges by an industrial discharger in such State into deep waters of the territorial seas, if the applicant demonstrates and the Administrator finds that —

(A) the facility for which modification is sought is covered at the time of the enactment of this subsection by National Pollutant Discharge Elimination System permit number CA0005894 or CA0005282;

(B) the energy and environmental costs of meeting such requirements of subsections (b)(1)(A) and (b)(2)(E) of this section and section 1343 of this title exceed by an unreasonable amount the benefits to be obtained, including the objectives of this chapter;

(C) the applicant has established a system for monitoring the impact of such discharges on a representative sample of aquatic biota;

(D) such modified requirements will not result in any additional requirements on any other point or nonpoint source;

(E) there will be no new or substantially increased discharges from the point source of the pollutant to which the modification applies above that volume of discharge specified in the permit;

(F) the discharge is into waters where there is strong tidal movement and other hydrological and geological characteristics which are necessary to allow compliance with this subsection and section 1251(a)(2) of this title;

(G) the applicant accepts as a condition to the permit a contractual obligation to use funds in the amount required (but not less than $250,000 per year for ten years) for research and development of water pollution control technology, including but not limited to closed cycle technology;

(H) the facts and circumstances present a unique situation which, if relief is granted, will not establish a precedent or the relaxation of the requirements of this chapter applicable to similarly situated discharges; and

(I) no owner or operator of a facility comparable to that of the applicant situated in the United States has demonstrated that it would be put at a competitive disadvantage to the applicant (or the parent company or any subsidiary thereof) as a result of the issuance of a permit under this subsection.

(2) The effluent limitations established under a permit issued under paragraph (1) shall be sufficient to implement the applicable State water quality standards, to assure the protection of public water supplies and protection and propagation of a balanced, indigenous population of shellfish, fish, fauna, wildlife, and other aquatic organisms, and to allow recreational activities in and on the water. In setting such limitations, the Administrator shall take into account any seasonal variations and the need for an adequate margin of safety, considering the lack of essential knowledge concerning the relationship between effluent limitations and water quality and the lack of essential knowledge of the effects of discharges on beneficial uses of the receiving waters.

(3) A permit under this subsection may be issued for a period not to exceed five years, and such a permit may be renewed for one additional period not to exceed five years upon a demonstration by the applicant and a finding by the Administrator at the time of application for any such renewal that the provisions of this subsection are met.

(4) The Administrator may terminate a permit issued under this subsection if the Administrator determines that there has been a decline in ambient water quality of the receiving waters during the period of the permit even if a direct cause and effect relationship cannot be shown: *Provided*, That if the effluent from a source with a permit issued under this subsection is contributing to a decline in ambient water quality of the receiving waters, the Administrator shall terminate such permit.

(n) FUNDAMENTALLY DIFFERENT FACTORS

(1) GENERAL RULE

The Administrator, with the concurrence of the State, may establish an alternative requirement under subsection (b)(2) of this section or section 1317(b) of this title for a facility that modifies the requirements of national effluent limitation guidelines or categorical pretreatment standards that would otherwise be applicable to such facility, if the owner or operator of such facility demonstrates to the satisfaction of the Administrator that —

(A) the facility is fundamentally different with respect to the factors (other than cost) specified in section 1314(b) or 1314(g) of this title and considered by the Administrator in establishing such national effluent limitation guidelines or categorical pretreatment standards;

Clean Water Act §1311

(B) the application —
(i) is based solely on information and supporting data submitted to the Administrator during the rulemaking for establishment of the applicable national effluent limitation guidelines or categorical pretreatment standard specifically raising the factors that are fundamentally different for such facility; or
(ii) is based on information and supporting data referred to in clause (i) and information and supporting data the applicant did not have a reasonable opportunity to submit during such rulemaking;

(C) the alternative requirement is no less stringent than justified by the fundamental difference; and

(D) the alternative requirement will not result in a non-water quality environmental impact which is markedly more adverse than the impact considered by the Administrator in establishing such national effluent limitation guideline or categorical pretreatment standard.

(2) TIME LIMIT FOR APPLICATIONS

An application for an alternative requirement which modifies the requirements of an effluent limitation or pretreatment standard under this subsection must be submitted to the Administrator within 180 days after the date on which such limitation or standard is established or revised, as the case may be.

(3) TIME LIMIT FOR DECISION

The Administrator shall approve or deny by final agency action an application submitted under this subsection within 180 days after the date such application is filed with the Administrator.

(4) SUBMISSION OF INFORMATION

The Administrator may allow an applicant under this subsection to submit information and supporting data until the earlier of the date the application is approved or denied or the last day that the Administrator has to approve or deny such application.

(5) TREATMENT OF PENDING APPLICATIONS

For the purposes of this subsection, an application for an alternative requirement based on fundamentally different factors which is pending on February 4, 1987, shall be treated as having been submitted to the Administrator on the 180th day following February 4, 1987. The applicant may amend the application to take into account the provisions of this subsection.

(6) EFFECT OF SUBMISSION OF APPLICATION

An application for an alternative requirement under this subsection shall not stay the applicant's obligation to comply with the effluent limitation guideline or categorical pretreatment standard which is the subject of the application.

(7) EFFECT OF DENIAL

If an application for an alternative requirement which modifies the requirements of an effluent limitation or pretreatment standard under this subsection is denied by the Administrator, the applicant must comply with such limitation or standard as established or revised, as the case may be.

(8) REPORTS

Every 6 months after February 4, 1987, the Administrator shall submit to the Committee on Environment and Public Works of the Senate and the Committee on Public Works and Transportation of the House of Representatives a report on the status of applications for alternative requirements which modify the requirements of effluent limitations under section 1311 or 1314 of this title or any national categorical pretreatment standard under section 1317(b) of this title filed before, on, or after February 4, 1987.

(o) APPLICATION FEES

The Administrator shall prescribe and collect from each applicant fees reflecting the reasonable administrative costs incurred in reviewing and processing applications for modifications submitted to the Administrator pursuant to subsections (c), (g), (i), (k), (m), and (n) of this section, section 1314(d)(4) of this title, and section 1326(a) of this title. All amounts collected by the Administrator under this subsection shall be deposited into a special fund of the Treasury entitled "Water Permits and Related Services" which shall thereafter be available for appropriation to carry out activities of the Environmental Protection Agency for which such fees were collected.

(p) MODIFIED PERMIT FOR COAL REMINING OPERATIONS

(1) IN GENERAL

Subject to paragraphs (2) through (4) of this subsection, the Administrator, or the State in any case which the State has an approved permit program under section 1342(b) of this title, may issue a permit under section 1342 of this title which modifies the requirements of subsection (b)(2)(A) of this section with respect to the pH level of any pre-existing discharge, and with respect to pre-existing discharges of iron and manganese from the remined area of any coal remining operation or with respect to the pH level or level of iron or manganese in any pre-existing discharge affected by the remining operation. Such modified requirements shall apply the best available technology economically achievable on a case-by-case basis, using best professional judgment, to set specific numerical effluent limitations in each permit.

(2) LIMITATIONS

The Administrator or the State may only issue a permit pursuant to paragraph (1) if the applicant demonstrates to the satisfaction of the Administrator or the State, as the case may be, that the coal remining operation will result in the potential for improved water quality from the remining operation but in no event shall such a permit allow the pH level of any discharge, and in no event shall such a permit allow the discharges of iron and manganese, to exceed the levels being discharged from the remined area before the coal remining operation begins. No discharge from, or affected by, the remining operation shall exceed State water quality standards established under section 1313 of this title.

(3) DEFINITIONS

For purposes of this subsection —

(A) COAL REMINING OPERATION

The term "coal remining operation" means a coal mining operation which begins after February 4, 1987 at a site on which coal mining was conducted before August 3, 1977.

(B) REMINED AREA

The term "remined area" means only that area of any coal remining operation on which coal mining was conducted before August 3, 1977.

(C) PRE-EXISTING DISCHARGE

The term "pre-existing discharge" means any discharge at the time of permit application under this subsection.

(4) APPLICABILITY OF STRIP MINING LAWS

Nothing in this subsection shall affect the application of the Surface Mining Control and Reclamation Act of 1977 [30 U.S.C. 1201 et seq.] to any coal remining operation, including the application of such Act to suspended solids.

§1312. WATER QUALITY RELATED EFFLUENT LIMITATIONS

(a) ESTABLISHMENT

Whenever, in the judgment of the Administrator or as identified under section 1314(l) of this title, discharges of pollutants from a point source or group of point sources, with the application of effluent limitations required under section 1311(b)(2) of this title, would interfere with the attainment or maintenance of that water quality in a specific portion of the navigable waters which shall assure protection of public health, public water supplies, agricultural and industrial uses, and the protection and propagation of a balanced population of shellfish, fish and wildlife, and allow recreational activities in and on the water, effluent limitations (including alternative effluent control strategies) for such point source or sources shall be established which can reasonably be expected to contribute to the attainment or maintenance of such water quality.

(b) MODIFICATIONS OF EFFLUENT LIMITATIONS

(1) NOTICE AND HEARING

Prior to establishment of any effluent limitation pursuant to subsection (a) of this section, the Administrator shall publish such proposed limitation and within 90 days of such publication hold a public hearing.

(2) PERMITS

(A) NO REASONABLE RELATIONSHIP

The Administrator, with the concurrence of the State, may issue a permit which modifies the effluent limitations required by subsection (a) of this section for pollutants other than toxic pollutants if the applicant demonstrates at such hearing that (whether or not technology or other alternative control strategies are available) there is no reasonable relationship between the economic and social costs and the benefits to be obtained (including attainment of the objective of this chapter) from achieving such limitation.

(B) REASONABLE PROGRESS

The Administrator, with the concurrence of the State, may issue a permit which modifies the effluent limitations required by subsection (a) of this section for toxic pollutants for a single period not to exceed 5 years if the applicant demonstrates to the satisfaction of the Administrator that such modified requirements (i) will represent the maximum degree of control within the economic capability of the owner and operator of the source, and (ii) will result in reasonable further progress beyond the requirements of section 1311(b)(2) of this title toward the requirements of subsection (a) of this section.

(c) DELAY IN APPLICATION OF OTHER LIMITATIONS

The establishment of effluent limitations under this section shall not operate to delay the application of any effluent limitation established under section 1311 of this title.

§1313. WATER QUALITY STANDARDS AND IMPLEMENTATION PLANS

(a) EXISTING WATER QUALITY STANDARDS

(1) In order to carry out the purpose of this chapter, any water quality standard applicable to interstate waters which was adopted by any State and submitted to, and approved by, or is a waiting approval by, the Administrator pursuant to this Act as in effect immediately prior to October 18, 1972, shall remain in effect unless the Administrator determined that such standard is not consistent with the applicable requirements of this Act as in effect immediately prior to October 18, 1972. If the Administrator makes such a determination he shall,

Clean Water Act §1313

within three months after October 18, 1972, notify the State and specify the changes needed to meet such requirements. If such changes are not adopted by the State within ninety days after the date of such notification, the Administrator shall promulgate such changes in accordance with subsection (b) of this section.

(2) Any State which, before October 18, 1972, has adopted, pursuant to its own law, water quality standards applicable to intrastate waters shall submit such standards to the Administrator within thirty days after October 18, 1972. Each such standard shall remain in effect, in the same manner and to the same extent as any other water quality standard established under this chapter unless the Administrator determines that such standard is inconsistent with the applicable requirements of this Act as in effect immediately prior to October 18, 1972. If the Administrator makes such a determination he shall not later than the one hundred and twentieth day after the date of submission of such standards, notify the State and specify the changes needed to meet such requirements. If such changes are not adopted by the State within ninety days after such notification, the Administrator shall promulgate such changes in accordance with subsection (b) of this section.

(3)(A) Any State which prior to October 18, 1972, has not adopted pursuant to its own laws water quality standards applicable to intrastate waters shall, not later than one hundred and eighty days after October 18, 1972, adopt and submit such standards to the Administrator.

(B) If the Administrator determines that any such standards are consistent with the applicable requirements of this Act as in effect immediately prior to October 18, 1972, he shall approve such standards.

(C) If the Administrator determines that any such standards are not consistent with the applicable requirements of this Act as in effect immediately prior to October 18, 1972, he shall, not later than the ninetieth day after the date of submission of such standards, notify the State and specify the changes to meet such requirements. If such changes are not adopted by the State within ninety days after the date of notification, the Administrator shall promulgate such standards pursuant to subsection (b) of this section.

(b) **PROPOSED REGULATIONS**

(1) The Administrator shall promptly prepare and publish proposed regulations setting forth water quality standards for a State in accordance with the applicable requirements of this Act as in effect immediately prior to October 18, 1972, if —

(A) the State fails to submit water quality standards within the times prescribed in subsection (a) of this section.

(B) a water quality standard submitted by such State under subsection (a) of this section is determined by the Administrator not to be consistent with the applicable requirements of subsection (a) of this section.

(2) The Administrator shall promulgate any water quality standard published in a proposed regulation not later than one hundred and ninety days after the date he publishes any such proposed standard, unless prior to such promul-

gation, such State has adopted a water quality standard which the Administrator determines to be in accordance with subsection (a) of this section.

(c) **REVIEW; REVISED STANDARDS; PUBLICATION**

(1) The Governor of a State or the State water pollution control agency of such State shall from time to time (but at least once each three year period beginning with October 18, 1972) hold public hearings for the purpose of reviewing applicable water quality standards and, as appropriate, modifying and adopting standards. Results of such review shall be made available to the Administrator.

(2)(A) Whenever the State revises or adopts a new standard, such revised or new standard shall be submitted to the Administrator. Such revised or new water quality standard shall consist of the designated uses of the navigable waters involved and the water quality criteria for such waters based upon such uses. Such standards shall be such as to protect the public health or welfare, enhance the quality of water and serve the purposes of this chapter. Such standards shall be established taking into consideration their use and value for public water supplies, propagation of fish and wildlife, recreational purposes, and agricultural, industrial, and other purposes, and also taking into consideration their use and value for navigation.

(B) Whenever a State reviews water quality standards pursuant to paragraph (1) of this subsection, or revises or adopts new standards pursuant to this paragraph, such State shall adopt criteria for all toxic pollutants listed pursuant to section 1317(a)(1) of this title for which criteria have been published under section 1314(a) of this title, the discharge or presence of which in the affected waters could reasonably be expected to interfere with those designated uses adopted by the State, as necessary to support such designated uses. Such criteria shall be specific numerical criteria for such toxic pollutants. Where such numerical criteria are not available, whenever a State reviews water quality standards pursuant to paragraph (1), or revises or adopts new standards pursuant to this paragraph, such State shall adopt criteria based on biological monitoring or assessment methods consistent with information published pursuant to section 1314(a)(8) of this title. Nothing in this section shall be construed to limit or delay the use of effluent limitations or other permit conditions based on or involving biological monitoring or assessment methods or previously adopted numerical criteria.

(3) If the Administrator, within sixty days after the date of submission of the revised or new standard, determines that such standard meets the requirements of this chapter, such standard shall thereafter be the water quality standard for the applicable waters of that State. If the Administrator determines that any such revised or new standard is not consistent with the applicable requirements of this chapter, he shall not later than the ninetieth day after the date of submission of such standard notify the State and specify the changes to meet such requirements. If such changes are not adopted by the State within ninety days after the date of notification, the Administrator shall promulgate such standard pursuant to paragraph (4) of this subsection.

Clean Water Act §1313

(4) The Administrator shall promptly prepare and publish proposed regulations setting forth a revised or new water quality standard for the navigable waters involved —

(A) if a revised or new water quality standard submitted by such State under paragraph (3) of this subsection for such waters is determined by the Administrator not to be consistent with the applicable requirements of this chapter, or

(B) in any case where the Administrator determines that a revised or new standard is necessary to meet the requirements of this chapter.

The Administrator shall promulgate any revised or new standard under this paragraph not later than ninety days after he publishes such proposed standards, unless prior to such promulgation, such State has adopted a revised or new water quality standard which the Administrator determines to be in accordance with this chapter.

(d) IDENTIFICATION OF AREAS WITH INSUFFICIENT CONTROLS; MAXIMUM DAILY LOAD; CERTAIN EFFLUENT LIMITATIONS REVISION

(1)(A) Each State shall identify those waters within its boundaries for which the effluent limitations required by section 1311(b)(1)(A) and section 1311(b)(1)(B) of this title are not stringent enough to implement any water quality standard applicable to such waters. The State shall establish a priority ranking for such waters, taking into account the severity of the pollution and the uses to be made of such waters.

(B) Each State shall identify those waters or parts thereof within its boundaries for which controls on thermal discharges under section 1311 of this title are not stringent enough to assure protection and propagation of a balanced indigenous population of shellfish, fish, and wildlife.

(C) Each State shall establish for the waters identified in paragraph (1)(A) of this subsection, and in accordance with the priority ranking, the total maximum daily load, for those pollutants which the Administrator identifies under section 1314(a)(2) of this title as suitable for such calculation. Such load shall be established at a level necessary to implement the applicable water quality standards with seasonal variations and a margin of safety which takes into account any lack of knowledge concerning the relationship between effluent limitations and water quality.

(D) Each State shall estimate for the waters identified in paragraph (1)(B) of this subsection the total maximum daily thermal load required to assure protection and propagation of a balanced, indigenous population of shellfish, fish, and wildlife. Such estimates shall take into account the normal water temperatures, flow rates, seasonal variations, existing sources of heat input, and the dissipative capacity of the identified waters or parts thereof. Such estimates shall include a calculation of the maximum heat input that can be made into each such part and shall include a margin of safety which takes into account any lack of knowledge concerning the development of thermal water quality criteria for such protection and propagation in the identified waters or parts thereof.

(2) Each State shall submit to the Administrator from time to time, with the first such submission not later than one hundred and eighty days after the date of publication of the first identification of pollutants under section 1314(a)(2)(D) of this title, for his approval the waters identified and the loads established under paragraphs (1)(A), (1)(B), (1)(C), and (1)(D) of this subsection. The Administrator shall either approve or disapprove such identification and load not later than thirty days after the date of submission. If the Administrator approves such identification and load, such State shall incorporate them into its current plan under subsection (e) of this section. If the Administrator disapproves such identification and load, he shall not later than thirty days after the date of such disapproval identify such waters in such State and establish such loads for such waters as he determines necessary to implement the water quality standards applicable to such waters and upon such identification and establishment the State shall incorporate them into its current plan under subsection (e) of this section.

(3) For the specific purpose of developing information, each State shall identify all waters within its boundaries which it has not identified under paragraph (1)(A) and (1)(B) of this subsection and estimate for such waters the total maximum daily load with seasonal variations and margins of safety, for those pollutants which the Administrator identifies under section 1314(a)(2) of this title as suitable for such calculation and for thermal discharges, at a level that would assure protection and propagation of a balanced indigenous population of fish, shellfish, and wildlife.

(4) Limitations on revision of certain effluent limitations. —

(A) Standard not attained. — For waters identified under paragraph (1)(A) where the applicable water quality standard has not yet been attained, any effluent limitation based on a total maximum daily load or other waste load allocation established under this section may be revised only if (i) the cumulative effect of all such revised effluent limitations based on such total maximum daily load or waste load allocation will assure the attainment of such water quality standard, or (ii) the designated use which is not being attained is removed in accordance with regulations established under this section.

(B) Standard attained. — For waters identified under paragraph (1)(A) where the quality of such waters equals or exceeds levels necessary to protect the designated use for such waters or otherwise required by applicable water quality standards, any effluent limitation based on a total maximum daily load or other waste load allocation established under this section, or any water quality standard established under this section, or any other permitting standard may be revised only if such revision is subject to and consistent with the antidegradation policy established under this section.

(e) CONTINUING PLANNING PROCESS

(1) Each State shall have a continuing planning process approved under paragraph (2) of this subsection which is consistent with this chapter.

(2) Each State shall submit not later than 120 days after October 18, 1972,

to the Administrator for his approval a proposed continuing planning process which is consistent with this chapter. Not later than thirty days after the date of submission of such a process the Administrator shall either approve or disapprove such process. The Administrator shall from time to time review each State's approved planning process for the purpose of insuring that such planning process is at all times consistent with this chapter. The Administrator shall not approve any State permit program under subchapter IV of this chapter for any State which does not have an approved continuing planning process under this section.

(3) The Administrator shall approve any continuing planning process submitted to him under this section which will result in plans for all navigable waters within such State, which include, but are not limited to, the following:

(A) effluent limitations and schedules of compliance at least as stringent as those required by section 1311(b)(1), section 1311(b)(2), section 1316, and section 1317 of this title, and at least as stringent as any requirements contained in any applicable water quality standard in effect under authority of this section;

(B) the incorporation of all elements of any applicable area-wide waste management plans under section 1288 of this title, and applicable basin plans under section 1289 of this title;

(C) total maximum daily load for pollutants in accordance with subsection (d) of this section;

(D) procedures for revision;

(E) adequate authority for intergovernmental cooperation;

(F) adequate implementation, including schedules of compliance, for revised or new water quality standards, under subsection (c) of this section;

(G) controls over the disposition of all residual waste from any water treatment processing;

(H) an inventory and ranking, in order of priority, of needs for construction of waste treatment works required to meet the applicable requirements of sections 1311 and 1312 of this title.

(f) **EARLIER COMPLIANCE**

Nothing in this section shall be construed to affect any effluent limitation, or schedule of compliance required by any State to be implemented prior to the dates set forth in sections 1311(b)(1) and 1311(b)(2) of this title nor to preclude any State from requiring compliance with any effluent limitation or schedule or compliance at dates earlier than such dates.

(g) **HEAT STANDARDS**

Water quality standards relating to heat shall be consistent with the requirements of section 1326 of this title.

(h) **THERMAL WATER QUALITY STANDARDS**

For the purposes of this chapter the term "water quality standards" includes thermal water quality standards.

§1313a. REVISED WATER QUALITY STANDARDS

The review, revision, and adoption or promulgation of revised or new water quality standards pursuant to section 303(c) of the Federal Water Pollution Control Act [33 U.S.C. 1313(c)] shall be completed by the date three years after December 29, 1981. No grant shall be made under title II of the Federal Water Pollution Control Act [33 U.S.C. 1281 et seq.] after such date until water quality standards are reviewed and revised pursuant to section 303(c), except where the State has in good faith submitted such revised water quality standards and the Administrator has not acted to approve or disapprove such submission within one hundred and twenty days of receipt.

§1314. INFORMATION AND GUIDELINES

(a) CRITERIA DEVELOPMENT AND PUBLICATION

(1) The Administrator, after consultation with appropriate Federal and State agencies and other interested persons, shall develop and publish, within one year after October 18, 1972 (and from time to time thereafter revise) criteria for water quality accurately reflecting the latest scientific knowledge (A) on the kind and extent of all identifiable effects on health and welfare including, but not limited to, plankton, fish, shellfish, wildlife, plant life, shorelines, beaches, esthetics, and recreation which may be expected from the presence of pollutants in any body of water, including ground water; (B) on the concentration and dispersal of pollutants, or their byproducts, through biological, physical, and chemical processes; and (C) on the effects of pollutants on biological community diversity, productivity, and stability, including information on the factors affecting rates of eutrophication and rates of organic and inorganic sedimentation for varying types of receiving waters.

(2) The Administrator, after consultation with appropriate Federal and State agencies and other interested persons, shall develop and publish, within one year after October 18, 1972 (and from time to time thereafter revise) information (A) on the factors necessary to restore and maintain the chemical, physical, and biological integrity of all navigable waters, ground waters, waters of the contiguous zone, and the oceans; (B) on the factors necessary for the protection and propagation of shellfish, fish, and wildlife for classes and categories of receiving waters and to allow recreational activities in and on the water; and (C) on the measurement and classification of water quality; and (D) for the purpose of section 1313 of this title, and on the identification of pollutants suitable for maximum daily load measurement correlated with the achievement of water quality objectives.

(3) Such criteria and information and revisions thereof shall be issued to the States and shall be published in the Federal Register and otherwise made available to the public.

(4) The Administrator shall, within 90 days after December 27, 1977, and from time to time thereafter, publish and revise as appropriate information identifying conventional pollutants, including but not limited to, pollutants classified

Clean Water Act §1314

as biological oxygen demanding, suspended solids, fecal coliform, and pH. The thermal component of any discharge shall not be identified as a conventional pollutant under this paragraph.

(5)(A) The Administrator, to the extent practicable before consideration of any request under section 1311(g) of this title and within six months after December 27, 1977, shall develop and publish information on the factors necessary for the protection of public water supplies, and the protection and propagation of a balanced population of shellfish, fish and wildlife, and to allow recreational activities, in and on the water.

(B) The Administrator, to the extent practicable before consideration of any application under section 1311(h) of this title and within six months after December 27, 1977, shall develop and publish information on the factors necessary for the protection of public water supplies, and the protection and propagation of a balanced indigenous population of shellfish, fish and wildlife, and to allow recreational activities, in and on the water.

(6) The Administrator shall, within three months after December 27, 1977, and annually thereafter, for purposes of section 1311(h) of this title publish and revise as appropriate information identifying each water quality standard in effect under this chapter or State law, the specific pollutants associated with such water quality standard, and the particular waters to which such water quality standard applies.

(7) Guidance to states. — The Administrator, after consultation with appropriate State agencies and on the basis of criteria and information published under paragraphs (1) and (2) of this subsection, shall develop and publish, within 9 months after February 4, 1987, guidance to the States on performing the identification required by subsection (l)(1) of this section.

(8) Information on water quality criteria. — The Administrator, after consultation with appropriate State agencies and within 2 years after February 4, 1987, shall develop and publish information on methods for establishing and measuring water quality criteria for toxic pollutants on other bases than pollutant-by-pollutant criteria, including biological monitoring and assessment methods.

(b) **EFFLUENT LIMITATION GUIDELINES**

For the purpose of adopting or revising effluent limitations under this chapter the Administrator shall, after consultation with appropriate Federal and State agencies and other interested persons, publish within one year of October 18, 1972, regulations, providing guidelines for effluent limitations, and, at least annually thereafter, revise, if appropriate, such regulations. Such regulations shall —

(1)(A) identify, in terms of amounts of constituents and chemical, physical, and biological characteristics of pollutants, the degree of effluent reduction attainable through the application of the best practicable control technology currently available for classes and categories of point sources (other than publicly owned treatment works); and

(B) specify factors to be taken into account in determining the control measures and practices to be applicable to point sources (other than publicly owned treatment works) within such categories or classes. Factors relating to the assessment of best practicable control technology currently available to comply with subsection (b)(1) of section 1311 of this title shall include consideration of the total cost of application of technology in relation to the effluent reduction benefits to be achieved from such application, and shall also take into account the age of equipment and facilities involved, the process employed, the engineering aspects of the application of various types of control techniques, process changes, non-water quality environmental impact (including energy requirements), and such other factors as the Administrator deems appropriate;

(2)(A) identify, in terms of amounts of constituents and chemical, physical, and biological characteristics of pollutants, the degree of effluent reduction attainable through the application of the best control measures and practices achievable including treatment techniques, process and procedure innovations, operating methods, and other alternatives for classes and categories of point sources (other than publicly owned treatment works); and

(B) specify factors to be taken into account in determining the best measures and practices available to comply with subsection (b)(2) of section 1311 of this title to be applicable to any point source (other than publicly owned treatment works) within such categories or classes. Factors relating to the assessment of best available technology shall take into account the age of equipment and facilities involved, the process employed, the engineering aspects of the application of various types of control techniques, process changes, the cost of achieving such effluent reduction, non-water quality environmental impact (including energy requirements), and such other factors as the Administrator deems appropriate;

(3) identify control measures and practices available to eliminate the discharge of pollutants from categories and classes of point sources, taking into account the cost of achieving such elimination of the discharge of pollutants; and

(4)(A) identify, in terms of amounts of constituents and chemical, physical, and biological characteristics of pollutants, the degree of effluent reduction attainable through the application of the best conventional pollutant control technology (including measures and practices) for classes and categories of point sources (other than publicly owned treatment works); and

(B) specify factors to be taken into account in determining the best conventional pollutant control technology measures and practices to comply with section 1311(b)(2)(E) of this title to be applicable to any point source (other than publicly owned treatment works) within such categories or classes. Factors relating to the assessment of best conventional pollutant control technology (including measures and practices) shall include consideration of the reasonableness of the relationship between the costs of attaining a reduction in effluents and the effluent reduction benefits derived, and the comparison of the cost and level of reduction of such pollutants from the discharge from publicly owned treatment works to the cost and level of reduction of such pollutants from a class or category of industrial sources, and shall take into account the age of equipment and facilities involved, the process employed, the engineering aspects of the application of various types of control techniques, process changes, non-water quality environmental impact (including energy requirements), and such other factors as the Administrator deems appropriate.

(c) POLLUTION DISCHARGE ELIMINATION PROCEDURES

The Administrator, after consultation, with appropriate Federal and State agencies and other interested persons, shall issue to the States and appropriate water pollution control agencies within 270 days after October 18, 1972 (and from time to time thereafter) information on the processes, procedures, or operating methods which result in the elimination or reduction of the discharge of pollutants to implement standards of performance under section 1316 of this title. Such information shall include technical and other data, including costs, as are available on alternative methods of elimination or reduction of the discharge of pollutants. Such information, and revisions thereof, shall be published in the Federal Register and otherwise shall be made available to the public.

(d) SECONDARY TREATMENT INFORMATION; ALTERNATIVE WASTE TREATMENT MANAGEMENT TECHNIQUES; INNOVATIVE AND ALTERNATIVE WASTEWATER TREATMENT PROCESSES; FACILITIES DEEMED EQUIVALENT OF SECONDARY TREATMENT

(1) The Administrator, after consultation with appropriate Federal and State agencies and other interested persons, shall publish within sixty days after October 18, 1972 (and from time to time thereafter) information, in terms of amounts of constituents and chemical, physical, and biological characteristics of pollutants, on the degree of effluent reduction attainable through the application of secondary treatment.

(2) The Administrator, after consultation with appropriate Federal and State agencies and other interested persons, shall publish within nine months after October 18, 1972 (and from time to time thereafter) information on alternative waste treatment management techniques and systems available to implement section 1281 of this title.

(3) The Administrator, after consultation with appropriate Federal and State agencies and other interested persons, shall promulgate within one hundred and eighty days after December 27, 1977, guidelines for identifying and evaluating innovative and alternative wastewater treatment processes and techniques referred to in section 1281(g)(5) of this title.

(4) For the purposes of this subsection, such biological treatment facilities as oxidation ponds, lagoons, and ditches and trickling filters shall be deemed the equivalent of secondary treatment. The Administrator shall provide guidance under paragraph (1) of this subsection on design criteria for such facilities, taking into account pollutant removal efficiencies and, consistent with the objectives of

§1314

this chapter, assuring that water quality will not be adversely affected by deeming such facilities as the equivalent of secondary treatment.

(e) BEST MANAGEMENT PRACTICES FOR INDUSTRY

The Administrator, after consultation with appropriate Federal and State agencies and other interested persons, may publish regulations, supplemental to any effluent limitations specified under subsections (b) and (c) of this section for a class or category of point sources, for any specific pollutant which the Administrator is charged with a duty to regulate as a toxic or hazardous pollutant under section 1317(a)(1) or 1321 of this title, to control plant site runoff, spillage or leaks, sludge or waste disposal, and drainage from raw material storage which the Administrator determines are associated with or ancillary to the industrial manufacturing or treatment process within such class or category of point sources and may contribute significant amounts of such pollutants to navigable waters. Any applicable controls established under this subsection shall be included as a requirement for the purposes of section 1311, 1312, 1316, 1317, or 1343 of this title, as the case may be, in any permit issued to a point source pursuant to section 1342 of this title.

(f) IDENTIFICATION AND EVALUATION OF NONPOINT SOURCES OF POLLUTION; PROCESSES, PROCEDURES, AND METHODS TO CONTROL POLLUTION

The Administrator, after consultation with appropriate Federal and State agencies and other interested persons, shall issue to appropriate Federal agencies, the States, water pollution control agencies, and agencies designated under section 1288 of this title, within one year after October 18, 1972 (and from time to time thereafter) information including (1) guidelines for identifying and evaluating the nature and extent of nonpoint sources of pollutants, and (2) processes, procedures, and methods to control pollution resulting from —

(A) agricultural and silvicultural activities, including runoff from fields and crop and forest lands;

(B) mining activities, including runoff and siltation from new, currently operating, and abandoned surface and underground mines;

(C) all construction activity, including runoff from the facilities resulting from such construction;

(D) the disposal of pollutants in wells or in subsurface excavations;

(E) salt water intrusion resulting from reductions of fresh water flow from any cause, including extraction of ground water, irrigation, obstruction, and diversion; and

(F) changes in the movement, flow, or circulation of any navigable waters or ground waters, including changes caused by the construction of dams, levees, channels, causeways, or flow diversion facilities.

Such information and revisions thereof shall be published in the Federal Register and otherwise made available to the public.

Clean Water Act §1314

(g) GUIDELINES FOR PRETREATMENT OF POLLUTANTS

(1) For the purpose of assisting States in carrying out programs under section 1342 of this title, the Administrator shall publish, within one hundred and twenty days after October 18, 1972, and review at least annually thereafter and, if appropriate, revise guidelines for pretreatment of pollutants which he determines are not susceptible to treatment by publicly owned treatment works. Guidelines under this subsection shall be established to control and prevent the discharge into the navigable waters, the contiguous zone, or the ocean (either directly or through publicly owned treatment works) of any pollutant which interferes with, passes through, or otherwise is incompatible with such works.

(2) When publishing guidelines under this subsection, the Administrator shall designate the category or categories of treatment works to which the guidelines shall apply.

(h) TEST PROCEDURES GUIDELINES

The Administrator shall, within one hundred and eighty days from October 18, 1972, promulgate guidelines establishing test procedures for the analysis of pollutants that shall include the factors which must be provided in any certification pursuant to section 1341 of this title or permit application pursuant to section 1342 of this title.

(i) GUIDELINES FOR MONITORING, REPORTING, ENFORCEMENT, FUNDING, PERSONNEL, AND MANPOWER

The Administrator shall (1) within sixty days after October 18, 1972, promulgate guidelines for the purpose of establishing uniform application forms and other minimum requirements for the acquisition of information from owners and operators of point-sources of discharge subject to any State program under section 1342 of this title, and (2) within sixty days from October 18, 1972, promulgate guidelines establishing the minimum procedural and other elements of any State program under section 1342 of this title, which shall include:

(A) monitoring requirements;

(B) reporting requirements (including procedures to make information available to the public);

(C) enforcement provisions; and

(D) funding, personnel qualifications, and manpower requirements (including a requirement that no board or body which approves permit applications or portions thereof shall include, as a member, any person who receives, or has during the previous two years received, a significant portion of his income directly or indirectly from permit holders or applicants for a permit).

(j) LAKE RESTORATION GUIDANCE MANUAL

The Administrator shall, within 1 year after February 4, 1987, and biennially thereafter, publish and disseminate a lake restoration guidance manual describing methods, procedures, and processes to guide State and local efforts to improve, restore, and enhance water quality in the Nation's publicly owned lakes.

(k) AGREEMENTS WITH SECRETARIES OF AGRICULTURE, ARMY, AND INTERIOR TO PROVIDE MAXIMUM UTILIZATION OF PROGRAMS TO ACHIEVE AND MAINTAIN WATER QUALITY; TRANSFER OF FUNDS; AUTHORIZATION OF APPROPRIATIONS

(1) The Administrator shall enter into agreements with the Secretary of Agriculture, the Secretary of the Army, and the Secretary of the Interior, and the heads of such other departments, agencies, and instrumentalities of the United States as the Administrator determines, to provide for the maximum utilization of other Federal laws and programs for the purpose of achieving and maintaining water quality through appropriate implementation of plans approved under section 1288 of this title and nonpoint source pollution management programs approved under section 1329 of this title.

(2) The Administrator is authorized to transfer to the Secretary of Agriculture, the Secretary of the Army, and the Secretary of the Interior and the heads of such other departments, agencies, and instrumentalities of the United States as the Administrator determines, any funds appropriated under paragraph (3) of this subsection to supplement funds otherwise appropriated to programs authorized pursuant to any agreement under paragraph (1).

(3) There is authorized to be appropriated to carry out the provisions of this subsection, $100,000,000 per fiscal year for the fiscal years 1979 through 1983 and such sums as may be necessary for fiscal years 1984 through 1990.

(l) INDIVIDUAL CONTROL STRATEGIES FOR TOXIC POLLUTANTS

(1) STATE LIST OF NAVIGABLE WATERS AND DEVELOPMENT OF STRATEGIES

Not later than 2 years after February 4, 1987, each State shall submit to the Administrator for review, approval, and implementation under this subsection —

(A) a list of those waters within the State which after the application of effluent limitations required under section 1311(b)(2) of this title cannot reasonably be anticipated to attain or maintain (i) water quality standards for such waters reviewed, revised, or adopted in accordance with section 1313(c)(2)(B) of this title, due to toxic pollutants, or (ii) that water quality which shall assure protection of public health, public water supplies, agricultural and industrial uses, and the protection and propagation of a balanced population of shellfish, fish and wildlife, and allow recreational activities in and on the water;

(B) a list of all navigable waters in such State for which the State does not expect the applicable standard under section 1313 of this title will be achieved after the requirements of sections 1311(b), 1316, and 1317(b) of this title are met, due entirely or substantially to discharges from point sources of any toxic pollutants listed pursuant to section 1317(a) of this title;

(C) for each segment of the navigable waters included on such lists, a determination of the specific point sources discharging any such toxic pollutant which is believed to be preventing or impairing such water quality and the amount of each such toxic pollutant discharged by each such source; and

(D) for each such segment, an individual control strategy which the State determines will produce a reduction in the discharge of toxic pollutants from point sources identified by the State under this paragraph through the establishment of effluent limitations under section 1342 of this title and water quality standards under section 1313(c)(2)(B) of this title, which reduction is sufficient, in combination with existing controls on point and nonpoint sources of pollution, to achieve the applicable water quality standard as soon as possible, but not later than 3 years after the date of the establishment of such strategy.

(2) APPROVAL OR DISAPPROVAL

Not later than 120 days after the last day of the 2-year period referred to in paragraph (1), the Administrator shall approve or disapprove the control strategies submitted under paragraph (1) by any State.

(3) ADMINISTRATOR'S ACTION

If a State fails to submit control strategies in accordance with paragraph (1) or the Administrator does not approve the control strategies submitted by such State in accordance with paragraph (1), then, not later than 1 year after the last day of the period referred to in paragraph (2), the Administrator, in cooperation with such State and after notice and opportunity for public comment, shall implement the requirements of paragraph (1) in such State. In the implementation of such requirements, the Administrator shall, at a minimum, consider for listing under this subsection any navigable waters for which any person submits a petition to the Administrator for listing not later than 120 days after such last day.

(m) SCHEDULE FOR REVIEW OF GUIDELINES

(1) PUBLICATION

Within 12 months after February 4, 1987, and biennially thereafter, the Administrator shall publish in the Federal Register a plan which shall —

(A) establish a schedule for the annual review and revision of promulgated effluent guidelines, in accordance with subsection (b) of this section;

(B) identify categories of sources discharging toxic or nonconventional pollutants for which guidelines under subsection (b)(2) of this section and section 1316 of this title have not previously been published; and

(C) establish a schedule for promulgation of effluent guidelines for categories identified in subparagraph (B), under which promulgation of such guidelines shall be no later than 4 years after February 4, 1987, for categories identified in the first published plan or 3 years after the publication of the plan for categories identified in later published plans.

(2) PUBLIC REVIEW

The Administrator shall provide for public review and comment on the plan prior to final publication.

§1315. STATE REPORTS ON WATER QUALITY; TRANSMITTAL TO CONGRESS

(a) Omitted

(b)(1) Each State shall prepare and submit to the Administrator by April 1, 1975, and shall bring up to date by April 1, 1976, and biennially thereafter, a report which shall include —

(A) a description of the water quality of all navigable waters in such State during the preceding year, with appropriate supplemental descriptions as shall be required to take into account seasonal, tidal, and other variations, correlated with the quality of water required by the objective of this chapter (as identified by the Administrator pursuant to criteria published under section 1314(a) of this title) and the water quality described in subparagraph (B) of this paragraph;

(B) an analysis of the extent to which all navigable waters of such State provide for the protection and propagation of a balanced population of shellfish, fish, and wildlife, and allow recreational activities in and on the water;

(C) an analysis of the extent to which the elimination of the discharge of pollutants and a level of water quality which provides for the protection and propagation of a balanced population of shellfish, fish, and wildlife and allows recreational activities in and on the water, have been or will be achieved by the requirements of this chapter, together with recommendations as to additional action necessary to achieve such objectives and for what waters such additional action is necessary;

(D) an estimate of (i) the environmental impact, (ii) the economic and social costs necessary to achieve the objective of this chapter in such State, (iii) the economic and social benefits of such achievement, and (iv) an estimate of the date of such achievement; and

(E) a description of the nature and extent of nonpoint sources of pollutants, and recommendations as to the programs which must be undertaken to control each category of such sources, including an estimate of the costs of implementing such programs.

(2) The Administrator shall transmit such State reports, together with an analysis thereof, to Congress on or before October 1, 1975, and October 1, 1976, and biennially thereafter.

Clean Water Act §1316

§1316. NATIONAL STANDARDS OF PERFORMANCE

(a) DEFINITIONS

For purposes of this section:

(1) The term "standard of performance" means a standard for the control of the discharge of pollutants which reflects the greatest degree of effluent reduction which the Administrator determines to be achievable through application of the best available demonstrated control technology, processes, operating methods, or other alternatives, including, where practicable, a standard permitting no discharge of pollutants.

(2) The term "new source" means any source, the construction of which is commenced after the publication of proposed regulations prescribing a standard of performance under this section which will be applicable to such source, if such standard is thereafter promulgated in accordance with this section.

(3) The term "source" means any building, structure, facility, or installation from which there is or may be the discharge of pollutants.

(4) The term "owner or operator" means any person who owns, leases, operates, controls, or supervises a source.

(5) The term "construction" means any placement, assembly, or installation of facilities or equipment (including contractual obligations to purchase such facilities or equipment) at the premises where such equipment will be used, including preparation work at such premises.

(b) CATEGORIES OF SOURCES; FEDERAL STANDARDS OF PERFORMANCE FOR NEW SOURCES

(1)(A) The Administrator shall, within ninety days after October 18, 1972, publish (and from time to time thereafter shall revise) a list of categories of sources, which shall, at the minimum, include:

pulp and paper mills;
paperboard, builders paper and board mills;
meat product and rendering processing;
dairy product processing;
grain mills;
canned and preserved fruits and vegetables processing;
canned and preserved seafood processing;
sugar processing;
textile mills;
cement manufacturing;
feedlots;
electroplating;
organic chemicals manufacturing;
inorganic chemicals manufacturing;
plastic and synthetic materials manufacturing;

soap and detergent manufacturing;
fertilizer manufacturing;
leather tanning and finishing;
glass and asbestos manufacturing;
rubber processing; and
timber products processing.

(B) As soon as practicable, but in no case more than one year, after a category of sources is included in a list under subparagraph (A) of this paragraph, the Administrator shall propose and publish regulations establishing Federal standards of performance for new sources within such category. The Administrator shall afford interested persons an opportunity for written comment on such proposed regulations. After considering such comments, he shall promulgate, within one hundred and twenty days after publication of such proposed regulations, such standards with such adjustments as he deems appropriate. The Administrator shall, from time to time, as technology and alternatives change, revise such standards following the procedure required by this subsection for promulgation of such standards. Standards of performance, or revisions thereof, shall become effective upon promulgation. In establishing or revising Federal standards of performance for new sources under this section, the Administrator shall take into consideration the cost of achieving such effluent reduction, and any nonwater quality, environmental impact and energy requirements.

(2) The Administrator may distinguish among classes, types, and sizes within categories of new sources for the purpose of establishing such standards and shall consider the type of process employed (including whether batch or continuous).

(3) The provisions of this section shall apply to any new source owned or operated by the United States.

(c) STATE ENFORCEMENT OF STANDARDS OF PERFORMANCE

Each State may develop and submit to the Administrator a procedure under State law for applying and enforcing standards of performance for new sources located in such State. If the Administrator finds that the procedure and the law of any State require the application and enforcement of standards of performance to at least the same extent as required by this section, such State is authorized to apply and enforce such standards of performance (except with respect to new sources owned or operated by the United States).

(d) PROTECTION FROM MORE STRINGENT STANDARDS

Notwithstanding any other provision of this chapter, any point source the construction of which is commenced after October 18, 1972, and which is so constructed as to meet all applicable standards of performance shall not be subject to any more stringent standard of performance during a ten-year period beginning on the date of completion of such construction or during the period of depreciation or amortization of such facility for the purposes of section 167 or 169 (or both) of title 26 whichever period ends first.

(e) ILLEGALITY OF OPERATION OF NEW SOURCES IN VIOLATION OF APPLICABLE STANDARDS OF PERFORMANCE

After the effective date of standards of performance promulgated under this section, it shall be unlawful for any owner or operator of any new source to operate such source in violation of any standard of performance applicable to such source.

§1317. TOXIC AND PRETREATMENT EFFLUENT STANDARDS

(a) TOXIC POLLUTANT LIST; REVISION; HEARING; PROMULGATION OF STANDARDS; EFFECTIVE DATE; CONSULTATION

(1) On and after December 27, 1977, the list of toxic pollutants or combination of pollutants subject to this chapter shall consist of those toxic pollutants listed in table 1 of Committee Print Numbered 95-30 of the Committee on Public Works and Transportation of the House of Representatives, and the Administrator shall publish, not later than the thirtieth day after December 27, 1977, that list. From time to time thereafter, the Administrator may revise such list and the Administrator is authorized to add to or remove from such list any pollutant. The Administrator in publishing any revised list, including the addition or removal of any pollutant from such list, shall take into account toxicity of the pollutant, its persistence, degradability, the usual or potential presence of the affected organisms in any waters, the importance of the affected organisms, and the nature and extent of the effect of the toxic pollutant on such organisms. A determination of the Administrator under this paragraph shall be final except that if, on judicial review, such determination was based on arbitrary and capricious action of the Administrator, the Administrator shall make a redetermination.

(2) Each toxic pollutant listed in accordance with paragraph (1) of this subsection shall be subject to effluent limitations resulting from the application of the best available technology economically achievable for the application category or class of point sources established in accordance with sections 1311(b)(2)(A) and 1314(b)(2) of this title. The Administrator, in his discretion, may publish in the Federal Register a proposed effluent standard (which may include a prohibition) establishing requirements for a toxic pollutant which, if an effluent limitation is applicable to a class or category of point sources, shall be applicable to such category or class only if such standard imposes more stringent requirements. Such published effluent standard (or prohibition) shall take into account the toxicity of the pollutant, its persistence, degradability, the usual or potential presence of the affected organisms in any waters, the importance of the affected organisms and the nature and extent of the effect of the toxic pol-

lutant on such organisms, and the extent to which effective control is being or may be achieved under other regulatory authority. The Administrator shall allow a period of not less than sixty days following publication of any such proposed effluent standard (or prohibition) for written comment by interested persons on such proposed standard. In addition, if within thirty days of publication of any such proposed effluent standard (or prohibition) any interested person so requests, the Administrator shall hold a public hearing in connection therewith. Such a public hearing shall provide an opportunity for oral and written presentations, such cross-examination as the Administrator determines is appropriate on disputed issues of material fact, and the transcription of a verbatim record which shall be available to the public. After consideration of such comments and any information and material presented at any public hearing held on such proposed standard or prohibition, the Administrator shall promulgate such standard (or prohibition) with such modification as the Administrator finds are justified. Such promulgation by the Administrator shall be made within two hundred and seventy days after publication of proposed standard (or prohibition). Such standard (or prohibition) shall be final except that if, on judicial review, such standard was not based on substantial evidence, the Administrator shall promulgate a revised standard. Effluent limitations shall be established in accordance with sections 1311(b)(2)(A) and 1314(b)(2) of this title for every toxic pollutant referred to in table 1 of Committee Print Numbered 95-30 of the Committee on Public Works and Transportation of the House of Representatives as soon as practicable after December 27, 1977, but no later than July 1, 1980. Such effluent limitations or effluent standards (or prohibitions) shall be established for every other toxic pollutant listed under paragraph (1) of this subsection as soon as practicable after it is so listed.

(3) Each such effluent standard (or prohibition) shall be reviewed and, if appropriate, revised at least every three years.

(4) Any effluent standard promulgated under this section shall be at that level which the Administrator determines provides an ample margin of safety.

(5) When proposing or promulgating any effluent standard (or prohibition) under this section, the Administrator shall designate the category or categories of sources to which the effluent standard (or prohibition) shall apply. Any disposal of dredged material may be included in such a category of sources after consultation with the Secretary of the Army.

(6) Any effluent standard (or prohibition) established pursuant to this section shall take effect on such date or dates as specified in the order promulgating such standard, but in no case, more than one year from the date of such promulgation. If the Administrator determines that compliance within one year from the date of promulgation is technologically infeasible for a category of sources, the Administrator may establish the effective date of the effluent standard (or prohibition) for such category at the earliest date upon which compliance can be feasibly attained by sources within such category, but in no event more than three years after the date of such promulgation.

Clean Water Act §1317

(7) Prior to publishing any regulations pursuant to this section the Administrator shall, to the maximum extent practicable within the time provided, consult with appropriate advisory committees, States, independent experts, and Federal departments and agencies.

(b) PRETREATMENT STANDARDS; HEARING; PROMULGATION; COMPLIANCE PERIOD; REVISION; APPLICATION TO STATE AND LOCAL LAWS

(1) The Administrator shall, within one hundred and eighty days after October 18, 1972, and from time to time thereafter, publish proposed regulations establishing pretreatment standards for introduction of pollutants into treatment works (as defined in section 1292 of this title) which are publicly owned for those pollutants which are determined not to be susceptible to treatment by such treatment works or which would interfere with the operation of such treatment works. Not later than ninety days after such publication, and after opportunity for public hearing, the Administrator shall promulgate such pretreatment standards. Pretreatment standards under this subsection shall specify a time for compliance not to exceed three years from the date of promulgation and shall be established to prevent the discharge of any pollutant through treatment works (as defined in section 1292 of this title) which are publicly owned, which pollutant interferes with, passes through, or otherwise is incompatible with such works. If, in the case of any toxic pollutant under subsection (a) of this section introduced by a source into a publicly owned treatment works, the treatment by such works removes all or any part of such toxic pollutant and the discharge from such works does not violate that effluent limitation or standard which would be applicable to such toxic pollutant if it were discharged by such source other than through a publicly owned treatment works, and does not prevent sludge use or disposal by such works in accordance with section 1345 of this title, then the pretreatment requirements for the sources actually discharging such toxic pollutant into such publicly owned treatment works may be revised by the owner or operator of such works to reflect the removal of such toxic pollutant by such works.

(2) The Administrator shall, from time to time, as control technology, processes, operating methods, or other alternatives change, revise such standards following the procedure established by this subsection for promulgation of such standards.

(3) When proposing or promulgating any pretreatment standard under this section, the Administrator shall designate the category or categories of sources to which such standard shall apply.

(4) Nothing in this subsection shall affect any pretreatment requirement established by any State or local law not in conflict with any pretreatment standard established under this subsection.

(c) NEW SOURCES OF POLLUTANTS INTO PUBLICLY OWNED TREATMENT WORKS

In order to insure that any source introducing pollutants into a publicly owned treatment works, which source would be a new source subject to section

§1317

Clean Water Act

1316 of this title if it were to discharge pollutants, will not cause a violation of the effluent limitations established for any such treatment works, the Administrator shall promulgate pretreatment standards for the category of such sources simultaneously with the promulgation of standards of performance under section 1316 of this title for the equivalent category of new sources. Such pretreatment standards shall prevent the discharge of any pollutant into such treatment works, which pollutant may interfere with, pass through, or otherwise be incompatible with such works.

(d) OPERATION IN VIOLATION OF STANDARDS UNLAWFUL

After the effective data of any effluent standard or prohibition or pretreatment standard promulgated under this section, it shall be unlawful for any owner or operator of any source to operate any source in violation of any such effluent standard or prohibition or pretreatment standard.

(e) COMPLIANCE DATE EXTENSION FOR INNOVATIVE PRETREATMENT SYSTEMS

In the case of any existing facility that proposes to comply with the pretreatment standards of subsection (b) of this section by applying an innovative system that meets the requirements of section 1311(k) of this title, the owner or operator of the publicly owned treatment works receiving the treated effluent from such facility may extend the date for compliance with the applicable pretreatment standard established under this section for a period not to exceed 2 years —

(1) if the Administrator determines that the innovative system has the potential for industrywide application, and

(2) if the Administrator (or the State in consultation with the Administrator, in any case in which the State has a pretreatment program approved by the Administrator) —

(A) determines that the proposed extension will not cause the publicly owned treatment works to be in violation of its permit under section 1342 of this title or of section 1345 of this title or to contribute to such a violation, and

(B) concurs with the proposed extension.

§1318. RECORDS AND REPORTS; INSPECTIONS

(a) MAINTENANCE; MONITORING EQUIPMENT; ENTRY; ACCESS TO INFORMATION

Whenever required to carry out the objective of this chapter, including but not limited to (1) developing or assisting in the development of any effluent limitation, or other limitation, prohibition, or effluent standard, pretreatment standard, or standard of performance under this chapter; (2) determining whether any person is in violation of any such effluent limitation, or other limitation, prohibition or effluent standard, pretreatment standard, or standard of performance; (3) any requirement established under this section; or (4) carrying out sections 1315, 1321, 1342, 1344 (relating to State permit programs), 1345, and 1364 of this title —

    (A) the Administrator shall require the owner or operator of any point source to (i) establish and maintain such records, (ii) make such reports, (iii) install, use, and maintain such monitoring equipment or methods (including where appropriate, biological monitoring methods), (iv) sample such effluents (in accordance with such methods, at such locations, at such intervals, and in such manner as the Administrator shall prescribe), and (v) provide such other information as he may reasonably require; and

    (B) the Administrator or his authorized representative (including an authorized contractor acting as a representative of the Administrator), upon presentation of his credentials —

        (i) shall have a right of entry to, upon, or through any premises in which an effluent source is located or in which any records required to be maintained under clause (A) of this subsection are located, and

        (ii) may at reasonable times have access to and copy any records, inspect any monitoring equipment or method required under clause (A), and sample any effluents which the owner or operator of such source is required to sample under such clause.

  (b) **AVAILABILITY TO PUBLIC; TRADE SECRETS EXCEPTION; PENALTY FOR DISCLOSURE OF CONFIDENTIAL INFORMATION**

    Any records, reports, or information obtained under this section (1) shall, in the case of effluent data, be related to any applicable effluent limitations, toxic, pretreatment, or new source performance standards, and (2) shall be available to the public, except that upon a showing satisfactory to the Administrator or by any person that records, reports, or information, or particular part thereof (other than effluent data), to which the Administrator has access under this section, if made public would divulge methods or processes entitled to protection as trade secrets of such person, the Administrator shall consider such record, report, or information, or particular portion thereof confidential in accordance with the purposes of section 1905 of title 18. Any authorized representative of the Administrator (including an authorized contractor acting as a representative of the Administrator) who knowingly or willfully publishes, divulges, discloses, or makes known in any manner or to any extent not authorized by law any information which is required to be considered confidential under this subsection shall be fined not more than $1,000 or imprisoned not more than 1 year, or both. Nothing in this subsection shall prohibit the Administrator or an authorized representative of the Administrator (including any authorized contractor acting as a representative of the Administrator) from disclosing records, reports, or information to other officers, employees, or authorized representatives of the United States concerned with carrying out this chapter or when relevant in any proceeding under this chapter.

(c) APPLICATION OF STATE LAW

Each State may develop and submit to the Administrator procedures under State law for inspection, monitoring, and entry with respect to point sources located in such State. If the Administrator finds that the procedures and the law of any State relating to inspection, monitoring, and entry are applicable to at least the same extent as those required by this section, such State is authorized to apply and enforce its procedures for inspection, monitoring, and entry with respect to point sources located in such State (except with respect to point sources owned or operated by the United States).

(d) ACCESS BY CONGRESS

Notwithstanding any limitation contained in this section or any other provision of law, all information reported to or otherwise obtained by the Administrator (or any representative of the Administrator) under this chapter shall be made available, upon written request of any duly authorized committee of Congress, to such committee.

§1319. ENFORCEMENT

(a) STATE ENFORCEMENT; COMPLIANCE ORDERS

(1) Whenever, on the basis of any information available to him, the Administrator finds that any person is in violation of any condition or limitation which implements section 1311, 1312, 1316, 1317, 1318, 1328, or 1345 of this title in a permit issued by a State under an approved permit program under section 1342 or 1344 of this title he shall proceed under his authority in paragraph (3) of this subsection or he shall notify the person in alleged violation and such State of such finding. If beyond the thirtieth day after the Administrator's notification the State has not commenced appropriate enforcement action, the Administrator shall issue an order requiring such person to comply with such condition or limitation or shall bring a civil action in accordance with subsection (b) of this section.

(2) Whenever, on the basis of information available to him, the Administrator finds that violations of permit conditions or limitations as set forth in paragraph (1) of this subsection are so widespread that such violations appear to result from a failure of the State to enforce such permit conditions or limitations effectively, he shall so notify the State. If the Administrator finds such failure extends beyond the thirtieth day after such notice, he shall give public notice of such finding. During the period beginning with such public notice and ending when such State satisfies the Administrator that it will enforce such conditions and limitations (hereafter referred to in this section as the period of "federally assumed enforcement"), except where an extension has been granted under paragraph (5)(B) of this subsection, the Administrator shall enforce any permit condition or limitation with respect to any person —

(A) by issuing an order to comply with such condition or limitation, or

(B) by bringing a civil action under subsection (b) of this section.

(3) Whenever on the basis of any information available to him the Administrator finds that any person is in violation of section 1311, 1312, 1316, 1317, 1318, 1328, or 1345 of this title, or is in violation of any permit condition or limitation implementing any of such sections in a permit issued under section 1342 of this title by him or by a State or in a permit issued under section 1344 of this title by a State, he shall issue an order requiring such person to comply with such section or requirement, or he shall bring a civil action in accordance with subsection (b) of this section.

(4) A copy of any order issued under this subsection shall be sent immediately by the Administrator to the State in which the violation occurs and other affected States. In any case in which an order under this subsection (or notice to a violator under paragraph (1) of this subsection) is issued to a corporation, a copy of such order (or notice) shall be served on any appropriate corporate officers. An order issued under this subsection relating to a violation of section 1318 of this title shall not take effect until the person to whom it is issued has had an opportunity to confer with the Administrator concerning the alleged violation.

(5)(A) Any order issued under this subsection shall be by personal service, shall state with reasonable specificity the nature of the violation, and shall specify a time for compliance not to exceed thirty days in the case of a violation of an interim compliance schedule or operation and maintenance requirement and not to exceed a time the Administrator determines to be reasonable in the case of a violation of a final deadline, taking into account the seriousness of the violation and any good faith efforts to comply with applicable requirements.

(B) The Administrator may, if he determines (i) that any person who is a violator of, or any person who is otherwise not in compliance with, the time requirements under this chapter or in any permit issued under this chapter, has acted in good faith, and has made a commitment (in the form of contracts or other securities) of necessary resources to achieve compliance by the earliest possible date after July 1, 1977, but not later than April 1, 1979; (ii) that any extension under this provision will not result in the imposition of any additional controls on any other point or nonpoint source; (iii) that an application for a permit under section 1342 of this title was filed for such person prior to December 31, 1974; and (iv) that the facilities necessary for compliance with such requirements are under construction, grant an extension of the date referred to in section 1311(b)(1)(A) of this title to a date which will achieve compliance at the earliest time possible but not later than April 1, 1979.

(6) Whenever, on the basis of information available to him, the Administrator finds (A) that any person is in violation of section 1311(b)(1)(A) or (C) of this title, (B) that such person cannot meet the requirements for a time extension under section 1311(i)(2) of this title, and (C) that the most expeditious and appropriate means of compliance with this chapter by such person is to discharge

§1319

into a publicly owned treatment works, then, upon request of such person, the Administrator may issue an order requiring such person to comply with this chapter at the earliest date practicable, but not later than July 1, 1983, by discharging into a publicly owned treatment works if such works concur with such order. Such order shall include a schedule of compliance.

(b) CIVIL ACTIONS

The Administrator is authorized to commence a civil action for appropriate relief, including a permanent or temporary injunction, for any violation for which he is authorized to issue a compliance order under subsection (a) of this section. Any action under this subsection may be brought in the district court of the United States for the district in which the defendant is located or resides or is doing business, and such court shall have jurisdiction to restrain such violation and to require compliance. Notice of the commencement of such action shall be given immediately to the appropriate State.

(c) CRIMINAL PENALTIES

(1) NEGLIGENT VIOLATIONS

Any person who —
(A) negligently violates section 1311, 1312, 1316, 1317, 1318, 1328, or 1345 of this title, or any permit condition or limitation implementing any of such sections in a permit issued under section 1342 of this title by the Administrator or by a State, or any requirement imposed in a pretreatment program approved under section 1342(a)(3) or 1342(b)(8) of this title or in a permit issued under section 1344 of this title by the Secretary of the Army or by a State; or
(B) negligently introduces into a sewer system or into a publicly owned treatment works any pollutant or hazardous substance which such person knew or reasonably should have known could cause personal injury or property damage or, other than in compliance with all applicable Federal, State, or local requirements or permits, which causes such treatment works to violate any effluent limitation or condition in any permit issued to the treatment works under section 1342 of this title by the Administrator or a State;

shall be punished by a fine of not less than $2,500 nor more than $25,000 per day of violation, or by imprisonment for not more than 1 year, or by both. If a conviction of a person is for a violation committed after a first conviction of such person under this paragraph, punishment shall be by a fine of not more than $50,000 per day of violation, or by imprisonment of not more than 2 years, or by both.

(2) KNOWING VIOLATIONS

Any person who —
(A) knowingly violates section 1311, 1312, 1316, 1317, 1318, 1328,

Clean Water Act §1319

or 1345 of this title, or any permit condition or limitation implementing any of such sections in a permit issued under section 1342 of this title by the Administrator or by a State, or any requirement imposed in a pretreatment program approved under section 1342(a)(3) or 1342(b)(8) of this title or in a permit issued under section 1344 of this title by the Secretary of the Army or by a State; or

(B) knowingly introduces into a sewer system or into a publicly owned treatment works any pollutant or hazardous substance which such person knew or reasonably should have known could cause personal injury or property damage or, other than in compliance with all applicable Federal, State, or local requirements or permits, which causes such treatment works to violate any effluent limitation or condition in a permit issued to the treatment works under section 1342 of this title by the Administrator or a State;

shall be punished by a fine of not less than $5,000 nor more than $50,000 per day of violation, or by imprisonment for not more than 3 years, or by both. If a conviction of a person is for a violation committed after a first conviction of such person under this paragraph, punishment shall be by a fine of not more than $100,000 per day of violation, or by imprisonment of not more than 6 years, or by both.

(3) KNOWING ENDANGERMENT

(A) GENERAL RULE

Any person who knowingly violates section 1311, 1312, 1313, 1316, 1317, 1318, 1328, or 1345 of this title, or any permit condition or limitation implementing any of such sections in a permit issued under section 1342 of this title by the Administrator or by a State, or in a permit issued under section 1344 of this title by the Secretary of the Army or by a State, and who knows at that time that he thereby places another person in imminent danger of death or serious bodily injury, shall, upon conviction, be subject to a fine of not more than $250,000 or imprisonment of not more than 15 years, or both. A person which is an organization shall, upon conviction of violating this subparagraph, be subject to a fine of not more than $1,000,000. If a conviction of a person is for a violation committed after a first conviction of such person under this paragraph, the maximum punishment shall be doubled with respect to both fine and imprisonment.

(B) ADDITIONAL PROVISIONS

For the purpose of subparagraph (A) of this paragraph —

(i) in determining whether a defendant who is an individual knew that his conduct placed another person in imminent danger of death or serious bodily injury —

(I) the person is responsible only for actual awareness or actual belief that he possessed; and

(II) knowledge possessed by a person other than the defendant but not by the defendant himself may not be attributed to the defendant;

except that in proving the defendant's possession of actual knowledge, circumstantial evidence may be used, including evidence that the defendant took affirmative steps to shield himself from relevant information;

(ii) it is an affirmative defense to prosecution that the conduct charged was consented to by the person endangered and that the danger and conduct charged were reasonably foreseeable hazards of —

(I) an occupation, a business, or a profession; or

(II) medical treatment or medical or scientific experimentation conducted by professionally approved methods and such other person had been made aware of the risks involved prior to giving consent;

and such defense may be established under this subparagraph by a preponderance of the evidence;

(iii) the term "organization" means a legal entity, other than a government, established or organized for any purpose, and such term includes a corporation, company, association, firm, partnership, joint stock company, foundation, institution, trust, society, union, or any other association of persons; and

(iv) the term "serious bodily injury" means bodily injury which involves a substantial risk of death, unconsciousness, extreme physical pain, protracted and obvious disfigurement, or protracted loss or impairment of the function of a bodily member, organ, or mental faculty.

(4) FALSE STATEMENTS

Any person who knowingly makes any false material statement, representation, or certification in any application, record, report, plan, or other document filed or required to be maintained under this chapter or who knowingly falsifies, tampers with, or renders inaccurate any monitoring device or method required to be maintained under this chapter, shall upon conviction, be punished by a fine of not more than $10,000, or by imprisonment for not more than 2 years, or by both. If a conviction of a person is for a violation committed after a first conviction of such person under this paragraph, punishment shall be by a fine of not more than $20,000 per day of violation, or by imprisonment of not more than 4 years, or by both.

(5) TREATMENT OF SINGLE OPERATIONAL UPSET

For purposes of this subsection, a single operational upset which leads to simultaneous violations of more than one pollutant parameter shall be treated as a single violation.

Clean Water Act §1319

(6) **RESPONSIBLE CORPORATE OFFICER AS "PERSON"**

For the purpose of this subsection, the term "person" means, in addition to the definition contained in section 1362(5) of this title, any responsible corporate officer.

(7) **HAZARDOUS SUBSTANCE DEFINED**

For the purpose of this subsection, the term "hazardous substance" means (A) any substance designated pursuant to section 1321(b)(2)(A) of this title, (B) any element, compound, mixture, solution, or substance designated pursuant to section 9602 of title 42, (C) any hazardous waste having the characteristics identified under or listed pursuant to section 3001 of the Solid Waste Disposal Act [42 U.S.C. 6921] (but not including any waste the regulation of which under the Solid Waste Disposal Act [42 U.S.C. 6901 et seq.] has been suspended by Act of Congress), (D) any toxic pollutant listed under section 1317(a) of this title, and (E) any imminently hazardous chemical substance or mixture with respect to which the Administrator has taken action pursuant to section 2606 of title 15.

(d) **CIVIL PENALTIES; FACTORS CONSIDERED IN DETERMINING AMOUNT**

Any person who violates section 1311, 1312, 1316, 1317, 1318, 1328, or 1345 of this title, or any permit condition or limitation implementing any of such sections in a permit issued under section 1342 of this title by the Administrator, or by a State, or in a permit issued under section 1344 of this title by a State,[2] or any requirement imposed in a pretreatment program approved under section 1342(a)(3) or 1342(b)(8) of this title, and any person who violates any order issued by the Administrator under subsection (a) of this section, shall be subject to a civil penalty not to exceed $25,000 per day for each violation. In determining the amount of a civil penalty the court shall consider the seriousness of the violation or violations, the economic benefit (if any) resulting from the violation, any history of such violations, any good-faith efforts to comply with the applicable requirements, the economic impact of the penalty on the violator, and such other matters as justice may require. For purposes of this subsection, a single operational upset which leads to simultaneous violations of more than one pollutant parameter shall be treated as a single violation.

(e) **STATE LIABILITY FOR JUDGMENTS AND EXPENSES**

Whenever a municipality is a party to a civil action brought by the United States under this section, the State in which such municipality is located shall be joined as a party. Such State shall be liable for payment of any judgment, or any expenses incurred as a result of complying with any judgment, entered against the municipality in such action to the extent that the laws of that State

---

2. So in original.

prevent the municipality from raising revenues needed to comply with such judgment.

(f) WRONGFUL INTRODUCTION OF POLLUTANTS INTO TREATMENT WORKS

Whenever, on the basis of any information available to him, the Administrator finds that an owner or operator of any source is introducing a pollutant into a treatment works in violation of subsection (d) of section 1317 of this title, the Administrator may notify the owner or operator of such treatment works and the State of such violation. If the owner or operator of the treatment works does not commence appropriate enforcement action within 30 days of the date of such notification, the Administrator may commence a civil action for appropriate relief, including but not limited to, a permanent or temporary injunction, against the owner or operator of such treatment works. In any such civil action the Administrator shall join the owner or operator of such source as a party to the action. Such action shall be brought in the district court of the United States in the district in which the treatment works is located. Such court shall have jurisdiction to restrain such violation and to require the owner or operator of the treatment works and the owner or operator of the source to take such action as may be necessary to come into compliance with this chapter. Notice of commencement of any such action shall be given to the State. Nothing in this subsection shall be construed to limit or prohibit any other authority the Administrator may have under this chapter.

(g) ADMINISTRATIVE PENALTIES

(1) VIOLATIONS

Whenever on the basis of any information available —
(A) the Administrator finds that any person has violated section 1311, 1312, 1316, 1317, 1318, 1328, or 1345 of this title, or has violated any permit condition or limitation implementing any of such sections in a permit issued under section 1342 of this title by the Administrator or by a State, or in a permit issued under section 1344 of this title by a State, or
(B) the Secretary of the Army (hereinafter in this subsection referred to as the "Secretary") finds that any person has violated any permit condition or limitation in a permit issued under section 1344 of this title by the Secretary,

the Administrator or Secretary, as the case may be, may, after consultation with the State in which the violation occurs, assess a class I civil penalty or a class II civil penalty under this subsection.

(2) CLASSES OF PENALTIES

(A) CLASS I

The amount of a class I civil penalty under paragraph (1) may not exceed $10,000 per violation, except that the maximum amount of any class I civil penalty under this subparagraph shall not exceed $25,000.

Before issuing an order assessing a civil penalty under this subparagraph, the Administrator or the Secretary, as the case may be, shall give to the person to be assessed such penalty written notice of the Administrator's or Secretary's proposal to issue such order and the opportunity to request, within 30 days of the date the notice is received by such person, a hearing on the proposed order. Such hearing shall not be subject to section 554 or 556 of title 5, but shall provide a reasonable opportunity to be heard and to present evidence.

(B) CLASS II

The amount of a class II civil penalty under paragraph (1) may not exceed $10,000 per day for each day during which the violation continues; except that the maximum amount of any class II civil penalty under this subparagraph shall not exceed $125,000. Except as otherwise provided in this subsection, a class II civil penalty shall be assessed and collected in the same manner, and subject to the same provisions, as in the case of civil penalties assessed and collected after notice and opportunity for a hearing on the record in accordance with section 554 of title 5. The Administrator and the Secretary may issue rules for discovery procedures for hearings under this subparagraph.

(3) DETERMINING AMOUNT

In determining the amount of any penalty assessed under this subsection, the Administrator or the Secretary, as the case may be, shall take into account the nature, circumstances, extent and gravity of the violation, or violations, and, with respect to the violator, ability to pay, any prior history of such violations, the degree of culpability, economic benefit or savings (if any) resulting from the violation, and such other matters as justice may require. For purposes of this subsection, a single operational upset which leads to simultaneous violations of more than one pollutant parameter shall be treated as a single violation.

(4) RIGHTS OF INTERESTED PERSONS

(A) PUBLIC NOTICE

Before issuing an order assessing a civil penalty under this subsection the Administrator or Secretary, as the case may be, shall provide public notice of and reasonable opportunity to comment on the proposed issuance of such order.

(B) PRESENTATION OF EVIDENCE

Any person who comments on a proposed assessment of a penalty under this subsection shall be given notice of any hearing held under this subsection and of the order assessing such penalty. In any hearing held under this subsection, such person shall have a reasonable opportunity to be heard and to present evidence.

(C) RIGHTS OF INTERESTED PERSONS TO A HEARING

If no hearing is held under paragraph (2) before issuance of an order assessing a penalty under this subsection, any person who commented on the proposed assessment may petition, within 30 days after the issuance of such order, the Administrator or Secretary, as the case may be, to set aside such order and to provide a hearing on the penalty. If the evidence presented by the petitioner in support of the petition is material and was not considered in the issuance of the order, the Administrator or Secretary shall immediately set aside such order and provide a hearing in accordance with paragraph (2)(A) in the case of a class I civil penalty and paragraph (2)(B) in the case of a class II civil penalty. If the Administrator or Secretary denies a hearing under this subparagraph, the Administrator or Secretary shall provide to the petitioner, and publish in the Federal Register, notice of and the reasons for such denial.

(5) FINALITY OF ORDER

An order issued under this subsection shall become final 30 days after its issuance unless a petition for judicial review is filed under paragraph (8) or a hearing is requested under paragraph (4)(C). If such a hearing is denied, such order shall become final 30 days after such denial.

(6) EFFECT OF ORDER

(A) LIMITATION ON ACTIONS UNDER OTHER SECTIONS

Action taken by the Administrator or the Secretary, as the case may be, under this subsection shall not affect or limit the Administrator's or Secretary's authority to enforce any provision of this chapter; except that any violation —

(i) with respect to which the Administrator or the Secretary has commenced and is diligently prosecuting an action under this subsection,

(ii) with respect to which a State has commenced and is diligently prosecuting an action under a State law comparable to this subsection, or

(iii) for which the Administrator, the Secretary, or the State has issued a final order not subject to further judicial review and the violator has paid a penalty assessed under this subsection, or such comparable State law, as the case may be,

shall not be the subject of a civil penalty action under subsection (d) of this section or section 1321(b) of this title or section 1365 of this title.

(B) APPLICABILITY OF LIMITATION WITH RESPECT TO CITIZEN SUITS

The limitations contained in subparagraph (A) on civil penalty actions under section 1365 of this title shall not apply with respect to any violation for which —

(i) a civil action under section 1365(a)(1) of this title has been filed prior to commencement of an action under this subsection, or

(ii) notice of an alleged violation of section 1356(a)(1) of this title has been given in accordance with section 1365(b)(1)(A) of this title prior to commencement of an action under this subsection and an action under section 1365(a)(1) of this title with respect to such alleged violation is filed before the 120th day after the date on which such notice is given.

(7) EFFECT OF ACTION ON COMPLIANCE

No action by the Administrator or the Secretary under this subsection shall affect any person's obligation to comply with any section of this chapter or with the terms and conditions of any permit issued pursuant to section 1342 or 1344 of this title.

(8) JUDICIAL REVIEW

Any person against whom a civil penalty is assessed under this subsection or who commented on the proposed assessment of such penalty in accordance with paragraph (4) may obtain review of such assessment —

(A) in the case of assessment of a class I civil penalty, in the United States District Court for the District of Columbia or in the district in which the violation is alleged to have occurred, or

(B) in the case of assessment of a class II civil penalty, in United States Court of Appeals for the District of Columbia Circuit or for any other circuit in which such person resides or transacts business.

by filing a notice of appeal in such court within the 30-day period beginning on the date the civil penalty order is issued and by simultaneously sending a copy of such notice by certified mail to the Administrator or the Secretary, as the case may be, and the Attorney General. The Administrator or the Secretary shall promptly file in such court a certified copy of the record on which the order was issued. Such court shall not set aside or remand such order unless there is not substantial evidence in the record, taken as a whole, to support the finding of a violation or unless the Administrator's or Secretary's assessment of the penalty constitutes an abuse of discretion and shall not impose additional civil penalties for the same violation unless the Administrator's or Secretary's assessment of the penalty constitutes an abuse of discretion.

(9) COLLECTION

If any person fails to pay an assessment of a civil penalty —

(A) after the order making the assessment has become final, or

(B) after a court in an action brought under paragraph (8) has entered a final judgment in favor of the Administrator or the Secretary, as the case may be,

the Administrator or the Secretary shall request the Attorney General to bring a civil action in an appropriate district court to recover the amount assessed (plus interest at currently prevailing rates from the date of the final order or the date of the final judgment, as the case may be). In such an action, the validity, amount, and appropriateness of such penalty shall not be subject to review. Any person who fails to pay on a timely basis the amount of an assessment of a civil penalty as described in the first sentence of this paragraph shall be required to pay, in addition to such amount and interest, attorneys fees and costs for collection proceedings and a quarterly nonpayment penalty for each quarter during which such failure to pay persists. Such nonpayment penalty shall be in an amount equal to 20 percent of the aggregate amount of such person's penalties and nonpayment penalties which are unpaid as of the beginning of such quarter.

(10) SUBPOENAS

The Administrator or Secretary, as the case may be, may issue subpoenas for the attendance and testimony of witnesses and the production of relevant papers, books, or documents in connection with hearings under this subsection. In case of contumacy or refusal to obey a subpoena issued pursuant to this paragraph and served upon any person, the district court of the United States for any district in which such person is found, resides, or transacts business, upon application by the United States and after notice to such person, shall have jurisdiction to issue an order requiring such person to appear and give testimony before the administrative law judge or to appear and produce documents before the administrative law judge, or both, and any failure to obey such order of the court may be punished by such court as a contempt thereof.

(11) PROTECTION OF EXISTING PROCEDURES

Nothing in this subsection shall change the procedures existing on the day before February 4, 1987, under other subsections of this section for issuance and enforcement of orders by the Administrator.

§1320. INTERNATIONAL POLLUTION ABATEMENT

(a) HEARING; PARTICIPATION BY FOREIGN NATIONS

Whenever the Administrator, upon receipts of reports, surveys, or studies from any duly constituted international agency, has reason to believe that pollution is occurring which endangers the health or welfare of persons in a foreign country, and the Secretary of State requests him to abate such pollution, he shall give formal notification thereof to the State water pollution control agency of the

Clean Water Act §1320

State or States in which such discharge or discharges originate and to the appropriate interstate agency, if any. He shall also promptly call such a hearing, if he believes that such pollution is occurring in sufficient quantity to warrant such action, and if such foreign country has given the United States essentially the same rights with respect to the prevention and control of pollution occurring in that country as is given that country by this subsection. The Administrator, through the Secretary of State, shall invite the foreign country which may be adversely affected by the pollution to attend and participate in the hearing, and the representative of such country shall, for the purpose of the hearing and any further proceeding resulting from such hearing, have all the rights of a State water pollution control agency. Nothing in this subsection shall be construed to modify, amend, repeal, or otherwise affect the provisions of the 1909 Boundary Waters Treaty between Canada and the United States or the Water Utilization Treaty of 1944 between Mexico and the United States (59 Stat. 1219), relative to the control and abatement of pollution in waters covered by those treaties.

(b) **FUNCTIONS AND RESPONSIBILITIES OF ADMINISTRATOR NOT AFFECTED**

The calling of a hearing under this section shall not be construed by the courts, the Administrator, or any person as limiting, modifying, or otherwise affecting the functions and responsibilities of the Administrator under this section to establish and enforce water quality requirements under this chapter.

(c) **HEARING BOARD; COMPOSITION; FINDINGS OF FACT; RECOMMENDATIONS; IMPLEMENTATION OF BOARD'S DECISION**

The Administrator shall publish in the Federal Register a notice of a public hearing before a hearing board of five or more persons appointed by the Administrator. A majority of the members of the board and the chairman who shall be designated by the Administrator shall not be officers or employees of Federal, State, or local governments. On the basis of the evidence presented at such hearing, the board shall within sixty days after completion of the hearing make findings of fact as to whether or not such pollution is occurring and shall thereupon by decision, incorporating its findings therein, make such recommendations to abate the pollution as may be appropriate and shall transmit such decision and the record of the hearings to the Administrator. All such decisions shall be public. Upon receipt of such decision, the Administrator shall promptly implement the board's decision in accordance with the provisions of this chapter.

(d) **REPORT BY ALLEGED POLLUTER**

In connection with any hearing called under this subsection, the board is authorized to require any person whose alleged activities result in discharges causing or contributing to pollution to file with it in such forms as it may prescribe, a report based on existing data, furnishing such information as may reasonably be required as to the character, kind, and quantity of such discharges and the use of facilities or other means to prevent or reduce such discharges by the person filing such a report. Such report shall be made under oath or otherwise, as the board may prescribe, and shall be filed with the board within such reasonable period as it may prescribe, unless additional time is granted by it. Upon a showing satisfactory to the board by the person filing such report that such report or portion thereof (other than effluent data), to which the Administrator has access under this section, if made public would divulge trade secrets or secret processes of such person, the board shall consider such report or portion thereof confidential for the purposes of section 1905 of title 18. If any person required to file any report under this paragraph shall fail to do so within the time fixed by the board for filing the same, and such failure shall continue for thirty days after notice of such default, such person shall forfeit to the United States the sum of $1,000 for each and every day of the continuance of such failure, which forfeiture shall be payable into the Treasury of the United States, and shall be recoverable in a civil suit in the name of the United States in the district court of the United States where such person has his principal office or in any district in which he does business. The Administrator may upon application therefor remit or mitigate any forfeiture provided under this subsection.

(e) COMPENSATION OF BOARD MEMBERS

Board members, other than officers or employees of Federal, State, or local governments, shall be for each day (including travel-time) during which they are performing board business, entitled to receive compensation at a rate fixed by the Administrator but not in excess of the maximum rate of pay for grade GS-18, as provided in the General Schedule under section 5332 of title 5, and shall, notwithstanding the limitations of sections 5703 and 5704 of title 5, be fully reimbursed for travel, subsistence and related expenses.

(f) ENFORCEMENT PROCEEDINGS

When any such recommendation adopted by the Administrator involves the institution of enforcement proceedings against any person to obtain the abatement of pollution subject to such recommendation, the Administrator shall institute such proceedings if he believes that the evidence warrants such proceedings. The district court of the United States shall consider and determine de novo all relevant issues, but shall receive in evidence the record of the proceedings before the conference or hearing board. The court shall have jurisdiction to enter such judgment and orders enforcing such judgment as it deems appropriate or to remand such proceedings to the Administrator for such further action as it may direct.

§1321. OIL AND HAZARDOUS SUBSTANCE LIABILITY

(a) DEFINITIONS

For the purpose of this section, the term —

(1) "oil" means oil of any kind or in any form, including, but not lim-

ited to, petroleum, fuel oil, sludge, oil refuse, and oil mixed with wastes other than dredged spoil;

(2) "discharge" includes, but is not limited to, any spilling, leaking, pumping, pouring, emitting, emptying or dumping, but excludes (A) discharges in compliance with a permit under section 1342 of this title, (B) discharges resulting from circumstances identified and reviewed and made a part of the public record with respect to a permit issued or modified under section 1342 of this title, and subject to a condition in such permit, and (C) continuous or anticipated intermittent discharges from a point source, identified in a permit or permit application under section 1342 of this title, which are caused by events occurring within the scope of relevant operating or treatment systems;

(3) "vessel" means every description of watercraft or other artificial contrivance used, or capable of being used, as a means of transportation on water other than a public vessel;

(4) "public vessel" means a vessel owned or bareboat-chartered and operated by the United States, or by a State or political subdivision thereof, or by a foreign nation, except when such vessel is engaged in commerce;

(5) "United States" means the States, the District of Columbia, the Commonwealth of Puerto Rico, the Commonwealth of the Northern Mariana Islands, Guam, American Samoa, the Virgin Islands, and the Trust Territory of the Pacific Islands;

(6) "owner or operator" means (A) in the case of a vessel, any person owning, operating, or chartering by demise, such vessel, and (B) in the case of an onshore facility, and an offshore facility, any person owning or operating such onshore facility or offshore facility, and (C) in the case of any abandoned offshore facility, the person who owned or operated such facility immediately prior to such abandonment;

(7) "person" includes an individual, firm, corporation, association, and a partnership.

(8) "remove" or "removal" refers to removal of the oil or hazardous substances from the water and shorelines or the taking of such other actions as may be necessary to minimize or mitigate damage to the public health or welfare, including, but not limited to, fish, shellfish, wildlife, and public and private property, shorelines, and beaches;

(9) "contiguous zone" means the entire zone established or to be established by the United States under article 24 of the Convention on the Territorial Sea and the Contiguous Zone;

(10) "onshore facility" means any facility (including, but not limited to, motor vehicles and rolling stock) of any kind located in, on, or under, any land within the United States other than submerged land;

(11) "offshore facility" means any facility of any kind located in, on, or under, any of the navigable waters of the United States, and any facility of any kind which is subject to the jurisdiction of the United States and is located in, on, or under any other waters, other than a vessel or a public vessel;

(12) "act of God" means an act occasioned by an unanticipated grave natural disaster;

(13) "barrel" means 42 United States gallons at 60 degrees Fahrenheit;

(14) "hazardous substance" means any substance designated pursuant to subsection (b)(2) of this section;

(15) "inland oil barge" means a non-self-propelled vessel carrying oil in bulk as cargo and certificated to operate only in the inland waters of the United States, while operating in such waters;

(16) "inland waters of the United States" means those waters of the United States lying inside the baseline from which the territorial sea is measured and those waters outside such baseline which are a part of the Gulf Intracoastal Waterway.[3]

(17) "Otherwise[4] subject to the jurisdiction of the United States" means subject to the jurisdiction of the United States by virtue of United States citizenship, United States vessel documentation or numbering, or as provided for by international agreement to which the United States is a party.

(b) CONGRESSIONAL DECLARATION OF POLICY AGAINST DISCHARGES OF OIL OR HAZARDOUS SUBSTANCES; DESIGNATION OF HAZARDOUS SUBSTANCES; STUDY OF HIGHER STANDARD OF CARE INCENTIVES AND REPORT TO CONGRESS; LIABILITY; PENALTIES; CIVIL ACTIONS; PENALTY LIMITATIONS, SEPARATE OFFENSES, JURISDICTION, MITIGATION OF DAMAGES AND COSTS, RECOVERY OF REMOVAL COSTS AND ALTERNATIVE REMEDIES

(1) The Congress hereby declares that it is the policy of the United States that there should be no discharges of oil or hazardous substances into or upon the navigable waters of the United States, adjoining shorelines, or into or upon the waters of the contiguous zone, or in connection with activities under the Outer Continental Shelf Lands Act [43 U.S.C. 1331 et seq.] or the Deepwater Port Act of 1974 [33 U.S.C. 1501 et seq.], or which may affect natural resources belonging to, appertaining to, or under the exclusive management authority of the United States (including resources under the Magnuson Fishery Conservation and Management Act [16 U.S.C. 1801 et seq.]).

(2)(A) The Administrator shall develop, promulgate, and revise as may be appropriate, regulations designating as hazardous substances, other than oil as defined in this section, such elements and compounds which, when discharged in any quantity into or upon the navigable waters of the United States or adjoining shorelines or the waters of the contiguous zone or in connection with activities under the Outer Continental Shelf Lands Act [43 U.S.C. 1331 et seq.] or the Deepwater Port Act of 1974 [33 U.S.C. 1501 et seq.], or which may affect natural resources belonging to, appertaining to, or under the exclusive management authority of the United States (including resources under the Magnuson Fishery Conservation and Management Act [16 U.S.C. 1801 et seq.]), present

---

3. So in original. The period probably should be a semicolon.
4. So in original. Probably should not be capitalized.

Clean Water Act §1321

an imminent and substantial danger to the public health or welfare, including, but not limited to, fish, shellfish, wildlife, shorelines, and beaches.

(B) The Administrator shall within 18 months after the date of enactment of this paragraph, conduct a study and report to the Congress on methods, mechanisms, and procedures to create incentives to achieve a higher standard of care in all aspects of the management and movement of hazardous substances on the part of owners, operators, or persons in charge of onshore facilities, offshore facilities, or vessels. The Administrator shall include in such study (1) limits of liability, (2) liability for third party damages, (3) penalties and fees, (4) spill prevention plans, (5) current practices in the insurance and banking industries, and (6) whether the penalty enacted in subclause (bb) of clause (iii) of subparagraph (B) of subsection (b)(2) of section 311 of Public Law 92-500 should be enacted.

(3) The discharge of oil or hazardous substances (i) into or upon the navigable waters of the United States, adjoining shorelines, or into or upon the waters of the contiguous zone, or (ii) in connection with activities under the Outer Continental Shelf Lands Act [43 U.S.C. 1331 et seq.] or the Deepwater Port Act of 1974 [33 U.S.C. 1501 et seq.], or which may affect natural resources belonging to, appertaining to, or under the exclusive management authority of the United States (including resources under the Magnuson Fishery Conservation and Management Act [16 U.S.C. 1801 et seq.]), in such quantities as may be harmful as determined by the President under paragraph (4) of this subsection, is prohibited, except (A) in the case of such discharges into the waters of the contiguous zone or which may affect natural resources belonging to, appertaining to, or under the exclusive management authority of the United States (including resources under the Magnuson Fishery Conservation and Management Act), where permitted under the Protocol of 1978 Relating to the International Convention for the Prevention of Pollution from Ships, 1973, and (B) where permitted in quantities and at times and locations or under such circumstances or conditions as the President may, by regulation, determine not to be harmful. Any regulations issued under this subsection shall be consistent with maritime safety and with marine and navigation laws and regulations and applicable water quality standards.

(4) The President shall by regulation, determine for the purposes of this section those quantities of oil and any hazardous substances the discharge of which may be harmful to the public health or welfare of the United States, including but not limited to fish, shellfish, wildlife, and public and private property, shorelines, and beaches.

(5) Any person in charge of a vessel or of an onshore facility or an offshore facility shall, as soon as he has knowledge of any discharge of oil or a hazardous substance from such vessel or facility in violation of paragraph (3) of this subsection, immediately notify the appropriate agency of the United States Government of such discharge. Any such person (A) in charge of a vessel from which oil or a hazardous substance is discharged in violation of paragraph (3)(i) of this

subsection, or (B) in charge of a vessel from which oil or a hazardous substance is discharged in violation of paragraph (3)(ii) of this subsection and who is otherwise subject to the jurisdiction of the United States at the time of the discharge, or (C) in charge of an onshore facility or an offshore facility, who fails to notify immediately such agency of such discharge shall, upon conviction, be fined not more than $10,000, or imprisoned for not more than one year, or both. Notification received pursuant to this paragraph or information obtained by the exploitation of such notification shall not be used against any such person in any criminal case, except a prosecution for personal injury or for giving a false statement.

(6)(A) Any owner, operator, or person in charge of any onshore facility or offshore facility from which oil or a hazardous substance is discharged in violation of paragraph (3) of this subsection shall be assessed a civil penalty by the Secretary of the department in which the Coast Guard is operating of not more than $5,000 for each offense. Any owner, operator, or person in charge of any vessel from which oil or a hazardous substance is discharged in violation of paragraph (3)(i) of this subsection, and any owner, operator, or person in charge of a vessel from which oil or a hazardous substance is discharged in violation of paragraph (3)(ii) who is otherwise subject to the jurisdiction of the United States at the time of the discharge, shall be assessed a civil penalty by the Secretary of the department in which the Coast Guard is operating of not more than $5,000 for each offense. No penalty shall be assessed unless the owner or operator charged shall have been given notice and opportunity for a hearing on such charge. Each violation is a separate offense. Any such civil penalty may be compromised by such Secretary. In determining the amount of the penalty, or the amount agreed upon in compromise, the appropriateness of such penalty to the size of the business of the owner or operator charged, the effect on the owner or operator's ability to continue in business, and the gravity of the violation, shall be considered by such Secretary. The Secretary of the Treasury shall withhold at the request of such Secretary the clearance required by section 91 of title 46, Appendix, of any vessel the owner or operator of which is subject to the foregoing penalty. Clearance may be granted in such cases upon the filing of a bond or other surety satisfactory to such Secretary.

> (B) The Administrator, taking into account the gravity of the offense, and the standard of care manifested by the owner, operator, or person in charge, may commence a civil action against any such person subject to the penalty under subparagraph (A) of this paragraph to impose a penalty based on consideration of the size of the business of the owner or operator, the effect on the ability of the owner or operator to continue in business, the gravity of the violation, and the nature, extent, and degree of success of any efforts made by the owner, operator, or person in charge to minimize or mitigate the effects of such discharge. The amount of such penalty shall not exceed $50,000, except that where the United States can show that such discharge was the result of willful negligence or willful misconduct within the privity and knowledge of the owner, operator, or person in charge, such penalty shall not

Clean Water Act §1321

exceed $250,000. Each violation is a separate offense. Any action under this subparagraph may be brought in the district court of the United States for the district in which the defendant is located or resides or is doing business, and such court shall have jurisdiction to assess such penalty. No action may be commenced under this clause where a penalty has been assessed under clause (A) of this paragraph.

(C) In addition to establishing a penalty for the discharge of a hazardous substance, the Administrator may act to mitigate the damage to the public health or welfare caused by such discharge. The cost of such mitigation shall be deemed a cost incurred under subsection (c) of this section for the removal of such substance by the United States Government.

(D) Any costs of removal incurred in connection with a discharge excluded by subsection (a)(2)(C) of this section shall be recoverable from the owner or operator of the source of the discharge in an action brought under section 1319(b) of this title.

(E) Civil penalties shall not be assessed under both this section and section 1319 of this title for the same discharge.

(c) REMOVAL OF DISCHARGED OIL OR HAZARDOUS SUBSTANCES; NATIONAL CONTINGENCY PLAN

(1) Whenever any oil or a hazardous substance is discharged, or there is a substantial threat of such discharge, into or upon the navigable waters of the United States, adjoining shorelines, or into or upon the waters of the contiguous zone, or in connection with activities under the Outer Continental Shelf Lands Act [43 U.S.C. 1331 et seq.] or the Deepwater Port Act of 1974 [33 U.S.C. 1501 et seq.], or which may affect natural resources belonging to, appertaining to, or under the exclusive management authority of the United States (including resources under the Magnuson Fishery Conservation and Management Act [16 U.S.C. 1801 et seq.]) the President is authorized to act to remove or arrange for the removal of such oil or substance at any time, unless he determines such removal will be done properly by the owner or operator of the vessel, onshore facility, or offshore facility from which the discharge occurs.

(2) Within sixty days after October 18, 1972, the President shall prepare and publish a National Contingency Plan for removal of oil and hazardous substances, pursuant to this subsection. Such National Contingency Plan shall provide for efficient, coordinated, and effective action to minimize damage from oil and hazardous substance discharges, including containment, dispersal, and removal of oil and hazardous substances, and shall include, but not be limited to —

(A) assignment of duties and responsibilities among Federal departments and agencies in coordination with State and local agencies, including, but not limited to, water pollution control, conservation, and port authorities;

(B) identification, procurement, maintenance, and storage of equipment and supplies;

(C) establishment or designation of a strike force consisting of personnel who shall be trained, prepared, and available to provide necessary services to carry out the Plan, including the establishment at major ports, to be determined by the President, of emergency task forces of trained personnel, adequate oil and hazardous substance pollution control equipment and material, and a detailed oil and hazardous substance pollution prevention and removal plan;

(D) a system of surveillance and notice designed to insure earliest possible notice of discharges of oil and hazardous substances and imminent threats of such discharges to the appropriate State and Federal agencies;

(E) establishment of a national center to provide coordination and direction for operations in carrying out the Plan;

(F) procedures and techniques to be employed in identifying, containing, dispersing, and removing oil and hazardous substances;

(G) a schedule, prepared in cooperation with the States, identifying (i) dispersants and other chemicals, if any, that may be used in carrying out the Plan, (ii) the waters in which such dispersants and chemicals may be used, and (iii) the quantities of such dispersant or chemical which can be used safely in such waters, which schedule shall provide in the case of any dispersant, chemical, or waters not specifically identified in such schedule that the President, or his delegate, may, on a case-by-case basis, identify the dispersants and other chemicals which may be used, the waters in which they may be used, and the quantities which can be used safely in such waters; and

(H) a system whereby the State or States affected by a discharge of oil or hazardous substance may act where necessary to remove such discharge and such State or States may be reimbursed from the fund established under subsection (k) of this section for the reasonable costs incurred in such removal.

The President may, from time to time, as he deems advisable revise or otherwise amend the National Contingency Plan. After publication of the National Contingency Plan, the removal of oil and hazardous substances and actions to minimize damage from oil and hazardous substance discharges shall, to the greatest extent possible, be in accordance with the National Contingency Plan.

(d) MARITIME DISASTER DISCHARGES

Whenever a marine disaster in or upon the navigable waters of the United States has created a substantial threat of a pollution hazard to the public health or welfare of the United States, including, but not limited to, fish, shellfish, and wildlife and the public and private shorelines and beaches of the United States, because of a discharge, or an imminent discharge, of large quantities of oil, or of a hazardous substance from a vessel the United States may (A) coordinate and direct all public and private efforts directed at the removal or elimination of such threat; and (B) summarily remove, and, if necessary, destroy such vessel by whatever means are available without regard to any provisions of law governing the employment of personnel or the expenditure of appropriated funds. Any expense incurred under this subsection or under the Intervention on the High Seas Act

[33 U.S.C. 1471 et seq.] (or the convention defined in section 2(3) thereof [33 U.S.C. 1471(3)]) shall be a cost incurred by the United States Government for the purposes of subsection (f) of this section in the removal of oil or hazardous substance.

(e) **JUDICIAL RELIEF**

In addition to any other action taken by a State or local government, when the President determines there is an imminent and substantial threat to the public health or welfare of the United States, including, but not limited to, fish, shellfish, and wildlife and public and private property, shorelines, and beaches within the United States, because of an actual or threatened discharge of oil or hazardous substance into or upon the navigable waters of the United States from an onshore or offshore facility, the President may require the United States attorney of the district in which the threat occurs to secure such relief as may be necessary to abate such threat, and the district courts of the United States shall have jurisdiction to grant such relief as the public interest and the equities of the case may require.

(f) **LIABILITY FOR ACTUAL COSTS OF REMOVAL**

(1) Except where an owner or operator can prove that a discharge was caused solely by (A) an act of God, (B) an act of war, (C) negligence on the part of the United States Government, or (D) an act or omission of a third party without regard to whether any such act or omission was or was not negligent, or any combination of the foregoing clauses, such owner or operator of any vessel from which oil or a hazardous substance is discharged in violation of subsection (b)(3) of this section shall, notwithstanding any other provision of law, be liable to the United States Government for the actual costs incurred under subsection (c) of this section for the removal of such oil or substance by the United States Government in an amount not to exceed, in the case of an inland oil barge $125 per gross ton of such barge, or $125,000, whichever is greater, and in the case of any other vessel, $150 per gross ton of such vessel (or, for a vessel carrying oil or hazardous substances as cargo, $250,000), whichever is greater, except that where the United States can show that such discharge was the result of willful negligence of willful misconduct within the privity and knowledge of the owner, such owner or operator shall be liable to the United States Government for the full amount of such costs. Such costs shall constitute a maritime lien on such vessel which may be recovered in an action in rem in the district court of the United States for any district within which any vessel may be found. The United States may also bring an action against the owner or operator of such vessel in any court of competent jurisdiction to recover such costs.

(2) Except where an owner or operator of an onshore facility can prove that a discharge was caused solely by (A) an act of God, (B) an act of war, (C) negligence on the part of the United States Government, or (D) an act or omission of a third party without regard to whether any such act or omission was or was not negligent, or any combination of the foregoing clauses, such owner or

operator of any such facility from which oil or a hazardous substance is discharged in violation of subsection (b)(3) of this section shall be liable to the United States Government for the actual costs incurred under subsection (c) of this section for the removal of such oil or substance by the United States Government in an amount not to exceed $50,000,000, except that where the United Sates can show that such discharge was the result of willful negligence or willful misconduct within the privity and knowledge of the owner, such owner or operator shall be liable to the United States Government for the full amount of such costs. The United States may bring an action against the owner or operator of such facility in any court of competent jurisdiction to recover such costs. The Administrator is authorized, by regulation, after consultation with the Secretary of Commerce and the Small Business Administration, to establish reasonable and equitable classifications of those onshore facilities having a total fixed storage capacity of 1,000 barrels or less which he determines because of size, type, and location do not present a substantial risk of the discharge of oil or a hazardous substance in violation of subsection (b)(3) of this section, and apply with respect to such classifications differing limits of liability which may be less than the amount contained in this paragraph.

(3) Except where an owner or operator of an offshore facility can prove that a discharge was caused solely by (A) an act of God, (B) an act of war, (C) negligence on the part of the United States Government, or (D) an act or omission of a third party without regard to whether any such act or omission was or was not negligent, or any combination of the foregoing clauses, such owner or operator of any such facility from which oil or a hazardous substance is discharged in violation of subsection (b)(3) of this section shall, notwithstanding any other provision of law, be liable to the United States Government for the actual costs incurred under subsection (c) of this section for the removal of such oil or substance by the United States Government in an amount not to exceed $50,000,000, except that where the United States can show that such discharge was the result of willful negligence or willful misconduct within the privity and knowledge of the owner, such owner or operator shall be liable to the United States Government for the full amount of such costs. The United States may bring an action against the owner or operator of such a facility in any court of competent jurisdiction to recover such costs.

(4) The costs of removal of oil or a hazardous substance for which the owner or operator of a vessel or onshore or offshore facility is liable under subsection (f) of this section shall include any costs or expenses incurred by the Federal Government or any State government in the restoration or replacement of natural resources damaged or destroyed as a result of a discharge of oil or a hazardous substance in violation of subsection (b) of this section.

(5) The President, or the authorized representative of any State, shall act on behalf of the public as trustee of the natural resources to recover for the costs of replacing or restoring such resources. Sums recovered shall be used to restore, rehabilitate, or acquire the equivalent of such natural resources by the appropriate agencies of the Federal Government, or the State government.

(g) THIRD PARTY LIABILITY

Where the owner or operator of a vessel (other than an inland oil barge) carrying oil or hazardous substances as cargo or an onshore or offshore facility which handles or stores oil or hazardous substances in bulk, from which oil or a hazardous substance is discharged in violation of subsection (b) of this section, alleges that such discharge was caused solely by an act or omission of a third party, such owner or operator shall pay to the United States Government the actual costs incurred under subsection (c) of this section for removal of such oil or substance and shall be entitled by subrogation to all rights of the United States Government to recover such costs from such third party under this subsection. In any case where an owner or operator of a vessel, of an onshore facility, or of an offshore facility, from which oil or a hazardous substance is discharged in violation of subsection (b)(3) of this section, proves that such discharge of oil or hazardous substance was caused solely by an act or omission of a third party, or was caused solely by such an act or omission in combination with an act of God, an act of war, or negligence on the part of the United States Government, such third party shall, notwithstanding any other provision of law, be liable to the United States Government for the actual costs incurred under subsection (c) of this section for removal of such oil or substance by the United States Government, except where such third party can prove that such discharge was caused solely by (A) an act of God, (B) an act of war, (C) negligence on the part of the United States Government, or (D) an act or omission of another party without regard to whether such act or omission was or was not negligent, or any combination of the foregoing clauses. If such third party was the owner or operator of a vessel which caused the discharge of oil or a hazardous substance in violation of subsection (b)(3) of this section, the liability of such third party under this subsection shall not exceed, in the case of an inland oil barge $125 per gross ton of such barge, or $125,000, whichever is greater, and in the case of any other vessel, $150 per gross ton of such vessel (or, for a vessel carrying oil or hazardous substances as cargo, $250,000), whichever is greater. In any other case the liability of such third party shall not exceed the limitation which would have been applicable to the owner or operator of the vessel or the onshore or offshore facility from which the discharge actually occurred if such owner or operator were liable. If the United States can show that the discharge of oil or a hazardous substance in violation of subsection (b)(3) of this section was the result of willful negligence or willful misconduct within the privity and knowledge of such third party, such third party shall be liable to the United States Government for the full amount of such removal costs. The United States may bring an action against the third party in any court of competent jurisdiction to recover such removal costs.

(h) RIGHTS AGAINST THIRD PARTIES WHO CAUSED OR CONTRIBUTED TO DISCHARGE

The liabilities established by this section shall in no way affect any rights which (1) the owner or operator of a vessel or of an onshore facility or an offshore facility may have against any third party whose acts may in any way have caused

§1321   Clean Water Act

or contributed to such discharge, or (2) the United States Government may have against any third party whose actions may in any way have caused or contributed to the discharge of oil or hazardous substance.

(i) **RECOVERY OF REMOVAL COSTS**

(1) In any case where an owner or operator of a vessel or an onshore facility or an offshore facility from which oil or a hazardous substance is discharged in violation of subsection (b)(3) of this section acts to remove such oil or substance in accordance with regulations promulgated pursuant to this section, such owner or operator shall be entitled to recover the reasonable costs incurred in such removal upon establishing, in a suit which may be brought against the United States Government in the United States Claims Court, that such discharge was caused solely by (A) an act of God, (B) an act of war, (C) negligence on the part of the United States Government, or (D) an act or omission of a third party without regard to whether such act or omission was or was not negligent, or of any combination of the foregoing causes.

(2) The provisions of this subsection shall not apply in any case where liability is established pursuant to the Outer Continental Shelf Lands Act [43 U.S.C. 1331 et seq.], or the Deepwater Port Act of 1974 [33 U.S.C. 1501 et seq.].

(3) Any amount paid in accordance with a judgment of the United States Claims Court pursuant to this section shall be paid from the funds established pursuant to subsection (k) of this section.

(j) **REGULATIONS; PENALTY**

(1) Consistent with the National Contingency Plan required by subsection (c)(2) of this section, as soon as practicable after October 18, 1972, and from time to time thereafter, the President shall issue regulations consistent with maritime safety and with marine and navigation laws (A) establishing methods and procedures for removal of discharged oil and hazardous substances. (B) establishing criteria for the development and implementation of local and regional oil and hazardous substance removal contingency plans, (C) establishing procedures, methods, and equipment and other requirements for equipment to prevent discharges of oil and hazardous substances from vessels and from onshore facilities and offshore facilities, and to contain such discharges, and (D) governing the inspection of vessels carrying cargoes of oil and hazardous substances and the inspection of such cargoes in order to reduce the likelihood of discharges of oil from vessels in violation of this section.

(2) Any owner or operator of a vessel or an onshore facility or an offshore facility and any other person subject to any regulation issued under paragraph (1) of this subsection who fails or refuses to comply with the provisions of any such regulations, shall be liable to a civil penalty of not more than $5,000 for each such violation. This paragraph shall not apply to any owner or operator of any vessel from which oil or a hazardous substance is discharged in violation of paragraph (3)(ii) of subsection (b) of this section unless such owner, operator, or

Clean Water Act §1321

person in charge is otherwise subject to the jurisdiction of the United States. Each violation shall be a separate offense. The President may assess and compromise such penalty. No penalty shall be assessed until the owner, operator, or other person charged shall have been given notice and an opportunity for a hearing on such charge. In determining the amount of the penalty, or the amount agreed upon in compromise, the gravity of the violation, and the demonstrated good faith of the owner, operator, or other person charged in attempting to achieve rapid compliance, after notification of a violation, shall be considered by the President.

(k) AUTHORIZATION OF APPROPRIATIONS; SUPPLEMENTAL APPROPRIATIONS

(1) There is hereby authorized to be appropriated to a revolving fund to be established in the Treasury such sums as may be necessary to maintain such fund at a level of $35,000,000 to carry out the provisions of subsections (c), (d), (i), and (l) of this section. Any other funds received by the United States under this section shall also be deposited in said fund for such purposes. All sums appropriated to, or deposited in, said fund shall remain available until expended.

(2) The Secretary of Transportation shall notify the Congress whenever the unobligated balance of the fund is less than $12,000,000, and shall include in such notification a recommendation for a supplemental appropriation relating to the sums that are needed to maintain the fund at the level provided in paragraph (1).

(l) ADMINISTRATION

The President is authorized to delegate the administration of this section to the heads of those Federal departments, agencies, and instrumentalities which he determines to be appropriate. Any moneys in the fund established by subsection (k) of this section shall be available to such Federal departments, agencies, and instrumentalities to carry out the provisions of subsections (c) and (i) of this section. Each such department, agency, and instrumentality, in order to avoid duplication of effort, shall, whenever appropriate, utilize the personnel, services, and facilities of other Federal departments, agencies, and instrumentalities.

(m) BOARDING AND INSPECTION OF VESSELS; ARREST; EXECUTION OF WARRANTS OR OTHER PROCESS

Anyone authorized by the President to enforce the provisions of this section may, except as to public vessels, (A) board and inspect any vessel upon the navigable waters of the United States or the waters of the contiguous zone, (B) with or without a warrant arrest any person who violates the provisions of this section or any regulation issued thereunder in his presence or view, and (C) execute any warrant or other process issued by an officer or court of competent jurisdiction.

(n) JURISDICTION

The several district courts of the United States are invested with jurisdiction for any actions, other than actions pursuant to subsection (i)(1) of this section, arising under this section. In the case of Guam and the Trust Territory of the Pacific Islands, such actions may be brought in the district court of Guam, and in the case of the Virgin Islands such actions may be brought in the district court of the Virgin Islands. In the case of American Samoa and the Trust Territory of the Pacific Islands, such actions may be brought in the District Court of the United States for the District of Hawaii and such court shall have jurisdiction of such actions. In the case of the Canal Zone, such actions may be brought in the United States District Court for the District of the Canal Zone.

(o) **OBLIGATION FOR DAMAGES UNAFFECTED; LOCAL AUTHORITY NOT PREEMPTED; EXISTING FEDERAL AUTHORITY NOT MODIFIED OR AFFECTED**

(1) Nothing in this section shall affect or modify in any way the obligations of any owner or operator of any vessel, or of any owner or operator of any onshore facility or offshore facility to any person or agency under any provision of law for damages to any publicly owned or privately owned property resulting from a discharge of any oil or hazardous substance or from the removal of any such oil or hazardous substance.

(2) Nothing in this section shall be construed as preempting any State or political subdivision thereof from imposing any requirement or liability with respect of the discharge of oil or hazardous substance into any waters within such State.

(3) Nothing in this section shall be construed as affecting or modifying any other existing authority of any Federal department, agency, or instrumentality, relative to onshore or offshore facilities under this chapter or any other provision of law, or to affect any State or local law not in conflict with this section.

(p) **FINANCIAL RESPONSIBILITY**

(1) Any vessel over three hundred gross tons, including any barge of equivalent size, but not including any barge that is not self-propelled and that does not carry oil or hazardous substances as cargo or fuel, using any port or place in the United States or the navigable waters of the United States for any purpose shall establish and maintain under regulations to be prescribed from time to time by the President, evidence of financial responsibility of, in the case of an inland oil barge $125 per gross ton of such barge, or $125,000, whichever is greater, and in the case of any other vessel, $150 per gross ton of such vessel (or, for a vessel carrying oil or hazardous substances as cargo, $250,000), whichever is greater, to meet the liability to the United States which such vessel could be subjected under this section. In cases where an owner or operator owns, operates, or charters more than one such vessel, financial responsibility need only be established to meet the maximum liability to which the largest of such vessels could be subjected. Financial responsibility may be established by any one of, or a combination of, the following methods acceptable to the President: (A) evidence of insurance, (B) surety bonds, (C) qualification as a self-insurer, or (D) other evidence of financial responsibility. Any bond filed shall be issued by a bonding company authorized to do business in the United States.

(2) The provisions of paragraph (1) of this subsection shall be effective April

3, 1971, with respect to oil and one year after October 18, 1972, with respect to hazardous substances. The President shall delegate the responsibility to carry out the provisions of this subsection to the appropriate agency head within sixty days after October 18, 1972. Regulations necessary to implement this subsection shall be issued within six months after October 18, 1972.

(3) Any claim for costs incurred by such vessel may be brought directly against the insurer or any other person providing evidence of financial responsibility as required under this subsection. In the case of any action pursuant to this subsection such insurer or other person shall be entitled to invoke all rights and defenses which would have been available to the owner or operator if an action had been brought against him by the claimant, and which would have been available to him if an action had been brought against him by the owner or operator.

(4) Any owner or operator of a vessel subject to this subsection, who fails to comply with the provisions of this subsection or any regulation issued thereunder, shall be subject to a fine of not more than $10,000.

(5) The Secretary of the Treasury may refuse the clearance required by section 91 of title 46, Appendix, to any vessel subject to this subsection, which does not have evidence furnished by the President that the financial responsibility provisions of paragraph (1) of this subsection have been complied with.

(6) The Secretary of the Department in which the Coast Guard is operated may (A) deny entry to any port or place in the United States or the navigable waters of the United States, to, and (B) detain at the port or place in the United States from which it is about to depart for any other port or place in the United States, any vessel subject to this subsection, which upon request, does not produce evidence furnished by the President that the financial responsibility provisions of paragraph (1) of this subsection have been complied with.

(q) **ESTABLISHMENT OF MAXIMUM LIMIT OF LIABILITY WITH RESPECT TO ONSHORE OR OFFSHORE FACILITIES**

The President is authorized to establish, with respect to any class or category of onshore or offshore facilities, a maximum limit of liability under subsections (f)(2) and (3) of this section of less than $50,000,000, but not less than $8,000,000.

(r) **LIABILITY LIMITATIONS NOT TO LIMIT LIABILITY UNDER OTHER LEGISLATION**

Nothing in this section shall be construed to impose, or authorize the imposition of, any limitation on liability under the Outer Continental Shelf Lands Act [43 U.S.C. 1331 et seq.] or the Deepwater Port Act of 1974 [33 U.S.C. 1501 et seq.].

§1322. MARINE SANITATION DEVICES

(a) **DEFINITIONS**

For the purpose of this section, the term —
  (1) "new vessel" includes every description of watercraft or other artifi-

cial contrivance used, or capable of being used, as a means of transportation on the navigable waters, the construction of which is initiated after promulgation of standards and regulations under this section;

(2) "existing vessel" includes every description of watercraft or other artificial contrivance used, or capable of being used, as a means of transportation on the navigable waters, the construction of which is initiated before promulgation of standards and regulations under this section;

(3) "public vessel" means a vessel owned or bareboat chartered and operated by the United States, by a State or political subdivision thereof, or by a foreign nation, except when such vessel is engaged in commerce;

(4) "United States" includes the States, the District of Columbia, the Commonwealth of Puerto Rico, the Virgin Islands, Guam, American Samoa, the Canal Zone, and the Trust Territory of the Pacific Islands;

(5) "marine sanitation device" includes any equipment for installation on board a vessel which is designed to receive, retain, treat, or discharge sewage, and any process to treat such sewage;

(6) "sewage" means human body wastes and the wastes from toilets and other receptacles intended to receive or retain body wastes except that, with respect to commercial vessels on the Great Lakes, such term shall include graywater;

(7) "manufacturer" means any person engaged in the manufacturing, assembling, or importation of marine sanitation devices or of vessels subject to standards and regulations promulgated under this section;

(8) "person" means an individual, partnership, firm, corporation, or association, but does not include an individual on board a public vessel;

(9) "discharge" includes, but is not limited to, any spilling, leaking, pumping, pouring, emitting, emptying or dumping;

(10) "commercial vessels" means those vessels used in the business of transporting property for compensation or hire, or in transporting property in the business of the owner, lessee, or operator of the vessel;

(11) "graywater" means galley, bath, and shower water.

(b) **FEDERAL STANDARDS OF PERFORMANCE**

(1) As soon as possible, after October 18, 1972, and subject to the provisions of section 1254(j) of this title, the Administrator, after consultation with the Secretary of the department in which the Coast Guard is operating, after giving appropriate consideration to the economic costs involved, and within the limits of available technology, shall promulgate Federal standards of performance for marine sanitation devices (hereafter in this section referred to as "standards") which shall be designed to prevent the discharge of untreated or inadequately treated sewage into or upon the navigable waters from new vessels and existing vessels, except vessels not equipped with installed toilet facilities. Such standards and standards established under subsection (c)(1)(B) of this section shall be consistent with maritime safety and the marine and navigation laws and regulations and shall be coordinated with the regulations issued under this

Clean Water Act §1322

subsection by the Secretary of the department in which the Coast Guard is operating. The Secretary of the department in which the Coast Guard is operating shall promulgate regulations, which are consistent with standards promulgated under this subsection and subsection (c) of this section and with maritime safety and the marine and navigation laws and regulations governing the design, construction, installation, and operation of any marine sanitation device on board such vessels.

(2) Any existing vessel equipped with a marine sanitation device on the date of promulgation of initial standards and regulations under this section, which device is in compliance with such initial standards and regulations, shall be deemed in compliance with this section until such time as the device is replaced or is found not to be in compliance with such initial standards and regulations.

(c) **INITIAL STANDARDS; EFFECTIVE DATES; REVISION; WAIVER**

(1)(A) Initial standards and regulations under this section shall become effective for new vessels two years after promulgation; and for existing vessels five years after promulgation. Revisions of standards and regulations shall be effective upon promulgation, unless another effective date is specified, except that no revision shall take effect before the effective date of the standard or regulation being revised.

(B) The Administrator shall, with respect to commercial vessels on the Great Lakes, establish standards which require at a minimum the equivalent of secondary treatment as defined under section 1314(d) of this title. Such standards and regulations shall take effect for existing vessels after such time as the Administrator determines to be reasonable for the upgrading of marine sanitation devices to attain such standard.

(2) The Secretary of the department in which the Coast Guard is operating with regard to his regulatory authority established by this section, after consultation with the Administrator, may distinguish among classes, type, and sizes of vessels as well as between new and existing vessels, and may waive applicability of standards and regulations as necessary or appropriate for such classes, types, and sizes of vessels (including existing vessels equipped with marine sanitation devices on the date of promulgation of the initial standards required by this section), and, upon application, for individual vessels.

(d) **VESSELS OWNED AND OPERATED BY THE UNITED STATES**

The provisions of this section and the standards and regulations promulgated hereunder apply to vessels owned and operated by the United States unless the Secretary of Defense finds that compliance would not be in the interest of national security. With respect to vessels owned and operated by the Department of Defense, regulations under the last sentence of subsection (b)(1) of this section and certifications under subsection (g)(2) of this section shall be promulgated and issued by the Secretary of Defense.

(e) **PRE-PROMULGATION CONSULTATION**

Before the standards and regulations under this section are promulgated, the Administrator and the Secretary of the department in which the Coast Guard is operating shall consult with the Secretary of State; the Secretary of Health and Human Services; the Secretary of Defense; the Secretary of the Treasury; the Secretary of Commerce; other interested Federal agencies; and the States and industries interested; and otherwise comply with the requirements of section 553 of title 5.

(f) **REGULATION BY STATES OR POLITICAL SUBDIVISIONS THEREOF; COMPLETE PROHIBITION UPON DISCHARGE OF SEWAGE**

(1)(A) Except as provided in subparagraph (B), after the effective date of the initial standards and regulations promulgated under this section, no State or political subdivision thereof shall adopt or enforce any statute or regulation of such State or political subdivision with respect to the design, manufacture, or installation or use of any marine sanitation device on any vessel subject to the provisions of this section.

(B) A State may adopt and enforce a statute or regulation with respect to the design, manufacture, or installation or use of any marine sanitation device on a houseboat, if such statute or regulation is more stringent than the standards and regulations promulgated under this section. For purposes of this paragraph, the term "houseboat" means a vessel which, for a period of time determined by the State in which the vessel is located, is used primarily as a residence and is not used primarily as a means of transportation.

(2) If, after promulgation of the initial standards and regulations and prior to their effective date, a vessel is equipped with a marine sanitation device in compliance with such standards and regulations and the installation and operation of such device is in accordance with such standards and regulations, such standards and regulations shall, for the purposes of paragraph (1) of this subsection, become effective with respect to such vessel on the date of such compliance.

(3) After the effective date of the initial standards and regulations promulgated under this section, if any State determines that the protection and enhancement of the quality of some or all of the waters within such State require greater environmental protection, such State may completely prohibit the discharge from all vessels of any sewage, whether treated or not, into such waters, except that no such prohibition shall apply until the Administrator determines that adequate facilities for the safe and sanitary removal and treatment of sewage from all vessels are reasonably available for such water to which such prohibition would apply. Upon application of the State, the Administrator shall make such determination within 90 days of the date of such application.

(4)(A) If the Administrator determines upon application by a State that the protection and enhancement of the quality of specified waters within such State requires such a prohibition, he shall by regulation completely prohibit the discharge from a vessel of any sewage (whether treated or not) into such waters.

(B) Upon application by a State, the Administrator shall, by regulation, establish a drinking water intake zone in any waters within such State and prohibit the discharge of sewage from vessels within that zone.

(g) SALES LIMITED TO CERTIFIED DEVICES; CERTIFICATION OF TEST DEVICE; RECORDKEEPING; REPORTS

(1) No manufacturer of a marine sanitation device shall sell, offer for sale, or introduce or deliver for introduction in interstate commerce, or import into the United States for sale or resale any marine sanitation device manufactured after the effective date of the standards and regulations promulgated under this section unless such device is in all material respects substantially the same as a test device certified under this subsection.

(2) Upon application of the manufacturer, the Secretary of the department in which the Coast Guard is operating shall so certify a marine sanitation device if he determines, in accordance with the provisions of this paragraph, that it meets the appropriate standards and regulations promulgated under this section. The Secretary of the department in which the Coast Guard is operating shall test or require such testing of the device in accordance with procedures set forth by the Administrator as to standards of performance and for such other purposes as may be appropriate. If the Secretary of the department in which the Coast Guard is operating determines that the device is satisfactory from the standpoint of safety and any other requirements of maritime law or regulation, and after consideration of the design, installation, operation, material, or other appropriate factors, he shall certify the device. Any device manufactured by such manufacturer which is in all material respects substantially the same as the certified test device shall be deemed to be in conformity with the appropriate standards and regulations established under this section.

(3) Every manufacturer shall establish and maintain such records, make such reports, and provide such information as the Administrator or the Secretary of the department in which the Coast Guard is operating may reasonably require to enable him to determine whether such manufacturer has acted or is acting in compliance with this section and regulations issued thereunder and shall, upon request of an officer or employee duly designated by the Administrator or the Secretary of the department in which the Coast Guard is operating, permit such officer or employee at reasonable times to have access to and copy such records. All information reported to or otherwise obtained by the Administrator or the Secretary of the Department in which the Coast Guard is operating or their representatives pursuant to this subsection which contains or relates to a trade secret or other matter referred to in section 1905 of title 18 shall be considered confidential for the purpose of that section, except that such information may be disclosed to other officers or employees concerned with carrying out this sec-

tion. This paragraph shall not apply in the case of the construction of a vessel by an individual for his own use.

(h) SALE AND RESALE OF PROPERLY EQUIPPED VESSELS; OPERABILITY OF CERTIFIED MARINE SANITATION DEVICES

After the effective date of standards and regulations promulgated under this section, it shall be unlawful —

(1) for the manufacturer of any vessel subject to such standards and regulations to manufacture for sale, to sell or offer for sale, or to distribute for sale or resale any such vessel unless it is equipped with a marine sanitation device which is in all material respects substantially the same as the appropriate test device certified pursuant to this section;

(2) for any person, prior to the sale or delivery of a vessel subject to such standards and regulations to the ultimate purchaser, wrongfully to remove or render inoperative any certified marine sanitation device or element of design of such device installed in such vessel;

(3) for any person to fail or refuse to permit access to or copying of records or to fail to make reports or provide information required under this section; and

(4) for a vessel subject to such standards and regulations to operate on the navigable waters of the United States, if such vessel is not equipped with an operable marine sanitation device certified pursuant to this section.

(i) JURISDICTION TO RESTRAIN VIOLATIONS; CONTEMPTS

The district courts of the United States shall have jurisdictions to restrain violations of subsection (g)(1) of this section and subsections (h)(1) through (3) of this section. Actions to restrain such violations shall be brought by, and in, the name of the United States. In case of contumacy or refusal to obey a subpena served upon any person under this subsection, the district court of the United States for any district in which such person is found or resides or transacts business, upon application by the United States and after notice to such person, shall have jurisdiction to issue an order requiring such person to appear and give testimony or to appear and produce documents, and any failure to obey such order of the court may be punished by such court as a contempt thereof.

(j) PENALTIES

Any person who violates subsection (g)(1) of this section or clause (1) or (2) of subsection (h) of this section shall be liable to a civil penalty of not more than $5,000 for each violation. Any person who violates clause (4) of subsection (h) of this section or any regulation issued pursuant to this section shall be liable to a civil penalty of not more than $2,000 for each violation. Each violation shall be a separate offense. The Secretary of the department in which the Coast Guard is operating may assess and compromise any such penalty. No penalty shall be assessed until the person charged shall have been given notice and an opportunity for a hearing on such charge. In determining the amount of the

Clean Water Act §1323

penalty, or the amount agreed upon in compromise, the gravity of the violation, and the demonstrated good faith of the person charged in attempting to achieve rapid compliance, after notification of a violation, shall be considered by said Secretary.

(k) ENFORCEMENT AUTHORITY

The provisions of this section shall be enforced by the Secretary of the department in which the Coast Guard is operating and he may utilize by agreement, with or without reimbursement, law enforcement officers or other personnel and facilities of the Administrator, other Federal agencies, or the States to carry out the provisions of this section. The provisions of this section may also be enforced by a State.

(l) BOARDING AND INSPECTION OF VESSELS; EXECUTION OF WARRANTS AND OTHER PROCESS

Anyone authorized by the Secretary of the department in which the Coast Guard is operating to enforce the provisions of this section may, except as to public vessels, (1) board and inspect any vessel upon the navigable waters of the United States and (2) execute any warrant or other process issued by an officer or court of competent jurisdiction.

(m) ENFORCEMENT IN UNITED STATES POSSESSIONS

In the case of Guam and the Trust Territory of the Pacific Islands, actions arising under this section may be brought in the district court of Guam, and in the case of the Virgin Islands such actions may be brought in the district court of the Virgin Islands. In the case of American Samoa and the Trust Territory of the Pacific Islands, such actions may be brought in the District Court of the United States for the District of Hawaii and such court shall have jurisdiction of such actions. In the case of the Canal Zone, such actions may be brought in the District Court for the District of the Canal Zone.

§1323. FEDERAL FACILITIES POLLUTION CONTROL

(a) Each department, agency, or instrumentality of the executive, legislative, and judicial branches of the Federal Government (1) having jurisdiction over any property or facility, or (2) engaged in any activity resulting, or which may result, in the discharge or runoff of pollutants, and each officer, agent, or employee thereof in the performance of his official duties, shall be subject to, and comply with, all Federal, State, interstate, and local requirements, administrative authority, and process and sanctions respecting the control and abatement of water pollution in the same manner, and to the same extent as any nongovernmental entity including the payment of reasonable service charges. The preceding sentence shall apply (A) to any requirement whether substantive or procedural (including any recordkeeping or reporting requirement, any requirement respecting permits and any other requirement, whatsoever), (B) to the

§1323

Clean Water Act

exercise of any Federal, State, or local administrative authority, and (C) to any process and sanction, whether enforced in Federal, State, or local courts or in any other manner. This subsection shall apply notwithstanding any immunity of such agencies, officers, agents, or employees under any law or rule of law. Nothing in this section shall be construed to prevent any department, agency, or instrumentality of the Federal Government, or any officer, agent, or employee thereof in the performance of his official duties, from removing to the appropriate Federal district court any proceeding to which the department, agency, or instrumentality or officer, agent, or employee thereof is subject pursuant to this section, and any such proceeding may be removed in accordance with section 1441 et seq. of title 28. No officer, agent, or employee of the United States shall be personally liable for any civil penalty arising from the performance of his official duties, for which he is not otherwise liable, and the United States shall be liable only for those civil penalties arising under Federal law or imposed by a State or local court to enforce an order or the process of such court. The President may exempt any effluent source of any department, agency, or instrumentality in the executive branch from compliance with any such a requirement if he determines it to be in the paramount interest of the United States to do so; except that no exemption may be granted from the requirements of section 1316 or 1317 of this title. No such exemptions shall be granted due to lack of appropriation unless the President shall have specifically requested such appropriation as a part of the budgetary process and the Congress shall have failed to make available such requested appropriation. Any exemption shall be for a period not in excess of one year, but additional exemptions may be granted for periods of not to exceed one year upon the President's making a new determination. The President shall report each January to the Congress all exemptions from the requirements of this section granted during the preceding calendar year, together with his reason for granting such exemption. In addition to any such exemption of a particular effluent source, the President may, if he determines it to be in the paramount interest of the United States to do so, issue regulations exempting from compliance with the requirements of this section any weaponry, equipment, aircraft, vessels, vehicles, or other classes or categories of property, and access to such property, which are owned or operated by the Armed Forces of the United States (including the Coast Guard) or by the National Guard of any State and which are uniquely military in nature. The President shall reconsider the need for such regulations at three-year intervals.

(b)(1) The Administrator shall coordinate with the head of each department, agency, or instrumentality of the Federal Government having jurisdiction over any property or facility utilizing federally owned wastewater facilities to develop a program of cooperation for utilizing wastewater control systems utilizing those innovative treatment processes and techniques for which guidelines have been promulgated under section 1314(d)(3) of this title. Such program shall include an inventory of property and facilities which could utilize such processes and techniques.

(2) Construction shall not be initiated for facilities for treatment of wastewater at any Federal property or facility after September 30, 1979, if

Clean Water Act §1324

alternative methods for wastewater treatment at such property or facility utilizing innovative treatment processes and techniques, including but not limited to methods utilizing recycle and reuse techniques and land treatment are not utilized, unless the life cycle cost of the alternative treatment works exceeds the life cycle cost of the most cost effective alternative by more than 15 per centum. The Administrator may waive the application of this paragraph in any case where the Administrator determines it to be in the public interest, or that compliance with this paragraph would interfere with the orderly compliance with conditions of a permit issued pursuant to section 1342 of this title.

§1324. CLEAN LAKES

(a) ESTABLISHMENT AND SCOPE OF PROGRAM

(1) STATE PROGRAM REQUIREMENTS

Each State on a biennial basis shall prepare and submit to the Administrator for his approval —

(A) an identification and classification according to eutrophic condition of all publicly owned lakes in such State;

(B) a description of procedures, processes, and methods (including land use requirements), to control sources of pollution of such lakes;

(C) a description of methods and procedures, in conjunction with appropriate Federal agencies, to restore the quality of such lakes;

(D) methods and procedures to mitigate the harmful effects of high acidity, including innovative methods of neutralizing and restoring buffering capacity of lakes and methods of removing from lakes toxic metals and other toxic substances mobilized by high acidity;

(E) a list and description of those publicly owned lakes in such State for which uses are known to be impaired, including those lakes which are known not to meet applicable water quality standards or which require implementation of control programs to maintain compliance with applicable standards and those lakes in which water quality has deteriorated as a result of high acidity that may reasonably be due to acid deposition; and

(F) an assessment of the status and trends of water quality in lakes in such State, including but not limited to, the nature and extent of pollution loading from point and nonpoint sources and the extent to which the use of lakes is impaired as a result of such pollution, particularly with respect to toxic pollution.

(2) SUBMISSION AS PART OF 1315(b)(1) REPORT

The information required under paragraph (1) shall be included in the report required under section 1315(b)(1) of this title, beginning with the report required under such section by April 1, 1988.

(3) REPORT OF ADMINISTRATOR

Not later than 180 days after receipt from the States of the biennial information required under paragraph (1), the Administrator shall submit to the Committee on Public Works and Transportation of the House of Representatives and the Committee on Environment and Public Works of the Senate a report on the status of water quality in lakes in the United States, including the effectiveness of the methods and procedures described in paragraph (1)(D).

(4) ELIGIBILITY REQUIREMENT

Beginning after April 1, 1988, a State must have submitted the information required under paragraph (1) in order to receive grant assistance under this section.

(b) FINANCIAL ASSISTANCE TO STATES

The Administrator shall provide financial assistance to States in order to carry out methods and procedures approved by him under subsection (a) of this section. The Administrator shall provide financial assistance to States to prepare the identification and classification surveys required in subsection (a)(1) of this section.

(c) MAXIMUM AMOUNT OF GRANT; AUTHORIZATION OF APPROPRIATIONS

(1) The amount granted to any State for any fiscal year under subsection (b) of this section shall not exceed 70 per centum of the funds expended by such State in such year for carrying out approved methods and procedures under subsection (a) of this section.

(2) There is authorized to be appropriated $50,000,000 for the fiscal year ending June 30, 1973; $100,000,000 for the fiscal year 1974; $150,000,000 for the fiscal year 1975, $50,000,000 for fiscal year 1977, $60,000,000 for fiscal year 1978, $60,000,000 for fiscal year 1979, $60,000,000 for fiscal year 1980, $30,000,000 for fiscal year 1981, $30,000,000 for fiscal year 1982, such sums as may be necessary for fiscal years 1983 through 1985, and $30,000,000 per fiscal year for each of the fiscal years 1986 through 1990 for grants to States under subsection (b) of this section which such sums shall remain available until expended. The Administrator shall provide for an equitable distribution of such sums to the States with approved methods and procedures under subsection (a) of this section.

(d) DEMONSTRATION PROGRAM

(1) GENERAL REQUIREMENTS

The Administrator is authorized and directed to establish and conduct at locations throughout the Nation a lake water quality demonstration program. The program shall, at a minimum —

(A) develop cost effective technologies for the control of pollutants to preserve or enhance lake water quality while optimizing multiple lakes uses;

(B) control nonpoint sources of pollution which are contributing to the degradation of water quality in lakes;

(C) Evaluate the feasibility of implementing regional consolidated pollution control strategies;

(D) demonstrate environmentally preferred techniques for the removal and disposal of contaminated lake sediments;

(E) develop improved methods for the removal of silt, stumps, aquatic growth, and other obstructions which impair the quality of lakes;

(F) construct and evaluate silt traps and other devices or equipment to prevent or abate the deposit of sediment in lakes; and

(G) demonstrate the costs and benefits of utilizing dredged material from lakes in the reclamation of despoiled land.

(2) GEOGRAPHICAL REQUIREMENTS

Demonstration projects authorized by this subsection shall be undertaken to reflect a variety of geographical and environmental conditions. As a priority, the Administrator shall undertake demonstration projects at Lake Houston, Texas; Beaver Lake, Arkansas; Greenwood Lake and Belcher Creek, New Jersey; Deal Lake, New Jersey; Alcyon Lake, New Jersey; Gorton's Pond, Rhode Island; Lake Washington, Rhode Island; Lake Bomoseen, Vermont; Sauk Lake, Minnesota; and Lake Worth, Texas.

(3) REPORTS

The Administrator shall report annually to the Committee on Public Works and Transportation of the House of Representatives and the Committee on Environment and Public Works of the Senate on work undertaken pursuant of this subsection. Upon completion of the program authorized by this subsection, the Administrator shall submit to such committees a final report on the results of such program, along with recommendations for further measures to improve the water quality of the Nation's lakes.

(4) AUTHORIZATION OF APPROPRIATIONS

(A) IN GENERAL

There is authorized to be appropriated to carry out this subsection not to exceed $40,000,000 for fiscal years beginning after September 30, 1986, to remain available until expended.

(B) SPECIAL AUTHORIZATIONS

(i) AMOUNT

There is authorized to be appropriated to carry out subsection (b) of this section with respect to subsection (a)(1)(D) of this section not to exceed $15,000,000 for fiscal years beginning after September 30, 1986, to remain available until expended.

(ii) **DISTRIBUTION OF FUNDS**

The Administrator shall provide for an equitable distribution of sums appropriated pursuant to this subparagraph among States carrying out approved methods and procedures. Such distribution shall be based on the relative needs of each such State for the mitigation of the harmful effects on lakes and other surface waters of high acidity that may reasonably be due to acid deposition or acid mine drainage.

(iii) **GRANTS AS ADDITIONAL ASSISTANCE**

The amount of any grant to a State under this subparagraph shall be in addition to, and not in lieu of, any other Federal financial assistance.

§1325. NATIONAL STUDY COMMISSION

(a) **ESTABLISHMENT**

There is established a National Study Commission, which shall make a full and complete investigation and study of all of the technological aspects of achieving, and all aspects of the total economic, social, and environmental effects of achieving or not achieving, the effluent limitations and goals set forth for 1983 in section 1311(b)(2) of this title.

(b) **MEMBERSHIP; CHAIRMAN**

Such Commission shall be composed of fifteen members, including five members of the Senate, who are members of the Environment and Public Works committee, appointed by the President of the Senate, five members of the House, who are members of the Public Works and Transportation committee, appointed by the Speaker of the House, and five members of the public appointed by the President. The Chairman of such Commission shall be elected from among its members.

(c) **CONTRACT AUTHORITY**

In the conduct of such study, the Commission is authorized to contract with the National Academy of Sciences and the National Academy of Engineering (acting through the National Research Council), the National Institute of Ecology, Brookings Institution, and other nongovernmental entities, for the investigation of matters within their competence.

(d) **COOPERATION OF DEPARTMENTS, AGENCIES, AND INSTRUMENTALITIES OF EXECUTIVE BRANCH**

The heads of the departments, agencies and instrumentalities of the executive branch of the Federal Government shall cooperate with the Commission in carrying out the requirements of this section, and shall furnish to the Commission such information as the Commission deems necessary to carry out this section.

(e) REPORT TO CONGRESS

A report shall be submitted to the Congress of the results of such investigation and study, together with recommendations, not later than three years after October 18, 1972.

(f) COMPENSATION AND ALLOWANCES

The members of the Commission who are not officers or employees of the United States, while attending conferences or meetings of the Commission or while otherwise serving at the request of the Chairman shall be entitled to receive compensation at a rate not in excess of the maximum rate of pay for Grade GS-18, as provided in the General Schedule under section 5332 of title 5, including traveltime and while away from their homes or regular places of business they may be allowed travel expenses, including per diem in lieu of subsistence as authorized by law for persons in the Government service employed intermittently.

(g) APPOINTMENT OF PERSONNEL

In addition to authority to appoint personnel subject to the provisions of title 5 governing appointments in the competitive service, and to pay such personnel in accordance with the provisions of chapter 51 and subchapter III of chapter 53 of such title relating to classification and General Schedule pay rates, the Commission shall have authority to enter into contracts with private or public organizations who shall furnish the Commission with such administrative and technical personnel as may be necessary to carry out the purpose of this section. Personnel furnished by such organizations under this subsection are not, and shall not be considered to be, Federal employees for any purposes, but in the performance of their duties shall be guided by the standards which apply to employees of the legislative branches under rules 41 and 43 of the Senate and House of Representatives, respectively.

(h) AUTHORIZATION OF APPROPRIATION

There is authorized to be appropriated, for use in carrying out this section, not to exceed $17,250,000.

§1326. THERMAL DISCHARGES

(a) EFFLUENT LIMITATIONS THAT WILL ASSURE PROTECTION AND PROPAGATION OF BALANCED, INDIGENOUS POPULATION OF SHELLFISH, FISH, AND WILDLIFE

With respect to any point source otherwise subject to the provisions of section 1311 of this title or section 1316 of this title, whenever the owner or operator of any such source, after opportunity for public hearing, can demonstrate to the satisfaction of the Administrator (or, if appropriate, the State) that any effluent limitation proposed for the control of the thermal component of any discharge from such source will require effluent limitations more stringent than necessary to assure the projection and propagation of a balanced, indigenous population of shellfish, fish, and wildlife in and on the body of water into which the discharge is to be made, the Administrator (or, if appropriate, the State) may impose an effluent limitation under such sections for such plant, with respect to the thermal component of such discharge (taking into account the interaction of such thermal component with other pollutants), that will assure the protection and propagation of a balanced, indigenous population of shellfish, fish, and wildlife in and on that body of water.

(b) COOLING WATER INTAKE STRUCTURES

Any standard established pursuant to section 1311 of this title or section 1316 of this title and applicable to a point source shall require that the location, design, construction, and capacity of cooling water intake structures reflect the best technology available for minimizing adverse environmental impact.

(c) PERIOD OF PROTECTION FROM MORE STRINGENT EFFLUENT LIMITATIONS FOLLOWING DISCHARGE POINT SOURCE MODIFICATION COMMENCED AFTER OCTOBER 18, 1972

Notwithstanding any other provision of this chapter, any point source of a discharge having a thermal component, the modification of which point source is commenced after October 18, 1972, and which, as modified, meets effluent limitations established under section 1311 of this title or, if more stringent, effluent limitations established under section 1313 of this title and which effluent limitations will assure protection and propagation of a balanced, indigenous population of shellfish, fish, and wildlife in or on the water into which the discharge is made, shall not be subject to any more stringent effluent limitation with respect to the thermal component of its discharge during a ten year period beginning on the date of completion of such modification or during the period of depreciation or amortization of such facility for the purpose of section 167 or 169 (or both) of title 26, whichever period ends first. . . .

§1329. NONPOINT SOURCE MANAGEMENT PROGRAMS

(a) STATE ASSESSMENT REPORTS

(1) CONTENTS

The Governor of each State shall, after notice and opportunity for public comment, prepare and submit to the Administrator for approval, a report which —

(A) identifies those navigable waters within the State which, without additional action to control nonpoint sources of pollution, cannot reasonably be expected to attain or maintain applicable water quality standards or the goals and requirements of this chapter;

(B) identifies those categories and subcategories of nonpoint sources or, where appropriate, particular nonpoint sources which add significant pollution to each portion of the navigable waters identified under subparagraph (A) in amounts which contribute to such portion not meeting such water quality standards or such goals and requirements;

(C) describes the process, including intergovernmental coordination and public participation, for identifying best management practices and measures to control each category and subcategory of nonpoint sources and, where appropriate, particular nonpoint sources identified under subparagraph (B) and to reduce, to the maximum extent practicable, the level of pollution resulting from such category, subcategory, or source; and

(D) identifies and describes State and local programs for controlling pollution added from nonpoint sources to, and improving the quality of, each such portion of the navigable waters, including but not limited to those programs which are receiving Federal assistance under subsections (h) and (i) of this section.

(2) INFORMATION USED IN PREPARATION

In developing the report required by this section, the State (A) may rely upon information developed pursuant to sections 1288, 1313(e), 1314(f), 1315(b), and 1324 of this title, and other information as appropriate, and (B) may utilize appropriate elements of the waste treatment management plans developed pursuant to sections 1288(b) and 1313 of this title, to the extent such elements are consistent with and fulfill the requirements of this section.

(b) STATE MANAGEMENT PROGRAMS

(1) IN GENERAL

The Governor of each State, for that State or in combination with adjacent States, shall, after notice and opportunity for public comment, prepare and submit to the Administrator for approval a management program which such State proposes to implement in the first four fiscal years beginning after the date of submission of such management program for controlling pollution added from nonpoint sources to the navigable waters within the State and improving the quality of such waters.

(2) SPECIFIC CONTENTS

Each management program proposed for implementation under this subsection shall include each of the following:

(A) An identification of the best management practices and measures which will be undertaken to reduce pollutant loadings resulting from each category, subcategory, or particular nonpoint source designated under paragraph (1)(B), taking into account the impact of the practice on ground water quality.

(B) An identification of programs (including, as appropriate, nonregulatory or regulatory programs for enforcement, technical assistance, financial assistance, education, training, technology transfer, and demonstration projects) to achieve implementation of the best management practices by the categories, subcategories, and particular nonpoint sources designated under subparagraph (A).

(C) A schedule containing annual milestones for (i) utilization of the program implementation methods identified in subparagraph (B), and (ii) implementation of the best management practices identified in subparagraph (A) by the categories, subcategories, or particular nonpoint sources designated under paragraph (1)(B). Such schedule shall provide for utilization of the best management practices at the earliest practicable date.

(D) A certification of the attorney general of the State or States (or the chief attorney of any State water pollution control agency which has independent legal counsel) that the laws of the State or States, as the case may be, provide adequate authority to implement such management program or, if there is not such adequate authority, a list of such additional authorities as will be necessary to implement such management program. A schedule and commitment by the State or States to seek such additional authorities as expeditiously as practicable.

(E) Sources of Federal and other assistance and funding (other than assistance provided under subsections (h) and (i) of this section) which will be available in each of such fiscal years for supporting implementation of such practices and measures and the purposes for which such assistance will be used in each of such fiscal years.

(F) An identification of Federal financial assistance programs and Federal development projects for which the State will review individual assistance applications or development projects for their effect on water quality pursuant to the procedures set forth in Executive Order 12372 as in effect on September 17, 1983, to determine whether such assistance applications or development projects would be consistent with the program prepared under this subsection; for the purposes of this subparagraph, identification shall not be limited to the assistance programs or development projects subject to Executive Order 12372 but may include any programs listed in the most recent Catalog of Federal Domestic Assistance which may have an effect on the purposes and objectives of the State's nonpoint source pollution management program.

(3) UTILIZATION OF LOCAL AND PRIVATE EXPERTS

In developing and implementing a management program under this subsection, a State shall, to the maximum extent practicable, involve local public and private agencies and organizations which have expertise in control of nonpoint sources of pollution.

(4) DEVELOPMENT ON WATERSHED BASIS

A State shall, to the maximum extent practicable, develop and implement a management program under this subsection on a watershed-by-watershed basis within such State.

Clean Water Act §1329

(c) ADMINISTRATIVE PROVISIONS

(1) COOPERATION REQUIREMENT

Any report required by subsection (a) of this section and any management program and report required by subsection (b) of this section shall be developed in cooperation with local, substate regional, and interstate entities which are actively planning for the implementation of nonpoint source pollution controls and have either been certified by the Administrator in accordance with section 1288 of this title, have worked jointly with the State on water quality management planning under section 1285(j) of this title, or have been designated by the State legislative body or Governor as water quality management planning agencies for their geographic areas.

(2) TIME PERIOD FOR SUBMISSION OF REPORTS AND MANAGEMENT PROGRAMS

Each report and management program shall be submitted to the Administrator during the 18-month period beginning on February 4, 1987.

(d) APPROVAL OR DISAPPROVAL OF REPORTS AND MANAGEMENT PROGRAMS

(1) DEADLINE

Subject to paragraph (2), not later than 180 days after the date of submission to the Administrator of any report or management program under this section (other than subsections (h), (i), and (k) of this section), the Administrator shall either approve or disapprove such report or management program, as the case may be. The Administrator may approve a portion of a management program under this subsection. If the Administrator does not disapprove a report, management program, or portion of a management program in such 180-day period, such report, management program, or portion shall be deemed approved for purposes of this section.

(2) PROCEDURE FOR DISAPPROVAL

If, after notice and opportunity for public comment and consultation with appropriate Federal and State agencies and other interested persons, the Administrator determines that —

(A) the proposed management program or any portion thereof does not meet the requirements of subsection (b)(2) of this section or is not likely to satisfy, in whole or in part, the goals and requirements of this chapter;

(B) adequate authority does not exist, or adequate resources are not available, to implement such program or portion;

(C) the schedule for implementing such program or portion is not sufficiently expeditious; or

(D) the practices and measures proposed in such program or portion are not adequate to reduce the level of pollution in navigable waters in the State resulting from nonpoint sources and to improve the quality of navigable waters in the State;

the Administrator shall within 6 months of the receipt of the proposed program notify the State of any revisions or modifications necessary to obtain approval. The State shall thereupon have an additional 3 months to submit its revised management program and the Administrator shall approve or disapprove such revised program within three months of receipt.

(3) FAILURE OF STATE TO SUBMIT REPORT

If a Governor of a State does not submit the report required by subsection (a) of this section within the period specified by subsection (c)(2) of this section, the Administrator shall, within 30 months after February 4, 1987, prepare a report for such State which makes the identifications required by paragraphs (1)(A) and (1)(B) of subsection (a) of this section. Upon completion of the requirement of the preceding sentence and after notice and opportunity for comment, the Administrator shall report to Congress on his actions pursuant to this section.

(e) LOCAL MANAGEMENT PROGRAMS; TECHNICAL ASSISTANCE

If a State fails to submit a management program under subsection (b) of this section or the Administrator does not approve such a management program, a local public agency or organization which has expertise in, and authority to, control water pollution resulting from nonpoint sources in any area of such State which the Administrator determines is of sufficient geographic size may, with approval of such State, request the Administrator to provide, and the Administrator shall provide, technical assistance to such agency or organization in developing for such area a management program which is described in subsection (b) of this section and can be approved pursuant to subsection (d) of this section. After development of such management program, such agency or organization shall submit such management program to the Administrator for approval. If the Administrator approves such management program, such agency or organization shall be eligible to receive financial assistance under subsection (h) of this section for implementation of such management program as if such agency or organization were a State for which a report submitted under subsection (a) of this section and a management program submitted under subsection (b) of this section were approved under this section. Such financial assistance shall be subject to the same terms and conditions as assistance provided to a State under subsection (h) of this section.

(f) TECHNICAL ASSISTANCE FOR STATES

Upon request of a State, the Administrator may provide technical assistance to such State in developing a management program approved under subsection (b) of this section for those portions of the navigable waters requested by such State.

Clean Water Act §1329

(g) INTERSTATE MANAGEMENT CONFERENCE

(1) CONVENING OF CONFERENCE; NOTIFICATION; PURPOSE

If any portion of the navigable waters in any State which is implementing a management program approved under this section is not meeting applicable water quality standards or the goals and requirements of this chapter as a result, in whole or in part, of pollution from nonpoint sources in another State, such State may petition the Administrator to convene, and the Administrator shall convene, a management conference of all States which contribute significant pollution resulting from nonpoint sources to such portion. If, on the basis of information available, the Administrator determines that a State is not meeting applicable water quality standards or the goals and requirements of this chapter as a result, in whole or in part, of significant pollution from nonpoint sources in another State, the Administrator shall notify such States. The Administrator may convene a management conference under this paragraph not later than 180 days after giving such notification, whether or not the State which is not meeting such standards requests such conference. The purpose of such conference shall be to develop an agreement among such States to reduce the level of pollution in such portion resulting from nonpoint sources and to improve the water quality of such portion. Nothing in such agreement shall supersede or abrogate rights to quantities of water which have been established by interstate water compacts, Supreme Court decrees, or State water laws. This subsection shall not apply to any pollution which is subject to the Colorado River Basin Salinity Control Act [43 U.S.C. 1571 et seq.]. The requirement that the Administrator convene a management conference shall not be subject to the provisions of section 1365 of this title.

(2) STATE MANAGEMENT PROGRAM REQUIREMENT

To the extent that the States reach agreement through such conference, the management programs of the States which are parties to such agreements and which contribute significant pollution to the navigable waters or portions thereof not meeting applicable water quality standards or goals and requirements of this chapter will be revised to reflect such agreement. Such management programs shall be consistent with Federal and State law.

(h) GRANT PROGRAM

(1) GRANTS FOR IMPLEMENTATION OF MANAGEMENT PROGRAMS

Upon application of a State for which a report submitted under subsection (a) of this section and a management program submitted under subsection (b) of this section is approved under this section, the Administrator shall make grants, subject to such terms and conditions as the Administrator considers appropriate, under this subsection to such State for the purpose of assisting the State in implementing such management program. Funds reserved pursuant to section 1285(j)(5) of this title may be used to develop and implement such management program.

(2) APPLICATIONS

An application for a grant under this subsection in any fiscal year shall be in such form and shall contain such other information as the Administrator may require, including an identification and description of the best management practices and measures which the State proposes to assist, encourage, or require in such year with the Federal assistance to be provided under the grant.

(3) FEDERAL SHARE

The Federal share of the cost of each management program implemented with Federal assistance under this subsection in any fiscal year shall not exceed 60 percent of the cost incurred by the State in implementing such management program and shall be made on condition that the non-Federal share is provided from non-Federal sources.

(4) LIMITATION ON GRANT AMOUNTS

Notwithstanding any other provision of this subsection, not more than 15 percent of the amount appropriated to carry out this subsection may be used to make grants to any one State, including any grants to any local public agency or organization with authority to control pollution from nonpoint sources in any area of such State.

(5) PRIORITY FOR EFFECTIVE MECHANISMS

For each fiscal year beginning after September 30, 1987, the Administrator may give priority in making grants under this subsection, and shall give consideration in determining the Federal share of any such grant, to States which have implemented or are proposing to implement management programs which will —

    (A) control particularly difficult or serious nonpoint source pollution problems, including, but not limited to, problems resulting from mining activities;

    (B) implement innovative methods or practices for controlling nonpoint sources of pollution, including regulatory programs where the Administrator deems appropriate;

    (C) control interstate nonpoint source pollution problems; or

    (D) carry out ground water quality protection activities which the Administrator determines are part of a comprehensive nonpoint source pollution control program, including research, planning, ground water assessments, demonstration programs, enforcement, technical assistance, education, and training to protect ground water quality from nonpoint sources of pollution.

Clean Water Act §1329

(6) AVAILABILITY FOR OBLIGATION

The funds granted to each State pursuant to this subsection in a fiscal year shall remain available for obligation by such State for the fiscal year for which appropriated. The amount of any such funds not obligated by the end of such fiscal year shall be available to the Administrator for granting to other States under this subsection in the next fiscal year.

(7) LIMITATION ON USE OF FUNDS

States may use funds from grants made pursuant to this section for financial assistance to persons only to the extent that such assistance is related to the costs of demonstration projects.

(8) SATISFACTORY PROGRESS

No grant may be made under this subsection in any fiscal year to a State which in the preceding fiscal year received a grant under this subsection unless the Administrator determines that such State made satisfactory progress in such preceding fiscal year in meeting the schedule specified by such State under subsection (b)(2) of this section.

(9) MAINTENANCE OF EFFORT

No grant may be made to a State under this subsection in any fiscal year unless such State enters into such agreements with the Administrator as the Administrator may require to ensure that such State will maintain its aggregate expenditures from all other sources for programs for controlling pollution added to the navigable waters in such State from nonpoint sources and improving the quality of such waters at or above the average level of such expenditures in its two fiscal years preceding February 4, 1987.

(10) REQUEST FOR INFORMATION

The Administrator may request such information, data, and reports as he considers necessary to make the determination of continuing eligibility for grants under this section.

(11) REPORTING AND OTHER REQUIREMENTS

Each State shall report to the Administrator on an annual basis concerning (A) its progress in meeting the schedule of milestones submitted pursuant to subsection (b)(2)(C) of this section, and (B) to the extent that appropriate information is available, reductions in nonpoint source pollutant loading and improvements in water quality for those navigable waters or watersheds within the State which were identified pursuant to subsection (a)(1)(A) of this section resulting from implementation of the management program.

(12) LIMITATION ON ADMINISTRATIVE COSTS

For purposes of this subsection, administrative costs in the form of salaries, overhead, or indirect costs for services provided and charged against activities and programs carried out with a grant under this subsection shall not exceed in any fiscal year 10 percent of the amount of the grant in such year, except that costs of implementing enforcement and regulatory activities, education, training, technical assistance, demonstration projects, and technology transfer programs shall not be subject to this limitation.

(i) GRANTS FOR PROTECTING GROUNDWATER QUALITY

(1) ELIGIBLE APPLICANTS AND ACTIVITIES

Upon application of a State for which a report submitted under subsection (a) of this section and a plan submitted under subsection (b) of this section is approved under this section, the Administrator shall make grants under this subsection to such State for the purpose of assisting such State in carrying out groundwater quality protection activities which the Administrator determines will advance the State toward implementation of a comprehensive nonpoint source pollution control program. Such activities shall include, but not be limited to, research, planning, groundwater assessments, demonstration programs, enforcement, technical assistance, education, and training to protect the quality of groundwater and to prevent contamination of groundwater from nonpoint sources of pollution.

(2) APPLICATIONS

An application for a grant under this subsection shall be in such form and shall contain such information as the Administrator may require.

(3) FEDERAL SHARE; MAXIMUM AMOUNT

The Federal share of the cost of assisting a State in carrying out groundwater protection activities in any fiscal year under this subsection shall be 50 percent of the costs incurred by the State in carrying out such activities, except that the maximum amount of Federal assistance which any State may receive under this subsection in any fiscal year shall not exceed $150,000.

(4) REPORT

The Administrator shall include in each report transmitted under subsection (m) of this section a report on the activities and programs implemented under this subsection during the preceding fiscal year.

(j) AUTHORIZATION OF APPROPRIATIONS

There is authorized to be appropriated to carry out subsections (h) and (i) of this section not to exceed $70,000,000 for fiscal year 1988, $100,000,000 per fiscal year for each of fiscal years 1989 and 1990, and $130,000,000 for fiscal year 1991; except that for each of such fiscal years not to exceed $7,500,000 may be made available to carry out subsection (i) of this section. Sums appropriated pursuant to this subsection shall remain available until expended.

(k) CONSISTENCY OF OTHER PROGRAMS AND PROJECTS WITH MANAGEMENT PROGRAMS

The Administrator shall transmit to the Office of Management and Budget and the appropriate Federal departments and agencies a list of those assistance programs and development projects identified by each State under subsection (b)(2)(F) of this section for which individual assistance applications and projects will be reviewed pursuant to the procedures set forth in Executive Order 12372 as in effect on September 17, 1983. Beginning not later than sixty days after receiving notification by the Administrator, each Federal department and agency shall modify existing regulations to allow States to review individual development projects and assistance applications under the identified Federal assistance programs and shall accommodate, according to the requirements and definitions of Executive Order 12372, as in effect on September 17, 1983, the concerns of the State regarding the consistency of such applications or projects with the State nonpoint source pollution management program.

(l) COLLECTION OF INFORMATION

The Administrator shall collect and make available, through publications and other appropriate means, information pertaining to management practices and implementation methods, including, but not limited to, (1) information concerning the costs and relative efficiencies of best management practices for reducing nonpoint source pollution; and (2) available data concerning the relationship between water quality and implementation of various management practices to control nonpoint sources of pollution.

(m) REPORTS OF ADMINISTRATOR

(1) ANNUAL REPORTS

Not later than January 1, 1988, and each January 1 thereafter, the Administrator shall transmit to the Committee on Public Works and Transportation of the House of Representatives and the Committee on Environment and Public Works of the Senate, a report for the preceding fiscal year on the activities and programs implemented under this section and the progress made in reducing pollution in the navigable waters resulting from nonpoint sources and improving the quality of such waters.

(2) FINAL REPORT

Not later than January 1, 1990, the Administrator shall transmit to Congress a final report on the activities carried out under this section. Such report, at a minimum, shall —

(A) describe the management programs being implemented by the States by types and amount of affected navigable waters, categories and subcategories of nonpoint sources, and types of best management practices being implemented;

(B) describe the experiences of the States in adhering to schedules and implementing best management practices;

(C) describe the amount and purpose of grants awarded pursuant to subsections (h) and (i) of this section;

(D) identify, to the extent that information is available, the progress made in reducing pollutant loads and improving water quality in the navigable waters;

(E) indicate what further actions need to be taken to attain and maintain in those navigable waters (i) applicable water quality standards, and (ii) the goals and requirements of this chapter;

(F) include recommendations of the Administrator concerning future programs (including enforcement programs) for controlling pollution from nonpoint sources; and

(G) identify the activities and programs of departments, agencies, and instrumentalities of the United States which are inconsistent with the management programs submitted by the States and recommend modifications so that such activities and programs are consistent with and assist the States in implementation of such management programs.

(n) SET ASIDE FOR ADMINISTRATIVE PERSONNEL

Not less than 5 percent of the funds appropriated pursuant to subsection (j) of this section for any fiscal year shall be available to the Administrator to maintain personnel levels at the Environmental Protection Agency at levels which are adequate to carry out this section in such year.

§1330. NATIONAL ESTUARY PROGRAM

(a) MANAGEMENT CONFERENCE

(1) NOMINATION OF ESTUARIES

The Governor of any State may nominate to the Administrator an estuary lying in whole or in part within the State as an estuary of national significance and request a management conference to develop a comprehensive management plan for the estuary. The nomination shall document the need for the conference, the likelihood of success, and information relating to the factors in paragraph (2).

(2) CONVENING OF CONFERENCE

(A) IN GENERAL

In any case where the Administrator determines, on his own initiative or upon nomination of a State under paragraph (1), that the attainment or maintenance of that water quality in an estuary which assures

Clean Water Act §1330

protection of public water supplies and the protection and propagation of a balanced, indigenous population of shellfish, fish, and wildlife, and allows recreational activities, in and on the water, requires the control of point and nonpoint sources of pollution to supplement existing controls of pollution in more than one State, the Administrator shall select such estuary and convene a management conference.

(B) PRIORITY CONSIDERATION

The Administrator shall give priority consideration under this section to Long Island Sound, New York and Connecticut; Narragansett Bay, Rhode Island; Buzzards Bay, Massachusetts; Massachusetts Bay, Massachusetts (including Cape Cod Bay and Boston Harbor); Puget Sound, Washington; New York-New Jersey Harbor, New York and New Jersey; Delaware Bay, Delaware and New Jersey; Delaware Inland Bays, Delaware; Albemarle Sound, North Carolina; Sarasota Bay, Florida; San Francisco Bay, California; Santa Monica Bay, California; Galveston Bay, Texas; Barataria-Terrebonne Bay estuary complex, Louisiana; Indian River Lagoon, Florida; and Peconic Bay, New York.

(3) BOUNDARY DISPUTE EXCEPTION

In any case in which a boundary between two States passes through an estuary and such boundary is disputed and is the subject of an action in any court, the Administrator shall not convene a management conference with respect to such estuary before a final adjudication has been made of such dispute.

(b) PURPOSES OF CONFERENCE

The purposes of any management conference convened with respect to an estuary under this subsection shall be to —

(1) assess trends in water quality, natural resources, and uses of the estuary;

(2) collect, characterize, and assess data on toxics, nutrients, and natural resources within the estaurine zone to identify the causes of environmental problems;

(3) develop the relationship between the inplace loads and point and nonpoint loadings of pollutants to the estuarine zone and the potential uses of the zone, water quality, and natural resources;

(4) develop a comprehensive conservation and management plan that recommends priority corrective actions and compliance schedules addressing point and nonpoint sources of pollution to restore and maintain the chemical, physical, and biological integrity of the estuary, including restoration and maintenance of water quality, a balanced indigenous population of shellfish, fish and wildlife, and recreational activities in the estuary, and assure that the designated uses of the estuary are protected;

(5) develop plans for the coordinated implementation of the plan by the States as well as Federal and local agencies participating in the conference;
(6) monitor the effectiveness of actions taken pursuant to the plan; and
(7) review all Federal financial assistance programs and Federal development projects in accordance with the requirements of Executive Order 12372, as in effect on September 17, 1983, to determine whether such assistance program or project would be consistent with and further the purposes and objectives of the plan prepared under this section.

For the purposes of paragraph (7), such programs and projects shall not be limited to the assistance programs and development projects subject to Executive Order 12372, but may include any programs listed in the most recent Catalog of Federal Domestic Assistance which may have an effect on the purposes and objectives of the plan developed under this section.

(c) MEMBERS OF CONFERENCE

The members of a management conference convened under this section shall include, at a minimum, the Administrator and representatives of —

(1) each State and foreign nation located in whole or in part in the estuarine zone of the estuary for which the conference is convened;

(2) international, interstate, or regional agencies or entities having jurisdiction over all or a significant part of the estuary;

(3) each interested Federal agency, as determined appropriate by the Administrator;

(4) local governments having jurisdiction over any land or water within the estuarine zone, as determined appropriate by the Administrator; and

(5) affected industries, public and private educational institutions, and the general public, as determined appropriate by the Administrator.

(d) UTILIZATION OF EXISTING DATA

In developing a conservation and management plan under this section, the management conference shall survey and utilize existing reports, data, and studies relating to the estuary that have been developed by or made available to Federal, Interstate, State, and local agencies.

(e) PERIOD OF CONFERENCE

A management conference convened under this section shall be convened for a period not to exceed 5 years. Such conference may be extended by the Administrator, and if terminated after the initial period, may be reconvened by the Administrator at any time thereafter, as may be necessary to meet the requirements of this section.

(f) APPROVAL AND IMPLEMENTATION OF PLANS

(1) APPROVAL

Not later than 120 days after the completion of a conservation and management plan and after providing for public review and comment, the Administrator shall approve such plan if the plan meets the requirements of this section and the affected Governor or Governors concur.

(2) IMPLEMENTATION

Upon approval of a conservation and management plan under this section, such plan shall be implemented. Funds authorized to be appropriated under subchapters II and VI of this chapter and section 1329 of this title may be used in accordance with the applicable requirements of this chapter to assist States with the implementation of such plan.

(g) GRANTS

(1) RECIPIENTS

The Administrator is authorized to make grants to State, interstate, and regional water pollution control agencies and entities, State coastal zone management agencies, interstate agencies, other public or nonprofit private agencies, institutions, organizations, and individuals.

(2) PURPOSES

Grants under this subsection shall be made to pay for assisting research, surveys, studies, and modeling and other technical work necessary for the development of a conservation and management plan under this section.

(3) FEDERAL SHARE

The amount of grants to any person (including a State, interstate, or regional agency or entity) under this subsection for a fiscal year shall not exceed 75 percent of the costs of such research, survey, studies, and work and shall be made on condition that the non-Federal share of such costs are provided from non-Federal sources.

(h) GRANT REPORTING

Any person (including a State, interstate, or regional agency or entity) that receives a grant under subsection (g) of this section shall report to the Administrator not later than 18 months after receipt of such grant and biennially thereafter on the progress being made under this section.

(i) AUTHORIZATION OF APPROPRIATIONS

There are authorized to be appropriated to the Administrator not to exceed $12,000,000 per fiscal year for each of fiscal years 1987, 1988, 1989, 1990, and 1991 for —

(1) expenses related to the administration of management conferences under this section, not to exceed 10 percent of the amount appropriated under this subsection;

(2) making grants under subsection (g) of this section; and

(3) monitoring the implementation of a conservation and management

plan by the management conference or by the Administrator, in any case in which the conference has been terminated.

The Administrator shall provide up to $5,000,000 per fiscal year of the sums authorized to be appropriated under this subsection to the Administrator of the National Oceanic and Atmospheric Administration to carry out subsection (j) of this section.

(j) RESEARCH

(1) PROGRAMS

In order to determine the need to convene a management conference under this section or at the request of such a management conference, the Administrator shall coordinate and implement, through the National Marine Pollution Program Office and the National Marine Fisheries Services of the National Oceanic and Atmospheric Administration, as appropriate, for one or more estuarine zones —

(A) a long-term program of trend assessment monitoring measuring variations in pollutant concentrations, marine ecology, and other physical or biological environmental parameters which may affect estuarine zones, to provide the Administrator the capacity to determine the potential and actual effects of alternative management strategies and measures;

(B) a program of ecosystem assessment assisting in the development of (i) baseline studies which determine the state of estuarine zones and the effects of natural and anthropogenic changes, and (ii) predictive models capable of translating information on specific discharges or general pollutant loadings within estuarine zones into a set of probable effects on such zones;

(C) a comprehensive water quality sampling program for the continuous monitoring of nutrients, chlorine, acid precipitation dissolved oxygen, and potentially toxic pollutants (including organic chemicals and metals) in estuarine zones, after consultation with interested State, local, interstate, or international agencies and review and analysis of all environmental sampling data presently collected from estuarine zones; and

(D) a program of research to identify the movements of nutrients, sediments and pollutants through estuarine zones and the impact of nutrients, sediments, and pollutants on water quality, the ecosystem, and designated or potential uses of the estuarine zones.

(2) REPORTS

The Administrator, in cooperation with the Administrator of the National Oceanic and Atmospheric Administration, shall submit to the Congress no less often than biennially a comprehensive report on the activities authorized under this subsection including —

(A) a listing of priority monitoring and research needs;

(B) an assessment of the state and health of the Nation's estuarine zones, to the extent evaluated under this subsection;

(C) a discussion of pollution problems and trends in pollutant concentrations with a direct or indirect effect on water quality, the ecosystem, and designated or potential uses of each estuarine zone, to the extent evaluated under this subsection; and

(D) an evaluation of pollution abatement activities and management measures so far implemented to determine the degree of improvement toward the objectives expressed in subsection (b)(4) of this section.

(k) DEFINITIONS

For purposes of this section, the terms "estuary" and "estuarine zone" have the meanings such terms have in section 1254(n)(4) of this title, except that the term "estuarine zone" shall also include associated aquatic ecosystems and those portions of tributaries draining into the estuary up to the historic height of migration of anadromous fish or the historic head of tidal influence, whichever is higher. . . .

SUBCHAPTER IV — PERMITS AND LICENSES

§1341. CERTIFICATION

(a) COMPLIANCE WITH APPLICABLE REQUIREMENTS; APPLICATION; PROCEDURES; LICENSE SUSPENSION

(1) Any applicant for a Federal license or permit to conduct any activity including, but not limited to, the construction or operation of facilities, which may result in any discharge into the navigable waters, shall provide the licensing or permitting agency a certification from the State in which the discharge originates or will originate, or, if appropriate, from the interstate water pollution control agency having jurisdiction over the navigable waters at the point where the discharge originates or will originate, that any such discharge will comply with the applicable provisions of sections 1311, 1312, 1313, 1316, and 1317 of this title. In the case of any such activity for which there is not an applicable effluent limitation or other limitation under sections 1311(b) and 1312 of this title, and there is not an applicable standard under sections 1316 and 1317 of this title, the State shall so certify, except that any such certification shall not be deemed to satisfy section 1371(c) of this title. Such State or Interstate agency shall establish procedures for public notice in the case of all applications for certification by it and, to the extent it deems appropriate, procedures for public hearings in connection with specific applications. In any case where a State or interstate agency has no authority to give such a certification, such certification shall be from the Administrator. If the State, interstate agency, or Administrator, as the case may be, fails or refuses to act on a request for certification, within a reasonable period of time (which shall not exceed one year) after receipt of such request, the certification requirements of this subsection shall be waived with respect to such Federal application. No license or permit shall be granted until the certification required by this section has been obtained or has been waived

as provided in the preceding sentence. No license or permit shall be granted if certification has been denied by the State, interstate agency, or the Administrator, as the case may be.

(2) Upon receipt of such application and certification the licensing or permitting agency shall immediately notify the Administrator of such application and certification. Whenever such a discharge may affect, as determined by the Administrator, the quality of the waters of any other State, the Administrator within thirty days of the date of notice of application for such Federal license or permit shall so notify such other State, the licensing or permitting agency, and the applicant. If, within sixty days after receipt of such notification, such other State determines that such discharge will affect the quality of its waters so as to violate any water quality requirements in such State, and within such sixty-day period notifies the Administrator and the licensing or permitting agency in writing of its objection to the issuance of such license or permit and requests a public hearing on such objection, the licensing or permitting agency shall hold such a hearing. The Administrator shall at such hearing submit his evaluation and recommendations with respect to any such objection to the licensing or permitting agency. Such agency, based upon the recommendations of such State, the Administrator, and upon any additional evidence, if any, presented to the agency at the hearing, shall condition such license or permit in such manner as may be necessary to insure compliance with applicable water quality requirements. If the imposition of conditions cannot insure such compliance such agency shall not issue such license or permit.

(3) The certification obtained pursuant to paragraph (1) of this subsection with respect to the construction of any facility shall fulfill the requirements of this subsection with respect to certification in connection with any other Federal license or permit required for the operation of such facility unless, after notice to the certifying State, agency, or Administrator, as the case may be, which shall be given by the Federal agency to whom application is made for such operating license or permit, the State, or if appropriate, the interstate agency or the Administrator, notifies such agency within sixty days after receipt of such notice that there is no longer reasonable assurance that there will be compliance with the applicable provisions of sections 1311, 1312, 1313, 1316, and 1317 of this title because of changes since the construction license or permit certification was issued in (A) the construction or operation of the facility, (B) the characteristics of the waters into which such discharge is made, (C) the water quality criteria applicable to such waters or (D) applicable effluent limitations or other requirements. This paragraph shall be inapplicable in any case where the applicant for such operating license or permit has failed to provide the certifying State, or, if appropriate, the interstate agency or the Administrator, with notice of any proposed changes in the construction or operation of the facility with respect to which a construction license or permit has been granted, which changes may result in violation of section 1311, 1312, 1313, 1316, or 1317 of this title.

(4) Prior to the initial operation of any federally licensed or permitted fa-

cility or activity which may result in any discharge into the navigable waters and with respect to which a certification has been obtained pursuant to paragraph (1) of this subsection, which facility or activity is not subject to a Federal operating license or permit, the licensee or permittee shall provide an opportunity for such certifying State, or, if appropriate, the interstate agency or the Administrator to review the manner in which the facility or activity shall be operated or conducted for the purposes of assuring that applicable effluent limitations or other limitations or other applicable water quality requirements will not be violated. Upon notification by the certifying State, or if appropriate, the interstate agency or the Administrator that the operation of any such federally licensed or permitted facility or activity will violate applicable effluent limitations or other limitations or other water quality requirements such Federal agency may, after public hearing, suspend such license or permit. If such license or permit is suspended, it shall remain suspended until notification is received from the certifying State, agency, or Administrator, as the case may be, that there is reasonable assurance that such facility or activity will not violate the applicable provisions of section 1311, 1312, 1313, 1316, or 1317 of this title.

(5) Any Federal license or permit with respect to which a certification has been obtained under paragraph (1) of this subsection may be suspended or revoked by the Federal agency issuing such license or permit upon the entering of a judgment under this chapter that such facility or activity has been operated in violation of the applicable provisions of section 1311, 1312, 1313, 1316, or 1317 of this title.

(6) Except with respect to a permit issued under section 1342 of this title, in any case where actual construction of a facility has been lawfully commenced prior to April 3, 1970, no certification shall be required under this subsection for a license or permit issued after April 3, 1970, to operate such facility, except that any such license or permit issued without certification shall terminate April 3, 1973, unless prior to such termination date the person having such license or permit submits to the Federal agency which issued such license or permit a certification and otherwise meets the requirements of this section.

(b) COMPLIANCE WITH OTHER PROVISIONS OF LAW SETTING APPLICABLE WATER QUALITY REQUIREMENTS

Nothing in this section shall be construed to limit the authority of any department or agency pursuant to any other provision of law to require compliance with any applicable water quality requirements. The Administrator shall, upon the request of any Federal department or agency, or State or interstate agency, or applicant, provide, for the purpose of this section, any relevant information on applicable effluent limitations, or other limitations, standards, regulations, or requirements, or water quality criteria, and shall, when requested by any such department or agency or State or interstate agency, or applicant, comment on any methods to comply with such limitations, standards, regulations, requirements, or criteria.

§1341

(c) AUTHORITY OF SECRETARY OF THE ARMY TO PERMIT USE OF SPOIL DISPOSAL AREAS BY FEDERAL LICENSEES OR PERMITTEES

In order to implement the provisions of this section, the Secretary of the Army, acting through the Chief of Engineers, is authorized, if he deems it to be in the public interest, to permit the use of spoil disposal areas under his jurisdiction by Federal licensees or permittees, and to make an appropriate charge for such use. Moneys received from such licensees or permittees shall be deposited in the Treasury as miscellaneous receipts.

(d) LIMITATIONS AND MONITORING REQUIREMENTS OF CERTIFICATION

Any certification provided under this section shall set forth any effluent limitations and other limitations, and monitoring requirements necessary to assure that any applicant for a Federal license or permit will comply with any applicable effluent limitations and other limitations, under section 1311 or 1312 of this title, standard of performance under section 1316 of this title, or prohibition, effluent standard, or pretreatment standard under section 1317 of this title, and with any other appropriate requirement of State law set forth in such certification, and shall become a condition on any Federal license or permit subject to the provisions of this section.

§1342. NATIONAL POLLUTANT DISCHARGE ELIMINATION SYSTEM

(a) PERMITS FOR DISCHARGE OF POLLUTANTS

(1) Except as provided in sections 1328 and 1344 of this title, the Administrator may, after opportunity for public hearing issue a permit for the discharge of any pollutant, or combination of pollutants, notwithstanding section 1311(a) of this title, upon condition that such discharge will meet either (A) all applicable requirements under sections 1311, 1312, 1316, 1317, 1318, and 1343 of this title, or (B) prior to the taking of necessary implementing actions relating to all such requirements, such conditions as the Administrator determines are necessary to carry out the provisions of this chapter.

(2) The Administrator shall prescribe conditions for such permits to assure compliance with the requirements of paragraph (1) of this subsection, including conditions on data and information collection, reporting, and such other requirements as he deems appropriate.

(3) The permit program of the Administrator under paragraph (1) of this subsection, and permits issued thereunder, shall be subject to the same terms, conditions, and requirements as apply to a State permit program and permits issued thereunder under subsection (b) of this section.

(4) All permits for discharges into the navigable waters issued pursuant to section 407 of this title shall be deemed to be permits issued under this subchapter, and permits issued under this subchapter shall be deemed to be permits issued under section 407 of this title, and shall continue in force and effect for their term unless revoked, modified, or suspended in accordance with the provisions of this chapter.

(5) No permit for a discharge into the navigable waters shall be issued under section 407 of this title after October 18, 1972. Each application for a permit under section 407 of this title, pending on October 18, 1972, shall be deemed to be an application for a permit under this section. The Administrator shall authorize a State, which he determines has the capability of administering a permit program which will carry out the objectives of this chapter to issue permits for discharges into the navigable waters within the jurisdiction of such State. The Administrator may exercise the authority granted him by the preceding sentence only during the period which begins on October 18, 1972, and ends either on the ninetieth day after the date of the first promulgation of guidelines required by section 1314(i)(2) of this title, or the date of approval by the Administrator of a permit program for such State under subsection (b) of this section, whichever date first occurs, and no such authorization to a State shall extend beyond the last day of such period. Each such permit shall be subject to such conditions as the Administrator determines are necessary to carry out the provisions of this chapter. No such permit shall issue if the Administrator objects to such issuance.

(b) STATE PERMIT PROGRAMS

At any time after the promulgation of the guidelines required by subsection (i)(2) of section 1314 of this title, the Governor of each State desiring to administer its own permit program for discharges into navigable waters within its jurisdiction may submit to the Administrator a full and complete description of the program it proposes to establish and administer under State law or under an interstate compact. In addition, such State shall submit a statement from the attorney general (or the attorney for those State water pollution control agencies which have independent legal counsel), or from the chief legal officer in the case of an interstate agency, that the laws of such State, or the interstate compact, as the case may be, provide adequate authority to carry out the described program. The Administrator shall approve each submitted program unless he determines that adequate authority does not exist:

(1) To issue permits which —

(A) apply, and insure compliance with, any applicable requirements of sections 1311, 1312, 1316, 1317, and 1343 of this title;

(B) are for fixed terms not exceeding five years; and

(C) can be terminated or modified for cause including, but not limited to, the following:

(i) violation of any condition of the permit;

(ii) obtaining a permit by misrepresentation, or failure to disclose fully all relevant facts;

(iii) change in any condition that requires either a temporary or permanent reduction or elimination of the permitted discharge;

(D) control the disposal of pollutants into wells;

(2)(A) To issue permits which apply, and insure compliance with, all applicable requirements of section 1318 of this title; or

(B) To inspect, monitor, enter, and require reports to at least the same extent as required in section 1318 of this title;

(3) To insure that the public, and any other State the waters of which may be affected, receive notice of each application for a permit and to provide an opportunity for public hearing before a ruling on each such application;

(4) To insure that the Administrator receives notice of each application (including a copy thereof) for a permit;

(5) To insure that any State (other than the permitting State), whose waters may be affected by the issuance of a permit may submit written recommendations to the permitting State (and the Administrator) with respect to any permit application and, if any part of such written recommendations are not accepted by the permitting State, that the permitting State will notify such affected State (and the Administrator) in writing of its failure to so accept such recommendations together with its reasons for so doing;

(6) To insure that no permit will be issued if, in the judgment of the Secretary of the Army acting through the Chief of Engineers, after consultation with the Secretary of the department in which the Coast Guard is operating, anchorage and navigation of any of the navigable waters would be substantially impaired thereby;

(7) To abate violations of the permit or the permit program, including civil and criminal penalties and other ways and means of enforcement;

(8) To insure that any permit for a discharge from a publicly owned treatment works includes conditions to require the identification in terms of character and volume of pollutants of any significant source introducing pollutants subject to pretreatment standards under section 1317(b) of this title into such works and a program to assure compliance with such pretreatment standards by each such source, in addition to adequate notice to the permitting agency of (A) new introductions into such works of pollutants from any source which would be a new source as defined in section 1316 of this title if such source were discharging pollutants, (B) new introductions of pollutants into such works from a source which would be subject to section 1311 of this title if it were discharging such pollutants, or (C) a substantial change in volume or character of pollutants being introduced into such works by a source introducing pollutants into such works at the time of issuance of the permit. Such notice shall include information on the quality and quantity of effluent to be introduced into such treatment works and any anticipated impact of such change in the quantity or quality of effluent to be discharged from such publicly owned treatment works; and

(9) To insure that any industrial user of any publicly owned treatment works will comply with sections 1284(b), 1317, and 1318 of this title.

(c) **SUSPENSION OF FEDERAL PROGRAM UPON SUBMISSION OF STATE PROGRAM; WITHDRAWAL OF APPROVAL OF STATE PROGRAM; RETURN OF STATE PROGRAM TO ADMINISTRATOR**

(1) Not later than ninety days after the date on which a State has submitted a program (or revision thereof) pursuant to subsection (b) of this section, the

Administrator shall suspend the issuance of permits under subsection (a) of this section as to those discharges subject to such program unless he determines that the State permit program does not meet the requirements of subsection (b) of this section or does not conform to the guidelines issued under section 1314(i)(2) of this title. If the Administrator so determines, he shall notify the State of any revisions or modifications necessary to conform to such requirements or guidelines.

(2) Any State permit program under this section shall at all times be in accordance with this section and guidelines promulgated pursuant to section 1314(i)(2) of this title.

(3) Whenever the Administrator determines after public hearing that a State is not administering a program approved under this section in accordance with requirements of this section, he shall so notify the State and, if appropriate corrective action is not taken within a reasonable time, not to exceed ninety days, the Administrator shall withdraw approval of such program. The Administrator shall not withdraw approval of any such program unless he shall first have notified the State, and made public, in writing, the reasons for such withdrawal.

(4) Limitations on partial permit program returns and withdrawals. — A State may return to the Administrator administration, and the Administrator may withdraw under paragraph (3) of this subsection approval, of —

(A) a State partial permit program approved under subsection (n)(3) of this section only if the entire permit program being administered by the State department or agency at the time is returned or withdrawn; and

(B) a State partial permit program approved under subsection (n)(4) of this section only if an entire phased component of the permit program being administered by the State at the time is returned or withdrawn.

(d) NOTIFICATION OF ADMINISTRATOR

(1) Each State shall transmit to the Administrator a copy of each permit application received by such State and provide notice to the Administrator of every action related to the consideration of such permit application, including each permit proposed to be issued by such State.

(2) No permit shall issue (A) if the Administrator within ninety days of the date of his notification under subsection (b)(5) of this section objects in writing to the issuance of such permit, or (B) if the Administrator within ninety days of the date of transmittal of the proposed permit by the State objects in writing to the issuance of such permit as being outside the guidelines and requirements of this chapter. Whenever the Administrator objects to the issuance of a permit under this paragraph such written objection shall contain a statement of the reasons for such objection and the effluent limitations and conditions which such permit would include if it were issued by the Administrator.

(3) The Administrator may, as to any permit application, waive paragraph (2) of this subsection.

(4) In any case where, after December 27, 1977, the Administrator, pursuant to paragraph (2) of this subsection, objects to the issuance of a permit, on request of the State, a public hearing shall be held by the Administrator on such

objection. If the State does not resubmit such permit revised to meet such objection within 30 days after completion of the hearing, or, if no hearing is requested within 90 days after the date of such objection, the Administrator may issue the permit pursuant to subsection (a) of this section for such source in accordance with the guidelines and requirements of this chapter.

(e) **WAIVER OF NOTIFICATION REQUIREMENT**

In accordance with guidelines promulgated pursuant to subsection (i)(2) of section 1314 of this title, the Administrator is authorized to waive the requirements of subsection (d) of this section at the time he approves a program pursuant to subsection (b) of this section for any category (including any class, type, or size within such category) of point sources within the State submitting such program.

(f) **POINT SOURCE CATEGORIES**

The Administrator shall promulgate regulations establishing categories of point sources which he determines shall not be subject to the requirements of subsection (d) of this section in any State with a program approved pursuant to subsection (b) of this section. The Administrator may distinguish among classes, types, and sizes within any category of point sources.

(g) **OTHER REGULATIONS FOR SAFE TRANSPORTATION, HANDLING, CARRIAGE, STORAGE, AND STOWAGE OF POLLUTANTS**

Any permit issued under this section for the discharge of pollutants into the navigable waters from a vessel or other floating craft shall be subject to any applicable regulations promulgated by the Secretary of the department in which the Coast Guard is operating, establishing specifications for safe transportation, handling, carriage, storage, and stowage of pollutants.

(h) **VIOLATION OF PERMIT CONDITIONS; RESTRICTION OR PROHIBITION UPON INTRODUCTION OF POLLUTANT BY SOURCE NOT PREVIOUSLY UTILIZING TREATMENT WORKS**

In the event any condition of a permit for discharges from a treatment works (as defined in section 1292 of this title) which is publicly owned is violated, a State with a program approved under subsection (b) of this section or the Administrator, where no State program is approved or where the Administrator determines pursuant to section 1319(a) of this title that a State with an approved program has not commenced appropriate enforcement action with respect to such permit, may proceed in a court of competent jurisdiction to restrict or prohibit the introduction of any pollutant into such treatment works by a source not utilizing such treatment works prior to the finding that such condition was violated.

(i) **FEDERAL ENFORCEMENT NOT LIMITED**

Nothing in this section shall be construed to limit the authority of the Administrator to take action pursuant to section 1319 of this title.

Clean Water Act §1342

(j) PUBLIC INFORMATION

A copy of each permit application and each permit issued under this section shall be available to the public. Such permit application or permit, or portion thereof, shall further be available on request for the purpose of reproduction.

(k) COMPLIANCE WITH PERMITS

Compliance with a permit issued pursuant to this section shall be deemed compliance, for purposes of sections 1319 and 1365 of this title, with sections 1311, 1312, 1316, 1317, and 1343 of this title, except any standard imposed under section 1317 of this title for a toxic pollutant injurious to human health. Until December 31, 1974, in any case where a permit for discharge has been applied for pursuant to this section, but final administrative disposition of such application has not been made, such discharge shall not be a violation of (1) section 1311, 1316, or 1342 of this title, or (2) section 407 of this title, unless the Administrator or other plaintiff proves that final administrative disposition of such application has not been made because of the failure of the applicant to furnish information reasonably required or requested in order to process the application. For the 180-day period beginning on October 18, 1972, in the case of any point source discharging any pollutant or combination of pollutants immediately prior to such date which source is not subject to section 407 of this title, the discharge by such source shall not be a violation of this chapter if such a source applies for a permit for discharge pursuant to this section within such 180-day period.

(l) LIMITATION ON PERMIT REQUIREMENT

(1) AGRICULTURAL RETURN FLOWS

The Administrator shall not require a permit under this section for discharges composed entirely of return flows from irrigated agriculture, nor shall the Administrator directly or indirectly, require any State to require such a permit.

(2) STORMWATER RUNOFF FROM OIL, GAS, AND MINING OPERATIONS

The Administrator shall not require a permit under this section, nor shall the Administrator directly or indirectly require any State to require a permit, for discharges of stormwater runoff from mining operations or oil and gas exploration, production, processing, or treatment operations or transmission facilities, composed entirely of flows which are from conveyances or systems of conveyances (including but not limited to pipes, conduits, ditches, and channels) used for collecting and conveying precipitation runoff and which are not contaminated by contact with, or do not come into contact with, any overburden, raw material, intermediate products, finished product, byproduct, or waste products located on the site of such operations.

(m) ADDITIONAL PRETREATMENT OF CONVENTIONAL POLLUTANTS NOT REQUIRED

To the extent a treatment works (as defined in section 1292 of this title) which is publicly owned is not meeting the requirements of a permit issued under this section for such treatment works as a result of inadequate design or operation of such treatment works, the Administrator, in issuing a permit under this section, shall not require pretreatment by a person introducing conventional pollutants identified pursuant to section 1314(a)(4) of this title into such treatment works other than pretreatment required to assure compliance with pretreatment standards under subsection (b)(8) of this section and section 1317(b)(1) of this title. Nothing in this subsection shall affect the Administrator's authority under sections 1317 and 1319 of this title, affect State and local authority under sections 1317(b)(4) and 1370 of this title, relieve such treatment works of its obligations to meet requirements established under this chapter, or otherwise preclude such works from pursuing whatever feasible options are available to meet its responsibility to comply with its permit under this section.

(n) PARTIAL PERMIT PROGRAM

(1) STATE SUBMISSION

The Governor of a State may submit under subsection (b) of this section a permit program for a portion of the discharges into the navigable waters in such State.

(2) MINIMUM COVERAGE

A partial permit program under this subsection shall cover, at a minimum, administration of a major category of the discharges into the navigable waters of the State or a major component of the permit program required by subsection (b) of this section.

(3) APPROVAL OF MAJOR CATEGORY PARTIAL PERMIT PROGRAMS

The Administrator may approve a partial permit program covering administration of a major category of discharges under this subsection if —

(A) such program represents a complete permit program and covers all of the discharges under the jurisdiction of a department or agency of the State; and

(B) the Administrator determines that the partial program represents a significant and identifiable part of the State program required by subsection (b) of this section.

(4) APPROVAL OF MAJOR COMPONENT PARTIAL PERMIT PROGRAMS

The Administrator may approve under this subsection a partial and phased permit program covering administration of a major component (including discharge categories) of a State permit program required by subsection (b) of this section if —

Clean Water Act §1342

(A) the Administrator determines that the partial program represents a significant and identifiable part of the State program required by subsection (b) of this section; and

(B) the State submits, and the Administrator approves, a plan for the State to assume administration by phases of the remainder of the State program required by subsection (b) of this section by a specified date not more than 5 years after submission of the partial program under this subsection and agrees to make all reasonable efforts to assume such administration by such date.

(o) ANTI-BACKSLIDING

(1) GENERAL PROHIBITION

In the case of effluent limitations established on the basis of subsection (a)(1)(B) of this section, a permit may not be renewed, reissued, or modified on the basis of effluent guidelines promulgated under section 1314(b) of this title subsequent to the original issuance of such permit, to contain effluent limitations which are less stringent than the comparable effluent limitations in the previous permit. In the case of effluent limitations established on the basis of section 1311(b)(1)(C) or section 1313(d) or (e) of this title, a permit may not be renewed, reissued, or modified to contain effluent limitations which are less stringent than the comparable effluent limitations in the previous permit except in compliance with section 1313(d)(4) of this title.

(2) EXCEPTIONS

A permit with respect to which paragraph (1) applies may be renewed, reissued, or modified to contain a less stringent effluent limitation applicable to a pollutant if —

(A) material and substantial alterations or additions to the permitted facility occurred after permit issuance which justify the application of a less stringent effluent limitation;

(B)(i) information is available which was not available at the time of permit issuance (other than revised regulations, guidance, or test methods) and which would have justified the application of a less stringent effluent limitation at the time of permit issuance; or

(ii) the Administrator determines that technical mistakes or mistaken interpretations of law were made in issuing the permit under subsection (a)(1)(B) of this section;

(C) a less stringent effluent limitation is necessary because of events over which the permittee has no control and for which there is no reasonably available remedy;

(D) the permittee has received a permit modification under section 1311(c), 1311(g), 1311(h), 1311(i), 1311(k), 1311(n), or 1326(a) of this title; or

(E) the permittee has installed the treatment facilities required to meet the effluent limitations in the previous permit and has properly operated and maintained the facilities but has nevertheless been unable to achieve the previous effluent limitations, in which case the limitations in the reviewed, reissued, or modified permit may reflect the level of pollutant control actually achieved (but shall not be less stringent than required by effluent guidelines in effect at the time of permit renewal, reissuance, or modification).

Subparagraph (B) shall not apply to any revised waste load allocations or any alternative grounds for translating water quality standards into effluent limitations, except where the cumulative effect of such revised allocations results in a decrease in the amount of pollutants discharged into the concerned waters, and such revised allocations are not the result of a discharger eliminating or substantially reducing its discharge of pollutants due to complying with the requirements of this chapter or for reasons otherwise unrelated to water quality.

(3) LIMITATIONS

In no event may a permit with respect to which paragraph (1) applies be renewed, reissued, or modified to contain an effluent limitation which is less stringent than required by effluent guidelines in effect at the time the permit is renewed, reissued, or modified. In no event may such a permit to discharge into waters be renewed, reissued, or modified to contain a less stringent effluent limitation if the implementation of such limitation would result in a violation of a water quality standard under section 1313 of this title applicable to such waters.

(p) MUNICIPAL AND INDUSTRIAL STORMWATER DISCHARGES

(1) GENERAL RULE

Prior to October 1, 1992, the Administrator or the State (in the case of a permit program approved under this section) shall not require a permit under this section for discharges composed entirely of stormwater.

(2) EXCEPTIONS

Paragraph (1) shall not apply with respect to the following stormwater discharges:

(A) A discharge with respect to which a permit has been issued under this section before February 4, 1987.

(B) A discharge associated with industrial activity.

(C) A discharge from a municipal separate storm sewer system serving a population of 250,000 or more.

(D) A discharge from a municipal separate storm sewer system serving a population of 100,000 or more but less than 250,000.

(E) A discharge for which the Administrator or the State, as the case may be, determines that the stormwater discharge contributes to a violation of a water quality standard or is a significant contributor of pollutants to waters of the United States.

(3) **PERMIT REQUIREMENTS**

(A) **INDUSTRIAL DISCHARGES**

Permits for discharges associated with industrial activity shall meet all applicable provisions of this section and section 1311 of this title.

(B) **MUNICIPAL DISCHARGE**

Permits for discharges from municipal storm sewers —
(i) may be issued on a system- or jurisdiction-wide basis;
(ii) shall include a requirement to effectively prohibit non-stormwater discharges into the storm sewers; and
(iii) shall require controls to reduce the discharge of pollutants to the maximum extent practicable, including management practices, control techniques and system, design and engineering methods, and such other provisions as the Administrator or the State determines appropriate for the control of such pollutants.

(4) **PERMIT APPLICATION REQUIREMENTS**

(A) **INDUSTRIAL AND LARGE MUNICIPAL DISCHARGES**

Not later than 2 years after February 4, 1987, the Administrator shall establish regulations setting forth the permit application requirements for stormwater discharges described in paragraphs (2)(B) and (2)(C). Applications for permits for such discharges shall be filed no later than 3 years after February 4, 1987. Not later than 4 years after February 4, 1987, the Administrator or the State, as the case may be, shall issue or deny each such permit. Any such permit shall provide for compliance as expeditiously as practicable, but in no event later than 3 years after the date of issuance of such permit.

(B) **OTHER MUNICIPAL DISCHARGES**

Not later than 4 years after February 4, 1987, the Administrator shall establish regulations setting forth the permit application requirements for stormwater discharges described in paragraph (2)(D). Applications for permits for such discharges shall be filed no later than 5 years after February 4, 1987. Not later than 6 years after February 4, 1987, the Administrator or the State, as the case may be, shall issue or deny each such permit. Any such permit shall provide for compliance as expeditiously as practicable, but in no event later than 3 years after the date of issuance of such permit.

(5) **STUDIES**

The Administrator, in consultation with the States, shall conduct a study for the purposes of —

(A) identifying those stormwater discharges or classes of stormwater discharges for which permits are not required pursuant to paragraphs (1) and (2) of this subsection;

(B) determining, to the maximum extent practicable, the nature and extent of pollutants in such discharges; and

(C) establishing procedures and methods to control stormwater discharges to the extent necessary to mitigate impacts on water quality.

Not later than October 1, 1988, the Administrator shall submit to Congress a report on the results of the study described in subparagraphs (A) and (B). Not later than October 1, 1989, the Administrator shall submit to Congress a report on the results of the study described in subparagraph (C).

(6) REGULATIONS

Not later than October 1, 1992, the Administrator, in consultation with State and local officials, shall issue regulations (based on the results of the studies conducted under paragraph (5)) which designate stormwater discharges, other than those discharges described in paragraph (2), to be regulated to protect water quality and shall establish a comprehensive program to regulate such designated sources. The program shall, at a minimum, (A) establish priorities, (B) establish requirements for State stormwater management programs, and (C) establish expeditious deadlines. The program may include performance standards, guidelines, guidance, and management practices and treatment requirements, as appropriate.

§1343. OCEAN DISCHARGE CRITERIA

(a) ISSUANCE OF PERMITS

No permit under section 1342 of this title for a discharge into the territorial sea, the waters of the contiguous zone, or the oceans shall be issued, after promulgation of guidelines established under subsection (c) of this section, except in compliance with such guidelines. Prior to the promulgation of such guidelines, a permit may be issued under such section 1342 of this title if the Administrator determines it to be in the public interest.

(b) WAIVER

The requirements of subsection (d) of section 1342 of this title may not be waived in the case of permits for discharges into the territorial sea.

(c) GUIDELINES FOR DETERMINING DEGRADATION OF WATERS

(1) The Administrator shall, within one hundred and eighty days after October 18, 1972 (and from time to time thereafter), promulgate guidelines for determining the degradation of the waters of the territorial seas, and contiguous zone, and the oceans, which shall include:

(A) the effect of disposal of pollutants on human health or welfare, including but not limited to plankton, fish, shellfish, wildlife, shorelines, and beaches;

(B) the effect of disposal of pollutants on marine life including the transfer, concentration, and dispersal of pollutants or their by-products through biological, physical, and chemical processes; changes in marine ecosystem diversity, productivity, and stability; and species and community population changes;

(C) the effect of disposal, of pollutants on esthetic, recreation, and economic values;

(D) the persistence and permanence of the effects of disposal of pollutants;

(E) the effect of the disposal of varying rates, of particular volumes and concentrations of pollutants;

(F) other possible locations and methods of disposal or recycling of pollutants including land-based alternatives; and

(G) the effect on alternate uses of the oceans, such as mineral exploitation and scientific study.

(2) In any event where insufficient information exists on any proposed discharge to make a reasonable judgment on any of the guidelines established pursuant to this subsection no permit shall be issued under section 1342 of this title.

§1344. PERMITS FOR DREDGED OR FILL MATERIAL

(a) DISCHARGE INTO NAVIGABLE WATERS AT SPECIFIED DISPOSAL SITES

The Secretary may issue permits, after notice and opportunity for public hearings for the discharge of dredged or fill material into the navigable waters at specified disposal sites. Not later than the fifteenth day after the date an applicant submits all the information required to complete an application for a permit under this subsection, the Secretary shall publish the notice required by this subsection.

(b) SPECIFICATION FOR DISPOSAL SITES

Subject to subsection (c) of this section, each such disposal site shall be specified for each such permit by the Secretary (1) through the application of guidelines developed by the Administrator, in conjunction with the Secretary, which guidelines shall be based upon criteria comparable to the criteria applicable to the territorial seas, the contiguous zone, and the ocean under section 1343(c) of this title, and (2) in any case where such guidelines under clause (1) alone would prohibit the specification of a site, through the application additionally of the economic impact of the site on navigation and anchorage.

(c) DENIAL OR RESTRICTION OF USE OF DEFINED AREAS AS DISPOSAL SITES

The Administrator is authorized to prohibit the specification (including the withdrawal of specification) of any defined area as a disposal site, and he is

§1344   Clean Water Act

authorized to deny or restrict the use of any defined area for specification (including the withdrawal of specification) as a disposal site, whenever he determines, after notice and opportunity for public hearings, that the discharge of such materials into such area will have an unacceptable adverse effect on municipal water supplies, shellfish beds and fishery areas (including spawning and breeding areas), wildlife, or recreational areas. Before making such determination, the Administrator shall consult with the Secretary. The Administrator shall set forth in writing and make public his findings and his reasons for making any determination under this subsection.

(d)   "SECRETARY" DEFINED

The term "Secretary" as used in this section means the Secretary of the Army, acting through the Chief of Engineers.

(e)   GENERAL PERMITS ON STATE, REGIONAL, OR NATIONWIDE BASIS

(1) In carrying out his functions relating to the discharge of dredged or fill material under this section, the Secretary may, after notice and opportunity for public hearing, issue general permits on a State, regional, or nationwide basis for any category of activities involving discharges of dredged or fill material if the Secretary determines that the activities in such category are similar in nature, will cause only minimal adverse environmental effects when performed separately, and will have only minimal cumulative adverse effect on the environment. Any general permit issued under this subsection shall (A) be based on the guidelines described in subsection (b)(1) of this section, and (B) set forth the requirements and standards which shall apply to any activity authorized by such general permit.

(2) No general permit issued under this subsection shall be for a period of more than five years after the date of its issuance and such general permit may be revoked or modified by the Secretary if, after opportunity for public hearing, the Secretary determines that the activities authorized by such general permit have an adverse impact on the environment or such activities are more appropriately authorized by individual permits.

(f)   NON-PROHIBITED DISCHARGE OF DREDGED OR FILL MATERIAL

(1) Except as provided in paragraph (2) of this subsection, the discharge of dredged or fill material —

    (A) from normal farming, silviculture, and ranching activities such as plowing, seeding, cultivating, minor drainage, harvesting for the production of food, fiber, and forest products, or upland soil and water conservation practices;

    (B) for the purpose of maintenance, including emergency reconstruction of recently damaged parts, of currently serviceable structures such as dikes, dams, levees, groins, riprap, breakwaters, causeways, and bridge abutments or approaches, and transportation structures;

(C) for the purpose of construction or maintenance of farm or stock ponds or irrigation ditches, or the maintenance of drainage ditches;

(D) for the purpose of construction of temporary sedimentation basins on a construction site which does not include placement of fill material into the navigable waters;

(E) for the purpose of construction or maintenance of farm roads or forest roads, or temporary roads for moving mining equipment, where such roads are constructed and maintained, in accordance with best management practices, to assure that flow and circulation patterns and chemical and biological characteristics of the navigable waters are not impaired, that the reach of the navigable waters is not reduced, and that any adverse effect on the aquatic environment will be otherwise minimized;

(F) resulting from any activity with respect to which a State has an approved program under section 1288(b)(4) of this title which meets the requirements of subparagraphs (B) and (C) of such section.

is not prohibited by or otherwise subject to regulation under this section or section 1311(a) or 1342 of this title (except for effluent standards or prohibitions under section 1317 of this title).

(2) Any discharge of dredged or fill material into the navigable waters incidental to any activity having as its purpose bringing an area of the navigable waters into a use to which it was not previously subject, where the flow or circulation of navigable waters may be impaired or the reach of such waters be reduced, shall be required to have a permit under this section.

(g) STATE ADMINISTRATION

(1) The Governor of any State desiring to administer its own individual and general permit program for the discharge of dredged or fill material into the navigable waters (other than those waters which are presently used, or are susceptible to use in their natural condition or by reasonable improvement as a means to transport interstate or foreign commerce shoreward to their ordinary high water mark, including all waters which are subject to the ebb and flow of the tide shoreward to their mean high water mark, or mean higher high water mark on the west coast, including wetlands adjacent thereto) within its jurisdiction may submit to the Administrator a full and complete description of the program it proposes to establish and administer under State law or under an interstate compact. In addition, such State shall submit a statement from the attorney general (or the attorney for those State agencies which have independent legal counsel), or from the chief legal officer in the case of an interstate agency, that the laws of such State, or the interstate compact, as the case may be, provide adequate authority to carry out the described program.

(2) Not later than the tenth day after the date of the receipt of the program and statement submitted by any State under paragraph (1) of this subsection, the Administrator shall provide copies of such program and statement to the Secretary and the Secretary of the Interior, acting through the Director of the United States Fish and Wildlife Service.

§1344   Clean Water Act

(3) Not later than the ninetieth day after the date of the receipt by the Administrator of the program and statement submitted by any State, under paragraph (1) of this subsection, the Secretary and the Secretary of the Interior, acting through the Director of the United States Fish and Wildlife Service, shall submit any comments with respect to such program and statement to the Administrator in writing.

(h) DETERMINATION OF STATE'S AUTHORITY TO ISSUE PERMITS UNDER STATE PROGRAM; APPROVAL; NOTIFICATION; TRANSFERS TO STATE PROGRAM

(1) Not later than the one-hundred-twentieth day after the date of the receipt by the Administrator of a program and statement submitted by any State under paragraph (1) of this subsection, the Administrator shall determine, taking into account any comments submitted by the Secretary and the Secretary of the Interior, acting through the Director of the United States Fish and Wildlife Service, pursuant to subsection (g) of this section, whether such State has the following authority with respect to the issuance of permits pursuant to such program:

(A) To issue permits which —

(i) apply, and assure compliance with, any applicable requirements of this section, including, but not limited to, the guidelines established under subsection (b)(1) of this section, and sections 1317 and 1343 of this title;

(ii) are for fixed terms not exceeding five years; and

(iii) can be terminated or modified for cause including, but not limited to, the following:

(I) violation of any condition of the permit;

(II) obtaining a permit by misrepresentation, or failure to disclose fully all relevant facts;

(III) change in any condition that requires either a temporary or permanent reduction or elimination of the permitted discharge.

(B) To issue permits which apply, and assure compliance with, all applicable requirements of section 1318 of this title, or to inspect, monitor, enter, and require reports to at least the same extent as required in section 1318 of this title.

(C) To assure that the public, and any other State the waters of which may be affected, receive notice of each application for a permit and to provide an opportunity for public hearing before a ruling on each such application.

(D) To assure that the Administrator receives notice of each application (including a copy thereof) for a permit.

(E) To assure that any State (other than the permitting State), whose waters may be affected by the issuance of a permit may submit written recommendations to the permitting State (and the Administrator) with respect to any permit application and, if any part of such written recommendations are not accepted by the permitting State, that the permitting State will notify such affected State (and the Administrator) in writing of its failure to so accept such recommendations together with its reasons for so doing.

Clean Water Act §1344

(F) To assure that no permit will be issued if, in the judgment of the Secretary, after consultation with the Secretary of the department in which the Coast Guard is operating, anchorage and navigation of any of the navigable waters would be substantially impaired thereby.

(G) To abate violations of the permit or the permit program, including civil and criminal penalties and other ways and means of enforcement.

(H) To assure continued coordination with Federal and Federal-State water-related planning and review processes.

(2) If, with respect to a State program submitted under subsection (g)(1) of this section, the Administrator determines that such State —

(A) has the authority set forth in paragraph (1) of this subsection, the Administrator shall approve the program and so notify (i) such State and (ii) the Secretary, who upon subsequent notification from such State that it is administering such program, shall suspend the issuance of permits under subsections (a) and (e) of this section for activities with respect to which a permit may be issued pursuant to such State program; or

(B) does not have the authority set forth in paragraph (1) of this subsection, the Administrator shall so notify such State, which notification shall also describe the revisions or modifications necessary so that such State may resubmit such program for a determination by the Administrator under this subsection.

(3) If the Administrator fails to make a determination with respect to any program submitted by a State under subsection (g)(1) of this section within one-hundred-twenty days after the date of the receipt of such program, such program shall be deemed approved pursuant to paragraph (2)(A) of this subsection and the Administrator shall so notify such State and the Secretary who, upon subsequent notification from such State that it is administering such program, shall suspend the issuance of permits under subsection (a) and (e) of this section for activities with respect to which a permit may be issued by such State.

(4) After the Secretary receives notification from the Administrator under paragraph (2) or (3) of this subsection that a State permit program has been approved, the Secretary shall transfer any applications for permits pending before the Secretary for activities with respect to which a permit may be issued pursuant to such State program to such State for appropriate action.

(5) Upon notification from a State with a permit program approved under this subsection that such State intends to administer and enforce the terms and conditions of a general permit issued by the Secretary under subsection (e) of this section with respect to activities in such State to which such general permit applies, the Secretary shall suspend the administration and enforcement of such general permit with respect to such activities.

(i) WITHDRAWAL OF APPROVAL

Whenever the Administrator determines after public hearing that a State is not administering a program approved under subsection (h)(2)(A) of this section, in accordance with this section, including, but not limited to, the guidelines established under subsection (b)(1) of this section, the Administrator shall so notify the State, and, if appropriate corrective action is not taken within a reasonable time, not to exceed ninety days after the date of the receipt of such notification, the Administrator shall (1) withdraw approval of such program until the Administrator determines such corrective action has been taken, and (2) notify the Secretary that the Secretary shall resume the program for the issuance of permits under subsections (a) and (e) of this section for activities with respect to which the State was issuing permits and that such authority of the Secretary shall continue in effect until such time as the Administrator makes the determination described in clause (1) of this subsection and such State again has an approved program.

(j) COPIES OF APPLICATIONS FOR STATE PERMITS AND PROPOSED GENERAL PERMITS TO BE TRANSMITTED TO ADMINISTRATOR

Each State which is administering a permit program pursuant to this section shall transmit to the Administrator (1) a copy of each permit application received by such State and provide notice to the Administrator of every action related to the consideration of such permit application, including each permit proposed to be issued by such State, and (2) a copy of each proposed general permit which such State intends to issue. Not later than the tenth day after the date of the receipt of such permit application or such proposed general permit, the Administrator shall provide copies of such permit application or such proposed general permit to the Secretary and the Secretary of the Interior, acting through the Director of the United States Fish and Wildlife Service. If the Administrator intends to provide written comments to such State with respect to such permit application or such proposed general permit, he shall so notify such State not later than the thirtieth day after the date of the receipt of such application or such proposed general permit and provide such written comments to such State, after consideration of any comments made in writing with respect to such application or such proposed general permit by the Secretary and the Secretary of the Interior, acting through the Director of the United States Fish and Wildlife Service, not later than the ninetieth day after the date of such receipt. If such State is so notified by the Administrator, it shall not issue the proposed permit until after the receipt of such comments from the Administrator, or after such ninetieth day, whichever first occurs. Such State shall not issue such proposed permit after such ninetieth day if it has received such written comments in which the Administrator objects (A) to the issuance of such proposed permit and such proposed permit is one that has been submitted to the Administrator pursuant to subsection (h)(1)(E) of this section, or (B) to the issuance of such proposed permit as being outside the requirements of this section, including, but not limited to, the guidelines developed under subsection (b)(1) of this section unless it modifies such proposed permit in accordance with such comments. Whenever the Administrator objects to the issuance of a permit under the preceding sentence such written objection shall contain a statement of the reasons for such objection and the conditions which such permit would include if it were issued by the Administrator. In any case where the Administrator objects to the issuance of a permit, on request of the State, a public hearing shall be

Clean Water Act §1344

held by the Administrator on such objection. If the State does not resubmit such permit revised to meet such objection within 30 days after completion of the hearing or, if no hearing is requested within 90 days after the date of such objection, the Secretary may issue the permit pursuant to subsection (a) or (e) of this section, as the case may be, for such source in accordance with the guidelines and requirements of this chapter.

(k) WAIVER

In accordance with guidelines promulgated pursuant to subsection (i)(2) of section 1314 of this title, the Administrator is authorized to waive the requirements of subsection (j) of this section at the time of the approval of a program pursuant to subsection (h)(2)(A) of this section for any category (including any class, type, or size within such category) of discharge within the State submitting such program.

(l) CATEGORIES OF DISCHARGES NOT SUBJECT TO REQUIREMENTS

The Administrator shall promulgate regulations establishing categories of discharges which he determines shall not be subject to the requirements of subsection (j) of this section in any State with a program approved pursuant to subsection (h)(2)(A) of this section. The Administrator may distinguish among classes, types, and sizes within any category of discharges.

(m) COMMENTS ON PERMIT APPLICATIONS OR PROPOSED GENERAL PERMITS BY SECRETARY OF THE INTERIOR ACTING THROUGH DIRECTOR OF UNITED STATES FISH AND WILDLIFE SERVICE

Not later than the ninetieth day after the date on which the Secretary notifies the Secretary of the Interior, acting through the Director of the United States Fish and Wildlife Service that (1) an application for a permit under subsection (a) of this section has been received by the Secretary, or (2) the Secretary proposes to issue a general permit under subsection (e) of this section, the Secretary of the Interior, acting through the Director of the United States Fish and Wildlife Service, shall submit any comments with respect to such application or such proposed general permit in writing to the Secretary.

(n) ENFORCEMENT AUTHORITY NOT LIMITED

Nothing in this section shall be construed to limit the authority of the Administrator to take action pursuant to section 1319 of this title.

(o) PUBLIC AVAILABILITY OF PERMITS AND PERMIT APPLICATIONS

A copy of each permit application and each permit issued under this section shall be available to the public. Such permit application or portion thereof, shall further be available on request for the purpose of reproduction.

(p) COMPLIANCE

Compliance with a permit issued pursuant to this section, including any activity carried out pursuant to a general permit issued under this section, shall be deemed compliance, for purposes of sections 1319 and 1365 of this title, with sections 1311, 1317, and 1343 of this title.

(q) MINIMIZATION OF DUPLICATION, NEEDLESS PAPERWORK, AND DELAYS IN ISSUANCE; AGREEMENTS

Not later than the one-hundred-eightieth day after December 27, 1977, the Secretary shall enter into agreements with the Administrator, the Secretaries of the Departments of Agriculture, Commerce, Interior, and Transportation, and the heads of other appropriate Federal agencies to minimize, to the maximum extent practicable, duplication, needless paperwork, and delays in the issuance of permits under this section. Such agreements shall be developed to assure that, to the maximum extent practicable, a decision with respect to an application for a permit under subsection (a) of this section will be made not later than the ninetieth day after the date the notice for such application is published under subsection (a) of this section.

(r) FEDERAL PROJECTS SPECIFICALLY AUTHORIZED BY CONGRESS

The discharge of dredged or fill material as part of the construction of a Federal project specifically authorized by Congress, whether prior to or on or after December 27, 1977, is not prohibited by or otherwise subject to regulation under this section, or a State program approved under this section, or section 1311(a) or 1342 of this title (except for effluent standards or prohibitions under section 1317 of this title), if information on the effects of such discharge, including consideration of the guidelines developed under subsection (b)(1) of this section, is included in an environmental impact statement for such project pursuant to the National Environmental Policy Act of 1969 [42 U.S.C. 4321 et seq.] and such environmental impact statement has been submitted to Congress before the actual discharge of dredged or fill material in connection with the construction of such project and prior to either authorization of such project or an appropriation of funds for such construction.

(s) VIOLATION OF PERMITS

(1) Whenever on the basis of any information available to him the Secretary finds that any person is in violation of any condition or limitation set forth in a permit issued by the Secretary under this section, the Secretary shall issue an order requiring such person to comply with such condition or limitation, or the Secretary shall bring a civil action in accordance with paragraph (3) of this subsection.

(2) A copy of any order issued under this subsection shall be sent immediately by the Secretary to the State in which the violation occurs and other affected States. Any order issued under this subsection shall be by personal service and shall state with reasonable specificity the nature of the violation, specify a time for compliance, not to exceed thirty days, which the Secretary determines is reasonable, taking into account the seriousness of the violation and any good faith efforts to comply with applicable requirements. In any case in which an

Clean Water Act §1345

order under this subsection is issued to a corporation, a copy of such order shall be served on any appropriate corporate officers.

(3) The Secretary is authorized to commence a civil action for appropriate relief, including a permanent or temporary injunction for any violation for which he is authorized to issue a compliance order under paragraph (1) of this subsection. Any action under this paragraph may be brought in the district court of the United States for the district in which the defendant is located or resides or is doing business, and such court shall have jurisdiction to restrain such violation and to require compliance. Notice of the commencement of such acton[1] shall be given immediately to the appropriate State.

(4) Any person who violates any condition or limitation in a permit issued by the Secretary under this section, and any person who violates any order issued by the Secretary under paragraph (1) of this subsection, shall be subject to a civil penalty not to exceed $25,000 per day for each violation. In determining the amount of a civil penalty the court shall consider the seriousness of the violation or violations, the economic benefit (if any) resulting from the violation, any history of such violations, any good-faith efforts to comply with the applicable requirements, the economic impact of the penalty on the violator, and such other matters as justice may require.

(t) NAVIGABLE WATERS WITHIN STATE JURISDICTION

Nothing in this section shall preclude or deny the right of any State or interstate agency to control the discharge of dredged or fill material in any portion of the navigable waters within the jurisdiction of such State, including any activity of any Federal agency, and each such agency shall comply with such State or interstate requirements both substantive and procedural to control the discharge of dredged or fill material to the same extent that any person is subject to such requirements. This section shall not be construed as affecting or impairing the authority of the Secretary to maintain navigation.

§1345. DISPOSAL OR USE OF SEWAGE SLUDGE

(a) PERMIT

Notwithstanding any other provision of this chapter or of any other law, in any case where the disposal of sewage sludge resulting from the operation of a treatment works as defined in section 1292 of this title (including the removal of in-place sewage sludge from one location and its deposit at another location) would result in any pollutant from such sewage sludge entering the navigable waters, such disposal is prohibited except in accordance with a permit issued by the Administrator under section 1342 of this title.

---

[1] So in original. Probably should be "action."

(b) ISSUANCE OF PERMIT; REGULATIONS

The Administrator shall issue regulations governing the issuance of permits for the disposal of sewage sludge subject to subsection (a) of this section and section 1342 of this title. Such regulations shall require the application to such disposal of each criterion, factor, procedure, and requirement applicable to a permit issued under section 1342 of this title.

(c) STATE PERMIT PROGRAM

Each State desiring to administer its own permit program for disposal of sewage sludge subject to subsection (a) of this section within its jurisdiction may do so in accordance with section 1342 of this title.

(d) REGULATIONS

(1) REGULATIONS

The Administrator, after consultation with appropriate Federal and State agencies and other interested persons, shall develop and publish, within one year after December 27, 1977, and from time to time thereafter, regulations providing guidelines for the disposal of sludge and the utilization of sludge for various purposes. Such regulations shall —

(A) identify uses for sludge, including disposal;

(B) specify factors to be taken into account in determining the measures and practices applicable to each such use or disposal (including publication of information on costs);

(C) identify concentrations of pollutants which interfere with each such use or disposal.

The Administrator is authorized to revise any regulation issued under this subsection.

(2) IDENTIFICATION AND REGULATION OF TOXIC POLLUTANTS

(A) ON BASIS OF AVAILABLE INFORMATION

(i) PROPOSED REGULATIONS

Not later than November 30, 1986, the Administrator shall identify those toxic pollutants which, on the basis of available information on their toxicity, persistence, concentration, mobility, or potential for exposure, may be present in sewage sludge in concentrations which may adversely affect public health or the environment, and propose regulations specifying acceptable management practices for sewage sludge containing each such toxic pollutant and establishing numerical limitations for each such pollutant for each use identified under paragraph (1)(A).

(ii) FINAL REGULATIONS

Not later than August 31, 1987, and after opportunity for public hearing, the Administrator shall promulgate the regulations required by subparagraph (A)(i).

(B) OTHERS

(i) PROPOSED REGULATIONS

Not later than July 31, 1987, the Administrator shall identify those toxic pollutants not identified under subparagraph (A)(i) which may be present in sewage sludge in concentrations which may adversely affect public health or the environment, and propose regulations specifying acceptable management practices for sewage sludge containing each such toxic pollutant and establishing numerical limitations for each pollutant for each such use identified under paragraph (1)(A).

(ii) FINAL REGULATIONS

Not later than June 15, 1988, the Administrator shall promulgate the regulations required by subparagraph (B)(i).

(C) REVIEW

From time to time, but not less often than every 2 years, the Administrator shall review the regulations promulgated under this paragraph for the purpose of identifying additional toxic pollutants and promulgating regulations for such pollutants consistent with the requirements of this paragraph.

(D) MINIMUM STANDARDS; COMPLIANCE DATE

The management practices and numerical criteria established under subparagraphs (A), (B), and (C) shall be adequate to protect public health and the environment from any reasonably anticipated adverse effects of each pollutant. Such regulations shall require compliance as expeditiously as practicable but in no case later than 12 months after their publication, unless such regulations require the construction of new pollution control facilities, in which case the regulations shall require compliance as expeditiously as practicable but in no case later than two years from the date of their publication.

(3) ALTERNATIVE STANDARDS

For purposes of this subsection, if, in the judgment of the Administrator, it is not feasible to prescribe or enforce a numerical limitation for a pollutant identified under paragraph (2), the Administrator may instead promulgate a design, equipment, management practice, or operational standard, or combination thereof, which in the Administrator's judgment is adequate to protect public health and the environment from any reasonably anticipated adverse effects of such pollutant. In the event the Administrator promulgates a design or equipment standard under this subsection, the Administrator shall include as part of such standard such requirements as will assure the proper operation and maintenance of any such element of design or equipment.

(4) CONDITIONS ON PERMITS

Prior to the promulgation of the regulations required by paragraph (2), the Administrator shall impose conditions in permits issued to publicly owned treatment works under section 1342 of this title or take such other measures as the Administrator deems appropriate to protect public health and the environment from any adverse effects which may occur from toxic pollutants in sewage sludge.

(5) LIMITATION ON STATUTORY CONSTRUCTION

Nothing in this section is intended to waive more stringent requirements established by this chapter or any other law.

(e) MANNER OF SLUDGE DISPOSAL

The determination of the manner of disposal or use of sludge is a local determination, except that it shall be unlawful for any person to dispose of sludge from a publicly owned treatment works or any other treatment works treating domestic sewage for any use for which regulations have been established pursuant to subsection (d) of this section, except in accordance with such regulations.

(f) IMPLEMENTATION OF REGULATIONS

(1) THROUGH SECTION 1342 PERMITS

Any permit issued under section 1342 of this title to a publicly owned treatment works or any other treatment works treating domestic sewage shall include requirements for the use and disposal of sludge that implement the regulations established pursuant to subsection (d) of this section, unless such requirements have been included in a permit issued under the appropriate provisions of subtitle C of the Solid Waste Disposal Act [42 U.S.C. 6921 et seq.], part C of the Safe Drinking Water Act [42 U.S.C. 300h et seq.], the Marine Protection, Research, and Sanctuaries Act of 1972 [33 U.S.C. 1401 et seq.], or the Clean Air Act [42 U.S.C. 7401 et seq.], or under State permit programs approved by the Administrator, where the Administrator determines that such programs assure compliance with any applicable requirements of this section. Not later than December 15, 1986, the Administrator shall promulgate procedures for approval of State programs pursuant to this paragraph.

(2) THROUGH OTHER PERMITS

In the case of a treatment works described in paragraph (1) that is not subject to section 1342 of this title and to which none of the other above listed permit programs nor approved State permit authority apply, the Administrator may issue a permit to such treatment works solely to impose requirements for the use and disposal of sludge that implement the regulations established pursuant to subsection (d) of this section. The Administrator shall include in the permit appropriate requirements to assure compliance with the regulations established pursuant to subsection (d) of this section. The Admin-

Clean Water Act §1361

istrator shall establish procedures for issuing permits pursuant to this paragraph.

(g) STUDIES AND PROJECTS

(1) GRANT PROGRAM; INFORMATION GATHERING

The Administrator is authorized to conduct or initiate scientific studies, demonstration projects, and public information and education projects which are designed to promote the safe and beneficial management or use of sewage sludge for such purposes as aiding the restoration of abandoned mine sites, conditioning soil for parks and recreation areas, agricultural and horticultural uses, and other beneficial purposes. For the purposes of carrying out this subsection, the Administrator may make grants to State water pollution control agencies, other public or nonprofit agencies, institutions, organizations, and individuals. In cooperation with other Federal departments and agencies, other public and private agencies, institutions, and organizations, the Administrator is authorized to collect and disseminate information pertaining to the safe and beneficial use of sewage sludge.

(2) AUTHORIZATION OF APPROPRIATIONS

For the purposes of carrying out the scientific studies, demonstration projects, and public information and education projects authorized in this section, there is authorized to be appropriated for fiscal years beginning after September 30, 1986, not to exceed $5,000,000. . . .

Subchapter V — General Provisions

§1361. ADMINISTRATION

(a) AUTHORITY OF ADMINISTRATOR TO PRESCRIBE REGULATIONS

The Administrator is authorized to prescribe such regulations as are necessary to carry out his functions under this chapter.

(b) UTILIZATION OF OTHER AGENCY OFFICERS AND EMPLOYEES

The Administrator, with the consent of the head of any other agency of the United States, may utilize such officers and employees of such agency as may be found necessary to assist in carrying out the purposes of this chapter.

(c) RECORDKEEPING

Each recipient of financial assistance under this chapter shall keep such records as the Administrator shall prescribe, including records which fully disclose the amount and disposition by such recipient of the proceeds of such assistance, the total cost of the project or undertaking in connection with which such assistance is given or used, and the amount of that portion of the cost of the project or undertaking supplied by other sources, and such other records as will facilitate effective audit.

(d) AUDIT

The Administrator and the Comptroller General of the United States, or any of their duly authorized representatives, shall have access, for the purpose of audit and examination, to any books, documents, papers, and records of the recipients that are pertinent to the grants received under this chapter. For the purpose of carrying out audits and examinations with respect to recipients of Federal assistance under this chapter, the Administrator is authorized to enter into noncompetitive procurement contracts with independent State audit organizations, consistent with chapter 75 of title 31. Such contracts may only be entered into to the extent and in such amounts as may be provided in advance in appropriation Acts.

(e) AWARDS FOR OUTSTANDING TECHNOLOGICAL ACHIEVEMENT OR INNOVATIVE PROCESSES, METHODS, OR DEVICES IN WASTE TREATMENT AND POLLUTION ABATEMENT PROGRAMS

(1) It is the purpose of this subsection to authorize a program which will provide official recognition by the United States Government to those industrial organizations and political subdivisions of States which during the preceding year demonstrated an outstanding technological achievement or an innovative process, method, or device in their waste treatment and pollution abatement programs. The Administrator shall, in consultation with the appropriate State water pollution control agencies, establish regulations under which such recognition may be applied for and granted, except that no applicant shall be eligible for an award under this subsection if such applicant is not in total compliance with all applicable water quality requirements under this chapter, or otherwise does not have a satisfactory record with respect to environmental quality.

(2) The Administrator shall award a certificate or plaque of suitable design to each industrial organization or political subdivision which qualifies for such recognition under regulations established under this subsection.

(3) The President of the United States, the Governor of the appropriate State, the Speaker of the House of Representatives, and the President pro tempore of the Senate shall be notified of the award by the Administrator and the awarding of such recognition shall be published in the Federal Register.

(f) DETAIL OF ENVIRONMENTAL PROTECTION AGENCY PERSONNEL TO STATE WATER POLLUTION CONTROL AGENCIES

Upon the request of a State water pollution control agency, personnel of the Environmental Protection Agency may be detailed to such agency for the purpose of carrying out the provisions of this chapter.

§1362. DEFINITIONS

Except as otherwise specifically provided, when used in this chapter.

(1) The term "State water pollution control agency" means the State agency designated by the Governor having responsibility for enforcing State laws relating to the abatement of pollution.

(2) The term "interstate agency" means an agency of two or more States established by or pursuant to an agreement or compact approved by the Congress, or any other agency of two or more States, having substantial powers or duties pertaining to the control of pollution as determined and approved by the Administrator.

(3) The term "State" means a State, the District of Columbia, the Commonwealth of Puerto Rico, the Virgin Islands, Guam, American Samoa, the Commonwealth of the Northern Mariana Islands, and the Trust Territory of the Pacific Islands.

(4) The term "municipality" means a city, town, borough, county, parish, district, association, or other public body created by or pursuant to State law and having jurisdiction over disposal of sewage, industrial wastes, or other wastes, or an Indian tribe or an authorized Indian tribal organization, or a designated and approved management agency under section 1288 of this title.

(5) The term "persons" means an individual, corporation, partnership, association, State, municipality, commission, or political subdivision of a State, or any interstate body.

(6) The term "pollutant" means dredged spoil, solid waste, incinerator residue, sewage, garbage, sewage sludge, munitions, chemical wastes, biological materials, radioactive materials, heat, wrecked or discarded equipment, rock, sand, cellar dirt and industrial, municipal, and agricultural waste discharged into water. This term does not mean (A) "sewage from vessels" within the meaning of section 1322 of this title; or (B) water, gas, or other material which is injected into a well to facilitate production of oil or gas, or water derived in association with oil or gas production and disposed of in a well, if the well used either to facilitate production or for disposal purposes is approved by authority of the State in which the well is located, and if such State determines that such injection or disposal will not result in the degradation of ground or surface water resources.

(7) The term "navigable waters" means the waters of the United States, including the territorial seas.

(8) The term "territorial seas" means the belt of the seas measured from the line of ordinary low water along that portion of the coast which is in direct contact with the open sea and the line marking the seaward limit of inland waters, and extending seaward a distance of three miles.

(9) The term "contiguous zone" means the entire zone established or to be established by the United States under article 24 of the Convention of the Territorial Sea and the Contiguous Zone.

(10) The term "ocean" means any portion of the high seas beyond the contiguous zone.

(11) The term "effluent limitation" means any restriction established by a State or the Administrator on quantities, rates, and concentrations of chemical, physical, biological, and other constituents which are discharged from point sources into navigable waters, the waters of the contiguous zone, or the ocean, including schedules of compliance.

(12) The term "discharge of a pollutant" and the term "discharge of

pollutants" each means (A) any addition of any pollutant to navigable waters from any point source, (B) any addition of any pollutant to the waters of the contiguous zone or the ocean from any point source other than a vessel or other floating craft.

(13) The term "toxic pollutant" means those pollutants, or combinations of pollutants, including disease-causing agents, which after discharge and upon exposure, ingestion, inhalation or assimilation into any organism, either directly from the environment or indirectly by ingestion through food chains will, on the basis of information available to the Administrator, cause death, disease, behavioral abnormalities, cancer, genetic mutations, physiological malfunctions (including malfunctions in reproduction) or physical deformations, in such organisms or their offspring.

(14) The term "point source" means any discernible, confined and discrete conveyance, including but not limited to any pipe, ditch, channel, tunnel, conduit, well, discrete fissure, container, rolling stock, concentrated animal feeding operation, or vessel or other floating craft, from which pollutants are or may be discharged. This term does not include agricultural stormwater discharges and return flows from irrigated agriculture.

(15) The term "biological monitoring" shall mean the determination of the effects on aquatic life, including accumulation of pollutants in tissue, in receiving waters due to the discharge of pollutants (A) by techniques and procedures, including sampling of organisms representative of appropriate levels of the food chain appropriate to the volume and the physical, chemical, and biological characteristics of the effluent, and (B) at appropriate frequencies and locations.

(16) The term "discharge" when used without qualification includes a discharge of a pollutant, and a discharge of pollutants.

(17) The term "schedule of compliance" means a schedule of remedial measures including an enforceable sequence of actions or operations leading to compliance with an effluent limitation, other limitation, prohibition, or standard.

(18) The term "industrial user" means those industries identified in the Standard Industrial Classification Manual, Bureau of the Budget, 1967, as amended and supplemented, under the category of "Division D — Manufacturing" and such other classes of significant waste producers as, by regulation, the Administrator deems appropriate.

(19) The term "pollution" means the man-made or man-induced alteration of the chemical, physical, biological, and radiological integrity of water.

(20) The term "medical waste" means isolation wastes; infectious agents; human blood and blood products; pathological wastes; sharps; body parts; contaminated bedding; surgical wastes and potentially contaminated laboratory wastes; dialysis wastes; and such additional medical items as the Administrator shall prescribe by regulation.

§1363. WATER POLLUTION CONTROL ADVISORY BOARD

(a) ESTABLISHMENT; COMPOSITION; TERMS OF OFFICE

(1) There is hereby established in the Environmental Protection Agency a Water Pollution Control Advisory Board, composed of the Administrator or his designee, who shall be Chairman, and nine members appointed by the President, none of whom shall be Federal officers or employees. The appointed members, having due regard for the purposes of this chapter, shall be selected from among representatives of various State, interstate, and local governmental agencies, of public or private interests contributing to, affected by, or concerned with pollution, and of other public and private agencies, organizations, or groups demonstrating an active interest in the field of pollution prevention and control, as well as other individuals who are expert in this field.

(2)(A) Each member appointed by the President shall hold office for a term of three years, except that (i) any member appointed to fill a vacancy occurring prior to the expiration of the term for which his predecessor was appointed shall be appointed for the remainder of such term, and (ii) the terms of office of the members first taking office after June 30, 1956, shall expire as follows: three at the end of one year after such date, three at the end of two years after such date, and three at the end of three years after such date, as designated by the President at the time of appointment, and (iii) the term of any member under the preceding provisions shall be extended until the date on which his successor's appointment is effective. None of the members appointed by the President shall be eligible for reappointment within one year after the end of his preceding term.

(B) The members of the Board who are not officers or employees of the United States, while attending conferences or meetings of the Board or while serving at the request of the Administrator, shall be entitled to receive compensation at a rate to be fixed by the Administrator, but not exceeding $100 per diem, including travel-time, and while away from their homes or regular places of business they may be allowed travel expenses, including per diem in lieu of subsistence, as authorized by law for persons in the Government service employed intermittently.

(b) FUNCTIONS

The Board shall advise, consult with, and make recommendations to the Administrator on matters of policy relating to the activities and functions of the Administrator under this chapter.

(c) CLERICAL AND TECHNICAL ASSISTANCE

Such clerical and technical assistance as may be necessary to discharge the duties of the Board shall be provided from the personnel of the Environmental Protection Agency.

§1364. EMERGENCY POWERS

(a) EMERGENCY POWERS

Notwithstanding any other provision of this chapter, the Administrator upon receipt of evidence that a pollution source or combination of sources is presenting an imminent and substantial endangerment to the health of persons or to the welfare of persons where such endangerment is to the livelihood of such persons, such as inability to market shellfish, may bring suit on behalf of the United States in the appropriate district court to immediately restrain any person causing or contributing to the alleged pollution to stop the discharge of pollutants causing or contributing to such pollution or to take such other action as may be necessary. . . .

§1365. CITIZEN SUITS

(a) AUTHORIZATION; JURISDICTION

Except as provided in subsection (b) of this section and section 1319 (g)(6) of this title, any citizen may commence a civil action on his own behalf —

(1) against any person (including (i) the United States, and (ii) any other governmental instrumentality or agency to the extent permitted by the eleventh amendment to the Constitution) who is alleged to be in violation of (A) an effluent standard or limitation under this chapter or (B) an order issued by the Administrator or a State with respect to such a standard or limitation, or

(2) against the Administrator where there is alleged a failure of the Administrator to perform any act or duty under this chapter which is not discretionary with the Administrator.

The district courts shall have jurisdiction, without regard to the amount in controversy or the citizenship of the parties, to enforce such an effluent standard or limitation, or such an order, or to order the Administrator to perform such act or duty, as the case may be, and to apply any appropriate civil penalties under section 1319(d) of this title.

(b) NOTICE

No action may be commenced —

(1) under subsection (a)(1) of this section —

(A) prior to sixty days after the plaintiff has given notice of the alleged violation (i) to the Administrator, (ii) to the State in which the alleged violation occurs, and (iii) to any alleged violator of the standard, limitation, or order, or

(B) if the Administrator or State has commenced and is diligently prosecuting a civil or criminal action in a court of the United States, or a State to require compliance with the standard, limitation, or order, but in any such action in a court of the United States any citizen may intervene as a matter of right.

Clean Water Act §1365

(2) under subsection (a)(2) of this section prior to sixty days after the plaintiff has given notice of such action to the Administrator,

except that such action may be brought immediately after such notification in the case of an action under this section respecting a violation of sections 1316 and 1317(a) of this title. Notice under this subsection shall be given in such manner as the Administrator shall prescribe by regulation.

(c) VENUE; INTERVENTION BY ADMINISTRATOR; UNITED STATES INTERESTS PROTECTED

(1) Any action respecting a violation by a discharge source of an effluent standard or limitation or an order respecting such standard or limitation may be brought under this section only in the judicial district in which such source is located.

(2) In such action under this section, the Administrator, if not a party, may intervene as a matter of right.

(3) Protection of interests of United States. — Whenever any action is brought under this section in a court of the United States, the plaintiff shall serve a copy of the complaint on the Attorney General and the Administrator. No consent judgment shall be entered in an action in which the United States is not a party prior to 45 days following the receipt of a copy of the proposed consent judgment by the Attorney General and the Administrator.

(d) LITIGATION COSTS

The court, in issuing any final order in any action brought pursuant to this section, may award costs of litigation (including reasonable attorney and expert witness fees) to any prevailing or substantially prevailing party, whenever the court determines such award is appropriate. The court may, if a temporary restraining order or preliminary injunction is sought, require the filing of a bond or equivalent security in accordance with the Federal Rules of Civil Procedure.

(e) STATUTORY OR COMMON LAW RIGHTS NOT RESTRICTED

Nothing in this section shall restrict any right which any person (or class of persons) may have under any statute or common law to seek enforcement of any effluent standard or limitation or to seek any other relief (including relief against the Administrator or a State agency).

(f) EFFLUENT STANDARD OR LIMITATION

For purposes of this section, the term "effluent standard or limitation under this chapter" means (1) effective July 1, 1973, an unlawful act under subsection (a) of section 1311 of this title, (2) an effluent limitation or other limitation under section 1311 or 1312 of this title; (3) standard of performance under section 1316 of this title; (4) prohibition, effluent standard or pretreatment standards under section 1317 of this title; (5) certification under section 1341 of this title; (6) a permit or condition thereof issued under section 1342 of this title, which is in effect under this chapter (including a requirement applicable by reason of section 1323 of this title); or (7) a regulation under section 1345(d) of this title,.[1]

(g) "CITIZEN" DEFINED

For the purposes of this section the term "citizen" means a person or persons having an interest which is or may be adversely affected.

(h) CIVIL ACTION BY STATE GOVERNORS

A Governor of a State may commence a civil action under subsection (a) of this section, without regard to the limitations of subsection (b) of this section, against the Administrator where there is alleged a failure of the Administrator to enforce an effluent standard or limitation under this chapter the violation of which is occurring in another State and is causing an adverse effect on the public health or welfare in his State, or is causing a violation of any water quality requirement in his State.

§1366. APPEARANCE

The Administrator shall request the Attorney General to appear and represent the United States in any civil or criminal action instituted under this chapter to which the Administrator is a party. Unless the Attorney General notifies the Administrator within a reasonable time, that he will appear in a civil action, attorneys who are officers or employees of the Environmental Protection Agency shall appear and represent the United States in such action.

§1367. EMPLOYEE PROTECTION

(a) DISCRIMINATION AGAINST PERSONS FILING, INSTITUTING, OR TESTIFYING IN PROCEEDINGS UNDER THIS CHAPTER PROHIBITED

No person shall fire, or in any other way discriminate against, or cause to be fired or discriminated against, any employee or any authorized representative of employees by reason of the fact that such employee or representative has filed, instituted, or caused to be filed or instituted any proceeding under this chapter, or has testified or is about to testify in any proceeding resulting from the administration or enforcement of the provisions of this chapter.

(b) APPLICATION FOR REVIEW; INVESTIGATION; HEARING; REVIEW

Any employee or a representative of employees who believes that he has been fired or otherwise discriminated against by any person in violation of subsection (a) of this section may, within thirty days after such alleged violation occurs, apply to the Secretary of Labor for a review of such firing or alleged discrimination. A copy of the application shall be sent to such person who shall be the respondent. Upon receipt of such application, the Secretary of Labor shall

1. So in original.

cause such investigation to be made as he deems appropriate. Such investigation shall provide an opportunity for a public hearing at the request of any party to such review to enable the parties to present information relating to such alleged violation. The parties shall be given written notice of the time and place of the hearing at least five days prior to the hearing. Any such hearing shall be of record and shall be subject to section 554 of title 5. Upon receiving the report of such investigation, the Secretary of Labor shall make findings of fact. If he finds that such violation did occur, he shall issue a decision, incorporating an order therein and his findings, requiring the party committing such violation to take such affirmative action to abate the violation as the Secretary of Labor deems appropriate, including, but not limited to, the rehiring or reinstatement of the employee or representative of employees to his former position with compensation. If he finds that there was no such violation, he shall issue an order denying the application. Such order issued by the Secretary of Labor under this subparagraph shall be subject to judicial review in the same manner as orders and decisions of the Administrator are subject to judicial review under this chapter.

(c) COSTS AND EXPENSES

Whenever an order is issued under this section to abate such violation, at the request of the applicant, a sum equal to the aggregate amount of all costs and expenses (including the attorney's fees), as determined by the Secretary of Labor, to have been reasonably incurred by the applicant for, or in connection with, the institution and prosecution of such proceedings, shall be assessed against the person committing such violation.

(d) DELIBERATE VIOLATIONS BY EMPLOYEE ACTING WITHOUT DIRECTION FROM HIS EMPLOYER OR HIS AGENT

This section shall have no application to any employee who, acting without direction from his employer (or his agent) deliberately violates any prohibition of effluent limitation or other limitation under section 1311 or 1312 of this title, standards of performance under section 1316 of this title, effluent standard, prohibition or pretreatment standard under section 1317 of this title, or any other prohibition or limitation established under this chapter.

(e) INVESTIGATIONS OF EMPLOYMENT REDUCTIONS

The Administrator shall conduct continuing evaluations of potential loss or shifts of employment which may result from the issuance of any effluent limitation or order under this chapter, including, where appropriate, investigating threatened plant closures or reductions in employment allegedly resulting from such limitation or order. Any employee who is discharged or laid-off, threatened with discharge or lay-off, or otherwise discriminated against by any person because of the alleged results of any effluent limitation or order issued under this chapter, or any representative of such employee, may request the Administrator to conduct a full investigation of the matter. The Administrator shall thereupon investigate the matter and, at the request of any party, shall hold public hearings on not less than five days notice, and shall at such hearings require the parties, including the employer involved, to present information relating to the actual or potential effect of such limitation or order on employment and on any alleged discharge, layoff, or other discrimination and the detailed reasons or justification therefor. Any such hearing shall be of record and shall be subject to section 554 of title 5. Upon receiving the report of such investigation, the Administrator shall make findings of fact as to the effect of such effluent limitation or order on employment and on the alleged discharge, lay-off, or discrimination and shall make such recommendations as he deems appropriate. Such report, findings, and recommendations shall be available to the public. Nothing in this subsection shall be construed to require or authorize the Administrator to modify or withdraw any effluent limitation or order issued under this chapter.

§1368. FEDERAL PROCUREMENT

(a) CONTRACTS WITH VIOLATORS PROHIBITED

No Federal agency may enter into any contract with any person, who has been convicted of any offense under section 1319(c) of this title, for the procurement of goods, materials, and services if such contract is to be performed at any facility at which the violation which gave rise to such conviction occurred, and if such facility is owned, leased, or supervised by such person. The prohibition in the preceding sentence shall continue until the Administrator certifies that the condition giving rise to such conviction has been corrected.

(b) NOTIFICATION OF AGENCIES

The Administrator shall establish procedures to provide all Federal agencies with the notification necessary for the purposes of subsection (a) of this section.

(c) OMITTED

(d) EXEMPTIONS

The President may exempt any contract, loan, or grant from all of part of the provisions of this section where he determines such exemption is necessary in the paramount interest of the United States and he shall notify the Congress of such exemption.

(e) ANNUAL REPORT TO CONGRESS

The President shall annually report to the Congress on measures taken in compliance with the purpose and intent of this section, including, but not limited to, the progress and problems associated with such compliance.

§1369. ADMINISTRATIVE PROCEDURE AND JUDICIAL REVIEW

(a) SUBPENAS

(1) For purposes of obtaining information under section 1315 of this title, or carrying out section 1367(e) of this title, the Administrator may issue subpenas for the attendance and testimony of witnesses and the production of relevant papers, books, and documents, and he may administer oaths. Except for effluent data, upon a showing satisfactory to the Administrator that such papers, books, documents, or information or particular part thereof, if made public, would divulge trade secrets or secret processes, the Administrator shall consider such record, report, or information or particular portion thereof confidential in accordance with the purposes of section 1905 of title 18, except that such paper, book, document, or information may be disclosed to other officers, employees, or authorized representatives of the United States concerned with carrying out this chapter, or when relevant in any proceeding under this chapter. Witnesses summoned shall be paid the same fees and mileage that are paid witnesses in the courts of the United States. In case of contumacy or refusal to obey a subpena served upon any person under this subsection, the district court of the United States for any district in which such person is found or resides or transacts business, upon application by the United States and after notice to such person, shall have jurisdiction to issue an order requiring such person to appear and give testimony before the Administrator, to appear and produce papers, books, and documents before the Administrator, or both, and any failure to obey such order of the court may be punished by such court as a contempt thereof.

(2) The district courts of the United States are authorized, upon application by the Administrator, to issue subpenas for attendance and testimony of witnesses and the production of relevant papers, books, and documents, for purposes of obtaining information under sections 1314(b) and (c) of this title. Any papers, books, documents, or other information or part thereof, obtained by reason of such a subpena shall be subject to the same requirements as are provided in paragraph (1) of this subsection.

(b) REVIEW OF ADMINISTRATOR'S ACTIONS; SELECTION OF COURT; FEES

(1) Review of the Administrator's action (A) in promulgating any standard of performance under section 1316 of this title, (B) in making any determination pursuant to section 1316(b)(1)(C) of this title, (C) in promulgating any effluent standard, prohibition, or pretreatment standard under section 1317 of this title, (D) in making any determination as to a State permit program submitted under section 1342(b) of this title, (E) in approving or promulgating any effluent limitation or other limitation under section 1311, 1312, 1316, or 1345 of this title, (F) in issuing or denying any permit under section 1342 of this title, and (G) in promulgating any individual control strategy under section 1314(l) of this title, may be had by any interested person in the Circuit Court of Appeals of the United States for the Federal judicial district in which such person resides or

transacts business which is directly affected by such action upon application by such person. Any such application shall be made within 120 days from the date of such determination, approval, promulgation, issuance or denial, or after such date only if such application is based solely on grounds which arose after such 120th day.

(2) Action of the Administrator with respect to which review could have been obtained under paragraph (1) of this subsection shall not be subject to judicial review in any civil or criminal proceeding for enforcement.

(3) Award of fees. — In any judicial proceeding under this subsection, the court may award costs of litigation (including reasonable attorney and expert witness fees) to any prevailing or substantially prevailing party whenever it determines that such award is appropriate.

(c) **ADDITIONAL EVIDENCE**

In any judicial proceeding brought under subsection (b) of this section in which review is sought of a determination under this chapter required to be made on the record after notice and opportunity for hearing, if any party applies to the court for leave to adduce additional evidence, and shows to the satisfaction of the court that such additional evidence is material and that there were reasonable grounds for the failure to adduce such evidence in the proceeding before the Administrator, the court may order such additional evidence (and evidence in rebuttal thereof) to be taken before the Administrator, in such manner and upon such terms and conditions as the court may deem proper. The Administrator may modify his findings as to the facts, or make new findings, by reason of the additional evidence so taken and he shall file such modified or new findings, and his recommendation, if any, for the modification or setting aside of his original determination, with the return of such additional evidence.

§1370. STATE AUTHORITY

Except as expressly provided in this chapter, nothing in his chapter shall (1) preclude or deny the right of any State or political subdivision thereof or interstate agency to adopt or enforce (A) any standard or limitation respecting discharges of pollutants, or (B) any requirement respecting control or abatement of pollution; except that if an effluent limitation, or other limitation, effluent standard, prohibition, pretreatment standard, or standard of performance is in effect under this chapter, such State or political subdivision or interstate agency may not adopt or enforce any effluent limitation, or other limitation, effluent standard, prohibition, pretreatment standard, or standard of performance which is less stringent than the effluent limitation, or other limitation, effluent standard, prohibition, pretreatment standard, or standard of performance under this chapter; or (2) be construed as impairing or in any manner affecting any right or jurisdiction of the States with respect to the waters (including boundary waters) of such States.

Clean Water Act §1371

§1371. AUTHORITY UNDER OTHER LAWS AND REGULATIONS

(a) IMPAIRMENT OF AUTHORITY OR FUNCTIONS OF OFFICIALS AND AGENCIES; TREATY PROVISIONS

This chapter shall not be construed as (1) limiting the authority or functions of any officer or agency of the United States under any other law or regulation not inconsistent with this chapter; (2) affecting or impairing the authority of the Secretary of the Army (A) to maintain navigation or (B) under the Act of March 3, 1899, (30 Stat. 1112); except that any permit issued under section 1344 of this title shall be conclusive as to the effect on water quality of any discharge resulting from any activity subject to section 403 of this title, or (3) affecting or impairing the provisions of any treaty of the United States.

(b) DISCHARGES OF POLLUTANTS INTO NAVIGABLE WATERS

Discharges of pollutants into the navigable waters subject to the Rivers and Harbors Act of 1910 (36 Stat. 593; 33 U.S.C. 421) and the Supervisory Harbors Act of 1888 (25 Stat. 209; 33 U.S.C. 441-451b) shall be regulated pursuant to this chapter, and not subject to such Act of 1910 and the Act of 1888 except as to effect on navigation and anchorage.

(c) ACTION OF THE ADMINISTRATOR DEEMED MAJOR FEDERAL ACTION; CONSTRUCTION OF THE NATIONAL ENVIRONMENTAL POLICY ACT OF 1969

(1) Except for the provision of Federal financial assistance for the purpose of assisting the construction of publicly owned treatment works as authorized by section 1281 of this title, and the issuance of a permit under section 1342 of this title for the discharge of any pollutant by a new source as defined in section 1316 of this title, no action of the Administrator taken pursuant to this chapter shall be deemed a major Federal action significantly affecting the quality of the human environment within the meaning of the National Environmental Policy Act of 1969 (83 Stat. 852) [42 U.S.C. 4321 et seq.]; and

(2) Nothing in the National Environmental Policy Act of 1969 (83 Stat. 852) shall be deemed to —

(A) authorize any Federal agency authorized to license or permit the conduct of any activity which may result in the discharge of a pollutant into the navigable waters to review any effluent limitation or other requirement established pursuant to this chapter or the adequacy of any certification under section 1341 of this title; or

(B) authorize any such agency to impose, as a condition precedent to the issuance of any license or permit, any effluent limitation other than any such limitation established pursuant to this chapter.

(d) CONSIDERATION OF INTERNATIONAL WATER POLLUTION CONTROL AGREEMENTS

Notwithstanding this chapter or any other provision of law, the Administrator (1) shall not require any State to consider in the development of the ranking in order of priority of needs for the construction of treatment works (as defined in subchapter II of this chapter), any water pollution control agreement which may have been entered into between the United States and any other nation, and (2) shall not consider any such agreement in the approval of any such priority ranking.

§1372. LABOR STANDARDS

The Administrator shall take such action as may be necessary to insure that all laborers and mechanics employed by contractors or subcontractors on treatment works for which grants are made under this chapter shall be paid wages at rates not less than those prevailing for the same type of work on similar construction in the immediate locality, as determined by the Secretary of Labor, in accordance with the Davis-Bacon Act (46 Stat. 1494; 40 U.S.C., sec. 276a through 276a-5). The Secretary of Labor shall have, with respect to the labor standards specified in this subsection, the authority and functions set forth in Reorganization Plan Numbered 14 of 1950 (15 F.R. 3176) and section 276c of title 40.

§1373. PUBLIC HEALTH AGENCY COORDINATION

The permitting agency under section 1342 of this title shall assist the applicant for a permit under such section in coordinating the requirements of this chapter with those of the appropriate public health agencies.

[Various sections establishing advisory commissions and mandating reports to Congress before 1990 are omitted.]

§1377. INDIAN TRIBES

(a) POLICY

Nothing in this section shall be construed to affect the application of section 1251(g) of this title, and all of the provisions of this section shall be carried out in accordance with the provisions of such section 1251(g) of this title. Indian tribes shall be treated as States for purposes of such section 1251(g) of this title.

(b) ASSESSMENT OF SEWAGE TREATMENT NEEDS; REPORT

The Administrator, in cooperation with the Director of the Indian Health Service, shall assess the need for sewage treatment works to serve Indian tribes, the degree to which such needs will be met through funds allotted to States under section 1285 of this title and priority lists under section 1296 of this title, and any obstacles which prevent such needs from being met. Not later than one year after February 4, 1987, the Administrator shall submit a report to Congress on the assessment under this subsection, along with recommendations specifying (1) how the Administrator intends to provide assistance to Indian tribes to devel-

Clean Water Act §1377

op waste treatment management plans and to construct treatment works under this chapter, and (2) methods by which the participation in and administration of programs under this chapter by Indian tribes can be maximized.

(c) **RESERVATION OF FUNDS**

The Administrator shall reserve each fiscal year beginning after September 30, 1986, before allotments to the States under section 1285(e) of this title, one-half of one percent of the sums appropriated under section 1287 of this title. Sums reserved under this subsection shall be available only for grants for the development of waste treatment management plans and for the construction of sewage treatment works to serve Indian tribes, as defined in subsection (h) of this section and former Indian reservations in Oklahoma (as determined by the Secretary of the Interior) and Alaska Native Villages as defined in Public Law 92-203 [43 U.S.C. 1601 et seq.].

(d) **COOPERATIVE AGREEMENTS**

In order to ensure the consistent implementation of the requirements of this chapter, an Indian tribe and the State or States in which the lands of such tribe are located may enter into a cooperative agreement, subject to the review and approval of the Administrator, to jointly plan and administer the requirements of this chapter.

(e) **TREATMENT AS STATES**

The Administrator is authorized to treat an Indian tribe as a State for purposes of subchapter II of this chapter and sections 1254, 1256, 1313, 1315, 1318, 1319, 1324, 1329, 1341, 1342, and 1344 of this title to the degree necessary to carry out the objectives of this section, but only if —

(1) the Indian tribe has a governing body carrying out substantial governmental duties and powers;

(2) the functions to be exercised by the Indian tribe pertain to the management and protection of water resources which are held by an Indian tribe, held by the United States in trust for Indians, held by a member of an Indian tribe if such property interest is subject to a trust restriction on alienation, or otherwise within the borders of an Indian reservation; and

(3) the Indian tribe is reasonably expected to be capable, in the Administrator's judgment, of carrying out the functions to be exercised in a manner consistent with the terms and purposes of this chapter and of all applicable regulations.

Such treatment as a State may include the direct provision of funds reserved under subsection (c) of this section to the governing bodies of Indian tribes, and the determination of priorities by Indian tribes, where not determined by the Administrator in cooperation with the Director of the Indian Health Service. The Administrator, in cooperation with the Director of the Indian Health Service, is authorized to make grants under subchapter II of this chapter in an amount not to exceed 100 percent of the cost of a project. Not later than 18 months after February 4, 1987, the Administrator shall, in consultation with Indian tribes, promulgate final regulations which specify how Indian tribes shall be treated as States for purposes of this chapter. The Administrator shall, in promulgating such regulations, consult affected States sharing common water bodies and provide a mechanism for the resolution of any unreasonable consequences that may arise as a result of differing water quality standards that may be set by States and Indian tribes located on common bodies of water. Such mechanism shall provide for explicit consideration of relevant factors including, but not limited to, the effects of differing water quality permit requirements on upstream and downstream dischargers, economic impacts, and present and historical uses and quality of the waters subject to such standards. Such mechanism should provide for the avoidance of such unreasonable consequences in a manner consistent with the objective of this chapter.

(f) GRANTS FOR NONPOINT SOURCE PROGRAMS

The Administrator shall make grants to an Indian tribe under section 1329 of this title as though such tribe was a State. Not more than one-third of one percent of the amount appropriated for any fiscal year under section 1329 of this title may be used to make grants under this subsection. In addition to the requirements of section 1329 of this title, an Indian tribe shall be required to meet the requirements of paragraphs (1), (2), and (3) of subsection (d) of this section in order to receive such a grant.

(g) ALASKA NATIVE ORGANIZATIONS

No provision of this chapter shall be construed to —

(1) grant, enlarge, or diminish, or in any way affect the scope of the governmental authority, if any, of any Alaska Native organization, including any federally-recognized tribe, traditional Alaska Native council, or Native council organized pursuant to the Act of June 18, 1934 (48 Stat. 987), over lands or persons in Alaska;

(2) create or validate any assertion by such organization or any form of governmental authority over lands or persons in Alaska; or

(3) in any way affect any assertion that Indian country, as defined in section 1151 of title 18, exists or does not exist in Alaska.

(h) DEFINITIONS

For purposes of this section, the term —

(1) "Federal Indian reservation" means all land within the limits of any Indian reservation under the jurisdiction of the United States Government, notwithstanding the issuance of any patent, and including rights-of-way running through the reservation; and

(2) "Indian tribe" means any Indian tribe, band, group, or community recognized by the Secretary of the Interior and exercising governmental authority over a Federal Indian reservation. . . .

Clean Water Act

Subchapter VI — State Water Pollution Control Revolving Funds

§1381. Grants to States for Establishment of Revolving Funds

(a) GENERAL AUTHORITY

Subject to the provisions of this subchapter, the Administrator shall make capitalization grants to each State for the purpose of establishing a water pollution control revolving fund for providing assistance (1) for construction of treatment works (as defined in section 1292 of this title) which are publicly owned, (2) for implementing a management program under section 1329 of this title, and (3) for developing and implementing a conservation and management plan under section 1330 of this title.

(b) SCHEDULE OF GRANT PAYMENTS

The Administrator and each State shall jointly establish a schedule of payments under which the Administrator will pay to the State the amount of each grant to be made to the State under this subchapter. Such schedule shall be based on the State's intended use plan under section 1386(c) of this title, except that —

(1) such payments shall be made in quarterly installments, and

(2) such payments shall be made as expeditiously as possible, but in no event later than the earlier of —

(A) 8 quarters after the date such funds were obligated by the State, or

(B) 12 quarters after the date such funds were allotted to the State.

§1382. Capitalization Grant Agreements

(a) GENERAL RULE

To receive a capitalization grant with funds made available under this subchapter and section 1285(m) of this title, a State shall enter into an agreement with the Administrator which shall include but not be limited to the specifications set forth in subsection (b) of this section.

(b) SPECIFIC REQUIREMENTS

The Administrator shall enter into an agreement under this section with a State only after the State has established to the satisfaction of the Administrator that —

(1) the State will accept grant payments with funds to be made available under this subchapter and section 1285(m) of this title in accordance with a payment schedule established jointly by the Administrator under section 1381(b) of this title and will deposit all such payments in the water pollution control revolving fund established by the State in accordance with this subchapter.

(2) the State will deposit in the fund from State moneys an amount equal to at least 20 percent of the total amount of all capitalization grants which will be made to the State with funds to be made available under this subchapter and section 1285(m) of this title on or before the date on which each quarterly grant payment will be made to the State under this subchapter;

(3) the State will enter into binding commitments to provide assistance in accordance with the requirements of this subchapter in an amount equal to 120 percent of the amount of each such grant payment within 1 year after the receipt of such grant payment;

(4) all funds in the fund will be expended in an expeditious and timely manner;

(5) all funds in the fund as a result of capitalization grants under this subchapter and section 1285(m) of this title will first be used to assure maintenance of progress, as determined by the Governor of the State, toward compliance with enforceable deadlines, goals, and requirements of this chapter, including the municipal compliance deadline;

(6) treatment works eligible under section 1383(c)(1) of this title which will be constructed in whole or in part before fiscal year 1995 with funds directly made available by capitalization grants under this subchapter and section 1285(m) of this title will meet the requirements of, or otherwise be treated (as determined by the Governor of the State) under sections 1281(b), 1281(g)(1), 1281(g)(2), 1281(g)(3), 1281(g)(5), 1281(g)(6), 1281(n)(1), 1281(o), 1284(a)(1), 1284(a)(2), 1284(b)(1), 1284(d)(2), 1291, 1298, 1371(c)(1), and 1372 of this title in the same manner as treatment works constructed with assistance under subchapter II of this chapter;

(7) in addition to complying with the requirements of this subchapter, the State will commit or expend each quarterly grant payment which it will receive under this subchapter in accordance with laws and procedures applicable to the commitment or expenditure of revenues of the State;

(8) in carrying out the requirements of section 1386 of this title, the State will use accounting, audit, and fiscal procedures conforming to generally accepted government accounting standards;

(9) the State will require as a condition of making a loan or providing other assistance, as described in section 1383(d) of this title, from the fund that the recipient of such assistance will maintain project accounts in accordance with generally accepted government accounting standards; and

(10) the State will make annual reports to the Administrator on the actual use of funds in accordance with section 1386(d) of this title.

§1383. WATER POLLUTION CONTROL REVOLVING LOAN FUNDS

(a) **REQUIREMENTS FOR OBLIGATION OF GRANT FUNDS**

Before a State may receive a capitalization grant with funds made available under this subchapter and section 1285(m) of this title, the State shall first establish a water pollution control revolving fund which complies with the requirements of this section.

(b) ADMINISTRATION

Each State water pollution control revolving fund shall be administered by an instrumentality of the State with such powers and limitations as may be required to operate such fund in accordance with the requirements and objectives of this chapter.

(c) PROJECTS ELIGIBLE FOR ASSISTANCE

The amounts of funds available to each State water pollution control revolving fund shall be used only for providing financial assistance (1) to any municipality, intermunicipal, interstate, or State agency for construction of publicly owned treatment works (as defined in section 1292 of this title), (2) for the implementation of a management program established under section 1329 of this title, and (3) for development and implementation of a conservation and management plan under section 1330 of this title. The fund shall be established, maintained, and credited with repayments, and the fund balance shall be available in perpetuity for providing such financial assistance.

(d) TYPES OF ASSISTANCE

Except as otherwise limited by State law, a water pollution control revolving fund of a State under this section may be used only —

(1) to make loans, on the condition that —

(A) such loans are made at or below market interest rates, including interest free loans, at terms not to exceed 20 years;

(B) annual principal and interest payments will commence not later than 1 year after completion of any project and all loans will be fully amortized not later than 20 years after project completion;

(C) the recipient of a loan will establish a dedicated source of revenue for repayment of loans; and

(D) the fund will be credited with all payments of principal and interest on all loans;

(2) to buy or refinance the debt obligation of municipalities and intermunicipal and interstate agencies within the State at or below market rates, where such debt obligations were incurred after March 7, 1985;

(3) to guarantee, or purchase insurance for, local obligations where such action would improve credit market access or reduce interest rates;

(4) as a source of revenue or security for the payment of principal and interest on revenue or general obligation bonds issued by the State if the proceeds of the sale of such bonds will be deposited in the fund;

(5) to provide loan guarantees for similar revolving funds established by municipalities or intermunicipal agencies;

(6) to earn interest on fund accounts; and

(7) for the reasonable costs of administering the fund and conducting

activities under this subchapter, except that such amounts shall not exceed 4 percent of all grant awards to such fund under this subchapter.

(e) **LIMITATION TO PREVENT DOUBLE BENEFITS**

If a State makes, from its water pollution revolving fund, a loan which will finance the cost of facility planning and the preparation of plans, specifications, and estimates for construction of publicly owned treatment works, the State shall ensure that if the recipient of such loan receives a grant under section 1281(g) of this title for construction of such treatment works and an allowance under section 1281(*l*)(1) of this title for non-Federal funds expended for such planning and preparation, such recipient will promptly repay such loan to the extent of such allowance.

(f) **CONSISTENCY WITH PLANNING REQUIREMENTS**

A State may provide financial assistance from its water pollution control revolving fund only with respect to a project which is consistent with plans, if any, developed under sections 1285(j), 1288, 1313(e), 1329, and 1330 of this title.

(g) **PRIORITY LIST REQUIREMENT**

The State may provide financial assistance from its water pollution control revolving fund only with respect to a project for construction of a treatment works described in subsection (c)(1) of this section if such project is on the State's priority list under section 1296 of this title. Such assistance may be provided regardless of the rank of such project on such list.

(h) **ELIGIBILITY OF NON-FEDERAL SHARE OF CONSTRUCTION GRANT PROJECTS**

A State water pollution control revolving fund may provide assistance (other than under subsection (d)(1) of this section) to a municipality or intermunicipal or interstate agency with respect to the non-Federal share of the costs of a treatment works project for which such municipality or agency is receiving assistance from the Administrator under any other authority only if such assistance is necessary to allow such project to proceed.

§1384. ALLOTMENT OF FUNDS

(a) **FORMULA**

Sums authorized to be appropriated to carry out this section for each of fiscal years 1989 and 1990 shall be allotted by the Administrator in accordance with section 1285(c) of this title.

(b) **RESERVATION OF FUNDS FOR PLANNING**

Each State shall reserve each fiscal year 1 percent of the sums allotted to such State under this section for such fiscal year, or $100,000, whichever amount is greater, to carry out planning under sections 1285(j) and 1313(e) of this title.

Clean Water Act

(c) ALLOTMENT PERIOD

(1) PERIOD OF AVAILABILITY FOR GRANT AWARD

Sums allotted to a State under this section for a fiscal year shall be available for obligation by the State during the fiscal year for which sums are authorized and during the following fiscal year.

(2) REALLOTMENT OF UNOBLIGATED FUNDS

The amount of any allotment not obligated by the State by the last day of the 2-year period of availability established by paragraph (1) shall be immediately reallotted by the Administrator on the basis of the same ratio as is applicable to sums allotted under subchapter II of this chapter for the second fiscal year of such 2-year period. None of the funds reallotted by the Administrator shall be reallotted to any State which has not obligated all sums allotted to such State in the first fiscal year of such 2-year period.

§1385. CORRECTIVE ACTION

(a) NOTIFICATION OF NONCOMPLIANCE

If the Administrator determines that a State has not complied with its agreement with the Administrator under section 1382 of this title or any other requirement of this subchapter, the Administrator shall notify the State of such noncompliance and the necessary corrective action.

(b) WITHHOLDING OF PAYMENTS

If a State does not take corrective action within 60 days after the date a State receives notification of such action under subsection (a) of this section, the Administrator shall withhold additional payments to the State until the Administrator is satisfied that the State has taken the necessary corrective action.

(c) REALLOTMENT OF WITHHELD PAYMENTS

If the Administrator is not satisfied that adequate corrective actions have been taken by the State within 12 months after the State is notified of such actions under subsection (a) of this section, the payments withheld from the State by the Administrator under subsection (b) of this section shall be made available for reallotment in accordance with the most recent formula for allotment of funds under this subchapter.

§1386. AUDITS, REPORTS, AND FISCAL CONTROLS; INTENDED USE PLAN

(a) FISCAL CONTROL AND AUDITING PROCEDURES

Each State electing to establish a water pollution control revolving fund under this subchapter shall establish fiscal controls and accounting procedures sufficient to assure proper accounting during appropriate accounting periods for —

(1) payments received by the fund;
(2) disbursements made by the fund; and
(3) fund balances at the beginning and end of the accounting period.

(b) ANNUAL FEDERAL AUDITS

The Administrator shall, at least on an annual basis, conduct or require each State to have independently conducted reviews and audits as may be deemed necessary or appropriate by the Administrator to carry out the objectives of this section. Audits of the use of funds deposited in the water pollution revolving fund established by such State shall be conducted in accordance with the auditing procedures of the General Accounting Office, including chapter 75 of title 31.

(c) INTENDED USE PLAN

After providing for public comment and review, each State shall annually prepare a plan identifying the intended uses of the amounts available to its water pollution control revolving fund. Such intended use plan shall include, but not be limited to —

(1) a list of those projects for construction of publicly owned treatment works on the State's priority list developed pursuant to section 1296 of this title and a list of activities eligible for assistance under sections 1329 and 1330 of this title;

(2) a description of the short- and long-term goals and objectives of its water pollution control revolving fund;

(3) information on the activities to be supported, including a description of project categories, discharge requirements under subchapters III and IV of this chapter, terms of financial assistance, and communities served;

(4) assurances and specific proposals for meeting the requirements of paragraphs (3), (4), (5), and (6) of section 1382(b) of this title; and

(5) the criteria and method established for the distribution of funds.

(d) ANNUAL REPORT

Beginning the first fiscal year after the receipt of payments under this subchapter, the State shall provide an annual report to the Administrator describing how the State has met the goals and objectives for the previous fiscal year as identified in the plan prepared for the previous fiscal year pursuant to subsection (c) of this section, including identification of loan recipients, loan amounts, and loan terms and similar details on other forms of financial assistance provided from the water pollution control revolving fund.

(e) ANNUAL FEDERAL OVERSIGHT REVIEW

The Administrator shall conduct an annual oversight review of each State plan prepared under subsection (c) of this section, each State report prepared under subsection (d) of this section, and other such materials as are considered necessary and appropriate in carrying out the purposes of this subchapter. After reasonable notice by the Administrator to the State or the recipient of a loan from a water pollution control revolving fund, the State or loan recipient shall make available to the Administrator such records as the Administrator reasonably requires to review and determine compliance with this subchapter.

(f) APPLICABILITY OF SUBCHAPTER II PROVISIONS

Except to the extent provided in this subchapter, the provisions of subchapter II of this chapter shall not apply to grants under this subchapter.

[Sections 1401-1416, which deal with ocean dumping, have been omitted.]

Endangered Species Act (ESA)
16 U.S.C. §§1531-1544

CHAPTER 35 — ENDANGERED SPECIES

Sec.
1531. Congressional findings and declaration of purposes and policy.
    (a) Findings.
    (b) Purposes.
    (c) Policy.
1532. Definitions.
1533. Determination of endangered species and threatened species.
    (a) Generally.
    (b) Basis for determinations.
    (c) Lists.
    (d) Protective regulations.
    (e) Similarity of appearance cases.
    (f) Recovery plans.
    (g) Monitoring.
    (h) Agency guidelines; publication in Federal Register; scope; proposals and amendments: notice and opportunity for comments.
    (i) Submission to State agency of justification for regulations inconsistent with State agency's comments or petition.
1534. Land acquisition.
    (a) Implementation of conservation program; authorization of Secretary and Secretary of Agriculture.
    (b) Availability of funds for acquisition of lands, waters, etc.
1535. Cooperation with States.
    (a) Generally.
    (b) Management agreements.
    (c) Cooperative agreements.
    (d) Allocation of funds.
    (e) Review of State programs.
    (f) Conflicts between Federal and State laws.
    (g) Transition.
    (h) Regulations.
    (i) Appropriations.
1536. Interagency cooperation.
    (a) Federal agency actions and consultations.
    (b) Opinion of Secretary.
    (c) Biological assessment.
    (d) Limitation on commitment of resources.
    (e) Endangered Species Committee.
    (f) Promulgation of regulations; form and contents of exemption application.

Endangered Species Act

(g) Application for exemption; report to Committee.
(h) Grant of exemption.
(i) Review of Secretary of State; violation of international treaty or other international obligation of United States.
(j) Exemption for national security reasons.
(k) Exemption decision not considered major Federal action; environmental impact statement.
(l) Committee order granting exemption; cost of mitigation and enhancement measures; report by applicant to Council on Environmental Quality.
(m) Notice requirement for citizen suits not applicable.
(n) Judicial review.
(o) Exemption as providing exception on taking of endangered species.
(p) Exemptions in Presidentially declared disaster areas.

1537. International cooperation.
(a) Financial assistance.
(b) Encouragement of foreign programs.
(c) Personnel.
(d) Investigations.

1537a. Convention implementation
(a) Management Authority and Scientific Authority.
(b) Management Authority functions.
(c) Scientific Authority functions; determinations.
(d) Reservations by the United States under Convention.
(e) Wildlife preservation in Western Hemisphere.

1538. Prohibited acts.
(a) Generally.
(b) Species held in captivity or controlled environment.
(c) Violation of Convention.
(d) Imports and exports.
(e) Reports.
(f) Designation of ports.
(g) Violations.

1539. Exceptions.
(a) Permits.
(b) Hardship exemptions.
(c) Notice and review.
(d) Permit and exemption policy.
(e) Alaska natives.
(f) Pre-Act endangered species parts exemption; application and certification; regulation; validity of sales contract; separability of provisions; renewal of exemption; expiration of renewal certification.
(g) Burden of proof.
(h) Certain antique articles; importation; port designation; application for return of articles.
(i) Noncommercial transshipments.
(j) Experimental populations.

1540. Penalties and enforcement.
(a) Civil penalties.

(b) Criminal violations.
(c) District court jurisdiction.
(d) Rewards and incidental expenses.
(e) Enforcement.
(f) Regulations.
(g) Citizen suits.
(h) Coordination with other laws.
1543. Construction with Marine Mammal Protection Act of 1972.
1544. Annual cost analysis by Fish and Wildlife Service.

§1531. *Congressional Findings and Declaration of Purposes and Policy*

(a) FINDINGS

The Congress finds and declares that —

(1) various species of fish, wildlife, and plants in the United States have been rendered extinct as a consequence of economic growth and development untempered by adequate concern and conservation;

(2) other species of fish, wildlife, and plants have been so depleted in numbers that they are in danger of or threatened with extinction;

(3) these species of fish, wildlife, and plants are of esthetic, ecological, educational, historical, recreational, and scientific value to the Nation and its people;

(4) the United States has pledged itself as a sovereign state in the international community to conserve to the extent practicable the various species of fish or wildlife and plants facing extinction, pursuant to —

(A) migratory bird treaties with Canada and Mexico;

(B) the Migratory and Endangered Bird Treaty with Japan;

(C) the Convention on Nature Protection and Wildlife Preservation in the Western Hemisphere;

(D) the International Convention for the Northwest Atlantic Fisheries;

(E) the International Convention for the High Seas Fisheries of the North Pacific Ocean;

(F) the Convention on International Trade in Endangered Species of Wild Fauna and Flora; and

(G) other international agreements; and

(5) encouraging the States and other interested parties, through Federal financial assistance and a system of incentives, to develop and maintain conservation programs which meet national and international standards is a key to meeting the Nation's international commitments and to better safeguarding, for the benefit of all citizens, the Nation's heritage in fish, wildlife, and plants.

(b) PURPOSES

The purposes of this chapter are to provide a means whereby the ecosystems upon which endangered species and threatened species depend may be conserved, to provide a program for the conservation of such endangered species and threatened species, and to take such steps as may be appropriate to achieve the purposes of the treaties and conventions set forth in subsection (a) of this section.

(c) POLICY

(1) It is further declared to be the policy of Congress that all Federal departments and agencies shall seek to conserve endangered species and threatened species and shall utilize their authorities in furtherance of the purposes of this chapter.

(2) It is further declared to be the policy of Congress that Federal agencies shall cooperate with State and local agencies to resolve water resource issues in concert with conservation of endangered species.

§1532. *Definitions*

For the purpose of this chapter —

(1) The term "alternative courses of action" means all alternatives and thus is not limited to original project objectives and agency jurisdiction.

(2) The term "commercial activity" means all activities of industry and trade, including, but not limited to, the buying or selling of commodities and activities conducted for the purpose of facilitating such buying and selling: *Provided, however,* That it does not include exhibition of commodities by museums or similar cultural or historical organizations.

(3) The terms "conserve," "conserving," and "conservation" mean to use and the use of all methods and procedures which are necessary to bring any endangered species or threatened species to the point at which the measures provided pursuant to this chapter are no longer necessary. Such methods and procedures include, but are not limited to, all activities associated with scientific resources management such as research, census, law enforcement, habitat acquisition and maintenance, propagation, live trapping, and transplantation, and, in the extraordinary case where population pressures within a given ecosystem cannot be otherwise relieved, may include regulated taking.

(4) The term "Convention" means the Convention on International Trade in Endangered Species of Wild Fauna and Flora, signed on March 3, 1973, and the appendices thereto.

(5)(A) The term "critical habitat" for a threatened or endangered species means —

(i) the specific areas within the geographical area occupied by the species, at the time it is listed in accordance with the provisions of section 1533 of this title, on which are found those physical or biological features (I) essential to the conservation of the species and (II) which may require special management considerations or protection; and

(ii) specific areas outside the geographical area occupied by the species at the time it is listed in accordance with the provisions of section 1533 of this title, upon a determination by the Secretary that such areas are essential for the conservation of the species.

(B) Critical habitat may be established for those species now listed as threatened or endangered species for which no critical habitat has heretofore been established as set forth in subparagraph (A) of this paragraph.

(C) Except in those circumstances determined by the Secretary, critical habitat shall not include the entire geographical area which can be occupied by the threatened or endangered species.

(6) The term "endangered species" means any species which is in danger of extinction throughout all or a significant portion of its range other than a species of the Class Insecta determined by the Secretary to constitute a pest whose protection under the provisions of this chapter would present an overwhelming and overriding risk to man.

(7) The term "Federal agency" means any department, agency, or instrumentality of the United States.

(8) The term "fish or wildlife" means any member of the animal kingdom, including without limitation any mammal, fish, bird (including any migratory, nonmigratory, or endangered bird for which protection is also afforded by treaty or other international agreement), amphibian, reptile, mollusk, crustacean, arthropod or other invertebrate, and includes any part, product, egg, or offspring thereof, or the dead body or parts thereof.

(9) The term "foreign commerce" includes, among other things, any transaction —

(A) between persons within one foreign country;

(B) between persons in two or more foreign countries;

(C) between a person within the United States and a person in a foreign country; or

(D) between persons within the United States, where the fish and wildlife in question are moving in any country or countries outside the United States.

(10) The term "import" means to land on, bring into, or introduce into, or attempt to land on, bring into, or introduce into, any place subject to the jurisdiction of the United States, whether or not such landing, bringing, or introduction constitutes an importation within the meaning of the customs laws of the United States.

(11) Repealed. Pub. L. 97-304, §4(b), Oct. 13, 1982, 96 Stat. 1420.

(12) The term "permit or license applicant" means, when used with respect to an action of a Federal agency for which exemption is sought under section 1536 of this title, any person whose application to such agency for a permit or license has been denied primarily because of the application of section 1536(a) of this title to such agency action.

(13) The term "person" means an individual, corporation, partnership, trust, association, or any other private entity; or any officer, employee, agent, department, or instrumentality of the Federal Government, of any State, municipality, or political subdivision of a State, or of any foreign government; any State, municipality, or political subdivision of a State; or any other entity subject to the jurisdiction of the United States.

(14) The term "plant" means any member of the plant kingdom, including seeds, roots and other parts thereof.

(15) The term "Secretary" means, except as otherwise herein provided, the Secretary of the Interior or the Secretary of Commerce as program responsibilities are vested pursuant to the provisions of Reorganization Plan Numbered 4 of 1970; except that with respect to the enforcement of the provisions of this chapter and the Convention which pertain to the importation or exportation of terrestrial plants, the term also means the Secretary of Agriculture.

(16) The term "species" includes any subspecies of fish or wildlife or plants, and any distinct population segment of any species of vertebrate fish or wildlife which interbreeds when mature.

(17) The term "State" means any of the several States, the District of Columbia, the Commonwealth of Puerto Rico, American Samoa, the Virgin Islands, Guam, and the Trust Territory of the Pacific Islands.

(18) The term "State agency" means any State agency, department, board, commission, or other governmental entity which is responsible for the management and conservation of fish, plant, or wildlife resources within a State.

(19) The term "take" means to harass, harm, pursue, hunt, shoot, wound, kill, trap, capture, or collect, or to attempt to engage in any such conduct.

(20) The term "threatened species" means any species which is likely to become an endangered species within the foreseeable future throughout all or a significant portion of its range.

(21) The term "United States," when used in a geographical context, includes all States.

§1533. Determination of Endangered Species and Threatened Species

(a) GENERALLY

(1) The Secretary shall by regulation promulgated in accordance with subsection (b) of this section determine whether any species is an endangered species or a threatened species because of any of the following factors:

(A) the present or threatened destruction, modification, or curtailment of its habitat or range;

(B) overutilization for commercial, recreational, scientific, or educational purposes;

(C) disease or predation;

(D) the inadequacy of existing regulatory mechanisms; or

(E) other natural or manmade factors affecting its continued existence.

(2) With respect to any species over which program responsibilities have been vested in the Secretary of Commerce pursuant to Reorganization Plan Numbered 4 of 1970 —

(A) in any case in which the Secretary of Commerce determines that such species should —

(i) be listed as an endangered species or a threatened species, or

(ii) be changed in status from a threatened species to an endangered species,

he shall so inform the Secretary of the Interior, who shall list such species in accordance with this section;

(B) in any case in which the Secretary of Commerce determines that such species should —

(i) be removed from any list published pursuant to subsection (c) of this section, or

(ii) be changed in status from an endangered species to a threatened species,

he shall recommend such action to the Secretary of the Interior, and the Secretary of the Interior, if he concurs in the recommendation, shall implement such action; and

(C) the Secretary of the Interior may not list or remove from any list any such species, and may not change the status of any such species which are listed, without a prior favorable determination made pursuant to this section by the Secretary of Commerce.

(3) The Secretary, by regulation promulgated in accordance with subsection (b) of this section and to the maximum extent prudent and determinable —

(A) shall, concurrently with making a determination under paragraph (1) that a species is an endangered species or a threatened species, designate any habitat of such species which is then considered to be critical habitat; and

(B) may, from time-to-time thereafter as appropriate, revise such designation.

(b) **BASIS FOR DETERMINATIONS**

(1)(A) The Secretary shall make determinations required by subsection (a)(1) of this section solely on the basis of the best scientific and commercial data available to him after conducting a review of the status of the species and after taking into account those efforts, if any, being made by any State or foreign nation, or any political subdivision of a State or foreign nation, to protect such species, whether by predator control, protection of habitat and food supply, or other conservation practices, within any area under its jurisdiction; or on the high seas.

(B) In carrying out this section, the Secretary shall give consideration to species which have been —

(i) designated as requiring protection from unrestricted commerce by any foreign nation, or pursuant to any international agreement; or

(ii) identified as in danger of extinction, or likely to become so within the foreseeable future, by any State agency or by any agency of a foreign nation that is responsible for the conservation of fish or wildlife or plants.

(2) The Secretary shall designate critical habitat, and make revisions thereto, under subsection (a)(3) of this section on the basis of the best scientific data available and after taking into consideration the economic impact, and any other relevant impact, of specifying any particular area as critical habitat. The Secretary may exclude any area from critical habitat if he determines that the benefits of such exclusion outweigh the benefits of specifying such area as part of the critical habitat, unless he determines, based on the best scientific and commercial data available, that the failure to designate such area as critical habitat will result in the extinction of the species concerned.

(3)(A) To the maximum extent practicable, within 90 days after receiving the petition of an interested person under section 553(e) of title 5, to add a species to, or to remove a species from, either of the lists published under subsection (c) of this section, the Secretary shall make a finding as to whether the petition presents substantial scientific or commercial information indicating that the petitioned action may be warranted. If such a petition is found to present such information, the Secretary shall promptly commence a review of the status of the species concerned. The Secretary shall promptly publish each finding made under this subparagraph in the Federal Register.

(B) Within 12 months after receiving a petition that is found under subparagraph (A) to present substantial information indicating that the petitioned action may be warranted, the Secretary shall make one of the following findings:

(i) The petitioned action is not warranted, in which case the Secretary shall promptly publish such finding in the Federal Register.

(ii) The petitioned action is warranted, in which case the Secretary shall promptly publish in the Federal Register a general notice and the complete text of a proposed regulation to implement such action in accordance with paragraph (5).

(iii) The petitioned action is warranted, but that —

(I) the immediate proposal and timely promulgation of a final regulation implementing the petitioned action in accordance with paragraphs (5) and (6) is precluded by pending proposals to determine whether any species is an endangered species or a threatened species, and

(II) expeditious progress is being made to add qualified species to either of the lists published under subsection (c) of this section and to remove from such lists species for which the protections of this chapter are no longer necessary,

in which case the Secretary shall promptly publish such finding in the

Federal Register, together with a description and evaluation of the reasons and data on which the finding is based.

(C)(i) A petition with respect to which a finding is made under subparagraph (B)(iii) shall be treated as a petition that is resubmitted to the Secretary under subparagraph (A) on the date of such finding and that presents substantial scientific or commercial information that the petitioned action may be warranted.

(ii) Any negative finding described in subparagraph (A) and any finding described in subparagraph (B)(i) or (iii) shall be subject to judicial review.

(iii) The Secretary shall implement a system to monitor effectively the status of all species with respect to which a finding is made under subparagraph (B)(iii) and shall make prompt use of the authority under paragraph 7[1] to prevent a significant risk to the well being of any such species.

(D)(i) To the maximum extent practicable, within 90 days after receiving the petition of an interested person under section 553(e) of title 5, to revise a critical habitat designation, the Secretary shall make a finding as to whether the petition presents substantial scientific information indicating that the revision may be warranted. The Secretary shall promptly publish such finding in the Federal Register.

(ii) Within 12 months after receiving a petition that is found under clause (i) to present substantial information indicating that the requested revision may be warranted, the Secretary shall determine how he intends to proceed with the requested revision, and shall promptly publish notice of such intention in the Federal Register.

(4) Except as provided in paragraphs (5) and (6) of this subsection, the provisions of section 553 of title 5 (relating to rulemaking procedures), shall apply to any regulation promulgated to carry out the purposes of this chapter.

(5) With respect to any regulation proposed by the Secretary to implement a determination, designation, or revision referred to in subsection (a)(1) or (3) of this section, the Secretary shall —

(A) not less than 90 days before the effective date of the regulation —

(i) publish a general notice and the complete text of the proposed regulation in the Federal Register, and

(ii) give actual notice of the proposed regulation (including the complete text of the regulation) to the State agency in each State in which the species is believed to occur, and to each county, or equivalent jurisdiction in which the species is believed to occur, and invite the comment of such agency, and each jurisdiction, thereon;

(B) insofar as practical, and in cooperation with the Secretary of State, give notice of the proposed regulation to each foreign nation in which the

---

1. So in original. Probably should be "(7)."

species is believed to occur or whose citizens harvest the species on the high seas, and invite the comment of such nation thereon;

(C) give notice of the proposed regulation to such professional scientific organizations as he deems appropriate;

(D) publish a summary of the proposed regulation in a newspaper of general circulation in each area of the United States in which the species is believed to occur; and

(E) promptly hold one public hearing on the proposed regulation if any person files a request for such a hearing within 45 days after the date of publication of general notice.

(6)(A) Within the one-year period beginning on the date on which general notice is published in accordance with paragraph (5)(A)(i) regarding a proposed regulation, the Secretary shall publish in the Federal Register —

(i) if a determination as to whether a species is an endangered species or a threatened species, or a revision of critical habitat, is involved, either —

(I) a final regulation to implement such determination,

(II) a final regulation to implement such revision or a finding that such revision should not be made,

(III) notice that such one-year period is being extended under subparagraph (B)(i), or

(IV) notice that the proposed regulation is being withdrawn under subparagraph (B)(ii), together with the finding on which such withdrawal is based; or

(ii) subject to subparagraph (C), if a designation of critical habitat is involved, either —

(I) a final regulation to implement such designation, or

(II) notice that such one-year period is being extended under such subparagraph.

(B)(i) If the Secretary finds with respect to a proposed regulation referred to in subparagraph (A)(i) that there is substantial disagreement regarding the sufficiency or accuracy of the available data relevant to the determination or revision concerned, the Secretary may extend the one-year period specified in subparagraph (A) for not more than six months for purposes of soliciting additional data.

(ii) If a proposed regulation referred to in subparagraph (A)(i) is not promulgated as a final regulation within such one-year period (or longer period if extension under clause (i) applies) because the Secretary finds that there is not sufficient evidence to justify the action proposed by the regulation, the Secretary shall immediately withdraw the regulation. The finding on which a withdrawal is based shall be subject to judicial review. The Secretary may not propose a regulation that has previously been withdrawn under this clause unless he determines that sufficient new information is available to warrant such proposal.

(iii) If the one-year period specified in subparagraph (A) is extended under clause (i) with respect to a proposed regulation, then before the close of such extended period the Secretary shall publish in the Federal Register either a final regulation to implement the determination or revision concerned, a finding that the revision should not be made, or a notice of withdrawal of the regulation under clause (ii), together with the finding on which the withdrawal is based.

(C) A final regulation designating critical habitat of an endangered species or a threatened species shall be published concurrently with the final regulation implementing the determination that such species is endangered or threatened, unless the Secretary deems that —

(i) it is essential to the conservation of such species that the regulation implementing such determination be promptly published; or

(ii) critical habitat of such species is not then determinable, in which case the Secretary, with respect to the proposed regulation to designate such habitat, may extend the one-year period specified in subparagraph (A) by not more than one additional year, but not later than the close of such additional year the Secretary must publish a final regulation, based on such data as may be available at that time, designating, to the maximum extent prudent, such habitat.

(7) Neither paragraph (4), (5), or (6) of this subsection nor section 553 of title 5 shall apply to any regulation issued by the Secretary in regard to any emergency posing a significant risk to the well-being of any species of fish or wildlife or plants, but only if —

(A) at the time of publication of the regulation in the Federal Register the Secretary publishes therein detailed reasons why such regulation is necessary; and

(B) in the case such regulation applies to resident species of fish or wildlife, or plants, the Secretary gives actual notice of such regulation to the State agency in each State in which such species is believed to occur.

Such regulation shall, at the discretion of the Secretary, take effect immediately upon the publication of the regulation in the Federal Register. Any regulation promulgated under the authority of this paragraph shall cease to have force and effect at the close of the 240-day period following the date of publication unless, during such 240-day period, the rulemaking procedures which would apply to such regulation without regard to this paragraph are complied with. If at any time after issuing an emergency regulation the Secretary determines, on the basis of the best appropriate data available to him, that substantial evidence does not exist to warrant such regulation, he shall withdraw it.

(8) The publication in the Federal Register of any proposed or final regulation which is necessary or appropriate to carry out the purposes of this chapter shall include a summary by the Secretary of the data on which such regulation is based and shall show the relationship of such data to such regulation; and if such regulation designates or revises critical habitat, such summary shall, to the maximum extent practicable, also include a brief description and evaluation of those activities (whether public or private) which, in the opinion of the Secretary,

if undertaken may adversely modify such habitat, or may be affected by such designation.

(c) LISTS

(1) The Secretary of the Interior shall publish in the Federal Register a list of all species determined by him or the Secretary of Commerce to be endangered species and a list of all species determined by him or the Secretary of Commerce to be threatened species. Each list shall refer to the species contained therein by scientific and common name or names, if any, specify with respect to each such species over what portion of its range it is endangered or threatened, and specify any critical habitat within such range. The Secretary shall from time to time revise each list published under the authority of this subsection to reflect recent determinations, designations, and revisions made in accordance with subsections (a) and (b) of this section.

(2) The Secretary shall —

(A) conduct, at least once every five years, a review of all species included in a list which is published pursuant to paragraph (1) and which is in effect at the time of such review; and

(B) determine on the basis of such review whether any such species should —

(i) be removed from such list;

(ii) be changed in status from an endangered species to a threatened species; or

(iii) be changed in status from a threatened species to an endangered species.

Each determination made under subparagraph (B) shall be made in accordance with the provisions of subsections (a) and (b) of this section.

(d) PROTECTIVE REGULATIONS

Whenever any species is listed as a threatened species pursuant to subsection (c) of this section, the Secretary shall issue such regulations as he deems necessary and advisable to provide for the conservation of such species. The Secretary may by regulation prohibit with respect to any threatened species any act prohibited under section 1538(a)(1) of this title, in the case of fish or wildlife, or section 1538(a)(2) of this title, in the case of plants, with respect to endangered species; except that with respect to the taking of resident species of fish or wildlife, such regulations shall apply in any State which has entered into a cooperative agreement pursuant to section 1535(c) of this title only to the extent that such regulations have also been adopted by such State.

(e) SIMILARITY OF APPEARANCE CASES

The Secretary may, by regulation of commerce or taking, and to the extent he deems advisable, treat any species as an endangered species or threatened species even though it is not listed pursuant to this section if he finds that —

(A) such species so closely resembles in appearance, at the point in question, a species which has been listed pursuant to such section that enforcement personnel would have substantial difficulty in attempting to differentiate between the listed and unlisted species;

(B) the effect of this substantial difficulty is an additional threat to an endangered or threatened species; and

(C) such treatment of an unlisted species will substantially facilitate the enforcement and further the policy of this chapter.

(f) **RECOVERY PLANS**

(1) The Secretary shall develop and implement plans (hereinafter in this subsection referred to as "recovery plans") for the conservation and survival of endangered species and threatened species listed pursuant to this section, unless he finds that such a plan will not promote the conservation of the species. The Secretary, in developing and implementing recovery plans, shall, to the maximum extent practicable —

(A) give priority to those endangered species or threatened species, without regard to taxonomic classification, that are most likely to benefit from such plans, particularly those species that are, or may be, in conflict with construction or other development projects or other forms of economic activity;

(B) incorporate in each plan —

(i) a description of such site-specific management actions as may be necessary to achieve the plan's goal for the conservation and survival of the species;

(ii) objective, measurable criteria which, when met, would result in a determination, in accordance with the provisions of this section, that the species be removed from the list; and

(iii) estimates of the time required and the cost to carry out those measures needed to achieve the plan's goal and to achieve intermediate steps toward that goal.

(2) The Secretary, in developing and implementing recovery plans, may procure the services and appropriate public and private agencies and institutions, and other qualified persons. Recovery teams appointed pursuant to this subsection shall not be subject to the Federal Advisory Committee Act.

(3) The Secretary shall report every two years to the Committee on Environment and Public Works of the Senate and the Committee on Merchant Marine and Fisheries of the House of Representatives on the status of efforts to develop and implement recovery plans for all species listed pursuant to this section and on the status of all species for which such plans have been developed.

(4) The Secretary shall, prior to final approval of a new or revised recovery plan, provide public notice and an opportunity for public review and comment on such plan. The Secretary shall consider all information presented during the public comment period prior to approval of the plan.

(5) Each Federal agency shall, prior to implementation of a new or revised

§1533   Endangered Species Act

recovery plan, consider all information presented during the public comment period under paragraph (4).

(g) MONITORING

(1) The Secretary shall implement a system in cooperation with the States to monitor effectively for not less than five years the status of all species which have recovered to the point at which the measures provided pursuant to this chapter are no longer necessary and which, in accordance with the provisions of this section, have been removed from either of the lists published under subsection (c) of this section.

(2) The Secretary shall make prompt use of the authority under paragraph 7[2] of subsection (b) of this section to prevent a significant risk to the well being of any such recovered species.

(h) AGENCY GUIDELINES; PUBLICATION IN FEDERAL REGISTER; SCOPE; PROPOSALS AND AMENDMENTS; NOTICE AND OPPORTUNITY FOR COMMENTS

The Secretary shall establish, and publish in the Federal Register, agency guidelines to insure that the purposes of this section are achieved efficiently and effectively. Such guidelines shall include, but are not limited to —

(1) procedures for recording the receipt and the disposition of petitions submitted under subsection (b)(3) of this section;

(2) criteria for making the findings required under such subsection with respect to petitions;

(3) a ranking system to assist in the identification of species that should receive priority review under subsection (a)(1) of this section; and

(4) a system for developing and implementing, on a priority basis, recovery plans under subsection (f) of this section.

The Secretary shall provide to the public notice of, and opportunity to submit written comments on, any guideline (including any amendment thereto) proposed to be established under this subsection.

(i) SUBMISSION TO STATE AGENCY OF JUSTIFICATION FOR REGULATIONS INCONSISTENT WITH STATE AGENCY'S COMMENTS OR PETITION

If, in the case of any regulation proposed by the Secretary under the authority of this section, a State agency to which notice thereof was given in accordance with subsection (b)(5)(A)(ii) of this section files comments disagreeing with all or part of the proposed regulation, and the Secretary issues a final regulation which is in conflict with such comments, or if the Secretary fails to adopt a regulation pursuant to an action petitioned by a State agency under subsection (b)(3) of this section, the Secretary shall submit to the State agency a written justification for his failure to adopt regulations consistent with the agency's comments or petition.

---

2. So in original. Probably should be "(7)."

§1534. Land Acquisition

(a) IMPLEMENTATION OF CONSERVATION PROGRAM; AUTHORIZATION OF SECRETARY AND SECRETARY OF AGRICULTURE

The Secretary, and the Secretary of Agriculture with respect to the National Forest System, shall establish and implement a program to conserve fish, wildlife, and plants, including those which are listed as endangered species or threatened species pursuant to section 1533 of this title. To carry out such a program, the appropriate Secretary —

(1) shall utilize the land acquisition and other authority under the Fish and Wildlife Act of 1956, as amended [16 U.S.C. 742a et seq.], the Fish and Wildlife Coordination Act, as amended [16 U.S.C. 661 et seq.], and the Migratory Bird Conservation Act [16 U.S.C. 715 et seq.], as appropriate; and

(2) is authorized to acquire by purchase, donation, or otherwise, lands, waters, or interest therein, and such authority shall be in addition to any other land acquisition authority vested in him.

(b) AVAILABILITY OF FUNDS FOR ACQUISITION OF LANDS, WATERS, ETC.

Funds made available pursuant to the Land and Water Conservation Fund Act of 1965, as amended [16 U.S.C. 460*l*-4 et seq.], may be used for the purpose of acquiring lands, waters, or interests therein under subsection (a) of this section.

§1535. Cooperation with States

(a) GENERALLY

In carrying out the program authorized by this chapter, the Secretary shall cooperate to the maximum extent practicable with the States. Such cooperation shall include consultation with the States concerned before acquiring any land or water, or interest therein, for the purpose of conserving any endangered species or threatened species.

(b) MANAGEMENT AGREEMENTS

The Secretary may enter into agreements with any State for the administration and management of any area established for the conservation of endangered species or threatened species. Any revenues derived from the administration of such areas under these agreements shall be subject to the provisions of section 715s of this title.

(c) COOPERATIVE AGREEMENTS

(1) In furtherance of the purposes of this chapter, the Secretary is authorized to enter into a cooperative agreement in accordance with this section with any State which establishes and maintains an adequate and active program for

the conservation of endangered species and threatened species. Within one hundred and twenty days after the Secretary receives a certified copy of such a proposed State program, he shall make a determination whether such program is in accordance with this chapter. Unless he determines, pursuant to this paragraph, that the State program is not in accordance with this chapter, he shall enter into a cooperative agreement with the State for the purpose of assisting in implementation of the State program. In order for a State program to be deemed an adequate and active program for the conservation of endangered species and threatened species, the Secretary must find, and annually thereafter reconfirm such finding, that under the State program —

(A) authority resides in the State agency to conserve resident species of fish or wildlife determined by the State agency or the Secretary to be endangered or threatened;

(B) the State agency has established acceptable conservation programs, consistent with the purposes and policies of this chapter, for all resident species of fish or wildlife in the State which are deemed by the Secretary to be endangered or threatened, and has furnished a copy of such plan and program together with all pertinent details, information, and data requested to the Secretary;

(C) the State agency is authorized to conduct investigations to determine the status and requirements for survival of resident species of fish and wildlife;

(D) the State agency is authorized to establish programs, including the acquisition of land or aquatic habitat or interests therein, for the conservation of resident endangered or threatened species of fish or wildlife; and

(E) provision is made for public participation in designating resident species of fish or wildlife as endangered or threatened; or

that under the State program —

(i) the requirements set forth in subparagraphs (C), (D), and (E) of this paragraph are complied with, and

(ii) plans are included under which immediate attention will be given to those resident species of fish and wildlife which are determined by the Secretary or the State agency to be endangered or threatened and which the Secretary and the State agency agree are most urgently in need of conservation programs; except that a cooperative agreement entered into with a State whose program is deemed adequate and active pursuant to clause (i) and this clause shall not affect the applicability of prohibitions set forth in or authorized pursuant to section 1533(d) of this title or section 1538(a)(1) of this title with respect to the taking of any resident endangered or threatened species.

(2) In furtherance of the purposes of this chapter the Secretary is authorized to enter into a cooperative agreement in accordance with this section with any State which establishes and maintains an adequate and active program for the conservation of endangered species and threatened species of plants. Within one hundred and twenty days after the Secretary receives a certified copy of such a proposed State program, he shall make a determination whether such program

Endangered Species Act §1535

is in accordance with this chapter. Unless he determines, pursuant to this paragraph, that the State program is not in accordance with this chapter, he shall enter into a cooperative agreement with the State for the purpose of assisting in implementation of the State program. In order for a State program to be deemed an adequate and active program for the conservation of endangered species of plants and threatened species of plants, the Secretary must find, and annually thereafter reconfirm such finding, that under the State program —

    (A) authority resides in the State agency to conserve resident species of plants determined by the State agency or the Secretary to be endangered or threatened;

    (B) the State agency has established acceptable conservation programs, consistent with the purposes and policies of this chapter, for all resident species of plants in the State which are deemed by the Secretary to be endangered or threatened, and has furnished a copy of such plan and program together with all pertinent details, information, and data requested to the Secretary;

    (C) the State agency is authorized to conduct investigations to determine the status and requirements for survival of resident species of plants; and

    (D) provision is made for public participation in designating resident species of plants as endangered or threatened; or

that under the State program —

    (i) the requirements set forth in subparagraphs (C) and (D) of this paragraph are complied with, and

    (ii) plans are included under which immediate attention will be given to those resident species of plants which are determined by the Secretary or the State agency to be endangered or threatened and which the Secretary and the State agency agree are most urgently in need of conservation programs; except that a cooperative agreement entered into with a State whose program is deemed adequate and active pursuant to clause (i) and this clause shall not affect the applicability of prohibitions set forth in or authorized pursuant to section 1533(d) or section 1538(a)(1) of this title with respect to the taking of any resident endangered or threatened species.

    (d)   ALLOCATION OF FUNDS

(1) The Secretary is authorized to provide financial assistance to any State, through its respective State agency, which has entered into a cooperative agreement pursuant to subsection (c) of this section to assist in development of programs for the conservation of endangered and threatened species or to assist in monitoring the status of candidate species pursuant to subparagraph (C) of section 1533(b)(3) of this title and recovered species pursuant to section 1533(g) of this title. The Secretary shall allocate each annual appropriation made in accordance with the provisions of subsection (i) of this section to such States based on consideration of —

    (A) the international commitments of the United States to protect endangered species or threatened species;

(B) the readiness of a State to proceed with a conservation program consistent with the objectives and purposes of this chapter;

(C) the number of endangered species and threatened species within a State;

(D) the potential for restoring endangered species and threatened species within a State;

(E) the relative urgency to initiate a program to restore and protect an endangered species or threatened species in terms of survival of the species;

(F) the importance of monitoring the status of candidate species within a State to prevent a significant risk to the well being of any such species; and

(G) the importance of monitoring the status of recovered species within a State to assure that such species do not return to the point at which the measures provided pursuant to this chapter are again necessary.

So much of the annual appropriation made in accordance with provisions of subsection (i) of this section allocated for obligation to any State for any fiscal year as remains unobligated at the close thereof is authorized to be made available to that State until the close of the succeeding fiscal year. Any amount allocated to any State which is unobligated at the end of the period during which it is available for expenditure is authorized to be made available for expenditure by the Secretary in conducting programs under this section.

(2) Such cooperative agreements shall provide for (A) the actions to be taken by the Secretary and the States; (B) the benefits that are expected to be derived in connection with the conservation of endangered or threatened species; (C) the estimated cost of these actions; and (D) the share of such costs to be borne by the Federal Government and by the States; except that —

(i) the Federal share of such program costs shall not exceed 75 percent of the estimated program cost stated in the agreement; and

(ii) the Federal share may be increased to 90 percent whenever two or more States having a common interest in one or more endangered or threatened species, the conservation of which may be enhanced by cooperation of such States, enter jointly into an agreement with the Secretary.

The Secretary may, in his discretion, and under such rules and regulations as he may prescribe, advance funds to the State for financing the United States pro rata share agreed upon in the cooperative agreement. For the purposes of this section, the non-Federal share may, in the discretion of the Secretary, be in the form of money or real property, the value of which will be determined by the Secretary, whose decision shall be final.

(e) **REVIEW OF STATE PROGRAMS**

Any action taken by the Secretary under this section shall be subject to his periodic review at no greater than annual intervals.

(f) **CONFLICTS BETWEEN FEDERAL AND STATE LAWS**

Any State law or regulation which applies with respect to the importation or exportation of, or interstate or foreign commerce in, endangered species or threatened species is void to the extent that it may effectively (1) permit what is prohibited by this chapter or by any regulation which implements this chapter, or (2) prohibit what is authorized pursuant to an exemption or permit provided for in this chapter or in any regulation which implements this chapter. This chapter shall not otherwise be construed to void any State law or regulation which is intended to conserve migratory, resident, or introduced fish or wildlife, or to permit or prohibit sale of such fish or wildlife. Any State law or regulation respecting the taking of an endangered species or threatened species may be more restrictive than the exemptions or permits provided for in this chapter or in any regulation which implements this chapter but not less restrictive than the prohibitions so defined.

(g) TRANSITION

(1) For purposes of this subsection, the term "establishment period" means, with respect to any State, the period beginning on December 28, 1973, and ending on whichever of the following dates first occurs: (A) the date of the close of the 120-day period following the adjournment of the first regular session of the legislature of such State which commences after December 28, 1973, or (B) the date of the close of the 15-month period following December 28, 1973.

(2) The prohibitions set forth in or authorized pursuant to sections 1533(d) and 1538(a)(1)(B) of this title shall not apply with respect to the taking of any resident endangered species or threatened species (other than species listed in Appendix I to the Convention or otherwise specifically covered by any other treaty or Federal law) within any State —

(A) which is then a party to a cooperative agreement with the Secretary pursuant to subsection (c) of this section (except to the extent that the taking of any such species is contrary to the law of such State); or

(B) except for any time within the establishment period when —

(i) the Secretary applies such prohibition to such species at the request of the State, or

(ii) the Secretary applies such prohibition after he finds, and publishes his finding, that an emergency exists posing a significant risk to the well-being of such species and that the prohibition must be applied to protect such species. The Secretary's finding and publication may be made without regard to the public hearing or comment provisions of section 553 of title 5 or any other provision of this chapter; but such prohibition shall expire 90 days after the date of its imposition unless the Secretary further extends such prohibition by publishing notice and a statement of justification of such extension.

(h) REGULATIONS

The Secretary is authorized to promulgate such regulations as may be appropriate to carry out the provisions of this section relating to financial assistance to States.

(i) APPROPRIATIONS

(1) To carry out the provisions of this section for fiscal years after September 30, 1988, there shall be deposited into a special fund known as the cooperative endangered species conservation fund, to be administered by the Secretary, an amount equal to 5 percent of the combined amounts covered each fiscal year into the Federal aid to wildlife restoration fund under section 669b of this title, and paid, transferred, or otherwise credited each fiscal year to the Sport Fishing Restoration Account established under 1016 of the Act of July 18, 1984.

(2) Amounts deposited into the special fund are authorized to be appropriated annually and allocated in accordance with subsection (d) of this section.

§1536. *Interagency Cooperation*

(a) FEDERAL AGENCY ACTIONS AND CONSULTATIONS

(1) The Secretary shall review other programs administered by him and utilize such programs in furtherance of the purposes of this chapter. All other Federal agencies shall, in consultation with and with the assistance of the Secretary, utilize their authorities in furtherance of the purposes of this chapter by carrying out programs for the conservation of endangered species and threatened species listed pursuant to section 1533 of this title.

(2) Each Federal agency shall, in consultation with and with the assistance of the Secretary, insure that any action authorized, funded, or carried out by such agency (hereinafter in this section referred to as an "agency action") is not likely to jeopardize the continued existence of any endangered species or threatened species or result in the destruction or adverse modification of habitat of such species which is determined by the Secretary, after consultation as appropriate with affected States, to be critical, unless such agency has been granted an exemption for such action by the Committee pursuant to subsection (h) of this section. In fulfilling the requirements of this paragraph each agency shall use the best scientific and commercial data available.

(3) Subject to such guidelines as the Secretary may establish, a Federal agency shall consult with the Secretary on any prospective agency action at the request of, and in cooperation with, the prospective permit or license applicant if the applicant has reason to believe that an endangered species or a threatened species may be present in the area affected by his project and that implementation of such action will likely affect such species.

(4) Each Federal agency shall confer with the Secretary on any agency action which is likely to jeopardize the continued existence of any species proposed to be listed under section 1533 of this title or result in the destruction or adverse modification of critical habitat proposed to be designated for such species. This paragraph does not require a limitation on the commitment of resources as described in subsection (d) of this section.

(b) OPINION OF SECRETARY

(1)(A) Consultation under subsection (a)(2) of this section with respect to any agency action shall be concluded within the 90-day period beginning on the date on which initiated or, subject to subparagraph (B), within such other period of time as is mutually agreeable to the Secretary and the Federal agency.

(B) In the case of an agency action involving a permit or license application, the Secretary and the Federal agency may not mutually agree to conclude consultation within a period exceeding 90 days unless the Secretary, before the close of the 90th day referred to in subparagraph (A) —

(i) if the consultation period proposed to be agreed to will end before the 150th day after the date on which consultation was initiated, submits to the applicant a written statement setting forth —

(I) the reasons why a longer period is required,

(II) the information that is required to complete the consultation, and

(III) the estimated date on which consultation will be completed;

or

(ii) if the consultation period proposed to be agreed to will end 150 or more days after the date on which consultation was initiated, obtains the consent of the applicant to such period.

The Secretary and the Federal agency may mutually agree to extend a consultation period established under the preceding sentence if the Secretary, before the close of such period, obtains the consent of the applicant to the extension.

(2) Consultation under subsection (a)(3) of this section shall be concluded within such period as is agreeable to the Secretary, the Federal agency, and the applicant concerned.

(3)(A) Promptly after conclusion of consultation under paragraph (2) or (3) of subsection (a) of this section, the Secretary shall provide to the Federal agency and the applicant, if any, a written statement setting forth the Secretary's opinion, and a summary of the information on which the opinion is based, detailing how the agency action affects the species or its critical habitat. If jeopardy or adverse modification is found, the Secretary shall suggest those reasonable and prudent alternatives which he believes would not violate subsection (a)(2) of this section and can be taken by the Federal agency or applicant in implementing the agency action.

(B) Consultation under subsection (a)(3) of this section, and an opinion issued by the Secretary incident to such consultation, regarding an agency action shall be treated respectively as a consultation under subsection (a)(2) of this section, and as an opinion issued after consultation under such subsection, regarding that action if the Secretary reviews the action before it is commenced by the Federal agency and finds, and notifies such agency, that no significant changes have been made with respect to the action and that no significant change has occurred regarding the information used during the initial consultation.

(4) If after consultation under subsection (a)(2) of this section, the Secretary concludes that —

(A) the agency action will not violate such subsection, or offers reasonable and prudent alternatives which the Secretary believes would not violate such subsection;

(B) the taking of an endangered species or a threatened species incidental to the agency action will not violate such subsection; and

(C) if an endangered species or threatened species of a marine mammal is involved, the taking is authorized pursuant to section 1371(a)(5) of this title; the Secretary shall provide the Federal agency and the applicant concerned, if any, with a written statement that —

(i) specifies the impact of such incidental taking on the species,

(ii) specifies those reasonable and prudent measures that the Secretary considers necessary or appropriate to minimize such impact,

(iii) in the case of marine mammals, specifies those measures that are necessary to comply with section 1371(a)(5) of this title with regard to the taking, and

(iv) sets forth the terms and conditions (including, but not limited to, reporting requirements) that must be complied with by the Federal agency or applicant (if any), or both, to implement the measures specified under clauses (ii) and (iii).

(c) **BIOLOGICAL ASSESSMENT**

(1) To facilitate compliance with the requirements of subsection (a)(2) of this section, each Federal agency shall, with respect to any agency action of such agency for which no contract for construction has been entered into and for which no construction has begun on November 10, 1978, request of the Secretary information whether any species which is listed or proposed to be listed may be present in the area of such proposed action. If the Secretary advises, based on the best scientific and commercial data available, that such species may be present, such agency shall conduct a biological assessment for the purpose of identifying any endangered species or threatened species which is likely to be affected by such action. Such assessment shall be completed within 180 days after the date on which initiated (or within such other period as is mutually agreed to by the Secretary and such agency, except that if a permit or license applicant is involved, the 180-day period may not be extended unless such agency provides the applicant, before the close of such period, with a written statement setting forth the estimated length of the proposed extension and the reasons therefor) and, before any contract for construction is entered into and before construction is begun with respect to such action. Such assessment may be undertaken as part of a Federal agency's compliance with the requirements of section 102 of the National Environmental Policy Act of 1969 (42 U.S.C. 4332).

(2) Any person who may wish to apply for an exemption under subsection (g) of this section for that action may conduct a biological assessment to identify any endangered species or threatened species which is likely to be affected by such action. Any such biological assessment must, however, be conducted in

cooperation with the Secretary and under the supervision of the appropriate Federal agency.

(d) LIMITATION ON COMMITMENT OF RESOURCES

After initiation of consultation required under subsection (a)(2) of this section, the Federal agency and the permit or license applicant shall not make any irreversible or irretrievable commitment of resources with respect to the agency action which has the effect of foreclosing the formulation or implementation of any reasonable and prudent alternative measures which would not violate subsection (a)(2) of this section.

(e) ENDANGERED SPECIES COMMITTEE

(1) There is established a committee to be known as the Endangered Species Committee (hereinafter in this section referred to as the "Committee").

(2) The Committee shall review any application submitted to it pursuant to this section and determine in accordance with subsection (h) of this section whether or not to grant an exemption from the requirements of subsection (a)(2) of this section for the action set forth in such application.

(3) The Committee shall be composed of seven members as follows:

(A) The Secretary of Agriculture.
(B) The Secretary of the Army.
(C) The Chairman of the Council of Economic Advisors.
(D) The Administrator of the Environmental Protection Agency.
(E) The Secretary of the Interior.
(F) The Administrator of the National Oceanic and Atmospheric Administration.
(G) The President, after consideration of any recommendations received pursuant to subsection (g)(2)(B) of this section shall appoint one individual from each affected State, as determined by the Secretary, to be a member of the Committee for the consideration of the application for exemption for an agency action with respect to which such recommendations are made, not later than 30 days after an application is submitted pursuant to this section.

(4)(A) Members of the Committee shall receive no additional pay on account of their service on the Committee.

(B) While away from their homes or regular places of business in the performance of services for the Committee, members of the Committee shall be allowed travel expenses, including per diem in lieu of subsistence, in the same manner as persons employed intermittently in the Government service are allowed expenses under section 5703 of title 5.

(5)(A) Five members of the Committee or their representatives shall constitute a quorum for the transaction of any function of the Committee, except that, in no case shall any representative be considered in determining the existence of a quorum for the transaction of any function of the Committee if that function involves a vote by the Committee on any matter before the Committee.

(B) The Secretary of the Interior shall be the Chairman of the Committee.

(C) The Committee shall meet at the call of the Chairman or five of its members.

(D) All meetings and records of the Committee shall be open to the public.

(6) Upon request of the Committee, the head of any Federal agency is authorized to detail, on a nonreimbursable basis, any of the personnel of such agency to the Committee to assist it in carrying out its duties under this section.

(7)(A) The Committee may for the purpose of carrying out its duties under this section hold such hearings, sit and act at such times and places, take such testimony, and receive such evidence, as the Committee deems advisable.

(B) When so authorized by the Committee, any member or agent of the Committee may take any action which the Committee is authorized to take by this paragraph.

(C) Subject to the Privacy Act [5 U.S.C. 552a], the Committee may secure directly from any Federal agency information necessary to enable it to carry out its duties under this section. Upon request of the Chairman of the Committee, the head of such Federal agency shall furnish such information to the Committee.

(D) The Committee may use the United States mails in the same manner and upon the same conditions as a Federal agency.

(E) The Administrator of General Services shall provide to the Committee on a reimbursable basis such administrative support services as the Committee may request.

(8) In carrying out its duties under this section, the Committee may promulgate and amend such rules, regulations, and procedures, and issue and amend such orders as it deems necessary.

(9) For the purpose of obtaining information necessary for the consideration of an application for an exemption under this section the Committee may issue subpenas for the attendance and testimony of witnesses and the production of relevant papers, books, and documents.

(10) In no case shall any representative, including a representative of a member designated pursuant to paragraph (3)(G) of this subsection, be eligible to cast a vote on behalf of any member.

(f) **PROMULGATION OF REGULATIONS; FORM AND CONTENTS OF EXEMPTION APPLICATION**

Not later than 90 days after November 10, 1978, the Secretary shall promulgate regulations which set forth the form and manner in which applications for exemption shall be submitted to the Secretary and the information to be contained in such applications. Such regulations shall require that information submitted in an application by the head of any Federal agency with respect to any agency action include, but not be limited to —

(1) a description of the consultation process carried out pursuant to sub-

Endangered Species Act §1536

section (a)(2) of this section between the head of the Federal agency and the Secretary; and

(2) a statement describing why such action cannot be altered or modified to conform with the requirements of subsection (a)(2) of this section.

(g) APPLICATION FOR EXEMPTION; REPORT TO COMMITTEE

(1) A Federal agency, the Governor of the State in which an agency action will occur, if any, or a permit or license applicant may apply to the Secretary for an exemption for an agency action of such agency if, after consultation under subsection (a)(2) of this section, the Secretary's opinion under subsection (b) of this section indicates that the agency action would violate subsection (a)(2) of this section. An application for an exemption shall be considered initially by the Secretary in the manner provided for in this subsection, and shall be considered by the Committee for a final determination under subsection (h) of this section after a report is made pursuant to paragraph (5). The applicant for an exemption shall be referred to as the "exemption applicant" in this section.

(2)(A) An exemption applicant shall submit a written application to the Secretary, in a form prescribed under subsection (f) of this section, not later than 90 days after the completion of the consultation process; except that, in the case of any agency action involving a permit or license applicant, such application shall be submitted not later than 90 days after the date on which the Federal agency concerned takes final agency action with respect to the issuance of the permit or license. For purposes of the preceding sentence, the term "final agency action" means (i) a disposition by an agency with respect to the issuance of a permit or license that is subject to administrative review, whether or not such disposition is subject to judicial review; or (ii) if administrative review is sought with respect to such disposition, the decision resulting after such review. Such application shall set forth the reasons why the exemption applicant considers that the agency action meets the requirements for an exemption under this subsection.

(B) Upon receipt of an application for exemption for an agency action under paragraph (1), the Secretary shall promptly (i) notify the Governor of each affected State, if any, as determined by the Secretary, and request the Governors so notified to recommend individuals to be appointed to the Endangered Species Committee for consideration of such application; and (ii) publish notice of receipt of the application in the Federal Register, including a summary of the information contained in the application and a description of the agency action with respect to which the application for exemption has been filed.

(3) The Secretary shall within 20 days after the receipt of an application for exemption, or within such other period of time as is mutually agreeable to the exemption applicant and the Secretary —

(A) determine that the Federal agency concerned and the exemption applicant have —

(i) carried out the consultation responsibilities described in subsection (a) of this section in good faith and made a reasonable and responsible effort to develop and fairly consider modifications or reasonable and prudent alternatives to the proposed agency action which would not violate subsection (a)(2) of this section;

(ii) conducted any biological assessment required by subsection (c) of this section; and

(iii) to the extent determinable within the time provided herein, refrained from making any irreversible or irretrievable commitment of resources prohibited by subsection (d) of this section; or

(B) deny the application for exemption because the Federal agency concerned or the exemption applicant have not met the requirements set forth in subparagraph (A)(i), (ii), and (iii).

The denial of an application under subparagraph (B) shall be considered final agency action for purposes of chapter 7 of title 5.

(4) If the Secretary determines that the Federal agency concerned and the exemption applicant have met the requirements set forth in paragraph (3)(A)(i), (ii), and (iii) he shall, in consultation with the Members of the Committee, hold a hearing on the application for exemption in accordance with sections 554, 555, and 556 (other than subsection (b)(1) and (2) thereof) of title 5 and prepare the report to be submitted pursuant to paragraph (5).

(5) Within 140 days after making the determinations under paragraph (3) or within such other period of time as is mutually agreeable to the exemption applicant and the Secretary, the Secretary shall submit to the Committee a report discussing —

(A) the availability of reasonable and prudent alternatives to the agency action, and the nature and extent of the benefits of the agency action and of alternative courses of action consistent with conserving the species or the critical habitat;

(B) a summary of the evidence concerning whether or not the agency action is in the public interest and is of national or regional significance;

(C) appropriate reasonable mitigation and enhancement measures which should be considered by the Committee; and

(D) whether the Federal agency concerned and the exemption applicant refrained from making any irreversible or irretrievable commitment of resources prohibited by subsection (d) of this section.

(6) To the extent practicable within the time required for action under subsection (g) of this section, and except to the extent inconsistent with the requirements of this section, the consideration of any application for an exemption under this section and the conduct of any hearing under this subsection shall be in accordance with sections 554, 555, and 556 (other than subsection (b)(3) of section 556) of title 5.

(7) Upon request of the Secretary, the head of any Federal agency is authorized to detail, on a nonreimbursable basis, any of the personnel of such agency to the Secretary to assist him in carrying out his duties under this section.

(8) All meetings and records resulting from activities pursuant to this subsection shall be open to the public.

(h) GRANT OF EXEMPTION

(1) The Committee shall make a final determination whether or not to grant an exemption within 30 days after receiving the report of the Secretary pursuant to subsection (g)(5) of this section. The Committee shall grant an exemption from the requirements of subsection (a)(2) of this section for an agency action if, by a vote of not less than five of its members voting in person —

(A) it determines on the record, based on the report of the Secretary, the record of the hearing held under subsection (g)(4) of this section and on such other testimony or evidence as it may receive, that —

(i) there are no reasonable and prudent alternatives to the agency action;

(ii) the benefits of such action clearly outweigh the benefits of alternative courses of action consistent with conserving the species or its critical habitat, and such action is in the public interest;

(iii) the action is of regional or national significance; and

(iv) neither the Federal agency concerned nor the exemption applicant made any irreversible or irretrievable commitment of resources prohibited by subsection (d) of this section; and

(B) it establishes such reasonable mitigation and enhancement measures, including, but not limited to, live propagation, transplantation, and habitat acquisition and improvement, as are necessary and appropriate to minimize the adverse effects of the agency action upon the endangered species, threatened species, or critical habitat concerned.

Any final determination by the Committee under this subsection shall be considered final agency action for purposes of chapter 7 of title 5.

(2)(A) Except as provided in subparagraph (B), an exemption for an agency action granted under paragraph (1) shall constitute a permanent exemption with respect to all endangered or threatened species for the purposes of completing such agency action —

(i) regardless whether the species was identified in the biological assessment; and

(ii) only if a biological assessment has been conducted under subsection (c) of this section with respect to such agency action.

(B) An exemption shall be permanent under subparagraph (A) unless —

(i) the Secretary finds, based on the best scientific and commercial data available, that such exemption would result in the extinction of a species that was not the subject of consultation under subsection (a)(2) of this section or was not identified in any biological assessment conducted under subsection (c) of this section, and

(ii) the Committee determines within 60 days after the date of the Secretary's finding that the exemption should not be permanent.

If the Secretary makes a finding described in clause (i), the Committee shall meet with respect to the matter within 30 days after the date of the finding.

(i) **REVIEW BY SECRETARY OF STATE; VIOLATION OF INTERNATIONAL TREATY OR OTHER INTERNATIONAL OBLIGATION OF UNITED STATES**

Notwithstanding any other provision of this chapter, the Committee shall be prohibited from considering for exemption any application made to it, if the Secretary of State, after a review of the proposed agency action and its potential implications, and after hearing, certifies, in writing, to the Committee within 60 days of any application made under this section that the granting of any such exemption and the carrying out of such action would be in violation of an international treaty obligation or other international obligation of the United States. The Secretary of State shall, at the time of such certification, publish a copy thereof in the Federal Register.

(j) **EXEMPTION FOR NATIONAL SECURITY REASONS**

Notwithstanding any other provision of this chapter, the Committee shall grant an exemption for any agency action if the Secretary of Defense finds that such exemption is necessary for reasons of national security.

(k) **EXEMPTION DECISION NOT CONSIDERED MAJOR FEDERAL ACTION; ENVIRONMENTAL IMPACT STATEMENT**

An exemption decision by the Committee under this section shall not be a major Federal action for purposes of the National Environmental Policy Act of 1969 [42 U.S.C. 4321 et seq.]: *Provided*, That an environmental impact statement which discusses the impacts upon endangered species or threatened species or their critical habitats shall have been previously prepared with respect to any agency action exempted by such order.

(*l*) **COMMITTEE ORDER GRANTING EXEMPTION; COST OF MITIGATION AND ENHANCEMENT MEASURES; REPORT BY APPLICANT TO COUNCIL ON ENVIRONMENTAL QUALITY**

(1) If the Committee determines under subsection (h) of this section that an exemption should be granted with respect to any agency action, the Committee shall issue an order granting the exemption and specifying the mitigation and enhancement measures established pursuant to subsection (h) of this section which shall be carried out and paid for by the exemption applicant in implementing the agency action. All necessary mitigation and enhancement measures shall be authorized prior to the implementing of the agency action and funded concurrently with all other project features.

(2) The applicant receiving such exemption shall include the costs of such mitigation and enhancement measures within the overall costs of continuing the proposed action. Notwithstanding the preceding sentence the costs of such

measures shall not be treated as project costs for the purpose of computing benefit-cost or other ratios for the proposed action. Any applicant may request the Secretary to carry out such mitigation and enhancement measures. The costs incurred by the Secretary in carrying out any such measures shall be paid by the applicant receiving the exemption. No later than one year after the granting of an exemption, the exemption applicant shall submit to the Council on Environmental Quality a report describing its compliance with the mitigation and enhancement measures prescribed by this section. Such a report shall be submitted annually until all such mitigation and enhancement measures have been completed. Notice of the public availability of such reports shall be published in the Federal Register by the Council on Environmental Quality.

(m) NOTICE REQUIREMENT FOR CITIZEN SUITS NOT APPLICABLE

The 60-day notice requirement of section 1540(g) of this title shall not apply with respect to review of any final determination of the Committee under subsection (h) of this section granting an exemption from the requirements of subsection (a)(2) of this section.

(n) JUDICIAL REVIEW

Any person, as defined by section 1532(13) of this title, may obtain judicial review, under chapter 7 of title 5, of any decision of the Endangered Species Committee under subsection (h) of this section in the United States Court of Appeals for (1) any circuit wherein the agency action concerned will be, or is being, carried out, or (2) in any case in which the agency action will be, or is being, carried out outside of any circuit, the District of Columbia, by filing in such court within 90 days after the date of issuance of the decision, a written petition for review. A copy of such petition shall be transmitted by the clerk of the court to the Committee and the Committee shall file in the court the record in the proceeding, as provided in section 2112 of title 28. Attorneys designated by the Endangered Species Committee may appear for, and represent the Committee in any action for review under this subsection.

(o) EXEMPTION AS PROVIDING EXCEPTION ON TAKING OF ENDANGERED SPECIES

Notwithstanding sections 1533(d) and 1538(a)(1)(B) and (C) of this title, sections 1371 and 1372 of this title, or any regulation promulgated to implement any such section —

(1) any action for which an exemption is granted under subsection (h) of this section shall not be considered to be a taking of any endangered species or threatened species with respect to any activity which is necessary to carry out such action; and

(2) any taking that is in compliance with the terms and conditions specified in a written statement provided under subsection (b)(4)(iv) of this section shall not be considered to be a prohibited taking of the species concerned.

(p) **EXEMPTIONS IN PRESIDENTIALLY DECLARED DISASTER AREAS**

In any area which has been declared by the President to be a major disaster area under the Disaster Relief and Emergency Assistance Act [42 U.S.C. 5121 et seq.], the President is authorized to make the determinations required by subsections (g) and (h) of this section for any project for the repair or replacement of a public facility substantially as it existed prior to the disaster under section 405 or 406 of the Disaster Relief and Emergency Assistance Act [42 U.S.C. 5171 or 5172], and which the President determines (1) is necessary to prevent the recurrence of such a natural disaster and to reduce the potential loss of human life, and (2) to involve an emergency situation which does not allow the ordinary procedures of this section to be followed. Notwithstanding any other provision of this section, the Committee shall accept the determinations of the President under this subsection.

§1537. *International Cooperation*

(a) **FINANCIAL ASSISTANCE**

As a demonstration of the commitment of the United States to the worldwide protection of endangered species and threatened species, the President may, subject to the provisions of section 1306 of title 31, use foreign currencies accruing to the United States Government under the Agricultural Trade Development and Assistance Act of 1954 [7 U.S.C. 1691 et seq.] or any other law to provide to any foreign country (with its consent) assistance in the development and management of programs in that country which the Secretary determines to be necessary or useful for the conservation of any endangered species or threatened species listed by the Secretary pursuant to section 1533 of this title. The President shall provide assistance (which includes, but is not limited to, the acquisition, by lease or otherwise, of lands, waters, or interests therein) to foreign countries under this section under such terms and conditions as he deems appropriate. Whenever foreign currencies are available for the provision of assistance under this section, such currencies shall be used in preference to funds appropriated under the authority of section 1542 of this title.

(b) **ENCOURAGEMENT OF FOREIGN PROGRAMS**

In order to carry out further the provisions of this chapter, the Secretary, through the Secretary of State, shall encourage —

(1) foreign countries to provide for the conservation of fish or wildlife and plants including endangered species and threatened species listed pursuant to section 1533 of this title;

(2) the entering into of bilateral or multilateral agreements with foreign countries to provide for such conservation; and

(3) foreign persons who directly or indirectly take fish or wildlife or plants in foreign countries or on the high seas for importation into the United

Endangered Species Act

States for commercial or other purposes to develop and carry out with such assistance as he may provide, conservation practices designed to enhance such fish or wildlife or plants and their habitat.

(c) PERSONNEL

After consultation with the Secretary of State, the Secretary may —

(1) assign or otherwise make available any officer or employee of his department for the purpose of cooperating with foreign countries and international organizations in developing personnel resources and programs which promote the conservation of fish or wildlife or plants; and

(2) conduct or provide financial assistance for the educational training of foreign personnel, in this country or abroad, in fish, wildlife, or plant management, research and law enforcement and to render professional assistance abroad in such matters.

(d) INVESTIGATIONS

After consultation with the Secretary of State and the Secretary of the Treasury, as appropriate, the Secretary may conduct or cause to be conducted such law enforcement investigations and research abroad as he deems necessary to carry out the purposes of this chapter.

§1537a. Convention Implementation

(a) MANAGEMENT AUTHORITY AND SCIENTIFIC AUTHORITY

The Secretary of the Interior (hereinafter in this section referred to as the "Secretary") is designated as the Management Authority and the Scientific Authority for purposes of the Convention and the respective functions of each such Authority shall be carried out through the United States Fish and Wildlife Service.

(b) MANAGEMENT AUTHORITY FUNCTIONS

The Secretary shall do all things necessary and appropriate to carry out the functions of the Management Authority under the Convention.

(c) SCIENTIFIC AUTHORITY FUNCTIONS; DETERMINATIONS

(1) The Secretary shall do all things necessary and appropriate to carry out the functions of the Scientific Authority under the Convention.

(2) The Secretary shall base the determinations and advice given by him under Article IV of the Convention with respect to wildlife upon the best available biological information derived from professionally accepted wildlife management practices; but is not required to make, or require any State to make, estimates of population size in making such determinations or giving such advice.

(d) **RESERVATIONS BY THE UNITED STATES UNDER CONVENTION**

If the United States votes against including any species in Appendix I or II of the Convention and does not enter a reservation pursuant to paragraph (3) of Article XV of the Convention with respect to that species, the Secretary of State, before the 90th day after the last day on which such a reservation could be entered, shall submit to the Committee on Merchant Marine and Fisheries of the House of Representatives, and to the Committee on the Environment and Public Works of the Senate, a written report setting forth the reasons why such a reservation was not entered.

(e) **WILDLIFE PRESERVATION IN WESTERN HEMISPHERE**

(1) The Secretary of the Interior (hereinafter in this subsection referred to as the "Secretary"), in cooperation with the Secretary of State, shall act on behalf of, and represent, the United States in all regards as required by the Convention on Nature Protection and Wildlife Preservation in the Western Hemisphere (56 Stat. 1354, T.S. 982, hereinafter in this subsection referred to as the "Western Convention"). In the discharge of these responsibilities, the Secretary and the Secretary of State shall consult with the Secretary of Agriculture, the Secretary of Commerce, and the heads of other agencies with respect to matters relating to or affecting their areas of responsibility.

(2) The Secretary and the Secretary of State shall, in cooperation with the contracting parties to the Western Convention and, to the extent feasible and appropriate, with the participation of State agencies, take such steps as are necessary to implement the Western Convention. Such steps shall include, but not be limited to —

(A) cooperation with contracting parties and international organizations for the purpose of developing personnel resources and programs that will facilitate implementation of the Western Convention;

(B) identification of those species of birds that migrate between the United States and other contracting parties, and the habitats upon which those species depend, and the implementation of cooperative measures to ensure that such species will not become endangered or threatened; and

(C) identification of measures that are necessary and appropriate to implement those provisions of the Western Convention which address the protection of wild plants.

(3) No later than September 30, 1985, the Secretary and the Secretary of State shall submit a report to Congress describing those steps taken in accordance with the requirements of this subsection and identifying the principal remaining actions yet necessary for comprehensive and effective implementation of the Western Convention.

(4) The provisions of this subsection shall not be construed as affecting the authority, jurisdiction, or responsibility of the several States to manage, control, or regulate resident fish or wildlife under State law or regulations.

§1538. *Prohibited Acts*

(a) GENERALLY

(1) Except as provided in sections 1535(g)(2) and 1539 of this title, with respect to any endangered species of fish or wildlife listed pursuant to section 1533 of this title it is unlawful for any person subject to the jurisdiction of the United States to —

(A) import any such species into, or export any such species from the United States;

(B) take any such species within the United States or the territorial sea of the United States;

(C) take any such species upon the high seas;

(D) possess, sell, deliver, carry, transport, or ship, by any means whatsoever, any such species taken in violation of subparagraphs (B) and (C);

(E) deliver, receive, carry, transport, or ship in interstate or foreign commerce, by any means whatsoever and in the course of commercial activity, any such species;

(F) sell or offer for sale in interstate or foreign commerce any such species; or

(G) violate any regulation pertaining to such species or to any threatened species of fish or wildlife listed pursuant to section 1533 of this title and promulgated by the Secretary pursuant to authority provided by this chapter.

(2) Except as provided in sections 1535(g)(2) and 1539 of this title, with respect to any endangered species of plants listed pursuant to section 1533 of this title, it is unlawful for any person subject to the jurisdiction of the United States to —

(A) import any such species into, or export any such species from, the United States;

(B) remove and reduce to possession any such species from areas under Federal jurisdiction; maliciously damage or destroy any such species on any such areas; or remove, cut, dig up, or damage or destroy any such species on any other area in knowing violation of any law or regulation of any State or in the course of any violation of a State criminal trespass law;

(C) deliver, receive, carry, transport, or ship in interstate or foreign commerce, by any means whatsoever and in the course of a commercial activity, any such species;

(D) sell or offer for sale in interstate or foreign commerce any such species; or

(E) violate any regulation pertaining to such species or to any threatened species of plants listed pursuant to section 1533 of this title and promulgated by the Secretary pursuant to authority provided by this chapter.

(b) SPECIES HELD IN CAPTIVITY OR CONTROLLED ENVIRONMENT

(1) The provisions of subsections (a)(1)(A) and (a)(1)(G) of this section shall not apply to any fish or wildlife which was held in captivity or in a controlled

environment on (A) December 28, 1973, or (B) the date of the publication in the Federal Register of a final regulation adding such fish or wildlife species to any list published pursuant to subsection (c) of section 1533 of this title; *Provided*, That such holding and any subsequent holding or use of the fish or wildlife was not in the course of a commercial activity. With respect to any act prohibited by subsections (a)(1)(A) and (a)(1)(G) of this section which occurs after a period of 180 days from (i) December 28, 1973, or (ii) the date of publication in the Federal Register of a final regulation adding such fish or wildlife species to any list published pursuant to subsection (c) of section 1533 of this title, there shall be a rebuttable presumption that the fish or wildlife involved in such act is not entitled to the exemption contained in this subsection.

(2)(A) The provisions of subsection (a)(1) of this section shall not apply to —

(i) any raptor legally held in captivity or in a controlled environment on November 10, 1978; or

(ii) any progeny of any raptor described in clause (i);

until such time as any such raptor or progeny is intentionally returned to a wild state.

(B) Any person holding any raptor or progeny described in subparagraph (A) must be able to demonstrate that the raptor or progeny does, in fact, qualify under the provisions of this paragraph, and shall maintain and submit to the Secretary, on request, such inventories, documentation, and records as the Secretary may by regulation require as being reasonably appropriate to carry out the purposes of this paragraph. Such requirements shall not unnecessarily duplicate the requirements of other rules and regulations promulgated by the Secretary.

(c) **VIOLATION OF CONVENTION**

(1) It is unlawful for any person subject to the jurisdiction of the United States to engage in any trade in any specimens contrary to the provisions of the Convention, or to possess any specimens traded contrary to the provisions of the Convention, including the definitions of terms in article I thereof.

(2) Any importation into the United States of fish or wildlife shall, if —

(A) such fish or wildlife is not an endangered species listed pursuant to section 1533 of this title but is listed in Appendix II to the Convention,

(B) the taking and exportation of such fish or wildlife is not contrary to the provisions of the Convention and all other applicable requirements of the Convention have been satisfied,

(C) the applicable requirements of subsections (d), (e), and (f) of this section have been satisfied, and

(D) such importation is not made in the course of a commercial activity, be presumed to be an importation not in violation of any provision of this chapter or any regulation issued pursuant to this chapter.

(d) IMPORTS AND EXPORTS

(1) IN GENERAL

It is unlawful for any person, without first having obtained permission from the Secretary, to engage in business —

(A) as an importer or exporter of fish or wildlife (other than shellfish and fishery products which (i) are not listed pursuant to section 1533 of this title as endangered species or threatened species, and (ii) are imported for purposes of human or animal consumption or taken in waters under the jurisdiction of the United States or on the high seas for recreational purposes) or plants; or

(B) as an importer or exporter of any amount of raw or worked African elephant ivory.

(2) REQUIREMENTS

Any person required to obtain permission under paragraph (1) of this subsection shall —

(A) keep such records as will fully and correctly disclose each importation or exportation of fish, wildlife, plants, or African elephant ivory made by him and the subsequent disposition made by him with respect to such fish, wildlife, plants, or ivory;

(B) at all reasonable times upon notice by a duly authorized representative of the Secretary, afford such representative access to his place of business, an opportunity to examine his inventory of imported fish, wildlife, plants, or African elephant ivory and the records required to be kept under subparagraph (A) of this paragraph, and to copy such records; and

(C) file such reports as the Secretary may require.

(3) REGULATIONS

The Secretary shall prescribe such regulations as are necessary and appropriate to carry out the purposes of this subsection.

(4) RESTRICTION ON CONSIDERATION OF VALUE OR AMOUNT OF AFRICAN ELEPHANT IVORY IMPORTED OR EXPORTED

In granting permission under this subsection for importation or exportation of African elephant ivory, the Secretary shall not vary the requirements for obtaining such permission on the basis of the value or amount of ivory imported or exported under such permission.

(e) REPORTS

It is unlawful for any person importing or exporting fish or wildlife (other than shellfish and fishery products which (1) are not listed pursuant to section 1533 of this title as endangered or threatened species, and (2) are imported for purposes of human or animal consumption or taken in waters under the juris-

§1538   Endangered Species Act

diction of the United States or on the high seas for recreational purposes) or plants to fail to file any declaration or report as the Secretary deems necessary to facilitate enforcement of this chapter or to meet the obligations of the Convention.

(f)   DESIGNATION OF PORTS

(1) It is unlawful for any person subject to the jurisdiction of the United States to import into or export from the United States any fish or wildlife (other than shellfish and fishery products which (A) are not listed pursuant to section 1533 of this title as endangered species or threatened species, and (B) are imported for purposes of human or animal consumption or taken in waters under the jurisdiction of the United States or on the high seas for recreational purposes) or plants, except at a port or ports designated by the Secretary of the Interior. For the purpose of facilitating enforcement of this chapter and reducing the costs thereof, the Secretary of the Interior, with approval of the Secretary of the Treasury and after notice and opportunity for public hearing, may, by regulation, designate ports and change such designations. The Secretary of the Interior, under such terms and conditions as he may prescribe, may permit the importation or exportation at nondesignated ports in the interest of the health or safety of the fish or wildlife or plants, or for other reasons, if, in his discretion, he deems it appropriate and consistent with the purpose of this subsection.

(2) Any port designated by the Secretary of the Interior under the authority of section 668cc-4(d) of this title, shall, if such designation is in effect on December 27, 1973, be deemed to be a port designated by the Secretary under paragraph (1) of this subsection until such time as the Secretary otherwise provides.

(g)   VIOLATIONS

It is unlawful for any person subject to the jurisdiction of the United States to attempt to commit, solicit another to commit, or cause to be committed, any offense defined in this section.

§1539. *Exceptions*

(a)   PERMITS

(1) The Secretary may permit, under such terms and conditions as he shall prescribe —

    (A) any act otherwise prohibited by section 1538 of this title for scientific purposes or to enhance the propagation or survival of the affected species, including, but not limited to, acts necessary for the establishment and maintenance of experimental populations pursuant to subsection (j) of this section; or

    (B) any taking otherwise prohibited by section 1538(a)(1)(B) of this title

Endangered Species Act §1539

if such taking is incidental to, and not the purpose of, the carrying out of an otherwise lawful activity.

(2)(A) No permit may be issued by the Secretary authorizing any taking referred to in paragraph (1)(B) unless the applicant therefor submits to the Secretary a conservation plan that specifies —

> (i) the impact which will likely result from such taking;
>
> (ii) what steps the applicant will take to minimize and mitigate such impacts, and the funding that will be available to implement such steps;
>
> (iii) what alternative actions to such taking the applicant considered and the reasons why such alternatives are not being utilized; and
>
> (iv) such other measures that the Secretary may require as being necessary or appropriate for purposes of the plan.

(B) If the Secretary finds, after opportunity for public comment, with respect to a permit application and the related conservation plan that —

> (i) the taking will be incidental;
>
> (ii) the applicant will, to the maximum extent practicable, minimize and mitigate the impacts of such taking;
>
> (iii) the applicant will ensure that adequate funding for the plan will be provided;
>
> (iv) the taking will not appreciably reduce the likelihood of the survival and recovery of the species in the wild; and
>
> (v) the measures, if any, required under subparagraph (A)(iv) will be met;

and he has received such other assurances as he may require that the plan will be implemented, the Secretary shall issue the permit. The permit shall contain such terms and conditions as the Secretary deems necessary or appropriate to carry out the purposes of this paragraph, including, but not limited to, such reporting requirements as the secretary deems necessary for determining whether such terms and conditions are being complied with.

(C) The Secretary shall revoke a permit issued under this paragraph if he finds that the permittee is not complying with the terms and conditions of the permit.

(b) **HARDSHIP EXEMPTIONS**

(1) If any person enters into a contract with respect to a species of fish or wildlife or plant before the date of the publication in the Federal Register of notice of consideration of that species as an endangered species and the subsequent listing of that species as an endangered species pursuant to section 1533 of this title will cause undue economic hardship to such person under the contract, the Secretary, in order to minimize such hardship, may exempt such person from the application of section 1538(a) of this title to the extent the Secretary deems appropriate if such person applies to him for such exemption and includes with such application such information as the Secretary may require to prove such hardship; except that (A) no such exemption shall be for a duration of more than one year from the date of publication in the Federal Register of notice of

consideration of the species concerned, or shall apply to a quantity of fish or wildlife or plants in excess of that specified by the Secretary; (B) the one-year period for those species of fish or wildlife listed by the Secretary as endangered prior to December 28, 1973, shall expire in accordance with the terms of section 668cc-3 of this title; and (C) no such exemption may be granted for the importation or exportation of a specimen listed in Appendix I of the Convention which is to be used in a commercial activity.

(2) As used in this subsection, the term "undue economic hardship" shall include, but not be limited to:

(A) substantial economic loss resulting from inability caused by this chapter to perform contracts with respect to species for fish and wildlife entered into prior to the date of publication in the Federal Register of a notice of consideration of such species as an endangered species;

(B) substantial economic loss to persons who, for the year prior to the notice of consideration of such species as an endangered species, derived a substantial portion of their income from the lawful taking of any listed species, which taking would be made unlawful under this chapter; or

(C) curtailment of subsistence taking made unlawful under this chapter by persons (i) not reasonably able to secure other sources of subsistence; and (ii) dependent to a substantial extent upon hunting and fishing for subsistence; and (iii) who must engage in such curtailed taking for subsistence purposes.

(3) The Secretary may make further requirements for a showing of undue economic hardship as he deems fit. Exceptions granted under this section may be limited by the Secretary in his discretion as to time, area, or other factor of applicability.

(c) **NOTICE AND REVIEW**

The Secretary shall publish notice in the Federal Register of each application for an exemption or permit which is made under this subsection. Each notice shall invite the submission from interested parties, within thirty days after the date of the notice, of written data, views, or arguments with respect to the application; except, that such thirty-day period may be waived by the Secretary in an emergency situation where the health or life of an endangered animal is threatened and no reasonable alternative is available to the applicant, but notice of any such waiver shall be published by the Secretary in the Federal Register within ten days following the issuance of the exemption or permit. Information received by the Secretary as a part of any application shall be available to the public as a matter of public record at every stage of the proceeding.

(d) **PERMIT AND EXEMPTION POLICY**

The Secretary may grant exceptions under subsections (a)(1)(A) and (b) of this section only if he finds and publishes his finding in the Federal Register that (1) such exceptions were applied for in good faith, (2) if granted and exercised will not operate to the disadvantage of such endangered species, and (3) will be consistent with the purposes and policy set forth in section 1531 of this title.

(e) **ALASKA NATIVES**

(1) Except as provided in paragraph (4) of this subsection the provisions of this chapter shall not apply with respect to the taking of any endangered species or threatened species, or the importation of any such species taken pursuant to this section, by —
    (A) any Indian, Aleut, or Eskimo who is an Alaskan Native who resides in Alaska; or
    (B) any non-native permanent resident of an Alaskan native village;
if such taking is primarily for subsistence purposes. Non-edible byproducts of species taken pursuant to this section may be sold in interstate commerce when made into authentic native articles of handicrafts and clothing; except that the provisions of this subsection shall not apply to any non-native resident of an Alaskan native village found by the Secretary to be not primarily dependent upon the taking of fish and wildlife for consumption or for the creation and sale of authentic native articles of handicrafts and clothing.

(2) Any taking under this subsection may not be accomplished in a wasteful manner.

(3) As used in this subsection —
    (i) The term "subsistence" includes selling any edible portion of fish or wildlife in native villages and towns in Alaska for native consumption within native villages or towns; and
    (ii) The term "authentic native articles of handicrafts and clothing" means items composed wholly or in some significant respect of natural materials, and which are produced, decorated, or fashioned in the exercise of traditional native handicrafts without the use of pantographs, multiple carvers, or other mass copying devices. Traditional native handicrafts include, but are not limited to, weaving, carving, stitching, sewing, lacing, beading, drawing, and painting.

(4) Notwithstanding the provisions of paragraph (1) of this subsection, whenever the Secretary determines that any species of fish or wildlife which is subject to taking under the provisions of this subsection is an endangered species or threatened species, and that such taking materially and negatively affects the threatened or endangered species, he may prescribe regulations upon the taking of such species by any such Indian, Aleut, Eskimo, or non-Native Alaskan resident of an Alaskan native village. Such regulations may be established with reference to species, geographical description of the area included, the season for taking, or any other factors related to the reason for establishing such regulations and consistent with the policy of this chapter. Such regulations shall be prescribed after a notice and hearings in the affected judicial districts of Alaska and as otherwise required by section 1373 of this title, and shall be removed as

soon as the Secretary determines that the need for their impositions has disappeared.

(f) **PRE-ACT ENDANGERED SPECIES PARTS EXEMPTION; APPLICATION AND CERTIFICATION; REGULATION; VALIDITY OF SALES CONTRACT; SEPARABILITY OF PROVISIONS; RENEWAL OF EXEMPTION; EXPIRATION OF RENEWAL CERTIFICATION**

(1) As used in this subsection —

(A) The term "pre-Act endangered species part" means —

(i) any sperm whale oil, including derivatives thereof, which was lawfully held within the United States on December 28, 1973, in the course of a commercial activity; or

(ii) any finished scrimshaw product, if such product or the raw material for such product was lawfully held within the United States on December 28, 1973, in the course of a commercial activity.

(B) The term "scrimshaw product" means any art form which involves the substantial etching or engraving of designs upon, or the substantial carving of figures, patterns, or designs from, any bone or tooth of any marine mammal of the order Cetacea. For purposes of this subsection, polishing or the adding of minor superficial markings does not constitute substantial etching, engraving, or carving.

(2) The Secretary, pursuant to the provisions of this subsection, may exempt, if such exemption is not in violation of the Convention, any pre-Act endangered species part from one or more of the following prohibitions:

(A) The prohibition on exportation from the United States set forth in section 1538(a)(1)(A) of this title.

(B) Any prohibition set forth in section 1538(a)(1)(E) or (F) of this title.

(3) Any person seeking an exemption described in paragraph (2) of this subsection shall make application therefor to the Secretary in such form and manner as he shall prescribe, but no such application may be considered by the Secretary unless the application —

(A) is received by the Secretary before the close of the one-year period beginning on the date on which regulations promulgated by the Secretary to carry out this subsection first take effect;

(B) contains a complete and detailed inventory of all pre-Act endangered species parts for which the applicant seeks exemption;

(C) is accompanied by such documentation as the Secretary may require to prove that any endangered species part or product claimed by the applicant to be a pre-Act endangered species part is in fact such a part; and

(D) contains such other information as the Secretary deems necessary and appropriate to carry out the purposes of this subsection.

(4) If the Secretary approves any application for exemption made under this subsection, he shall issue to the applicant a certificate of exemption which shall specify —

(A) any prohibition in section 1538(a) of this title which is exempted;

(B) the pre-Act endangered species parts to which the exemption applies;

(C) the period of time during which the exemption is in effect, but no exemption made under this subsection shall have force and effect after the close of the three-year period beginning on the date of issuance of the certificate unless such exemption is renewed under paragraph (8); and

(D) any term or condition prescribed pursuant to paragraph (5)(A) or (B), or both, which the Secretary deems necessary or appropriate.

(5) The Secretary shall prescribe such regulations as he deems necessary and appropriate to carry out the purposes of this subsection. Such regulations may set forth —

(A) terms and conditions which may be imposed on applicants for exemptions under this subsection (including, but not limited to, requirements that applicants register inventories, keep complete sales records, permit duly authorized agents of the Secretary to inspect such inventories and records, and periodically file appropriate reports with the Secretary); and

(B) terms and conditions which may be imposed on any subsequent purchaser of any pre-Act endangered species part covered by an exemption granted under this subsection;

to insure that any such part so exempted is adequately accounted for and not disposed of contrary to the provisions of this chapter. No regulation prescribed by the Secretary to carry out the purposes of this subsection shall be subject to section 1533(f)(2)(A)(i) of this title.

(6)(A) Any contract for the sale of pre-Act endangered species parts which is entered into by the Administrator of General Services prior to the effective date of this subsection and pursuant to the notice published in the Federal Register on January 9, 1973, shall not be rendered invalid by virtue of the fact that fulfillment of such contract may be prohibited under section 1538(a)(1)(F) of this title.

(B) In the event that this paragraph is held invalid, the validity of the remainder of this chapter, including the remainder of this subsection, shall not be affected.

(7) Nothing in this subsection shall be construed to —

(A) exonerate any person from any act committed in violation of paragraphs (1)(A), (1)(E), or (1)(F) of section 1538(a) of this title prior to July 12, 1976; or

(B) immunize any person from prosecution for any such act.

(8)(A)(i)[3] Any valid certificate of exemption which was renewed after October 13, 1982, and was in effect on March 31, 1988, shall be deemed to be renewed for a six-month period beginning on October 7, 1988. Any person holding such a certificate may apply to the Secretary for one additional renewal of such certificate for a period not to exceed 5 years beginning on October 7, 1988.

(B) If the Secretary approves any application for renewal of an exemp-

---

3. So in original. No cl. (ii) has been enacted.

tion under this paragraph, he shall issue to the applicant a certificate of renewal of such exemption which shall provide that all terms, conditions, prohibitions, and other regulations made applicable by the previous certificate shall remain in effect during the period of the renewal.

(C) No exemption or renewal of such exemption made under this subsection shall have force and effect after the expiration date of the certificate of renewal of such exemption issued under this paragraph.

(D) No person may, after January 31, 1984, sell or offer for sale in interstate or foreign commerce, any pre-Act finished scrimshaw product unless such person holds a valid certificate of exemption issued by the Secretary under this subsection, and unless such product or the raw material for such product was held by such person on October 13, 1982.

(g) BURDEN OF PROOF

In connection with any action alleging a violation of section 1538 of this title, any person claiming the benefit of any exemption or permit under this chapter shall have the burden of proving that the exemption or permit is applicable, has been granted, and was valid and in force at the time of the alleged violation.

(h) CERTAIN ANTIQUE ARTICLES; IMPORTATION; PORT DESIGNATION; APPLICATION FOR RETURN OF ARTICLES

(1) Sections 1533(d) and 1538(a) and (c) of this title do not apply to any article which —

(A) is not less than 100 years of age;

(B) is composed in whole or in part of any endangered species or threatened species listed under section 1533 of this title;

(C) has not been repaired or modified with any part of any such species on or after December 28, 1973; and

(D) is entered at a port designated under paragraph (3).

(2) Any person who wishes to import an article under the exception provided by this subsection shall submit to the customs officer concerned at the time of entry of the article such documentation as the Secretary of the Treasury, after consultation with the Secretary of the Interior, shall by regulation require as being necessary to establish that the article meets the requirements set forth in paragraph (1)(A), (B), and (C).

(3) The Secretary of the Treasury, after consultation with the Secretary of the Interior, shall designate one port within each customs region at which articles described in paragraph (1)(A), (B), and (C) must be entered into the customs territory of the United States.

(4) Any person who imported, after December 27, 1973, and on or before November 10, 1978, any article described in paragraph (1) which —

(A) was not repaired or modified after the date of importation with any part of any endangered species or threatened species listed under section 1533 of this title;

(B) was forfeited to the United States before November 10, 1978, or is subject to forfeiture to the United States on such date of enactment, pursuant to the assessment of a civil penalty under section 1540 of this title; and

(C) is in the custody of the United States on November 10, 1978;

may, before the close of the one-year period beginning on November 10, 1978, make application to the Secretary for return of the article. Application shall be made in such form and manner, and contain such documentation, as the Secretary prescribes. If on the basis of any such application which is timely filed, the Secretary is satisfied that the requirements of this paragraph are met with respect to the article concerned, the Secretary shall return the article to the applicant and the importation of such article shall, on and after the date of return, be deemed to be a lawful importation under this chapter.

(i) NONCOMMERCIAL TRANSSHIPMENTS

Any importation into the United States of fish or wildlife shall, if —

(1) such fish or wildlife was lawfully taken and exported from the country of origin and country of reexport, if any;

(2) such fish or wildlife is in transit or transshipment through any place subject to the jurisdiction of the United States en route to a country where such fish or wildlife may be lawfully imported and received;

(3) the exporter or owner of such fish or wildlife gave explicit instructions not to ship such fish or wildlife through any place subject to the jurisdiction of the United States, or did all that could have reasonably been done to prevent transshipment, and the circumstances leading to the transshipment were beyond the exporter's or owner's control;

(4) the applicable requirements of the Convention have been satisfied; and

(5) such importation is not made in the course of a commercial activity,

be an importation not in violation of any provision of this chapter or any regulation issued pursuant to this chapter while such fish or wildlife remains in the control of the United States Customs Service.

(j) EXPERIMENTAL POPULATIONS

(1) For purposes of this subsection, the term "experimental population" means any population (including any offspring arising solely therefrom) authorized by the Secretary for release under paragraph (2), but only when, and at such times as, the population is wholly separate geographically from nonexperimental populations of the same species.

(2)(A) The Secretary may authorize the release (and the related transportation) of any population (including eggs, propagules, or individuals) of an endangered species or a threatened species outside the current range of such species if the Secretary determines that such release will further the conservation of such species.

(B) Before authorizing the release of any population under subparagraph (A), the Secretary shall by regulation identify the population and determine, on the basis of the best available information, whether or not such population is essential to the continued existence of an endangered species or a threatened species.

(C) For the purposes of this chapter, each member of an experimental population shall be treated as a threatened species; except that —

(i) solely for purposes of section 1536 of this title (other than subsection (a)(1) thereof), an experimental population determined under subparagraph (B) to be not essential to the continued existence of a species shall be treated, except when it occurs in an area within the National Wildlife Refuge System or the National Park System, as a species proposed to be listed under section 1533 of this title; and

(ii) critical habitat shall not be designated under this chapter for any experimental population determined under subparagraph (B) to be not essential to the continued existence of a species.

(3) The Secretary, with respect to populations of endangered species or threatened species that the Secretary authorized, before October 13, 1982, for release in geographical areas separate from the other populations of such species, shall determine by regulation which of such populations are an experimental population for the purposes of this subsection and whether or not each is essential to the continued existence of an endangered species or a threatened species.

§1540. Penalties and Enforcement

(a) CIVIL PENALTIES

(1) Any person who knowingly violates, and any person engaged in business as an importer or exporter of fish, wildlife, or plants who violates, any provision of this chapter, or any provision of any permit or certificate issued hereunder, or of any regulation issued in order to implement subsection (a)(1)(A), (B), (C), (D), (E), or (F), (a)(2)(A), (B), (C), or (D), (c), (d) (other than regulation relating to recordkeeping or filing of reports), (f) or (g) of section 1538 of this title, may be assessed a civil penalty by the Secretary of not more than $25,000 for each violation. Any person who knowingly violates, and any person engaged in business as an importer or exporter of fish, wildlife, or plants who violates, any provision of any other regulation issued under this chapter may be assessed a civil penalty by the Secretary of not more than $12,000 for each such violation. Any person who otherwise violates any provision of this chapter, or any regulation, permit, or certificate issued hereunder, may be assessed a civil penalty by the Secretary of not more than $500 for each such violation. No penalty may be assessed under this subsection unless such person is given notice and opportunity for a hearing with respect to such violation. Each violation shall be a separate offense. Any such civil penalty may be remitted or mitigated by the Secretary. Upon any failure to pay a penalty assessed under this subsection, the Secretary may request the Attorney General to institute a civil action in a district

Endangered Species Act								§1540

court of the United States for any district in which such person is found, resides, or transacts business to collect the penalty and such court shall have jurisdiction to hear and decide any such action. The court shall hear such action on the record made before the Secretary and shall sustain his action if it is supported by substantial evidence on the record considered as a whole.

(2) Hearings held during proceedings for the assessment of civil penalties authorized by paragraph (1) of this subsection shall be conducted in accordance with section 554 of title 5. The Secretary may issue subpenas for the attendance and testimony of witnesses and the production of relevant papers, books, and documents, and administer oaths. Witnesses summoned shall be paid the same fees and mileage that are paid to witnesses in the courts of the United States. In case of contumacy or refusal to obey a subpena served upon any person pursuant to this paragraph, the district court of the United States for any district in which such person is found or resides or transacts business, upon application by the United States and after notice to such person, shall have jurisdiction to issue an order requiring such person to appear and give testimony before the Secretary or to appear and produce documents before the Secretary, or both, and any failure to obey such order of the court may be punished by such court as a contempt thereof.

(3) Notwithstanding any other provision of this chapter, no civil penalty shall be imposed if it can be shown by a preponderance of the evidence that the defendant committed an act based on a good faith belief that he was acting to protect himself or herself, a member of his or her family, or any other individual from bodily harm, from any endangered or threatened species.

(b) **CRIMINAL VIOLATIONS**

(1) Any person who knowingly violates any provision of this chapter, of any permit or certificate issued hereunder, or of any regulation issued in order to implement subsection (a)(1)(A), (B), (C), (D), (E), or (F), (a)(2)(A), (B), (C), or (D), (c), (d) (other than a regulation relating to recordkeeping, or filing of reports), (f), or (g) of section 1538 of this title shall, upon conviction, be fined not more than $50,000 or imprisoned for not more than one year, or both. Any person who knowingly violates any provision of any other regulation issued under this chapter shall, upon conviction, be fined not more than $25,000 or imprisoned for not more than six months, or both.

(2) The head of any Federal agency which has issued a lease, license, permit, or other agreement authorizing a person to import or export fish, wildlife, or plants, or to operate a quarantine station for imported wildlife, or authorizing the use of Federal lands, including grazing of domestic livestock, to any person who is convicted of a criminal violation of this chapter or any regulation, permit, or certificate issued hereunder may immediately modify, suspend, or revoke each lease, license, permit, or other agreement. The Secretary shall also suspend for a period of up to one year, or cancel, any Federal hunting or fishing permits or stamps issued to any person who is convicted of a criminal violation of any provision of this chapter or any regulation, permit, or certificate

issued hereunder. The United States shall not be liable for the payments of any compensation, reimbursement, or damages in connection with the modification, suspension, or revocation of any leases, licenses, permits, stamps, or other agreements pursuant to this section.

(3) Notwithstanding any other provision of this chapter, it shall be a defense to prosecution under this subsection if the defendant committed the offense based on a good faith belief that he was acting to protect himself or herself, a member of his or her family, or any other individual, from bodily harm from any endangered or threatened species.

(c) **DISTRICT COURT JURISDICTION**

The several district courts of the United States, including the courts enumerated in section 460 of title 28, shall have jurisdiction over any actions arising under this chapter. For the purpose of this chapter, American Samoa shall be included within the judicial district of the District Court of the United States for the District of Hawaii.

(d) **REWARDS AND INCIDENTAL EXPENSES**

The Secretary or the Secretary of the Treasury shall pay, from sums received as penalties, fines, or forfeitures of property for any violation of this chapter or any regulation issued hereunder (1) a reward to any person who furnishes information which leads to an arrest, a criminal conviction, civil penalty assessment, or forfeiture of property for any violation of this chapter or any regulation issued hereunder. The amount of the reward, if any, is to be designated by the Secretary or the Secretary of the Treasury, as appropriate. Any officer or employee of the United States or any State or local government who furnishes information or renders service in the performance of his official duties is ineligible for payment under this subsection, and (2) the reasonable and necessary costs incurred by any person in providing temporary care for any fish, wildlife, or plant pending the disposition of any civil or criminal proceeding alleging a violation of this chapter with respect to that fish, wildlife, or plant. Whenever the balance of sums received under this section and section 3375(d) of this title, as penalties or fines, or from forfeitures of property, exceed $500,000, the Secretary of the Treasury shall deposit an amount equal to such excess balance in the cooperative endangered species conservation fund established under section 1535(i) of this title.

(e) **ENFORCEMENT**

(1) The provisions of this chapter and any regulations or permits issued pursuant thereto shall be enforced by the Secretary, the Secretary of the Treasury, or the Secretary of the Department in which the Coast Guard is operating, or all such Secretaries. Each such Secretary may utilize by agreement, with or without reimbursement, the personnel, services, and facilities of any other Federal agency or any State agency for purposes of enforcing this chapter.

(2) The judges of the district courts of the United States and the United States magistrates may, within their respective jurisdictions, upon proper oath or affirmation showing probable cause, issue such warrants or other process as may be required for enforcement of this chapter and any regulation issued thereunder.

(3) Any person authorized by the Secretary, the Secretary of the Treasury, or the Secretary of the Department in which the Coast Guard is operating, to enforce this chapter may detain for inspection and inspect any package, crate, or other container, including its contents, and all accompanying documents, upon importation or exportation. Such person may make arrests without a warrant for any violation of this chapter if he has reasonable grounds to believe that the person to be arrested is committing the violation in his presence or view, and may execute and serve any arrest warrant, search warrant, or other warrant or civil or criminal process issued by any officer or court of competent jurisdiction for enforcement of this chapter. Such person so authorized may search and seize, with or without a warrant, as authorized by law. Any fish, wildlife, property, or item so seized shall be held by any person authorized by the Secretary, the Secretary of the Treasury, or the Secretary of the Department in which the Coast Guard is operating pending disposition of civil or criminal proceedings, or the institution of an action in rem for forfeiture of such fish, wildlife, property, or item pursuant to paragraph (4) of this subsection; except that the Secretary may, in lieu of holding such fish, wildlife, property, or item, permit the owner or consignee to post a bond or other surety satisfactory to the Secretary, but upon forfeiture of any such property to the United States, or the abandonment or waiver of any claim to any such property, it shall be disposed of (other than by sale to the general public) by the Secretary in such a manner, consistent with the purposes of this chapter, as the Secretary shall by regulation prescribe.

(4)(A) All fish or wildlife or plants taken, possessed, sold, purchased, offered for sale or purchase, transported, delivered, received, carried, shipped, exported, or imported contrary to the provisions of this chapter, any regulation made pursuant thereto, or any permit or certificate issued hereunder shall be subject to forfeiture to the United States.

(B) All guns, traps, nets, and other equipment, vessels, vehicles, aircraft, and other means of transportation used to aid the taking, possessing, selling, purchasing, offering for sale or purchase, transporting, delivering, receiving, carrying, shipping, exporting, or importing of any fish or wildlife or plants in violation of this chapter, any regulation made pursuant thereto, or any permit or certificate issued thereunder shall be subject to forfeiture to the United States upon conviction of a criminal violation pursuant to subsection (b)(1) of this section.

(5) All provisions of law relating to the seizure, forfeiture, and condemnation of a vessel for violation of the customs laws, the disposition of such vessel or the proceeds from the sale thereof, and the remission or mitigation of such forfeiture, shall apply to the seizures and forfeitures incurred, or alleged to have been incurred, under the provisions of this chapter, insofar as such provisions of

law are applicable and not inconsistent with the provisions of this chapter; except that all powers, rights, and duties conferred or imposed by the customs laws upon any officer or employee of the Treasury Department shall, for the purposes of this chapter, be exercised or performed by the Secretary or by such persons as he may designate.

(6) The Attorney General of the United States may seek to enjoin any person who is alleged to be in violation of any provision of this chapter or regulation issued under authority thereof.

(f) REGULATIONS

The Secretary, the Secretary of the Treasury, and the Secretary of the Department in which the Coast Guard is operating, are authorized to promulgate such regulations as may be appropriate to enforce this chapter, and charge reasonable fees for expenses to the Government connected with permits or certificates authorized by this chapter including processing applications and reasonable inspections, and with the transfer, board, handling, or storage of fish or wildlife or plants and evidentiary items seized and forfeited under this chapter. All such fees collected pursuant to this subsection shall be deposited in the Treasury to the credit of the appropriation which is current and chargeable for the cost of furnishing the services. Appropriated funds may be expended pending reimbursement from parties in interest.

(g) CITIZEN SUITS

(1) Except as provided in paragraph (2) of this subsection any person may commence a civil suit on his own behalf —

(A) to enjoin any person, including the United States and any other governmental instrumentality or agency (to the extent permitted by the eleventh amendment to the Constitution), who is alleged to be in violation of any provision of this chapter or regulation issued under the authority thereof; or

(B) to compel the Secretary to apply, pursuant to section 1535 (g)(2)(B)(ii) of this title, the prohibitions set forth in or authorized pursuant to section 1533(d) or 1538(a)(1)(B) of this title with respect to the taking of any resident endangered species or threatened species within any State; or

(C) against the Secretary where there is alleged a failure of the Secretary to perform any act or duty under section 1533 of this title which is not discretionary with the Secretary.

The district courts shall have jurisdiction, without regard to the amount in controversy or the citizenship of the parties, to enforce any such provision or regulation, or to order the Secretary to perform such act or duty, as the case may be. In any civil suit commenced under subparagraph (B) the district court shall compel the Secretary to apply the prohibition sought if the court finds that the allegation that an emergency exists is supported by substantial evidence.

(2)(A) No action may be commenced under subparagraph (1)(A) of this section —

(i) prior to sixty days after written notice of the violation has been given to the Secretary, and to any alleged violator of any such provision or regulation;

(ii) if the Secretary has commenced action to impose a penalty pursuant to subsection (a) of this section; or

(iii) if the United States has commenced and is diligently prosecuting a criminal action in a court of the United States or a State to redress a violation of any such provision or regulation.

(B) No action may be commenced under subparagraph (1)(B) of this section —

(i) prior to sixty days after written notice has been given to the Secretary setting forth the reasons why an emergency is thought to exist with respect to an endangered species or a threatened species in the State concerned; or

(ii) if the Secretary has commenced and is diligently prosecuting action under section 1535(g)(2)(B)(ii) of this title to determine whether any such emergency exists.

(C) No action may be commenced under subparagraph (1)(C) of this section prior to sixty days after written notice has been given to the Secretary; except that such action may be brought immediately after such notification in the case of an action under this section respecting an emergency posing a significant risk to the well-being of any species of fish or wildlife or plants.

(3)(A) Any suit under this subsection may be brought in the judicial district in which the violation occurs.

(B) In any such suit under this subsection in which the United States is not a party, the Attorney General, at the request of the Secretary, may intervene on behalf of the United States as a matter of right.

(4) The court, in issuing any final order in any suit brought pursuant to paragraph (1) of this subsection, may award costs of litigation (including reasonable attorney and expert witness fees) to any party, whenever the court determines such award is appropriate.

(5) The injunctive relief provided by this subsection shall not restrict any right which any person (or class of persons) may have under any statute or common law to seek enforcement of any standard or limitation or to seek any other relief (including relief against the Secretary or a State agency).

(h) COORDINATION WITH OTHER LAWS

The Secretary of Agriculture and the Secretary shall provide for appropriate coordination of the administration of this chapter with the administration of the animal quarantine laws (21 U.S.C. 101-105, 111-135b, and 612-614) and section 306 of the Tariff Act of 1930 (19 U.S.C. 1306). Nothing in this chapter or any amendment made by this chapter shall be construed as superseding or limiting in any manner the functions of the Secretary of Agriculture under any other law relating to prohibited or restricted importations or possession of animals and other articles and no proceeding or determination under this chapter shall preclude any proceeding or be considered determinative of any issue of fact or law in any proceeding under any Act administered by the Secretary of Agriculture. Nothing in this chapter shall be construed as superseding or limiting in any manner the functions and responsibilities of the Secretary of the Treasury under the Tariff Act of 1930 [19 U.S.C. 1202 et seq.], including, without limitation, section 527 of that Act (19 U.S.C. 1527), relating to the importation of wildlife taken, killed, possessed, or exported to the United States in violation of the laws or regulations of a foreign country. . . .

§1543. Construction with Marine Mammal Protection Act of 1972

Except as otherwise provided in this chapter, no provision of this chapter shall take precedence over any more restrictive conflicting provision of the Marine Mammal Protection Act of 1972 [16 U.S.C. 1361 et seq.].

§1544. Annual Cost Analysis by Fish and Wildlife Service

On or before January 15, 1990, and each January 15 thereafter, the Secretary of the Interior, acting through the Fish and Wildlife Service, shall submit to the Congress an annual report covering the preceding fiscal year which shall contain —

(1) an accounting on a species by species basis of all reasonably identifiable Federal expenditures made primarily for the conservation of endangered or threatened species pursuant to this chapter; and

(2) an accounting on a species by species basis of all reasonably identifiable expenditures made primarily for the conservation of endangered or threatened species pursuant to this chapter by States receiving grants under section 1535 of this title.

Comprehensive Environmental Response, Compensation, and Liability Act of 1980 (CERCLA)
42 U.S.C. §§9601-9675

SUBCHAPTER I — HAZARDOUS SUBSTANCES RELEASES, LIABILITY, COMPENSATION

Sec.
9601. Definitions.
9602. Designation of additional hazardous substances and establishment of reportable released quantities; regulations.
9603. Notification requirements respecting released substances.
    (a) Notice to National Response Center upon release from vessel or offshore or onshore facility by person in charge; conveyance of notice by Center.
    (b) Penalties for failure to notify; use of notice or information pursuant to notice in criminal case.
    (c) Notice to Administrator of EPA of existence of storage, etc., facility by owner or operator; exception; time, manner, and form of notice; penalties for failure to notify; use of notice or information pursuant to notice in criminal case.
    (d) Recordkeeping requirements; promulgation of rules and regulations by Administrator of EPA; penalties for violations; waiver of retention requirements.
    (e) Applicability to registered pesticide product.
    (f) Exemptions from notice and penalty provisions for substances reported under other Federal law or is in continuous release, etc.
9604. Response authorities.
    (a) Removal and other remedial action by President; applicability of national contingency plan; response by potentially responsible parties; public health threats; limitations on response; exception.
    (b) Investigations, monitoring, coordination, etc, by President.
    (c) Criteria for continuance of obligations from Fund over specified amount for response actions; consultation by President with affected States; contracts or cooperative agreements by States with President prior to remedial actions; cost-sharing agreements; selection by President of remedial actions; State credits: granting of credit, expenses before listing or agreement, response actions between 1978 and 1980, State expenses after December 11, 1980, in excess of 10 percent of costs, item-by-item approval, use of credits; operation and maintenance; limitation on source of funds for O&M; recontracting; siting
    (d) Contracts or cooperative agreements by President with States or political subdivisions or Indian tribes; State applications, terms and conditions; reimbursements; cost-sharing provisions; enforcement requirements and procedures.
    (e) Information gathering and access.

- (f) Contracts for response actions; compliance with Federal health and safety standards.
- (g) Rates for wages and labor standards applicable to covered work.
- (h) Emergency procurement powers; exercise by President.
- (i) Agency for Toxic Substances and Disease Registry; establishment, functions, etc.
- (j) Acquisition of property.

9605. National contingency plan; preparation, contents, etc.
- (a) Revision and republication.
- (b) Revision of plan.
- (c) Hazard banking system.
- (d) Petition for assessment of release.
- (e) Releases from earlier sites.
- (f) Minority contractors.
- (g) Special study wastes.

9606. Abatement actions.
- (a) Maintenance, jurisdiction, etc.
- (b) Fines; reimbursement.
- (c) Guidelines for using imminent hazard, enforcement, and emergency response authorities; promulgation by Administrator of EPA, scope, etc.

9607. Liability.
- (a) Covered persons; scope; recoverable costs and damages; interest rate; "comparable maturity" date.
- (b) Defenses.
- (c) Determination of amounts.
- (d) Rendering care or advice.
- (e) Indemnification, hold harmless, etc., agreements or conveyances; subrogation rights.
- (f) Natural resources liability; designation of public trustees of natural resources.
- (g) Federal agencies.
- (h) Owner or operator of vessel.
- (i) Application of a registered pesticide product.
- (j) Obligations or liability pursuant to federally permitted release
- (k) Transfer to, and assumption by, Post-Closure Liability Fund of liability of owner or operator of hazardous waste disposal facility in receipt of permit under applicable solid waste disposal law; time, criteria applicable, procedures, etc.; monitoring costs; reports
- (l) Federal lien.
- (m) Maritime lien.

9608. Financial responsibility.
- (a) Establishment and maintenance by owner or operator of vessel; amount; failure to obtain certification of compliance.
- (b) Establishment and maintenance by owner or operator of production, etc., facilities; amount; adjustment; consolidated form of responsibility; coverage of motor carriers.
- (c) Direct action.
- (d) Limitation of guarantor liability.

CERCLA

9609. Civil penalties and awards.
  (a) Class I administrative penalty.
  (b) Class II administrative penalty.
  (c) Judicial assessment.
  (d) Awards.
  (e) Procurement procedures.
  (f) Savings clause.
9610. Employee protection.
  (a) Activities of employee subject to protection.
  (b) Administrative grievance procedure in cases of alleged violations.
  (c) Assessment of costs and expenses against violator subsequent to issuance of order of abatement.
  (d) Defenses.
  (e) Presidential evaluations of potential loss of shifts of employment resulting from administration or enforcement of provisions; investigations; procedures applicable, etc.
9611. Use of Fund.
  (a) In general.
  (b) Additional authorized purposes.
  (c) Peripheral matters and limitations.
  (d) Additional limitations.
  (e) Funding requirements respecting moneys in Fund; limitation on certain claims; Fund use outside Federal property boundaries.
  (f) Obligation of moneys by Federal officials; obligation of moneys or settlement of claims by State officials or Indian tribe.
  (g) Notice to potential injured parties by owner and operator of vessel or facility causing release of substance; rules and regulations.
  (h) Repealed. Pub. L. 99-499, title I, §111(c)(2), Oct. 17, 1986, 100 Stat. 1643.
  (i) Restoration, etc., of natural resources.
  (j) Use of Post-closure Liability Fund.
  (k) Inspector General.
  (l) Foreign claimants.
  (m) Agency for Toxic Substances and Disease Registry.
  (n) Limitations on research, development, and demonstration program.
  (o) Notification procedures for limitations on certain payments.
  (p) General revenue share of Superfund.
9612. Claims procedure.
  (a) Claims against Fund for response costs.
  (b) Forms and procedures applicable.
  (c) Subrogation rights; actions maintainable.
  (d) Statute of limitations.
  (e) Other statutory or common law claims not waived, etc.
  (f) Double recovery prohibited.
9613. Civil proceedings.
  (a) Review of regulations in Circuit Court of Appeals of the United States for the District of Columbia.
  (b) Jurisdiction; venue.

- (c) Controversies or other matters resulting from tax collection or tax regulation review.
- (d) Litigation commenced prior to December 11, 1980.
- (e) Nationwide service of process.
- (f) Contribution.
- (g) Period in which action may be brought.
- (h) Timing of review.
- (i) Intervention.
- (j) Judicial review.
- (k) Administrative record and participation procedures.
- (l) Notice of actions.

9614. Relationship to other law.
- (a) Additional State liability or requirements with respect to release of substances within State.
- (b) Recovery under other State or Federal law of compensation for removal costs or damages, or payment of claims.
- (c) Recycled oil.
- (d) Financial responsibility of owner or operator of vessel or facility under State or local law, rule, or regulation.

9615. Presidential delegation and assignment of duties or powers and promulgation of regulations.

9616. Schedules.
- (a) Assessment and listing of facilities.
- (b) Evaluation.
- (c) Explanations.
- (d) Commencement of RI/FS.
- (e) Commencement of remedial action.

9617. Public participation.
- (a) Proposed plan.
- (b) Final plan.
- (c) Explanation of differences.
- (d) Publication.
- (e) Grants for technical assistance.

9618. High priority for drinking water supplies.

9619. Response action contractors.
- (a) Liability of response action contractors.
- (b) Savings provisions.
- (c) Indemnification.
- (d) Exception.
- (e) Definitions.
- (f) Competition.

9620. Federal facilities.
- (a) Application of chapter to Federal Government.
- (b) Notice.
- (c) Federal Agency Hazardous Waste Compliance Docket.
- (d) Assessment and evaluation.
- (e) Required action by department.
- (f) State and local participation.
- (g) Transfer of authorities.

CERCLA

        (h)   Property transferred by Federal agencies.
        (i)   Obligations under Solid Waste Disposal Act.
        (j)   National security.
9621.   Cleanup standards.
        (a)   Selection of remedial action.
        (b)   General rules.
        (c)   Review.
        (d)   Degree of cleanup.
        (e)   Permits and enforcement.
        (f)   State involvement.
9622.   Settlements.
        (a)   Authority to enter into agreements.
        (b)   Agreements with potentially responsible parties.
        (c)   Effect of agreement.
        (d)   Enforcement.
        (e)   Special notice procedures.
        (f)   Covenant not to sue.
        (g)   De minimis settlements.
        (h)   Cost recovery settlement authority.
        (i)   Settlement procedures.
        (j)   Natural resources.
        (k)   Section not applicable to vessels.
        (*l*)   Civil penalties.
        (m)   Applicability of general principles of law.
9623.   Reimbursement to local governments.
        (a)   Application.
        (b)   Reimbursement.
        (c)   Amount.
        (d)   Procedure.
9624.   Methane recovery.
        (a)   In general.
        (b)   Exceptions.
9625.   Section 6921(b)(3)(A)(i) waste.
        (a)   Revision of hazard ranking system.
        (b)   Inclusion prohibited.
9626.   Indian tribes.
        (a)   Treatment generally.
        (b)   Community relocation.
        (c)   Study.
        (d)   Limitation.

SUBCHAPTER III — MISCELLANEOUS PROVISIONS

9657.   Separability of provisions; contribution.
9658.   Actions under State law for damages from exposure to hazardous substances.
        (a)   State statutes of limitations for hazardous substance cases.
        (b)   Definitions.
9659.   Citizens suits.
        (a)   Authority to bring civil actions.

(b) Venue.
(c) Relief.
(d) Rules applicable to subsection (a)(1) actions.
(e) Rules applicable to subsection (a)(2) actions.
(f) Costs.
(g) Intervention.
(h) Other rights.
(i) Definitions.

SUBCHAPTER IV — POLLUTION INSURANCE

9671. Definitions.
    (1) Insurance.
    (2) Pollution liability.
    (3) Risk retention group.
    (4) Purchasing group.
    (5) State.
9672. State laws; scope of title.
    (a) State laws.
    (b) Scope of title.
9673. Risk retention groups.
    (a) Exemption.
    (b) Exceptions.
    (c) Application of exemptions.
    (d) Agents or brokers.
9674. Purchasing groups.
    (a) Exemption.
    (b) Application of exemptions.
    (c) Agents or brokers.
9675. Applicability of securities laws.
    (a) Ownership interests.
    (b) Investment Company Act.
    (c) Blue sky law.

Subchapter I — Hazardous Substances Releases, Liability, Compensation

§9601. Definitions

For purpose of this subchapter —

(1) The term "act of God" means an unanticipated grave natural disaster or other natural phenomenon of an exceptional, inevitable, and irresistible character, the effects of which could not have been prevented or avoided by the exercise of due care or foresight.

(2) The term "Administrator" means the Administrator of the United States Environmental Protection Agency.

(3) The term "barrel" means forty-two United States gallons at sixty degrees Fahrenheit.

(4) The term "claim" means a demand in writing for a sum certain.

(5) The term "claimant" means any person who presents a claim for compensation under this chapter.

(6) The term "damages" means damages for injury or loss of natural resources as set forth in section 9607(a) or 9611(b) of this title.

(7) The term "drinking water supply" means any raw or finished water source that is or may be used by a public water system (as defined in the Safe Drinking Water Act [42 U.S.C. 300f et seq.]) or as drinking water by one or more individuals.

(8) The term "environment" means (A) the navigable waters, the waters of the contiguous zone, and the ocean waters of which the natural resources are under the exclusive management authority of the United States under the Magnuson Fishery Conservation and Management Act [16 U.S.C. 1801 et seq.], and (B) any other surface water, ground water, drinking water supply, land surface or subsurface strata, or ambient air within the United States or under the jurisdiction of the United States.

(9) The term "facility" means (A) any building, structure, installation, equipment, pipe or pipeline (including any pipe into a sewer or publicly owned treatment works), well, pit, pond, lagoon, impoundment, ditch, landfill, storage container, motor vehicle, rolling stock, or aircraft, or (B) any site or area where a hazardous substance has been deposited, stored, disposed of, or placed, or otherwise come to be located; but does not include any consumer product in consumer use or any vessel.

(10) The term "federally permitted release" means (A) discharges in compliance with a permit under section 1342 of title 33, (B) discharges resulting from circumstances identified and reviewed and made part of the public record with respect to a permit issued or modified under section 1342 of title 33 and subject to a condition of such permit, (C) continuous or anticipated intermittent discharges from a point source, identified in a permit or permit application under section 1342 of title 33, which are caused by events occurring within the scope of relevant operating or treatment systems, (D) discharges in compliance with a legally enforceable permit under section 1344 of title 33, (E) releases in compliance with a legally enforceable final permit issued pursuant to section 3005(a) through (d) of the Solid Waste Disposal Act [42 U.S.C. 6925(a)-(d)] from a hazardous waste treatment, storage, or disposal facility when such permit specifically identifies the hazardous substances and makes such substances subject to a standard of practice, control procedure or bioassay limitation or condition, or other control on the hazardous substances in such releases, (F) any release in compliance with a legally enforceable permit issued under section 1412 of title 33 of[1] section 1413 of

---

1. So in original. Probably should be "or."

title 33, (G) any injection of fluids authorized under Federal underground injection control programs or State programs submitted for Federal approval (and not disapproved by the Administrator of the Environmental Protection Agency) pursuant to part C of the Safe Drinking Water Act [42 U.S.C. 300h et seq.], (H) any emission into the air subject to a permit or control regulation under section 111 [42 U.S.C. 7411], section 112 [42 U.S.C. 7412], title I part C [42 U.S.C. 7470 et seq.], title I part D [42 U.S.C. 7501 et seq.], or State implementation plans submitted in accordance with section 110 of the Clean Air Act [42 U.S.C. 7410] (and not disapproved by the Administrator of the Environmental Protection Agency), including any schedule or waiver granted, promulgated, or approved under these sections, (I) any injection of fluids or other materials authorized under applicable State law (i) for the purpose of stimulating or treating wells for the production of crude oil, natural gas, or water, (ii) for the purpose of secondary, tertiary, or other enhanced recovery of crude oil or natural gas, or (iii) which are brought to the surface in conjunction with the production of crude oil or natural gas and which are reinjected, (J) the introduction of any pollutant into a publicly owned treatment works when such pollutant is specified in and in compliance with applicable pretreatment standards of section 1317 (b) or (c) of title 33 and enforceable requirements in a pretreatment program submitted by a State or municipality for Federal approval under section 1342 of title 33, and (K) any release of source, special nuclear, or byproduct material, as those terms are defined in the Atomic Energy Act of 1954 [42 U.S.C. 2011 et seq.], in compliance with a legally enforceable license, permit, regulation, or order issued pursuant to the Atomic Energy Act of 1954.

(11) The term "Fund" or "Trust Fund" means the Hazardous Substance Superfund established by section 9507 of title 26.

(12) The term "ground water" means water in a saturated zone or stratum beneath the surface of land or water.

(13) The term "guarantor" means any person, other than the owner or operator, who provides evidence of financial responsibility for an owner or operator under this chapter.

(14) The term "hazardous substance" means (A) any substance designated pursuant to section 1321(b)(2)(A) of title 33, (B) any element, compound, mixture, solution, or substance designated pursuant to section 9602 of this title, (C) any hazardous waste having the characteristics identified under or listed pursuant to section 3001 of the Solid Waste Disposal Act [42 U.S.C. 6921] (but not including any waste the regulation of which under the Solid Waste Disposal Act [42 U.S.C. 6901 et seq.] has been suspended by Act of Congress), (D) any toxic pollutant listed under section 1317(a) of title 33, (E) any hazardous air pollutant listed under section 112 of the Clean Air Act [42 U.S.C. 7412], and (F) any imminently hazardous chemical substance or mixture with respect to which the Administrator has taken action pursuant to section 2606 of title 15. The term does not include petroleum, including crude oil or any fraction thereof which is not otherwise specifically listed or

designated as a hazardous substance under subparagraphs (A) through (F) of this paragraph, and the term does not include natural gas, natural gas liquids, liquefied natural gas, or synthetic gas usable for fuel (or mixtures of natural gas and such synthetic gas).

(15) The term "navigable waters" or "navigable waters of the United States" means the waters of the United States, including the territorial seas.

(16) The term "natural resources" means land, fish, wildlife, biota, air, water, ground water, drinking water supplies, and other such resources belonging to, managed by, held in trust by, appertaining to, or otherwise controlled by the United States (including the resources of the fishery conservation zone established by the Magnuson Fishery Conservation and Management Act [16 U.S.C. 1801 et seq.]), any State or local government, any foreign government, any Indian tribe, or, if such resources are subject to a trust restriction on alienation, any member of an Indian tribe.

(17) The term "offshore facility" means any facility of any kind located in, on, or under, any of the navigable waters of the United States, and any facility of any kind which is subject to the jurisdiction of the United States and is located in, on, or under any other waters, other than a vessel or a public vessel.

(18) The term "onshore facility" means any facility (including, but not limited to, motor vehicles and rolling stock) of any kind located in, on, or under, any land or nonnavigable waters within the United States.

(19) The term "otherwise subject to the jurisdiction of the United States" means subject to the jurisdiction of the United States by virtue of United States citizenship, United States vessel documentation or numbering, or as provided by international agreement to which the United States is a party.

(20)(A) The term "owner or operator" means (i) in the case of a vessel, any person owning, operating, or chartering by demise, such vessel, (ii) in the case of an onshore facility or an offshore facility, any person owning or operating such facility, and (iii) in the case of any facility, title or control of which was conveyed due to bankruptcy, foreclosure, tax delinquency, abandonment, or similar means to a unit of State or local government, any person who owned, operated, or otherwise controlled activities at such facility immediately beforehand. Such term does not include a person, who, without participating in the management of a vessel or facility, holds indicia of ownership primarily to protect his security interest in the vessel or facility.

(B) In the case of a hazardous substance which has been accepted for transportation by a common or contract carrier and except as provided in section 9607(a)(3) or (4) of this title, (i) the term "owner or operator" shall mean such common carrier or other bona fide for hire carrier acting as an independent contractor during such transportation, (ii) the shipper of such hazardous substance shall not be considered to have caused or contributed to any release during such transportation which resulted solely from circumstances or conditions beyond his control.

(C) In the case of a hazardous substance which has been delivered by a common or contract carrier to a disposal or treatment facility and except as provided in section 9607(a)(3) or (4) of this title, (i) the term "owner or operator" shall not include such common or contract carrier, and (ii) such common or contract carrier shall not be considered to have caused or contributed to any release at such disposal or treatment facility resulting from circumstances or conditions beyond its control.

(D) The term "owner or operator" does not include a unit of State or local government which acquired ownership or control involuntarily through bankruptcy, tax delinquency, abandonment, or other circumstances in which the government involuntarily acquires title by virtue of its function as sovereign. The exclusion provided under this paragraph shall not apply to any State or local government which has caused or contributed to the release or threatened release of a hazardous substance from the facility, and such a State or local government shall be subject to the provisions of this chapter in the same manner and to the same extent, both procedurally and substantively, as any nongovernmental entity, including liability under section 9607 of this title.

(21) The term "person" means an individual, firm, corporation, association, partnership, consortium, joint venture, commercial entity, United States Government, State, municipality, commission, political subdivision of a State, or any interstate body.

(22) The term "release" means any spilling, leaking, pumping, pouring, emitting, emptying, discharging, injecting, escaping, leaching, dumping, or disposing into the environment (including the abandonment or discarding of barrels, containers, and other closed receptacles containing any hazardous substance or pollutant or contaminant), but excludes (A) any release which results in exposure to persons solely within a workplace, with respect to a claim which such persons may assert against the employer of such persons, (B) emissions from the engine exhaust of a motor vehicle, rolling stock, aircraft, vessel, or pipeline pumping station engine, (C) release of source, byproduct, or special nuclear material from a nuclear incident, as those terms are defined in the Atomic Energy Act of 1954 [42 U.S.C. 2011 et seq.], if such release is subject to requirements with respect to financial protection established by the Nuclear Regulatory Commission under section 170 of such Act [42 U.S.C. 2210], or, for the purposes of section 9604 of this title or any other response action, any release of source byproduct, or special nuclear material from any processing site designated under section 7912(a)(1) or 7942(a) of this title, and (D) the normal application of fertilizer.

(23) The terms "remove" or "removal" means[2] the cleanup or removal of released hazardous substances from the environment, such actions as may be necessary taken in the event of the threat of release of hazardous substances into the environment, such actions as may be necessary to monitor, assess,

---

2. So in original. Probably should be "mean."

and evaluate the release or threat of release of hazardous substances, the disposal of removed material, or the taking of such other actions as may be necessary to prevent, minimize, or mitigate damage to the public health or welfare or to the environment, which may otherwise result from a release or threat of release. The term includes, in addition, without being limited to, security fencing or other measures to limit access, provision of alternative water supplies, temporary evacuation and housing of threatened individuals not otherwise provided for, action taken under section 9604(b) of this title, and any emergency assistance which may be provided under the Disaster Relief and Emergency Assistance Act [42 U.S.C. 5121 et seq.].

(24) The terms "remedy" or "remedial action" means[2] those actions consistent with permanent remedy taken instead of or in addition to removal actions in the event of a release or threatened release of a hazardous substance into the environment, to prevent or minimize the release of hazardous substances so that they do not migrate to cause substantial danger to present or future public health or welfare or the environment. The term includes, but is not limited to, such actions at the location of the release as storage, confinement, perimeter protection using dikes, trenches, or ditches, clay cover, neutralization, cleanup of released hazardous substances and associated contaminated materials, recycling or reuse, diversion, destruction, segregation of reactive wastes, dredging or excavations, repair or replacement of leaking containers, collection of leachate and runoff, onsite treatment or incineration, provision of alternative water supplies, and any monitoring reasonably required to assure that such actions protect the public health and welfare and the environment. The term includes the costs of permanent relocation of residents and businesses and community facilities where the President determines that, alone or in combination with other measures, such relocation is more cost-effective than and environmentally preferable to the transportation, storage, treatment, destruction, or secure disposition offsite of hazardous substances, or may otherwise be necessary to protect the public health or welfare; the term includes offsite transport and offsite storage, treatment, destruction, or secure disposition of hazardous substances and associated contaminated materials.

(25) The terms "respond" or "response" means[2] remove, removal, remedy, and remedial action;,[3] all such terms (including the terms "removal" and "remedial action") include enforcement activities related thereto.

(26) The terms "transport" or "transportation" means[2] the movement of a hazardous substance by any mode, including pipeline (as defined in the Pipeline Safety Act), and in the case of a hazardous substance which has been accepted for transportation by a common or contract carrier, the term "transport" or "transportation" shall include any stoppage in transit which is temporary, incidental to the transportation movement, and at the ordinary operating convenience of a common or contract carrier, and any such stop-

3. So in original.

page shall be considered as a continuity of movement and not as the storage of a hazardous substance.

(27) The terms "United States" and "State" include the several States of the United States, the District of Columbia, the Commonwealth of Puerto Rico, Guam, American Samoa, the United States Virgin Islands, the Commonwealth of the Northern Marianas, and any other territory or possession over which the United States has jurisdiction.

(28) The term "vessel" means every description of watercraft or other artificial contrivance used, or capable of being used, as a means of transportation on water.

(29) The terms "disposal," "hazardous waste," and "treatment" shall have the meaning provided in section 1004 of the Solid Waste Disposal Act [42 U.S.C. 6903].

(30) The terms "territorial sea" and "contiguous zone" shall have the meaning provided in section 1362 of title 33.

(31) The term "national contingency plan" means the national contingency plan published under section 1321(c) of title 33 or revised pursuant to section 9605 of this title.

(32) The terms "liable" or "liability" under this subchapter shall be construed to be the standard of liability which obtains under section 1321 of title 33.

(33) The term "pollutant or contaminant" shall include, but not be limited to, any element, substance, compound, or mixture, including disease-causing agents, which after release into the environment and upon exposure, ingestion, inhalation, or assimilation into any organism, either directly from the environment or indirectly by ingestion through food chains, will or may reasonably be anticipated to cause death, disease, behavioral abnormalities, cancer, genetic mutation, physiological malfunctions (including malfunctions in reproduction) or physical deformations, in such organisms or their offspring; except that the term "pollutant or contaminant" shall not include petroleum, including crude oil or any fraction thereof which is not otherwise specifically listed or designated as a hazardous substance under subparagraphs (A) through (F) of paragraph (14) and shall not include natural gas, liquefied natural gas, or synthetic gas of pipeline quality (or mixtures of natural gas and such synthetic gas).

(34) The term "alternative water supplies" includes, but is not limited to, drinking water and household water supplies.

(35)(A) The term "contractual relationship," for the purpose of section 9607(b)(3) of this title, includes, but is not limited to, land contracts, deeds or other instruments transferring title or possession, unless the real property on which the facility concerned is located was acquired by the defendant after the disposal or placement of the hazardous substance on, in, or at the facility, and one or more of the circumstances described in clause (i), (ii), or (iii) is also established by the defendant by a preponderance of the evidence:

(i) At the time the defendant acquired the facility the defendant did not know and had no reason to know that any hazardous substance which is the subject of the release or threatened release was disposed of on, in, or at the facility.

(ii) The defendant is a government entity which acquired the facility by escheat, or through any other involuntary transfer or acquisition, or through the exercise of eminent domain authority by purchase or condemnation.

(iii) The defendant acquired the facility by inheritance or bequest.

In addition to establishing the foregoing, the defendant must establish that he has satisfied the requirements of section 9607(b)(3)(a) and (b) of this title.

(B) To establish that the defendant had no reason to know, as provided in clause (i) of subparagraph (A) of this paragraph, the defendant must have undertaken, at the time of acquisition, all appropriate inquiry into the previous ownership and uses of the property consistent with good commercial or customary practice in an effort to minimize liability. For purposes of the preceding sentence the court shall take into account any specialized knowledge or experience on the part of the defendant, the relationship of the purchase price to the value of the property if uncontaminated, commonly known or reasonably ascertainable information about the property, the obviousness of the presence or likely presence of contamination at the property, and the ability to detect such contamination by appropriate inspection.

(C) Nothing in this paragraph or in section 9607(b)(3) of this title shall diminish the liability of any previous owner or operator of such facility who would otherwise be liable under this chapter. Notwithstanding this paragraph, if the defendant obtained actual knowledge of the release or threatened release of a hazardous substance at such facility when the defendant owned the real property and then subsequently transferred ownership of the property to another person without disclosing such knowledge, such defendant shall be treated as liable under section 9607(a)(1) of this title and no defense under section 9607(b)(3) of this title shall be available to such defendant.

(D) Nothing in this paragraph shall affect the liability under this chapter of a defendant who, by any act or omission, caused or contributed to the release or threatened release of a hazardous substance which is the subject of the action relating to the facility.

(36) The term "Indian tribe" means any Indian tribe, band, nation, or other organized group or community, including any Alaska Native village but not including any Alaska Native regional or village corporation, which is recognized as eligible for the special programs and services provided by the United States to Indians because of their status as Indians.

(37)(A) The term "service station dealer" means any person —

(i) who owns or operates a motor vehicle service station, filling station, garage, or similar retail establishment engaged in the business of selling, repairing, or servicing motor vehicles, where a significant percentage of the gross revenue of the establishment is derived from the fueling, repairing, or servicing of motor vehicles, and

(ii) who accepts for collection, accumulation, and delivery to an oil recycling facility, recycled oil that (I) has been removed from the engine of a light duty motor vehicle or household appliances by the owner of such vehicle or appliances, and (II) is presented, by such owner, to such person for collection, accumulation, and delivery to an oil recycling facility.

(B) For purposes of section 9614(c) of this title, the term "service station dealer" shall, notwithstanding the provisions of subparagraph (A), include any government agency that establishes a facility solely for the purpose of accepting recycled oil that satisfies the criteria set forth in subclauses (I) and (II) of subparagraph (A)(ii), and, with respect to recycled oil that satisfies the criteria set forth in subclauses (I) and (II), owners or operators of refuse collection services who are compelled by State law to collect, accumulate, and deliver such oil to an oil recycling facility.

(C) The President shall promulgate regulations regarding the determination of what constitutes a significant percentage of the gross revenues of an establishment for purposes of this paragraph.

(38) The term "incineration vessel" means any vessel which carries hazardous substances for the purpose of incineration of such substances, so long as such substances or residues of such substances are on board.

§9602. DESIGNATION OF ADDITIONAL HAZARDOUS SUBSTANCES AND ESTABLISHMENT OF REPORTABLE RELEASED QUANTITIES; REGULATIONS

(a) The Administrator shall promulgate and revise as may be appropriate, regulations designating as hazardous substances, in addition to those referred to in section 9601(14) of this title, such elements, compounds, mixtures, solutions, and substances which, when released into the environment may present substantial danger to the public health or welfare or the environment, and shall promulgate regulations establishing that quantity of any hazardous substance the release of which shall be reported pursuant to section 9603 of this title. The Administrator may determine that one single quantity shall be the reportable quantity for any hazardous substance, regardless of the medium into which the hazardous substance is released. For all hazardous substances for which proposed regulations establishing reportable quantities were published in the Federal Register under this subsection on or before March 1, 1986, the Administrator shall promulgate under this subsection final regulations establishing reportable quantities not later than December 31, 1986. For all hazardous substances for which proposed regulations establishing reportable quantities were not published in the Federal Register under this subsection on or before March 1, 1986, the Administrator shall publish under this subsection proposed regulations establishing reportable quantities not later than December 31, 1986, and promulgate final regulations under this subsection establishing reportable quantities not later than April 30, 1988.

(b) Unless and until superseded by regulations establishing a reportable quantity under subsection (a) of this section for any hazardous substance as defined in section 9601(14) of this title, (1) a quantity of one pound, or (2) for those hazardous substances for which reportable quantities have been established pursuant to section 1321(b)(4) of title 33, such reportable quantity, shall be deemed that quantity, the release of which requires notification pursuant to section 9603(a) or (b) of this title.

§9603. Notification Requirements Respecting Released Substances

(a) NOTICE TO NATIONAL RESPONSE CENTER UPON RELEASE FROM VESSEL OR OFFSHORE OR ONSHORE FACILITY BY PERSON IN CHARGE; CONVEYANCE OF NOTICE BY CENTER

Any person in charge of a vessel or an offshore or an onshore facility shall, as soon as he has knowledge of any release (other than a federally permitted release) of a hazardous substance from such vessel or facility in quantities equal to or greater than those determined pursuant to section 9602 of this title, immediately notify the National Response Center established under the Clean Water Act [33 U.S.C. 1251 et seq.] of such release. The National Response Center shall convey the notification expeditiously to all appropriate Government agencies, including the Governor of any affected State.

(b) PENALTIES FOR FAILURE TO NOTIFY; USE OF NOTICE OR INFORMATION PURSUANT TO NOTICE IN CRIMINAL CASE

Any person —
  (1) in charge of a vessel from which a hazardous substance is released, other than a federally permitted release, into or upon the navigable waters of the United States, adjoining shorelines, or into or upon the waters of the contiguous zone, or
  (2) in charge of a vessel from which a hazardous substance is released, other than a federally permitted release, which may affect natural resources belonging to, appertaining to, or under the exclusive management authority of the United States (including resources under the Magnuson Fishery Conservation and Management Act [16 U.S.C. 1801 et seq.]), and who is otherwise subject to the jurisdiction of the United States at the time of the release, or
  (3) in charge of a facility from which a hazardous substance is released, other than a federally permitted release,
in a quantity equal to or greater than that determined pursuant to section 9602 of this title who fails to notify immediately the appropriate agency of the United States Government as soon as he has knowledge of such release or who submits in such a notification any information which he knows to be false or misleading shall, upon conviction, be fined in accordance with the applicable provisions of title 18 or imprisoned for not more than 3 years (or not more than 5 years in the

case of a second or subsequent conviction), or both. Notification received pursuant to this subsection or information obtained by the exploitation of such notification shall not be used against any such person in any criminal case, except a prosecution for perjury or for giving a false statement.

(c) **NOTICE TO ADMINISTRATOR OF EPA OF EXISTENCE OF STORAGE, ETC., FACILITY BY OWNER OR OPERATOR; EXCEPTION; TIME, MANNER, AND FORM OF NOTICE; PENALTIES FOR FAILURE TO NOTIFY; USE OF NOTICE OR INFORMATION PURSUANT TO NOTICE IN CRIMINAL CASE**

Within one hundred and eighty days after December 11, 1980, any person who owns or operates or who at the time of disposal owned or operated, or who accepted hazardous substances for transport and selected, a facility at which hazardous substances (as defined in section 9601(14)(C) of this title) are or have been stored, treated, or disposed of shall, unless such facility has a permit issued under, or has been accorded interim status under, subtitle C of the Solid Waste Disposal Act [42 U.S.C. 6921 et seq.], notify the Administrator of the Environmental Protection Agency of the existence of such facility, specifying the amount and type of any hazardous substance to be found there, and any known, suspected, or likely releases of such substances from such facility. The Administrator may prescribe in greater detail the manner and form of the notice and the information included. The Administrator shall notify the affected State agency, or any department designated by the Governor to receive such notice, of the existence of such facility. Any person who knowingly fails to notify the Administrator of the existence of any such facility shall, upon conviction, be fined not more than $10,000, or imprisoned for not more than one year, or both. In addition, any such person who knowingly fails to provide the notice required by this subsection shall not be entitled to any limitation of liability or to any defenses to liability set out in section 9607 of this title: *Provided, however,* That notification under this subsection is not required for any facility which would be reportable hereunder solely as a result of any stoppage in transit which is temporary, incidental to the transportation movement, or at the ordinary operating convenience of a common or contract carrier, and such stoppage shall be considered as a continuity of movement and not as the storage of a hazardous substance. Notification received pursuant to this subsection or information obtained by the exploitation of such notification shall not be used against any such person in any criminal case, except a prosecution for perjury or for giving a false statement.

(d) **RECORDKEEPING REQUIREMENTS; PROMULGATION OF RULES AND REGULATIONS BY ADMINISTRATOR OF EPA; PENALTIES FOR VIOLATIONS; WAIVER OF RETENTION REQUIREMENTS**

(1) The Administrator of the Environmental Protection Agency is authorized to promulgate rules and regulations specifying, with respect to —

    (A) the location, title, or condition of a facility, and

    (B) the identity, characteristics, quantity, origin, or condition (including

containerization and previous treatment) of any hazardous substances contained or deposited in a facility;
the records which shall be retained by any person required to provide the notification of a facility set out in subsection (c) of this section. Such specification shall be in accordance with the provisions of this subsection.

(2) Beginning with December 11, 1980, for fifty years thereafter or for fifty years after the date of establishment of a record (whichever is later), or at any such earlier time as a waiver if obtained under paragraph (3) of this subsection, it shall be unlawful for any such person knowingly to destroy, mutilate, erase, dispose of, conceal, or otherwise render unavailable or unreadable or falsify any records identified in paragraph (1) of this subsection. Any person who violates this paragraph shall, upon conviction, be fined in accordance with the applicable provisions of title 18 or imprisoned for not more than 3 years (or not more than 5 years in the case of a second or subsequent conviction), or both.

(3) At any time prior to the date which occurs fifty years after December 11, 1980, any person identified under paragraph (1) of this subsection may apply to the Administrator of the Environmental Protection Agency for a waiver of the provisions of the first sentence of paragraph (2) of this subsection. The Administrator is authorized to grant such waiver if, in his discretion, such waiver would not unreasonably interfere with the attainment of the purposes and provisions of this chapter. The Administrator shall promulgate rules and regulations regarding such a waiver so as to inform parties of the proper application procedure and conditions for approval of such a waiver.

(4) Notwithstanding the provisions of this subsection, the Administrator of the Environmental Protection Agency may in his discretion require any such person to retain any record identified pursuant to paragraph (1) of this subsection for such a time period in excess of the period specified in paragraph (2) of this subsection as the Administrator determines to be necessary to protect the public health or welfare.

(e) **APPLICABILITY TO REGISTERED PESTICIDE PRODUCT**

This section shall not apply to the application of a pesticide registered under the Federal Insecticide, Fungicide, and Rodenticide Act [7 U.S.C. 136 et seq.] or to the handling and storage of such a pesticide product by an agricultural producer.

(f) **EXEMPTIONS FROM NOTICE AND PENALTY PROVISIONS FOR SUBSTANCES REPORTED UNDER OTHER FEDERAL LAW OR IS IN CONTINUOUS RELEASE, ETC.**

No notification shall be required under subsection (a) or (b) of this section for any release of a hazardous substance —

(1) which is required to be reported (or specifically exempted from a requirement for reporting) under subtitle C of the Solid Waste Disposal Act

[42 U.S.C. 6921 et seq.] or regulations thereunder and which has been reported to the National Response Center, or

 (2) which is a continuous release, stable in quantity and rate, and is —
  (A) from a facility for which notification has been given under subsection (c) of this section, or
  (B) a release of which notification has been given under subsections (a) and (b) of this section for a period sufficient to establish the continuity, quantity, and regularity of such release:

Provided, That notification in accordance with subsections (a) and (b) of this paragraph shall be given for releases subject to this paragraph annually, or at such time as there is any statistically significant increase in the quantity of any hazardous substance or constituent thereof released, above that previously reported or occurring.

§9604. RESPONSE AUTHORITIES

(a) REMOVAL AND OTHER REMEDIAL ACTION BY PRESIDENT; APPLICABILITY OF NATIONAL CONTINGENCY PLAN; RESPONSE BY POTENTIALLY RESPONSIBLE PARTIES; PUBLIC HEALTH THREATS; LIMITATIONS ON RESPONSE; EXCEPTION

(1) Whenever (A) any hazardous substance is released or there is a substantial threat of such a release into the environment, or (B) there is a release or substantial threat of release into the environment of any pollutant or contaminant which may present an imminent and substantial danger to the public health or welfare, the President is authorized to act, consistent with the national contingency plan, to remove or arrange for the removal of, and provide for remedial action relating to such hazardous substance, pollutant, or contaminant at any time (including its removal from any contaminated natural resource), or take any other response measure consistent with the national contingency plan which the President deems necessary to protect the public health or welfare or the environment. When the President determines that such action will be done properly and promptly by the owner or operator of the facility or vessel or by any other responsible party, the President may allow such person to carry out the action, conduct the remedial investigation, or conduct the feasibility study in accordance with section 9622 of this title. No remedial investigation or feasibility study (RI/FS) shall be authorized except on a determination by the President that the party is qualified to conduct the RI/FS and only if the President contracts with or arranges for a qualified person to assist the President in overseeing and reviewing the conduct of such RI/FS and if the responsible party agrees to reimburse the Fund for any cost incurred by the President under, or in connection with, the oversight contract or arrangement. In no event shall a potentially responsible party be subject to a lesser standard of liability, receive preferential treatment, or in any other way, whether direct or indirect, benefit from any such arrangements as a response action contractor, or as a person hired or retained by such a response action contractor, with respect to the release or facility in ques-

tion. The President shall give primary attention to those releases which the President deems may present a public health threat.

(2) Removal action. — Any removal action undertaken by the President under this subsection (or by any other person referred to in section 9622 of this title) should, to the extent the President deems practicable, contribute to the efficient performance of any long term remedial action with respect to the release or threatened release concerned.

(3) Limitations on response. — The President shall not provide for a removal or remedial action under this section in response to a release or threat of release —

 (A) of a naturally occurring substance in its unaltered form, or altered solely through naturally occurring processes or phenomena, from a location where it is naturally found;

 (B) from products which are part of the structure of, and result in exposure within, residential buildings or business or community structures; or

 (C) into public or private drinking water supplies due to deterioration of the system through ordinary use.

(4) Exception to limitations. — Notwithstanding paragraph (3) of this subsection, to the extent authorized by this section, the President may respond to any release or threat of release if in the President's discretion, it constitutes a public health or environmental emergency and no other person with the authority and capability to respond to the emergency will do so in a timely manner.

 (b) **INVESTIGATIONS, MONITORING, COORDINATION, ETC., BY PRESIDENT**

  (1) **INFORMATION; STUDIES AND INVESTIGATIONS**

Whenever the President is authorized to act pursuant to subsection (a) of this section, or whenever the President has reason to believe that a release has occurred or is about to occur, or that illness, disease, or complaints thereof may be attributable to exposure to a hazardous substance, pollutant, or contaminant and that a release may have occurred or be occurring, he may undertake such investigations, monitoring, surveys, testing, and other information gathering as he may deem necessary or appropriate to identify the existence and extent of the release or threat thereof, the source and nature of the hazardous substances, pollutants or contaminants involved, and the extent of danger to the public health or welfare or to the environment. In addition, the President may undertake such planning, legal, fiscal, economic, engineering, architectural, and other studies or investigations as he may deem necessary or appropriate to plan and direct response actions, to recover the costs thereof, and to enforce the provisions of this chapter.

  (2) **COORDINATION OF INVESTIGATIONS**

The President shall promptly notify the appropriate Federal and State natural resource trustees of potential damages to natural resources resulting from releases under investigation pursuant to this section and shall seek to coordinate the assessments, investigations, and planning under this section with such Federal and State trustees.

(c) CRITERIA FOR CONTINUANCE OF OBLIGATIONS FROM FUND OVER SPECIFIED AMOUNT FOR RESPONSE ACTIONS; CONSULTATION BY PRESIDENT WITH AFFECTED STATES; CONTRACTS OR COOPERATIVE AGREEMENTS BY STATES WITH PRESIDENT PRIOR TO REMEDIAL ACTIONS; COST-SHARING AGREEMENTS; SELECTION BY PRESIDENT OF REMEDIAL ACTIONS; STATE CREDITS: GRANTING OF CREDIT, EXPENSES BEFORE LISTING OR AGREEMENT, RESPONSE ACTIONS BETWEEN 1978 AND 1980, STATE EXPENSES AFTER DECEMBER 11, 1980, IN EXCESS OF 10 PERCENT OF COSTS, ITEM-BY-ITEM APPROVAL, USE OF CREDITS; OPERATION AND MAINTENANCE; LIMITATION ON SOURCE OF FUNDS FOR O&M; RECONTRACTING; SITING

(1) Unless (A) the President finds that (i) continued response actions are immediately required to prevent, limit, or mitigate an emergency, (ii) there is an immediate risk to public health or welfare or the environment, and (iii) such assistance will not otherwise be provided on a timely basis, or (B) the President has determined the appropriate remedial actions pursuant to paragraph (2) of this subsection and the State or States in which the source of the release is located have complied with the requirements of paragraph (3) of this subsection, or (C) continued response action is otherwise appropriate and consistent with the remedial action to be taken[4] obligations from the Fund, other than those authorized by subsection (b) of this section, shall not continue after $2,000,000 has been obligated for response actions or 12 months has elapsed from the date of initial response to a release or threatened release of hazardous substances.

(2) The President shall consult with the affected State or States before determining any appropriate remedial action to be taken pursuant to the authority granted under subsection (a) of this section.

(3) The President shall not provide any remedial actions pursuant to this section unless the State in which the release occurs first enters into a contract or cooperative agreement with the President providing assurances deemed adequate by the President that (A) the State will assure all future maintenance of the removal and remedial actions provided for the expected life of such actions as determined by the President; (B) the State will assure the availability of a hazardous waste disposal facility acceptable to the President and in compliance with the requirements of subtitle C of the Solid Waste Disposal Act [42 U.S.C. 6921 et seq.] for any necessary offsite storage, destruction, treatment, or secure disposition of the hazardous substances; and (C) the State will pay or assure payment of (i) 10 per centum of the costs of the remedial action, including all future maintenance, or (ii) 50 percent (or such greater amount as the President may determine appropriate, taking into account the degree of responsibility of the State or political subdivision for the release) of any sums expended in response to a release at a facility, that was operated by the State or a political subdivision thereof, either directly or through a contractual relationship or otherwise, at the time of any disposal of hazardous substances therein. For the purpose of clause

---

4. So in original. Probably should be followed by a comma.

(ii) of this subparagraph, the term "facility" does not include navigable waters or the beds underlying those waters. In the case of remedial action to be taken on land or water held by an Indian tribe, held by the United States in trust for Indians, held by a member of an Indian tribe (if such land or water is subject to a trust restriction on alienation), or otherwise within the borders of an Indian reservation, the requirements of this paragraph for assurances regarding future maintenance and cost-sharing shall not apply, and the President shall provide the assurance required by this paragraph regarding the availability of a hazardous waste disposal facility.

(4) Selection of remedial action. — The President shall select remedial actions to carry out this section in accordance with section 9621 of this title (relating to cleanup standards).

(5) State credits. —

(A) GRANTING OF CREDIT

The President shall grant a State a credit against the share of the costs, for which it is responsible under paragraph (3) with respect to a facility listed on the National Priorities List under the National Contingency Plan, for amounts expended by a State for remedial action at such facility pursuant to a contract or cooperative agreement with the President. The credit under this paragraph shall be limited to those State expenses which the President determines to be reasonable, documented, direct out-of-pocket expenditures of non-Federal funds.

(B) EXPENSES BEFORE LISTING OR AGREEMENT

The credit under this paragraph shall include expenses for remedial action at a facility incurred before the listing of the facility on the National Priorities List or before a contract or cooperative agreement is entered into under subsection (d) of this section for the facility if —

(i) after such expenses are incurred the facility is listed on such list and a contract or cooperative agreement is entered into for the facility, and

(ii) the President determines that such expenses would have been credited to the State under subparagraph (A) had the expenditures been made after listing of the facility on such list and after the date on which such contract or cooperative agreement is entered into.

(C) RESPONSE ACTIONS BETWEEN 1978 AND 1980

The credit under this paragraph shall include funds expended or obligated by the State or a political subdivision thereof after January 1, 1978, and before December 11, 1980, for cost-eligible response actions and claims for damages compensable under section 9611 of this title.

(D) STATE EXPENSES AFTER DECEMBER 11, 1980, IN EXCESS OF 10 PERCENT OF COSTS

The credit under this paragraph shall include 90 percent of State expenses incurred at a facility owned, but not operated, by such State or by a political subdivision thereof. Such credit applies only to expenses incurred pursuant to a contract or cooperative agreement under subsection (d) of this section and only to expenses incurred after December 11, 1980, but before October 17, 1986.

(E) ITEM-BY-ITEM APPROVAL

In the case of expenditures made after October 17, 1986, the President may require prior approval of each item of expenditure as a condition of granting a credit under this paragraph.

(F) USE OF CREDITS

Credits granted under this paragraph for funds expended with respect to a facility may be used by the State to reduce all or part of the share of costs otherwise required to be paid by the State under paragraph (3) in connection with remedial actions at such facility. If the amount of funds for which credit is allowed under this paragraph exceeds such share of costs for such facility, the State may use the amount of such excess to reduce all or part of the share of such costs at other facilities in that State. A credit shall not entitle the State to any direct payment.

(6) Operation and maintenance. — For the purposes of paragraph (3) of this subsection, in the case of ground or surface water contamination, completed remedial action includes the completion of treatment or other measures, whether taken onsite or offsite, necessary to restore ground and surface water quality to a level that assures protection of human health and the environment. With respect to such measures, the operation of such measures for a period of up to 10 years after the construction or installation and commencement of operation shall be considered remedial action. Activities required to maintain the effectiveness of such measures following such period or the completion of remedial action, whichever is earlier, shall be considered operation or maintenance.

(7) Limitation on source of funds for O&M. — During any period after the availability of funds received by the Hazardous Substance Superfund established under subchapter A of chapter 98 of Title 26 from tax revenues or appropriations from general revenues, the Federal share of the payment of the cost of operation or maintenance pursuant to paragraph (3)(C)(i) or paragraph (6) of this subsection (relating to operation and maintenance) shall be from funds received by the Hazardous Substance Superfund from amounts recovered on behalf of such fund under this chapter.

(8) Recontracting. — The President is authorized to undertake or continue whatever interim remedial actions the President determines to be appropriate to reduce risks to public health or the environment where the performance of a complete remedial action requires recontracting because of the discovery of sources, types, or quantities of hazardous substances not known at the time of entry into the original contract. The total cost of interim actions undertaken at a facility pursuant to this paragraph shall not exceed $2,000,000.

(9) Siting. — Effective 3 years after October 17, 1986, the President shall not provide any remedial actions pursuant to this section unless the State in which the release occurs first enters into a contract or cooperative agreement with the President providing assurances deemed adequate by the President that the State will assure the availability of hazardous waste treatment or disposal facilities which —

(A) have adequate capacity for the destruction, treatment, or secure disposition of all hazardous wastes that are reasonably expected to be generated within the State during the 20-year period following the date of such contract or cooperative agreement and to be disposed of, treated, or destroyed.

(B) are within the State or outside the State in accordance with an interstate agreement or regional agreement or authority,

(C) are acceptable to the President, and

(D) are in compliance with the requirements of subtitle C of the Solid Waste Disposal Act [42 U.S.C. 6921 et seq.].

(d) CONTRACTS OR COOPERATIVE AGREEMENTS BY PRESIDENT WITH STATES OR POLITICAL SUBDIVISIONS OR INDIAN TRIBES; STATE APPLICATIONS, TERMS AND CONDITIONS; REIMBURSEMENTS; COST-SHARING PROVISIONS; ENFORCEMENT REQUIREMENTS AND PROCEDURES

(1) Cooperative agreements. —

(A) STATE APPLICATIONS

A State or political subdivision thereof or Indian tribe may apply to the President to carry out actions authorized in this section. If the President determines that the State or political subdivision or Indian tribe has the capability to carry out any or all of such actions in accordance with the criteria and priorities established pursuant to section 9605(a)(8) of this title and to carry out related enforcement actions, the President may enter into a contract or cooperative agreement with the State or political subdivision or Indian tribe to carry out such actions. The President shall make a determination regarding such an application within 90 days after the President receives the application.

(B) TERMS AND CONDITIONS

A contract or cooperative agreement under this paragraph shall be subject to such terms and conditions as the President may prescribe. The contract or cooperative agreement may cover a specific facility or specific facilities.

(C) REIMBURSEMENTS

Any State which expended funds during the period beginning September 30, 1985, and ending on October 17, 1986, for response actions at any site included on the National Priorities List and subject to a cooperative agreement under this chapter shall be reimbursed for the share of costs of such actions for which the Federal Government is responsible under this chapter.

(2) If the President enters into a cost-sharing agreement pursuant to sub-

section (c) of this section or a contract or cooperative agreement pursuant to this subsection, and the State or political subdivision thereof fails to comply with any requirements of the contract, the President may, after providing sixty days notice, seek in the appropriate Federal district court to enforce the contract or to recover any funds advanced or any costs incurred because of the breach of the contract by the State or political subdivision.

(3) Where a State or a political subdivision thereof is acting in behalf of the President, the President is authorized to provide technical and legal assistance in the administration and enforcement of any contract or subcontract in connection with response actions assisted under this subchapter, and to intervene in any civil action involving the enforcement of such contract or subcontract.

(4) Where two or more noncontiguous facilities are reasonably related on the basis of geography, or on the basis of the threat, or potential threat to the public health or welfare or the environment, the President may, in his discretion, treat these related facilities as one for purposes of this section.

(e) INFORMATION GATHERING AND ACCESS

(1) ACTION AUTHORIZED

Any officer, employee, or representative of the President, duly designated by the President, is authorized to take action under paragraph (2), (3), or (4) (or any combination thereof) at a vessel, facility, establishment, place, property, or location or, in the case of paragraph (3) or (4), at any vessel, facility, establishment, place, property, or location which is adjacent to the vessel, facility, establishment, place, property, or location referred to in such paragraph (3) or (4). Any duly designated officer, employee, or representative of a State or political subdivision under a contract or cooperative agreement under subsection (d)(1) of this section is also authorized to take such action. The authority of paragraphs (3) and (4) may be exercised only if there is a reasonable basis to believe there may be a release or threat of release of a hazardous substance or pollutant or contaminant. The authority of this subsection may be exercised only for the purposes of determining the need for response, or choosing or taking any response action under this subchapter, or otherwise enforcing the provisions of this subchapter.

(2) ACCESS TO INFORMATION

Any officer, employee, or representative described in paragraph (1) may require any person who has or may have information relevant to any of the following to furnish, upon reasonable notice, information or documents relating to such matter:

(A) The identification, nature, and quantity of materials which have been or are generated, treated, stored, or disposed of at a vessel or facility or transported to a vessel or facility.

(B) The nature or extent of a release or threatened release of a hazardous substance or pollutant or contaminant at or from a vessel or facility.

(C) Information relating to the ability of a person to pay for or to perform a cleanup.

In addition, upon reasonable notice, such person either (i) shall grant any such officer, employee, or representative access at all reasonable times to any vessel, facility, establishment, place, property, or location to inspect and copy all documents or records relating to such matters or (ii) shall copy and furnish to the officer, employee, or representative all such documents or records, at the option and expense of such person.

(3) ENTRY

Any officer, employee, or representative described in paragraph (1) is authorized to enter at reasonable times any of the following:

(A) Any vessel, facility, establishment, or other place or property where any hazardous substance or pollutant or contaminant may be or has been generated, stored, treated, disposed of, or transported from.

(B) Any vessel, facility, establishment, or other place or property from which or to which a hazardous substance or pollutant or contaminant has been or may have been released.

(C) Any vessel, facility, establishment, or other place or property where such release is or may be threatened.

(D) Any vessel, facility, establishment, or other place or property where entry is needed to determine the need for response or the appropriate response or to effectuate a response action under this subchapter.

(4) INSPECTION AND SAMPLES

(A) AUTHORITY

Any officer, employee or representative described in paragraph (1) is authorized to inspect and obtain samples from any vessel, facility, establishment, or other place or property referred to in paragraph (3) or from any location of any suspected hazardous substance or pollutant or contaminant. Any such officer, employee, or representative is authorized to inspect and obtain samples of any containers or labeling for suspected hazardous substances or pollutants or contaminants. Each such inspection shall be completed with reasonable promptness.

(B) SAMPLES

If the officer, employee, or representative obtains any samples, before leaving the premises he shall give to the owner, operator, tenant, or other person in charge of the place from which the samples were obtained a receipt describing the sample obtained and, if requested, a portion of each such sample. A copy of the results of any analysis made of such samples shall be furnished promptly to the owner, operator, tenant, or other person in charge, if such person can be located.

(5) COMPLIANCE ORDERS

(A) ISSUANCE

If consent is not granted regarding any request made by an officer, employee, or representative under paragraph (2), (3), or (4), the President may issue an order directing compliance with the request. The order may be issued after such notice and opportunity for consultation as is reasonably appropriate under the circumstances.

(B) COMPLIANCE

The President may ask the Attorney General to commence a civil action to compel compliance with a request or order referred to in subparagraph (A). Where there is a reasonable basis to believe there may be a release or threat of a release of a hazardous substance or pollutant or contaminant, the court shall take the following actions:

(i) In the case of interference with entry or inspection, the court shall enjoin such interference or direct compliance with orders to prohibit interference with entry or inspection unless under the circumstances of the case the demand for entry or inspection is arbitrary and capricious, an abuse of discretion, or otherwise not in accordance with law.

(ii) In the case of information or document requests or orders, the court shall enjoin interference with such information or document requests or orders or direct compliance with the requests or orders to provide such information or documents unless under the circumstances of the case the demand for information or documents is arbitrary and capricious, an abuse of discretion, or otherwise not in accordance with law.

The court may assess a civil penalty not to exceed $25,000 for each day of noncompliance against any person who unreasonably fails to comply with the provisions of paragraph (2), (3), or (4) or an order issued pursuant to subparagraph (A) of this paragraph.

(6) OTHER AUTHORITY

Nothing in this subsection shall preclude the President from securing access or obtaining information in any other lawful manner.

(7) CONFIDENTIALITY OF INFORMATION

(A) Any records, reports, or information obtained from any person under this section (including records, reports, or information obtained by representatives of the President) shall be available to the public, except that upon a showing satisfactory to the President (or the State, as the case may be) by any person that records, reports, or information, or particular part thereof (other than health or safety effects data), to which the President (or the State, as the case may be) or any officer, employee, or representative has access under this section if made public would divulge information entitled to protection under section 1905 of title 18, such information or particular portion thereof shall be considered confidential in accordance with the purposes of that section, except that such record, report, document or information may be disclosed to other officers, employees, or authorized representatives of the United States concerned with carrying out this chapter, or when relevant in any proceeding under this chapter.

(B) Any person not subject to the provisions of section 1905 of title 18 who knowingly and willfully divulges or discloses any information entitled to protection under this subsection shall, upon conviction, be subject to a fine of not more than $5,000 or to imprisonment not to exceed one year, or both.

(C) In submitting data under this chapter, a person required to provide such data may (i) designate the data which such person believes is entitled to protection under this subsection and (ii) submit such designated data separately from other data submitted under this chapter. A designation under this paragraph shall be made in writing and in such manner as the President may prescribe by regulation.

(D) Notwithstanding any limitation contained in this section or any other provision of law, all information reported to or otherwise obtained by the President (or any representative of the President) under this chapter shall be made available, upon written request of any duly authorized committee of the Congress, to such committee.

(E) No person required to provide information under this chapter may claim that the information is entitled to protection under this paragraph unless such person shows each of the following:

(i) Such person has not disclosed the information to any other person, other than a member of a local emergency planning committee established under title III of the Amendments and Reauthorization Act of 1986 [42 U.S.C. 11001 et seq.], an officer or employee of the United States or a State or local government, an employee of such person, or a person who is bound by a confidentiality agreement, and such person has taken reasonable measures to protect the confidentiality of such information and intends to continue to take such measures.

(ii) The information is not required to be disclosed, or otherwise made available, to the public under any other Federal or State law.

(iii) Disclosure of the information is likely to cause substantial harm to the competitive position of such person.

(iv) The specific chemical identity, if sought to be protected, is not readily discoverable through reverse engineering.

(F) The following information with respect to any hazardous substance at the facility or vessel shall not be entitled to protection under this paragraph:

(i) The trade name, common name, or generic class or category of the hazardous substance.

(ii) The physical properties of the substance, including its boiling point, melting point, flash point, specific gravity, vapor density, solubility in water, and vapor pressure at 20 degrees celsius.

(iii) The hazards to health and the environment posed by the substance, including physical hazards (such as explosion) and potential acute and chronic health hazards.

(iv) The potential routes of human exposure to the substance at the facility, establishment, place, or property being investigated, entered, or inspected under this subsection.

(v) The location of disposal of any waste stream.

(vi) Any monitoring data or analysis of monitoring data pertaining to disposal activities.

(vii) Any hydrogeologic or geologic data.

(viii) Any groundwater monitoring data.

(f) **CONTRACTS FOR RESPONSE ACTIONS; COMPLIANCE WITH FEDERAL HEALTH AND SAFETY STANDARDS**

In awarding contracts to any person engaged in response actions, the President or the State, in any case where it is awarding contracts pursuant to a contract entered into under subsection (d) of this section, shall require compliance with Federal health and safety standards established under section 9651(f) of this title by contractors and subcontractors as a condition of such contracts.

(g) **RATES FOR WAGES AND LABOR STANDARDS APPLICABLE TO COVERED WORK**

(1) All laborers and mechanics employed by contractors or subcontractors in the performance of construction, repair, or alteration work funded in whole or in part under this section shall be paid wages at rates not less than those prevailing on projects of a character similar in the locality as determined by the Secretary of Labor in accordance with the Davis-Bacon Act [40 U.S.C. 276a et seq.]. The President shall not approve any such funding without first obtaining adequate assurance that required labor standards will be maintained upon the construction work.

(2) The Secretary of Labor shall have, with respect to the labor standards specified in paragraph (1), the authority and functions set forth in Reorganization Plan Numbered 14 of 1950 (15 F.R. 3176; 64 Stat. 1267) and section 276c of title 40.

(h) **EMERGENCY PROCUREMENT POWERS; EXERCISE BY PRESIDENT**

Notwithstanding any other provision of law, subject to the provisions of section 9611 of this title, the President may authorize the use of such emergency procurement powers as he deems necessary to effect the purpose of this chapter. Upon determination that such procedures are necessary, the President shall promulgate regulations prescribing the circumstances under which such authority shall be used and the procedures governing the use of such authority.

CERCLA §9604

(i) AGENCY FOR TOXIC SUBSTANCES AND DISEASE REGISTRY; ESTABLISHMENT, FUNCTIONS, ETC.

(1) There is hereby established within the Public Health Service an agency, to be known as the Agency for Toxic Substances and Disease Registry, which shall report directly to the Surgeon General of the United States. The Administrator of said Agency shall, with the cooperation of the Administrator of the Environmental Protection Agency, the Commissioner of the Food and Drug Administration, the Directors of the National Institute of Medicine, National Institute of Environmental Health Sciences, National Institute of Occupational Safety and Health, Centers for Disease Control, the Administrator of the Occupational Safety and Health Administration, the Administrator of the Social Security Administration, the Secretary of Transportation, and appropriate State and local health officials, effectuate and implement the health related authorities of this chapter. In addition, said Administrator shall—

(A) in cooperation with the States, establish and maintain a national registry of serious diseases and illnesses and a national registry of persons exposed to toxic substances;

(B) establish and maintain inventory of literature, research, and studies on the health effects of toxic substances;

(C) in cooperation with the States, and other agencies of the Federal Government, establish and maintain a complete listing of areas closed to the public or otherwise restricted in use because of toxic substance contamination;

(D) in cases of public health emergencies caused or believed to be caused by exposure to toxic substances, provide medical care and testing to exposed individuals, including but not limited to tissue sampling, chromosomal testing where appropriate, epidemiological studies, or any other assistance appropriate under the circumstances; and

(E) either independently or as part of other health status survey, conduct periodic survey and screening programs to determine relationships between exposure to toxic substances and illness. In cases of public health emergencies, exposed persons shall be eligible for admission to hospitals and other facilities and services operated or provided by the Public Health Service.

(2)(A) Within 6 months after October 17, 1986, the Administrator of the Agency for Toxic Substances and Disease Registry (ATSDR) and the Administrator of the Environmental Protection Agency ("EPA") shall prepare a list, in order of priority, of at least 100 hazardous substances which are most commonly found at facilities on the National Priorities List and which, in their sole discretion, they determine are posing the most significant potential threat to human health due to their known or suspected toxicity to humans and the potential for human exposure to such substances at facilities on the National Priorities List or at facilities to which a response to a release or a threatened release under this section is under consideration.

(B) Within 24 months after October 17, 1986, the Administrator of

ATSDR and the Administrator of EPA shall revise the list prepared under subparagraph (A). Such revision shall include, in order of priority, the addition of 100 or more such hazardous substances. In each of the 3 consecutive 12-month periods that follow, the Administrator of ATSDR and the Administrator of EPA shall revise, in the same manner as provided in the 2 preceding sentences, such list to include not fewer than 25 additional hazardous substances per revision. The Administrator of ATSDR and the Administrator of EPA shall not less often than once every year thereafter revise such list to include additional hazardous substances in accordance with the criteria in subparagraph (A).

(3) Based on all available information, including information maintained under paragraph (1)(B) and data developed and collected on the health effects of hazardous substances under this paragraph, the Administrator of ATSDR shall prepare toxicological profiles of each of the substances listed pursuant to paragraph (2). The toxicological profiles shall be prepared in accordance with guidelines developed by the Administrator of ATSDR and the Administrator of EPA. Such profiles shall include, but not be limited to each of the following:

(A) An examination, summary, and interpretation of available toxicological information and epidemiologic evaluations on a hazardous substance in order to ascertain the levels of significant human exposure for the substance and the associated acute, subacute, and chronic health effects.

(B) A determination of whether adequate information on the health effects of each substance is available or in the process of development to determine levels of exposure which present a significant risk to human health of acute, subacute, and chronic health effects.

(C) Where appropriate, an identification of toxicological testing needed to identify the types of levels of exposure that may present significant risk of adverse health effects in humans.

Any toxicological profile or revision thereof shall reflect the Administrator of ATSDR's assessment of all relevant toxicological testing which has been peer reviewed. The profiles required to be prepared under this paragraph for those hazardous substances listed under subparagraph (A) of paragraph (2) shall be completed, at a rate of no fewer than 25 per year, within 4 years after October 17, 1986. A profile required on a substance listed pursuant to subparagraph (B) of paragraph (2) shall be completed within 3 years after addition to the list. The profiles prepared under this paragraph shall be of those substances highest on the list of priorities under paragraph (2) for which profiles have not previously been prepared. Profiles required under this paragraph shall be revised and republished as necessary, but no less often than once every 3 years. Such profiles shall be provided to the States and made available to other interested parties.

(4) The Administrator of the ATSDR shall provide consultations upon request on health issues relating to exposure to hazardous or toxic substances, on the basis of available information, to the Administrator of EPA, State officials, and local officials. Such consultations to individuals may be provided by States under cooperative agreements established under this chapter.

(5)(A) For each hazardous substance listed pursuant to paragraph (2), the Administrator of ATSDR (in consultation with the Administrator of EPA and other agencies and programs of the Public Health Service) shall assess whether adequate information on the health effects of such substance is available. For any such substance for which adequate information is not available (or under development), the Administrator of ATSDR, in cooperation with the Director of the National Toxicology Program, shall assure the initiation of a program of research designed to determine the health effects (and techniques for development of methods to determine such health effects) of such substance. Where feasible, such program shall seek to develop methods to determine the health effects of such substance in combination with other substances with which it is commonly found. Before assuring the initiation of such program, the Administrator of ATSDR shall consider recommendations of the Interagency Testing Committee established under section 4(e) of the Toxic Substances Control Act [15 U.S.C. 2603(e)] on the types of research that should be done. Such program shall include, to the extent necessary to supplement existing information, but shall not be limited to —

(i) laboratory and other studies to determine short, intermediate, and long-term health effects;

(ii) laboratory and other studies to determine organ-specific, site-specific, and system-specific acute and chronic toxicity;

(iii) laboratory and other studies to determine the manner in which such substances are metabolized or to otherwise develop an understanding of the biokinetics of such substances, and

(iv) where there is a possibility of obtaining human data, the collection of such information.

(B) In assessing the need to perform laboratory and other studies, as required by subparagraph (A), the Administrator of ATSDR shall consider —

(i) the availability and quality of existing test data concerning the substance on the suspected health effect in question;

(ii) the extent to which testing already in progress will, in a timely fashion, provide data that will be adequate to support the preparation of toxicological profiles as required by paragraph (3); and

(iii) such other scientific and technical factors as the Administrator of ATSDR may determine are necessary for the effective implementation of this subsection.

(C) In the development and implementation of any research program under this paragraph, the Administrator of ATSDR and the Administrator of EPA shall coordinate such research program implemented under this paragraph with the National Toxicology Program and with programs of toxicological testing established under the Toxic Substances Control Act [15 U.S.C. 2601 et seq.] and the Federal Insecticide, Fungicide and Rodenticide Act [7 U.S.C. 136 et seq.]. The purpose of such coordination shall be to avoid duplication of effort and to assure that the hazardous substances listed pursuant to this subsection are tested thoroughly at the earliest practicable date.

Where appropriate, consistent with such purpose, a research program under this paragraph may be carried out using such programs of toxicological testing.

(D) It is the sense of the Congress that the costs of research programs under this paragraph be borne by the manufacturers and processors of the hazardous substance in question, as required in programs of toxicological testing under the Toxic Substances Control Act [15 U.S.C. 2601 et seq.]. Within 1 year after October 17, 1986, the Administrator of EPA shall promulgate regulations which provide, where appropriate, for payment of such costs by manufacturers and processors under the Toxic Substances Control Act, and registrants under the Federal Insecticide, Fungicide, and Rodenticide Act [7 U.S.C. 136 et seq.], and recovery of such costs from responsible parties under this chapter.

(6)(A) The Administrator of ATSDR shall perform a health assessment for each facility on the National Priorities List established under section 9605 of this title. Such health assessment shall be completed not later than December 10, 1988, for each facility proposed for inclusion on such list prior to October 17, 1986, or not later than one year after the date of proposal for inclusion on such list for each facility proposed for inclusion on such list after October 17, 1986.

(B) The Administrator of ATSDR may perform health assessments for releases or facilities where individual persons or licensed physicians provide information that individuals have been exposed to a hazardous substance, for which the probable source of such exposure is a release. In addition to other methods (formal or informal) of providing such information, such individual persons or licensed physicians may submit a petition to the Administrator of ATSDR providing such information and requesting a health assessment. If such a petition is submitted and the Administrator of ATSDR does not initiate a health assessment, the Administrator of ATSDR shall provide a written explanation of why a health assessment is not appropriate.

(C) In determining the priority in which to conduct health assessments under this subsection, the Administrator of ATSDR, in consultation with the Administrator of EPA, shall give priority to those facilities at which there is documented evidence of the release of hazardous substances, at which the potential risk to human health appears highest, and for which in the judgment of the Administrator of ATSDR existing health assessment data are inadequate to assess the potential risk to human health as provided in subparagraph (F). In determining the priorities for conducting health assessments under this subsection, the Administrator of ATSDR shall consider the National Priorities List schedules and the needs of the Environmental Protection Agency and other Federal agencies pursuant to schedules for remedial investigation and feasibility studies.

(D) Where a health assessment is done at a site on the National Priorities List, the Administrator of ATSDR shall complete such assessment promptly and, to the maximum extent practicable, before the completion of the remedial investigation and feasibility study at the facility concerned.

(E) Any State or political subdivision carrying out a health assessment for a facility shall report the results of the assessment to the Administrator of ATSDR and the Administrator of EPA and shall include recommendations with respect to further activities which need to be carried out under this section. The Administrator of ATSDR shall state such recommendation in any report on the results of any assessment carried out directly by the Administrator of ATSDR for such facility and shall issue periodic reports which include the results of all the assessments carried out under this subsection.

(F) For the purposes of this subsection and section 9611(c)(4) of this title, the term "health assessments," shall include preliminary assessments of the potential risk to human health posed by individual sites and facilities, based on such factors as the nature and extent of contamination, the existence of potential pathways of human exposure (including ground or surface water contamination, air emissions, and food chain contamination), the size and potential susceptibility of the community within the likely pathways of exposure, the comparison of expected human exposure levels to the short-term and long-term health effects associated with identified hazardous substances and any available recommended exposure or tolerance limits for such hazardous substances, and the comparison of existing morbidity and mortality data on diseases that may be associated with the observed levels of exposure. The Administrator of ATSDR shall use appropriate data, risk assessments, risk evaluations and studies available from the Administrator of EPA.

(G) The purpose of health assessments under this subsection shall be to assist in determining whether actions under paragraph (11) of this subsection should be taken to reduce human exposure to hazardous substances from a facility and whether additional information on human exposure and associated health risks is needed and should be acquired by conducting epidemiological studies under paragraph (7), establishing a registry under paragraph (8), establishing a health surveillance program under paragraph (9), or through other means. In using the results of health assessments for determining additional actions to be taken under this section, the Administrator of ATSDR may consider additional information on the risks to the potentially affected population from all sources of such hazardous substances including known point or nonpoint sources other than those from the facility in question.

(H) At the completion of each health assessment, the Administrator of ATSDR shall provide the Administrator of EPA and each affected State with the results of such assessment, together with any recommendations for further actions under this subsection or otherwise under this chapter. In addition, if the health assessment indicates that the release or threatened release concerned may pose a serious threat to human health or the environment, the Administrator of ATSDR shall so notify the Administrator of EPA who shall promptly evaluate such release or threatened release in accordance with the hazard ranking system referred to in section 9605(a)(8)(A) of this title to determine whether the site shall be placed on the National Priorities List or, if the site is already on the list, the Administrator of ATSDR may recommend to the Administrator of EPA that the site be accorded a higher priority.

(7)(A) Whenever in the judgment of the Administrator of ATSDR it is appropriate on the basis of the results of a health assessment, the Administrator of ATSDR shall conduct a pilot study of health effects for selected groups of exposed individuals in order to determine the desirability of conducting full scale epidemiological or other health studies of the entire exposed population.

(B) Whenever in the judgment of the Administrator of ATSDR it is appropriate on the basis of the results of such pilot study or other study or health assessment, the Administrator of ATSDR shall conduct such full scale epidemiological or other health studies as may be necessary to determine the health effects on the population exposed to hazardous substances from a release or threatened release. If a significant excess of disease in a population is identified, the letter of transmittal of such study shall include an assessment of other risk factors, other than a release, that may, in the judgment of the peer review group, be associated with such disease, if such risk factors were not taken into account in the design or conduct of the study.

(8) In any case in which the results of a health assessment indicate a potential significant risk to human health, the Administrator of ATSDR shall consider whether the establishment of a registry of exposed persons would contribute to accomplishing the purposes of this subsection, taking into account circumstances bearing on the usefulness of such a registry, including the seriousness or unique character of identified diseases or the likelihood of population migration from the affected area.

(9) Where the Administrator of ATSDR has determined that there is a significant increased risk of adverse health effects in humans from exposure to hazardous substances based on the results of a health assessment conducted under paragraph (6), an epidemiologic study conducted under paragraph (7), or an exposure registry that has been established under paragraph (8), and the Administrator of ATSDR has determined that such exposure is the result of a release from a facility, the Administrator of ATSDR shall initiate a health surveillance program for such population. This program shall include but not be limited to —

(A) periodic medical testing where appropriate of population subgroups to screen for diseases for which the population or subgroup is at significant increased risk; and

(B) a mechanism to refer for treatment those individuals within such population who are screened positive for such diseases.

(10) Two years after October 17, 1986, and every 2 years thereafter, the Administrator of ATSDR shall prepare and submit to the Administrator of EPA and to the Congress a report on the results of the activities of ATSDR regarding —

(A) health assessments and pilot health effects studies conducted;

(B) epidemiologic studies conducted;

(C) hazardous substances which have been listed under paragraph (2), toxicological profiles which have been developed, and toxicologic testing which has been conducted or which is being conducted under this subsection;

(D) registries established under paragraph (8); and

(E) an overall assessment, based on the results of activities conducted by the Administrator of ATSDR, of the linkage between human exposure to individual or combinations of hazardous substances due to releases from facilities covered by this chapter or the Solid Waste Disposal Act [42 U.S.C. 6901 et seq.] and any increased incidence or prevalence of adverse health effects in humans.

(11) If a health assessment or other study carried out under this subsection contains a finding that the exposure concerned presents a significant risk to human health, the President shall take such steps as may be necessary to reduce such exposure and eliminate or substantially mitigate the significant risk to human health. Such steps may include the use of any authority under this chapter, including, but not limited to —

(A) provision of alternative water supplies, and

(B) permanent or temporary relocation of individuals.

In any case in which information is insufficient, in the judgment of the Administrator of ATSDR or the President to determine a significant human exposure level with respect to a hazardous substance, the President may take such steps as may be necessary to reduce the exposure of any person to such hazardous substance to such level as the President deems necessary to protect human health.

(12) In any case which is the subject of a petition, a health assessment or study, or a research program under this subsection, nothing in this subsection shall be construed to delay or otherwise affect or impair the authority of the President, the Administrator of ATSDR, or the Administrator of EPA to exercise any authority vested in the President, the Administrator of ATSDR or the Administrator of EPA under any other provision of law (including, but not limited to, the imminent hazard authority of section 7003 of the Solid Waste Disposal Act [42 U.S.C. 6973]) or the response and abatement authorities of this chapter.

(13) All studies and results of research conducted under this subsection (other than health assessments) shall be reported or adopted only after appropriate peer review. Such peer review shall be completed, to the maximum extent practicable, within a period of 60 days. In the case of research conducted under the National Toxicology Program, such peer review may be conducted by the Board of Scientific Counselors. In the case of other research, such peer review shall be conducted by panels consisting of no less than three nor more than seven members, who shall be disinterested scientific experts selected for such purpose by the Administrator of ATSDR or the Administrator of EPA, as appropriate, on the basis of their reputation for scientific objectivity and the lack of institutional ties with any person involved in the conduct of the study or research under review. Support services for such panels shall be provided by the Agency for Toxic Substances and Disease Registry, or by the Environmental Protection Agency, as appropriate.

(14) In the implementation of this subsection and other health-related au-

thorities of this chapter, the Administrator of ATSDR shall assemble, develop as necessary, and distribute to the States, and upon request to medical colleges, physicians, and other health professionals, appropriate educational materials (including short courses) on the medical surveillance, screening, and methods of diagnosis and treatment of injury or disease related to exposure to hazardous substances (giving priority to those listed in paragraph (2)), through such means as the Administrator of ATSDR deems appropriate.

(15) The activities of the Administrator of ATSDR described in this subsection and section 9611(c)(4) of this title shall be carried out by the Administrator of ATSDR, either directly or through cooperative agreements with States (or political subdivisions thereof) which the Administrator of ATSDR determines are capable of carrying out such activities. Such activities shall include provision of consultations on health information, the conduct of health assessments, including those required under section 3019(b) of the Solid Waste Disposal Act [42 U.S.C. 6939a(b)], health studies, registries, and health surveillance.

(16) The President shall provide adequate personnel for ATSDR, which shall not be fewer than 100 employees. For purposes of determining the number of employees under this subsection, an employee employed by ATSDR on a part-time career employment basis shall be counted as a fraction which is determined by dividing 40 hours into the average number of hours of such employee's regularly scheduled workweek.

(17) In accordance with section 9620 of this title (relating to Federal facilities), the Administrator of ATSDR shall have the same authorities under this section with respect to facilities owned or operated by a department, agency, or instrumentality of the United States as the Administrator of ATSDR has with respect to any nongovernmental entity.

(18) If the Administrator of ATSDR determines that it is appropriate for purposes of this section to treat a pollutant or contaminant as a hazardous substance, such pollutant or contaminant shall be treated as a hazardous substance for such purpose.

(j) ACQUISITION OF PROPERTY

(1) AUTHORITY

The President is authorized to acquire, by purchase, lease, condemnation, donation, or otherwise, any real property or any interest in real property that the President in his discretion determines is needed to conduct a remedial action under this chapter. There shall be no cause of action to compel the President to acquire any interest in real property under this chapter.

(2) STATE ASSURANCE

The President may use the authority of paragraph (1) for a remedial action only if, before an interest in real estate is acquired under this subsection, the State in which the interest to be acquired is located assures the President, through a contract or cooperative agreement or otherwise, that the

State will accept transfer of the interest following completion of the remedial action.

(3) EXEMPTION

No Federal, State, or local government agency shall be liable under this chapter solely as a result of acquiring an interest in real estate under this subsection.

§9605. NATIONAL CONTINGENCY PLAN

(a) REVISION AND REPUBLICATION

Within one hundred and eighty days after December 11, 1980, the President shall, after notice and opportunity for public comments, revise and republish the national contingency plan for the removal of oil and hazardous substances, originally prepared and published pursuant to section 1321 of title 33, to reflect and effectuate the responsibilities and powers created by this chapter, in addition to those matters specified in section 1321(c)(2) of title 33. Such revision shall include a section of the plan to be known as the national hazardous substance response plan which shall establish procedures and standards for responding to releases of hazardous substances, pollutants, and contaminants, which shall include at a minimum:

(1) methods for discovering and investigating facilities at which hazardous substances have been disposed of or otherwise come to be located;

(2) methods for evaluating, including analyses of relative cost, and remedying any releases or threats of releases from facilities which pose substantial danger to the public health or the environment;

(3) methods and criteria for determining the appropriate extent of removal, remedy, and other measures authorized by this chapter;

(4) appropriate roles and responsibilities for the Federal, State, and local governments and for interstate and nongovernmental entities in effectuating the plan;

(5) provision for identification, procurement, maintenance, and storage of response equipment and supplies;

(6) a method for and assignment of responsibility for reporting the existence of such facilities which may be located on federally owned or controlled properties and any releases of hazardous substances from such facilities;

(7) means of assuring that remedial action measures are cost-effective over the period of potential exposure to the hazardous substances or contaminated materials;

(8)(A) criteria for determining priorities among releases or threatened releases throughout the United States for the purpose of taking remedial action and, to the extent practicable taking into account the potential urgency of such action, for the purpose of taking removal action. Criteria and priorities under this paragraph shall be based upon relative risk or danger to public health or welfare or the environment, in the judgment of the President, taking into account to the extent possible the population at risk, the hazard potential of the hazardous substances at such facilities, the potential for contamination of drinking water supplies, the potential for direct human contact, the potential for destruction of sensitive ecosystems, the damage to natural resources which may affect the human food chain and which is associated with any release or threatened release, the contamination or potential contamination of the ambient air which is associated with the release or threatened release, State preparedness to assume State costs and responsibilities, and other appropriate factors;

(B) Based upon the criteria set forth in subparagraph (A) of this paragraph, the President shall list as part of the plan national priorities among the known releases or threatened releases throughout the United States and shall revise the list no less often than annually. Within one year after December 11, 1980, and annually thereafter, each State shall establish and submit for consideration by the President priorities for remedial action among known releases and potential releases in that State based upon the criteria set forth in subparagraph (A) of this paragraph. In assembling or revising the national list, the President shall consider any priorities established by the States. To the extent practicable, the highest priority facilities shall be designated individually and shall be referred to as the "top priority among known response targets," and, to the extent practicable, shall include among the one hundred highest priority facilities one such facility from each State which shall be the facility designated by the State as presenting the greatest danger to public health or welfare or the environment among the known facilities in such State. A State shall be allowed to designate its highest priority facility only once. Other priority facilities or incidents may be listed singly or grouped for response priority purposes;

(9) specified roles for private organizations and entities in preparation for response and in responding to releases of hazardous substances, including identification of appropriate qualifications and capacity therefor and including consideration of minority firms in accordance with subsection (f) of this section; and

(10) standards and testing procedures by which alternative or innovative treatment technologies can be determined to be appropriate for utilization in response actions authorized by this chapter.

The plan shall specify procedures, techniques, materials, equipment, and methods to be employed in identifying, removing, or remedying releases of hazardous substances comparable to those required under section 1321(c)(2)(F) and (G) and (j)(1) of title 33. Following publication of the revised national contingency plan, the response to and actions to minimize damage from hazardous substances releases shall, to the greatest extent possible, be in accordance with the provisions of the plan. The President may, from time to time, revise and republish the national contingency plan.

(b) REVISION OF PLAN

Not later than 18 months after the enactment of the Superfund Amendments and Reauthorization Act of 1986 [October 17, 1986], the President shall revise the National Contingency Plan to reflect the requirements of such amendments. The portion of such Plan known as "the National Hazardous Substance Response Plan" shall be revised to provide procedures and standards for remedial actions undertaken pursuant to this chapter which are consistent with amendments made by the Superfund Amendments and Reauthorization Act of 1986 relating to the selection of remedial action.

(c) HAZAED RANKING SYSTEM

(1) REVISION

Not later than 18 months after October 17, 1986, and after publication of notice and opportunity for submission of comments in accordance with section 553 of title 5, the President shall by rule promulgate amendments to the hazard ranking system in effect on September 1, 1984. Such amendments shall assure, to the maximum extent feasible, that the hazard ranking system accurately assesses the relative degree of risk to human health and the environment posed by sites and facilities subject to review. The President shall establish an effective date for the amended hazard ranking system which is not later than 24 months after October 17, 1986. Such amended hazard ranking system shall be applied to any site or facility to be newly listed on the National Priorities List after the effective date established by the President. Until such effective date of the regulations, the hazard ranking system in effect on September 1, 1984, shall continue in full force and effect.

(2) HEALTH ASSESSMENT OF WATER CONTAMINATION RISKS

In carrying out this subsection, the President shall ensure that the human health risks associated with the contamination or potential contamination (either directly or as a result of the runoff of any hazardous substance or pollutant or contaminant from sites or facilities) of surface water are appropriately assessed where such surface water is, or can be, used for recreation or potable water consumption. In making the assessment required pursuant to the preceding sentence, the President shall take into account the potential migration of any hazardous substance or pollutant or contaminant through such surface water to downstream sources of drinking water.

(3) REEVALUATION NOT REQUIRED

The President shall not be required to reevaluate, after October 17, 1986, the hazard ranking of any facility which was evaluated in accordance with the criteria under this section before the effective date of the amendments to the hazard ranking system under this subsection and which was assigned a national priority under the National Contingency Plan.

(4) NEW INFORMATION

Nothing in paragraph (3) shall preclude the President from taking new information into account in undertaking response actions under this chapter.

(d) PETITION FOR ASSESSMENT OF RELEASE

Any person who is, or may be, affected by a release or threatened release of a hazardous substance or pollutant or contaminant, may petition the President to conduct a preliminary assessment of the hazards to public health and the environment which are associated with such release or threatened release. If the President has not previously conducted a preliminary assessment of such release, the President shall, within 12 months after the receipt of any such petition, complete such assessment or provide an explanation of why the assessment is not appropriate. If the preliminary assessment indicates that the release or threatened release concerned may pose a threat to human health or the environment, the President shall promptly evaluate such release or threatened release in accordance with the hazard ranking system referred to in paragraph (8)(A) of subsection (a) of this section to determine the national priority of such release or threatened release.

(e) RELEASES FROM EARLIER SITES

Whenever there has been, after January 1, 1985, a significant release of hazardous substances or pollutants or contaminants from a site which is listed by the President as a "Site Cleaned Up To Date" on the National Priorities List (revised edition, December 1984) the site shall be restored to the National Priorities List, without application of the hazard ranking system.

(f) MINORITY CONTRACTORS

In awarding contracts under this chapter, the President shall consider the availability of qualified minority firms. The President shall describe, as part of any annual report submitted to the Congress under this chapter, the participation of minority firms in contracts carried out under this chapter. Such report shall contain a brief description of the contracts which have been awarded to minority firms under this chapter and of the efforts made by the President to encourage the participation of such firms in programs carried out under this chapter.

(g) SPECIAL STUDY WASTES

(1) APPLICATION

This subsection applies to facilities —
    (A) which as of October 17, 1986, were not included on, or proposed for inclusion on, the National Priorities List; and
    (B) at which special study wastes described in paragraph (2), (3)(A)(ii) or (3)(A)(iii) of section 6921(b) of this title are present in significant quantities, including any such facility from which there has been a release of a special study waste.

(2) CONSIDERATIONS IN ADDING FACILITIES TO NPL

Pending revision of the hazard ranking system under subsection (c) of this section, the President shall consider each of the following factors in adding facilities covered by this section to the National Priorities List:

(A) The extent to which hazard ranking system score for the facility is affected by the presence of any special study waste at, or any release from, such facility.

(B) Available information as to the quantity, toxicity, and concentration of hazardous substances that are constituents of any special study waste at, or released from such facility, the extent of or potential for release of such hazardous constituents, the exposure or potential exposure to human population and the environment, and the degree of hazard to human health or the environment posed by the release of such hazardous constituents at such facility. This subparagraph refers only to available information on actual concentrations of hazardous substances and not on the total quantity of special study waste at such facility.

(3) SAVINGS PROVISIONS

Nothing in this subsection shall be construed to limit the authority of the President to remove any facility which as of October 17, 1986, is included on the National Priorities List from such List, or not to list any facility which as of such date is proposed for inclusion on such list.

(4) INFORMATION GATHERING AND ANALYSIS

Nothing in this chapter shall be construed to preclude the expenditure of monies from the Fund for gathering and analysis of information which will enable the President to consider the specific factors required by paragraph (2).

§9606. ABATEMENT ACTIONS

(a) MAINTENANCE, JURISDICTION, ETC.

In addition to any other action taken by a State or local government, when the President determines that there may be an imminent and substantial endangerment to the public health or welfare or the environment because of an actual or threatened release of a hazardous substance from a facility, he may require the Attorney General of the United States to secure such relief as may be necessary to abate such danger or threat, and the district court of the United States in the district in which the threat occurs shall have jurisdiction to grant such relief as the public interest and the equities of the case may require. The President may also, after notice to the affected State, take other action under this section including, but not limited to, issuing such orders as may be necessary to protect public health and welfare and the environment.

(b) FINES; REIMBURSEMENT

(1) Any person who, without sufficient cause, willfully violates, or fails or refuses to comply with, any order of the President under subsection (a) of this section may, in an action brought in the appropriate United States district court to enforce such order, be fined not more than $25,000 for each day in which such violation occurs or such failure to comply continues.

(2)(A) Any person who receives and complies with the terms of any order issued under subsection (a) of this section may, within 60 days after completion of the required action, petition the President for reimbursement from the Fund for the reasonable costs of such action, plus interest. Any interest payable under this paragraph shall accrue on the amounts expended from the date of expenditure at the same rate as specified for interest on investments of the Hazardous Substance Superfund established under subchapter A of chapter 98 of title 26.

(B) If the President refuses to grant all or part of a petition made under this paragraph, the petitioner may within 30 days of receipt of such refusal file an action against the President in the appropriate United States district court seeking reimbursement from the Fund.

(C) Except as provided in subparagraph (D), to obtain reimbursement, the petitioner shall establish by a preponderance of the evidence that it is not liable for response costs under section 9607(a) of this title and that costs for which it seeks reimbursement are reasonable in light of the action required by the relevant order.

(D) A petitioner who is liable for response costs under section 9607(a) of this title may also recover its reasonable costs of response to the extent that it can demonstrate, on the administrative record, that the President's decision in selecting the response action ordered was arbitrary and capricious or was otherwise not in accordance with law. Reimbursement awarded under this subparagraph shall include all reasonable response costs incurred by the petitioner pursuant to the portions of the order found to be arbitrary and capricious or otherwise not in accordance with law.

(E) Reimbursement awarded by a court under subparagraph (C) or (D) may include appropriate costs, fees, and other expenses in accordance with subsections (a) and (d) of section 2412 of title 28.

(c) GUIDELINES FOR USING IMMINENT HAZARD, ENFORCEMENT, AND EMERGENCY RESPONSE AUTHORITIES; PROMULGATION BY ADMINISTRATOR OF EPA, SCOPE, ETC.

Within one hundred and eighty days after December 11, 1980, the Administrator of the Environmental Protection Agency shall, after consultation with the Attorney General, establish and publish guidelines for using the imminent hazard, enforcement, and emergency response authorities of this section and other existing statutes administered by the Administrator of the Environmental Protection Agency to effectuate the responsibilities and powers created by this chapter. Such guidelines shall to the extent practicable be consistent with the national hazardous substance response plan, and shall include, at a minimum, the assignment of responsibility for coordinating response actions with the issuance of administrative orders, enforcement of standards and permits, the gathering of information, and other imminent hazard and emergency powers authorized by (1) sections 1321(c)(2), 1318, 1319, and 1364(a) of title 33, (2) sections 6927, 6928, 6934, and 6973 of this title, (3) sections 300j-4 and 300i of this title, (4) sections 7413, 7414, and 7603 of this title, and (5) section 2606 of title 15.

§9607. LIABILITY

(a) COVERED PERSONS; SCOPE; RECOVERABLE COSTS AND DAMAGES; INTEREST RATE; "COMPARABLE MATURITY" DATE

Notwithstanding any other provision or rule of law, and subject only to the defenses set forth in subsection (b) of this section —

(1) the owner and operator of a vessel or a facility,

(2) any person who at the time of disposal of any hazardous substance owned or operated any facility at which such hazardous substances were disposed of,

(3) any person who by contract, agreement, or otherwise arranged for disposal or treatment, or arranged with a transporter for transport for disposal or treatment, of hazardous substances owned or possessed by such person, by any other party or entity, at any facility or incineration vessel owned or operated by another party or entity and containing such hazardous substances, and

(4) any person who accepts or accepted any hazardous substances for transport to disposal or treatment facilities, incineration vessels or sites selected by such person, from which there is a release, or a threatened release which causes the incurrence of response costs, of a hazardous substance, shall be liable for —

(A) all costs of removal or remedial action incurred by the United States Government or a State or an Indian tribe not inconsistent with the national contingency plan;

(B) any other necessary costs of response incurred by any other person consistent with the national contingency plan;

(C) damages for injury to, destruction of, or loss of natural resources, including the reasonable costs of assessing such injury, destruction, or loss resulting from such a release; and

(D) the costs of any health assessment or health effects study carried out under section 9604(i) of this title.

The amounts recoverable in an action under this section shall include interest on the amounts recoverable under subparagraphs (A) through (D). Such interest shall accrue from the later of (i) the date payment of a specified amount is demanded in writing, or (ii) the date of the expenditure concerned. The rate of interest on the outstanding unpaid balance of the amounts recoverable under this section shall be the same rate as is specified for interest on investments of the Hazardous Substance Superfund established under subchapter A of chapter 98 of title 26. For purposes of applying such amendments to interest under this subsection, the term "comparable maturity" shall be determined with reference to the date on which interest accruing under this subsection commences.

(b) DEFENSES

There shall be no liability under subsection (a) of this section for a person otherwise liable who can establish by a preponderance of the evidence that the release or threat of release of a hazardous substance and the damages resulting therefrom were caused solely by —

(1) an act of God;

(2) an act of war;

(3) an act or omission of a third party other than an employee or agent of the defendant, or than one whose act or omission occurs in connection with a contractual relationship, existing directly or indirectly, with the defendant (except where the sole contractual arrangement arises from a published tariff and acceptance for carriage by a common carrier by rail), if the defendant establishes by a preponderance of the evidence that (a) he exercised due care with respect to the hazardous substance concerned, taking into consideration the characteristics of such hazardous substance, in light of all relevant facts and circumstances, and (b) he took precautions against foreseeable acts or omissions of any such third party and the consequences that could foreseeably result from such acts or omissions; or

(4) any combination of the foregoing paragraphs.

(c) DETERMINATION OF AMOUNTS

(1) Except as provided in paragraph (2) of this subsection, the liability under this section of an owner or operator or other responsible person for each release of a hazardous substance or incident involving release of a hazardous substance shall not exceed —

(A) for any vessel, other than an incineration vessel, which carries any hazardous substance as cargo or residue, $300 per gross ton, or $5,000,000, whichever is greater;

(B) for any other vessel, other than an incineration vessel, $300 per gross ton, or $500,000, whichever is greater;

(C) for any motor vehicle, aircraft, pipeline (as defined in the Hazardous Liquid Pipeline Safety Act of 1979 [49 App. U.S.C. 2001 et seq.]), or rolling stock, $50,000,000 or such lesser amount as the President shall establish by regulation, but in no event less than $5,000,000 (or, for releases of hazardous substances as defined in section 9601(14)(A) of this title into the navigable waters, $8,000,000). Such regulations shall take into account the size, type, location, storage, and handling capacity and other matters relating to the likelihood of release in each such class and to the economic impact of such limits on each such class; or

(D) for any incineration vessel or any facility other than those specified in subparagraph (C) of this paragraph, the total of all costs of response plus $50,000,000 for any damages under this subchapter.

(2) Notwithstanding the limitations in paragraph (1) of this subsection, the liability of an owner or operator or other responsible person under this section shall be the full and total costs of response and damages, if (A)(i) the release or threat of release of a hazardous substance was the result of willful misconduct or willful negligence within the privity or knowledge of such person, or (ii) the primary cause of the release was a violation (within the privity or knowledge of such person) of applicable safety, construction, or operating standards or regulations; or (B) such person fails or refuses to provide all reasonable cooperation and assistance requested by a responsible public official in connection with response activities under the national contingency plan with respect to regulated carriers subject to the provisions of title 49 or vessels subject to the provisions of title 33, 46, or 46 Appendix, subparagraph (A)(ii) of this paragraph shall be deemed to refer to Federal standards or regulations.

(3) If any person who is liable for a release or threat of release of a hazardous substance fails without sufficient cause to properly provide removal or remedial action upon order of the President pursuant to section 9604 or 9606 of this title, such person may be liable to the United States for punitive damages in an amount at least equal to, and not more than three times, the amount of any costs incurred by the Fund as a result of such failure to take proper action. The President is authorized to commence a civil action against any such person to recover the punitive damages, which shall be in addition to any costs recovered from such person pursuant to section 9612(c) of this title. Any moneys received by the United States pursuant to this subsection shall be deposited in the Fund.

(d) RENDERING CARE OR ADVICE

(1) IN GENERAL

Except as provided in paragraph (2), no person shall be liable under this subchapter for costs or damages as a result of actions taken or omitted in the course of rendering care, assistance, or advice in accordance with the National Contingency Plan ("NCP") or at the direction of an onscene coordinator appointed under such plan, with respect to an incident creating a danger to public health or welfare or the environment as a result of any releases of a hazardous substance or the threat thereof. This paragraph shall not preclude liability for costs or damages as the result of negligence on the part of such person.

(2) STATE AND LOCAL GOVERNMENTS

No State or local government shall be liable under this subchapter for costs or damages as a result of actions taken in response to an emergency created by the release or threatened release of a hazardous substance generated by or from a facility owned by another person. This paragraph shall not preclude liability for costs or damages as a result of gross negligence or intentional misconduct by the State or local government. For the purpose of the preceding sentence, reckless, willful, or wanton misconduct shall constitute gross negligence.

(3) SAVINGS PROVISION

This subsection shall not alter the liability of any person covered by the provisions of paragraph (1), (2), (3), or (4) of subsection (a) of this section with respect to the release or threatened release concerned.

(e) INDEMNIFICATION, HOLD HARMLESS, ETC., AGREEMENTS OR CONVEYANCES; SUBROGATION RIGHTS

(1) No indemnification, hold harmless, or similar agreement or conveyance shall be effective to transfer from the owner or operator of any vessel or facility or from any person who may be liable for a release or threat of release under this section, to any other person the liability imposed under this section. Nothing in this subsection shall bar any agreement to insure, hold harmless, or indemnify a party to such agreement for any liability under this section.

(2) Nothing in this subchapter, including the provisions of paragraph (1) of this subsection, shall bar a cause of action that an owner or operator or any other person subject to liability under this section, or a guarantor, has or would have, by reason of subrogation or otherwise against any person.

(f) NATURAL RESOURCES LIABILITY; DESIGNATION OF PUBLIC TRUSTEES OF NATURAL RESOURCES

(1) NATURAL RESOURCES LIABILITY

In the case of an injury to, destruction of, or loss of natural resources under subparagraph (C) of subsection (a) of this section liability shall be to the United States Government and to any State for natural resources within the State or belonging to, managed by, controlled by, or appertaining to such State and to any Indian tribe for natural resources belonging to, managed by, controlled by, or appertaining to such tribe, or held in trust for the benefit of such tribe, or belonging to a member of such tribe if such resources are subject to a trust restriction on alienation: *Provided, however,* That no liability to the United States or State or Indian tribe shall be imposed under subparagraph (C) of subsection (a) of this section, where the party sought to be charged has demonstrated that the damages to natural resources complained of were specifically identified as an irreversible and irretrievable commitment of natural resources in an environmental impact statement, or other comparable environment analysis, and the decision to grant a permit or license authorizes such commitment of natural resources, and the facility or project was otherwise operating within the terms of its permit or license, so long as, in the case of damages to an Indian tribe occurring pursuant to a Federal permit or license, the issuance of that permit or license was not inconsistent with the fiduciary duty of the United States with respect to such Indian tribe. The President, or the authorized representative of any State, shall act on behalf of the public as trustee of such natural resources to recover for such damages. Sums recovered by the United States Government as trustee under this subsection shall be retained by the trustee, without further appropriation, for use only to restore, replace, or acquire the equivalent of such natural resources. Sums recovered by a State as trustee under this subsection shall be available for use only to restore, replace, or acquire the equivalent of such natural resources by the State. The measure of damages in any action under subparagraph (C) of subsection (a) of this section shall not be limited by the sums which can be used to restore or replace such resources. There shall be no double recovery under this chapter for natural resource damages, including the costs of damage assessment or restoration, rehabilitation, or acquisition for the same release and natural resource. There shall be no recovery under the authority of subparagraph (C) of subsection (a) of this section where such damages and the release of a hazardous substance from which such damages resulted have occurred wholly before December 11, 1980.

(2) DESIGNATION OF FEDERAL AND STATE OFFICIALS

(A) FEDERAL

The president shall designate in the National Contingency Plan published under section 9605 of this title the Federal officials who shall act on behalf of the public as trustees for natural resources under this chapter and section 1321 of title 33. Such officials shall assess damages for injury to, destruction of, or loss of natural resources for purposes of this chapter and such section 1321 of title 33 for those resources under their trusteeship and may, upon request of and reimbursement from a State and at the Federal officials' discretion, assess damages for those natural resources under the State's trusteeship.

(B) STATE

The Governor of each State shall designate State officials who may act on behalf of the public as trustees for natural resources under this chapter and section 1321 of title 33 and shall notify the President of such designations. Such State officials shall assess damages to natural resources for the purposes of this chapter and such section 1321 of title 33 for those natural resources under their trusteeship.

(C) REBUTTABLE PRESUMPTION

Any determination or assessment of damages to natural resources for the purposes of this chapter and section 1321 of title 33 made by a Federal or State trustee in accordance with the regulations promulgated under section 9651(c) of this title shall have the force and effect of a rebuttable presumption on behalf of the trustee in any administrative or judicial proceeding under this chapter or section 1321 of title 33.

(g) **FEDERAL AGENCIES**

For provisions relating to Federal agencies, see section 9620 of this title.

(h) **OWNER OR OPERATOR OF VESSEL**

The owner or operator of a vessel shall be liable in accordance with this section, under maritime tort law, and as provided under section 9614 of this title notwithstanding any provision of the Act of March 3, 1851 (46 U.S.C. 183ff) [46 App. U.S.C. 182, 183, 184-188] or the absence of any physical damage to the proprietary interest of the claimant.

(i) **APPLICATION OF A REGISTERED PESTICIDE PRODUCT**

No person (including the United States or any State or Indian tribe) may recover under the authority of this section for any response costs or damages resulting from the application of a pesticide product registered under the Federal Insecticide, Fungicide, and Rodenticide Act [7 U.S.C. 136 et seq.]. Nothing in this paragraph shall affect or modify in any way the obligations or liability of any person under any other provision of State or Federal law, including common law, for damages, injury, or loss resulting from a release of any hazardous substance or for removal or remedial action or the costs of removal or remedial action of such hazardous substance.

(j) **OBLIGATIONS OR LIABILITY PURSUANT TO FEDERALLY PERMITTED RELEASE**

Recovery by any person (including the United States or any State or Indian tribe) for response costs or damages resulting from a federally permitted release shall be pursuant to existing law in lieu of this section. Nothing in this paragraph shall affect or modify in any way the obligations or liability of any person under any other provision of State or Federal law, including common law, for damages, injury, or loss resulting from a release of any hazardous substance or for removal or remedial action or the costs of removal or remedial action of such hazardous substance. In addition, costs of response incurred by the Federal Government in connection with a discharge specified in section 9601(10)(B) or (C) of this title shall be recoverable in an action brought under section 1319(b) of title 33.

(k) **TRANSFER TO, AND ASSUMPTION BY, POST-CLOSURE LIABILITY FUND OF LIABILITY OF OWNER OR OPERATOR OF HAZARDOUS WASTE DISPOSAL FACILITY IN RECEIPT OF PERMIT UNDER APPLICABLE SOLID WASTE DISPOSAL LAW; TIME, CRITERIA APPLICABLE, PROCEDURES, ETC.; MONITORING COSTS; REPORTS**

(1) The liability established by this section or any other law for the owner or operator of a hazardous waste disposal facility which has received a permit under subtitle C of the Solid Waste Disposal Act [42 U.S.C. 6921 et seq.], shall be transferred to and assumed by the Post-closure Liability Fund established by section 9641[5] of this title when —

5. See References in Text note below.

(A) such facility and the owner and operator thereof has complied with the requirements of subtitle C of the Solid Waste Disposal Act [42 U.S.C. 6921 et seq.] and regulations issued thereunder, which may affect the performance of such facility after closure; and

(B) such facility has been closed in accordance with such regulations and the conditions of such permit, and such facility and the surrounding area have been monitored as required by such regulations and permit conditions for a period not to exceed five years after closure to demonstrate that there is no substantial likelihood that any migration off-site or release from confinement of any hazardous substance or other risk to public health or welfare will occur.

(2) Such transfer of liability shall be effective ninety days after the owner or operator of such facility notifies the Administrator of the Environmental Protection Agency (and the State where it has an authorized program under section 3006(b) of the Solid Waste Disposal Act [42 U.S.C. 6926(b)]) that the conditions imposed by this subsection have been satisfied. If within such ninety-day period the Administrator of the Environmental Protection Agency or such State determines that any such facility has not complied with all the conditions imposed by this subsection or that insufficient information has been provided to demonstrate such compliance, the Administrator or such State shall so notify the owner and operator of such facility and the administrator of the Fund established by section 9641[5] of this title, and the owner and operator of such facility shall continue to be liable with respect to such facility under this section and other law until such time as the Administrator and such State determines that such facility has complied with all conditions imposed by this subsection. A determination by the Administrator or such State that a facility has not complied with all conditions imposed by this subsection or that insufficient information has been supplied to demonstrate compliance, shall be a final administrative action for purposes of judicial review. A request for additional information shall state in specific terms the data required.

(3) In addition to the assumption of liability of owners and operators under paragraph (1) of this subsection, the Post-closure Liability Fund established by section 9641[5] of this title may be used to pay costs of monitoring and care and maintenance of a site incurred by other persons after the period of monitoring required by regulations under subtitle C of the Solid Waste Disposal Act [42 U.S.C. 6921 et seq.] for hazardous waste disposal facilities meeting the conditions of paragraph (1) of this subsection.

(4)(A) Not later than one year after December 11, 1980, the Secretary of the Treasury shall conduct a study and shall submit a report thereon to the Congress on the feasibility of establishing or qualifying an optional system of private insurance for postclosure financial responsibility for hazardous waste disposal facilities to which this subsection applies. Such study shall include a specification of adequate and realistic minimum standards to assure that any such privately placed insurance will carry out the purposes of this subsection in a reliable, enforceable, and practical manner. Such a study shall include an examination of the public and private incentives, programs, and actions necessary to make privately placed insurance a practical and effective option to the financing system for the Post-closure Liability Fund provided in subchapter II[6] of this chapter.

(B) Not later than eighteen months after December 11, 1980, and after a public hearing, the President shall by rule determine whether or not it is feasible to establish or qualify an optional system of private insurance for postclosure financial responsibility for hazardous waste disposal facilities to which this subsection applies. If the President determines the establishment or qualification of such a system would be infeasible, he shall promptly publish an explanation of the reasons for such a determination. If the President determines the establishment or qualification of such a system would be feasible, he shall promptly publish notice of such determination. Not later than six months after an affirmative determination under the preceding sentence and after a public hearing, the President shall by rule promulgate adequate and realistic minimum standards which must be met by any such privately placed insurance, taking into account the purposes of this chapter and this subsection. Such rules shall also specify reasonably expeditious procedures by which privately placed insurance plans can qualify as meeting such minimum standards.

(C) In the event any privately placed insurance plan qualifies under subparagraph (B), any person enrolled in, and complying with the terms of, such plan shall be excluded from the provisions of paragraphs (1), (2), and (3) of this subsection and exempt from the requirements to pay any tax or fee to the Post-closure Liability Fund under subchapter II[6] of this chapter.

(D) The President may issue such rules and take such other actions as are necessary to effectuate the purposes of this paragraph.

(5) Suspension of liability transfer. — Notwithstanding paragraphs (1), (2), (3), and (4) of this subsection and subsection (j) of section 9611 of this title, no liability shall be transferred to or assumed by the Post-Closure Liability Trust Fund established by section 9641[6] of this title prior to completion of the study required under paragraph (6) of this subsection, transmission of a report of such study to both Houses of Congress, and authorization of such a transfer or assumption by Act of Congress following receipt of such study and report.

(6) Study of options for post-closure program. —

(A) STUDY

The Comptroller General shall conduct a study of options for a program for the management of the liabilities associated with hazardous waste treatment, storage, and disposal sites after their closure which complements the policies set forth in the Hazardous and Solid Waste Amendments of 1984 and assures the protection of human health and the environment.

6. See References in Text note below.

CERCLA §9607

(B) PROGRAM ELEMENTS

The program referred to in subparagraph (A) shall be designed to assure each of the following:

(i) Incentives are created and maintained for the safe management and disposal of hazardous wastes so as to assure protection of human health and the environment.

(ii) Members of the public will have reasonable confidence that hazardous wastes will be managed and disposed of safely and that resources will be available to address any problems that may arise and to cover costs of long-term monitoring, care, and maintenance of such sites.

(iii) Persons who are or seek to become owners and operators of hazardous waste disposal facilities will be able to manage their potential future liabilities and to attract the investment capital necessary to build, operate, and close such facilities in a manner which assures protection of human health and the environment.

(C) ASSESSMENTS

The study under this paragraph shall include assessments of treatment, storage, and disposal facilities which have been or are likely to be issued a permit under section 3005 of the Solid Waste Disposal Act [42 U.S.C. 6925] and the likelihood of future insolvency on the part of owners and operators of such facilities. Separate assessments shall be made for different classes of facilities and for different classes of land disposal facilities and shall include but not be limited to —

(i) the current and future financial capabilities of facility owners and operators;

(ii) the current and future costs associated with facilities, including the costs of routine monitoring and maintenance, compliance monitoring, corrective action, natural resource damages, and liability for damages to third parties; and

(iii) the availability of mechanisms by which owners and operators of such facilities can assure that current and future costs, including post-closure costs, will be financed.

(D) PROCEDURES

In carrying out the responsibilities of this paragraph, the Comptroller General shall consult with the Administrator, the Secretary of Commerce, the Secretary of the Treasury, and the heads of other appropriate Federal agencies.

(E) CONSIDERATION OF OPTIONS

In conducting the study under this paragraph, the Comptroller General shall consider various mechanisms and combinations of mechanisms to complement the policies set forth in the Hazardous and Solid Waste Amendments of 1984 to serve the purposes set forth in subparagraph (B) and to assure that the current and future costs associated with hazardous waste facilities, including post-closure costs, will be adequately financed and to the greatest extent possible, borne by the owners and operators of such facilities. Mechanisms to be considered include, but are not limited to —

(i) revisions to closure, post-closure, and financial responsibility requirements under subtitles C and I of the Solid Waste Disposal Act [42 U.S.C. 6921 et seq., 6991 et seq.];

(ii) voluntary risk pooling by owners and operators;

(iii) legislation to require risk pooling by owners and operators;

(iv) modification of the Post-Closure Liability Trust Fund previously established by section 9641[6] of this title, and the conditions for transfer of liability under this subsection, including limiting the transfer of some or all liability under this subsection only in the case of insolvency of owners and operators;

(v) private insurance;

(vi) insurance provided by the Federal Government;

(vii) coinsurance, reinsurance, or pooled-risk insurance, whether provided by the private sector or provided or assisted by the Federal Government; and

(viii) creation of a new program to be administered by a new or existing Federal agency or by a federally chartered corporation.

(F) RECOMMENDATIONS

The Comptroller General shall consider options for funding any program under this section and shall, to the extent necessary, make recommendations to the appropriate committees of Congress for additional authority to implement such program.

(*l*) FEDERAL LIEN

(1) IN GENERAL

All costs and damages for which a person is liable to the United States under subsection (a) of this section (other than the owner or operator of a vessel under paragraph (1) of subsection (a) of this section) shall constitute a lien in favor of the United States upon all real property and rights to such property which —

(A) belong to such person; and

(B) are subject to or affected by a removal or remedial action.

(2) DURATION

The lien imposed by this subsection shall arise at the later of the following:

(A) The time costs are first incurred by the United States with respect to a response action under this chapter.

(B) The time that the person referred to in paragraph (1) is provided (by certified or registered mail) written notice of potential liability.

Such lien shall continue until the liability for the costs (or a judgment against the person arising out of such liability) is satisfied or becomes unenforceable through operation of the statute of limitations provided in section 9613 of this title.

(3) NOTICE AND VALIDITY

The lien imposed by this subsection shall be subject to the rights of any purchaser, holder of a security interest, or judgment lien creditor whose interest is perfected under applicable State law before notice of the lien has been filed in the appropriate office within the State (or county or other governmental subdivision), as designated by State law, in which the real property subject to the lien is located. Any such purchaser, holder of a security interest, or judgment lien creditor shall be afforded the same protections against the lien imposed by this subsection as are afforded under State law against a judgment lien which arises out of an unsecured obligation and which arises as of the time of the filing of the notice of the lien imposed by this subsection. If the State has not by law designated one office for the receipt of such notices of liens, the notice shall be filed in the office of the clerk of the United States district court for the district in which the real property is located. For purposes of this subsection, the terms "purchaser" and "security interest" shall have the definitions provided under section 6323(h) of title 26.

(4) ACTION IN REM

The costs constituting the lien may be recovered in an action in rem in the United States district court for the district in which the removal or remedial action is occurring or has occurred. Nothing in this subsection shall affect the right of the United States to bring an action against any person to recover all costs and damages for which such person is liable under subsection (a) of this section.

(m) MARITIME LIEN

All costs and damages for which the owner or operator of a vessel is liable under subsection (a)(1) of this section with respect to a release or threatened release from such vessel shall constitute a maritime lien in favor of the United States on such vessel. Such costs may be recovered in an action in rem in the district court of the United States for the district in which the vessel may be found. Nothing in this subsection shall affect the right of the United States to bring an action against the owner or operator of such vessel in any court of competent jurisdiction to recover such costs.

§9608. Financial Responsibility

(a) ESTABLISHMENT AND MAINTENANCE BY OWNER OR OPERATOR OF VESSEL; AMOUNT; FAILURE TO OBTAIN CERTIFICATION OF COMPLIANCE

(1) The owner or operator of each vessel (except a nonself-propelled barge that does not carry hazardous substances as cargo) over three hundred gross tons that uses any port or place in the United States or the navigable waters or any offshore facility, shall establish and maintain, in accordance with regulations promulgated by the President, evidence of financial responsibility of $300 per gross ton (or for a vessel carrying hazardous substances as cargo, or $5,000,000, whichever is greater) to cover the liability prescribed under paragraph (1) of section 9607(a) of this title. Financial responsibility may be established by any one, or any combination, of the following: insurance, guarantee, surety bond, or qualification as a self-insurer. Any bond filed shall be issued by a bonding company authorized to do business in the United States. In cases where an owner or operator owns, operates, or charters more than one vessel subject to this subsection, evidence of financial responsibility need be established only to meet the maximum liability applicable to the largest of such vessels.

(2) The Secretary of the Treasury shall withhold or revoke the clearance required by section 91 of title 46, Appendix, of any vessel subject to this subsection that does not have certification furnished by the President that the financial responsibility provisions of paragraph (1) of this subsection have been complied with.

(3) The Secretary of Transportation, in accordance with regulations issued by him, shall (A) deny entry to any port or place in the United States or navigable waters to, and (B) detain at the port or place in the United States from which it is about to depart for any other port or place in the United States, any vessel subject to this subsection that, upon request, does not produce certification furnished by the President that the financial responsibility provisions of paragraph (1) of this subsection have been complied with.

(4) In addition to the financial responsibility provisions of paragraph (1) of this subsection, the President shall require additional evidence of financial responsibility for incineration vessels in such amounts, and to cover such liabilities recognized by law, as the President deems appropriate, taking into account the potential risks posed by incineration and transport for incineration, and any other factors deemed relevant.

(b) ESTABLISHMENT AND MAINTENANCE BY OWNER OR OPERATOR OF PRODUCTION, ETC., FACILITIES; AMOUNT; ADJUSTMENT; CONSOLIDATED FORM OF RESPONSIBILITY; COVERAGE OF MOTOR CARRIERS

(1) Beginning not earlier than five years after December 11, 1980, the President shall promulgate requirements (for facilities in addition to those under subtitle C of the Solid Waste Disposal Act [42 U.S.C. 6921 et seq.] and other Federal law) that classes of facilities establish and maintain evidence of financial

responsibility consistent with the degree and duration of risk associated with the production, transportation, treatment, storage, or disposal of hazardous substances. Not later than three years after December 11, 1980, the President shall identify those classes for which requirements will be first developed and publish notice of such identification in the Federal Register. Priority in the development of such requirements shall be accorded to those classes of facilities, owners, and operators which the President determines present the highest level of risk of injury.

(2) The level of financial responsibility shall be initially established, and, when necessary, adjusted to protect against the level of risk which the President in his discretion believes is appropriate based on the payment experience of the Fund, commercial insurers, courts settlements and judgments, and voluntary claims satisfaction. To the maximum extent practicable, the President shall cooperate with and seek the advice of the commercial insurance industry in developing financial responsibility requirements. Financial responsibility may be established by any one, or any combination, of the following: insurance, guarantee, surety bond, letter of credit, or qualification as a self-insurer. In promulgating requirements under this section, the President is authorized to specify policy or other contractual terms, conditions, or defenses which are necessary, or which are unacceptable, in establishing such evidence of financial responsibility in order to effectuate the purposes of this chapter.

(3) Regulations promulgated under this subsection shall incrementally impose financial responsibility requirements as quickly as can reasonably be achieved but in no event more than 4 years after the date of promulgation. Where possible, the level of financial responsibility which the President believes appropriate as a final requirement shall be achieved through incremental, annual increases in the requirements.

(4) Where a facility is owned or operated by more than one person, evidence of financial responsibility covering the facility may be established and maintained by one of the owners or operators, or, in consolidated form, by or on behalf of two or more owners or operators. When evidence of financial responsibility is established in a consolidated form, the proportional share of each participant shall be shown. The evidence shall be accompanied by a statement authorizing the applicant to act for and in behalf of each participant in submitting and maintaining the evidence of financial responsibility.

(5) The requirements for evidence of financial responsibility for motor carriers covered by this chapter shall be determined under section 30 of the Motor Carrier Act of 1980, Public Law 96-296.

(c) **DIRECT ACTION**

(1) **RELEASES FROM VESSELS**

In the case of a release or threatened release from a vessel, any claim authorized by section 9607 or 9611 of this title may be asserted directly against any guarantor providing evidence of financial responsibility for such vessel under subsection (a) of this section. In defending such a claim, the guarantor may invoke all rights and defenses which would be available to the owner or operator under this subchapter. The guarantor may also invoke the defense that the incident was caused by the willful misconduct of the owner or operator, but the guarantor may not invoke any other defense that the guarantor might have been entitled to invoke in a proceeding brought by the owner or operator against him.

(2) RELEASES FROM FACILITIES

In the case of a release or threatened release from a facility, any claim authorized by section 9607 or 9611 of this title may be asserted directly against any guarantor providing evidence of financial responsibility for such facility under subsection (b) of this section, if the person liable under section 9607 of this title is in bankruptcy, reorganization, or arrangement pursuant to the Federal Bankruptcy Code, or if, with reasonable diligence, jurisdiction in the Federal courts cannot be obtained over a person liable under section 9607 of this title who is likely to be solvent at the time of judgment. In the case of any action pursuant to this paragraph, the guarantor shall be entitled to invoke all rights and defenses which would have been available to the person liable under section 9607 of this title if any action had been brought against such person by the claimant and all rights and defenses which would have been available to the guarantor if an action had been brought against the guarantor by such person.

(d) LIMITATION OF GUARANTOR LIABILITY

(1) TOTAL LIABILITY

The total liability of any guarantor in a direct action suit brought under this section shall be limited to the aggregate amount of the monetary limits of the policy of insurance, guarantee, surety bond, letter of credit, or similar instrument obtained from the guarantor by the person subject to liability under section 9607 of this title for the purpose of satisfying the requirement for evidence of financial responsibility.

(2) OTHER LIABILITY

Nothing in this subsection shall be construed to limit any other State or Federal statutory, contractual, or common law liability of a guarantor, including, but not limited to, the liability of such guarantor for bad faith either in negotiating or in failing to negotiate the settlement of any claim. Nothing in this subsection shall be construed, interpreted, or applied to diminish the liability of any person under section 9607 of this title or other applicable law.

CERCLA §9609

§9609. Civil Penalties and Awards

(a) Class I Administrative Penalty

(1) Violations

A civil penalty of not more than $25,000 per violation may be assessed by the President in the case of any of the following —

(A) A violation of the requirements of section 9603(a) or (b) of this title (relating to notice).

(B) A violation of the requirements of section 9603(d)(2) of this title (relating to destruction of records, etc.).

(C) A violation of the requirements of section 9608 of this title (relating to financial responsibility, etc.), the regulations issued under section 9608 of this title, or with any denial or detention order under section 9608 of this title.

(D) A violation of an order under section 9622(d)(3) of this title (relating to settlement agreements for action under section 9604(b) of this title).

(E) Any failure or refusal referred to in section 9622(*l*) of this title (relating to violations of administrative orders, consent decrees, or agreements under section 9620 of this title).

(2) Notice and Hearings

No civil penalty may be assessed under this subsection unless the person accused of the violation is given notice and opportunity for a hearing with respect to the violation.

(3) Determining Amount

In determining the amount of any penalty assessed pursuant to this subsection, the President shall take into account the nature, circumstances, extent and gravity of the violation or violations and, with respect to the violator, ability to pay, any prior history of such violations, the degree of culpability, economic benefit or savings (if any) resulting from the violation, and such other matters as justice may require.

(4) Review

Any person against whom a civil penalty is assessed under this subsection may obtain review thereof in the appropriate district court of the United States by filing a notice of appeal in such court within 30 days from the date of such order and by simultaneously sending a copy of such notice by certified mail to the President. The President shall promptly file in such court a certified copy of the record upon which such violation was found or such penalty imposed. If any person fails to pay an assessment of a civil penalty after it has become a final and unappealable order or after the appropriate court has entered final judgment in favor of the United States, the President may request the Attorney General of the United States to institute a civil action in an appropriate district court of the United States to collect the penalty, and such court shall have jurisdiction to hear and decide any such action. In hearing such action, the court shall have authority to review the violation and the assessment of the civil penalty on the record.

(5) SUBPOENAS

The President may issue subpoenas for the attendance and testimony of witnesses and the production of relevant papers, books, or documents in connection with hearings under this subsection. In case of contumacy or refusal to obey a subpoena issued pursuant to this paragraph and served upon any person, the district court of the United States for any district in which such person is found, resides, or transacts business, upon application by the United States and after notice to such person, shall have jurisdiction to issue an order requiring such person to appear and give testimony before the administrative law judge or to appear and produce documents before the administrative law judge, or both, and any failure to obey such order of the court may be punished by such court as a contempt thereof.

(b) CLASS II ADMINISTRATIVE PENALTY

A civil penalty of not more than $25,000 per day for each day during which the violation continues may be assessed by the President in the case of any of the following —

(1) A violation of the notice requirements of section 9603(a) or (b) of this title.

(2) A violation of section 9603(d)(2) of this title (relating to destruction of records, etc.).

(3) A violation of the requirements of section 9608 of this title (relating to financial responsibility, etc.), the regulations issued under section 9608 of this title, or with any denial or detention order under section 9608 of this title.

(4) A violation of an order under section 9622(d)(3) of this title (relating to settlement agreements for action under section 9604(b) of this title).

(5) Any failure or refusal referred to in section 9622(l) of this title (relating to violations of administrative orders, consent decrees, or agreements under section 9620 of this title).

In the case of a second or subsequent violation the amount of such penalty may be not more than $75,000 for each day during which the violation continues. Any civil penalty under this subsection shall be assessed and collected in the same manner, and subject to the same provisions, as in the case of civil penalties assessed and collected after notice and opportunity for hearing on the record in accordance with section 554 of title 5. In any proceeding for the assessment of a civil penalty under this subsection the President may issue subpoenas for the attendance and testimony of witnesses and the production of relevant papers, books, and documents and may promulgate rules for discovery procedures. Any person who requested a hearing with respect to a civil penalty under this subsection and who is aggrieved by an order assessing the civil penalty may file a petition for judicial review of such order with the United States Court of Appeals for the District of Columbia Circuit or for any other circuit in which such person resides or transacts business. Such a petition may only be filed within the 30-day period beginning on the date the order making such assessment was issued.

(c) JUDICIAL ASSESSMENT

The President may bring an action in the United States district court for the appropriate district to assess and collect a penalty of not more than $25,000 per day for each day during which the violation (or failure or refusal) continues in the case of any of the following —

(1) A violation of the notice requirements of section 9603(a) or (b) of this title.

(2) A violation of section 9603(d)(2) of this title (relating to destruction of records, etc.).

(3) A violation of the requirements of section 9608 of this title (relating to financial responsibility, etc.), the regulations issued under section 9608 of this title, or with any denial or detention order under section 9608 of this title.

(4) A violation of an order under section 9622(d)(3) of this title (relating to settlement agreements for action under section 9604(b) of this title).

(5) Any failure or refusal referred to in section 9622(*l*) of this title (relating to violations of administrative orders, consent decrees, or agreements under section 9620 of this title).

In the case of a second or subsequent violation (or failure or refusal), the amount of such penalty may be not more than $75,000 for each day during which the violation (or failure or refusal) continues. For additional provisions providing for judicial assessment of civil penalties for failure to comply with a request or order under section 9604(e) of this title (relating to information gathering and access authorities), see section 9604(e) of this title.

(d) AWARDS

The President may pay an award of up to $10,000 to any individual who provides information leading to the arrest and conviction of any person for a violation subject to a criminal penalty under this chapter, including any violation of section 9603 of this title and any other violation referred to in this section. The President shall, by regulation, prescribe criteria for such an award and may pay any award under this subsection from the Fund, as provided in section 9611 of this title.

(e) PROCUREMENT PROCEDURES

Notwithstanding any other provision of law, any executive agency may use competitive procedures or procedures other than competitive procedures to procure the services of experts for use in preparing or prosecuting a civil or criminal action under this chapter, whether or not the expert is expected to testify at trial. The executive agency need not provide any written justification for the use of procedures other than competitive procedures when procuring such expert services under this chapter and need not furnish for publication in the Commerce Business Daily or otherwise any notice of solicitation or synopsis with respect to such procurement.

(f) SAVINGS CLAUSE

Action taken by the President pursuant to this section shall not affect or limit the President's authority to enforce any provisions of this chapter.

§9610. EMPLOYEE PROTECTION

(a) ACTIVITIES OF EMPLOYEE SUBJECT TO PROTECTION

No person shall fire or in any other way discriminate against, or cause to be fired or discriminated against, any employee or any authorized representative of employees by reason of the fact that such employee or representative has provided information to a State or to the Federal Government, filed, instituted, or caused to be filed or instituted any proceeding under this chapter, or has testified or is about to testify in any proceeding resulting from the administration or enforcement of the provisions of this chapter.

(b) ADMINISTRATIVE GRIEVANCE PROCEDURE IN CASES OF ALLEGED VIOLATIONS

Any employee or a representative of employees who believes that he has been fired or otherwise discriminated against by any person in violation of subsection (a) of this section may, within thirty days after such alleged violation occurs, apply to the Secretary of Labor for a review of such firing or alleged discrimination. A copy of the application shall be sent to such person, who shall be the respondent. Upon receipt of such application, the Secretary of Labor shall cause such investigation to be made as he deems appropriate. Such investigation shall provide an opportunity for a public hearing at the request of any party to such review to enable the parties to present information relating to such alleged violation. The parties shall be given written notice of the time and place of the hearing at least five days prior to the hearing. Any such hearing shall be of record and shall be subject to section 554 of title 5. Upon receiving the report of such investigation, the Secretary of Labor shall make findings of fact. If he finds that such violation did occur, he shall issue a decision, incorporating an order therein and his findings, requiring the party committing such violation to take such affirmative action to abate the violation as the Secretary of Labor deems appropriate, including, but not limited to, the rehiring or reinstatement of the employee or representative of employees to his former position with compensation. If he finds that there was no such violation, he shall issue an order denying the application. Such order issued by the Secretary of Labor under this subparagraph shall be subject to judicial review in the same manner as orders and decisions are subject to judicial review under this chapter.

(c) ASSESSMENT OF COSTS AND EXPENSES AGAINST VIOLATOR SUBSEQUENT TO ISSUANCE OF ORDER OF ABATEMENT

Whenever an order is issued under this section to abate such violation, at the request of the applicant a sum equal to the aggregate amount of all costs and expenses (including the attorney's fees) determined by the Secretary of Labor to have been reasonably incurred by the applicant for, or in connection with, the institution and prosecution of such proceedings, shall be assessed against the person committing such violation.

(d) DEFENSES

This section shall have no application to any employee who acting without discretion from his employer (or his agent) deliberately violates any requirement of this chapter.

(e) PRESIDENTIAL EVALUATIONS OF POTENTIAL LOSS OF SHIFTS OF EMPLOYMENT RESULTING FROM ADMINISTRATION OR ENFORCEMENT OF PROVISIONS; INVESTIGATIONS; PROCEDURES APPLICABLE, ETC.

The President shall conduct continuing evaluations of potential loss of shifts of employment which may result from the administration or enforcement of the provisions of this chapter, including, where appropriate, investigating threatened plant closures or reductions in employment allegedly resulting from such administration or enforcement. Any employee who is discharged, or laid off, threatened with discharge or layoff, or otherwise discriminated against by any person because of the alleged results of such administration or enforcement, or any representative of such employee, may request the President to conduct a full investigation of the matter and, at the request of any party, shall hold public hearings, require the parties, including the employer involved, to present information relating to the actual or potential effect of such administration or enforcement on employment and any alleged discharge, layoff, or other discrimination, and the detailed reasons or justification therefore.[7] Any such hearing shall be of record and shall be subject to section 554 of title 5. Upon receiving the report of such investigation, the President shall make findings of fact as to the effect of such administration or enforcement on employment and on the alleged discharge, layoff, or discrimination and shall make such recommendations as he deems appropriate. Such report, findings, and recommendations shall be available to the public. Nothing in this subsection shall be construed to require or authorize the President or any State to modify or withdraw any action, standard, limitation, or any other requirement of this chapter.

---

7. So in original.

§9611. USE OF FUND

(a) IN GENERAL

For the purposes specified in this section there is authorized to be appropriated from the Hazardous Substance Superfund established under subchapter A of chapter 98 of title 26 not more than $8,500,000,000 for the 5-year period beginning on October 17, 1986, and such sums shall remain available until expended. The preceding sentence constitutes a specific authorization for the funds appropriated under title II of Public Law 99-160 (relating to payment to the Hazardous Substances Trust Fund). The President shall use the money in the Fund for the following purposes:

(1) Payment of governmental response costs incurred pursuant to section 9604 of this title, including costs incurred pursuant to the Intervention on the High Seas Act [33 U.S.C. 1471 et seq.].

(2) Payment of any claim for necessary response costs incurred by any other person as a result of carrying out the national contingency plan established under section 1321(c) of title 33 and amended by section 9605 of this title: *Provided, however,* That such costs must be approved under said plan and certified by the responsible Federal official.

(3) Payment of any claim authorized by subsection (b) of this section and finally decided pursuant to section 9612 of this title, including those costs set out in subsection 9612(c)(3) of this title.

(4) Payment of costs specified under subsection (c) of this section.

(5) Grants for technical assistance. — The cost of grants under section 9617(e) of this title (relating to public participation grants for technical assistance).

(6) Lead contaminated soil. — Payment of not to exceed $15,000,000 for the costs of a pilot program for removal, decontamination, or other action with respect to lead-contaminated soil in one to three different metropolitan areas.

The President shall not pay for any administrative costs or expenses out of the Fund unless such costs and expenses are reasonably necessary for and incidental to the implementation of this subchapter.

(b) ADDITIONAL AUTHORIZED PURPOSES

(1) IN GENERAL

Claims asserted and compensable but unsatisfied under provisions of section 1321 of title 33, which are modified by section 304 of this Act may be asserted against the Fund under this subchapter; and other claims resulting from a release or threat of release of a hazardous substance from a vessel or a facility may be asserted against the Fund under this subchapter for injury to, or destruction or loss of, natural resources, including cost for damage assessment: *Provided, however,* That any such claim may be asserted only by the President, as trustee, for natural resources over which the United States has sovereign rights, or natural resources within the territory or the fishery conservation zone of the United States to the extent they are managed or protected by the United States, or by any State for natural resources within the boundary of that State belonging to, managed by, controlled by, or appertaining to the State, or by any Indian tribe or by the United States acting on behalf of any Indian tribe for natural resources belonging to, managed by, controlled by, or appertaining to such tribe, or held in trust for the benefit of such tribe, or belonging to a member of such tribe if such resources are subject to a trust restriction on alienation.

(2) LIMITATION ON PAYMENT OF NATURAL RESOURCE CLAIMS

(A) GENERAL REQUIREMENTS

No natural resource claim may be paid from the Fund unless the President determines that the claimant has exhausted all administrative and judicial remedies to recover the amount of such claim from persons who may be liable under section 9607 of this title.

(B) DEFINITION

As used in this paragraph, the term "natural resource claim" means any claim for injury to, or destruction or loss of, natural resources. The term does not include any claim for the costs of natural resource damage assessment.

(c) PERIPHERAL MATTERS AND LIMITATIONS

Uses of the Fund under subsection (a) of this section include —

(1) The costs of assessing both short-term and long-term injury to, destruction of, or loss of any natural resources resulting from a release of a hazardous substance.

(2) The costs of Federal or State or Indian tribe efforts in the restoration, rehabilitation, or replacement or acquiring the equivalent of any natural resources injured, destroyed, or lost as a result of a release of a hazardous substance.

(3) Subject to such amounts as are provided in appropriation Acts, the costs of a program to identify, investigate, and take enforcement and abatement action against releases of hazardous substances.

(4) Any costs incurred in accordance with subsection (m) of this section (relating to ATSDR) and section 9604(i) of this title, including the costs of epidemiologic and laboratory studies, health assessments, preparation of toxicologic profiles, development and maintenance of a registry of persons exposed to hazardous substances to allow long-term health effect studies, and diagnostic services not otherwise available to determine whether persons in populations exposed to hazardous substances in connection with a release or a suspected release are suffering from long-latency diseases.

(5) Subject to such amounts as are provided in appropriation Acts, the

costs of providing equipment and similar overhead, related to the purposes of this chapter and section 1321 of title 33, and needed to supplement equipment and services available through contractors or other non-Federal entities, and of establishing and maintaining damage assessment capability, for any Federal agency involved in strike forces, emergency task forces, or other response teams under the national contingency plan.

(6) Subject to such amounts as are provided in appropriation Acts, the costs of a program to protect the health and safety of employees involved in response to hazardous substance releases. Such program shall be developed jointly by the Environmental Protection Agency, the Occupational Safety and Health Administration, and the National Institute for Occupational Safety and Health and shall include, but not be limited to, measures for identifying and assessing hazards to which persons engaged in removal, remedy, or other response to hazardous substances may be exposed, methods to protect workers from such hazards, and necessary regulatory and enforcement measures to assure adequate protection of such employees.

(7) Evaluation costs under petition provisions of section 9605(d). — Costs incurred by the President in evaluating facilities pursuant to petitions under section 9605(d) of this title (relating to petitions for assessment of release).

(8) Contract costs under section 9604(a)(1). — The costs of contracts or arrangements entered into under section 9604(a)(1) of this title to oversee and review the conduct of remedial investigations and feasibility studies undertaken by persons other than the President and the costs of appropriate Federal and State oversight of remedial activities at National Priorities List sites resulting from consent orders or settlement agreements.

(9) Acquisition costs under section 9604(j). — The costs incurred by the President in acquiring real estate or interests in real estate under section 9604(j) of this title (relating to acquisition of property).

(10) Research, development, and demonstration costs under section 9660. — The cost of carrying out section 9660 of this title (relating to research, development, and demonstration), except that the amounts available for such purposes shall not exceed the amounts specified in subsection (n) of this section.

(11) Local government reimbursement. — Reimbursements to local governments under section 9623 of this title, except that during the 5-fiscal-year period beginning October 1, 1986, not more than 0.1 percent of the total amount appropriated from the Fund may be used for such reimbursements.

(12) Worker training and education grants. — The costs of grants under section 9660a of this title for training and education of workers to the extent that such costs do not exceed $10,000,000 for each of the fiscal years 1987, 1988, 1989, 1990, and 1991.

(13) Awards under section 9609. — The costs of any awards granted under section 9609(d) of this title.

(14) Lead poisoning study. — The cost of carrying out the study under

subsection (f) of section 118 of the Superfund Amendments and Reauthorization Act of 1986 (relating to lead poisoning in children).

(d) ADDITIONAL LIMITATIONS

(1) No money in the Fund may be used under subsection (c)(1) and (2) of this section, nor for the payment of any claim under subsection (b) of this section, where the injury, destruction, or loss of natural resources and the release of a hazardous substance from which such damages resulted have occurred wholly before December 11, 1980.

(2) No money in the Fund may be used for the payment of any claim under subsection (b) of this section where such expenses are associated with injury or loss resulting from long-term exposure to ambient concentrations of air pollutants from multiple or diffuse sources.

(e) FUNDING REQUIREMENTS RESPECTING MONEYS IN FUND; LIMITATION ON CERTAIN CLAIMS; FUND USE OUTSIDE FEDERAL PROPERTY BOUNDARIES

(1) Claims against or presented to the Fund shall not be valid or paid in excess of the total money in the Fund at any one time. Such claims become valid only when additional money is collected, appropriated, or otherwise added to the Fund. Should the total claims outstanding at any time exceed the current balance of the Fund, the President shall pay such claims, to the extent authorized under this section, in full in the order in which they were finally determined.

(2) In any fiscal year, 85 percent of the money credited to the Fund under subchapter II[8] of this chapter shall be available only for the purposes specified in paragraphs (1), (2), and (4) of subsection (a) of this section. No money in the Fund may be used for the payment of any claim under subsection (a)(3) or subsection (b) of this section in any fiscal year for which the President determines that all of the Fund is needed for response to threats to public health from releases or threatened releases of hazardous substances.

(3) No money in the Fund shall be available for remedial action, other than actions specified in subsection (c) of this section, with respect to federally owned facilities; except that money in the Fund shall be available for the provision of alternative water supplies (including the reimbursement of costs incurred by a municipality) in any case involving groundwater contamination outside the boundaries of a federally owned facility in which the federally owned facility is not the only potentially responsible party.

(4) Paragraphs (1) and (4) of subsection (a) of this section shall in the aggregate be subject to such amounts as are provided in appropriation Acts.

(f) OBLIGATION OF MONEYS BY FEDERAL OFFICIALS; OBLIGATION OF MONEYS OR SETTLEMENT OF CLAIMS BY STATE OFFICIALS OR INDIAN TRIBE

The President is authorized to promulgate regulations designating one or more Federal officials who may obligate money in the Fund in accordance with

---

8. See References in Text note below.

this section or portions thereof. The President is also authorized to delegate authority to obligate money in the Fund or to settle claims to officials of a State or Indian tribe operating under a contract or cooperative agreement with the Federal Government pursuant to section 9604(d) of this title.

(g) **NOTICE TO POTENTIAL INJURED PARTIES BY OWNER AND OPERATOR OF VESSEL OR FACILITY CAUSING RELEASE OF SUBSTANCE; RULES AND REGULATIONS**

The President shall provide for the promulgation of rules and regulations with respect to the notice to be provided to potential injured parties by an owner and operator of any vessel, or facility from which a hazardous substance has been released. Such rules and regulations shall consider the scope and form of the notice which would be appropriate to carry out the purposes of this subchapter. Upon promulgation of such rules and regulations, the owner and operator of any vessel or facility from which a hazardous substance has been released shall provide notice in accordance with such rules and regulations. With respect to releases from public vessels, the President shall provide such notification as is appropriate to potential injured parties. Until the promulgation of such rules and regulations, the owner and operator of any vessel or facility from which a hazardous substance has been released shall provide reasonable notice to potential injured parties by publication in local newspapers serving the affected area.

(h) **REPEALED. PUB. L. 99-499, TITLE I, §111(c)(2), OCT. 17, 1986, 100 STAT. 1643**

(i) **RESTORATION, ETC., OF NATURAL RESOURCES**

Except in a situation requiring action to avoid an irreversible loss of natural resources or to prevent or reduce any continuing danger to natural resources or similar need for emergency action, funds may not be used under this chapter for the restoration, rehabilitation, or replacement or acquisition of the equivalent of any natural resources until a plan for the use of such funds for such purposes has been developed and adopted by affected Federal agencies and the Governor or Governors of any State having sustained damage to natural resources within its borders, belonging to, managed by or appertaining to such State, and by the governing body of any Indian tribe having sustained damage to natural resources belonging to, managed by, controlled by, or appertaining to such tribe, or held in trust for the benefit of such tribe, or belonging to a member of such tribe if such resources are subject to a trust restriction on alienation, after adequate public notice and opportunity for hearing and consideration of all public comment.

(j) **USE OF POST-CLOSURE LIABILITY FUND**

The President shall use the money in the Post-closure Liability Fund for any of the purposes specified in subsection (a) of this section with respect to a hazardous waste disposal facility for which liability has transferred to such fund under section 9607(k) of this title, and, in addition, for payment of any claim or appropriate request for costs of response, damages, or other compensation for injury or loss under section 9607 of this title or any other State or Federal law, resulting from a release of a hazardous substance from such a facility.

(k) INSPECTOR GENERAL

In each fiscal year, the Inspector General of each department, agency, or instrumentality of the United States which is carrying out any authority of this chapter shall conduct an annual audit of all payments, obligations, reimbursements, or other uses of the Fund in the prior fiscal year, to assure that the Fund is being properly administered and that claims are being appropriately and expeditiously considered. The audit shall include an examination of a sample of agreements with States (in accordance with the provisions of the Single Audit Act [31 U.S.C. 7501 et seq.]) carrying out response actions under this subchapter and an examination of remedial investigations and feasibility studies prepared for remedial actions. The Inspector General shall submit to the Congress an annual report regarding the audit report required under this subsection. The report shall contain such recommendations as the Inspector General deems appropriate. Each department, agency, or instrumentality of the United States shall cooperate with its inspector general in carrying out this subsection.

(*l*) FOREIGN CLAIMANTS

To the extent that the provisions of this chapter permit, a foreign claimant may assert a claim to the same extent that a United States claimant may assert a claim if —

(1) the release of a hazardous substance occurred (A) in the navigable waters or (B) in or on the territorial sea or adjacent shoreline of a foreign country of which the claimant is a resident;

(2) the claimant is not otherwise compensated for his loss;

(3) the hazardous substance was released from a facility or from a vessel located adjacent to or within the navigable waters or was discharged in connection with activities conducted under the Outer Continental Shelf Lands Act, as amended (43 U.S.C. 1331 et seq.) or the Deepwater Port Act of 1974, as amended (33 U.S.C. 1501 et seq.); and

(4) recovery is authorized by a treaty or an executive agreement between the United States and foreign country involved, or if the Secretary of State, in consultation with the Attorney General and other appropriate officials, certifies that such country provides a comparable remedy for United States claimants.

(m) AGENCY FOR TOXIC SUBSTANCES AND DISEASE REGISTRY

There shall be directly available to the Agency for Toxic Substances and Disease Registry to be used for the purpose of carrying out activities described in subsection (c)(4) of this section and section 9604(i) of this title not less than $50,000,000 per fiscal year for each of fiscal years 1987 and 1988, not less than $55,000,000 for fiscal year 1989, and not less than $60,000,000 per fiscal year for each of fiscal years 1990 and 1991. Any funds so made available which are not obligated by the end of the fiscal year in which made available shall be returned to the Fund.

(n) LIMITATIONS ON RESEARCH, DEVELOPMENT, AND DEMONSTRATION PROGRAM

(1) SECTION 9660(b)

For each of the fiscal years 1987, 1988, 1989, 1990, and 1991, not more than $20,000,000 of the amounts available in the Fund may be used for the purposes of carrying out the applied research, development, and demonstration program for alternative or innovative technologies and training program authorized under section 9660(b) of this title (relating to research, development, and demonstration) other than basic research. Such amounts shall remain available until expended.

(2) SECTION 9660(a)

From the amounts available in the Fund, not more than the following amounts may be used for the purposes of section 9660(a) of this title (relating to hazardous substance research, demonstration, and training activities):

(A) For the fiscal year 1987, $3,000,000.
(B) For the fiscal year 1988, $10,000,000.
(C) For the fiscal year 1989, $20,000,000.
(D) For the fiscal year 1990, $30,000,000.
(E) For the fiscal year 1991, $35,000,000.

No more than 10 percent of such amounts shall be used for training under section 9660(a) of this title in any fiscal year.

(3) SECTION 9660(d)

For each of the fiscal years 1987, 1988, 1989, 1990, and 1991, not more than $5,000,000 of the amounts available in the Fund may be used for the purposes of section 9660(d) of this title (relating to university hazardous substance research centers).

(o) NOTIFICATION PROCEDURES FOR LIMITATIONS ON CERTAIN PAYMENTS

Not later than 90 days after October 17, 1986, the President shall develop and implement procedures to adequately notify, as soon as practicable after a site is included on the National Priorities List, concerned local and State officials and other concerned persons of the limitations, set forth in subsection (a)(2) of this section, on the payment of claims for necessary response costs incurred with respect to such site.

(p) GENERAL REVENUE SHARE OF SUPERFUND

(1) IN GENERAL

The following sums are authorized to be appropriated, out of any money in the Treasury not otherwise appropriated, to the Hazardous Substance Superfund:

(A) For fiscal year 1987, $212,500,000.
(B) For fiscal year 1988, $212,500,000.
(C) For fiscal year 1989, $212,500,000.
(D) For fiscal year 1990, $212,500,000.
(E) For fiscal year 1991, $212,500,000.

In addition there is authorized to be appropriated to the Hazardous Substance Superfund for each fiscal year an amount equal to so much of the aggregate amount authorized to be appropriated under this subsection (and paragraph (2) of section 9631(b))[9] of this title) as has not been appropriated before the beginning of the fiscal year involved.

(2) COMPUTATION

The amounts authorized to be appropriated under paragraph (1) of this subsection in a given fiscal year shall be available only to the extent that such amount exceeds the amount determined by the Secretary under section 9507(b)(2) of title 26 for the prior fiscal year.

§9612. CLAIMS PROCEDURE

(a) CLAIMS AGAINST FUND FOR RESPONSE COSTS

No claim may be asserted against the Fund pursuant to section 9611(a) of this title unless such claim is presented in the first instance to the owner, operator, or guarantor of the vessel or facility from which a hazardous substance has been released, if known to the claimant, and to any other person known to the claimant who may be liable under section 9607 of this title. In any case where the claim has not been satisfied within 60 days of presentation in accordance with this subsection, the claimant may present the claim to the Fund for payment. No claim against the Fund may be approved or certified during the pendency of an action by the claimant in court to recover costs which are the subject of the claim.

(b) · FORMS AND PROCEDURES APPLICABLE

(1) PRESCRIBING FORMS AND PROCEDURES

The President shall prescribe appropriate forms and procedures for claims filed hereunder, which shall include a provision requiring the claimant to make a sworn verification of the claim to the best of his knowledge. Any person who knowingly gives or causes to be given any false information as a part of any such claim shall, upon conviction, be fined in accordance with the applicable provisions of title 18 or imprisoned for not more than 3 years (or not more than 5 years in the case of a second or subsequent conviction), or both.

---

9. See References in Text note below.

(2) **PAYMENT OR REQUEST FOR HEARING**

The President may, if satisfied that the information developed during the processing of the claim warrants it, make and pay an award of the claim, except that no claim may be awarded to the extent that a judicial judgment has been made on the costs that are the subject of the claim. If the President declines to pay all or part of the claim, the claimant may, within 30 days after receiving notice of the President's decision, request an administrative hearing.

(3) **BURDEN OF PROOF**

In any proceeding under this subsection, the claimant shall bear the burden of proving his claim.

(4) **DECISIONS**

All administrative decisions made hereunder shall be in writing, with notification to all appropriate parties, and shall be rendered within 90 days of submission of a claim to an administrative law judge, unless all the parties to the claim agree in writing to an extension or unless the President, in his discretion, extends the time limit for a period not to exceed sixty days.

(5) **FINALITY AND APPEAL**

All administrative decisions hereunder shall be final, and any party to the proceeding may appeal a decision within 30 days of notification of the award or decision. Any such appeal shall be made to the Federal district court for the district where the release or threat of release took place. In any such appeal, the decision shall be considered binding and conclusive, and shall not be overturned except for arbitrary or capricious abuse of discretion.

(6) **PAYMENT**

Within 20 days after the expiration of the appeal period for any administrative decision concerning an award, or within 20 days after the final judicial determination of any appeal taken pursuant to this subsection, the President shall pay any such award from the Fund. The President shall determine the method, terms, and time of payment.

(c) **SUBROGATION RIGHTS; ACTIONS MAINTAINABLE**

(1) Payment of any claim by the Fund under this section shall be subject to the United States Government acquiring by subrogation the rights of the claimant to recover those costs of removal or damages for which it has compensated the claimant from the person responsible or liable for such release.

(2) Any person, including the Fund, who pays compensation pursuant to this chapter to any claimant for damages or costs resulting from a release of a hazardous substance shall be subrogated to all rights, claims, and causes of action for such damages and costs of removal that the claimant has under this chapter or any other law.

(3) Upon request of the President, the Attorney General shall commence an action on behalf of the Fund to recover any compensation paid by the Fund to any claimant pursuant to this subchapter, and, without regard to any limitation of liability, all interest, administrative and adjudicative costs, and attorney's fees incurred by the Fund by reason of the claim. Such an action may be commenced against any owner, operator, or guarantor, or against any other person who is liable, pursuant to any law, to the compensated claimant or to the Fund, for the damages or costs for which compensation was paid.

(d) STATUTE OF LIMITATIONS

(1) CLAIMS FOR RECOVERY OF COSTS

No claim may be presented under this section for recovery of the costs referred to in section 9607(a) of this title after the date 6 years after the date of completion of all response action.

(2) CLAIMS FOR RECOVERY OF DAMAGES

No claim may be presented under this section for recovery of the damages referred to in section 9607(a) of this title unless the claim is presented within 3 years after the later of the following:

(A) The date of the discovery of the loss and its connection with the release in question.

(B) The date on which final regulations are promulgated under section 9651(c) of this title.

(3) MINORS AND INCOMPETENTS

The time limitations contained herein shall not begin to run—

(A) against a minor until the earlier of the date when such minor reaches 18 years of age or the date on which a legal representative is duly appointed for the minor, or

(B) against an incompetent person until the earlier of the date on which such person's incompetency ends or the date on which a legal representative is duly appointed for such incompetent person.

(e) OTHER STATUTORY OR COMMON LAW CLAIMS NOT WAIVED, ETC.

Regardless of any State statutory or common law to the contrary, no person who asserts a claim against the Fund pursuant to this subchapter shall be deemed or held to have waived any other claim not covered or assertable against the Fund under this subchapter arising from the same incident, transaction, or set of circumstances, nor to have split a cause of action. Further, no person asserting a claim against the Fund pursuant to this subchapter shall as a result of any determination of a question of fact or law made in connection with that claim be deemed or held to be collaterally estopped from raising such question in connection with any other claim not covered or assertable against the Fund under this subchapter arising from the same incident, transaction, or set of circumstances.

(f) DOUBLE RECOVERY PROHIBITED

Where the President has paid out of the Fund for any response costs or any costs specified under section 9611(c)(1) and (2) of this title, no other claim may be paid out of the Fund for the same costs.

§9613. CIVIL PROCEEDINGS

(a) REVIEW OF REGULATIONS IN CIRCUIT COURT OF APPEALS OF THE UNITED STATES FOR THE DISTRICT OF COLUMBIA

Review of any regulation promulgated under this chapter may be had upon application by any interested person only in the Circuit Court of Appeals of the United States for the District of Columbia. Any such application shall be made within ninety days from the date of promulgation of such regulations. Any matter with respect to which review could have been obtained under this subsection shall not be subject to judicial review in any civil or criminal proceeding for enforcement or to obtain damages or recovery of response costs.

(b) JURISDICTION; VENUE

Except as provided in subsections (a) and (h) of this section, the United States district courts shall have exclusive original jurisdiction over all controversies arising under this chapter, without regard to the citizenship of the parties or the amount in controversy. Venue shall lie in any district in which the release or damages occurred, or in which the defendant resides, may be found, or has his principal office. For the purposes of this section, the Fund shall reside in the District of Columbia.

(c) CONTROVERSIES OR OTHER MATTERS RESULTING FROM TAX COLLECTION OR TAX REGULATION REVIEW

The provisions of subsections (a) and (b) of this section shall not apply to any controversy or other matter resulting from the assessment of collection of any tax, as provided by subchapter II[10] of this chapter, or to the review of any regulation promulgated under title 26.

(d) LITIGATION COMMENCED PRIOR TO DECEMBER 11, 1980

No provision of this chapter shall be deemed or held to moot any litigation concerning any release of any hazardous substance, or any damages associated therewith, commenced prior to December 11, 1980.

10. See References in Text note below.

CERCLA §9613

(e) NATIONWIDE SERVICE OF PROCESS

In any action by the United States under this chapter, process may be served in any district where the defendant is found, resides, transacts business, or has appointed an agent for the service of process.

(f) CONTRIBUTION

(1) CONTRIBUTION

Any person may seek contribution from any other person who is liable or potentially liable under section 9607(a) of this title, during or following any civil action under section 9606 of this title or under section 9607(a) of this title. Such claims shall be brought in accordance with this section and the Federal Rules of Civil Procedure, and shall be governed by Federal law. In resolving contribution claims, the court may allocate response costs among liable parties using such equitable factors as the court determines are appropriate. Nothing in this subsection shall diminish the right of any person to bring an action for contribution in the absence of a civil action under section 9606 of this title or section 9607 of this title.

(2) SETTLEMENT

A person who has resolved its liability to the United States or a State in an administrative or judicially approved settlement shall not be liable for claims for contribution regarding matters addressed in the settlement. Such settlement does not discharge any of the other potentially liable persons unless its terms so provide, but it reduces the potential liability of the others by the amount of the settlement.

(3) PERSONS NOT PARTY TO SETTLEMENT

(A) If the United States or a State has obtained less than complete relief from a person who has resolved its liability to the United States or the State in an administrative or judicially approved settlement, the United States or the State may bring an action against any person who has not so resolved its liability.

(B) A person who has resolved its liability to the United States or a State for some or all of a response action or for some or all of the costs of such action in an administrative or judicially approved settlement may seek contribution from any person who is not party to a settlement referred to in paragraph (2).

(C) In any action under this paragraph, the rights of any person who has resolved its liability to the United States or a State shall be subordinate to the rights of the United States or the State. Any contribution action brought under this paragraph shall be governed by Federal law.

§9613 CERCLA

(g) PERIOD IN WHICH ACTION MAY BE BROUGHT

(1) ACTIONS FOR NATURAL RESOURCE DAMAGES

Except as provided in paragraphs (3) and (4), no action may be commenced for damages (as defined in section 9601(6) of this title) under this chapter, unless that action is commenced within 3 years after the later of the following:

(A) The date of the discovery of the loss and its connection with the release in question.

(B) The date on which regulations are promulgated under section 9651(c) of this title.

With respect to any facility listed on the National Priorities List (NPL), any Federal facility identified under section 9620 of this title (relating to Federal facilities), or any vessel or facility at which a remedial action under this chapter is otherwise scheduled, an action for damages under this chapter must be commenced within 3 years after the completion of the remedial action (excluding operation and maintenance activities) in lieu of the dates referred to in subparagraph (A) or (B). In no event may an action for damages under this chapter with respect to such a vessel or facility be commenced (i) prior to 60 days after the Federal or State natural resource trustee provides to the President and the potentially responsible party a notice of intent to file suit, or (ii) before selection of the remedial action if the President is diligently proceeding with a remedial investigation and feasibility study under section 9604(b) of this title or section 9620 of this title (relating to Federal facilities). The limitation in the preceding sentence on commencing an action before giving notice or before selection of the remedial action does not apply to actions filed on or before October 17, 1986.

(2) ACTIONS FOR RECOVERY OF COSTS

An initial action for recovery of the costs referred to in section 9607 of this title must be commenced—

(A) for a removal action, within 3 years after completion of the removal action, except that such cost recovery action must be brought within 6 years after a determination to grant a waiver under section 9604(c)(1)(C) of this title for continued response action; and

(B) for a remedial action, within 6 years after initiation of physical on-site construction of the remedial action, except that, if the remedial action is initiated within 3 years after the completion of the removal action, costs incurred in the removal action may be recovered in the cost recovery action brought under this subparagraph.

In any such action described in this subsection, the court shall enter a declaratory judgment on liability for response costs or damages that will be binding on any subsequent action or actions to recover further response costs or damages. A subsequent action or actions under section 9607 of this title for further response costs at the vessel or facility may be maintained at any time during the response action, but must be commenced no later than 3 years after the date of completion of all response action. Except as otherwise provided in this paragraph, an action may be commenced under section 9607 of this title for recovery of costs at any time after such costs have been incurred.

(3) CONTRIBUTION

No action for contribution for any response costs or damages may be commenced more than 3 years after—

(A) the date of judgement in any action under this chapter for recovery of such costs or damages, or

(B) the date of an administrative order under section 9622(g) of this title (relating to de minimis settlements) or 9622(h) of this title (relating to cost recovery settlements) or entry of a judicially approved settlement with respect to such costs or damages.

(4) SUBROGATION

No action based on rights subrogated pursuant to this section by reason of payment of a claim may be commenced under this subchapter more than 3 years after the date of payment of such claim.

(5) ACTIONS TO RECOVER INDEMNIFICATION PAYMENTS

Notwithstanding any other provision of this subsection, where a payment pursuant to an indemnification agreement with a response action contractor is made under section 9619 of this title, an action under section 9607 of this title for recovery of such indemnification payment from a potentially responsible party may be brought at any time before the expiration of 3 years from the date on which such payment is made.

(6) MINORS AND INCOMPETENTS

The time limitations contained herein shall not begin to run—

(A) against a minor until the earlier of the date when such minor reaches 18 years of age or the date on which a legal representative is duly appointed for such minor, or

(B) against an incompetent person until the earlier of the date on which such incompetent's incompetency ends or the date on which a legal representative is duly appointed for such incompetent.

(h) TIMING OF REVIEW

No Federal court shall have jurisdiction under Federal law other than under section 1332 of title 28 (relating to diversity of citizenship jurisdiction) or under State law which is applicable or relevant and appropriate under section 9621 of this title (relating to cleanup standards) to review any challenges to removal or remedial action selected under section 9604 of this title, or to review any order issued under section 9606(a) of this title, in any action except one of the following:

(1) An action under section 9607 of this title to recover response costs or damages or for contribution.

(2) An action to enforce an order issued under section 9606(a) of this title or to recover a penalty for violation of such order.

(3) An action for reimbursement under section 9606(b)(2) of this title.

(4) An action under section 9659 of this title (relating to citizens suits) alleging that the removal or remedial action taken under section 9604 of this title or secured under section 9606 of this title was in violation of any requirement of this chapter. Such an action may not be brought with regard to a removal where a remedial action is to be undertaken at the site.

(5) An action under section 9606 of this title in which the United States has moved to compel a remedial action.

(i) INTERVENTION

In any action commenced under this chapter or under the Solid Waste Disposal Act [42 U.S.C. 6901 et seq.] in a court of the United States, any person may intervene as a matter of right when such person claims an interest relating to the subject of the action and is so situated that the disposition of the action may, as a practical matter, impair or impede the person's ability to protect that interest, unless the President or the State shows that the person's interest is adequately represented by existing parties.

(j) JUDICIAL REVIEW

(1) LIMITATION

In any judicial action under this chapter, judicial review of any issues concerning the adequacy of any response action taken or ordered by the President shall be limited to the administrative record. Otherwise applicable principles of administrative law shall govern whether any supplemental materials may be considered by the court.

(2) STANDARD

In considering objections raised in any judicial action under this chapter, the court shall uphold the President's decision in selecting the response action unless the objecting party can demonstrate, on the administrative record, that the decision was arbitrary and capricious or otherwise not in accordance with law.

(3) REMEDY

If the court finds that the selection of the response action was arbitrary and capricious or otherwise not in accordance with law, the court shall award (A) only the response costs or damages that are not inconsistent with the national contingency plan, and (B) such other relief as is consistent with the National Contingency Plan.

(4) PROCEDURAL ERRORS

In reviewing alleged procedural errors, the court may disallow costs or damages only if the errors were so serious and related to matters of such central relevance to the action that the action would have been significantly changed had such errors not been made.

(k) ADMINISTRATIVE RECORD AND PARTICIPATION PROCEDURES

(1) ADMINISTRATIVE RECORD

The President shall establish an administrative record upon which the President shall base the selection of a response action. The administrative record shall be available to the public at or near the facility at issue. The President also may place duplicates of the administrative record at any other location.

(2) PARTICIPATION PROCEDURES

(A) REMOVAL ACTION

The President shall promulgate regulations in accordance with chapter 5 of title 5 establishing procedures for the appropriate participation of interested persons in the development of the administrative record on which the President will base the selection of removal actions and on which judicial review of removal actions will be based.

(B) REMEDIAL ACTION

The President shall provide for the participation of interested persons, including potentially responsible parties, in the development of the administrative record on which the President will base the selection of remedial actions and on which judicial review of remedial actions will be based. The procedures developed under this subparagraph shall include, at a minimum, each of the following:

(i) Notice to potentially affected persons and the public, which shall be accompanied by a brief analysis of the plan and alternative plans that were considered.

(ii) A reasonable opportunity to comment and provide information regarding the plan.

(iii) An opportunity for a public meeting in the affected area, in accordance with section 9617(a)(2) of this title (relating to public participation).

(iv) A response to each of the significant comments, criticisms, and new data submitted in written or oral presentations.

(v) A statement of the basis and purpose of the selected action.

For purposes of this subparagraph, the administrative record shall include all items developed and received under this subparagraph and all items described in the second sentence of section 9617(d) of this title. The President shall promulgate regulations in accordance with chapter 5 of title 5 to carry out the requirements of this subparagraph.

(C) INTERIM RECORD

Until such regulations under subparagraphs (A) and (B) are promulgated, the administrative record shall consist of all items developed and received pursuant to current procedures for selection of the response action, including procedures for the participation of interested parties and the public. The development of an administrative record and the selection of response action under this chapter shall not include an adjudicatory hearing.

(D) POTENTIALLY RESPONSIBLE PARTIES

The President shall make reasonable efforts to identify and notify potentially responsible parties as early as possible before selection of a response action. Nothing in this paragraph shall be construed to be a defense to liability.

(*l*) NOTICE OF ACTIONS

Whenever any action is brought under this chapter in a court of the United States by a plaintiff other than the United States, the plaintiff shall provide a copy of the complaint to the Attorney General of the United States and to the Administrator of the Environmental Protection Agency.

§9614. RELATIONSHIP TO OTHER LAW

(a) ADDITIONAL STATE LIABILITY OR REQUIREMENTS WITH RESPECT TO RELEASE OF SUBSTANCES WITHIN STATE

Nothing in this chapter shall be construed or interpreted as preempting any State from imposing any additional liability or requirements with respect to the release of hazardous substances within such State.

(b) RECOVERY UNDER OTHER STATE OR FEDERAL LAW OF COMPENSATION FOR REMOVAL COSTS OR DAMAGES, OR PAYMENT OF CLAIMS

Any person who receives compensation for removal costs or damages or claims pursuant to this chapter shall be precluded from recovering compensation for the same removal costs or damages or claims pursuant to any other State or Federal law. Any person who receives compensation for removal costs or damages or claims pursuant to any other Federal or State law shall be precluded from

CERCLA §9614

receiving compensation for the same removal costs or damages or claims as provided in this chapter.

(c) RECYCLED OIL

(1) SERVICE STATION DEALERS, ETC.

No person (including the United States or any State) may recover, under the authority of subsection (a)(3) or (a)(4) of section 9607 of this title, from a service station dealer for any response costs or damages resulting from a release or threatened release of recycled oil, or use the authority of section 9606 of this title against a service station dealer other than a person described in subsection (a)(1) or (a)(2) of section 9607 of this title, if such recycled oil—

(A) is not mixed with any other hazardous substance, and

(B) is stored, treated, transported, or otherwise managed in compliance with regulations or standards promulgated pursuant to section 3014 of the Solid Waste Disposal Act [42 U.S.C. 6935] and other applicable authorities.

Nothing in this paragraph shall affect or modify in any way the obligations or liability of any person under any other provision of State or Federal law, including common law, for damages, injury, or loss resulting from a release or threatened release of any hazardous substance or for removal or remedial action or the costs of removal or remedial action.

(2) PRESUMPTION

Solely for the purposes of this subsection, a service station dealer may presume that a small quantity of used oil is not mixed with other hazardous substances if it—

(A) has been removed from the engine of a light duty motor vehicle or household appliances by the owner of such vehicle or appliances, and

(B) is presented, by such owner, to the dealer for collection, accumulation, and delivery to an oil recycling facility.

(3) DEFINITION

For purposes of this subsection, the terms "used oil" and "recycled oil" have the same meanings as set forth in sections 1004(36) and 1004(37) of the Solid Waste Disposal Act [42 U.S.C. 6903(36), (37)] and regulations promulgated pursuant to that Act [42 U.S.C. 6901 et seq.].

(4) EFFECTIVE DATE

The effective date of paragraphs (1) and (2) of this subsection shall be the effective date of regulations or standards promulgated under section 3014 of the Solid Waste Disposal Act [42 U.S.C. 6935] that include, among other provisions, a requirement to conduct corrective action to respond to any releases of recycled oil under subtitle C or subtitle I of such Act [42 U.S.C. 6921 et seq., 6991 et seq.].

(d) FINANCIAL RESPONSIBILITY OF OWNER OR OPERATOR OF VESSEL OR FACILITY UNDER STATE OR LOCAL LAW, RULE, OR REGULATION

Except as provided in this subchapter, no owner or operator of a vessel or facility who establishes and maintains evidence of financial responsibility in accordance with this subchapter shall be required under any State or local law, rule, or regulation to establish or maintain any other evidence of financial responsibility in connection with liability for the release of a hazardous substance from such vessel or facility. Evidence of compliance with the financial responsibility requirements of this subchapter shall be accepted by a State in lieu of any other requirement of financial responsibility imposed by such State in connection with liability for the release of a hazardous substance from such vessel or facility.

§9615. PRESIDENTIAL DELEGATION AND ASSIGNMENT OF DUTIES OR POWERS AND PROMULGATION OF REGULATIONS

The President is authorized to delegate and assign any duties or powers imposed upon or assigned to him and to promulgate any regulations necessary to carry out the provisions of this subchapter.

§9616. SCHEDULES

(a) ASSESSMENT AND LISTING OF FACILITIES

It shall be a goal of this chapter that, to the maximum extent practicable—

(1) not later than January 1, 1988, the President shall complete preliminary assessments of all facilities that are contained (as of October 17, 1986) on the Comprehensive Environmental Response, Compensation, and Liability Information System (CERCLIS) including in each assessment a statement as to whether a site inspection is necessary and by whom it should be carried out; and

(2) not later than January 1, 1989, the President shall assure the completion of site inspections at all facilities for which the President has stated a site inspection is necessary pursuant to paragraph (1).

(b) EVALUATION

Within 4 years after October 17, 1986, each facility listed (as of October 17, 1986) in the CERCLIS shall be evaluated if the President determines that such evaluation is warranted on the basis of a site inspection or preliminary assessment. The evaluation shall be in accordance with the criteria established in section 9605 of this title under the National Contingency Plan for determining priorities among release for inclusion on the National Priorities List. In the case of a facility listed in the CERCLIS after October 17, 1986, the facility shall be evaluated within 4 years after the date of such listing if the President determines that such evaluation is warranted on the basis of a site inspection or preliminary assessment.

(c) EXPLANATIONS

If any of the goals established by subsection (a) or (b) of this section are not achieved, the President shall publish an explanation of why such action could not be completed by the specified date.

(d) COMMENCEMENT OF RI/FS

The President shall assure that remedial investigations and feasibility studies (RI/FS) are commenced for facilities listed on the National Priorities List, in addition to those commenced prior to October 17, 1986, in accordance with the following schedule:

(1) not fewer than 275 by the date 36 months after October 17, 1986, and

(2) if the requirement of paragraph (1) is not met, not fewer than an additional 175 by the date 4 years after October 17, 1986, an additional 200 by the date 5 years after October 17, 1986, and a total of 650 by the date 5 years after October 17, 1986.

(e) COMMENCEMENT OF REMEDIAL ACTION

The President shall assure that substantial and continuous physical on-site remedial action commences at facilities on the National Priorities List, in addition to those facilities on which remedial action has commenced prior to October 17, 1986, at a rate not fewer than:

(1) 175 facilities during the first 36-month period after October 17, 1986; and

(2) 200 additional facilities during the following 24 months after such 36-month period.

§9617. PUBLIC PARTICIPATION

(a) PROPOSED PLAN

Before adoption of any plan for remedial action to be undertaken by the President, by a State, or by any other person, under section 9604, 9606, 9620, or 9622 of this title, the President or State, as appropriate, shall take both of the following actions:

(1) Publish a notice and brief analysis of the proposed plan and make such plan available to the public.

(2) Provide a reasonable opportunity for submission of written and oral comments and an opportunity for a public meeting at or near the facility at issue regarding the proposed plan and regarding any proposed findings under section 9621(d)(4) of this title (relating to cleanup standards). The President

or the State shall keep a transcript of the meeting and make such transcript available to the public.

The notice and analysis published under paragraph (1) shall include sufficient information as may be necessary to provide a reasonable explanation of the proposed plan and alternative proposals considered.

(b) FINAL PLAN

Notice of the final remedial action plan adopted shall be published and the plan shall be made available to the public before commencement of any remedial action. Such final plan shall be accompanied by a discussion of any significant changes (and the reasons for such changes) in the proposed plan and a response to each of the significant comments, criticisms, and new data submitted in written or oral presentations under subsection (a) of this section.

(c) EXPLANATION OF DIFFERENCES

After adoption of a final remedial action plan—

(1) if any remedial action is taken,

(2) if any enforcement action under section 9606 of this title is taken, or

(3) if any settlement or consent decree under section 9606 of this title or section 9622 of this title is entered into,

and if such action, settlement, or decree differs in any significant respects from the final plan, the President or the State shall publish an explanation of the significant differences and the reasons such changes were made.

(d) PUBLICATION

For the purposes of this section, publication shall include, at a minimum, publication in a major local newspaper of general circulation. In addition, each item developed, received, published, or made available to the public under this section shall be available for public inspection and copying at or near the facility at issue.

(e) GRANTS FOR TECHNICAL ASSISTANCE

(1) AUTHORITY

Subject to such amounts as are provided in appropriations Acts and in accordance with rules promulgated by the President, the President may make grants available to any group of individuals which may be affected by a release or threatened release at any facility which is listed on the National Priorities List under the National Contingency Plan. Such grants may be used to obtain technical assistance in interpreting information with regard to the nature of the hazard, remedial investigation and feasibility study, record of decision, remedial design, selection and construction of remedial action, operation and maintenance, or removal action at such facility.

(2) AMOUNT

The amount of any grant under this subsection may not exceed $50,000 for a single grant recipient. The President may waive the $50,000 limitation in any case where such waiver is necessary to carry out the purposes of this subsection. Each grant recipient shall be required, as a condition of the grant, to contribute at least 20 percent of the total of costs of the technical assistance for which such grant is made. The President may waive the 20 percent contribution requirement if the grant recipient demonstrates financial need and such waiver is necessary to facilitate public participation in the selection of remedial action at the facility. Not more than one grant may be made under this subsection with respect to a single facility, but the grant may be renewed to facilitate public participation at all stages of remedial action.

§9618. HIGH PRIORITY FOR DRINKING WATER SUPPLIES

For purposes of taking action under section 9604 or 9606 of this title and listing facilities on the National Priorities List, the President shall give a high priority to facilities where the release of hazardous substances or pollutants or contaminants has resulted in the closing of drinking water wells or has contaminated a principal drinking water supply.

§9619. RESPONSE ACTION CONTRACTORS

(a) LIABILITY OF RESPONSE ACTION CONTRACTORS

(1) RESPONSE ACTION CONTRACTORS

A person who is a response action contractor with respect to any release or threatened release of a hazardous substance or pollutant or contaminant from a vessel or facility shall not be liable under this subchapter or under any other Federal law to any person for injuries, costs, damages, expenses, or other liability (including but not limited to claims for indemnification or contribution and claims by third parties for death, personal injury, illness or loss of or damage to property or economic loss) which results from such release or threatened release.

(2) NEGLIGENCE, ETC.

Paragraph (1) shall not apply in the case of a release that is caused by conduct of the response action contractor which is negligent, grossly negligent, or which constitutes intentional misconduct.

(3) EFFECT ON WARRANTIES; EMPLOYER LIABILITY

Nothing in this subsection shall affect the liability of any person under any warranty under Federal, State, or common law. Nothing in this subsection shall affect the liability of an employer who is a response action contractor to any employee of such employer under any provision of law, including any provision of any law relating to worker's compensation.

(4) GOVERNMENTAL EMPLOYEES

A state employee or an employee of a political subdivision who provides services relating to response action while acting within the scope of his authority as a governmental employee shall have the same exemption from liability (subject to the other provisions of this section) as is provided to the response action contractor under this section.

(b) SAVINGS PROVISIONS

(1) LIABILITY OF OTHER PERSONS

The defense provided by section 9607(b)(3) of this title shall not be available to any potentially responsible party with respect to any costs or damages caused by any act or omission of a response action contractor. Except as provided in subsection (a)(4) of this section and the preceding sentence, nothing in this section shall affect the liability under this chapter or under any other Federal or State law of any person, other than a response action contractor.

(2) BURDEN OF PLAINTIFF

Nothing in this section shall affect the plaintiff's burden of establishing liability under this subchapter.

(c) INDEMNIFICATION

(1) IN GENERAL

The President may agree to hold harmless and indemnify any response action contractor meeting the requirements of this subsection against any liability (including the expenses of litigation or settlement) for negligence arising out of the contractor's performance in carrying out response action activities under this subchapter, unless such liability was caused by conduct of the contractor which was grossly negligent or which constituted intentional misconduct.

(2) APPLICABILITY

This subsection shall apply only with respect to a response action carried out under written agreement with—

(A) the President;
(B) any Federal agency;
(C) a State or political subdivision which has entered into a contract or cooperative agreement in accordance with section 9604(d)(1) of this title; or

(D) any potentially responsible party carrying out any agreement under section 9622 of this title (relating to settlements) or section 9606 of this title (relating to abatement).

(3) SOURCE OF FUNDING

This subsection shall not be subject to section 1301 or 1341 of title 31 or section 11 of title 41 or to section 9662 of this title. For purposes of section 9611 of this title, amounts expended pursuant to this subsection for indemnification of any response action contractor (except with respect to federally owned or operated facilities) shall be considered governmental response costs incurred pursuant to section 9604 of this title. If sufficient funds are unavailable in the Hazardous Substance Superfund established under subchapter A of chapter 98 of title 26 to make payments pursuant to such indemnification or if the Fund is repealed, there are authorized to be appropriated such amounts as may be necessary to make such payments.

(4) REQUIREMENTS

An indemnification agreement may be provided under this subsection only if the President determines that each of the following requirements are met:

(A) The liability covered by the indemnification agreement exceeds or is not covered by insurance available, at a fair and reasonable price, to the contractor at the time the contractor enters into the contract to provide response action, and adequate insurance to cover such liability is not generally available at the time the response action contract is entered into.

(B) The response action contractor has made diligent efforts to obtain insurance coverage from non-Federal sources to cover such liability.

(C) In the case of a response action contract covering more than one facility, the response action contractor agrees to continue to make such diligent efforts each time the contractor begins work under the contract at a new facility.

(5) LIMITATIONS

(A) LIABILITY COVERED

Indemnification under this subsection shall apply only to response action contractor liability which results from a release of any hazardous substance or pollutant or contaminant if such release arises out of response action activities.

(B) DEDUCTIBLES AND LIMITS

An indemnification agreement under this subsection shall include deductibles and shall place limits on the amount of indemnification to be made available.

(C) CONTRACTS WITH POTENTIALLY RESPONSIBLE PARTIES

(i) DECISION TO INDEMNIFY

In deciding whether to enter into an indemnification agreement with a response action contractor carrying out a written contract or agreement with any potentially responsible party, the President shall determine an amount which the potentially responsible party is able to indemnify the contractor. The President may enter into such an indemnification agreement only if the President determines that such amount of indemnification is inadequate to cover any reasonable potential liability of the contractor arising out of the contractor's negligence in performing the contract or agreement with such party. The President shall make the determinations in the preceding sentences (with respect to the amount and the adequacy of the amount) taking into account the total net assets and resources of potentially responsible parties with respect to the facility at the time of such determinations.

(ii) CONDITIONS

The President may pay a claim under an indemnification agreement referred to in clause (i) for the amount determined under clause (i) only if the contractor has exhausted all administrative, judicial, and common law claims for indemnification against all potentially responsible parties participating in the clean-up of the facility with respect to the liability of the contractor arising out of the contractor's negligence in performing the contract or agreement with such party. Such indemnification agreement shall require such contractor to pay any deductible established under subparagraph (B) before the contractor may recover any amount from the potentially responsible party or under the indemnification agreement.

(D) RCRA FACILITIES

No owner or operator of a facility regulated under the Solid Waste Disposal Act [42 U.S.C. 6901 et seq.] may be indemnified under this subsection with respect to such facility.

(E) PERSONS RETAINED OR HIRED

A person retained or hired by a person described in subsection (e)(2)(B) of this section shall be eligible for indemnification under this subsection only if the President specifically approves of the retaining or hiring of such person.

(6) COST RECOVERY

For purposes of section 9607 of this title, amounts expended pursuant to this subsection for indemnification of any person who is a response action contractor with respect to any release or threatened release shall be considered a cost of response incurred by the United States Government with respect to such release.

(7) REGULATIONS

The President shall promulgate regulations for carrying out the provisions of this subsection. Before promulgation of the regulations, the President shall develop guidelines to carry out this section. Development of such guidelines shall include reasonable opportunity for public comment.

(8) STUDY

The Comptroller General shall conduct a study in the fiscal year ending September 30, 1989, on the application of this subsection, including whether indemnification agreements under this subsection are being used, the number of claims that have been filed under such agreements, and the need for this subsection. The Comptroller General shall report the findings of the study to Congress no later than September 30, 1989.

(d) EXCEPTION

The exemption provided under subsection (a) of this section and the authority of the President to offer indemnification under subsection (c) of this section shall not apply to any person covered by the provisions of paragraph (1), (2), (3), or (4) of section 9607(a) of this title with respect to the release or threatened release concerned if such person would be covered by such provisions even if such person had not carried out any actions referred to in subsection (e) of this section.

(e) DEFINITIONS

For purposes of this section—

(1) RESPONSE ACTION CONTRACT

The term "response action contract" means any written contract or agreement entered into by a response action contractor (as defined in paragraph (2)(A) of this subsection) with—

(A) the President;

(B) any Federal agency;

(C) a State or political subdivision which has entered into a contract or cooperative agreement in accordance with section 9604(d)(1) of this title; or

(D) any potentially responsible party carrying out an agreement under section 9606 or 9622 of this title;

to provide any remedial action under this chapter at a facility listed on the National Priorities List, or any removal under this chapter, with respect to any release or threatened release of a hazardous substance or pollutant or contaminant from the facility or to provide any evaluation, planning, engineering, surveying and mapping, design, construction, equipment, or any ancillary services thereto for such facility.

§9619

(2) RESPONSE ACTION CONTRACTOR

The term "response action contractor" means—

(A) any—

(i) person who enters into a response action contract with respect to any release or threatened release of a hazardous substance or pollutant or contaminant from a facility and is carrying out such contract; and[11]

(ii) person, public or nonprofit private entity, conducting a field demonstration pursuant to section 9660(b) of this title; and

(iii) Recipients[12] of grants (including sub-grantees) under section 9660a[13] of this title for the training and education of workers who are or may be engaged in activities related to hazardous waste removal, containment, or emergency response under this chapter; and

(B) any person who is retained or hired by a person described in subparagraph (A) to provide any services relating to a response action.

(3) INSURANCE

The term "insurance" means liability insurance which is fair and reasonably priced, as determined by the President, and which is made available at the time the contractor enters into the response action contract to provide response action.

(f) COMPETITION

Response action contractors and subcontractors for program management, construction management, architectural and engineering, surveying and mapping, and related services shall be selected in accordance with title IX of the Federal Property and Administrative Services Act of 1949 [40 U.S.C. 541 et seq.]. The Federal selection procedures shall apply to appropriate contracts negotiated by all Federal governmental agencies involved in carrying out this chapter. Such procedures shall be followed by response action contractors and subcontractors.

§9620. FEDERAL FACILITIES

(a) APPLICATION OF CHAPTER TO FEDERAL GOVERNMENT

(1) IN GENERAL

Each department, agency, and instrumentality of the United States (including the executive, legislative, and judicial branches of government) shall be subject to, and comply with, this chapter in the same manner and to the same extent, both procedurally and substantively, as any nongovernmental

11. So in original. The word "and" probably should not appear.
12. So in original. Probably should not be capitalized.
13. See References in Text note below.

entity, including liability under section 9607 of this title. Nothing in this section shall be construed to affect the liability of any person or entity under sections 9606 and 9607 of this title.

(2) APPLICATION OF REQUIREMENTS TO FEDERAL FACILITIES

All guidelines, rules, regulations, and criteria which are applicable to preliminary assessments carried out under this chapter for facilities at which hazardous substances are located, applicable to evaluations of such facilities under the National Contingency Plan, applicable to inclusion on the National Priorities List, or applicable to remedial actions at such facilities shall also be applicable to facilities which are owned or operated by a department, agency, or instrumentality of the United States in the same manner and to the extent as such guidelines, rules, regulations, and criteria are applicable to other facilities. No department, agency, or instrumentality of the United States may adopt or utilize any such guidelines, rules, regulations, or criteria which are inconsistent with the guidelines, rules, regulations, and criteria established by the Administrator under this chapter.

(3) EXCEPTIONS

This subsection shall not apply to the extent otherwise provided in this section with respect to applicable time periods. This subsection shall also not apply to any requirements relating to bonding, insurance, or financial responsibility. Nothing in this chapter shall be construed to require a State to comply with section 9604(c)(3) of this title in the case of a facility which is owned or operated by any department, agency, or instrumentality of the United States.

(4) STATE LAWS

State laws concerning removal and remedial action, including State laws regarding enforcement, shall apply to removal and remedial action at facilities owned or operated by a department, agency, or instrumentality of the United States when such facilities are not included on the National Priorities List. The preceding sentence shall not apply to the extent a State law would apply any standard or requirement to such facilities which is more stringent than the standards and requirements applicable to facilities which are not owned or operated by any such department, agency, or instrumentality.

(b) NOTICE

Each department, agency, and instrumentality of the United States shall add to the inventory of Federal agency hazardous waste facilities required to be submitted under section 3016 of the Solid Waste Disposal Act [42 U.S.C. 6937] (in addition to the information required under section 3016(a)(3) of such Act [42 U.S.C. 6937(a)(3)]) information on contamination from each facility owned or operated by the department, agency, or instrumentality if such contamination affects contiguous or adjacent property owned by the department, agency, or instrumentality or by any other person, including a description of the monitoring data obtained.

(c) **FEDERAL AGENCY HAZARDOUS WASTE COMPLIANCE DOCKET**

The Administrator shall establish a special Federal Agency Hazardous Waste Compliance Docket (hereinafter in this section referred to as the "docket") which shall contain each of the following:

(1) All information submitted under section 3016 of the Solid Waste Disposal Act [42 U.S.C. 6937] and subsection (b) of this section regarding any Federal facility and notice of each subsequent action taken under this chapter with respect to the facility.

(2) Information submitted by each department, agency, or instrumentality of the United States under section 3005 or 3010 of such Act [42 U.S.C. 6925, 6930].

(3) Information submitted by the department, agency, or instrumentality under section 9603 of this title.

The docket shall be available for public inspection at reasonable times. Six months after establishment of the docket and every 6 months thereafter, the Administrator shall publish in the Federal Register a list of the Federal facilities which have been included in the docket during the immediately preceding 6-month period. Such publication shall also indicate where in the appropriate regional office of the Environmental Protection Agency additional information may be obtained with respect to any facility on the docket. The Administrator shall establish a program to provide information to the public with respect to facilities which are included in the docket under this subsection.

(d) **ASSESSMENT AND EVALUATION**

Not later than 18 months after October 17, 1986, the Administrator shall take steps to assure that a preliminary assessment is conducted for each facility on the docket. Following such preliminary assessment, the Administrator shall, where appropriate—

(1) evaluate such facilities in accordance with the criteria established in accordance with section 9605 of this title under the National Contingency Plan for determining priorities among releases; and

(2) include such facilities on the National Priorities List maintained under such plan if the facility meets such criteria.

Such criteria shall be applied in the same manner as the criteria are applied to facilities which are owned or operated by other persons. Evaluation and listing under this subsection shall be completed not later than 30 months after October 17, 1986. Upon the receipt of a petition from the Governor of any State, the Administrator shall make such an evaluation of any facility included in the docket.

(e) REQUIRED ACTION BY DEPARTMENT

(1) RI/FS

Not later than 6 months after the inclusion of any facility on the National Priorities List, the department, agency, or instrumentality which owns or operates such facility shall, in consultation with the Administrator and appropriate State authorities, commence a remedial investigation and feasibility study for such facility. In the case of any facility which is listed on such list before October 17, 1986, the department, agency, or instrumentality which owns or operates such facility shall, in consultation with the Administrator and appropriate State authorities, commence such an investigation and study for such facility within one year after October 17, 1986. The Administrator and appropriate State authorities shall publish a timetable and deadlines for expeditious completion of such investigation and study.

(2) COMMENCEMENT OF REMEDIAL ACTION; INTERAGENCY AGREEMENT

The Administrator shall review the results of each investigation and study conducted as provided in paragraph (1). Within 180 days thereafter, the head of the department, agency, or instrumentality concerned shall enter into an interagency agreement with the Administrator for the expeditious completion by such department, agency, or instrumentality of all necessary remedial action at such facility. Substantial continuous physical onsite remedial action shall be commenced at each facility not later than 15 months after completion of the investigation and study. All such interagency agreements, including review of alternative remedial action plans and selection of remedial action, shall comply with the public participation requirements of section 9617 of this title.

(3) COMPLETION OF REMEDIAL ACTIONS

Remedial actions at facilities subject to interagency agreements under this section shall be completed as expeditiously as practicable. Each agency shall include in its annual budget submissions to the Congress a review of alternative agency funding which could be used to provide for the costs of remedial action. The budget submission shall also include a statement of the hazard posed by the facility to human health, welfare, and the environment and identify the specific consequences of failure to begin and complete remedial action.

(4) CONTENTS OF AGREEMENT

Each interagency agreement under this subsection shall include, but shall not be limited to, each of the following:

(A) A review of alternative remedial actions and selection of a remedial action by the head of the relevant department, agency, or instrumentality and the Administrator or, if unable to reach agreement on selection of a remedial action, selection by the Administrator.

(B) A schedule for the completion of each such remedial action.

(C) Arrangements for long-term operation and maintenance of the facility.

(5) ANNUAL REPORT

Each department, agency, or instrumentality responsible for compliance with this section shall furnish an annual report to the Congress concerning its progress in implementing the requirements of this section. Such reports shall include, but shall not be limited to, each of the following items:

(A) A report on the progress in reaching interagency agreements under this section.

(B)The specific cost estimates and budgetary proposals involved in each interagency agreement.

(C) A brief summary of the public comments regarding each proposed interagency agreement.

(D) A description of the instances in which no agreement was reached.

(E) A report on progress in conducting investigations and studies under paragraph (1).

(F) A report on progress in conducting remedial actions.

(G) A report on progress in conducting remedial action at facilities which are not listed on the National Priorities List.

With respect to instances in which no agreement was reached within the required time period, the department, agency, or instrumentality filing the report under this paragraph shall include in such report an explanation of the reasons why no agreement was reached. The annual report required by this paragraph shall also contain a detailed description on a State-by-State basis of the status of each facility subject to this section, including a description of the hazard presented by each facility, plans and schedules for initiating and completing response action, enforcement status (where appropriate), and an explanation of any postponements or failure to complete response action. Such reports shall also be submitted to the affected States.

(6) SETTLEMENTS WITH OTHER PARTIES

If the Administrator, in consultation with the head of the relevant department, agency, or instrumentality of the United States, determines that remedial investigations and feasibility studies or remedial action will be done properly at the Federal facility by another potentially responsible party within the deadlines provided in paragraphs (1), (2), and (3) of this subsection, the Administrator may enter into an agreement with such party under section 9622 of this title (relating to settlements). Following approval by the Attorney General of any such agreement relating to a remedial action, the agreement

CERCLA §9620

shall be entered in the appropriate United States district court as a consent decree under section 9606 of this title.

(f) STATE AND LOCAL PARTICIPATION

The Administrator and each department, agency, or instrumentality responsible for compliance with this section shall afford to relevant State and local officials the opportunity to participate in the planning and selection of the remedial action, including but not limited to the review of all applicable data as it becomes available and the development of studies, reports, and action plans. In the case of State officials, the opportunity to participate shall be provided in accordance with section 9621 of this title.

(g) TRANSFER OF AUTHORITIES

Except for authorities which are delegated by the Administrator to an officer or employee of the Environmental Protection Agency, no authority vested in the Administrator under this section may be transferred, by executive order of the President or otherwise, to any other officer or employee of the United States or to any other person.

(h) PROPERTY TRANSFERRED BY FEDERAL AGENCIES

(1) NOTICE

After the last day of the 6-month period beginning on the effective date of regulations under paragraph (2) of this subsection, whenever any department, agency, or instrumentality of the United States enters into any contract for the sale or other transfer of real property which is owned by the United States and on which any hazardous substance was stored for one year or more, known to have been released, or disposed of, the head of such department, agency, or instrumentality shall include in such contract notice of the type and quantity of such hazardous substance and notice of the time at which such storage, release, or disposal took place, to the extent such information is available on the basis of a complete search of agency files.

(2) FORM OF NOTICE; REGULATIONS

Notice under this subsection shall be provided in such form and manner as may be provided in regulations promulgated by the Administrator. As promptly as practicable after October 17, 1986, but not later than 18 months after October 17, 1986, and after consultation with the Administrator of the General Services Administration, the Administrator shall promulgate regulations regarding the notice required to be provided under this subsection.

(3) CONTENTS OF CERTAIN DEEDS

After the last day of the 6-month period beginning on the effective date of regulations under paragraph (2) of this subsection, in the case of any real property owned by the United States on which any hazardous substance was stored for one year or more, known to have been released, or disposed of, each deed entered into for the transfer of such property by the United States to any other person or entity shall contain—

 (A) to the extent such information is available on the basis of a complete search of agency files—

  (i) a notice of the type and quantity of such hazardous substances,

  (ii) notice of the time at which such storage, release, or disposal took place, and

  (iii) a description of the remedial action taken, if any, and

 (B) a covenant warranting that—

  (i) all remedial action necessary to protect human health and the environment with respect to any such substance remaining on the property has been taken before the date of such transfer, and

  (ii) any additional remedial action found to be necessary after the date of such transfer shall be conducted by the United States.

The requirements of subparagraph (B) shall not apply in any case in which the person or entity to whom the property is transferred is a potentially responsible party with respect to such real property.

 (i) **OBLIGATIONS UNDER SOLID WASTE DISPOSAL ACT**

Nothing in this section shall affect or impair the obligation of any department, agency, or instrumentality of the United States to comply with any requirement of the Solid Waste Disposal Act [42 U.S.C. 6901 et seq.] (including corrective action requirements).

 (j) **NATIONAL SECURITY**

  (1) **SITE SPECIFIC PRESIDENTIAL ORDERS**

The President may issue such orders regarding response actions at any specified site or facility of the Department of Energy or the Department of Defense as may be necessary to protect the national security interests of the United States at that site or facility. Such orders may include, where necessary to protect such interests, an exemption from any requirement contained in this subchapter or under title III of the Superfund Amendments and Reauthorization Act of 1986 [42 U.S.C. 11001 et seq.] with respect to the site or facility concerned. The President shall notify the Congress within 30 days of the issuance of an order under this paragraph providing for any such exemption. Such notification shall include a statement of the reasons for the granting of the exemption. An exemption under this paragraph shall be for a specified period which may not exceed one year. Additional exemptions may be granted, each upon the President's issuance of a new order under this paragraph for the site or facility concerned. Each such additional exemption shall be for a specified period which may not exceed one year. It is the intention of the Congress that whenever an exemption is issued under this paragraph the response action shall proceed as expeditiously as practicable. The Congress shall be notified periodically on the progress of any response action with respect to which an exemption has been issued under this paragraph. No exemption shall be granted under this paragraph due to lack of appropriation unless the President shall have specifically requested such appropriation as a part of the budgetary process and the Congress shall have failed to make available such requested appropriation.

(2) CLASSIFIED INFORMATION

Notwithstanding any other provision of law, all requirements of the Atomic Energy Act [42 U.S.C. 2011 et seq.] and all Executive orders concerning the handling of restricted data and national security information, including "need to know" requirements, shall be applicable to any grant of access to classified information under the provisions of this chapter or under title III of the Superfund Amendments and Reauthorization Act of 1986 [42 U.S.C. 11001 et seq.].

§9621. CLEANUP STANDARDS

(a) SELECTION OF REMEDIAL ACTION

The President shall select appropriate remedial actions determined to be necessary to be carried out under section 9604 of this title or secured under section 9606 of this title which are in accordance with this section and, to the extent practicable, the national contingency plan, and which provide for cost-effective response. In evaluating the cost effectiveness of proposed alternative remedial actions, the President shall take into account the total short- and long-term costs of such actions, including the costs of operation and maintenance for the entire period during which such activities will be required.

(b) GENERAL RULES

(1) Remedial actions in which treatment which permanently and significantly reduces the volume, toxicity or mobility of the hazardous substances, pollutants, and contaminants is a principal element, are to be preferred over remedial actions not involving such treatment. The offsite transport and disposal of hazardous substances or contaminated materials without such treatment should be the least favored alternative remedial action where practicable treatment technologies are available. The President shall conduct an assessment of permanent solutions and alternative treatment technologies or resource recovery technologies that, in whole or in part, will result in a permanent and significant decrease in the toxicity, mobility, or volume of the hazardous substance, pollutant, or contaminant. In making such assessment, the President shall specifically

address the long-term effectiveness of various alternatives. In assessing alternative remedial actions, the President shall, at a minimum, take into account:

(A) the long-term uncertainties associated with land disposal;

(B) the goals, objectives, and requirements of the Solid Waste Disposal Act [42 U.S.C. 6901 et seq.];

(C) the persistence, toxicity, mobility, and propensity to bioaccumulate of such hazardous substances and their constituents;

(D) short- and long-term potential for adverse health effects from human exposure;

(E) long-term maintenance costs;

(F) the potential for future remedial action costs if the alternative remedial action in question were to fall; and

(G) the potential threat to human health and the environment associated with excavation, transportation, and redisposal, or containment.

The President shall select a remedial action that is protective of human health and the environment, that is cost effective, and that utilizes permanent solutions and alternative treatment technologies or resource recovery technologies to the maximum extent practicable. If the President selects a remedial action not appropriate for a preference under this subsection, the President shall publish an explanation as to why a remedial action involving such reductions was not selected.

(2) The President may select an alternative remedial action meeting the objectives of this subsection whether or not such action has been achieved in practice at any other facility or site that has similar characteristics. In making such a selection, the President may take into account the degree of support for such remedial action by parties interested in such site.

(c) **REVIEW**

If the President selects a remedial action that results in any hazardous substances, pollutants, or contaminants remaining at the site, the President shall review such remedial action no less often than each 5 years after the initiation of such remedial action to assure that human health and the environment are being protected by the remedial action being implemented. In addition, if upon such review it is the judgment of the President that action is appropriate at such site in accordance with section 9604 or 9606 of this title, the President shall take or require such action. The President shall report to the Congress a list of facilities for which such review is required, the results of all such reviews, and any actions taken as a result of such reviews.

(d) **DEGREE OF CLEANUP**

(1) Remedial actions selected under this section or otherwise required or agreed to by the President under this chapter shall attain a degree of cleanup of hazardous substances, pollutants, and contaminants released into the environment and of control of further release at a minimum which assures protection of human health and the environment. Such remedial actions shall be relevant

CERCLA §9621

and appropriate under the circumstances presented by the release or threatened release of such substance, pollutant, or contaminant.

(2)(A) With respect to any hazardous substance, pollutant or contaminant that will remain onsite, if—

> (i) any standard, requirement, criteria, or limitation under any Federal environmental law, including, but not limited to, the Toxic Substances Control Act [15 U.S.C. 2601 et seq.], the Safe Drinking Water Act [42 U.S.C. 300f et seq.], the Clean Air Act [42 U.S.C. 7401 et seq.], the Clean Water Act [33 U.S.C. 1251 et seq.], the Marine Protection, Research and Sanctuaries Act [33 U.S.C. 1401 et seq.], or the Solid Waste Disposal Act [42 U.S.C. 6901 et seq.]; or
>
> (ii) any promulgated standard, requirement, criteria, or limitation under a State environmental or facility siting law that is more stringent than any Federal standard, requirement, criteria, or limitation, including each such State standard, requirement, criteria, or limitation contained in a program approved, authorized or delegated by the Administrator under a statute cited in subparagraph (A), and that has been identified to the President by the State in a timely manner,

is legally applicable to the hazardous substance or pollutant or contaminant concerned or is relevant and appropriate under the circumstances of the release or threatened release of such hazardous substance or pollutant or contaminant, the remedial action selected under section 9604 of this title or secured under section 9606 of this title shall require, at the completion of the remedial action, a level or standard of control for such hazardous substance or pollutant or contaminant which at least attains such legally applicable or relevant and appropriate standard, requirement, criteria, or limitation. Such remedial action shall require a level or standard of control which at least attains Maximum Contaminant Level Goals established under the Safe Drinking Water Act [42 U.S.C. 300f et seq.] and water quality criteria established under section 304 or 303 of the Clean Water Act [33 U.S.C. 1314, 1313], where such goals or criteria are relevant and appropriate under the circumstances of the release or threatened release.

> (B)(i) In determining whether or not any water quality criteria under the Clean Water Act [33 U.S.C. 1251 et seq.] is relevant and appropriate under the circumstances of the release or threatened release, the President shall consider the designated or potential use of the surface or groundwater, the environmental media affected, the purposes for which such criteria were developed, and the latest information available.
>
> (ii) For the purposes of this section, a process for establishing alternate concentration limits to those otherwise applicable for hazardous constituents in groundwater under subparagraph (A) may not be used to establish applicable standards under this paragraph if the process assumes a point of human exposure beyond the boundary of the facility, as defined at the conclusion of the remedial investigation and feasibility study, except where—

(I) there are known and projected points of entry of such groundwater into surface water; and

(II) on the basis of measurements or projections, there is or will be no statistically significant increase of such constituents from such groundwater in such surface water at the point of entry or at any point where there is reason to believe accumulation of constituents may occur downstream; and

(III) the remedial action includes enforceable measures that will preclude human exposure to the contaminated groundwater at any point between the facility boundary and all known and projected points of entry of such groundwater into surface water

then the assumed point of human exposure may be at such known and projected points of entry.

(C)(i) Clause (ii) of this subparagraph shall be applicable only in cases where, due to the President's selection, in compliance with subsection (b)(1) of this section, of a proposed remedial action which does not permanently and significantly reduce the volume, toxicity, or mobility of hazardous substances, pollutants, or contaminants, the proposed disposition of waste generated by or associated with the remedial action selected by the President is land disposal in a State referred to in clause (ii).

(ii) Except as provided in clauses (iii) and (iv), a State standard, requirement, criteria, or limitation (including any State siting standard or requirement) which could effectively result in the statewide prohibition of land disposal of hazardous substances, pollutants, or contaminants shall not apply.

(iii) Any State standard, requirement, criteria, or limitation referred to in clause (ii) shall apply where each of the following conditions is met:

(I) The State standard, requirement, criteria, or limitation is of general applicability and was adopted by formal means.

(II) The State standard, requirement, criteria, or limitation was adopted on the basis of hydrologic, geologic, or other relevant considerations and was not adopted for the purpose of precluding onsite remedial actions or other land disposal for reasons unrelated to protection of human health and the environment.

(III) The State arranges for, and assures payment of the incremental costs of utilizing, a facility for disposition of the hazardous substances, pollutants, or contaminants concerned.

(iv) Where the remedial action selected by the President does not conform to a State standard and the State has initiated a law suit against the Environmental Protection Agency prior to May 1, 1986, to seek to have the remedial action conform to such standard, the President shall conform the remedial action to the State standard. The State shall assure the availability of an offsite facility for such remedial action.

(3) In the case of any removal or remedial action involving the transfer of

any hazardous substance or pollutant or contaminant offsite, such hazardous substance or pollutant or contaminant shall only be transferred to a facility which is operating in compliance with section 3004 and 3005 of the Solid Waste Disposal Act [42 U.S.C. 6924, 6925] (or, where applicable, in compliance with the Toxic Substances Control Act [15 U.S.C. 2601 et seq.] or other applicable Federal law) and all applicable State requirements. Such substance or pollutant or contaminant may be transferred to a land disposal facility only if the President determines that both of the following requirements are met:

(A) The unit to which the hazardous substance or pollutant or contaminant is transferred is not releasing any hazardous waste, or constituent thereof, into the groundwater or surface water or soil.

(B) All such releases from other units at the facility are being controlled by a corrective action program approved by the Administrator under subtitle C of the Solid Waste Disposal Act [42 U.S.C. 6921 et seq.].

The President shall notify the owner or operator of such facility of determinations under this paragraph.

(4) The President may select a remedial action meeting the requirements of paragraph (1) that does not attain a level or standard of control at least equivalent to a legally applicable or relevant and appropriate standard, requirement, criteria, or limitation as required by paragraph (2) (including subparagraph (B) thereof), if the President finds that—

(A) the remedial action selected is only part of a total remedial action that will attain such level or standard of control when completed;

(B) compliance with such requirement at that facility will result in greater risk to human health and the environment than alternative options;

(C) compliance with such requirements is technically impracticable from an engineering perspective;

(D) the remedial action selected will attain a standard of performance that is equivalent to that required under the otherwise applicable standard, requirement, criteria, or limitation, through use of another method or approach;

(E) with respect to a State standard, requirement, criteria, or limitation, the State has not consistently applied (or demonstrated the intention to consistently apply) the standard, requirement, criteria, or limitation in similar circumstances at other remedial actions within the State; or

(F) in the case of a remedial action to be undertaken solely under section 9604 of this title using the Fund, selection of a remedial action that attains such level or standard of control will not provide a balance between the need for protection of public health and welfare and the environment at the facility under consideration, and the availability of amounts from the Fund to respond to other sites which present or may present a threat to public health or welfare or the environment, taking into consideration the relative immediacy of such threats.

The President shall publish such findings, together with an explanation and appropriate documentation.

(e) **PERMITS AND ENFORCEMENT**

(1) No Federal, State, or local permit shall be required for the portion of any removal or remedial action conducted entirely onsite, where such remedial action is selected and carried out in compliance with this section.

(2) A State may enforce any Federal or State standard, requirement, criteria, or limitation to which the remedial action is required to conform under this chapter in the United States district court for the district in which the facility is located. Any consent decree shall require the parties to attempt expeditiously to resolve disagreements concerning implementation of the remedial action informally with the appropriate Federal and State agencies. Where the parties agree, the consent decree may provide for administrative enforcement. Each consent decree shall also contain stipulated penalties for violations of the decree in an amount not to exceed $25,000 per day, which may be enforced by either the President or the State. Such stipulated penalties shall not be construed to impair or affect the authority of the court to order compliance with the specific terms of any such decree.

(f) **STATE INVOLVEMENT**

(1) The President shall promulgate regulations providing for substantial and meaningful involvement by each State in initiation, development, and selection of remedial actions to be undertaken in that State. The regulations, at a minimum, shall include each of the following:

(A) State involvement in decisions whether to perform a preliminary assessment and site inspection.

(B) Allocation of responsibility for hazard ranking system scoring.

(C) State concurrence in deleting sites from the National Priorities List.

(D) State participation in the long-term planning process for all remedial sites within the State.

(E) A reasonable opportunity for States to review and comment on each of the following:

(i) The remedial investigation and feasibility study and all data and technical documents leading to its issuance.

(ii) The planned remedial action identified in the remedial investigation and feasibility study.

(iii) The engineering design following selection of the final remedial action.

(iv) Other technical data and reports relating to implementation of the remedy.

(v) Any proposed finding or decision by the President to exercise the authority of subsection (d)(4) of this section.

(F) Notice to the State of negotiations with potentially responsible parties regarding the scope of any response action at a facility in the State and an opportunity to participate in such negotiations and, subject to paragraph (2), be a party to any settlement.

(G) Notice to the State and an opportunity to comment on the President's proposed plan for remedial action as well as on alternative plans under consideration. The President's proposed decision regarding the selection of remedial action shall be accompanied by a response to the comments submitted by the State, including an explanation regarding any decision under subsection (d)(4) of this section on compliance with promulgated State standards. A copy of such response shall also be provided to the State.

(H) Prompt notice and explanation of each proposed action to the State in which the facility is located.

Prior to the promulgation of such regulations, the President shall provide notice to the State of negotiations with potentially responsible parties regarding the scope of any response action at a facility in the State, and such State may participate in such negotiations and, subject to paragraph (2), any settlements.

(2)(A) This paragraph shall apply to remedial actions secured under section 9606 of this title. At least 30 days prior to the entering of any consent decree, if the President proposes to select a remedial action that does not attain a legally applicable or relevant and appropriate standard, requirement, criteria, or limitation, under the authority of subsection (d)(4) of this section, the President shall provide an opportunity for the State to concur or not concur in such selection. If the State concurs, the State may become a signatory to the consent decree.

(B) If the State does not concur in such selection, and the State desires to have the remedial action conform to such standard, requirement, criteria, or limitation, the State shall intervene in the action under section 9606 of this title before entry of the consent decree, to seek to have the remedial action so conform. Such intervention shall be a matter of right. The remedial action shall conform to such standard, requirement, criteria, or limitation if the State establishes, on the administrative record, that the finding of the President was not supported by substantial evidence. If the court determines that the remedial action shall conform to such standard, requirement, criteria, or limitation, the remedial action shall be so modified and the State may become a signatory to the decree. If the court determines that the remedial action need not conform to such standard, requirement, criteria, or limitation, and the State pays or assures the payment of the additional costs attributable to meeting such standard, requirement, criteria, or limitation, the remedial action shall be so modified and the State shall become a signatory to the decree.

(C) The President may conclude settlement negotiations with potentially responsible parties without State concurrence.

(3)(A) This paragraph shall apply to remedial actions at facilities owned or operated by a department, agency, or instrumentality of the United States. At least 30 days prior to the publication of the President's final remedial action plan, if the President proposes to select a remedial action that does not attain a legally applicable or relevant and appropriate standard, requirement, criteria, or limitation, under the authority of subsection (d)(4) of this section, the President shall provide an opportunity for the State to concur or not concur in such selection.

If the State concurs, or does not act within 30 days, the remedial action may proceed.

(B) If the State does not concur in such selection as provided in subparagraph (A), and desires to have the remedial action conform to such standard, requirement, criteria, or limitation, the State may maintain an action as follows:

(i) If the President has notified the State of selection of such a remedial action, the State may bring an action within 30 days of such notification for the sole purpose of determining whether the finding of the President is supported by substantial evidence. Such action shall be brought in the United States district court for the district in which the facility is located.

(ii) If the State establishes, on the administrative record, that the President's finding is not supported by substantial evidence, the remedial action shall be modified to conform to such standard, requirement, criteria, or limitation.

(iii) If the State fails to establish that the President's finding was not supported by substantial evidence and if the State pays, within 60 days of judgment, the additional costs attributable to meeting such standard, requirement, criteria, or limitation, the remedial action shall be selected to meet such standard, requirement, criteria, or limitation. If the State fails to pay within 60 days, the remedial action selected by the President shall proceed through completion.

(C) Nothing in this section precludes, and the court shall not enjoin, the Federal agency from taking any remedial action unrelated to or not inconsistent with such standard, requirement, criteria, or limitation.

§9622. Settlements

(a) Authority to Enter into Agreements

The President, in his discretion, may enter into an agreement with any person (including the owner or operator of the facility from which a release or substantial threat of release emanates, or any other potentially responsible person), to perform any response action (including any action described in section 9604(b) of this title) if the President determines that such action will be done properly by such person. Whenever practicable and in the public interest, as determined by the President, the President shall act to facilitate agreements under this section that are in the public interest and consistent with the National Contingency Plan in order to expedite effective remedial actions and minimize litigation. If the President decides not to use the procedures in this section, the President shall notify in writing potentially responsible parties at the facility of such decision and the reasons why use of the procedures is inappropriate. A

CERCLA §9622

decision of the President to use or not to use the procedures in this section is not subject to judicial review.

(b) AGREEMENTS WITH POTENTIALLY RESPONSIBLE PARTIES

(1) MIXED FUNDING

An agreement under this section may provide that the President will reimburse the parties to the agreement from the Fund, with interest, for certain costs of actions under the agreement that the parties have agreed to perform but which the President has agreed to finance. In any case in which the President provides such reimbursement, the President shall make all reasonable efforts to recover the amount of such reimbursement under section 9607 of this title or under other relevant authorities.

(2) REVIEWABILITY

The President's decisions regarding the availability of fund financing under this subsection shall not be subject to judicial review under subsection (d) of this section.

(3) RETENTION OF FUNDS

If, as part of any agreement, the President will be carrying out any action and the parties will be paying amounts to the President, the President may, notwithstanding any other provision of law, retain and use such amounts for purposes of carrying out the agreement.

(4) FUTURE OBLIGATION OF FUND

In the case of a completed remedial action pursuant to an agreement described in paragraph (1), the Fund shall be subject to an obligation for subsequent remedial actions at the same facility but only to the extent that such subsequent actions are necessary by reason of the failure of the original remedial action. Such obligation shall be in a proportion equal to, but not exceeding, the proportion contributed by the Fund for the original remedial action. The Fund's obligation for such future remedial action may be met through Fund expenditures or through payment, following settlement or enforcement action, by parties who were not signatories to the original agreement.

(c) EFFECT OF AGREEMENT

(1) LIABILITY

Whenever the President has entered into an agreement under this section, the liability to the United States under this chapter of each party to the agreement, including any future liability to the United States, arising from the release or threatened release that is the subject of the agreement shall be limited as provided in the agreement pursuant to a covenant not to sue in accordance with subsection (f) of this section. A covenant not to sue may provide that future liability to the United States of a settling potentially responsible party under the agreement may be limited to the same proportion as that established in the original settlement agreement. Nothing in this section shall limit or otherwise affect the authority of any court to review in the consent decree process under subsection (d) of this section any covenant not to sue contained in an agreement under this section. In determining the extent to which the liability of parties to an agreement shall be limited pursuant to a covenant not to sue, the President shall be guided by the principle that a more complete covenant not to sue shall be provided for a more permanent remedy undertaken by such parties.

(2) ACTIONS AGAINST OTHER PERSONS

If an agreement has been entered into under this section, the President may take any action under section 9606 of this title against any person who is not a party to the agreement, once the period for submitting a proposal under subsection (e)(2)(B) of this section has expired. Nothing in this section shall be construed to affect either of the following:

(A) The liability of any person under section 9606 or 9607 of this title with respect to any costs or damages which are not included in the agreement.

(B) The authority of the President to maintain an action under this chapter against any person who is not a party to the agreement.

(d) ENFORCEMENT

(1) CLEANUP AGREEMENTS

(A) CONSENT DECREE

Whenever the President enters into an agreement under this section with any potentially responsible party with respect to remedial action under section 9606 of this title, following approval of the agreement by the Attorney General, except as otherwise provided in the case of certain administrative settlements referred to in subsection (g) of this section, the agreement shall be entered in the appropriate United States district court as a consent decree. The President need not make any finding regarding an imminent and substantial endangerment to the public health or the environment in connection with any such agreement or consent decree.

(B) EFFECT

The entry of any consent decree under this subsection shall not be construed to be an acknowledgment by the parties that the release or threatened release concerned constitutes an imminent and substantial endangerment to the public health or welfare or the environment. Except as otherwise provided in the Federal Rules of Evidence, the participation by any party in the process under this section shall not be considered an admission of liability for any purpose, and the fact of such participation shall not be admissible in any judicial or administrative proceeding, including a subsequent proceeding under this section.

(C) STRUCTURE

The President may fashion a consent decree so that the entering of such decree and compliance with such decree or with any determination or agreement made pursuant to this section shall not be considered an admission of liability for any purpose.

(2) PUBLIC PARTICIPATION

(A) FILING OF PROPOSED JUDGMENT

At least 30 days before a final judgment is entered under paragraph (1), the proposed judgement shall be filed with the court.

(B) OPPORTUNITY FOR COMMENT

The Attorney General shall provide an opportunity to persons who are not named as parties to the action to comment on the proposed judgment before its entry by the court as a final judgment. The Attorney General shall consider, and file with the court, any written comments, views, or allegations relating to the proposed judgment. The Attorney General may withdraw or withhold its consent to the proposed judgment if the comments, views, and allegations concerning the judgment disclose facts or considerations which indicate that the proposed judgment is inappropriate, improper, or inadequate.

(3) 9604(b) AGREEMENTS

Whenever the President enters into an agreement under this section with any potentially responsible party with respect to action under section 9604(b) of this title, the President shall issue an order or enter into a decree setting forth the obligations of such party. The United States district court for the district in which the release or threatened release occurs may enforce such order or decree.

(e) SPECIAL NOTICE PROCEDURES

(1) NOTICE

Whenever the President determines that a period of negotiation under this subsection would facilitate an agreement with potentially responsible parties for taking response action (including any action described in section 9604(b) of this title) and would expedite remedial action, the President shall so notify all such parties and shall provide them with information concerning each of the following:

(A) The names and addresses of potentially responsible parties (including owners and operators and other persons referred to in section 9607(a) of this title), to the extent such information is available.

(B) To the extent such information is available, the volume and nature of substances contributed by each potentially responsible party identified at the facility.

(C) A ranking by volume of the substances at the facility, to the extent such information is available.

The President shall make the information referred to in this paragraph available in advance of notice under this paragraph upon the request of a potentially responsible party in accordance with procedures provided by the President. The provisions of subsection (e) of section 9604 of this title regarding protection of confidential information apply to information provided under this paragraph. Disclosure of information generated by the President under this section to persons other than the Congress, or any duly authorized Committee thereof, is subject to other privileges or protections provided by law, including (but not limited to) those applicable to attorney work product. Nothing contained in this paragraph or in other provisions of this chapter shall be construed, interpreted, or applied to diminish the required disclosure of information under other provisions of this or other Federal or State laws.

(2) NEGOTIATION

(A) MORATORIUM

Except as provided in this subsection, the President may not commence action under section 9604(a) of this title or take any action under section 9606 of this title for 120 days after providing notice and information under this subsection with respect to such action. Except as provided in this subsection, the President may not commence a remedial investigation and feasibility study under section 9604(b) of this title for 90 days after providing notice and information under this subsection with respect to such action. The President may commence any additional studies or investigations authorized under section 9604(b) of this title, including remedial design, during the negotiation period.

(B) PROPOSALS

Persons receiving notice and information under paragraph (1) of this subsection with respect to action under section 9606 of this title shall have 60 days from the date of receipt of such notice to make a proposal to the President for undertaking or financing the action under section 9606 of this title. Persons receiving notice and information under paragraph (1) of this subsection with respect to action under section 9604(b) of this title shall have 60 days from the date of receipt of such notice to make a proposal to the President for undertaking or financing the action under section 9604(b) of this title.

(C) ADDITIONAL PARTIES

If an additional potentially responsible party is identified during the negotiation period or after an agreement has been entered into under this subsection concerning a release or threatened release, the President may bring the additional party into the negotiation or enter into a separate agreement with such party.

(3) PRELIMINARY ALLOCATION OF RESPONSIBILITY

(A) IN GENERAL

The President shall develop guidelines for preparing nonbinding preliminary allocations of responsibility. In developing these guidelines the President may include such factors as the President considers relevant, such as: volume, toxicity, mobility, strength of evidence, ability to pay, litigative risks, public interest considerations, precedential value, and inequities and aggravating factors. When it would expedite settlements under this section and remedial action, the President may, after completion of the remedial investigation and feasibility study, provide a nonbinding preliminary allocation of responsibility which allocates percentages of the total cost of response among potentially responsible parties at the facility.

(B) COLLECTION OF INFORMATION

To collect information necessary or appropriate for performing the allocation under subparagraph (A) or for otherwise implementing this section, the President may by subpoena require the attendance and testimony of witnesses and the production of reports, papers, documents, answers to questions, and other information that the President deems necessary. Witnesses shall be paid the same fees and mileage that are paid witnesses in the courts of the United States. In the event of contumacy or failure or refusal of any person to obey any such subpoena, any district court of the United States in which venue is proper shall have jurisdiction to order any such person to comply with such subpoena. Any failure to obey such an order of the court is punishable by the court as a contempt thereof.

(C) EFFECT

The nonbinding preliminary allocation of responsibility shall not be admissible as evidence in any proceeding, and no court shall have jurisdiction to review the nonbinding preliminary allocation of responsibility. The nonbinding preliminary allocation of responsibility shall not constitute an apportionment or other statement on the divisibility of harm or causation.

(D) COSTS

The costs incurred by the President in producing the nonbinding preliminary allocation of responsibility shall be reimbursed by the potentially responsible parties whose offer is accepted by the President. Where an offer under this section is not accepted, such costs shall be considered costs of response.

(E) DECISION TO REJECT OFFER

Where the President, in his discretion, has provided a nonbinding preliminary allocation of responsibility and the potentially responsible parties have made a substantial offer providing for response to the President which he rejects, the reasons for the rejection shall be provided in a written explanation. The President's decision to reject such an offer shall not be subject to judicial review.

(4) FAILURE TO PROPOSE

If the President determines that a good faith proposal for undertaking or financing action under section 9606 of this title has not been submitted within 60 days of the provision of notice pursuant to this subsection, the President may thereafter commence action under section 9604(a) of this title or take an action against any person under section 9606 of this title. If the President determines that a good faith proposal for undertaking or financing action under section 9604(b) of this title has not been submitted within 60 days after the provision of notice pursuant to this subsection, the President may thereafter commence action under section 9604(b) of this title.

(5) SIGNIFICANT THREATS

Nothing in this subsection shall limit the President's authority to undertake response or enforcement action regarding a significant threat to public health or the environment within the negotiation period established by this subsection.

(6) INCONSISTENT RESPONSE ACTION

When either the President, or a potentially responsible party pursuant to an administrative order or consent decree under this chapter, has initiated a remedial investigation and feasibility study for a particular facility under this chapter, no potentially responsible party may undertake any remedial action at the facility unless such remedial action has been authorized by the President.

(f) COVENANT NOT TO SUE

(1) DISCRETIONARY COVENANTS

The President may, in his discretion, provide any person with a covenant not to sue concerning any liability to the United States under this chapter, including future liability, resulting from a release or threatened release of a hazardous substance addressed by a remedial action, whether that action is onsite of offsite, if each of the following conditions is met:

(A) The covenant not to sue is in the public interest.

(B) The covenant not to sue would expedite response action consistent with the National Contingency Plan under section 9605 of this title.

(C) The person is in full compliance with a consent decree under section 9606 of this title (including a consent decree entered into in accordance with this section) for response to the release or threatened release concerned.

(D) The response action has been approved by the President.

(2) SPECIAL COVENANTS NOT TO SUE

In the case of any person to whom the President is authorized under paragraph (1) of this subsection to provide a covenant not to sue, for the portion of remedial action —

(A) which involves the transport and secure disposition offsite of hazardous substances in a facility meeting the requirements of sections 6924(c), (d), (e), (f), (g), (m), (o), (p), (u), and (v) and 6925 (c) of this title, where the President has rejected a proposed remedial action that is consistent with the National Contingency Plan that does not include such offsite disposition and has thereafter required offsite disposition; or

(B) which involves the treatment of hazardous substances so as to destroy, eliminate, or permanently immobilize the hazardous constituents of such substances, such that, in the judgment of the President, the substances no longer present any current or currently foreseeable future significant risk to public health, welfare or the environment, no byproduct of the treatment or destruction process presents any significant hazard to public health, welfare or the environment, and all byproducts are themselves treated, destroyed, or contained in a manner which assures that such byproducts do not present any current or currently foreseeable future significant risk to public health, welfare or the environment,

the President shall provide such person with a covenant not to sue with respect to future liability to the United States under this chapter for a future release or threatened release of hazardous substances from such facility, and a person provided such covenant not to sue shall not be liable to the United States under section 9606 or 9607 of this title with respect to such release or threatened release at a future time.

(3) REQUIREMENT THAT REMEDIAL ACTION BE COMPLETED

A covenant not to sue concerning future liability to the United States shall not take effect until the President certifies that remedial action has been completed in accordance with the requirements of this chapter at the facility that is the subject of such covenant.

(4) FACTORS

In assessing the appropriateness of a covenant not to sue under paragraph (1) and any condition to be included in a covenant not to sue under paragraph (1) or (2), the President shall consider whether the covenant or condition is in the public interest on the basis of such factors as the following:

(A) The effectiveness and reliability of the remedy, in light of the other alternative remedies considered for the facility concerned.

(B) The nature of the risks remaining at the facility.

(C) The extent to which performance standards are included in the order or decree.

(D) The extent to which the response action provides a complete remedy for the facility, including a reduction in the hazardous nature of the substances at the facility.

(E) The extent to which the technology used in the response action is demonstrated to be effective.

(F) Whether the Fund or other sources of funding would be available for any additional remedial actions that might eventually be necessary at the facility.

(G) Whether the remedial action will be carried out, in whole or in significant part, by the responsible parties themselves.

(5) SATISFACTORY PERFORMANCE

Any covenant not to sue under this subsection shall be subject to the satisfactory performance by such party of its obligations under the agreement concerned.

(6) ADDITIONAL CONDITION FOR FUTURE LIABILITY

(A) Except for the portion of the remedial action which is subject to a covenant not to sue under paragraph (2) or under subsection (g) of this section (relating to de minimis settlements), a covenant not to sue a person concerning future liability to the United States shall include an exception to the covenant that allows the President to sue such person concerning future liability resulting from the release or threatened release that is the subject of the covenant where such liability arises out of conditions which are unknown at the time the President certifies under paragraph (3) that remedial action has been completed at the facility concerned.

(B) In extraordinary circumstances, the President may determine, after assessment of relevant factors such as those referred to in paragraph (4) and volume, toxicity, mobility, strength of evidence, ability to pay, litigative risks, public interest considerations, precedential value, and inequities and aggravating factors, not to include the exception referred to in subparagraph (A) if other terms, conditions, or requirements of the agreement containing the covenant not to sue are sufficient to provide all reasonable assurances that public health and the environment will be protected from any future releases at or from the facility.

(C) The President is authorized to include any provisions allowing future enforcement action under section 9606 or 9607 of this title that in the discretion of the President are necessary and appropriate to assure protection of public health, welfare, and the environment.

(g) DE MINIMIS SETTLEMENTS

(1) EXPEDITED FINAL SETTLEMENT

Whenever practicable and in the public interest, as determined by the President, the President shall as promptly as possible reach a final settlement with a potentially responsible party in an administrative or civil action under section 9606 or 9607 of this title if such settlement involves only a minor portion of the response costs at the facility concerned and, in the judgment of the President, the conditions in either of the following subparagraph (A) or (B) are met:

(A) Both of the following are minimal in comparison to other hazardous substances at the facility:

(i) The amount of the hazardous substances contributed by that party to the facility.

(ii) The toxic or other hazardous effects of the substances contributed by that party to the facility.

(B) The potentially responsible party —

(i) is the owner of the real property on or in which the facility is located;

(ii) did not conduct or permit the generation, transportation, storage, treatment, or disposal of any hazardous substance at the facility; and

(iii) did not contribute to the release or threat of release of a hazardous substance at the facility through any action or omission.

This subparagraph (B) does not apply if the potentially responsible party purchased the real property with actual or constructive knowledge that the property was used for the generation, transportation, storage, treatment, or disposal of any hazardous substance.

(2) COVENANT NOT TO SUE

The President may provide a covenant not to sue with respect to the facility concerned to any party who has entered into a settlement under this subsection unless such a covenant would be inconsistent with the public interest as determined under subsection (f) of this section.

(3) EXPEDITED AGREEMENT

The President shall reach any such settlement or grant any such covenant not to sue as soon as possible after the President has available the information necessary to reach such a settlement or grant such a covenant.

(4) CONSENT DECREE OR ADMINISTRATIVE ORDER

A settlement under this subsection shall be entered as a consent decree or embodied in an administrative order setting forth the terms of the settlement. In the case of any facility where the total response costs exceed $500,000 (excluding interest), if the settlement is embodied as an administrative order, the order may be issued only with the prior written approval of the Attorney General. If the Attorney General or his designee has not approved or disapproved the order within 30 days of this referral, the order shall be deemed to be approved unless the Attorney General and the Administrator have agreed to extend the time. The district court for the district in which the release or threatened release occurs may enforce any such administrative order.

(5) EFFECT OF AGREEMENT

A party who has resolved its liability to the United States under this subsection shall not be liable for claims for contribution regarding matters addressed in the settlement. Such settlement does not discharge any of the other potentially responsible parties unless its terms so provide, but it reduces the potential liability of the others by the amount of the settlement.

(6) SETTLEMENTS WITH OTHER POTENTIALLY RESPONSIBLE PARTIES

Nothing in this subsection shall be construed to affect the authority of the President to reach settlements with other potentially responsible parties under this chapter.

(h) COST RECOVERY SETTLEMENT AUTHORITY

(1) AUTHORITY TO SETTLE

The head of any department or agency with authority to undertake a response action under this chapter pursuant to the national contingency plan may consider, compromise, and settle a claim under section 9607 of this title for costs incurred by the United States Government if the claim has not been referred to the Department of Justice for further action. In the case of any facility where the total response costs exceed $500,000 (excluding interest), any claim referred to in the preceding sentence may be compromised and settled only with the prior written approval of the Attorney General.

(2) USE OF ARBITRATION

Arbitration in accordance with regulations promulgated under this subsection may be used as a method of settling claims of the United States where the total response costs for the facility concerned did not exceed $500,000 (excluding interest). After consultation with the Attorney General, the department or agency head may establish and publish regulations for the use of arbitration or settlement under this subsection.

(3) RECOVERY OF CLAIMS

If any person fails to pay a claim that has been settled under this subsection, the department or agency head shall request the Attorney General to bring a civil action in an appropriate district court to recover the amount of such claim, plus costs, attorneys' fees, and interest from the date of the settlement. In such an action, the terms of the settlement shall not be subject to review.

(4) CLAIMS FOR CONTRIBUTION

A person who has resolved its liability to the United States under this subsection shall not be liable for claims for contribution regarding matters addressed in the settlement. Such settlement shall not discharge any of the other potentially liable persons unless its terms so provide, but it reduces the potential liability of the others by the amount of the settlement.

(i) SETTLEMENT PROCEDURES

(1) PUBLICATION IN FEDERAL REGISTER

At least 30 days before any settlement (including any settlement arrived at through arbitration) may become final under subsection (h) of this section, or under subsection (g) of this section in the case of a settlement embodied in an administrative order, the head of the department or agency which has jurisdiction over the proposed settlement shall publish in the Federal Register notice of the proposed settlement. The notice shall identify the facility concerned and the parties to the proposed settlement.

(2) COMMENT PERIOD

For a 30-day period beginning on the date of publication of notice under paragraph (1) of a proposed settlement, the head of the department or agency which has jurisdiction over the proposed settlement shall provide an opportunity for persons who are not parties to the proposed settlement to file written comments relating to the proposed settlement.

(3) CONSIDERATION OF COMMENTS

The head of the department or agency shall consider any comments filed under paragraph (2) in determining whether or not to consent to the proposed settlement and may withdraw or withhold consent to the proposed settlement if such comments disclose facts or considerations which indicate the proposed settlement is inappropriate, improper, or inadequate.

(j) NATURAL RESOURCES

(1) NOTIFICATION OF TRUSTEE

Where a release or threatened release of any hazardous substance that is the subject of negotiations under this section may have resulted in damages to natural resources under the trusteeship of the United States, the President shall notify the Federal natural resource trustee of the negotiations and shall encourage the participation of such trustee in the negotiations.

(2) COVENANT NOT TO SUE

An agreement under this section may contain a covenant not to sue under section 9607(a)(4)(C) of this title for damages to natural resources under

§9622 CERCLA

the trusteeship of the United States resulting from the release or threatened release of hazardous substances that is the subject of the agreement, but only if the Federal natural resource trustee has agreed in writing to such covenant. The Federal natural resource trustee may agree to such covenant if the potentially responsible party agrees to undertake appropriate actions necessary to protect and restore the natural resources damaged by such release or threatened release of hazardous substances.

(k) SECTION NOT APPLICABLE TO VESSELS

The provisions of this section shall not apply to releases from a vessel.

(l) CIVIL PENALTIES

A potentially responsible party which is a party to an administrative order or consent decree entered pursuant to an agreement under this section or section 9620 of this title (relating to Federal facilities) or which is a party to an agreement under section 9620 of this title and which fails or refuses to comply with any term or condition of the order, decree or agreement shall be subject to a civil penalty in accordance with section 9609 of this title.

(m) APPLICABILITY OF GENERAL PRINCIPLES OF LAW

In the case of consent decrees and other settlements under this section (including covenants not to sue), no provision of this chapter shall be construed to preclude or otherwise affect the applicability of general principles of law regarding the setting aside or modification of consent decrees or other settlements.

§9623. REIMBURSEMENT TO LOCAL GOVERNMENTS

(a) APPLICATION

Any general purpose unit of local government for a political subdivision which is affected by a release or threatened release at any facility may apply to the President for reimbursement under this section.

(b) REIMBURSEMENT

(1) TEMPORARY EMERGENCY MEASURES

The President is authorized to reimburse local community authorities for expenses incurred (before or after October 17, 1986) in carrying out temporary emergency measures necessary to prevent or mitigate injury to human health or the environment associated with the release or threatened release of any hazardous substance or pollutant or contaminant. Such measures may include, where appropriate, security fencing to limit access, response to fires and explosions, and other measures which require immediate response at the local level.

CERCLA §9624

(2) LOCAL FUNDS NOT SUPPLANTED

Reimbursement under this section shall not supplant local funds normally provided for response.

(c) AMOUNT

The amount of any reimbursement to any local authority under subsection (b)(1) of this section may not exceed $25,000 for a single response. The reimbursement under this section with respect to a single facility shall be limited to the units of local government having jurisdiction over the political subdivision in which the facility is located.

(d) PROCEDURE

Reimbursements authorized pursuant to this section shall be in accordance with rules promulgated by the Administrator within one year after October 17, 1986.

§9624. METHANE RECOVERY

(a) IN GENERAL

In the case of a facility at which equipment for the recovery or processing (including recirculation of condensate) of methane has been installed, for purposes of this chapter:

(1) The owner or operator of such equipment shall not be considered an "owner or operator", as defined in section 9601(20) of this title, with respect to such facility.

(2) The owner or operator of such equipment shall not be considered to have arranged for disposal or treatment of any hazardous substance at such facility pursuant to section 9607 of this title.

(3) The owner or operator of such equipment shall not be subject to any action under section 9606 of this title with respect to such facility.

(b) EXCEPTIONS

Subsection (a) of this section does not apply with respect to a release or threatened release of a hazardous substance from a facility described in subsection (a) of this section if either of the following circumstances exist:

(1) The release or threatened release was primarily caused by activities of the owner or operator of the equipment described in subsection (a) of this section.

(2) The owner or operator of such equipment would be covered by paragraph (1), (2), (3), or (4) of subsection (a) of section 9607 of this title with respect to such release or threatened release if he were not the owner or operator of such equipment.

In the case of any release or threatened release referred to in paragraph (1), the owner or operator of the equipment described in subsection (a) of this section shall be liable under this chapter only for costs or damages primarily caused by the activities of such owner or operator.

§9625. SECTION 6921(b)(3)(A)(i) WASTE

(a) REVISION OF HAZARD RANKING SYSTEM

This section shall apply only to facilities which are not included or proposed for inclusion on the National Priorities List and which contain substantial volumes of waste described in section 6921(b)(3)(A)(i) of this title. As expeditiously as practicable, the President shall revise the hazard ranking system in effect under the National Contingency Plan with respect to such facilities in a manner which assures appropriate consideration of each of the following site-specific characteristics of such facilities:

(1) The quantity, toxicity, and concentrations of hazardous constituents which are present in such waste and a comparison thereof with other wastes.

(2) The extent of, and potential for, release of such hazardous constituents into the environment.

(3) The degree of risk to human health and the environment posed by such constituents.

(b) INCLUSION PROHIBITED

Until the hazard ranking system is revised as required by this section, the President may not include on the National Priorities List any facility which contains substantial volumes of waste described in section 6921(b)(3)(A)(i) of this title on the basis of an evaluation made principally on the volume of such waste and not on the concentrations of the hazardous constituents of such waste. Nothing in this section shall be construed to affect the President's authority to include any such facility on the National Priorities List based on the presence of other substances at such facility or to exercise any other authority of this chapter with respect to such other substances.

§9626. INDIAN TRIBES

(a) TREATMENT GENERALLY

The governing body of an Indian tribe shall be afforded substantially the same treatment as a State with respect to the provisions of section 9603(a) of this title (regarding notification of releases), section 9604(c)(2) of this title (regarding consultation on remedial actions), section 9604(e) of this title (regarding access to information), section 9604(i) of this title (regarding health authorities) and section 9605 of this title (regarding roles and responsibilities under the national contingency plan and submittal of priorities for remedial action, but not includ-

(b) COMMUNITY RELOCATION

Should the President determine that proper remedial action is the permanent relocation of tribal members away from a contaminated site because it is cost effective and necessary to protect their health and welfare, such finding must be concurred in by the affected tribal government before relocation shall occur. The President, in cooperation with the Secretary of the Interior, shall also assure that all benefits of the relocation program are provided to the affected tribe and that alternative land of equivalent value is available and satisfactory to the tribe. Any lands acquired for relocation of tribal members shall be held in trust by the United States for the benefit of the tribe.

(c) STUDY

The President shall conduct a survey, in consultation with the Indian tribes, to determine the extent of hazardous waste sites on Indian lands. Such survey shall be included within a report which shall make recommendations on the program needs of tribes under this chapter, with particular emphasis on how tribal participation in the administration of such programs can be maximized. Such report shall be submitted to Congress along with the President's budget request for fiscal year 1988.

(d) LIMITATION

Notwithstanding any other provision of this chapter, no action under this chapter by an Indian tribe shall be barred until the later of the following:

(1) The applicable period of limitations has expired.

(2) 2 years after the United States, in its capacity as trustee for the tribe, gives written notice to the governing body of the tribe that it will not present a claim or commence an action on behalf of the tribe or fails to present a claim or commence an action within the time limitations specified in this chapter. . . .

Subchapter III — Miscellaneous Provisions

§9657. SEPARABILITY OF PROVISIONS; CONTRIBUTION

If any provision of this chapter, or the application of any provision of this chapter to any person or circumstance, is held invalid, the application of such provision to other persons or circumstances and the remainder of this chapter shall not be affected thereby. If an administrative settlement under section 9622 of this title has the effect of limiting any person's right to obtain contribution from any party to such settlement, and if the effect of such limitation would constitute a taking without just compensation in violation of the fifth amendment of the Constitution of the United States, such person shall not be entitled, under other laws of the United States, to recover compensation from the United States for such taking, but in any such case, such limitation on the right to obtain contribution shall be treated as having no force and effect.

§9658. Actions Under State Law for Damages from Exposure to Hazardous Substances

(a) STATE STATUTES OF LIMITATIONS FOR HAZARDOUS SUBSTANCE CASES

(1) EXCEPTION TO STATE STATUTES

In the case of any action brought under State law for personal injury, or property damages, which are caused or contributed to by exposure to any hazardous substance, or pollutant or contaminant, released into the environment from a facility, if the applicable limitations period for such action (as specified in the State statute of limitations or under common law) provides a commencement date which is earlier than the federally required commencement date, such period shall commence at the federally required commencement date in lieu of the date specified in such State statute.

(2) STATE LAW GENERALLY APPLICABLE

Except as provided in paragraph (1), the statute of limitations established under State law shall apply in all actions brought under State law for personal injury, or property damages, which are caused or contributed to by exposure to any hazardous substance, or pollutant or contaminant, released into the environment from a facility.

(3) ACTIONS UNDER SECTION 9607

Nothing in this section shall apply with respect to any cause of action brought under section 9607 of this title.

(b) DEFINITIONS

As used in this section —

(1) SUBCHAPTER I TERMS

The terms used in this section shall have the same meaning as when used in subchapter I of this chapter.

(2) APPLICABLE LIMITATIONS PERIOD

The term "applicable limitations period" means the period specified in a statute of limitations during which a civil action referred to in subsection (a)(1) of this section may be brought.

CERCLA §9659

(3) COMMENCEMENT DATE

The term "commencement date" means the date specified in a statute of limitations as the beginning of the applicable limitations period.

(4) FEDERALLY REQUIRED COMMENCEMENT DATE

(A) IN GENERAL

Except as provided in subparagraph (B), the term "federally required commencement date" means the date the plaintiff knew (or reasonably should have known) that the personal injury or property damages referred to in subsection (a)(1) of this section were caused or contributed to by the hazardous substance or pollutant or contaminant concerned.

(B) SPECIAL RULES

In the case of a minor or incompetent plaintiff, the term "federally required commencement date" means the later of the date referred to in subparagraph (A) or the following:

(i) In the case of a minor, the date on which the minor reaches the age of majority, as determined by State law, or has a legal representative appointed.

(ii) In the case of an incompetent individual, the date on which such individual becomes competent or has had a legal representative appointed.

§9659. CITIZENS SUITS

(a) AUTHORITY TO BRING CIVIL ACTIONS

Except as provided in subsections (d) and (e) of this section and in section 9613(h) of this title (relating to timing of judicial review), any person may commence a civil action on his own behalf —

(1) against any person (including the United States and any other governmental instrumentality or agency, to the extent permitted by the eleventh amendment to the Constitution) who is alleged to be in violation of any standard, regulation, condition, requirement, or order which has become effective pursuant to this chapter (including any provision of an agreement under section 9620 of this title, relating to Federal facilities); or

(2) against the President or any other officer of the United States (including the Administrator of the Environmental Protection Agency and the Administrator of the ATSDR) where there is alleged a failure of the President or of such other officer to perform any act or duty under this chapter, including an act or duty under section 9620 of this title (relating to Federal facilities), which is not discretionary with the President or such other officer.

Paragraph (2) shall not apply to any act or duty under the provisions of section 9660 of this title (relating to research, development, and demonstration).

(b) VENUE

(1) ACTIONS UNDER SUBSECTION (a)(1)

Any action under subsection (a)(1) of this section shall be brought in the district court for the district in which the alleged violation occurred.

(2) ACTIONS UNDER SUBSECTION (a)(2)

Any action brought under subsection (a)(2) of this section may be brought in the United States District Court for the District of Columbia.

(c) RELIEF

The district court shall have jurisdiction in actions brought under subsection (a)(1) of this section to enforce the standard, regulation, condition, requirement, or order concerned (including any provision of an agreement under section 9620 of this title), to order such action as may be necessary to correct the violation, and to impose any civil penalty provided for the violation. The district court shall have jurisdiction in actions brought under subsection (a)(2) of this section to order the President or other officer to perform the act or duty concerned.

(d) RULES APPLICABLE TO SUBSECTION (a)(1) ACTIONS

(1) NOTICE

No action may be commenced under subsection (a)(1) of this section before 60 days after the plaintiff has given notice of the violation to each of the following:
  (A) The President.
  (B) The State in which the alleged violation occurs.
  (C) Any alleged violator of the standard, regulation, condition, requirement, or order concerned (including any provision of an agreement under section 9620 of this title).
Notice under this paragraph shall be given in such manner as the President shall prescribe by regulation.

(2) DILIGENT PROSECUTION

No action may be commenced under paragraph (1) of subsection (a) of this section if the President has commenced and is diligently prosecuting an action under this chapter, or under the Solid Waste Disposal Act [42 U.S.C. 6901 et seq.] to require compliance with the standard, regulation, condition, requirement, or order concerned (including any provision of an agreement under section 9620 of this title).

(e) RULES APPLICABLE TO SUBSECTION (a)(2) ACTIONS

No action may be commenced under paragraph (2) of subsection (a) of this section before the 60th day following the date on which the plaintiff gives notice to the Administrator or other department, agency, or instrumentality that the plaintiff will commence such action. Notice under this subsection shall be given in such manner as the President shall prescribe by regulation.

(f) COSTS

The court, in issuing any final order in any action brought pursuant to this section, may award costs of litigation (including reasonable attorney and expert witness fees) to the prevailing or the substantially prevailing party whenever the court determines such an award is appropriate. The court may, if a temporary restraining order or preliminary injunction is sought, require the filing of a bond or equivalent security in accordance with the Federal Rules of Civil Procedure.

(g) INTERVENTION

In any action under this section, the United States or the State, or both, if not a party may intervene as a matter of right. For other provisions regarding intervention, see section 9613 of this title.

(h) OTHER RIGHTS

This chapter does not affect or otherwise impair the rights of any person under Federal, State, or common law, except with respect to the timing of review as provided in section 9613(h) of this title or as otherwise provided in section 9658 of this title (relating to actions under State law).

(i) DEFINITIONS

The terms used in this section shall have the same meanings as when used in subchapter I of this chapter. . . .

Subchapter IV — Pollution Insurance

§9671. DEFINITIONS

As used in this subchapter —

(1) INSURANCE

The term "insurance" means primary insurance, excess insurance, reinsurance, surplus lines insurance, and any other arrangement for shifting and distributing risk which is determined to be insurance under applicable State or Federal law.

(2) POLLUTION LIABILITY

The term "pollution liability" means liability for injuries arising from the release of hazardous substances or pollutants or contaminants.

(3) RISK RETENTION GROUP

The term "risk retention group" means any corporation or other limited liability association taxable as a corporation, or as an insurance company, formed under the laws of any State —

(A) whose primary activity consists of assuming and spreading all, or any portion, of the pollution liability of its group members;

(B) which is organized for the primary purpose of conducting the activity described under subparagraph (A);

(C) which is chartered or licensed as an insurance company and authorized to engage in the business of insurance under the laws of any State; and

(D) which does not exclude any person from membership in the group solely to provide for members of such a group a competitive advantage over such a person.

(4) PURCHASING GROUP

The term "purchasing group" means any group of persons which has as one of its purposes the purchase of pollution liability insurance on a group basis.

(5) STATE

The term "State" means any State of the United States, the District of Columbia, the Commonwealth of Puerto Rico, Guam, American Samoa, the Virgin Islands, the Commonwealth of the Northern Marianas, and any other territory or possession over which the United States has jurisdiction.

§9672. STATE LAWS; SCOPE OF SUBCHAPTER

(a) STATE LAWS

Nothing in this subchapter shall be construed to affect either the tort law or the law governing the interpretation of insurance contracts of any State. The definitions of pollution liability and pollution liability insurance under any State law shall not be applied for the purposes of this subchapter, including recognition or qualification of risk retention groups or purchasing groups.

(b) SCOPE OF SUBCHAPTER

The authority to offer or to provide insurance under this subchapter shall be limited to coverage of pollution liability risks and this subchapter does not authorize a risk retention group or purchasing group to provide coverage of any other line of insurance.

§9673. Risk Retention Groups

(a) EXEMPTION

Except as provided in this section, a risk retention group shall be exempt from the following:

(1) A State law, rule, or order which makes unlawful, or regulates, directly or indirectly, the operation of a risk retention group.

(2) A State law, rule, or order which requires or permits a risk retention group to participate in any insurance insolvency guaranty association to which an insurer licensed in the State is required to belong.

(3) A State law, rule, or order which requires any insurance policy issued to a risk retention group or any member of the group to be countersigned by an insurance agent or broker residing in the State.

(4) A State law, rule, or order which otherwise discriminates against a risk retention group or any of its members.

(b) EXCEPTIONS

(1) STATE LAWS GENERALLY APPLICABLE

Nothing in subsection (a) of this section shall be construed to affect the applicability of State laws generally applicable to persons or corporations. The State in which a risk retention group is chartered may regulate the formation and operation of the group.

(2) STATE REGULATIONS NOT SUBJECT TO EXEMPTION

Subsection (a) of this section shall not apply to any State law which requires a risk retention group to do any of the following:

(A) Comply with the unfair claim settlement practices law of the State.

(B) Pay, on a nondiscriminatory basis, applicable premium and other taxes which are levied on admitted insurers and surplus line insurers, brokers, or policyholders under the laws of the State.

(C) Participate, on a nondiscriminatory basis, in any mechanism established or authorized under the law of the State for the equitable apportionment among insurers of pollution liability insurance losses and expenses incurred on policies written through such mechanism.

(D) Submit to the appropriate authority reports and other information required of licensed insurers under the laws of a State relating solely to pollution liability insurance losses and expenses.

(E) Register with and designate the State insurance commissioner as its agent solely for the purpose of receiving service of legal documents or process.

(F) Furnish, upon request, such commissioner a copy of any financial report submitted by the risk retention group to the commissioner of the chartering or licensing jurisdiction.

(G) Submit to an examination by the State insurance commissioner in any State in which the group is doing business to determine the group's financial condition, if —

   (i) the commissioner has reason to believe the risk retention group is in a financially impaired condition; and

   (ii) the commissioner of the jurisdiction in which the group is chartered has not begun or has refused to initiate an examination of the group.

(H) Comply with a lawful order issued in a delinquency proceeding commenced by the State insurance commissioner if the commissioner of the jurisdiction in which the group is chartered has failed to initiate such a proceeding after notice of a finding of financial impairment under subparagraph (G).

(c) APPLICATION OF EXEMPTIONS

The exemptions specified in subsection (a) of this section apply to —

(1) pollution liability insurance coverage provided by a risk retention group for —

   (A) such group; or

   (B) any person who is a member of such group;

(2) the sale of pollution liability insurance coverage for a risk retention group; and

(3) the provision of insurance related services or management services for a risk retention group or any member of such a group.

(d) AGENTS OR BROKERS

A State may require that a person acting, or offering to act, as an agent or broker for a risk retention group obtain a license from that State, except that a State may not impose any qualification or requirement which discriminates against a nonresident agent or broker.

§9674. PURCHASING GROUPS

(a) EXEMPTION

Except as provided in this section, a purchasing group is exempt from the following:

(1) A State law, rule, or order which prohibits the establishment of a purchasing group.

(2) A State law, rule, or order which makes it unlawful for an insurer to provide or offer to provide insurance on a basis providing, to a purchasing group or its member, advantages, based on their loss and expense experience, not afforded to other persons with respect to rates, policy forms, coverages, or other matters.

(3) A State law, rule, or order which prohibits a purchasing group or its

CERCLA §9675

members from purchasing insurance on the group basis described in paragraph (2) of this subsection.

(4) A State law, rule, or order which prohibits a purchasing group from obtaining insurance on a group basis because the group has not been in existence for a minimum period of time or because any member has not belonged to the group for a minimum period of time.

(5) A State law, rule, or order which requires that a purchasing group must have a minimum number of members, common ownership or affiliation, or a certain legal form.

(6) A State law, rule, or order which requires that a certain percentage of a purchasing group must obtain insurance on a group basis.

(7) A State law, rule, or order which requires that any insurance policy issued to a purchasing group or any members of the group be countersigned by an insurance agent or broker residing in that State.

(8) A State law, rule, or order which otherwise discriminate[1] against a purchasing group or any of its members.

(b) APPLICATION OF EXEMPTIONS

The exemptions specified in subsection (a) of this section apply to the following:

(1) Pollution liability insurance, and comprehensive general liability insurance which includes this coverage, provided to —

(A) a purchasing group; or

(B) any person who is a member of a purchasing group.

(2) The sale of any one of the following to a purchasing group or a member of the group:

(A) Pollution liability insurance and comprehensive general liability coverage.

(B) Insurance related services.

(C) Management services.

(c) AGENTS OR BROKERS

A State may require that a person acting, or offering to act, as an agent or broker for a purchasing group obtain a license from that State, except that a State may not impose any qualification or requirement which discriminates against a nonresident agent or broker.

§9675. APPLICABILITY OF SECURITIES LAWS

(a) OWNERSHIP INTERESTS

The ownership interests of members of a risk retention group shall be considered to be —

---

1. So in original. Probably should be "discriminates."

§9675

(1) exempted securities for purposes of section 77e of title 15 and for purposes of section 78*l* of title 15; and

(2) securities for purposes of the provisions of section 77q of title 15 and the provisions of section 78j of title 15.

(b) **INVESTMENT COMPANY ACT**

A risk retention group shall not be considered to be an investment company for purposes of the Investment Company Act of 1940 (15 U.S.C. 80a-1 et seq.).

(c) **BLUE SKY LAW**

The ownership interests of members in a risk retention group shall not be considered securities for purposes of any State blue sky law.

Resource Conservation and Recovery Act (RCRA)
42 U.S.C. §§6901-6922i

SUBCHAPTER I — GENERAL PROVISIONS

Sec.
- 6901. Congressional findings.
    - (a) Solid waste.
    - (b) Environment and health.
    - (c) Materials.
    - (d) Energy.
- 6901a. Congressional findings: used oil recycling.
- 6092. Objectives and national policy.
    - (a) Objectives.
    - (b) National policy.
- 6903. Definitions.
- 6904. Governmental cooperation.
    - (a) Interstate cooperation.
    - (b) Consent of Congress to compacts.
- 6905. Application of chapter and integration with other Acts.
    - (a) Application of chapter.
    - (b) Integration with other Acts.
    - (c) Integration with the Surface Mining Control and Reclamation Act of 1977.
- 6906. Financial disclosure.
    - (a) Statement.
    - (b) Action by Administrator.
    - (c) Exemption.
    - (d) Penalty.
- 6907. Solid waste management information and guidelines.
    - (a) Guidelines
    - (b) Notice

SUBCHAPTER II — OFFICE OF SOLID WASTE; AUTHORITIES OF THE ADMINISTRATOR

- 6911. Office of Solid Waste and Interagency Coordinating Committee.
    - (a) Office of Solid Waste.
    - (b) Interagency Coordinating Committee.
- 6911a. Assistant Administrator of Environmental Protection Agency; Appointment, etc.
- 6912. Authorities of Administrator.
    - (a) Authorities.
    - (b) Revision of Regulations.
    - (c) Criminal investigations.
- 6913. Resource Recovery and Conservation Panels.

Resource Conservation and Recovery Act

6914. Grants for discarded tire disposal.
    (a) Grants.
    (b) Authorization of appropriations.
6914a. Labeling of lubricating oil.
6914b. Degradable plastic ring carriers; definitions.
6914b-1. Regulation of plastic ring carriers.
6915. Annual report.

SUBCHAPTER III — HAZARDOUS WASTE MANAGEMENT

6921. Identification and listing of hazardous waste.
    (a) Criteria for identification or listing.
    (b) Identification and listing.
    (c) Petition by State Governor.
    (d) Small quantity generator waste.
    (e) Specified wastes.
    (f) Delisting procedures.
    (g) EP toxicity.
    (h) Additional characteristics.
    (i) Clarification of household waste exclusion.
6922. Standards applicable to generators of hazardous waste.
    (a) In general.
    (b) Waste minimization.
6923. Standards applicable to transporters of hazardous waste.
    (a) Standards.
    (b) Coordination with regulations of Secretary of Transportation.
    (c) Fuel from hazardous waste.
6924. Standards applicable to owners and operators of hazardous waste treatment, storage, and disposal facilities.
    (a) In general.
    (b) Salt dome formations, salt bed formations, underground mines and caves.
    (c) Liquids in landfills.
    (d) Prohibitions on land disposal of specified wastes.
    (e) Solvents and dioxins.
    (f) Disposal into deep injection wells; specified subsection (d) wastes, solvents and dioxins.
    (g) Additional land disposal prohibition determinations.
    (h) Variance from land disposal prohibitions.
    (i) Publication of determination.
    (j) Storage of hazardous waste prohibited from land disposal.
    (k) "Land disposal" defined.
    (*l*) Ban on dust suppression.
    (m) Treatment standards for wastes subject to land disposal prohibition.
    (n) Air emissions.
    (o) Minimum technological requirements.
    (p) Ground water monitoring.
    (q) Hazardous waste used as fuel.
    (r) Labeling.

Resource Conservation and Recovery Act

       (s) Recordkeeping.
       (t) Financial responsibility provisions.
       (u) Continuing releases at permitted facilities.
       (v) Corrective action beyond facility boundary.
       (w) Underground tanks.
       (x) Mining and other special wastes.

6925. Permits for treatment, storage, or disposal of hazardous waste.
       (a) Permit requirements.
       (b) Requirements of permit application.
       (c) Permit issuance.
       (d) Permit revocation.
       (e) Interim status.
       (f) Coal mining wastes and reclamation permits.
       (g) Research, development and demonstration permits.
       (h) Waste minimization.
       (i) Interim status facilities receiving wastes after July 26, 1982.
       (j) Interim status surface impoundments.

6926. Authorized State hazardous waste programs.
       (a) Federal guidelines.
       (b) Authorization of State program.
       (c) Interim authorization.
       (d) Effect of State permit.
       (e) Withdrawal of authorization.
       (f) Availability of information.
       (g) Amendments made by 1984 act.
       (h) State programs for used oil.

6927. Inspections.
       (a) Access Entry.
       (b) Availability to public.
       (c) Federal facility inspections.
       (d) State-operated facilities.
       (e) Mandatory inspections.

6928. Federal enforcement.
       (a) Compliance orders.
       (b) Public hearing.
       (c) Violation of compliance orders.
       (d to g) [See main volume for text].
       (h) Interim status corrective action orders.

6929. Retention of State authority.

6930. Effective date.
       (a) Preliminary notification.
       (b) Effective date of regulation.

6931. Authorization of assistance to States.
       (a) Authorization of appropriations.
       (b) Allocation.
       (c) Activities included.

6932. Transferred.

6933. Hazardous waste site inventory.
       (a) State inventory programs.

Resource Conservation and Recovery Act

          (b) Environmental Protection Agency program.
          (c) Grants.
          (d) No impediment to immediate remedial action.
6934. Monitoring, analysis, and testing.
          (a) Authority of Administrator.
          (b) Previous owners and operators.
          (c) Proposal.
          (d) Monitoring, etc., carried out by Administrator.
          (e) Enforcement.
6935. Restrictions on recycled oil.
          (a) In general.
          (b) Identification or listing of used oil as hazardous waste.
          (c) Used oil which is recycled.
          (d) Permits.
6936. Expansion during interim status.
          (a) Waste piles.
          (b) Landfills and surface impoundments.
6937. Inventory of Federal agency hazardous waste facilities.
          (a) Program requirement; submission; availability; contents.
          (b) Environmental Protection Agency program.
6938. Export of hazardous wastes.
          (a) In general.
          (b) Regulations.
          (c) Notification.
          (d) Procedures for requesting consent of the receiving country.
          (e) Conveyance of written consent to exporter.
          (f) International agreements.
          (g) Reports.
          (h) Other standards.
6939. Domestic sewage.
          (a) Report.
          (b) Revisions of regulations.
          (c) Report on wastewater lagoon.
          (d) Application of sections 6927 and 6930.
6939a. Exposure information and health assessments.
          (a) Exposure information.
          (b) Health assessments.
          (c) Members of the public.
          (d) Priority.
          (e) Periodic reports.
          (f) "Health assessments" defined.
          (g) Cost recovery.
6939b. Interim control of hazardous waste injection.
          (a) Underground source of drinking water.
          (b) Actions under Comprehensive Environmental Response, Compensation and Liability Act.
          (c) Enforcement.
          (d) Definitions.

SUBCHAPTER IV — STATE OR REGIONAL SOLID WASTE PLAN

- 6941. Objectives of subchapter.
- 6941a. Energy and materials conservation and recovery; Congressional findings.
- 6942. Federal guidelines for plans.
  - (a) Guidelines for identification of regions.
  - (b) Guidelines for State plans.
  - (c) Considerations for State plan guidelines.
- 6943. Requirements for approval of plans.
  - (a) Minimum requirements.
  - (b) Discretionary plan provisions relating to recycled oil.
  - (c) Energy and materials conservation and recovery feasibility planning and assistance.
  - (d) Size of waste-to-energy facilities.
- 6944. Criteria for sanitary landfills; sanitary landfills required for all disposal.
  - (a) Criteria for sanitary landfills.
  - (b) Disposal required to be in sanitary landfills, etc.
  - (c) Effective date.
- 6945. Upgrading of open dumps.
  - (a) Closing or upgrading of existing open dumps.
  - (b) Inventory.
  - (c) Control of hazardous disposal.
- 6946. Procedure for development and implementation of State plan.
  - (a) Identification of regions.
  - (b) Identification of State and local agencies and responsibilities.
  - (c) Interstate regions.
- 6947. Approval of State plan; Federal assistance.
  - (a) Plan approval.
  - (b) Eligibility of States for Federal financial assistance.
  - (c) Existing activities.
- 6949a. Adequacy of certain guidelines and criteria.
  - (a) Study.
  - (b) Report.
  - (c) Revisions of guidelines and criteria.

SUBCHAPTER VI — FEDERAL RESPONSIBILITIES

- 6961. Application of Federal, State, and local law to Federal facilities.
- 6963. Cooperation with Environmental Protection Agency.
  - (a) General rule.
  - (b) Information relating to energy and materials conservation and recovery.
- 6964. Applicability of solid waste disposal guidelines to Executive agencies.
  - (a) Compliance.
  - (b) Licenses and permits.

SUBCHAPTER VII — MISCELLANEOUS PROVISIONS

- 6972. Citizen suits.

Resource Conservation and Recovery Act

       (a) In general.
       (b) Actions prohibited.
       (c) Notice.
       (d) Intervention.
       (e) Costs.
       (f) Other rights preserved.
       (g) Transporters.
6973. Imminent hazard.
       (a) Authority of Administrator.
       (b) Violations.
       (c) Immediate notice.
       (d) Public participation in settlements.
6974. Petition for regulations; public participation.
       (a) Petition.
       (b) Public participation.
6975. Separability of provisions.
6976. Judicial review.
       (a) Review of final regulations and certain petitions.
       (b) Review of certain actions under sections 6925 and 6926 of this title.

SUBCHAPTER IX — REGULATION OF UNDERGROUND STORAGE TANKS

6991. Definitions and exemptions.
6991a. Notification.
       (a) Underground storage tanks.
       (b) Agency designation.
       (c) State inventories.
6991b. Release, detection, prevention, and correction regulations.
       (a) Regulations.
       (b) Distinctions in regulations.
       (c) Requirements.
       (d) Financial responsibility.
       (e) New tank performance standards.
       (f) Effective dates.
       (g) Interim prohibition.
       (h) EPA Response Program for Petroleum.
6991c. Approval of State programs.
       (a) Elements of State program.
       (b) Federal standards.
       (c) Financial responsibility.
       (d) EPA determination.
       (e) Withdrawal of authorization.
6991d. Inspections, monitoring, testing and corrective action.
       (a) Furnishing information.
       (b) Confidentiality.
6991e. Federal enforcement.
       (a) Compliance orders.

Resource Conservation and Recovery Act

          (b)   Procedure.
          (c)   Contents of order.
          (d)   Civil penalties.
6991f.   Federal facilities.
          (a)   Application of subchapter.
          (b)   Presidential exemption.
6991g. State authority.
6991h. Study of underground storage tanks.
          (a)   Petroleum tanks.
          (b)   Other tanks.
          (c)   Elements of studies.
          (d)   Farm and heating oil tanks.
          (e)   Reports.
          (f)   Reimbursement.
6991i.   Authorization of appropriations.

        SUBCHAPTER X — DEMONSTRATION MEDICAL WASTE
                          TRACKING PROGRAM

6992c. Inspections.
          (a)   Requirements for Access.
          (b)   Procedures.
          (c)   Availability to Public.
6992d. Enforcement.
          (a)   Compliance Orders.
          (b)   Criminal Penalties.
          (c)   Knowing Endangerment.
          (d)   Civil Penalties.
          (e)   Civil Penalty Policy.
6992e. Federal facilities.
          (a)   In General.
          (b)   "Person" defined.
6992f.   Relationship to State law.
          (a)   State Inspections and Enforcement.
          (b)   Retention of State Authority.
          (c)   State Forms.
6992g. . Report to Congress.
          (a)   Final Report.
          (b)   Interim Reports.
          (c)   Consultation.
6992h. Health impacts report.
6992i.   General provisions.
          (a)   Consultation.
          (b)   Public Comment.
          (c)   Relationship to Subchapter III.

[Various sections that mandate reports and fund demonstration projects are omitted.]

Subchapter I — General Provisions

§6901. Congressional Findings

(a) **SOLID WASTE**

The Congress finds with respect to solid waste —

(1) that the continuing technological progress and improvement in methods of manufacture, packaging, and marketing of consumer products has resulted in an evermounting increase, and in a change in the characteristics, of the mass material discarded by the purchaser of such products;

(2) that the economic and population growth of our Nation, and the improvements in the standard of living enjoyed by our population, have required increased industrial production to meet our needs, and have made necessary the demolition of old buildings, the construction of new buildings, and the provision of highways and other avenues of transportation, which, together with related industrial, commercial, and agricultural operations, have resulted in a rising tide of scrap, discarded, and waste materials;

(3) that the continuing concentration of our population in expanding metropolitan and other urban areas has presented these communities with serious financial, management, intergovernmental, and technical problems in the disposal of solid wastes resulting from the industrial, commercial, domestic, and other activities carried on in such areas;

(4) that while the collection and disposal of solid wastes should continue to be primarily the function of State, regional, and local agencies, the problems of waste disposal as set forth above have become a matter national in scope and in concern and necessitate Federal action through financial and technical assistance and leadership in the development, demonstration, and application of new and improved methods and processes to reduce the amount of waste and unsalvageable materials and to provide for proper and economical solid waste disposal practices.

(b) **ENVIRONMENT AND HEALTH**

The Congress finds with respect to the environment and health, that —

(1) although land is too valuable a national resource to be needlessly polluted by discarded materials, most solid waste is disposed of on land in open dumps and sanitary landfills;

(2) disposal of solid waste and hazardous waste in or on the land without careful planning and management can present a danger to human health and the environment;

(3) as a result of the Clean Air Act [42 U.S.C. 7401 et seq.], the Water Pollution Control Act [33 U.S.C. 1251 et seq.], and other Federal and State laws respecting public health and the environment, greater amounts of solid waste (in the form of sludge and other pollution treatment residues) have been created. Similarly, inadequate and environmentally unsound practices for the

disposal or use of solid waste have created greater amounts of air and water pollution and other problems for the environment and for health;

(4) open dumping is particularly harmful to health, contaminates drinking water from underground and surface supplies, and pollutes the air and the land;

(5) the placement of inadequate controls on hazardous waste management will result in substantial risks to human health and the environment;

(6) if hazardous waste management is improperly performed in the first instance, corrective action is likely to be expensive, complex, and time consuming;

(7) certain classes of land disposal facilities are not capable of assuring long-term containment of certain hazardous wastes, and to avoid substantial risk to human health and the environment, reliance on land disposal should be minimized or eliminated, and land disposal, particularly landfill and surface impoundment, should be the least favored method for managing hazardous wastes; and

(8) alternatives to existing methods of land disposal must be developed since many of the cities in the United States will be running out of suitable solid waste disposal sites within five years unless immediate action is taken.

(c) MATERIALS

The Congress finds with respect to materials, that —

(1) millions of tons of recoverable material which could be used are needlessly buried each year;

(2) methods are available to separate usable materials from solid waste; and

(3) the recovery and conservation of such materials can reduce the dependence of the United States on foreign resources and reduce the deficit in its balance of payments.

(d) ENERGY

The Congress finds with respect to energy, that —

(1) solid waste represents a potential source of solid fuel, oil, or gas that can be converted into energy;

(2) the need exists to develop alternative energy sources for public and private consumption in order to reduce our dependence on such sources as petroleum products, natural gas, nuclear and hydroelectric generation; and

(3) technology exists to produce usable energy from solid waste.

§6901a. CONGRESSIONAL FINDINGS: USED OIL RECYCLING

The Congress finds and declares that —

(1) used oil is a valuable source of increasingly scarce energy and materials;

(2) technology exists to re-refine, reprocess, reclaim, and otherwise recycle used oil;

(3) used oil constitutes a threat to public health and the environment when reused or disposed of improperly; and

that, therefore, it is in the national interest to recycle used oil in a manner which does not constitute a threat to public health and the environment and which conserves energy and materials.

§6902. OBJECTIVES AND NATIONAL POLICY

(a) OBJECTIVES

The objectives of this chapter are to promote the protection of health and the environment and to conserve valuable material and energy resources by —

(1) providing technical and financial assistance to State and local governments and interstate agencies for the development of solid waste management plans (including resource recovery and resource conservation systems) which will promote improved solid waste management techniques (including more effective organizational arrangements), new and improved methods of collection, separation, and recovery of solid waste, and the environmentally safe disposal of nonrecoverable residues;

(2) providing training grants in occupations involving the design, operation, and maintenance of solid waste disposal systems;

(3) prohibiting future open dumping on the land and requiring the conversion of existing open dumps to facilities which do not pose a danger to the environment or to health;

(4) assuring that hazardous waste management practices are conducted in a manner which protects human health and the environment;

(5) requiring that hazardous waste be properly managed in the first instance thereby reducing the need for corrective action at a future date;

(6) minimizing the generation of hazardous waste and the land disposal of hazardous waste by encouraging process substitution, materials recovery, properly conducted recycling and reuse, and treatment;

(7) establishing a viable Federal-State partnership to carry out the purposes of this chapter and insuring that the Administrator will, in carrying out the provisions of subchapter III of this chapter, give a high priority to assisting and cooperating with States in obtaining full authorization of State programs under subchapter III of this chapter;

(8) providing for the promulgation of guidelines for solid waste collection, transport, separation, recovery, and disposal practices and systems;

(9) promoting a national research and development program for improved solid waste management and resource conservation techniques, more effective organizational arrangements, and new and improved methods of collection, separation, and recovery, and recycling of solid wastes and environmentally safe disposal of nonrecoverable residues;

(10) promoting the demonstration, construction, and application of solid waste management, resource recovery, and resource conservation systems which preserve and enhance the quality of air, water, and land resources; and

(11) establishing a cooperative effort among the Federal, State, and local governments and private enterprise in order to recover valuable materials and energy from solid waste.

(b) NATIONAL POLICY

The Congress hereby declares it to be the national policy of the United States that, wherever feasible, the generation of hazardous waste is to be reduced or eliminated as expeditiously as possible. Waste that is nevertheless generated should be treated, stored, or disposed of so as to minimize the present and future threat to human health and the environment.

§6903. DEFINITIONS

As used in this chapter:

(1) The term "Administrator" means the Administrator of the Environmental Protection Agency.

(2) The term "construction," with respect to any project of construction under this chapter, means (A) the erection or building of new structures and acquisition of lands or interests therein, or the acquisition, replacement, expansion, remodeling, alteration, modernization, or extension of existing structures, and (B) the acquisition and installation of initial equipment of, or required in connection with, new or newly acquired structures or the expanded, remodeled, altered, modernized or extended part of existing structures (including trucks and other motor vehicles, and tractors, cranes, and other machinery) necessary for the proper utilization and operation of the facility after completion of the project; and includes preliminary planning to determine the economic and engineering feasibility and the public health and safety aspects of the project, the engineering, architectural, legal, fiscal, and economic investigations and studies, and any surveys, designs, plans, working drawings, specifications, and other action necessary for the carrying out of the project, and (C) the inspection and supervision of the process of carrying out the project to completion.

(2A) The term "demonstration" means the initial exhibition of a new technology process or practice or a significantly new combination or use of technologies, processes or practices, subsequent to the development stage, for the purpose of proving technological feasibility and cost effectiveness.

(3) The term "disposal" means the discharge, deposit, injection, dumping, spilling, leaking, or placing of any solid waste or hazardous waste into or on any land or water so that such solid waste or hazardous waste or any constituent thereof may enter the environment or be emitted into the air or discharged into any waters, including ground waters.

(4) The term "Federal agency" means any department, agency, or other

instrumentality of the Federal Government, any independent agency or establishment of the Federal Government including any Government corporation, and the Government Printing Office.

(5) The term "hazardous waste" means a solid waste, or combination of solid wastes, which because of its quantity, concentration, or physical, chemical, or infectious characteristics may —

    (A) cause, or significantly contribute to an increase in mortality or an increase in serious irreversible, or incapacitating reversible, illness; or

    (B) pose a substantial present or potential hazard to human health or the environment when improperly treated, stored, transported, or disposed of, or otherwise managed.

(6) The term "hazardous waste generation" means the act or process of producing hazardous waste.

(7) The term "hazardous waste management" means the systematic control of the collection, source separation, storage, transportation, processing, treatment, recovery, and disposal of hazardous wastes.

(8) For purposes of Federal financial assistance (other than rural communities assistance), the term "implementation" does not include the acquisition, leasing, construction, or modification of facilities or equipment or the acquisition, leasing, or improvement of land.

(9) The term "intermunicipal agency" means an agency established by two or more municipalities with responsibility for planning or administration of solid waste.

(10) The term "interstate agency" means an agency of two or more municipalities in different States, or an agency established by two or more States, with authority to provide for the management of solid wastes and serving two or more municipalities located in different States.

(11) The term "long-term contract" means, when used in relation to solid waste supply, a contract of sufficient duration to assure the viability of a resource recovery facility (to the extent that such viability depends upon solid waste supply).

(12) The term "manifest" means the form used for identifying the quantity, composition, and the origin, routing, and destination of hazardous waste during its transportation from the point of generation to the point of disposal, treatment, or storage.

(13) The term "municipality" (A) means a city, town, borough, county, parish, district, or other public body created by or pursuant to State law, with responsibility for the planning or administration of solid waste management, or an Indian tribe or authorized tribal organization or Alaska Native village or organization, and (B) includes any rural community or unincorporated town or village or any other public entity for which an application for assistance is made by a State or political subdivision thereof.

(14) The term "open dump" means any facility or site where solid waste is disposed of which is not a sanitary landfill which meets the criteria promulgated

under section 6944 of this title and which is not a facility for disposal of hazardous waste.

(15) The term "person" means an individual, trust, firm, joint stock company, corporation (including a government corporation), partnership, association, State, municipality, commission, political subdivision of a State, or any interstate body.

(16) The term "procurement item" means any device, good, substance, material, product, or other item whether real or personal property which is the subject of any purchase, barter, or other exchange made to procure such item.

(17) The term "procuring agency" means any Federal agency, or any State agency or agency of a political subdivision of a State which is using appropriated Federal funds for such procurement, or any person contracting with any such agency with respect to work performed under such contract.

(18) The term "recoverable" refers to the capability and likelihood of being recovered from solid waste for a commercial or industrial use.

(19) The term "recovered material" means waste material and byproducts which have been recovered or diverted from solid waste, but such term does not include those materials and byproducts generated from, and commonly reused within, an original manufacturing process.

(20) The term "recovered resources" means material or energy recovered from solid waste.

(21) The term "resource conservation" means reduction of the amounts of solid waste that are generated, reduction of overall resource consumption, and utilization of recovered resources.

(22) The term "resource recovery" means the recovery of material or energy from solid waste.

(23) The term "resource recovery system" means a solid waste management system which provides for collection, separation, recycling, and recovery of solid wastes, including disposal of nonrecoverable waste residues.

(24) The term "resource recovery facility" means any facility at which solid waste is processed for the purpose of extracting, converting to energy, or otherwise separating and preparing solid waste for reuse.

(25) The term "regional authority" means the authority established or designated under section 6946 of this title.

(26) The term "sanitary landfill" means a facility for the disposal of solid waste which meets the criteria published under section 6944 of this title.

(26A) The term "sludge" means any solid, semisolid or liquid waste generated from a municipal, commercial, or industrial wastewater treatment plant, water supply treatment plant, or air pollution control facility or any other such waste having similar characteristics and effects.

(27) The term "solid waste" means any garbage, refuse, sludge from a waste treatment plant, water supply treatment plant, or air pollution control facility and other discarded material, including solid, liquid, semisolid, or contained gaseous material resulting from industrial, commercial, mining, and agricultural

operations, and from community activities, but does not include solid or dissolved material in domestic sewage, or solid or dissolved materials in irrigation return flows or industrial discharges which are point sources subject to permits under section 1342 of title 33, or source, special nuclear, or byproduct material as defined by the Atomic Energy Act of 1954, as amended (68 Stat. 923) [42 U.S.C. 2011 et seq.].

(28) The term "solid waste management" means the systematic administration of activities which provide for the collection, source separation, storage, transportation, transfer, processing, treatment, and disposal of solid waste.

(29) The term "solid waste management facility" includes —

(A) any resource recovery system or component thereof,

(B) any system, program, or facility for resource conservation, and

(C) any facility for the collection, source separation, storage, transportation, transfer, processing, treatment or disposal of solid wastes, including hazardous wastes, whether such facility is associated with facilities generating such wastes or otherwise.

(30) The terms "solid waste planning," "solid waste management," and "comprehensive planning" include planning or management respecting resource recovery and resource conservation.

(31) The term "State" means any of the several States, the District of Columbia, the Commonwealth of Puerto Rico, the Virgin Islands, Guam, American Samoa, and the Commonwealth of the Northern Mariana Islands.

(32) The term "State authority" means the agency established or designated under section 6947 of this title.

(33) The term "storage," when used in connection with hazardous waste, means the containment of hazardous waste, either on a temporary basis or for a period of years, in such a manner as not to constitute disposal of such hazardous waste.

(34) The term "treatment," when used in connection with hazardous waste, means any method, technique, or process, including neutralization, designed to change the physical, chemical, or biological character or composition of any hazardous waste so as to neutralize such waste or so as to render such waste nonhazardous, safer for transport, amendable for recovery, amenable for storage, or reduced in volume. Such term includes any activity or processing designed to change the physical form or chemical composition of hazardous waste so as to render it nonhazardous.

(35) The term "virgin material" means a raw material, including previously unused copper, aluminum, lead, zinc, iron, or other metal or metal ore, any undeveloped resource that is, or with new technology will become, a source of raw materials.

(36) The term "used oil" means any oil which has been —

(A) refined from crude oil,

(B) used, and

(C) as a result of such use, contaminated by physical or chemical impurities.

(37) The term "recycled oil" means any used oil which is reused, following its original use, for any purpose (including the purpose for which the oil was originally used). Such term includes oil which is re-refined, reclaimed, burned, or reprocessed.

(38) The term "lubricating oil" means the fraction of crude oil which is sold for purposes of reducing friction in any industrial or mechanical device. Such term includes re-refined oil.

(39) The term "re-refined oil" means used oil from which the physical and chemical contaminants acquired through previous use have been removed through a refining process.

(40) Except as otherwise provided in this paragraph, the term "medical waste" means any solid waste which is generated in the diagnosis, treatment, or immunization of human beings or animals, in research pertaining thereto, or in the production or testing of biologicals. Such term does not include any hazardous waste identified or listed under subchapter III of this chapter or any household waste as defined in regulations under subchapter III of this chapter.

§6904. GOVERNMENTAL COOPERATION

(a) INTERSTATE COOPERATION

The provisions of this chapter to be carried out by States may be carried out by interstate agencies and provisions applicable to States may apply to interstate regions where such agencies and regions have been established by the respective States and approved by the Administrator. In any such case, action required to be taken by the Governor of a State, respecting regional designation shall be required to be taken by the Governor of each of the respective States with respect to so much of the interstate region as is within the jurisdiction of that State.

(b) CONSENT OF CONGRESS TO COMPACTS

The consent of the Congress is hereby given to two or more States to negotiate and enter into agreements or compacts, not in conflict with any law or treaty of the United States, for —

(1) cooperative effort and mutual assistance for the management of solid waste or hazardous waste (or both) and the enforcement of their respective laws relating thereto, and

(2) the establishment of such agencies, joint or otherwise, as they may deem desirable for making effective such agreements or compacts.

No such agreement or compact shall be binding or obligatory upon any State party thereto unless it is agreed upon by all parties to the agreement and until it has been approved by the Administrator and the Congress.

§6905. Application of Chapter and Integration with Other Acts

(a) APPLICATION OF CHAPTER

Nothing in this chapter shall be construed to apply to (or to authorize any State, interstate, or local authority to regulate) any activity or substance which is subject to the Federal Water Pollution Control Act [33 U.S.C. 1251 et seq.], the Safe Drinking Water Act [42 U.S.C. 300f et seq.], the Marine Protection, Research and Sanctuaries Act of 1972 [33 U.S.C. 1401 et seq.], or the Atomic Energy Act of 1954 [42 U.S.C. 2011 et seq.] except to the extent that such application (or regulation) is not inconsistent with the requirements of such Acts.

(b) INTEGRATION WITH OTHER ACTS

(1) The Administrator shall integrate all provisions of this chapter for purposes of administration and enforcement and shall avoid duplication, to the maximum extent practicable, with the appropriate provisions of the Clean Air Act [42 U.S.C. 7401 et seq.], the Federal Water Pollution Control Act [33 U.S.C. 1251 et seq.], the Federal Insecticide, Fungicide, and Rodenticide Act [7 U.S.C. 136 et seq.], the Safe Drinking Water Act [42 U.S.C. 300f et seq.], the Marine Protection, Research and Sanctuaries Act of 1972 [33 U.S.C. 1401 et seq.], and such other Acts of Congress as grant regulatory authority to the Administrator. Such integration shall be effected only to the extent that it can be done in a manner consistent with the goals and policies expressed in this chapter and in the other acts referred to in this subsection.

(2)(A) As promptly as practicable after November 8, 1984, the Administrator shall submit a report describing —

(i) the current data and information available on emissions of polychlorinated dibenzo-p-dioxins from resource recovery facilities burning municipal solid waste;

(ii) any significant risks to human health posed by these emissions; and

(iii) operating practices appropriate for controlling these emissions.

(B) Based on the report under subparagraph (A) and on any future information on such emissions, the Administrator may publish advisories or guidelines regarding the control of dioxin emissions from such facilities. Nothing in this paragraph shall be construed to preempt or otherwise affect the authority of the Administrator to promulgate any regulations under the Clean Air Act [42 U.S.C. 7401 et seq.] regarding emissions of polychlorinated dibenzo-p-dioxins.

(3) Notwithstanding any other provisions of law, in developing solid waste plans, it is the intention of this chapter that in determining the size of a waste-to-energy facility, adequate provisions shall be given to the present and reasonably anticipated future needs, including those needs created by thorough implementation of section 6962(h) of this title, of the recycling and resource recovery interests within the area encompassed by the solid waste plan.

(c) **INTEGRATION WITH THE SURFACE MINING CONTROL AND RECLAMATION ACT OF 1977**

(1) No later than 90 days after October 21, 1980, the Administrator shall review any regulations applicable to the treatment, storage, or disposal of any coal mining wastes or overburden promulgated by the Secretary of the Interior under the Surface Mining and Reclamation Act of 1977 [30 U.S.C. 1201 et seq.]. If the Administrator determines that any requirement of final regulations promulgated under any section of subchapter III of this chapter relating to mining wastes or overburden is not adequately addressed in such regulations promulgated by the Secretary, the Administrator shall promptly transmit such determination, together with suggested revisions and supporting documentation, to the Secretary.

(2) The Secretary of the Interior shall have exclusive responsibility for carrying out any requirement of subchapter III of this chapter with respect to coal mining wastes or overburden for which a surface coal mining and reclamation permit is issued or approved under the Surface Mining Control and Reclamation Act of 1977 [30 U.S.C. 1201 et seq.]. The Secretary shall, with the concurrence of the Administrator, promulgate such regulations as may be necessary to carry out the purposes of this subsection and shall integrate such regulations with regulations promulgated under the Surface Mining Control and Reclamation Act of 1977.

§6906. Financial Disclosure

(a) **STATEMENT**

Each officer or employee of the Administrator who —

(1) performs any function or duty under this chapter; and

(2) has any known financial interest in any person who applies for or receives financial assistance under this chapter

shall, beginning on February 1, 1977, annually file with the Administrator a written statement concerning all such interests held by such officer or employee during the preceding calendar year. Such statement shall be available to the public.

(b) **ACTION BY ADMINISTRATOR**

The Administrator shall —

(1) act within ninety days after October 21, 1976 —

(A) to define the term "known financial interest" for purposes of subsection (a) of this section; and

(B) to establish the methods by which the requirement to file written statements specified in subsection (a) of this section will be monitored and enforced, including appropriate provision for the filing by such officers and employees of such statements and the review by the Administrator of such statements; and

§6906

(2) report to the Congress on June 1, 1978, and of each succeeding calendar year with respect to such disclosures and the actions taken in regard thereto during the preceding calendar year.

(c) EXEMPTION

In the rules prescribed under subsection (b) of this section, the Administrator may identify specific positions within the Environmental Protection Agency which are of a nonpolicy-making nature and provide that officers or employees occupying such positions shall be exempt from the requirements of this section.

(d) PENALTY

Any officer or employee who is subject to, and knowingly violates, this section shall be fined not more than $2,500 or imprisoned not more than one year, or both.

§6907. SOLID WASTE MANAGEMENT INFORMATION AND GUIDELINES

(a) GUIDELINES

Within one year of October 21, 1976, and from time to time thereafter, the Administrator shall, in cooperation with appropriate Federal, State, municipal, and intermunicipal agencies, and in consultation with other interested persons, and after public hearings, develop and publish suggested guidelines for solid waste management. Such suggested guidelines shall —

(1) provide a technical and economic description of the level of performance that can be attained by various available solid waste management practices (including operating practices) which provide for the protection of public health and the environment;

(2) not later than two years after October 21, 1976, describe levels of performance, including appropriate methods and degrees of control, that provide at a minimum for (A) protection of public health and welfare; (B) protection of the quality of ground waters and surface waters from leachates; (C) protection of the quality of surface waters from runoff through compliance with effluent limitations under the Federal Water Pollution Control Act, as amended [33 U.S.C. 1251 et seq.]; (D) protection of ambient air quality through compliance with new source performance standards or requirements of air quality implementation plans under the Clean Air Act, as amended [42 U.S.C. 7401 et seq.]; (E) disease and vector control; (F) safety; and (G) esthetics; and

(3) provide minimum criteria to be used by the States to define those solid waste management practices which constitute the open dumping of solid waste or hazardous waste and are to be prohibited under subchapter IV of this chapter.

Where appropriate, such suggested guidelines also shall include minimum information for use in deciding the adequate location, design, and construction of facilities associated with solid waste management practices, including the consideration of regional, geographic, demographic, and climatic factors.

(b) NOTICE

The Administrator shall notify the Committee on Environment and Public Works of the Senate and the Committee on Energy and Commerce of the House of Representatives a reasonable time before publishing any suggested guidelines or proposed regulations under this chapter of the content of such proposed suggested guidelines or proposed regulations under this chapter.

Subchapter II — Office of Solid Waste; Authorities of the Administrator.

§6911. OFFICE OF SOLID WASTE AND INTERAGENCY COORDINATING COMMITTEE

(a) OFFICE OF SOLID WASTE

The Administrator shall establish within the Environmental Protection Agency an Office of Solid Waste (hereinafter referred to as the "Office") to be headed by an Assistant Administrator of the Environmental Protection Agency. The duties and responsibilities (other than duties and responsibilities relating to research and development) of the Administrator under this chapter (as modified by applicable reorganization plans) shall be carried out through the Office.

(b) INTERAGENCY COORDINATING COMMITTEE

(1) There is hereby established an Interagency Coordinating Committee on Federal Resource Conservation and Recovery Activities which shall have the responsibility for coordinating all activities dealing with resource conservation and recovery from solid waste carried out by the Environmental Protection Agency, the Department of Energy, the Department of Commerce, and all other Federal agencies which conduct such activities pursuant to this chapter or any other Act. For purposes of this subsection, the term "resource conservation and recovery activities" shall include, but not be limited to, all research, development and demonstration projects on resource conservation or energy, or material, recovery from solid waste, and all technical or financial assistance for State or local planning for, or implementation of, projects related to resource conservation or energy or material, recovery from solid waste. The Committee shall be chaired by the Administrator of the Environmental Protection Agency or such person as the Administrator may designate. Members of the Committee shall include representatives of the Department of Energy, the Department of Commerce, the Department of the Treasury, and each other Federal agency which the Administrator determines to have programs or responsibilities affecting resource conservation or recovery.

(2) The Interagency Coordinating Committee shall include oversight of the implementation of

(A) the May 1979 Memorandum of Understanding on Energy Recovery from Municipal Solid Waste between the Environmental Protection Agency and the Department of Energy;

(B) the May 30, 1978, Interagency Agreement between the Department of Commerce and the Environmental Protection Agency on the Implementation of the Resource Conservation and Recovery Act [42 U.S.C. 6901 et seq.]; and

(C) any subsequent agreements between these agencies or other Federal agencies which address Federal resource recovery or conservation activities.

(3) The Interagency Coordinating Committee shall submit to the Congress by March 1, 1981, and on March 1 each year thereafter, a five-year action plan for Federal resource conservation or recovery activities which shall identify means and propose programs to encourage resource conservation or material and energy recovery and increase private and municipal investment in resource conservation or recovery systems, especially those which provide for material conservation or recovery as well as energy conservation or recovery. Such plan shall describe, at a minimum, a coordinated and nonduplicatory plan for resource recovery and conservation activities for the Environmental Protection Agency, the Department of Energy, the Department of Commerce, and all other Federal agencies which conduct such activities.

§6911a. ASSISTANT ADMINISTRATOR OF ENVIRONMENTAL PROTECTION AGENCY; APPOINTMENT, ETC.

The Assistant Administrator of the Environmental Protection Agency appointed to head the Office of Solid Waste shall be in addition to the five Assistant Administrators of the Environmental Protection Agency provided for in section 1(d) of Reorganization Plan Numbered 3 of 1970 and the additional Assistant Administrator provided by the Toxic Substances Control Act [15 U.S.C. 2601 et seq.], shall be appointed by the President by and with the advice and consent of the Senate.

§6912. AUTHORITIES OF ADMINISTRATOR

(a) **AUTHORITIES**

In carrying out this chapter, the Administrator is authorized to —

(1) prescribe, in consultation with Federal, State, and regional authorities, such regulations as are necessary to carry out his functions under this chapter;

(2) consult with or exchange information with other Federal agencies undertaking research, development, demonstration projects, studies, or investigations relating to solid waste;

(3) provide technical and financial assistance to States or regional agencies in the development and implementation of solid waste plans and hazardous waste management programs;

(4) consult with representatives of science, industry, agriculture, labor, environmental protection and consumer organizations, and other groups, as he deems advisable;

(5) utilize the information, facilities, personnel and other resources of Federal agencies, including the National Institute of Standards and Technology and the National Bureau of the Census, on a reimbursable basis, to perform research and analyses and conduct studies and investigations related to resource recovery and conservation and to otherwise carry out the Administrator's functions under this chapter; and

(6) to delegate to the Secretary of Transportation the performance of any inspection or enforcement function under this chapter relating to the transportation of hazardous waste where such delegation would avoid unnecessary duplication of activity and would carry out the objectives of this chapter and of the Hazardous Materials Transportation Act [49 App. U.S.C. 1801 et seq.].

(b) **REVISION OF REGULATIONS**

Each regulation promulgated under this chapter shall be reviewed and, where necessary, revised not less frequently than every three years.

(c) **CRIMINAL INVESTIGATIONS**

In carrying out the provisions of this chapter, the Administrator, and duly-designated agents and employees of the Environmental Protection Agency, are authorized to initiate and conduct investigations under the criminal provisions of this chapter, and to refer the results of these investigations to the Attorney General for prosecution in appropriate cases.

§6913. Resource Recovery and Conservation Panels

The Administrator shall provide teams of personnel, including Federal, State, and local employees or contractors (hereinafter referred to as "Resource Conservation and Recovery Panels") to provide Federal agencies, States and local governments upon request with technical assistance on solid waste management, resource recovery, and resource conservation. Such teams shall include technical, marketing, financial, and institutional specialists, and the services of such teams shall be provided without charge to States or local governments.

§6914. Grants for Discarded Tire Disposal

(a) **GRANTS**

The Administrator shall make available grants equal to 5 percent of the purchase price of tire shredders (including portable shredders attached to tire collection trucks) to those eligible applicants best meeting criteria promulgated under this section. An eligible applicant may be any private purchaser, public body, or public-private joint venture. Criteria for receiving grants shall be promulgated under this section and shall include the policy to offer any private purchaser the first option to receive a grant, the policy to develop widespread geographic distribution of tire shredding facilities, the need for such facilities within a geographic area, and the projected risk and viability of any such venture. In the case of an application under this section from a public body, the Administrator shall first make a determination that there are no private purchasers interested in making an application before approving a grant to a public body.

(b) AUTHORIZATION OF APPROPRIATIONS

There is authorized to be appropriated $750,000 for each of the fiscal years 1978 and 1979 to carry out this section.

§6914a. LABELING OF LUBRICATING OIL

For purposes of any provision of law which requires the labeling of commodities, lubricating oil shall be treated as lawfully labeled only if it bears the following statement, prominently displayed:

"DON'T POLLUTE — CONSERVE RESOURCES; RETURN USED OIL TO COLLECTION CENTERS."

§6914b. DEGRADABLE PLASTIC RING CARRIERS; DEFINITIONS

As used in this title —
(1) the term "regulated item" means any plastic ring carrier device that contains at least one hole greater than 1¾ inches in diameter which is made, used, or designed for the purpose of packaging, transporting, or carrying multipackaged cans or bottles, and which is of a size, shape, design, or type capable, when discarded, of becoming entangled with fish or wildlife; and
(2) the term "naturally degradable material" means a material which, when discarded, will be reduced to environmentally benign subunits under the action of normal environmental forces, such as, among others, biological decomposition, photodegradation, or hydrolysis.

§6914b-1. REGULATION OF PLASTIC RING CARRIERS

Not later than 24 months after October 28, 1988 (unless the Administrator of the Environmental Protection Agency determines that it is not feasible or that the byproducts of degradable regulated items present a greater threat to the environment than nondegradable regulated items), the Administrator of the Environmental Protection Agency shall require, by regulation, that any regulated item intended for use in the United States shall be made of naturally degradable material which, when discarded, decomposes within a period established by such regulation. The period within which decomposition must occur after being discarded shall be the shortest period of time consistent with the intended use of the item and the physical integrity required for such use. Such regulation shall allow a reasonable time for affected parties to come into compliance, including the use of existing inventories.

§6915. ANNUAL REPORT

The Administrator shall transmit to the Congress and the President, not later than ninety days after the end of each fiscal year, a comprehensive and detailed report on all activities of the Office during the preceding fiscal year. Each such report shall include —

(1) a statement of specific and detailed objectives for the activities and programs conducted and assisted under this chapter;

(2) statements of the Administrator's conclusions as to the effectiveness of such activities and programs in meeting the stated objectives and the purposes of this chapter, measured through the end of such fiscal year;

(3) a summary of outstanding solid waste problems confronting the Administrator, in order of priority;

(4) recommendations with respect to such legislation which the Administrator deems necessary or desirable to assist in solving problems respecting solid waste;

(5) all other information required to be submitted to the Congress pursuant to any other provision of this chapter; and

(6) the Administrator's plans for activities and programs respecting solid waste during the next fiscal year. . . .

Subchapter III — Hazardous Waste Management.

§6921. IDENTIFICATION AND LISTING OF HAZARDOUS WASTE

(a) CRITERIA FOR IDENTIFICATION OR LISTING

Not later than eighteen months after October 21, 1976, the Administrator shall, after notice and opportunity for public hearing, and after consultation with appropriate Federal and State agencies, develop and promulgate criteria for identifying the characteristics of hazardous waste, and for listing hazardous waste, which should be subject to the provisions of this subchapter, taking into account toxicity, persistence, and degradability in nature, potential for accumulation in tissue, and other related factors such as flammability, corrosiveness, and other hazardous characteristics. Such criteria shall be revised from time to time as may be appropriate.

(b) **IDENTIFICATION AND LISTING**

(1) Not later than eighteen months after October 21, 1976, and after notice and opportunity for public hearing, the Administrator shall promulgate regulations identifying the characteristics of hazardous waste, and listing particular hazardous wastes (within the meaning of section 6903(5) of this title), which shall be subject to the provisions of this subchapter. Such regulations shall be based on the criteria promulgating under subsection (a) of this section and shall be revised from time to time thereafter as may be appropriate. The Administrator, in cooperation with the Agency for Toxic Substances and Disease Registry and the National Toxicology Program, shall also identify or list those hazardous wastes which shall be subject to the provisions of this subchapter solely because of the presence in such wastes of certain constituents (such as identified carcinogens, mutagens, or teratagens) at levels in excess of levels which endanger human health.

(2)(A) Notwithstanding the provisions of paragraph (1) of this subsection, drilling fluids, produced waters, and other wastes associated with the exploration, development, or production of crude oil or natural gas or geothermal energy shall be subject only to existing State or Federal regulatory programs in lieu of this subchapter until at least 24 months after October 21, 1980, and after promulgation of the regulations in accordance with subparagraphs (B) and (C) of this paragraph. It is the sense of the Congress that such State or Federal programs should include, for waste disposal sites which are to be closed, provisions requiring at least the following:

(i) The identification through surveying, platting, or other measures, together with recordation of such information on the public record, so as to assure that the location where such wastes are disposed of can be located in the future; except however, that no such surveying, platting, or other measure identifying the location of a disposal site for drilling fluids and associated wastes shall be required if the distance from the disposal site to the surveyed or platted location to the associated well is less than two hundred lineal feet; and

(ii) A chemical and physical analysis of a produced water and a composition of a drilling fluid suspected to contain a hazardous material, with such information to be acquired prior to closure and to be placed on the public record.

(B) Not later than six months after completion and submission of the study required by section 6982(m) of this title, the Administrator shall, after public hearings and opportunity for comment, determine either to promulgate regulations under this subchapter for drilling fluids, produced waters, and other wastes associated with the exploration, development, or production of crude oil or natural gas or geothermal energy or that such regulations are unwarranted. The Administrator shall publish his decision in the Federal Register accompanied by an explanation and justification of the reasons for it. In making the decision under this paragraph, the Administrator shall utilize the information developed or accumulated pursuant to the study required under section 6982(m) of this title.

(C) The Administrator shall transmit his decision, along with any regulations, if necessary, to both Houses of Congress. Such regulations shall take effect only when authorized by Act of Congress.

(3)(A) Notwithstanding the provisions of paragraph (1) of this subsection, each waste listed below shall, except as provided in subparagraph (B) of this paragraph, be subject only to regulation under other applicable provisions of Federal or State law in lieu of this subchapter until at least six months after the date of submission of the applicable study required to be conducted under subsection (f), (n), (o), or (p) of section 6982 of this title and after promulgation of regulations in accordance with subparagraph (C) of this paragraph:

(i) Fly ash waste, bottom ash waste, slag waste, and flue gas emission control waste generated primarily from the combustion of coal or other fossil fuels.

(ii) Solid waste from the extraction, beneficiation, and processing of ores and minerals, including phosphate rock and overburden from the mining of uranium ore.

(iii) Cement kiln dust waste.

(B)(i) Owners and operators of disposal sites for wastes listed in subparagraph (A) may be required by the Administrator, through regulations prescribed under authority of section 6912 of this title —

(I) as to disposal sites for such wastes which are to be closed, to identify the locations of such sites through surveying, platting, or other measures, together with recordation of such information on the public record, to assure that the locations where such wastes are disposed of are known and can be located in the future, and

(II) to provide chemical and physical analysis and composition of such wastes, based on available information, to be placed on the public record.

(ii)(I) In conducting any study under subsection (f), (n), (o), or (p), of section 6982 of this title, any officer, employee, or authorized representative of the Environmental Protection Agency, duly designated by the Administrator, is authorized, at reasonable times and as reasonably necessary for the purposes of such study, to enter any establishment where any waste subject to such study is generated, stored, treated, disposed of, or transported from; to inspect, take samples, and conduct monitoring and testing; and to have access to and copy records relating to such waste. Each such inspection shall be commenced and completed with reasonable promptness. If the officer, employee, or authorized representative obtains any samples prior to leaving the premises, he shall give to the owner, operator, or agent in charge a receipt describing the sample obtained and if requested a portion of each such sample equal in volume or weight to the portion retained. If any analysis is made of such samples, or monitoring and testing performed, a copy of the results shall be furnished promptly to the owner, operator, or agent in charge.

(II) Any records, reports, or information obtained from any person under subclause (I) shall be available to the public, except that upon a showing satisfactory to the Administrator by any person that records, reports, or information, or particular part thereof, to which the Administrator has access under this subparagraph is made public, would divulge information entitled to protection under section 1905 of title 18, the Administrator shall consider such information or particular portion thereof confidential in accordance with the purposes of that section, except that such record, report, document, or information may be disclosed to other officers, employees, or authorized representatives of the United States concerned with carrying out this chapter. Any person not subject to the provisions of section 1905 of title 18 who knowingly and willfully divulges or discloses any information entitled to protection under this subparagraph shall, upon conviction, be subject to a fine of not more than $5,000 or to imprisonment not to exceed one year, or both.

(iii) The Administrator may prescribe regulations, under the authority of this chapter, to prevent radiation exposure which presents an unreasonable risk to human health from the use in construction or land reclamation (with or without revegetation) of (I) solid waste from the extraction, beneficiation, and processing of phosphate rock or (II) overburden from the mining of uranium ore.

(iv) Whenever on the basis of any information the Administrator determines that any person is in violation of any requirement of this subparagraph, the Administrator shall give notice to the violator of his failure to comply with such requirement. If such violation extends beyond the thirtieth day after the Administrator's notification, the Administrator may issue an order requiring compliance within a specified time period or the Administrator may commence a civil action in the United States district court in the district in which the violation occurred for appropriate relief, including a temporary or permanent injunction.

(C) Not later than six months after the date of submission of the applicable study required to be conducted under subsection (f), (n), (o), or (p), of section 6982 of this title, the Administrator shall, after public hearings and opportunity for comment, either determine to promulgate regulations under this subchapter for each waste listed in subparagraph (A) of this paragraph or determine that such regulations are unwarranted. The Administrator shall publish his determination, which shall be based on information developed or accumulated pursuant to such study, public hearings, and comment, in the Federal Register accompanied by an explanation and justification of the reasons for it.

(c) PETITION BY STATE GOVERNOR

At any time after the date eighteen months after October 21, 1976, the Governor of any State may petition the Administrator to identify or list a material as a hazardous waste. The Administrator shall act upon such petition within ninety days following his receipt thereof and shall notify the Governor of such action. If the Administrator denies such petition because of financial considerations, in providing such notice to the Governor he shall include a statement concerning such considerations.

(d) SMALL QUANTITY GENERATOR WASTE

(1) By March 31, 1986, the Administrator shall promulgate standards under sections 6922, 6923, and 6924 of this title for hazardous waste generated by a generator in a total quantity of hazardous waste greater than one hundred kilograms but less than one thousand kilograms during a calendar month.

(2) The standards referred to in paragraph (1), including standards applicable to the legitimate use, reuse, recycling, and reclamation of such wastes, may vary from the standards applicable to hazardous waste generated by larger quantity generators, but such standards shall be sufficient to protect human health and the environment.

(3) Not later than two hundred and seventy days after November 8, 1984, any hazardous waste which is part of a total quantity generated by a generator generating greater than one hundred kilograms but less than one thousand kilograms during one calendar month and which is shipped off the premises on which such waste is generated shall be accompanied by a copy of the Environmental Protection Agency Uniform Hazardous Waste Manifest form signed by the generator. This form shall contain the following information:

(A) the name and address of the generator of the waste;

(B) the United States Department of Transportation description of the waste, including the proper shipping name, hazard class, and identification number (UN/NA), if applicable;

(C) the number and type of containers;

(D) the quantity of waste being transported; and

(E) the name and address of the facility designated to receive the waste.

If subparagraph (B) is not applicable, in lieu of the description referred to in such subparagraph (B), the form shall contain the Environmental Protection Agency identification number, or a generic description of the waste, or a description of the waste by hazardous waste characteristic. Additional requirements related to the manifest form shall apply only if determined necessary by the Administrator to protect human health and the environment.

(4) The Administrator's responsibility under this subchapter to protect human health and the environment may require the promulgation of standards under this subchapter for hazardous wastes which are generated by any generator who does not generate more than one hundred kilograms of hazardous waste in a calendar month.

(5) Until the effective date of standards required to be promulgated under paragraph (1), any hazardous waste identified or listed under this section generated by any generator during any calendar month in a total quantity greater than one hundred kilograms but less than one thousand kilograms, which is not treated, stored, or disposed of at a hazardous waste treatment, storage, or disposal facility with a permit under section 6925 of this title, shall be disposed of only in a facility which is permitted, licensed, or registered by a State to manage municipal or industrial solid waste.

(6) Standards promulgated as provided in paragraph (1) shall, at a minimum, require that all treatment, storage, or disposal of hazardous wastes generated by generators referred to in paragraph (1) shall occur at a facility with interim status or a permit under this subchapter, except that onsite storage of hazardous waste generated by a generator generating a total quantity of hazardous waste greater than one hundred kilograms, but less than one thousand kilograms during a calendar month, may occur without the requirement of a permit for up to one hundred and eighty days. Such onsite storage may occur without the requirement of a permit for not more than six thousand kilograms for up to two hundred and seventy days if such generator must ship or haul such waste over two hundred miles.

(7)(A) Nothing in this subsection shall be construed to affect or impair the validity of regulations promulgated by the Secretary of Transportation pursuant to the Hazardous Materials Transportation Act [49 App. U.S.C. 1801 et seq.].

(B) Nothing in this subsection shall be construed to affect, modify, or render invalid any requirements in regulations promulgated prior to January 1, 1983 applicable to any acutely hazardous waste identified or listed under this section which is generated by any generator during any calendar month in a total quantity less than one thousand kilograms.

(8) Effective March 31, 1986, unless the Administrator promulgates standards as provided in paragraph (1) of this subsection prior to such date, hazardous waste generated by any generator in a total quantity greater than one hundred kilograms but less than one thousand kilograms during a calendar month shall be subject to the following requirements until the standards referred to in paragraph (1) of this subsection have become effective:

(A) the notice requirements of paragraph (3) of this subsection shall apply and in addition, the information provided in the form shall include the name of the waste transporters and the name and address of the facility designated to receive the waste;

(B) except in the case of the onsite storage referred to in paragraph (6) of this subsection, the treatment, storage, or disposal of such waste shall occur at a facility with interim status or a permit under this subchapter;

(C) generators of such waste shall file manifest exception reports as required of generators producing greater amounts of hazardous waste per month except that such reports shall be filed by January 31, for any waste shipment occurring in the last half of the preceding calendar year, and by July 31, for any waste shipment occurring in the first half of the calendar year; and

(D) generators of such waste shall retain for three years a copy of the manifest signed by the designated facility that has received the waste.

Nothing in this paragraph shall be construed as a determination of the standards appropriate under paragraph (1).

(9) The last sentence of section 6930(b) of this title shall not apply to regulations promulgated under this subsection.

(e) SPECIFIED WASTES

(1) Not later than 6 months after November 8, 1984, the Administrator shall, where appropriate, list under subsection (b)(1) of this section, additional wastes containing chlorinated dioxins or chlorinated-dibenzofurans. Not later than one year after November 8, 1984, the Administrator shall, where appropriate, list under subsection (b)(1) of this section wastes containing remaining halogenated dioxins and halogenated-dibenzofurans.

(2) Not later than fifteen months after November 8, 1984, the Administrator shall make a determination of whether or not to list under subsection (b)(1) of this section the following wastes: Chlorinated Aliphatics, Dioxin, Dimethyl Hydrazine, TDI (toluene diisocyanate), Carbamates, Bromacil, Linuron, Organo-bromines, solvents, refining wastes, chlorinated aromatics, dyes and pigments, inorganic chemical industry wastes, lithium batteries, coke byproducts, paint production wastes, and coal slurry pipeline effluent.

(f) DELISTING PROCEDURES

(1) When evaluating a petition to exclude a waste generated at a particular facility from listing under this section, the Administrator shall consider factors (including additional constituents) other than those for which the waste was listed if the Administrator has a reasonable basis to believe that such additional factors could cause the waste to be a hazardous waste. The Administrator shall provide notice and opportunity for comment on these additional factors before granting or denying such petition.

(2)(A) To the maximum extent practicable the Administrator shall publish in the Federal Register a proposal to grant or deny a petition referred to in paragraph (1) within twelve months after receiving a complete application to exclude a waste generated at a particular facility from being regulated as a hazardous waste and shall grant or deny such a petition within twenty-four months after receiving a complete application.

(B) The temporary granting of such a petition prior to November 8, 1984, without the opportunity for public comment and the full consideration of such comments shall not continue for more than twenty-four months after November 8, 1984. If a final decision to grant or deny such a petition has not been promulgated after notice and opportunity for public comment within the time limit prescribed by the preceding sentence, any such temporary granting of such petition shall cease to be in effect.

(g) EP TOXICITY

Not later than twenty-eight months after November 8, 1984, the Administrator shall examine the deficiencies of the extraction procedure toxicity characteristic as a predictor of the leaching potential of wastes and make changes in the extraction procedure toxicity characteristics, including changes in the leaching media, as are necessary to insure that it accurately predicts the leaching potential of wastes which pose a threat to human health and the environment when mismanaged.

(h) ADDITIONAL CHARACTERISTICS

Not later than two years after November 8, 1984, the Administrator shall promulgate regulations under this section identifying additional characteristics of hazardous waste, including measures or indicators of toxicity.

(i) CLARIFICATION OF HOUSEHOLD WASTE EXCLUSION

A resource recovery facility recovering energy from the mass burning of municipal solid waste shall not be deemed to be treating, storing, disposing of, or otherwise managing hazardous wastes for the purposes of regulation under this subchapter, if —

(1) such facility —

(A) receives and burns only —

(i) household waste (from single and multiple dwellings, hotels, motels, and other residential sources), and

(ii) solid waste from commercial or industrial sources that does not contain hazardous waste identified or listed under this section, and

(B) does not accept hazardous wastes identified or listed under this section, and

(2) the owner or operator of such facility has established contractual requirements or other appropriate notification or inspection procedures to assure that hazardous wastes are not received at or burned in such facility.

§6922. STANDARDS APPLICABLE TO GENERATORS OF HAZARDOUS WASTE

(a) IN GENERAL

Not later than eighteen months after October 21, 1976, and after notice and opportunity for public hearings and after consultation with appropriate Federal and State agencies, the Administrator shall promulgate regulations establishing such standards, applicable to generators of hazardous waste identified or listed under this subchapter, as may be necessary to protect human health and the environment. Such standards shall establish requirements respecting —

(1) recordkeeping practices that accurately identify the quantities of such hazardous waste generated, the constituents thereof which are significant in quantity or in potential harm to human health or the environment, and the disposition of such wastes;

(2) labeling practices for any containers used for the storage, transport, or disposal of such hazardous waste such as will identify accurately such waste;

(3) use of appropriate containers for such hazardous waste;

(4) furnishing of information on the general chemical composition of such hazardous waste to persons transporting, treating, storing, or disposing of such wastes;

(5) use of a manifest system and any other reasonable means necessary to assure that all such hazardous waste generated is designated for treatment, storage, or disposal in, and arrives at, treatment, storage, or disposal facilities (other than facilities on the premises where the waste is generated) for which a permit has been issued as provided in this subchapter, or pursuant to title I of the Marine Protection, Research, and Sanctuaries Act (86 Stat. 1052) [33 U.S.C. 1411 et seq.]; and

(6) submission of reports to the Administrator (or the State agency in any case in which such agency carries out a permit program pursuant to this subchapter) at least once every two years, setting out —

(A) the quantities and nature of hazardous waste identified or listed under this subchapter that he has generated during the year;

(B) the disposition of all hazardous waste reported under subparagraph (A);

(C) the efforts undertaken during the year to reduce the volume and toxicity of waste generated; and

(D) the changes in volume and toxicity of waste actually achieved during the year in question in comparison with previous years, to the extent such information is available for years prior to November 8, 1984.

(b) **WASTE MINIMIZATION**

Effective September 1, 1985, the manifest required by subsection (a)(5) of this section shall contain a certification by the generator that —

(1) the generator of the hazardous waste has a program in place to reduce the volume or quantity and toxicity of such waste to the degree determined by the generator to be economically practicable; and

(2) the proposed method of treatment, storage, or disposal is that practicable method currently available to the generator which minimizes the present and future threat to human health and the environment.

§6923. STANDARDS APPLICABLE TO TRANSPORTERS OF HAZARDOUS WASTE

(a) **STANDARDS**

Not later than eighteen months after October 21, 1976, and after opportunity for public hearings, the Administrator, after consultation with the Secretary of Transportation and the States, shall promulgate regulations establishing such standards, applicable to transporters of hazardous waste identified or listed under this subchapter, as may be necessary to protect human health and the environment. Such standards shall include but need not be limited to requirements respecting —

(1) recordkeeping concerning such hazardous waste transported, and their source and delivery points;

(2) transportation of such waste only if properly labeled;

(3) compliance with the manifest system referred to in section 6922(5)[1] of this title; and

(4) transportation of all such hazardous waste only to the hazardous waste treatment, storage, or disposal facilities which the shipper designates on the manifest form to be a facility holding a permit issued under this subchapter, or pursuant to title I of the Marine Protection, Research, and Sanctuaries Act (86 Stat. 1052) [33 U.S.C. 1411 et seq.].

(b) COORDINATION WITH REGULATIONS OF SECRETARY OF TRANSPORTATION

In case of any hazardous waste identified or listed under this subchapter which is subject to the Hazardous Materials Transportation Act (88 Stat. 2156) [49 App. U.S.C. 1801 et seq.], the regulations promulgated by the Administrator under this section shall be consistent with the requirements of such Act and the regulations thereunder. The Administrator is authorized to make recommendations to the Secretary of Transportation respecting the regulations of such hazardous waste under the Hazardous Materials Transportation Act and for addition of materials to be covered by such Act.

(c) FUEL FROM HAZARDOUS WASTE

Not later than two years after November 8, 1984, and after opportunity for public hearing, the Administrator shall promulgate regulations establishing standards, applicable to transporters of fuel produced (1) from any hazardous waste identified or listed under section 6921 of this title, or (2) from any hazardous waste identified or listed under section 6921 of this title and any other material, as may be necessary to protect human health and the environment. Such standards may include any of the requirements set forth in paragraphs (1) through (4) of subsection (a) of this section as may be appropriate.

§6924. STANDARDS APPLICABLE TO OWNERS AND OPERATORS OF HAZARDOUS WASTE TREATMENT, STORAGE, AND DISPOSAL FACILITIES

(a) IN GENERAL

Not later than eighteen months after October 21, 1976, and after opportunity for public hearings and after consultation with appropriate Federal and State agencies, the Administrator shall promulgate regulations establishing such performance standards, applicable to owners and operators of facilities for the

---

1. See References in Text note below.

treatment, storage, or disposal of hazardous waste identified or listed under this subchapter, as may be necessary to protect human health and the environment. In establishing such standards the Administrator shall, where appropriate, distinguish in such standards between requirements appropriate for new facilities and for facilities in existence on the date of promulgation of such regulations. Such standards shall include, but need not be limited to, requirements respecting —

(1) maintaining records of all hazardous wastes identified or listed under this chapter which is treated, stored, or disposed of, as the case may be, and the manner in which such wastes were treated, stored, or disposed of;

(2) satisfactory reporting, monitoring, and inspection and compliance with the manifest system referred to in section 6922(5)[2] of this title;

(3) treatment, storage, or disposal of all such waste received by the facility pursuant to such operating methods, techniques, and practices as may be satisfactory to the Administrator;

(4) the location, design, and construction of such hazardous waste treatment, disposal, or storage facilities;

(5) contingency plans for effective action to minimize unanticipated damage from any treatment, storage, or disposal of any such hazardous waste;

(6) the maintenance of operation of such facilities and requiring such additional qualifications as to ownership, continuity of operation, training for personnel, and financial responsibility (including financial responsibility for corrective action) as may be necessary or desirable; and

(7) compliance with the requirements of section 6925 of this title respecting permits for treatment, storage, or disposal.

No private entity shall be precluded by reason of criteria established under paragraph (6) from the ownership or operation of facilities providing hazardous waste treatment, storage, or disposal services where such entity can provide assurances of financial responsibility and continuity of operation consistent with the degree and duration of risks associated with the treatment, storage, or disposal of specified hazardous waste.

(b) SALT DOME FORMATIONS, SALT BED FORMATIONS, UNDERGROUND MINES AND CAVES

(1) Effective on November 8, 1984, the placement of any noncontainerized or bulk liquid hazardous waste in any salt dome formation, salt bed formation, underground mine, or cave is prohibited until such time as —

(A) the Administrator has determined, after notice and opportunity for hearings on the record in the affected areas, that such placement is protective of human health and the environment;

(B) the Administrator has promulgated performance and permitting standards for such facilities under this subchapter, and;

(C) a permit has been issued under section 6925(c) of this title for the facility concerned.

2. See References in Text note below.

(2) Effective on November 8, 1984, the placement to any hazardous waste other than a hazardous waste referred to in paragraph (1) in a salt dome formation, salt bed formation, underground mine, or cave is prohibited until such time as a permit has been issued under section 6925(c) of this title for the facility concerned.

(3) No determination made by the Administrator under subsection (d), (e), or (g) of this section regarding any hazardous waste to which such subsection (d), (e), or (g) of this section applies shall affect the prohibition contained in paragraph (1) or (2) of this subsection.

(4) Nothing in this subsection shall apply to the Department of Energy Waste Isolation Pilot Project in New Mexico.

(c) **LIQUIDS IN LANDFILLS**

(1) Effective 6 months after November 8, 1984, the placement of bulk or noncontainerized liquid hazardous waste or free liquids contained in hazardous waste (whether or not absorbents have been added) in any landfill is prohibited. Prior to such date the requirements (as in effect on April 30, 1983) promulgated under this section by the Administrator regarding liquid hazardous waste shall remain in force and effect to the extent such requirements are applicable to the placement of bulk or noncontainerized liquid hazardous waste, or free liquids contained in hazardous waste, in landfills.

(2) Not later than fifteen months after November 8, 1984, the Administrator shall promulgate final regulations which —

(A) minimize the disposal of containerized liquid hazardous waste in landfills, and

(B) minimize the presence of free liquids in containerized hazardous waste to be disposed of in landfills.

Such regulations shall also prohibit the disposal in landfills of liquids that have been absorbed in materials that biodegrade or that release liquids when compressed as might occur during routine landfill operations. Prior to the date on which such final regulations take effect, the requirements (as in effect on April 30, 1983) promulgated under this section by the Administrator shall remain in force and effect to the extent such requirements are applicable to the disposal of containerized liquid hazardous waste, or free liquids contained in hazardous waste, in landfills.

(3) Effective twelve months after November 8, 1984, the placement of any liquid which is not a hazardous waste in a landfill for which a permit is required under section 6925(c) of this title or which is operating pursuant to interim status granted under section 6925(e) of this title is prohibited unless the owner or operator of such landfill demonstrates to the Administrator, or the Administrator determines, that —

(A) the only reasonably available alternative to the placement in such landfill is placement in a landfill or unlined surface impoundment, whether or not permitted under section 6925(c) of this title or operating pursuant to interim status under section 6925(e) of this title, which contains, or may reasonably be anticipated to contain, hazardous waste; and

(B) placement in such owner or operator's landfill will not present a risk of contamination of any underground source of drinking water.

As used in subparagraph (B), the term "underground source of drinking water" has the same meaning as provided in regulations under the Safe Drinking Water Act (title XIV of the Public Health Service Act) [42 U.S.C. 300f et seq.].

(4) No determination made by the Administrator under subsection (d), (e), or (g) of this section regarding any hazardous waste to which such subsection (d), (e), or (g) of this section applies shall affect the prohibition contained in paragraph (1) of this subsection.

(d) PROHIBITIONS ON LAND DISPOSAL OF SPECIFIED WASTES

(1) Effective 32 months after November 8, 1984 (except as provided in subsection (f) of this section with respect to underground injection into deep injection wells), the land disposal of the hazardous wastes referred to in paragraph (2) is prohibited unless the Administrator determines the prohibition on one or more methods of land disposal of such waste is not required in order to protect human health and the environment for as long as the waste remains hazardous, taking into account —

(A) the long-term uncertainties associated with land disposal,

(B) the goal of managing hazardous waste in an appropriate manner in the first instance, and

(C) the persistence, toxicity, mobility, and propensity to bioaccumulate of such hazardous wastes and their hazardous constituents.

For the purposes of this paragraph, a method of land disposal may not be determined to be protective of human health and the environment for a hazardous waste referred to in paragraph (2) (other than a hazardous waste which has complied with the pretreatment regulations promulgated under subsection (m) of this section), unless, upon application by an interested person, it has been demonstrated to the Administrator, to a reasonable degree of certainty, that there will be no migration of hazardous constituents from the disposal unit or injection zone for as long as the wastes remain hazardous.

(2) Paragraph (1) applies to the following hazardous wastes listed or identified under section 6921 of this title:

(A) Liquid hazardous wastes, including free liquids associated with any solid or sludge, containing free cyanides at concentrations greater than or equal to 1,000 mg/l.

(B) Liquid hazardous wastes, including free liquids associated with any solid or sludge, containing the following metals (or elements) or compounds of these metals (or elements) at concentrations greater than or equal to those specified below:

(i) arsenic and/or compounds (as As) 500 mg/l;
(ii) cadmium and/or compounds (as Cd) 100 mg/l;
(iii) chromium (VI and/or compounds (as Cr VI)) 500 mg/l;
(iv) lead and/or compounds (as Pb) 500 mg/l;
(v) mercury and/or compounds (as Hg) 20 mg/l;
(vi) nickel and/or compounds (as Ni) 134 mg/l;

(vii) selenium and/or compounds (as Se) 100 mg/l; and
(viii) thallium and/or compounds (as Th) 130 mg/l.

(C) Liquid hazardous waste having a pH less than or equal to two (2.0).

(D) Liquid hazardous wastes containing polychlorinated biphenyls at concentrations greater than or equal to 50 ppm.

(E) Hazardous wastes containing halogenated organic compounds in total concentration greater than or equal to 1,000 mg/kg.

When necessary to protect human health and the environment, the Administrator shall substitute more stringent concentration levels than the levels specified in subparagraphs (A) through (E).

(3) During the period ending forty-eight months after November 8, 1984, this subsection shall not apply to any disposal of contaminated soil or debris resulting from a response action taken under section 9604 or 9606 of this title or a corrective action required under this subchapter.

(e) **SOLVENTS AND DIOXINS**

(1) Effective twenty-four months after November 8, 1984 (except as provided in subsection (f) of this section with respect to underground injection into deep injection wells), the land disposal of the hazardous wastes referred to in paragraph (2) is prohibited unless the Administrator determines the prohibition of one or more methods of land disposal of such waste is not required in order to protect human health and the environment for as long as the waste remains hazardous, taking into account the factors referred to in subparagraph (A) through (C) of subsection (d)(1) of this section. For the purposes of this paragraph, a method of land disposal may not be determined to be protective of human health and the environment for a hazardous waste referred to in paragraph (2) (other than a hazardous waste which has complied with the pretreatment regulations promulgated under subsection (m) of this section), unless upon application by an interested person it has been demonstrated to the Administrator, to a reasonable degree of certainty, that there will be no migration of hazardous constituents from the disposal unit or injection zone for as long as the wastes remain hazardous.

(2) The hazardous wastes to which the prohibition under paragraph (1) applies are as follows —

(A) dioxin-containing hazardous wastes numbered F020, F021, F022, and F023 (as referred to in the proposed rule published by the Administrator in the Federal Register for April 4, 1983), and

(B) those hazardous wastes numbered F001, F002, F003, F004, and F005 in regulations promulgated by the Administrator under section 6921 of this title (40 C.F.R. 261.31 (July 1, 1983)), as those regulations are in effect on July 1, 1983.

(3) During the period ending forty-eight months after November 8, 1984, this subsection shall not apply to any disposal of contaminated soil or debris resulting from a response action taken under section 9604 or 9606 of this title or a corrective action required under this subchapter.

Resource Conservation and Recovery Act §6924

(f) DISPOSAL INTO DEEP INJECTION WELLS; SPECIFIED SUBSECTION (d) WASTES; SOLVENTS AND DIOXINS

(1) Not later than forty-five months after November 8, 1984, the Administrator shall complete a review of the disposal of all hazardous wastes referred to in paragraph (2) of subsection (d) of this section and in paragraph (2) of subsection (e) of this section by underground injection into deep injection wells.

(2) Within forty-five months after November 8, 1984, the Administrator shall make a determination regarding the disposal by underground injection into deep injection wells of the hazardous wastes referred to in paragraph (2) of subsection (d) of this section and the hazardous wastes referred to in paragraph (2) of subsection (e) of this section. The Administrator shall promulgate final regulations prohibiting the disposal of such wastes into such wells if it may reasonably be determined that such disposal may not be protective of human health and the environment for as long as the waste remains hazardous, taking into account the factors referred to in subparagraphs (A) through (C) of subsection (d)(1) of this section. In promulgating such regulations, the Administrator shall consider each hazardous waste referred to in paragraph (2) of subsection (d) of this section or in paragraph (2) of subsection (e) of this section which is prohibited from disposal into such wells by any State.

(3) If the Administrator fails to make a determination under paragraph (2) for any hazardous waste referred to in paragraph (2) of subsection (d) of this section or in paragraph (2) of subsection (e) of this section within forty-five months after November 8, 1984, such hazardous waste shall be prohibited from disposal into any deep injection well.

(4) As used in this subsection, the term "deep injection well" means a well used for the underground injection of hazardous waste other than a well to which section 6979a(a)[3] of this title applies.

(g) ADDITIONAL LAND DISPOSAL PROHIBITION DETERMINATIONS

(1) Not later than twenty-four months after November 8, 1984, the Administrator shall submit a schedule to Congress for —

(A) reviewing all hazardous wastes listed (as of November 8, 1984) under section 6921 of this title other than those wastes which are referred to in subsection (d) or (e) of this section; and

(B) taking action under paragraph (5) of this subsection with respect to each such hazardous waste.

(2) The Administrator shall base the schedule on a ranking of such listed wastes considering their intrinsic hazard and their volume such that decisions regarding the land disposal of high volume hazardous wastes with high intrinsic hazard shall, to the maximum extent possible, be made by the date forty-five months after November 8, 1984. Decisions regarding low volume hazardous wastes with lower intrinsic hazard shall be made by the date sixty-six months after November 8, 1984.

3. See References in Text note below.

(3) The preparation and submission of the schedule under this subsection shall not be subject to the Paperwork Reduction Act of 1980 [44 U.S.C. 3501 et seq.]. No hearing on the record shall be required for purposes of preparation or submission of the schedule. The schedule shall not be subject to judicial review.

(4) The schedule under this subsection shall require that the Administrator shall promulgate regulations in accordance with paragraph (5) or make a determination under paragraph (5) —

(A) for at least one-third of all hazardous wastes referred to in paragraph (1) by the date forty-five months after November 8, 1984;

(B) for at least two-thirds of all such listed wastes by the date fifty-five months after November 8, 1984; and

(C) for all such listed wastes and for all hazardous wastes identified under section 6921 of this title by the date sixty-six months after November 8, 1984.

In the case of any hazardous waste identified or listed under section 6921 of this title after November 8, 1984, the Administrator shall determine whether such waste shall be prohibited from one or more methods of land disposal in accordance with paragraph (5) within six months after the date of such identification or listing.

(5) Not later than the date specified in the schedule published under this subsection, the Administrator shall promulgate final regulations prohibiting one or more methods of land disposal of the hazardous wastes listed on such schedule except for methods of land disposal which the Administrator determines will be protective of human health and the environment for as long as the waste remains hazardous, taking into account the factors referred to in subparagraph[4] (A) through (C) of subsection (d)(1) of this section. For the purposes of this paragraph, a method of land disposal may not be determined to be protective of human health and the environment (except with respect to a hazardous waste which has complied with the pretreatment regulations promulgated under subsection (m) of this section) unless, upon application by an interested person, it has been demonstrated to the Administrator, to a reasonable degree of certainty, that there will be no migration of hazardous constituents from the disposal unit or injection zone for as long as the wastes remain hazardous.

(6)(A) If the Administrator fails (by the date forty-five months after November 8, 1984) to promulgate regulations or make a determination under paragraph (5) for any hazardous waste which is included in the first one-third of the schedule published under this subsection, such hazardous waste may be disposed of in a landfill or surface impoundment only if —

(i) such facility is in compliance with the requirements of subsection (o) of this section which are applicable to new facilities (relating to minimum technological requirements); and

(ii) prior to such disposal, the generator has certified to the Admin-

---

4. So in original. Probably should be "subparagraphs."

istrator that such generator has investigated the availability of treatment capacity and has determined that the use of such landfill or surface impoundment is the only practical alternative to treatment currently available to the generator.

The prohibition contained in this subparagraph shall continue to apply until the Administrator promulgates regulations or makes a determination under paragraph (5) for the waste concerned.

(B) If the Administrator fails (by the date 55 months after November 8, 1984) to promulgate regulations or make a determination under paragraph (5) for any hazardous waste which is included in the first two-thirds of the schedule published under this subsection, such hazardous waste may be disposed of in a landfill or surface impoundment only if —

(i) such facility is in compliance with the requirements of subsection (o) of this section which are applicable to new facilities (relating to minimum technological requirements); and

(ii) prior to such disposal, the generator has certified to the Administrator that such generator has investigated the availability of treatment capacity and has determined that the use of such landfill or surface impoundment is the only practical alternative to treatment currently available to the generator.

The prohibition contained in this subparagraph shall continue to apply until the Administrator promulgates regulations or makes a determination under paragraph (5) for the waste concerned.

(C) If the Administrator fails to promulgate regulations, or make a determination under paragraph (5) for any hazardous waste referred to in paragraph (1) within 66 months after November 8, 1984, such hazardous waste shall be prohibited from land disposal.

(h) VARIANCE FROM LAND DISPOSAL PROHIBITIONS

(1) A prohibition in regulations under subsection (d), (e), (f), or (g) of this section shall be effective immediately upon promulgation.

(2) The Administrator may establish an effective date different from the effective date which would otherwise apply under subsection (d), (e), (f), or (g) of this section with respect to a specific hazardous waste which is subject to a prohibition under subsection (d), (e), (f), or (g) of this section or under regulations under subsection (d), (e), (f), or (g) of this section. Any such other effective date shall be established on the basis of the earliest date on which adequate alternative treatment, recovery, or disposal capacity which protects human health and the environment will be available. Any such other effective date shall in no event be later than 2 years after the effective date of the prohibition which would otherwise apply under subsection (d), (e), (f), or (g) of this section.

(3) The Administrator, after notice and opportunity for comment and after consultation with appropriate State agencies in all affected States, may on a case-by-case basis grant an extension of the effective date which would otherwise apply under subsection (d), (e), (f), or (g) of this section or under paragraph (2)

for up to one year, where the applicant demonstrates that there is a binding contractual commitment to construct or otherwise provide such alternative capacity but due to circumstances beyond the control of such applicant such alternative capacity cannot reasonably be made available by such effective date. Such extension shall be renewable once for no more than one additional year.

(4) Whenever another effective date (hereinafter referred to as a "variance") is established under paragraph (2), or an extension is granted under paragraph (3), with respect to any hazardous waste, during the period for which such variance or extension is in effect, such hazardous waste may be disposed of in a landfill or surface impoundment only if such facility is in compliance with the requirements of subsection (o) of this section.

(i) PUBLICATION OF DETERMINATION

If the Administrator determines that a method of land disposal will be protective of human health and the environment, he shall promptly publish in the Federal Register notice of such determination, together with an explanation of the basis for such determination.

(j) STORAGE OF HAZARDOUS WASTE PROHIBITED FROM LAND DISPOSAL

In the case of any hazardous waste which is prohibited from one or more methods of land disposal under this section (or under regulations promulgated by the Administrator under any provision of this section) the storage of such hazardous waste is prohibited unless such storage is solely for the purpose of the accumulation of such quantities of hazardous waste as are necessary to facilitate proper recovery, treatment or disposal.

(k) "LAND DISPOSAL" DEFINED

For the purposes of this section, the term "land disposal", when used with respect to a specified hazardous waste, shall be deemed to include, but not be limited to, any placement of such hazardous waste in a landfill, surface impoundment, waste pile, injection well, land treatment facility, salt dome formation, salt bed formation, or underground mine or cave.

(l) BAN ON DUST SUPPRESSION

The use of waste or used oil or other material, which is contaminated or mixed with dioxin or any other hazardous waste identified or listed under section 6921 of this title (other than a waste identified solely on the basis of ignitability), for dust suppression or road treatment is prohibited.

(m) TREATMENT STANDARDS FOR WASTES SUBJECT TO LAND DISPOSAL PROHIBITION

(1) Simultaneously with the promulgation of regulations under subsection (d), (e), (f), or (g) of this section prohibiting one or more methods of land disposal of a particular hazardous waste, and as appropriate thereafter, the Administrator shall, after notice and an opportunity for hearings and after consultation with

appropriate Federal and State agencies, promulgate regulations specifying those levels or methods of treatment, if any, which substantially diminish the toxicity of the waste or substantially reduce the likelihood of migration of hazardous constituents from the waste so that short-term and long-term threats to human health and the environment are minimized.

(2) If such hazardous waste has been treated to the level or by a method specified in regulations promulgated under this subsection, such waste or residue thereof shall not be subject to any prohibition promulgated under subsection (d), (e), (f), or (g) of this section and may be disposed of in a land disposal facility which meets the requirements of this subchapter. Any regulation promulgated under this subsection for a particular hazardous waste shall become effective on the same date as any applicable prohibition promulgated under subsection (d), (e), (f), or (g) of this section.

(n) AIR EMISSIONS

Not later than thirty months after November 8, 1984, the Administrator shall promulgate such regulations for the monitoring and control of air emissions at hazardous waste treatment, storage, and disposal facilities, including but not limited to open tanks, surface impoundments, and landfills, as may be necessary to protect human health and the environment.

(o) MINIMUM TECHNOLOGICAL REQUIREMENTS

(1) The regulations under subsection (a) of this section shall be revised from time to time to take into account improvements in the technology of control and measurement. At a minimum, such regulations shall require, and a permit issued pursuant to section 6925(c) of this title after November 8, 1984, by the Administrator or a State shall require —

(A) for each new landfill or surface impoundment, each new landfill or surface impoundment unit at an existing facility, each replacement of an existing landfill or surface impoundment unit, and each lateral expansion of an existing landfill or surface impoundment unit, for which an application for a final determination regarding issuance of a permit under section 6925(c) of this title is received after November 8, 1984 —

(i) the installation of two or more liners and a leachate collection system above (in the case of a landfill) and between such liners; and

(ii) ground water monitoring; and

(B) for each incinerator which receives a permit under section 6925(c) of this title after November 8, 1984, the attainment of the minimum destruction and removal efficiency required by regulations in effect on June 24, 1982. The requirements of this paragraph shall apply with respect to all waste received after the issuance of the permit.

(2) Paragraph (1)(A)(i) shall not apply if the owner or operator demonstrates to the Administrator, and the Administrator finds for such landfill or surface impoundment, that alternative design and operating practices, together with location characteristics, will prevent the migration of any hazardous constituents

into the ground water or surface water at least as effectively as such liners and leachate collection systems.

(3) The double-liner requirement set forth in paragraph (1)(A)(i) may be waived by the Administrator for any monofill, if —

(A) such monofill contains only hazardous wastes from foundry furnace emission controls or metal casting molding sand,

(B) such wastes do not contain constituents which would render the wastes hazardous for reasons other than the Extraction Procedure ("EP") toxicity characteristics set forth in regulations under this subchapter, and

(C) such monofill meets the same requirements as are applicable in the case of a waiver under section 6925(j)(2) or (4) of this title.

(4)(A) Not later than thirty months after November 8, 1984, the Administrator shall promulgate standards requiring that new landfill units, surface impoundment units, waste piles, underground tanks and land treatment units for the storage, treatment, or disposal of hazardous waste identified or listed under section 6921 of this title shall be required to utilize approved leak detection systems.

(B) For the purposes of subparagraph (A) —

(i) the term "approved leak detection system" means a system or technology which the Administrator determines to be capable of detecting leaks of hazardous constituents at the earliest practicable time; and

(ii) the term "new units" means units on which construction commences after the date of promulgation of regulations under this paragraph.

(5)(A) The Administrator shall promulgate regulations or issue guidance documents implementing the requirements of paragraph (1)(A) within two years after November 8, 1984.

(B) Until the effective date of such regulations or guidance documents, the requirement for the installation of two or more liners may be satisfied by the installation of a top liner designed, operated, and constructed of materials to prevent the migration of any constituent into such liner during the period such facility remains in operation (including any post-closure monitoring period), and a lower liner designed, operated[5] and constructed to prevent the migration of any constituent through such liner during such period. For the purpose of the preceding sentence, a lower liner shall be deemed to satisfy such requirement if it is constructed of at least a 3-foot thick layer of recompacted clay or other natural material with a permeability of no more than 1×10^{-7} centimeter per second.

(6) Any permit under section 6925 of this title which is issued for a landfill located within the State of Alabama shall require the installation of two or more liners and a leachate collection system above and between such liners, notwithstanding any other provision of this chapter.

(7) In addition to the requirements set forth in this subsection, the regulations referred to in paragraph (1) shall specify criteria for the acceptable loca-

---

5. So in original. Probably should be followed by a comma.

Resource Conservation and Recovery Act §6924

tion of new and existing treatment, storage, or disposal facilities as necessary to protect human health and the environment. Within 18 months after November 8, 1984, the Administrator shall publish guidance criteria identifying areas of vulnerable hydrogeology.

(p) GROUND WATER MONITORING

The standards under this section concerning ground water monitoring which are applicable to surface impoundments, waste piles, land treatment units, and landfills shall apply to such a facility whether or not —

(1) the facility is located above the seasonal high water table;

(2) two liners and a leachate collection system have been installed at the facility; or

(3) the owner or operator inspects the liner (or liners) which has been installed at the facility.

This subsection shall not be construed to affect other exemptions or waivers from such standards provided in regulations in effect on November 8, 1984, or as may be provided in revisions to those regulations, to the extent consistent with this subsection. The Administrator is authorized on a case-by-case basis to exempt from ground water monitoring requirements under this section (including subsection (o) of this section) any engineered structure which the Administrator finds does not receive or contain liquid waste (nor waste containing free liquids), is designed and operated to exclude liquid from precipitation or other runoff, utilizes multiple leak detection systems within the outer layer of containment, and provides for continuing operation and maintenance of these leak detection systems during the operating period, closure, and the period required for post-closure monitoring and for which the Administrator concludes on the basis of such findings that there is a reasonable certainty hazardous constituents will not migrate beyond the outer layer of containment prior to the end of the period required for post-closure monitoring.

(q) HAZARDOUS WASTE USED AS FUEL

(1) Not later than two years after November 8, 1984, and after notice and opportunity for public hearing, the Administrator shall promulgate regulations establishing such —

(A) standards applicable to the owners and operators of facilities which produce a fuel —

(i) from any hazardous waste identified or listed under section 6921 of this title, or

(ii) from any hazardous waste identified or listed under section 6921 of this title and any other material;

(B) standards applicable to the owners and operators of facilities which burn, for purposes of energy recovery, any fuel produced as provided in subparagraph (A) or any fuel which otherwise contains any hazardous waste identified or listed under section 6921 of this title; and

(C) standards applicable to any person who distributes or markets any

fuel which is produced as provided in subparagraph (A) or any fuel which otherwise contains any hazardous waste identified or listed under section 6921 of this title[6]
as may be necessary to protect human health and the environment. Such standards may include any of the requirements set forth in paragraphs (1) through (7) of subsection (a) of this section as may be appropriate. Nothing in this subsection shall be construed to affect or impair the provisions of section 6921(b)(3) of this title. For purposes of this subsection, the term "hazardous waste listed under section 6921 of this title" includes any commercial chemical product which is listed under section 6921 of this title and which, in lieu of its original intended use, is (i) produced for use as (or as a component of) a fuel, (ii) distributed for use as a fuel, or (iii) burned as a fuel.

(2)(A) This subsection, subsection (r) of this section, and subsection (s) of this section shall not apply to petroleum refinery wastes containing oil which are converted into petroleum coke at the same facility at which such wastes were generated, unless the resulting coke product would exceed one or more characteristics by which a substance would be identified as a hazardous waste under section 6921 of this title.

(B) The Administrator may exempt from the requirements of this subsection, subsection (r) of this section, or subsection (s) of this section facilities which burn de minimis quantities of hazardous waste as fuel, as defined by the Administrator, if the wastes are burned at the same facility at which such wastes are generated; the waste is burned to recover useful energy, as determined by the Administrator on the basis of the design and operating characteristics of the facility and the heating value and other characteristics of the waste; and the waste is burned in a type of device determined by the Administrator to be designed and operated at a destruction and removal efficiency sufficient such that protection of human health and environment is assured.

(C)(i) After November 8, 1984, and until standards are promulgated and in effect under paragraph (2) of this subsection, no fuel which contains any hazardous waste may be burned in any cement kiln which is located within the boundaries of any incorporated municipality with a population greater than five hundred thousand (based on the most recent census statistics) unless such kiln fully complies with regulations (as in effect on November 8, 1984) under this subchapter which are applicable to incinerators.

(ii) Any person who knowingly violates the prohibition contained in clause (i) shall be deemed to have violated section 6928(d)(2) of this title.

(r) LABELING

(1) Notwithstanding any other provision of law, until such time as the Administrator promulgates standards under subsection (q) of this section specifically superceding this requirement, it shall be unlawful for any person who is required to file a notification in accordance with paragraph (1) or (3) of section

---

6. So in original. Probably should be followed by a semicolon.

6930 of this title to distribute or market any fuel which is produced from any hazardous waste identified or listed under section 6921 of this title, or any fuel which otherwise contains any hazardous waste identified or listed under section 6921 of this title if the invoice or the bill of sale fails —

(A) to bear the following statement: "WARNING: THIS FUEL CONTAINS HAZARDOUS WASTES," and

(B) to list the hazardous wastes contained therein.

Beginning ninety days after November 8, 1984, such statement shall be located in a conspicuous place on every such invoice or bill of sale and shall appear in conspicuous and legible type in contrast by typography, layouts, or color with other printed matter on the invoice or bill of sale.

(2) Unless the Administrator determines otherwise as may be necessary to protect human health and the environment, this subsection shall not apply to fuels produced from petroleum refining waste containing oil if —

(A) such materials are generated and reinserted onsite into the refining process;

(B) contaminants are removed; and

(C) such refining waste containing oil is converted along with normal process streams into pertroleum-derived[7] fuel products at a facility at which crude oil is refined into petroleum products and which is classified as a number SIC 2911 facility under the Office of Management and Budget Standard Industrial Classification Manual.

(3) Unless the Administrator determines otherwise as may be necessary to protect human health and the environment, this subsection shall not apply to fuels produced from oily materials, resulting from normal petroleum refining, production and transportation practices, if (A) contaminants are removed; and (B) such oily materials are converted along with normal process streams into petroleum-derived fuel products at a facility at which crude oil is refined into petroleum products and which is classified as a number SIC 2911 facility under the Office of Management and Budget Standard[8] Classification Manual.

(s) **RECORDKEEPING**

Not later than fifteen months after November 8, 1984, the Administrator shall promulgate regulations requiring that any person who is required to file a notification in accordance with subparagraph (1), (2), or (3), of section 6930(a) of this title shall maintain such records regarding fuel blending, distribution, or use as may be necessary to protect human health and the environment.

(t) **FINANCIAL RESPONSIBILITY PROVISIONS**

(1) Financial responsibility required by subsection (a) of this section may be established in accordance with regulations promulgated by the Administrator by any one, or any combination, of the following: insurance, guarantee, surety

---

7. So in original. Probably should be "petroleum-derived."
8. So in original. Probably should be "Standard Industrial."

bond, letter of credit, or qualification as a self-insurer. In promulgating requirements under this section, the Administrator is authorized to specify policy or other contractual terms, conditions, or defenses which are necessary or are unacceptable in establishing such evidence of financial responsibility in order to effectuate the purposes of this chapter.

(2) In any case where the owner or operator is in bankruptcy, reorganization, or arrangement pursuant to the Federal Bankruptcy Code or where (with reasonable diligence) jurisdiction in any State court or any Federal Court cannot be obtained over an owner or operator likely to be solvent at the time of judgment, any claim arising from conduct for which evidence of financial responsibility must be provided under this section may be asserted directly against the guarantor providing such evidence of financial responsibility. In the case of any action pursuant to this subsection, such guarantor shall be entitled to invoke all rights and defenses which would have been available to the owner or operator if any action had been brought against the owner or operator by the claimant and which would have been available to the guarantor if an action had been brought against the guarantor by the owner or operator.

(3) The total liability of any guarantor shall be limited to the aggregate amount which the guarantor has provided as evidence of financial responsibility to the owner or operator under this chapter. Nothing in this subsection shall be construed to limit any other State or Federal statutory, contractual or common law liability of a guarantor to its owner or operator including, but not limited to, the liability of such guarantor for bad faith either in negotiating or in failing to negotiate the settlement of any claim. Nothing in this subsection shall be construed to diminish the liability of any person under section 9607 or 9611 of this title or other applicable law.

(4) For the purpose of this subsection, the term "guarantor" means any person, other than the owner or operator, who provides evidence of financial responsibility for an owner or operator under this section.

(u) CONTINUING RELEASES AT PERMITTED FACILITIES

Standards promulgated under this section shall require, and a permit issued after November 8, 1984, by the Administrator or a State shall require, corrective action for all releases of hazardous waste or constituents from any solid waste management unit at a treatment, storage, or disposal facility seeking a permit under this subchapter, regardless of the time at which waste was placed in such unit. Permits issued under section 6925 of this title shall contain schedules of compliance for such corrective action (where such corrective action cannot be completed prior to issuance of the permit) and assurances of financial responsibility for completing such corrective action.

(v) CORRECTIVE ACTION BEYOND FACILITY BOUNDARY

As promptly as practicable after November 8, 1984, the Administrator shall amend the standards under this section regarding corrective action required at facilities for the treatment, storage, or disposal, of hazardous waste listed or identified under section 6921 of this title to require that corrective action be taken beyond the facility boundary where necessary to protect human health and the environment unless the owner or operator of the facility concerned demonstrates to the satisfaction of the Administrator that, despite the owner or operator's best efforts, the owner or operator was unable to obtain the necessary permission to undertake such action. Such regulations shall take effect immediately upon promulgation, notwithstanding section 6930(b) of this title, and shall apply to —

    (1) all facilities operating under permits issued under subsection (c) of this section, and

    (2) all landfills, surface impoundments, and waste pile units (including any new units, replacements of existing units, or lateral expansions of existing units) which receive hazardous waste after July 26, 1982.

Pending promulgation of such regulations, the Administrator shall issue corrective action orders for facilities referred to in paragraphs (1) and (2), on a case-by-case basis, consistent with the purposes of this subsection.

(w) UNDERGROUND TANKS

Not later than March 1, 1985, the Administrator shall promulgate final permitting standards under this section for underground tanks that cannot be entered for inspection. Within forty-eight months after November 8, 1984, such standards shall be modified, if necessary, to cover at a minimum all requirements and standards described in section 6991b of this title.

(x) MINING AND OTHER SPECIAL WASTES

If (1) solid waste from the extraction, beneficiation or processing of ores and minerals, including phosphate rock and overburden from the mining of uranium, (2) fly ash waste, bottom ash waste, slag waste, and flue gas emission control waste generated primarily from the combustion of coal or other fossil fuels, or (3) cement kiln dust waste, is subject to regulation under this subchapter, the Administrator is authorized to modify the requirements of subsections (c), (d), (e), (f), (g), (o), and (u) of this section and section 6925(j) of this title, in the case of landfills or surface impoundments receiving such solid waste, to take into account the special characteristics of such wastes, the practical difficulties associated with implementation of such requirements, and site-specific characteristics, including but not limited to the climate, geology, hydrology and soil chemistry at the site, so long as such modified requirements assure protection of human health and the environment.

§6925. PERMITS FOR TREATMENT, STORAGE, OR DISPOSAL OF HAZARDOUS WASTE

(a) PERMIT REQUIREMENTS

Not later than eighteen months after October 21, 1976, the Administrator shall promulgate regulations requiring each person owning or operating an existing facility or planning to construct a new facility for the treatment, storage, or disposal of hazardous waste identified or listed under this subchapter to have a permit issued pursuant to this section. Such regulations shall take effect on the date provided in section 6930 of this title and upon and after such date the treatment, storage, or disposal of any such hazardous waste and the construction of any new facility for the treatment, storage, or disposal of any such hazardous waste is prohibited except in accordance with such a permit. No permit shall be required under this section in order to construct a facility if such facility is constructed pursuant to an approval issued by the Administrator under section 2605(e) of title 15 for the incineration of polycholorinated[9] biphenyls and any person owning or operating such a facility may, at any time after operation or construction of such facility has begun, file an application for a permit pursuant to this section authorizing such facility to incinerate hazardous waste identified or listed under this subchapter.

(b) **REQUIREMENTS OF PERMIT APPLICATION**

Each application for a permit under this section shall contain such information as may be required under regulations promulgated by the Administrator, including information respecting —

(1) estimates with respect to the composition, quantities, and concentrations of any hazardous waste identified or listed under this subchapter, or combinations of any such hazardous waste and any other solid waste, proposed to be disposed of, treated, transported, or stored, and the time, frequency, or rate of which such waste is proposed to be disposed of, treated, transported, or stored; and

(2) the site at which such hazardous waste or the products of treatment of such hazardous waste will be disposed of, treated, transported to, or stored.

(c) **PERMIT ISSUANCE**

(1) Upon a determination by the Administrator (or a State, if applicable), of compliance by a facility for which a permit is applied for under this section with the requirements of this section and section 6924 of this title, the Administrator (or the State) shall issue a permit for such facilities. In the event permit applicants propose modification of their facilities, or in the event the Administrator (or the State) determines that modifications are necessary to conform to the requirements under this section and section 6924 of this title, the permit shall specify the time allowed to complete the modifications.

(2)(A)(i) Not later than the date four years after November 8, 1984, in the case of each application under this subsection for a permit for a land disposal facility which was submitted before such date, the Administrator shall issue a final permit pursuant to such application or issue a final denial of such application.

9. So in original. Probably should be "polychlorinated."

Resource Conservation and Recovery Act §6925

(ii) Not later than the date five years after November 8, 1984, in the case of each application for a permit under this subsection for an incinerator facility which was submitted before such date, the Administrator shall issue a final permit pursuant to such application or issue a final denial of such application.

(B) Not later than the date eight years after November 8, 1984, in the case of each application for a permit under this subsection for any facility (other than a facility referred to in subparagraph (A)) which was submitted before such date, the Administrator shall issue a final permit pursuant to such application or issue a final denial of such application.

(C) The time periods specified in this paragraph shall also apply in the case of any State which is administering an authorized hazardous waste program under section 6926 of this title. Interim status under subsection (e) of this section shall terminate for each facility referred to in subparagraph (A)(ii) or (B) on the expiration of the five- or eight-year period referred to in subparagraph (A) or (B), whichever is applicable, unless the owner or operator of the facility applies for a final determination regarding the issuance of a permit under this subsection within —

(i) two years after November 8, 1984 (in the case of a facility referred to in subparagraph (A)(ii)), or

(ii) four years after November 8, 1984 (in the case of a facility referred to in subparagraph (B)).

(3) Any permit under this section shall be for a fixed term, not to exceed 10 years in the case of any land disposal facility, storage facility, or incinerator or other treatment facility. Each permit for a land disposal facility shall be reviewed five years after date of issuance or reissuance and shall be modified as necessary to assure that the facility continues to comply with the currently applicable requirements of this section and section 6924 of this title. Nothing in this subsection shall preclude the Administrator from reviewing and modifying a permit at any time during its term. Review of any application for a permit renewal shall consider improvements in the state of control and measurement technology as well as changes in applicable regulations. Each permit issued under this section shall contain such terms and conditions as the Administrator (or the State) determines necessary to protect human health and the environment.

(d) **PERMIT REVOCATION**

Upon a determination by the Administrator (or by a State, in the case of a State having an authorized hazardous waste program under section 6926 of this title) of noncompliance by a facility having a permit under this chapter with the requirements of this section or section 6924 of this title, the Administrator (or State, in the case of a State having an authorized hazardous waste program under section 6926 of this title) shall revoke such permit.

(e) **INTERIM STATUS**

(1) Any person who —

(A) owns or operates a facility required to have a permit under this section which facility —

(i) was in existence on November 19, 1980, or

(ii) is in existence on the effective date of statutory or regulatory changes under this chapter that render the facility subject to the requirement to have a permit under this section,

(B) has complied with the requirements of section 6930(a) of this title, and

(C) has made an application for a permit under this section[10]

shall be treated as having been issued such permit until such time as final administrative disposition of such application is made, unless the Administrator or other plaintiff proves that final administrative disposition of such application has not been made because of the failure of the applicant to furnish information reasonably required or requested in order to process the application. This paragraph shall not apply to any facility which has been previously denied a permit under this section or if authority to operate the facility under this section has been previously terminated.

(2) In the case of each land disposal facility which has been granted interim status under this subsection before November 8, 1984, interim status shall terminate on the date twelve months after November 8, 1984, unless the owner or operator of such facility —

(A) applies for a final determination regarding the issuance of a permit under subsection (c) of this section for such facility before the date twelve months after November 8, 1984; and

(B) certifies that such facility is in compliance with all applicable groundwater monitoring and financial responsibility requirements.

(3) In the case of each land disposal facility which is in existence on the effective date of statutory or regulatory changes under this chapter that render the facility subject to the requirement to have a permit under this section and which is granted interim status under this subsection, interim status shall terminate on the date twelve months after the date on which the facility first becomes subject to such permit requirement unless the owner or operator of such facility —

(A) applies for a final determination regarding the issuance of a permit under subsection (c) of this section for such facility before the date twelve months after the date on which the facility first becomes subject to such permit requirement; and

(B) certifies that such a facility is in compliance with all applicable groundwater monitoring and financial responsibility requirements.

---

10. So in original. Probably should be followed by a comma.

Resource Conservation and Recovery Act §6925

(f) COAL MINING WASTES AND RECLAMATION PERMITS

Notwithstanding subsection (a) through (e) of this section, any surface coal mining and reclamation permit covering any coal mining wastes or overburden which has been issued or approved under the Surface Mining Control and Reclamation Act of 1977 [30 U.S.C. 1201 et seq.] shall be deemed to be a permit issued pursuant to this section with respect to the treatment, storage, or disposal of such wastes or overburden. Regulations promulgated by the Administrator under this subchapter shall not be applicable to treatment, storage, or disposal of coal mining wastes and overburden which are covered by such a permit.

(g) RESEARCH, DEVELOPMENT, AND DEMONSTRATION PERMITS

(1) The Administrator may issue a research, development, and demonstration permit for any hazardous waste treatment facility which proposes to utilize an innovative and experimental hazardous waste treatment technology or process for which permit standards for such experimental activity have not been promulgated under this subchapter. Any such permit shall include such terms and conditions as will assure protection of human health and the environment. Such permits —

(A) shall provide for the construction of such facilities, as necessary, and for operation of the facility for not longer than one year (unless renewed as provided in paragraph (4)), and

(B) shall provide for the receipt and treatment by the facility of only those types and quantities of hazardous waste which the Administrator deems necessary for purposes of determining the efficacy and performance capabilities of the technology or process and the effects of such technology or process on human health and the environment, and

(C) shall include such requirements as the Administrator deems necessary to protect human health and the environment (including, but not limited to, requirements regarding monitoring, operation, insurance or bonding, financial responsibility, closure, and remedial action), and such requirements as the Administrator deems necessary regarding testing and providing of information to the Administrator with respect to the operation of the facility. The Administrator may apply the criteria set forth in this paragraph in establishing the conditions of each permit without separate establishment of regulations implementing such criteria.

(2) For the purpose of expediting review and issuance of permits under this subsection, the Administrator may, consistent with the protection of human health and the environment, modify or waive permit application and permit issuance requirements established in the Administrator's general permit regulations except that there may be no modification or waiver of regulations regarding financial responsibility (including insurance) or of procedures established under section 6974(b)(2) of this title regarding public participation.

(3) The Administrator may order an immediate termination of all opera-

tions at the facility at any time he determines that termination is necessary to protect human health and the environment.

(4) Any permit issued under this subsection may be renewed not more than three times. Each such renewal shall be for a period of not more than 1 year.

(h) WASTE MINIMIZATION

Effective September 1, 1985, it shall be a condition of any permit issued under this section for the treatment, storage, or disposal of hazardous waste on the premises where such waste was generated that the permittee certify, no less often than annually, that —

(1) the generator of the hazardous waste has a program in place to reduce the volume or quantity and toxicity of such waste to the degree determined by the generator to be economically practicable; and

(2) the proposed method of treatment, storage, or disposal is that practicable method currently available to the generator which minimizes the present and future threat to human health and the environment.

(i) INTERIM STATUS FACILITIES RECEIVING WASTES AFTER JULY 26, 1982

The standards concerning ground water monitoring, unsaturated zone monitoring, and corrective action, which are applicable under section 6924 of this title to new landfills, surface impoundments, land treatment units, and waste-pile units required to be permitted under subsection (c) of this section shall also apply to any landfill, surface impoundment, land treatment unit, or waste-pile unit qualifying for the authorization to operate under subsection (e) of this section which receives hazardous waste after July 26, 1982.

(j) INTERIM STATUS SURFACE IMPOUNDMENTS

(1) Except as provided as paragraph (2), (3), or (4), each surface impoundment in existence on November 8, 1984, and qualifying for the authorization to operate under subsection (e) of this section shall not receive, store, or treat hazardous waste after the date four years after November 8, 1984, unless such surface impoundment is in compliance with the requirements of section 6924(o)(1)(A) of this title which would apply to such impoundment if it were new.

(2) Paragraph (1) of this subsection shall not apply to any surface impoundment which (A) has at least one liner, for which there is no evidence that such liner is leaking; (B) is located more than one-quarter mile from an underground source of drinking water; and (C) is in compliance with generally applicable ground water monitoring requirements for facilities with permits under subsection (c) of this section.

(3) Paragraph (1) of this subsection shall not apply to any surface impoundment which (A) contains treated waste water during the secondary or subsequent phases of an aggressive biological treatment facility subject to a permit issued under section 1342 of title 33 (or which holds such treated waste water after treatment and prior to discharge); (B) is in compliance with generally applicable

ground water monitoring requirements for facilities with permits under subsection (c) of this section; and (C)(i) is part of a facility in compliance with section 1311(b)(2) of title 33, or (ii) in the case of a facility for which no effluent guidelines required under section 1314(b)(2) of title 33 are in effect and no permit under section 1342(a)(1) of title 33 implementing section 1311(b)(2) of title 33 has been issued, is part of a facility in compliance with a permit under section 1342 of title 33, which is achieving significant degradation of toxic pollutants and hazardous constituents contained in the untreated waste stream and which has identified those toxic pollutants and hazardous constituents in the untreated waste stream to the appropriate permitting authority.

(4) The Administrator (or the State, in the case of a State with an authorized program), after notice and opportunity for comment, may modify the requirements of paragraph (1) for any surface impoundment if the owner or operator demonstrates that such surface impoundment is located, designed and operated so as to assure that there will be no migration of any hazardous constitutent[11] into ground water or surface water at any future time. The Administrator or the State shall take into account locational criteria established under section 6924(o)(7) of this title.

(5) The owner or operator of any surface impoundment potentially subject to paragraph (1) who has reason to believe that on the basis of paragraph (2), (3), or (4) such surface impoundment is not required to comply with the requirements of paragraph (1), shall apply to the Administrator (or the State, in the case of a State with an authorized program) not later than twenty-four months after November 8, 1984, for a determination of the applicability of paragraph (1) (in the case of paragraph (2) or (3)) or for a modification of the requirements of paragraph (1) (in the case of paragraph (4)), with respect to such surface impoundment. Such owner or operator shall provide, with such application, evidence pertinent to such decision, including:

(A) an application for a final determination regarding the issuance of a permit under subsection (c) of this section for such facility, if not previously submitted;

(B) evidence as to compliance with all applicable ground water monitoring requirements and the information and analysis from such monitoring;

(C) all reasonably ascertainable evidence as to whether such surface impoundment is leaking; and

(D) in the case of applications under paragraph (2) or (3), a certification by a registered professional engineer with academic training and experience in ground water hydrology that —

(i) under paragraph (2), the liner of such surface impoundment is designed, constructed, and operated in accordance with applicable requirements, such surface impoundment is more than one-quarter mile from an underground source of drinking water and there is no evidence such liner is leaking; or

---

11. So in original. Probably should be "constituent."

(ii) under paragraph (3), based on analysis of those toxic pollutants and hazardous constituents that are likely to be present in the untreated waste stream, such impoundment satisfies the conditions of paragraph (3). In the case of any surface impoundment for which the owner or operator fails to apply under this paragraph within the time provided by this paragraph or paragraph (6), such surface impoundment shall comply with paragraph (1) notwithstanding paragraph (2), (3), or (4). Within twelve months after receipt of such application and evidence and not later than thirty-six months after November 8, 1984, and after notice and opportunity to comment, the Administrator (or, if appropriate, the State) shall advise such owner or operator on the applicability of paragraph (1) to such surface impoundment or as to whether and how the requirements of paragraph (1) shall be modified and applied to such surface impoundment.

(6)(A) In any case in which a surface impoundment becomes subject to paragraph (1) after November 8, 1984, due to the promulgation of additional listings or characteristics for the identification of hazardous waste under section 6921 of this title, the period for compliance in paragraph (1) shall be four years after the date of such promulgation, the period for demonstrations under paragraph (4) and for submission of evidence under paragraph (5) shall be not later than twenty-four months after the date of such promulgation, and the period for the Administrator (or if appropriate, the State) to advise such owners or operators under paragraph (5) shall be not later than thirty-six months after the date of promulgation.

(B) In any case in which a surface impoundment is initially determined to be excluded from the requirements of paragraph (1) but due to a change in condition (including the existence of a leak) no longer satisfies the provisions of paragraph (2), (3), or (4) and therefore becomes subject to paragraph (1), the period for compliance in paragraph (1) shall be two years after the date of discovery of such change of condition, or in the case of a surface impoundment excluded under paragraph (3) three years after such date of discovery.

(7)(A) The Administrator shall study and report to the Congress on the number, range of size, construction, likelihood of hazardous constituents migrating into ground water, and potential threat to human health and the environment of existing surface impoundments excluded by paragraph (3) from the requirements of paragraph (1). Such report shall address the need, feasibility, and estimated costs of subjecting such existing surface impoundments to the requirements of paragraph (1).

(B) In the case of any existing surface impoundment or class of surface impoundments from which the Administrator (or the State, in the case of a State with an authorized program) determines hazardous constituents are likely to migrate into ground water, the Administrator (or if appropriate, the State) is authorized to impose such requirements as may be necessary to protect human health and the environment, including the requirements of section 6924(o) of this title which would apply to such impoundments if they were new.

(C) In the case of any surface impoundment excluded by paragraph (3) from the requirements of paragraph (1) which is subsequently determined to be leaking, the Administrator (or, if appropriate, the State) shall require compliance with paragraph (1), unless the Administrator (or, if appropriate, the State) determines that such compliance is not necessary to protect human health and the environment.

(8) In the case of any surface impoundment in which the liners and leak detection system have been installed pursuant to the requirements of paragraph (1) and in good faith compliance with section 6924(o) of this title and the Administrator's regulations and guidance documents governing liners and leak detection systems, no liner or leak detection system which is different from that which was so installed pursuant to paragraph (1) shall be required for such unit by the Administrator when issuing the first permit under this section to such facility. Nothing in this paragraph shall preclude the Administrator from requiring installation of a new liner when the Administrator has reason to believe that any liner installed pursuant to the requirements of this subsection is leaking.

(9) In the case of any surface impoundment which has been excluded by paragraph (2) on the basis of a liner meeting the definition under paragraph (12)(A)(ii), at the closure of such impoundment the Administrator shall require the owner or operator of such impoundment to remove or decontaminate all waste residues, all contaminated liner material, and contaminated soil to the extent practicable. If all contaminated soil is not removed or decontaminated, the owner or operator of such impoundment shall be required to comply with appropriate post-closure requirements, including but not limited to ground water monitoring and corrective action.

(10) Any incremental cost attributable to the requirements of this subsection or section 6924(o) of this title shall not be considered by the Administrator (or the State, in the case of a State with an authorized program under section 1342 of title 33) —

(A) in establishing effluent limitations and standards under section 1311, 1314, 1316, 1317, or 1342 of title 33 based on effluent limitations guidelines and standards promulgated any time before twelve months after November 8, 1984; or

(B) in establishing any other effluent limitations to carry out the provisions of section 1311, 1317, or 1342 of title 33 on or before October 1, 1986.

(11)(A) If the Administrator allows a hazardous waste which is prohibited from one or more methods of land disposal under subsection (d), (e), or (g) of section 6924 of this title (or under regulations promulgated by the Administrator under such subsections) to be placed in a surface impoundment (which is operating pursuant to interim status) for storage or treatment, such impoundment shall meet the requirements that are applicable to new surface impoundments under section 6924(o)(1) of this title, unless such impoundment meets the requirements of paragraph (2) or (4).

(B) In the case of any hazardous waste which is prohibited from one or more methods of land disposal under subsection (d), (e), or (g) of section 6924 of this title (or under regulations promulgated by the Administrator under such subsection) the placement or maintenance of such hazardous waste in a surface impoundment for treatment is prohibited as of the effective date of such prohibition unless the treatment residues which are hazardous are, at a minimum, removed for subsequent management within one year of the entry of the waste into the surface impoundment.

(12)(A) For the purposes of paragraph (2)(A) of this subsection, the term "liner" means —

(i) a liner designed, constructed, installed, and operated to prevent hazardous waste from passing into the liner at any time during the active life of the facility; or

(ii) a liner designed, constructed, installed, and operated to prevent hazardous waste from migrating beyond the liner to adjacent subsurface soil, ground water, or surface water at any time during the active life of the facility.

(B) For the purposes of this subsection, the term "aggressive biological treatment facility" means a system of surface impoundments in which the initial impoundment of the secondary treatment segment of the facility utilizes intense mechanical aeration to enhance biological activity to degrade waste water pollutants and

(i) the hydraulic retention time in such initial impoundment is no longer than 5 days under normal operating conditions, on an annual average basis;

(ii) the hydraulic retention time in such initial impoundment is no longer than thirty days under normal operating conditions, on an annual average basis: *Provided*, That the sludge in such impoundment does not constitute a hazardous waste as identified by the extraction procedure toxicity characteristic in effect on November 8, 1984; or

(iii) such system utilizes activated sludge treatment in the first portion of secondary treatment.

(C) For the purposes of this subsection, the term "underground source or[12] drinking water" has the same meaning as provided in regulations under the Safe Drinking Water Act (title XIV of the Public Health Service Act [42 U.S.C. 300f et seq.]).

(13) The Administrator may modify the requirements of paragraph (1) in the case of a surface impoundment for which the owner or operator, prior to October 1, 1984, has entered into, and is in compliance with, a consent order, decree, or agreement with the Administrator or a State with an authorized program mandating corrective action with respect to such surface impoundment that provides a degree of protection of human health and the environment which is at a minimum equivalent to that provided by paragraph (1).

---

12. So in original. Probably should be "of."

§6926. Authorized State Hazardous Waste Programs

(a) FEDERAL GUIDELINES

Not later than eighteen months after October 21, 1976, the Administrator, after consultation with State authorities, shall promulgate guidelines to assist States in the Development of State hazardous waste programs.

(b) AUTHORIZATION OF STATE PROGRAM

Any State which seeks to administer and enforce a hazardous waste program pursuant to this subchapter may develop and, after notice and opportunity for public hearing, submit to the Administrator an application in such form as he shall require, for authorization of such program. Within ninety days following submission of an application under this subsection, the Administrator shall issue a notice as to whether or not he expects such program to be authorized, and within ninety days following such notice (and after opportunity for public hearing) he shall publish his findings as to whether or not the conditions listed in items (1), (2), and (3) below have been met. Such State is authorized to carry out such program in lieu of the Federal program under this subchapter in such State and to issue and enforce permits for the storage, treatment, or disposal of hazardous waste (and to enforce permits deemed to have been issued under section 6935(d)(1)[13] of this title) unless, within ninety days following submission of the application the Administrator notifies such State that such program may not be authorized and, within ninety days following such notice and after opportunity for public hearing, he finds that (1) such State program is not equivalent to the Federal program under this subchapter, (2) such program is not consistent with the Federal or State programs applicable in other States, or (3) such program does not provide adequate enforcement of compliance with the requirements of this subchapter. In authorizing a State program, the Administrator may base his findings on the Federal program in effect one year prior to submission of a State's application or in effect on January 26, 1983, whichever is later.

(c) INTERIM AUTHORIZATION

(1) Any State which has in existence a hazardous waste program pursuant to State law before the date ninety days after the date of promulgation of regulations under sections 6922, 6923, 6924, and 6925 of this title, may submit to the Administrator evidence of such existing program and may request a temporary authorization to carry out such program under this subchapter. The Administrator shall, if the evidence submitted shows the existing State program to be substantially equivalent to the Federal program under this subchapter, grant an interim authorization to the State to carry out such program in lieu of the

---

13. See References in Text note below.

Federal program pursuant to this subchapter for a period ending no later than January 31, 1986.

(2) The Administrator shall, by rule, establish a date for the expiration of interim authorization under this subsection.

(3) Pending interim or final authorization of a State program for any State which reflects the amendments made by the Hazardous and Solid Waste Amendments of 1984, the State may enter into an agreement with the Administrator under which the State may assist in the administration of the requirements and prohibitions which take effect pursuant to such Amendments.

(4) In the case of a State permit program for any State which is authorized under subsection (b) of this section or under this subsection, until such program is amended to reflect the amendments made by the Hazardous and Solid Waste Amendments of 1984 and such program amendments receive interim or final authorization, the Administrator shall have the authority in such State to issue or deny permits or those portions of permits affected by the requirements and prohibitions established by the Hazardous and Solid Waste Amendments of 1984. The Administrator shall coordinate with States the procedures for issuing such permits.

(d) **EFFECT OF STATE PERMIT**

Any action taken by a State under a hazardous waste program authorized under this section shall have the same force and effect as action taken by the Administrator under this subchapter.

(e) **WITHDRAWAL OF AUTHORIZATION**

Whenever the Administrator determines after public hearing that a State is not administering and enforcing a program authorized under this section in accordance with requirements of this section, he shall so notify the State and, if appropriate corrective action is not taken within a reasonable time, not to exceed ninety days, the Administrator shall withdraw authorization of such program and establish a Federal program pursuant to this subchapter. The Administrator shall not withdraw authorization of any such program unless he shall first have notified the State, and made public, in writing, the reasons for such withdrawal.

(f) **AVAILABILITY OF INFORMATION**

No State program may be authorized by the Administrator under this section unless —

(1) such program provides for the public availability of information obtained by the State regarding facilities and sites for the treatment, storage, and disposal of hazardous waste; and

(2) such information is available to the public in substantially the same manner, and to the same degree, as would be the case if the Administrator was carrying out the provisions of this subchapter in such State.

Resource Conservation and Recovery Act §6927

(g) AMENDMENTS MADE BY 1984 ACT

(1) Any requirement or prohibition which is applicable to the generation, transportation, treatment, storage, or disposal of hazardous waste and which is imposed under this subchapter pursuant to the amendments made by the Hazardous and Solid Waste Amendments of 1984 shall take effect in each State having an interim or finally authorized State program on the same date as such requirement takes effect in other States. The Administrator shall carry out such requirement directly in each such State unless the State program is finally authorized (or is granted interim authorization as provided in paragraph (2)) with respect to such requirement.

(2) Any State which, before November 8, 1984, has an existing hazardous waste program which has been granted interim or final authorization under this section may submit to the Administrator evidence that such existing program contains (or has been amended to include) any requirement which is substantially equivalent to a requirement referred to in paragraph (1) and may request interim authorization to carry out that requirement under this subchapter. The Administrator shall, if the evidence submitted shows the State requirement to be substantially equivalent to the requirement referred to in paragraph (1), grant an interim authorization to the State to carry out such requirement in lieu of direct administration in the State by the Administrator of such requirement.

(h) STATE PROGRAMS FOR USED OIL

In the case of used oil which is not listed or identified under this subchapter as a hazardous waste but which is regulated under section 6935 of this title, the provisions of this section regarding State programs shall apply in the same manner and to the same extent as such provisions apply to hazardous waste identified or listed under this subchapter.

§6927. INSPECTIONS

(a) ACCESS ENTRY

For purposes of developing or assisting in the development of any regulation or enforcing the provisions of this chapter, any person who generates, stores, treats, transports, disposes of, or otherwise handles or has handled hazardous wastes shall, upon request of any officer, employee or representative of the Environmental Protection Agency, duly designated by the Administrator, or upon request of any duly designated officer, employee or representative of a State having an authorized hazardous waste program, furnish information relating to such wastes and permit such person at all reasonable times to have access to, and to copy all records relating to such wastes. For the purposes of developing or assisting in the development of any regulation or enforcing the provisions of this chapter, such officers, employees or representatives are authorized —

(1) to enter at reasonable times any establishment or other place where hazardous wastes are or have been generated, stored, treated, disposed of, or transported from:

(2) to inspect and obtain samples from any person of any such wastes and samples of any containers or labeling for such wastes.

Each such inspection shall be commenced and completed with reasonable promptness. If the officer, employee or representative obtains any samples, prior to leaving the premises, he shall give to the owner, operator, or agent in charge a receipt describing the sample obtained and if requested a portion of each such sample equal in volume or weight to the portion retained. If any analysis is made of such samples, a copy of the results of such analysis shall be furnished promptly to the owner, operator, or agent in charge.

(b) AVAILABILITY TO PUBLIC

(1) Any records, reports, or information (including records, reports, or information obtained by representatives of the Environmental Protection Agency) obtained from any person under this section shall be available to the public, except that upon a showing satisfactory to the Administrator (or the State, as the case may be) by any person that records, reports, or information, or particular part thereof, to which the Administrator (or the State, as the case may be) or any officer, employee or representative thereof has access under this section if made public, would divulge information entitled to protection under section 1905 of title 18, such information or particular portion thereof shall be considered confidential in accordance with the purposes of that section, except that such record, report, document, or information may be disclosed to other officers, employees, or authorized representatives of the United States concerned with carrying out this chapter, or when relevant in any proceeding under this chapter.

(2) Any person not subject to the provisions of section 1905 of title 18 who knowingly and willfully divulges or discloses any information entitled to protection under this subsection shall, upon conviction, be subject to a fine of not more than $5,000 or to imprisonment not to exceed one year, or both.

(3) In submitting data under this chapter, a person required to provide such data may —

(A) designate the data which such person believes is entitled to protection under this subsection, and

(B) submit such designated data separately from other data submitted under this subchapter.

A designation under this paragraph shall be made in writing and in such manner as the Administrator may prescribe.

(4) Notwithstanding any limitation contained in this section or any other provision of law, all information reported to, or otherwise obtained by, the Administrator (or any representative of the Administrator) under this chapter shall be made available, upon written request of any duly authorized committee of the Congress, to such committee.

Resource Conservation and Recovery Act   §6927

(c) FEDERAL FACILITY INSPECTIONS

Beginning twelve months after November 8, 1984, the Administrator shall, or in the case of a State with an authorized hazardous waste program the State may, undertake on an annual basis a thorough inspection of each facility for the treatment, storage, or disposal of hazardous waste which is owned or operated by a Federal agency to enforce its compliance with this subchapter and the regulations promulgated thereunder. The records of such inspections shall be available to the public as provided in subsection (b) of this section.

(d) STATE-OPERATED FACILITIES

The Administrator shall annually undertake a thorough inspection of every facility for the treatment, storage, or disposal of hazardous waste which is operated by a State or local government for which a permit is required under section 6925 of this title. The records of such inspection shall be available to the public as provided in subsection (b) of this section.

(e) MANDATORY INSPECTIONS

(1) The Administrator (or the State in the case of a State having an authorized hazardous waste program under this subchapter) shall commence a program to thoroughly inspect every facility for the treatment, storage, or disposal of hazardous waste for which a permit is required under section 6925 of this title no less often than every two years as to its compliance with this subchapter (and the regulations promulgated under this subchapter). Such inspections shall commence not later than twelve months after November 8, 1984. The Administrator shall, after notice and opportunity for public comment, promulgate regulations governing the minimum frequency and manner of such inspections, including the manner in which records of such inspections shall be maintained and the manner in which reports of such inspections shall be filed. The Administrator may distinguish between classes and categories of facilities commensurate with the risks posed by each class or category.

(2) Not later than six months after November 8, 1984, the Administrator shall submit to the Congress a report on the potential for inspections of hazardous waste treatment, storage, or disposal facilities by nongovernmental inspectors as a supplement to inspections conducted by officers, employees, or representatives of the Environmental Protection Agency or States having authorized hazardous waste programs or operating under a cooperative agreement with the Administrator. Such report shall be prepared in cooperation with the States, insurance companies offering environmental impairment insurance, independent companies providing inspection services, and other such groups as appropriate. Such report shall contain recommendations on provisions and requirements for a program of private inspections to supplement governmental inspections.

§6928. Federal Enforcement

(a) COMPLIANCE ORDERS

(1) Except as provided in paragraph (2), whenever on the basis of any information the Administrator determines that any person has violated or is in violation of any requirement of this subchapter, the Administrator may issue an order assessing a civil penalty for any past or current violation, requiring compliance immediately or within a specified time period, or both, or the Administrator may commence a civil action in the United States district court in the district in which the violation occurred for appropriate relief, including a temporary or permanent injunction.

(2) In the case of a violation of any requirement of this subchapter where such violation occurs in a State which is authorized to carry out a hazardous waste program under section 6926 of this title, the Administrator shall give notice to the State in which such violation has occurred prior to issuing an order or commencing a civil action under this section.

(3) Any order issued pursuant to this subsection may include a suspension or revocation of any permit issued by the Administrator or a State under this subchapter and shall state with reasonable specificity the nature of the violation. Any penalty assessed in the order shall not exceed $25,000 per day of noncompliance for each violation of a requirement of this subchapter. In assessing such a penalty, the Administrator shall take into account the seriousness of the violation and any good faith efforts to comply with applicable requirements.

(b) PUBLIC HEARING

Any order issued under this section shall become final unless, no later than thirty days after the order is served, the person or persons named therein request a public hearing. Upon such request the Administrator shall promptly conduct a public hearing. In connection with any proceeding under this section the Administrator may issue subpenas for the attendance and testimony of witnesses and the production of relevant papers, books, and documents, and may promulgate rules for discovery procedures.

(c) VIOLATION OF COMPLIANCE ORDERS

If a violator fails to take corrective action within the time specified in a compliance order, the Administrator may assess a civil penalty of not more than $25,000 for each day of continued noncompliance with the order and the Administrator may suspend or revoke any permit issued to the violator (whether issued by the Administrator or the State).

(d) CRIMINAL PENALTIES

Any person who —
(1) knowingly transports or causes to be transported any hazardous waste identified or listed under this subchapter to a facility which does not have a

permit under this subchapter, or pursuant to title I of the Marine Protection, Research, and Sanctuaries Act (86 Stat. 1052) [33 U.S.C. 1411 et seq.],

(2) knowingly treats, stores, or disposes of any hazardous waste identified or listed under this subchapter —

(A) without a permit under this subchapter or pursuant to title I of the Marine Protection, Research, and Sanctuaries Act (86 Stat. 1052) [33 U.S.C. 1411 et seq.]; or

(B) in knowing violation of any material condition or requirement of such permit; or

(C) in knowing violation of any material condition or requirement of any applicable interim status regulations or standards;

(3) knowingly omits material information or makes any false material statement or representation in any application, label, manifest, record, report, permit, or other document filed, maintained, or used for purposes of compliance with regulations promulgated by the Administrator (or by a State in the case of an authorized State program) under this subchapter;

(4) knowingly generates, stores, treats, transports, disposes of, exports, or otherwise handles any hazardous waste or any used oil not identified or listed as a hazardous waste under this subchapter (whether such activity took place before or takes place after November 8, 1984) and who knowingly destroys, alters, conceals, or fails to file any record, application, manifest, report, or other document required to be maintained or filed for purposes of compliance with regulations promulgated by the Administrator (or by a State in the case of an authorized State program) under this subchapter;

(5) knowingly transports without a manifest, or causes to be transported without a manifest, any hazardous waste or any used oil not identified or listed as a hazardous waste under this subchapter required by regulations promulgated under this subchapter (or by a State in the case of a State program authorized under this subchapter) to be accompanied by a manifest;

(6) knowingly exports a hazardous waste identified or listed under this subchapter (A) without the consent of the receiving country or, (B) where there exists an international agreement between the United States and the government of the receiving country establishing notice, export, and enforcement procedures for the transportation, treatment, storage, and disposal of hazardous wastes, in a manner which is not in conformance with such agreement; or

(7) knowingly stores, treats, transports, or causes to be transported, disposes of, or otherwise handles any used oil not identified or listed as a hazardous waste under this subchapter —

(A) in knowing violation of any material condition or requirement of a permit under this subchapter; or

(B) in knowing violation of any material condition or requirement of any applicable regulations or standards under this chapter;

shall, upon conviction, be subject to a fine of not more than $50,000 for each day of violation, or imprisonment not to exceed two years (five years in the case of a violation of paragraph (1) or (2)), or both. If the conviction is for a violation committed after a first conviction of such person under this paragraph, the maximum punishment under the respective paragraph shall be doubled with respect to both fine and imprisonment.

(e) **KNOWING ENDANGERMENT**

Any person who knowingly transports, treats, stores, disposes of, or exports any hazardous waste identified or listed under this subchapter or used oil not identified or listed as a hazardous waste under this subchapter in violation of paragraph (1), (2), (3), (4), (5), (6), or (7) of subsection (d) of this section who knows at that time that he thereby places another person in imminent danger of death or serious bodily injury, shall, upon conviction, be subject to a fine of not more than $250,000 or imprisonment for not more than fifteen years, or both. A defendant that is an organization shall, upon conviction of violating this subsection, be subject to a fine of not more than $1,000,000.

(f) **SPECIAL RULES**

For the purposes of subsection (e) of this section —
   (1) A person's state of mind is knowing with respect to —
      (A) his conduct, if he is aware of the nature of his conduct;
      (B) an existing circumstance, if he is aware or believes that the circumstance exists; or
      (C) a result of his conduct, if he is aware or believes that his conduct is substantially certain to cause danger of death or serious bodily injury.
   (2) In determining whether a defendant who is a natural person knew that his conduct placed another person in imminent danger of death or serious bodily injury —
      (A) the person is responsible only for actual awareness or actual belief that he possessed; and
      (B) knowledge possessed by a person other than the defendant but not by the defendant himself may not be attributed to the defendant;
Provided, That in proving the defendant's possession of actual knowledge, circumstantial evidence may be used, including evidence that the defendant took affirmative steps to shield himself from relevant information.
   (3) It is an affirmative defense to a prosecution that the conduct charged was consented to by the person endangered and that the danger and conduct charged were reasonably foreseeable hazards of —
      (A) an occupation, a business, or a profession; or
      (B) medical treatment or medical or scientific experimentation conducted by professionally approved methods and such other person had been made aware of the risks involved prior to giving consent.
The defendant may establish an affirmative defense under this subsection by a preponderance of the evidence.

(4) All general defenses, affirmative defenses, and bars to prosecution that may apply with respect to other Federal criminal offenses may apply under subsection (e) of this section and shall be determined by the courts of the United States according to the principles of common law as they may be interpreted in the light of reason and experience. Concepts of justification and excuse applicable under this section may be developed in the light of reason and experience.

(5) The term "organization" means a legal entity, other than a government, established, or organized for any purpose, and such term includes a corporation, company, association, firm, partnership, joint stock company, foundation, institution, trust, society, union, or any other association of persons.

(6) The term "serious bodily injury" means —

(A) bodily injury which involves a substantial risk of death;

(B) unconsciousness;

(C) extreme physical pain;

(D) protracted and obvious disfigurement; or

(E) protracted loss or impairment of the function of a bodily member, organ, or mental faculty.

(g) CIVIL PENALTY

Any person who violates any requirement of this subchapter shall be liable to the United States for a civil penalty in an amount not to exceed $25,000 for each such violation. Each day of such violation shall, for purposes of this subsection, constitute a separate violation.

(h) INTERIM STATUS CORRECTIVE ACTION ORDERS

(1) Whenever on the basis of any information the Administrator determines that there is or has been a release of hazardous waste into the environment from a facility authorized to operate under section 6925(e) of this title, the Administrator may issue an order requiring corrective action or such other response measure as he deems necessary to protect human health or the environment or the Administrator may commence a civil action in the United States district court in the district in which the facility is located for appropriate relief, including a temporary or permanent injunction.

(2) Any order issued under this subsection may include a suspension or revocation of authorization to operate under section 6925(e) of this title, shall state with reasonable specificity the nature of the required corrective action or other response measure, and shall specify a time for compliance. If any person named in an order fails to comply with the order, the Administrator may assess, and such person shall be liable to the United States for, a civil penalty in an amount not to exceed $25,000 for each day of noncompliance with the order.

§6929. Retention of State Authority

Upon the effective date of regulations under this subchapter no State or political subdivision may impose any requirements less stringent than those authorized under this subchapter respecting the same matter as governed by such regulations, except that if application of a regulation with respect to any matter under this subchapter is postponed or enjoined by the action of any court, no State or political subdivision shall be prohibited from acting with respect to the same aspect of such matter until such time as such regulation takes effect. Nothing in this chapter shall be construed to prohibit any State or political subdivision thereof from imposing any requirements, including those for site selection, which are more stringent than those imposed by such regulations. Nothing in this chapter (or in any regulation adopted under this chapter) shall be construed to prohibit any State from requiring that the State be provided with a copy of each manifest used in connection with hazardous waste which is generated within that State or transported to a treatment, storage, or disposal facility within that State.

§6930. Effective Date

(a) PRELIMINARY NOTIFICATION

Not later than ninety days after promulgation of regulations under section 6921 of this title identifying by its characteristics or listing any substance as hazardous waste subject to this subchapter, any person generating or transporting such substance or owning or operating a facility for treatment, storage, or disposal of such substance shall file with the Administrator (or with States having authorized hazardous waste permit programs under section 6926 of this title) a notification stating the location and general description of such activity and the identified or listed hazardous wastes handled by such person. Not later than fifteen months after November 8, 1984 —

(1) the owner or operator of any facility which produces a fuel (A) from any hazardous waste identified or listed under section 6921 of this title, (B) from such hazardous waste identified or listed under section 6921 of this title and any other material, (C) from used oil, or (D) from used oil and any other material;

(2) the owner or operator of any facility (other than a single- or two-family residence) which burns for purposes of energy recovery any fuel produced as provided in paragraph (1) or any fuel which otherwise contains used oil or any hazardous waste identified or listed under section 6921 of this title; and

(3) any person who distributes or markets any fuel which is produced as provided in paragraph (1) or any fuel which otherwise contains used

oil or any hazardous waste identified or listed under section 6921 of this title[14] shall file with the Administrator (and with the State in the case of a State with an authorized hazardous waste program) a notification stating the location and general description of the facility, together with a description of the identified or listed hazardous waste involved and, in the case of a facility referred to in paragraph (1) or (2), a description of the production or energy recovery activity carried out at the facility and such other information as the Administrator deems necessary. For purposes of the preceding provisions, the term "hazardous waste listed under section 6921 of this title" also includes any commercial chemical product which is listed under section 6921 of this title and which, in lieu of its original intended use, is (i) produced for use as (or as a component of) a fuel, (ii) distributed for use as a fuel, or (iii) burned as a fuel. Notification shall not be required under the second sentence of this subsection in the case of facilities (such as residential boilers) where the Administrator determines that such notification is not necessary in order for the Administrator to obtain sufficient information respecting current practices of facilities using hazardous waste for energy recovery. Nothing in this subsection shall be construed to affect or impair the provisions of section 6921(b)(3) of this title. Nothing in this subsection shall affect regulatory determinations under section 6935 of this title. In revising any regulation under section 6921 of this title identifying additional characteristics of hazardous waste or listing any additional substance as hazardous waste subject to this subchapter, the Administrator may require any person referred to in the preceding provisions to file with the Administrator (or with States having authorized hazardous waste permit programs under section 6926 of this title) the notification described in the preceding provisions. Not more than one such notification shall be required to be filed with respect to the same substance. No identified or listed hazardous waste subject to this subchapter may be transported, treated, stored, or disposed of unless notification has been given as required under this subsection.

(b) **EFFECTIVE DATE OF REGULATION**

The regulations under this subchapter respecting requirements applicable to the generation, transportation, treatment, storage, or disposal of hazardous waste (including requirements respecting permits for such treatment, storage, or disposal) shall take effect on the date six months after the date of promulgation thereof (or six months after the date of revision in the case of any regulation which is revised after the date required for promulgation thereof). At the time a regulation is promulgated, the Administrator may provide for a shorter period prior to the effective date, or an immediate effective date for:

(1) a regulation with which the Administrator finds the regulated community does not need six months to come into compliance;

14. So in original. Probably should be followed by a semicolon.

(2) a regulation which responds to an emergency situation; or
(3) other good cause found and published with the regulation.

§6931. Authorization of Assistance to States

(a) **AUTHORIZATION OF APPROPRIATIONS**

There is authorized to be appropriated $25,000,000 for each of the fiscal years 1978 and 1979[15] $20,000,000 for fiscal year 1980, $35,000,000 for fiscal year 1981, $40,000,000 for the fiscal year 1982, $55,000,000 for the fiscal year 1985, $60,000,000 for the fiscal year 1986, $60,000,000 for the fiscal year 1987, and $60,000,000 for the fiscal year 1988 to be used to make grants to the States for purposes of assisting the States in the development and implementation of authorized State hazardous waste programs.

(b) **ALLOCATION**

Amounts authorized to be appropriated under subsection (a) of this section shall be allocated among the States on the basis of regulations promulgated by the Administrator, after consultation with the States, which take into account, the extent to which hazardous waste is generated, transported, treated, stored, and disposed of within such State, the extent of exposure of human beings and the environment within such State to such waste, and such other factors as the Administrator deems appropriate.

(c) **ACTIVITIES INCLUDED**

State hazardous waste programs for which grants may be made under subsection (a) of this section may include (but shall not be limited to) planning for hazardous waste treatment, storage and disposal facilities, and the development and execution of programs to protect health and the environment from inactive facilities which may contain hazardous waste.

§6932. Transferred

§6933. Hazardous Waste Site Inventory

(a) **STATE INVENTORY PROGRAMS**

Each State shall, as expeditiously as practicable, undertake a continuing program to compile, publish, and submit to the Administrator an inventory describing the location of each site within such State at which hazardous waste has at any time been stored or disposed of. Such inventory shall contain —
   (1) a description of the location of the sites at which any such storage

---

15. So in original. Probably should be followed by a comma.

or disposal has taken place before the date on which permits are required under section 6925 of this title for such storage or disposal;

(2) such information relating to the amount, nature, and toxicity of the hazardous waste at each such site as may be practicable to obtain and as may be necessary to determine the extent of any health hazard which may be associated with such site;

(3) the name and address, or corporate headquarters of, the owner of each such site, determined as of the date of preparation of the inventory;

(4) an identification of the types or techniques of waste treatment or disposal which have been used at each such site; and

(5) information concerning the current status of the site, including information respecting whether or not hazardous waste is currently being treated or disposed of at such site (and if not, the date on which such activity ceased) and information respecting the nature of any other activity currently carried out at such site.

For purposes of assisting the States in compiling information under this section, the Administrator shall make available to each State undertaking a program under this section such information as is available to him concerning the items specified in paragraphs (1) through (5) with respect to the sites within such State, including such information as the Administrator is able to obtain from other agencies or departments of the United States and from surveys and studies carried out by any committee or subcommittee of the Congress. Any State may exercise the authority of section 6927 of this title for purposes of this section in the same manner and to the same extent as provided in such section in the case of States having an authorized hazardous waste program, and any State may by order require any person to submit such information as may be necessary to compile the data referred to in paragraphs (1) through (5).

(b) **ENVIRONMENTAL PROTECTION AGENCY PROGRAM**

If the Administrator determines that any State program under subsection (a) of this section is not adequately providing information respecting the sites in such State referred to in subsection (a) of this section, the Administrator shall notify the State. If within ninety days following such notification, the State program has not been revised or amended in such manner as will adequately provide such information, the Administrator shall carry out the inventory program in such State. In any such case —

(1) the Administrator shall have the authorities provided with respect to State programs under subsection (a) of this section;

(2) the funds allocated under subsection (c) of this section for grants to States under this section may be used by the Administrator for carrying out such program in such State; and

(3) no further expenditure may be made for grants to such State under this section until such time as the Administrator determines that such State is carrying out, or will carry out, an inventory program which meets the requirements of this section.

(c) GRANTS

(1) Upon receipt of an application submitted by any State to carry out a program under this section, the Administrator may make grants to the States for purposes of carrying out such a program. Grants under this section shall be allocated among the several States by the Administrator based upon such regulations as he prescribes to carry out the purposes of this section. The Administrator may make grants to any State which has conducted an inventory program which effectively carried out the purposes of this section before October 21, 1980, to reimburse such State for all, or any portion of, the costs incurred by such State in conducting such program.

(2) There are authorized to be appropriated to carry out this section $25,000,000 for each of the fiscal years 1985 through 1988.

(d) NO IMPEDIMENT TO IMMEDIATE REMEDIAL ACTION

Nothing in this section shall be construed to provide that the Administrator or any State should, pending completion of the inventory required under this section, postpone undertaking any enforcement or remedial action with respect to any site at which hazardous waste has been treated, stored, or disposed of.

§6934. MONITORING, ANALYSIS, AND TESTING

(a) AUTHORITY OF ADMINISTRATOR

If the Administrator determines, upon receipt of any information, that

(1) the presence of any hazardous waste at a facility or site at which hazardous waste is, or has been, stored, treated, or disposed of, or

(2) the release of any such waste from such facility or site

may present a substantial hazard to human health or the environment, he may issue an order requiring the owner or operator of such facility or site to conduct such monitoring, testing, analysis, and reporting with respect to such facility or site as the Administrator deems reasonable to ascertain the nature and extent of such hazard.

(b) PREVIOUS OWNERS AND OPERATORS

In the case of any facility or site not in operation at the time a determination is made under subsection (a) of this section with respect to the facility or site, if the Administrator finds that the owner of such facility or site could not reasonably be expected to have actual knowledge of the presence of hazardous waste at such facility or site and of its potential for release, he may issue an order requiring the most recent previous owner or operator of such facility or site who could reasonably be expected to have such actual knowledge to carry out the actions referred to in subsection (a) of this section.

(c) PROPOSAL

An order under subsection (a) or (b) of this section shall require the person to whom such order is issued to submit to the Administrator within 30 days from the issuance of such order a proposal for carrying out the required monitoring, testing, analysis, and reporting. The Administrator may, after providing such person with an opportunity to confer with the Administrator respecting such proposal, require such person to carry out such monitoring, testing, analysis, and reporting in accordance with such proposal, and such modifications in such proposal as the Administrator deems reasonable to ascertain the nature and extent of the hazard.

(d) MONITORING, ETC., CARRIED OUT BY ADMINISTRATOR

(1) If the Administrator determines that no owner or operator referred to in subsection (a) or (b) of this section is able to conduct monitoring, testing, analysis, or reporting satisfactory to the Administrator, if the Administrator deems any such action carried out by an owner or operator to be unsatisfactory, or if the Administrator cannot initially determine that there is an owner or operator referred to in subsection (a) or (b) of this section who is able to conduct such monitoring, testing, analysis, or reporting, he may —

  (A) conduct monitoring, testing, or analysis (or any combination thereof) which he deems reasonable to ascertain the nature and extent of the hazard associated with the site concerned, or

  (B) authorize a State or local authority or other person to carry out any such action,

and require, by order, the owner or operator referred to in subsection (a) or (b) of this section to reimburse the Administrator or other authority or person for the costs of such activity.

(2) No order may be issued under this subsection, requiring reimbursement of the costs of any action carried out by the Administrator which confirms the results of an order issued under subsection (a) or (b) of this section.

(3) For purposes of carrying out this subsection, the Administrator or any authority or other person authorized under paragraph (1), may exercise the authorities set forth in section 6927 of this title.

(e) ENFORCEMENT

The Administrator may commence a civil action against any person who fails or refuses to comply with any order issued under this section. Such action shall be brought in the United States district court in which the defendant is located, resides, or is doing business. Such court shall have jurisdiction to require compliance with such order and to assess a civil penalty of not to exceed $5,000 for each day during which such failure or refusal occurs.

§6935. Restrictions on Recycled Oil

(a) IN GENERAL

Not later than one year after October 15, 1980, the Administrator shall promulgate regulations establishing such performance standards and other requirements as may be necessary to protect the public health and the environment from hazards associated with recycled oil. In developing such regulations, the Administrator shall conduct an analysis of the economic impact of the regulations on the oil recycling industry. The Administrator shall ensure that such regulations do not discourage the recovery or recycling of used oil, consistent with the protection of human health and the environment.

(b) IDENTIFICATION OR LISTING OF USED OIL AS HAZARDOUS WASTE

Not later than twelve months after November 8, 1984, the Administrator shall propose whether to list or identify used automobile and truck crankcase oil as hazardous waste under section 6921 of this title. Not later than twenty-four months after November 8, 1984, the Administrator shall make a final determination whether to list or identify used automobile and truck crankcase oil and other used oil as hazardous wastes under section 6921 of this title.

(c) USED OIL WHICH IS RECYCLED

(1) With respect to generators and transporters of used oil identified or listed as a hazardous waste under section 6921 of this title, the standards promulgated under section[16] 6921(d), 6922, and 6923 of this title shall not apply to such used oil if such used oil is recycled.

(2)(A) In the case of used oil which is exempt under paragraph (1), not later than twenty-four months after November 8, 1984, the Administrator shall promulgate such standards under this subsection regarding the generation and transportation of used oil which is recycled as may be necessary to protect human health and the environment. In promulgating such regulations with respect to generators, the Administrator shall take into account the effect of such regulations on environmentally acceptable types of used oil recycling and the effect of such regulations on small quantity generators and generators which are small businesses (as defined by the Administrator).

(B) The regulations promulgated under this subsection shall provide that no generator of used oil which is exempt under paragraph (1) from the standards promulgated under section[16] 6921(d), 6922, and 6923 of this title shall be subject to any manifest requirement or any associated recordkeeping and reporting requirement with respect to such used oil if such generator —
    (i) either —
        (I) enters into an agreement or other arrangement (including an agreement or arrangement with an independent transporter or with an agent of the recycler) for delivery of such used oil to a recycling facility

---

16. So in original. Probably should be "sections."

which has a permit under section 6925(c) of this title (or for which a valid permit is deemed to be in effect under subsection (d) of this section), or

(II) recycles such used oil at one or more facilities of the generator which has such a permit under section 6925 of this title (or for which a valid permit is deemed to have been issued under subsection (d) of this section);

(ii) such used oil is not mixed by the generator with other types of hazardous wastes; and

(iii) the generator maintains such records relating to such used oil, including records of agreements or other arrangements for delivery of such used oil to any recycling facility referred to in clause (i)(I), as the Administrator deems necessary to protect human health and the environment.

(3) The regulations under this subsection regarding the transportation of used oil which is exempt from the standards promulgated under section[16] 6921(d), 6922, and 6923 of this title under paragraph (1) shall require the transporters of such used oil to deliver such used oil to a facility which has a valid permit under section 6925 of this title or which is deemed to have a valid permit under subsection (d) of this section. The Administrator shall also establish other standards for such transporters as may be necessary to protect human health and the environment.

(d) PERMITS

(1) The owner or operator of a facility which recycles used oil which is exempt under subsection (c)(1) of this section, shall be deemed to have a permit under this subsection for all such treatment or recycling (and any associated tank or container storage) if such owner and operator comply with standards promulgated by the Administrator under section 6924 of this title; except that the Administrator may require such owners and operators to obtain an individual permit under section 6925(c) of this title if he determines that an individual permit is necessary to protect human health and the environment.

(2) Notwithstanding any other provision of law, any generator who recycles used oil which is exempt under subsection (c)(1) of this section shall not be required to obtain a permit under section 6925(c) of this title with respect to such used oil until the Administrator has promulgated standards under section 6924 of this title regarding the recycling of such used oil.

§6936. EXPANSION DURING INTERIM STATUS

(a) WASTE PILES

The owner or operator of a waste pile qualifying for the authorization to operate under section 6925(e) of this title shall be subject to the same requirements for liners and leachate collection systems or equivalent protection provided in regulations promulgated by the Administrator under section 6924 of this title before October 1, 1982, or revised under section 6924(o) of this title (relating to minimum technological requirements), for new facilities receiving individual permits under subsection (c) of section 6925 of this title, with respect to each new unit, replacement of an existing unit, or lateral expansion of an existing unit that is within the waste management area identified in the permit application submitted under section 6925 of this title, and with respect to waste received beginning six months after November 8, 1984.

(b) LANDFILLS AND SURFACE IMPOUNDMENTS

(1) The owner or operator of a landfill or surface impoundment qualifying for the authorization to operate under section 6925(e) of this title shall be subject to the requirements of section 6924(o) of this title (relating to minimum technological requirements), with respect to each new unit, replacement of an existing unit, or lateral expansion of an existing unit that is within the waste management area identified in the permit application submitted under this section, and with respect to waste received beginning 6 months after November 8, 1984.

(2) The owner or operator of each unit referred to in paragraph (1) shall notify the Administrator (or the State, if appropriate) at least sixty days prior to receiving waste. The Administrator (or the State) shall require the filing, within six months of receipt of such notice, of an application for a final determination regarding the issuance of a permit for each facility submitting such notice.

(3) In the case of any unit in which the liner and leachate collection system has been installed pursuant to the requirements of this section and in good faith compliance with the Administrator's regulations and guidance documents governing liners and leachate collection systems, no liner or leachate collection system which is different from that which was so installed pursuant to this section shall be required for such unit by the Administrator when issuing the first permit under section 6925 of this title to such facility, except that the Administrator shall not be precluded from requiring installation of a new liner when the Administrator has reason to believe that any liner installed pursuant to the requirements of this section is leaking. The Administrator may, under section 6924 of this title, amend the requirements for liners and leachate collection systems required under this section as may be necessary to provide additional protection for human health and the environment.

§6937. INVENTORY OF FEDERAL AGENCY HAZARDOUS WASTE FACILITIES

(a) PROGRAM REQUIREMENT; SUBMISSION; AVAILABILITY; CONTENTS

Each Federal agency shall undertake a continuing program to compile, publish, and submit to the Administrator (and to the State in the case of sites in States having an authorized hazardous waste program) an inventory of each site which the Federal agency owns or operates or has owned or operated at which hazardous waste is stored, treated, or disposed of or has been disposed of at any time. The inventory shall be submitted every two years beginning January 31, 1986. Such inventory shall be available to the public as provided in section 6927(b) of this title. Information previously submitted by a Federal agency under section 9603 of this title, or under section 6925 or 6930 of this title, or under this section need not be resubmitted except that the agency shall update any previous submission to reflect the latest available data and information. The inventory shall include each of the following:

(1) A description of the location of each site at which any such treatment, storage, or disposal has taken place before the date on which permits are required under section 6925 of this title for such storage, treatment, or disposal, and where hazardous waste has been disposed, a description of hydrogeology of the site and the location of withdrawal wells and surface water within one mile of the site.

(2) Such information relating to the amount, nature, and toxicity of the hazardous waste in each site as may be necessary to determine the extent of any health hazard which may be associated with any site.

(3) Information on the known nature and extent of environmental contamination at each site, including a description of the monitoring data obtained.

(4) Information concerning the current status of the site, including information respecting whether or not hazardous waste is currently being treated, stored, or disposed of at such site (and if not, the date on which such activity ceased) and information respecting the nature of any other activity currently carried out at such site.

(5) A list of sites at which hazardous waste has been disposed and environmental monitoring data has not been obtained, and the reasons for the lack of monitoring data at each site.

(6) A description of response actions undertaken or contemplated at contaminated sites.

(7) An identification of the types of techniques of waste treatment, storage, or disposal which have been used at each site.

(8) The name and address and responsible Federal agency for each site, determined as of the date of preparation of the inventory.

(b) ENVIRONMENTAL PROTECTION AGENCY PROGRAM

If the Administrator determines that any Federal agency under subsection (a) of this section is not adequately providing information respecting the sites referred to in subsection (a) of this section, the Administrator shall notify the chief official of such agency. If within ninety days following such notification, the Federal agency has not undertaken a program to adequately provide such information, the Administrator shall carry out the inventory program for such agency.

§6938. Export of Hazardous Wastes

(a) IN GENERAL

Beginning twenty-four months after November 8, 1984, no person shall export any hazardous waste identified or listed under this subchapter unless[17]

(1)(A) such person has provided the notification required in subsection (c) of this section,

(B) the government of the receiving country has consented to accept such hazardous waste,

(C) a copy of the receiving country's written consent is attached to the manifest accompanying each waste shipment, and

(D) the shipment conforms with the terms of the consent of the government of the receiving country required pursuant to subsection (e) of this section, or

(2) the United States and the government of the receiving country have entered into an agreement as provided for in subsection (f) of this section and the shipment conforms with the terms of such agreement.

(b) REGULATIONS

Not later than twelve months after November 8, 1984, the Administrator shall promulgate the regulations necessary to implement this section. Such regulations shall become effective one hundred and eighty days after promulgation.

(c) NOTIFICATION

Any person who intends to export a hazardous waste identified or listed under this subchapter beginning twelve months after November 8, 1984, shall, before such hazardous waste is scheduled to leave the United States, provide notification to the Administrator. Such notification shall contain the following information:

(1) the name and address of the exporter;

(2) the types and estimated quantities of hazardous waste to be exported;

(3) the estimated frequency or rate at which such waste is to be exported; and the period of time over which such waste is to be exported;

(4) the ports of entry;

(5) a description of the manner in which such hazardous waste will be transported to and treated, stored, or disposed in the receiving country; and

(6) the name and address of the ultimate treatment, storage or disposal facility.

(d) PROCEDURES FOR REQUESTING CONSENT OF THE RECEIVING COUNTRY

Within thirty days of the Administrator's receipt of a complete notification under this section, the Secretary of State, acting on behalf of the Administrator, shall —

---

17. So in original. Probably should be followed by a dash.

Resource Conservation and Recovery Act §6939

(1) forward a copy of the notification to the government of the receiving country;

(2) advise the government that United States law prohibits the export of hazardous waste unless the receiving country consents to accept the hazardous waste;

(3) request the government to provide the Secretary with a written consent or objection to the terms of the notification; and

(4) forward to the government of the receiving country a description of the Federal regulations which would apply to the treatment, storage, and disposal of the hazardous waste in the United States.

(e) **CONVEYANCE OF WRITTEN CONSENT TO EXPORTER**

Within thirty days of receipt by the Secretary of State of the receiving country's written consent or objection (or any subsequent communication withdrawing a prior consent or objection), the Administrator shall forward such a consent, objection, or other communication to the exporter.

(f) **INTERNATIONAL AGREEMENTS**

Where there exists an international agreement between the United States and the government of the receiving country establishing notice, export, and enforcement procedures for the transportation, treatment, storage, and disposal of hazardous wastes, only the requirements of subsections (a)(2) and (g) of this section shall apply.

(g) **REPORTS**

After November 8, 1984, any person who exports any hazardous waste identified or listed under section 6921 of this title shall file with the Administrator no later than March 1 of each year, a report summarizing the types, quantities, frequency, and ultimate destination of all such hazardous waste exported during the previous calendar year.

(h) **OTHER STANDARDS**

Nothing in this section shall preclude the Administrator from establishing other standards for the export of hazardous wastes under section 6922 of this title or section 6923 of this title.

§6939. Domestic Sewage

(a) **REPORT**

The Administrator shall, not later than 15 months after November 8, 1984, submit a report to the Congress concerning those substances identified or listed under section 6921 of this title which are not regulated under this subchapter by reason of the exclusion for mixtures of domestic sewage and other wastes that pass through a sewer system to a publicly owned treatment works.

Such report shall include the types, size and number of generators which dispose of such substances in this manner, the types and quantities disposed of in this manner, and the identification of significant generators, wastes, and waste constituents not regulated under existing Federal law or regulated in a manner sufficient to protect human health and the environment.

(b) REVISIONS OF REGULATIONS

Within eighteen months after submitting the report specified in subsection (a) of this section, the Administrator shall revise existing regulations and promulgate such additional regulations pursuant to this subchapter (or any other authority of the Administrator, including section 1317 of title 33) as are necessary to assure that substances identified or listed under section 6921 of this title which pass through a sewer system to a publicly owned treatment works are adequately controlled to protect human health and the environment.

(c) REPORT ON WASTEWATER LAGOONS

The Administrator shall, within thirty-six months after November 8, 1984, submit a report to Congress concerning wastewater lagoons at publicly owned treatment works and their effect on groundwater quality. Such report shall include —

(1) the number and size of such lagoons;
(2) the types and quantities of waste contained in such lagoons;
(3) the extent to which such waste has been or may be released from such lagoons and contaminate ground water; and
(4) available alternatives for preventing or controlling such releases.

The Administrator may utilize the authority of sections 6927 and 6934 of this title for the purpose of completing such report.

(d) APPLICATION OF SECTIONS 6927 AND 6930

The provisions of sections 6927 and 6930 of this title shall apply to solid or dissolved materials in domestic sewage to the same extent and in the same manner as such provisions apply to hazardous waste.

§6939a. Exposure Information and Health Assessments

(a) EXPOSURE INFORMATION

Beginning on the date nine months after November 8, 1984, each application for a final determination regarding a permit under section 6925(c) of this title for a landfill or surface impoundment shall be accompanied by information reasonably ascertainable by the owner or operator on the potential for the public to be exposed to hazardous wastes or hazardous constituents through releases related to the unit. At a minimum, such information must address:

(1) reasonably foreseeable potential releases from both normal operations and accidents at the unit, including releases associated with transportation to or from the unit;

(2) the potential pathways of human exposure to hazardous wastes or constituents resulting from the releases described under paragraph (1); and

(3) the potential magnitude and nature of the human exposure resulting from such releases.

The owner or operator of a landfill or surface impoundment for which an application for such a final determination under section 6925(c) of this title has been submitted prior to November 8, 1984, shall submit the information required by this subsection to the Administrator (or the State, in the case of a State with an authorized program) no later than the date nine months after November 8, 1984.

(b) **HEALTH ASSESSMENTS**

(1) The Administrator (or the State, in the case of a State with an authorized program) shall make the information required by subsection (a) of this section, together with other relevant information, available to the Agency for Toxic Substances and Disease Registry established by section 9604(i) of this title.

(2) Whenever in the judgment of the Administrator, or the State (in the case of a State with an authorized program), a landfill or a surface impoundment poses a substantial potential risk to human health, due to the existence of releases of hazardous constituents, the magnitude of contamination with hazardous constituents which may be the result of a release, or the magnitude of the population exposed to such release or contamination, the Administrator or the State (with the concurrence of the Administrator) may request the Administrator of the Agency for Toxic Substances and Disease Registry to conduct a health assessment in connection with such facility and take other appropriate action with respect to such risks as authorized by section 9604(b) and (i) of this title. If funds are provided in connection with such request the Administrator of such Agency shall conduct such health assessment.

(c) **MEMBERS OF THE PUBLIC**

Any member of the public may submit evidence of releases of or exposure to hazardous constituents from such a facility, or as to the risks or health effects associated with such releases or exposure, to the Administrator of the Agency for Toxic Substances and Disease Registry, the Administrator, or the State (in the case of a State with an authorized program).

(d) **PRIORITY**

In determining the order in which to conduct health assessments under this subsection, the Administrator of the Agency for Toxic Substances and Disease Registry shall give priority to those facilities or sites at which there is documented evidence of release of hazardous constituents, at which the potential risk to human health appears highest, and for which in the judgment of the Administrator of such Agency existing health assessment data is inadequate to assess the potential risk to human health as provided in subsection (f) of this section.

(e) **PERIODIC REPORTS**

The Administrator of such Agency shall issue periodic reports which include the results of all the assessments carried out under this section. Such assessments or other activities shall be reported after appropriate peer review.

(f) **"HEALTH ASSESSMENTS" DEFINED**

For the purposes of this section, the term "health assessments" shall include preliminary assessments of the potential risk to human health posed by individual sites and facilities subject to this section, based on such factors as the nature and extent of contamination, the existence of potential for pathways of human exposure (including ground or surface water contamination, air emissions, and food chain contamination), the size and potential susceptibility of the community within the likely pathways of exposure, the comparison of expected human exposure levels to the short-term and long-term health effects associated with identified contaminants and any available recommended exposure or tolerance limits for such contaminants, and the comparison of existing morbidity and mortality data on diseases that may be associated with the observed levels of exposure. The assessment shall include an evaluation of the risks to the potentially affected population from all sources of such contaminants, including known point or nonpoint sources other than the site or facility in question. A purpose of such preliminary assessments shall be to help determine whether full-scale health or epidemiological studies and medical evaluations of exposed populations shall be undertaken.

(g) **COST RECOVERY**

In any case in which a health assessment performed under this section discloses the exposure of a population to the release of a hazardous substance, the costs of such health assessment may be recovered as a cost of response under section 9607 of this title from persons causing or contributing to such release of such hazardous substance or, in the case of multiple releases contributing to such exposure, to all such release.

§6939b. INTERIM CONTROL OF HAZARDOUS WASTE INJECTION

(a) **UNDERGROUND SOURCE OF DRINKING WATER**

No hazardous waste may be disposed of by underground injection —

(1) into a formation which contains (within one-quarter mile of the well used for such underground injection) an underground source of drinking water; or

(2) above such a formation.

The prohibitions established under this section shall take effect 6 months after November 8, 1984, except in the case of any State in which identical or more stringent prohibitions are in effect before such date under the Safe Drinking Water Act [42 U.S.C. 300f et seq.].

(b) ACTIONS UNDER COMPREHENSIVE ENVIRONMENTAL RESPONSE, COMPENSATION, AND LIABILITY ACT

Subsection (a) of this section shall not apply to the injection of contaminated ground water into the aquifer from which it was withdrawn, if —

(1) such injection is —

(A) a response action taken under section 9604 or 9606 of this title, or

(B) part of corrective action required under this chapter[18]

intended to clean up such contamination;

(2) such contaminated ground water is treated to substantially reduce hazardous constituents prior to such injection; and

(3) such response action or corrective action will, upon completion, be sufficient to protect human health and the environment.

(c) ENFORCEMENT

In addition to enforcement under the provisions of this chapter, the prohibitions established under paragraphs (1) and (2) of subsection (a) of this section shall be enforceable under the Safe Drinking Water Act [42 U.S.C. 300f et seq.] in any State —

(1) which has adopted identical or more stringent prohibitions under part C of the Safe Drinking Water Act [42 U.S.C. 300h et seq.] and which has assumed primary enforcement responsibility under that Act for enforcement of such prohibitions; or

(2) in which the Administrator has adopted identical or more stringent prohibitions under the Safe Drinking Water Act [42 U.S.C. 300f et seq.] and is exercising primary enforcement responsibility under that Act for enforcement of such prohibitions.

(d) DEFINITIONS

The terms "primary enforcement responsibility," "underground source of drinking water," "formation," and "well" have the same meanings as provided in regulations of the Administrator under the Safe Drinking Water Act [42 U.S.C. 300f et seq.]. The term "Safe Drinking Water Act" means title XIV of the Public Health Service Act.

Subchapter IV — State or Regional Solid Waste Plans

§6941. OBJECTIVES OF SUBCHAPTER

The objectives of this subchapter are to assist in developing and encouraging methods for the disposal of solid waste which are environmentally sound and which maximize the utilization of valuable resources including energy and

---

18. So in original. Probably should be followed by a comma.

materials which are recoverable from solid waste and to encourage resource conservation. Such objectives are to be accomplished through Federal technical and financial assistance to States or regional authorities for comprehensive planning pursuant to Federal guidelines designed to foster cooperation among Federal, State, and local governments and private industry. In developing such comprehensive plans, it is the intention of this chapter that in determining the size of the waste-to-energy facility, adequate provision shall be given to the present and reasonably anticipated future needs, including those needs created by thorough implementation of section 6962(h) of this title, of the recycling and resource recovery interest within the area encompassed by the planning process.

§6941a. ENERGY AND MATERIALS CONSERVATION AND RECOVERY; CONGRESSIONAL FINDINGS

The Congress finds that —

(1) significant savings could be realized by conserving materials in order to reduce the volume or quantity of material which ultimately becomes waste;

(2) solid waste contains valuable energy and material resources which can be recovered and used thereby conserving increasingly scarce and expensive fossil fuels and virgin materials;

(3) the recovery of energy and materials from municipal waste, and the conservation of energy and materials contributing to such waste streams, can have the effect of reducing the volume of the municipal waste stream and the burden of disposing of increasing volumes of solid waste;

(4) the technology to conserve resources exists and is commercially feasible to apply;

(5) the technology to recover energy and materials from solid waste is of demonstrated commercial feasibility; and

(6) various communities throughout the nation have different needs and different potentials for conserving resources and for utilizing techniques for the recovery of energy and materials from waste, and Federal assistance in planning and implementing such energy and materials conservation and recovery programs should be available to all such communities on an equitable basis in relation to their needs and potential.

§6942. FEDERAL GUIDELINES FOR PLANS

(a) GUIDELINES FOR IDENTIFICATION OF REGIONS

For purposes of encouraging and facilitating the development of regional planning for solid waste management, the Administrator, within one hundred and eighty days after October 21, 1976, and after consultation with appropriate Federal, State, and local authorities, shall by regulation publish guidelines for the identification of those areas which have common solid waste management problems and are appropriate units for planning regional solid waste management services. Such guidelines shall consider —

(1) the size and location of areas which should be included,

(2) the volume of solid waste which should be included, and

(3) the available means of coordinating regional planning with other related regional planning and for coordination of such regional planning into the State plan.

(b) GUIDELINES FOR STATE PLANS

Not later than eighteen months after October 21, 1976, and after notice and hearing, the Administrator shall, after consultation with appropriate Federal, State, and local authorities, promulgate regulations containing guidelines to assist in the development and implementation of State solid waste management plans (hereinafter in this chapter referred to as "State plans"). The guidelines shall contain methods for achieving the objectives specified in section 6941 of this title. Such guidelines shall be reviewed from time to time, but not less frequently than every three years, and revised as may be appropriate.

(c) CONSIDERATIONS FOR STATE PLAN GUIDELINES

The guidelines promulgated under subsection (b) of this section shall consider —

(1) the varying regional, geologic, hydrologic, climatic, and other circumstances under which different solid waste practices are required in order to insure the reasonable protection of the quality of the ground and surface waters from leachate contamination, the reasonable protection of the quality of the surface waters from surface runoff contamination, and the reasonable protection of ambient air quality;

(2) characteristics and conditions of collection, storage, processing, and disposal operating methods, techniques and practices, and location of facilities where such operating methods, techniques, and practices are conducted, taking into account the nature of the material to be disposed;

(3) methods for closing or upgrading open dumps for purposes of eliminating potential health hazards;

(4) population density, distribution, and projected growth;

(5) geographic, geologic, climatic, and hydrologic characteristics;

(6) the type and location of transportation;

(7) the profile of industries;

(8) the constituents and generation rates of waste;

(9) the political, economic, organizational, financial, and management problems affecting comprehensive solid waste management;

(10) types of resource recovery facilities and resource conservation systems which are appropriate; and

(11) available new and additional markets for recovered material and energy and energy resources recovered from solid waste as well as methods for conserving such materials and energy.

§6943. Requirements for Approval of Plans

(a) MINIMUM REQUIREMENTS

In order to be approved under section 6947 of this title, each State plan must comply with the following minimum requirements —

(1) The plan shall identify (in accordance with section 6946(b) of this title) (A) the responsibilities of State, local, and regional authorities in the implementation of the State plan, (B) the distribution of Federal funds to the authorities responsible for development and implementation of the State plan, and (C) the means for coordinating regional planning and implementation under the State plan.

(2) The plan shall, in accordance with sections 6944(b) and 6945(a) of this title, prohibit the establishment of new open dumps within the State, and contain requirements that all solid waste (including solid waste originating in other States, but not including hazardous waste) shall be (A) utilized for resource recovery or (B) disposed of in sanitary landfills (within the meaning of section 6944(a) of this title) or otherwise disposed of in an environmentally sound manner.

(3) The plan shall provide for the closing or upgrading of all existing open dumps within the State pursuant to the requirements of section 6945 of this title.

(4) The plan shall provide for the establishment of such State regulatory powers as may be necessary to implement the plan.

(5) The plan shall provide that no State or local government within the State shall be prohibited under State or local law from negotiating and entering into long-term contracts for the supply of solid waste to resource recovery facilities, from entering into long-term contracts for the operation of such facilities, or from securing long-term markets for material and energy recovered from such facilities or for conserving materials or energy by reducing the volume of waste.

(6) The plan shall provide for such resource conservation or recovery and for the disposal of solid waste in sanitary landfills or any combination of practices so as may be necessary to use or dispose of such waste in a manner that is environmentally sound.

(b) DISCRETIONARY PLAN PROVISIONS RELATING TO RECYCLED OIL

Any State plan submitted under this subchapter may include, at the option of the State, provisions to carry out each of the following:

(1) Encouragement, to the maximum extent feasible and consistent with the protection of the public health and the environment, of the use of recycled oil in all appropriate areas of State and local government.

(2) Encouragement of persons contracting with the State to use recycled oil to the maximum extent feasible, consistent with protection of the public health and the environment.

(3) Informing the public of the uses of recycled oil.

(4) Establishment and implementation of a program (including any necessary licensing of persons and including the use, where appropriate, of manifests) to assure that used oil is collected, transported, treated, stored, reused, and disposed of, in a manner which does not present a hazard to the public health or the environment.

Any plan submitted under this chapter before October 15, 1980, may be amended, at the option of the State, at any time after such date to include any provision referred to in this subsection.

(c) ENERGY AND MATERIALS CONSERVATION AND RECOVERY FEASIBILITY PLANNING AND ASSISTANCE

(1) A State which has a plan approved under this subchapter or which has submitted a plan for such approval shall be eligible for assistance under section 6948(a)(3) of this title if the Administrator determines that under such plan the State will —

(A) analyze and determine the economic and technical feasibility of facilities and programs to conserve resources which contribute to the waste stream or to recover energy and materials from municipal waste;

(B) analyze the legal, institutional, and economic impediments to the development of systems and facilities for conservation of energy or materials which contribute to the waste stream or for the recovery of energy and materials from municipal waste and make recommendations to appropriate governmental authorities for overcoming such impediments;

(C) assist municipalities within the State in developing plans, programs, and projects to conserve resources or recover energy and materials from municipal waste; and

(D) coordinate the resource conservation and recovery planning under subparagraph (C).

(2) The analysis referred to in paragraph (1)(A) shall include —

(A) the evaluation of, and establishment of priorities among, market opportunities for industrial and commercial users of all types (including public utilities and industrial parks) to utilize energy and materials recovered from municipal waste;

(B) comparisons of the relative costs of energy recovered from municipal waste in relation to the costs of energy derived from fossil fuels and other sources;

(C) studies of the transportation and storage problems and other problems associated with the development of energy and materials recovery technology, including curbside source separation;

(D) the evaluation and establishment of priorities among ways of conserving energy or materials which contribute to the waste stream;

(E) comparison of the relative total costs between conserving resources and disposing of or recovering such waste; and

(F) studies of impediments to resource conservation or recovery, including business practices, transportation requirements, or storage difficulties.

Such studies and analyses shall also include studies of other sources of solid waste from which energy and materials may be recovered or minimized.

(d) SIZE OF WASTE-TO-ENERGY FACILITIES

Notwithstanding any of the above requirements, it is the intention of this chapter and the planning process developed pursuant to this chapter that in determining the size of the waste-to-energy facility, adequate provision shall be given to the present and reasonably anticipated future needs of the recycling and resource recovery interest within the area encompassed by the planning process.

§6944. CRITERIA FOR SANITARY LANDFILLS; SANITARY LANDFILLS REQUIRED FOR ALL DISPOSAL

(a) CRITERIA FOR SANITARY LANDFILLS

Not later than one year after October 21, 1976, after consultation with the States, and after notice and public hearings, the Administrator shall promulgate regulations containing criteria for determining which facilities shall be classified as sanitary landfills and which shall be classified as open dumps within the meaning of this chapter. At a minimum, such criteria shall provide that a facility may be classified as a sanitary landfill and not an open dump only if there is no reasonable probability of adverse effects on health or the environment from disposal of solid waste at such facility. Such regulations may provide for the classification of the types of sanitary landfills.

(b) DISPOSAL REQUIRED TO BE IN SANITARY LANDFILLS, ETC.

For purposes of complying with section 6943(2)[1] of this title each State plan shall prohibit the establishment of open dumps and contain a requirement that disposal of all solid waste within the State shall be in compliance with such section 6943(2)[1] of this title.

(c) EFFECTIVE DATE

The prohibition contained in subsection (b) of this section shall take effect on the date six months after the date of promulgation of regulations under subsection (a) of this section.

§6945. UPGRADING OF OPEN DUMPS

(a) CLOSING OR UPGRADING OF EXISTING OPEN DUMPS

Upon promulgation of criteria under section 6907(a)(3) of this title, any solid waste management practice or disposal of solid waste or hazardous waste which constitutes the open dumping of solid waste or hazardous waste is prohibited, except in the case of any practice or disposal of solid waste under a timetable

1. See References in Text note below.

or schedule for compliance established under this section. The prohibition contained in the preceding sentence shall be enforceable under section 6972 of this title against persons engaged in the act of open dumping. For purposes of complying with section 6943(a)(2) and 6943(a)(3) of this title, each State plan shall contain a requirement that all existing disposal facilities or sites for solid waste in such State which are open dumps listed in the inventory under subsection (b) of this section shall comply with such measures as may be promulgated by the Administrator to eliminate health hazards and minimize potential health hazards. Each such plan shall establish, for any entity which demonstrates that it has considered other public or private alternatives for solid waste management to comply with the prohibition on open dumping and is unable to utilize such alternatives to so comply, a timetable or schedule for compliance for such practice or disposal of solid waste which specifies a schedule of remedial measures, including an enforceable sequence of actions or operations, leading to compliance with the prohibition on open dumping of solid waste within a reasonable time (not to exceed 5 years from the date of publication of criteria under section 6907(a)(3) of this title).

(b) INVENTORY

To assist the States in complying with section 6943(a)(3) of this title, not later than one year after promulgation of regulations under section 6944 of this title, the Administrator, with the cooperation of the Bureau of the Census shall publish an inventory of all disposal facilities or sites in the United States which are open dumps within the meaning of this chapter.

(c) CONTROL OF HAZARDOUS DISPOSAL

(1)(A) Not later than 36 months after November 8, 1984, each State shall adopt and implement a permit program or other system of prior approval and conditions to assure that each solid waste management facility within such State which may receive hazardous household waste or hazardous waste due to the provision of section 6921(d) of this title for small quantity generators (otherwise not subject to the requirement for a permit under section 6925 of this title) will comply with the applicable criteria promulgated under section 6944(a) and 6907(a)(3) of this title.

(B) Not later than eighteen months after the promulgation of revised criteria under subsection[2] 6944(a) of this title (as required by section 6949a(c) of this title), each State shall adopt and implement a permit program or other system or[3] prior approval and conditions, to assure that each solid waste management facility within such State which may receive hazardous household waste or hazardous waste due to the provision of section 6921(d) of this title for small quantity generators (otherwise not subject to the requirement for a

---

2. So in original. Probably should be "section."
3. So in original. Probably should be "of."

permit under section 6925 of this title) will comply with the criteria revised under section 6944(a) of this title.

(C) The Administrator shall determine whether each State has developed an adequate program under this paragraph. The Administrator may make such a determination in conjunction with approval, disapproval or partial approval of a State plan under section 6947 of this title.

(2)(A) In any State that the Administrator determines has not adopted an adequate program for such facilities under paragraph (1)(B) by the date provided in such paragraph, the Administrator may use the authorities available under sections 6927 and 6928 of this title to enforce the prohibition contained in subsection (a) of this section with respect to such facilities.

(B) For purposes of this paragraph, the term "requirement of this subchapter" in section 6928 of this title shall be deemed to include criteria promulgated by the Administrator under sections 6907(a)(3) and 6944(a) of this title, and the term "hazardous wastes" in section 6927 of this title shall be deemed to include solid waste at facilities that may handle hazardous household wastes or hazardous wastes from small quantity generators.

§6946. Procedure for Development and Implementation of State Plan

(a) IDENTIFICATION OF REGIONS

Within one hundred and eighty days after publication of guidelines under section 6942(a) of this title (relating to identification of regions), the Governor of each State, after consultation with local elected officials, shall promulgate regulations based on such guidelines identifying the boundaries of each area within the State which, as a result of urban concentrations, geographic conditions, markets, and other factors, is appropriate for carrying out regional solid waste management. Such regulations may be modified from time to time (identifying additional or different regions) pursuant to such guidelines.

(b) IDENTIFICATION OF STATE AND LOCAL AGENCIES AND RESPONSIBILITIES

(1) Within one hundred and eighty days after the Governor promulgates regulations under subsection (a) of this section, for purposes of facilitating the development and implementation of a State plan which will meet the minimum requirements of section 6943 of this title, the State, together with appropriate elected officials of general purpose units of local government, shall jointly (A) identify an agency to develop the State plan and identify one or more agencies to implement such plan, and (B) identify which solid waste management activities will, under such State plan, be planned for and carried out by the State and which such management activities will, under such State plan, be planned for and carried out by a regional or local authority or a combination of regional or local and State authorities. If a multi-functional regional agency authorized by State law to conduct solid waste planning and management (the members of which are appointed by the Governor) is in existence on October 21, 1976, the

Governor shall identify such authority for purposes of carrying out within such region clause (A) of this paragraph. Where feasible, designation of the agency for the affected area designated under section 1288 of title 33 shall be considered. A State agency identified under this paragraph shall be established or designated by the Governor of such State. Local or regional agencies identified under this paragraph shall be composed of individuals at least a majority of whom are elected local officials.

(2) If planning and implementation agencies are not identified and designated or established as required under paragraph (1) for any affected area, the governor shall, before the date two hundred and seventy days after promulgation of regulations under subsection (a) of this section, establish or designate a State agency to develop and implement the State plan for such area.

(c) INTERSTATE REGIONS

(1) In the case of any region which, pursuant to the guidelines published by the Administrator under section 6942(a) of this title (relating to identification of regions), would be located in two or more States, the Governors of the respective States, after consultation with local elected officials, shall consult, cooperate, and enter into agreements identifying the boundaries of such region pursuant to subsection (a) of this section.

(2) Within one hundred and eighty days after an interstate region is identified by agreement under paragraph (1), appropriate elected officials of general purpose units of local government within such region shall jointly establish or designate an agency to develop a plan for such region. If no such agency is established or designated within such period by such officials, the Governors of the respective States may, by agreement, establish or designate for such purpose a single representative organization including elected officials of general purpose units of local government within such region.

(3) Implementation of interstate regional solid waste management plans shall be conducted by units of local government for any portion of a region within their jurisdiction, or by multijurisdictional agencies or authorities designated in accordance with State law, including those designated by agreement by such units of local government for such purpose. If no such unit, agency, or authority is so designated, the respective Governors shall designate or establish a single interstate agency to implement such plan.

(4) For purposes of this subchapter, so much of an interstate regional plan as is carried out within a particular State shall be deemed part of the State plan for such State.

§6947. APPROVAL OF STATE PLAN; FEDERAL ASSISTANCE

(a) PLAN APPROVAL

The Administrator shall, within six months after a State plan has been submitted for approval, approve or disapprove the plan. The Administrator shall approve a plan if he determines that —

(1) it meets the requirements of paragraphs (1), (2), (3), and (5) of section 6943[4] of this title; and

(2) it contains provision for revision of such plan, after notice and public hearing, whenever the Administrator, by regulation, determines —

(A) that revised regulations respecting minimum requirements have been promulgated under paragraphs (1), (2), (3), and (5) of section 6943[4] of this title with which the State plan is not in compliance;

(B) that information has become available which demonstrates the inadequacy of the plan to effectuate the purposes of this subchapter; or

(C) that such revision is otherwise necessary.

The Administrator shall review approved plans from time to time and if he determines that revision or corrections are necessary to bring such plan into compliance with the minimum requirements promulgated under section 6943 of this title (including new or revised requirements), he shall, after notice and opportunity for public hearing, withdraw his approval of such plan. Such withdrawal of approval shall cease to be effective upon the Administrator's determination that such complies with such minimum requirements.

(b) ELIGIBILITY OF STATES FOR FEDERAL FINANCIAL ASSISTANCE

(1) The Administrator shall approve a State application for financial assistance under this subchapter, and make grants to such State, if such State and local and regional authorities within such State have complied with the requirements of section 6946 of this title within the period required under such section and if such State has a State plan which has been approved by the Administrator under this subchapter.

(2) The Administrator shall approve a State application for financial assistance under this subchapter, and make grants to such State, for fiscal years 1978 and 1979 if the Administrator determines that the State plan continues to be eligible for approval under subsection (a) of this section and is being implemented by the State.

(3) Upon withdrawal of approval of a State plan under subsection (a) of this section, the Administrator shall withhold Federal financial and technical assistance under this subchapter (other than such technical assistance as may be necessary to assist in obtaining the reinstatement of approval) until such time as such approval is reinstated.

(c) EXISTING ACTIVITIES

Nothing in this subchapter shall be construed to prevent or affect any activities respecting solid waste planning or management which are carried out by State, regional, or local authorities unless such activities are inconsistent with a State plan approved by the Administrator under this subchapter. . . .

4. See References in Text note below.

§6949a. ADEQUACY OF CERTAIN GUIDELINES AND CRITERIA

(a) STUDY

The Administrator shall conduct a study of the extent to which the guidelines and criteria under this chapter (other than guidelines and criteria for facilities to which subchapter III of this chapter applies) which are applicable to solid waste management and disposal facilities, including, but not limited to landfills and surface impoundments, are adequate to protect human health and the environment from ground water contamination. Such study shall include a detailed assessment of the degree to which the criteria under section 6907(a) of this title and the criteria under section 6944 of this title regarding monitoring, prevention of contamination, and remedial action are adequate to protect ground water and shall also include recommendation with respect to any additional enforcement authorities which the Administrator, in consultation with the Attorney General, deems necessary for such purposes.

(b) REPORT

Not later than thirty-six months after November 8, 1984, the Administrator shall submit a report to the Congress setting forth the results of the study required under this section, together with any recommendations made by the Administrator on the basis of such study.

(c) REVISIONS OF GUIDELINES AND CRITERIA

Not later than March 31, 1988, the Administrator shall promulgate revisions of the criteria promulgated under paragraph (1) of section 6944(a) of this title and under section 6907(a)(3) of this title for facilities that may receive hazardous household wastes or hazardous wastes from small quantity generators under section 6921(d) of this title. The criteria shall be those necessary to protect human health and the environment and may take into account the practicable capability of such facilities. At a minimum such revisions for facilities potentially receiving such wastes should require ground water monitoring as necessary to detect contamination, establish criteria for the acceptable location of new or existing facilities, and provide for corrective action as appropriate. . . .

Subchapter VI — Federal Responsibilities.

§6961. APPLICATION OF FEDERAL, STATE, AND LOCAL LAW
TO FEDERAL FACILITIES

Each department, agency, and instrumentality of the executive, legislative, and judicial branches of the Federal Government (1) having jurisdiction over any solid waste management facility or disposal site, or (2) engaged in any activity resulting, or which may result, in the disposal or management of solid waste or hazardous waste shall be subject to, and comply with, all Federal, State, interstate, and local requirements, both substantive and procedural (including any requirement for permits or reporting or any provisions for injunctive relief and such sanctions as may be imposed by a court to enforce such relief), respecting control and abatement of solid waste or hazardous waste disposal in the same manner, and to the same extent, as any person is subject to such requirements, including the payment of reasonable service charges. Neither the United States, nor any agent, employee, or officer thereof, shall be immune or exempt from any process or sanction of any State or Federal Court with respect to the enforcement of any such injunctive relief. The President may exempt any solid waste management facility of any department, agency, or instrumentality in the executive branch from compliance with such a requirement if he determines it to be in the paramount interest of the United States to do so. No such exemption shall be granted due to lack of appropriation unless the President shall have specifically requested such appropriation as a part of the budgetary process and the Congress shall have failed to make available such requested appropriation. Any exemption shall be for a period not in excess of one year, but additional exemptions may be granted for periods not to exceed one year upon the President's making a new determination. The President shall report each January to the Congress all exemptions from the requirements of this section granted during the preceding calendar year, together with his reason for granting each such exemption. . . .

§6963. COOPERATION WITH ENVIRONMENTAL PROTECTION AGENCY

(a) GENERAL RULE

All Federal agencies shall assist the Administrator in carrying out his functions under this chapter and shall promptly make available all requested information concerning past or present Agency waste management practices and past or present Agency owned, leased, or operated solid or hazardous waste facilities. This information shall be provided in such format as may be determined by the Administrator.

(b) INFORMATION RELATING TO ENERGY AND MATERIALS CONSERVATION AND RECOVERY

The Administrator shall collect, maintain, and disseminate information concerning the market potential of energy and materials recovered from solid waste, including materials obtained through source separation, and information concerning the savings potential of conserving resources contributing to the waste stream. The Administrator shall identify the regions in which the increased substitution of such energy for energy derived from fossil fuels and other sources is most likely to be feasible, and provide information on the technical and economic aspects of developing integrated resource conservation or recovery systems which provide for the recovery of source-separated materials to be recycled or the conservation of resources. The Administrator shall utilize the authorities of subsection (a) of this section in carrying out this subsection.

§6964. Applicability of Solid Waste Disposal Guidelines to Executive Agencies

(a) COMPLIANCE

(1) If —

(A) an Executive agency (as defined in section 105 of title 5) or any unit of the legislative branch of the Federal Government has jurisdiction over any real property or facility the operation or administration of which involves such agency in solid waste management activities, or

(B) such an agency enters into a contract with any person for the operation by such person of any Federal property or facility, and the performance of such contract involves such person in solid waste management activities,

then such agency shall insure compliance with the guidelines recommended under section 6907 of this title and the purposes of this chapter in the operation or administration of such property or facility, or the performance of such contract, as the case may be.

(2) Each Executive agency or any unit of the legislative branch of the Federal Government which conducts any activity —

(A) which generates solid waste, and

(B) which, if conducted by a person other than such agency, would require a permit or license from such agency in order to dispose of such solid waste,

shall insure compliance with such guidelines and the purposes of this chapter in conducting such activity.

(3) Each Executive agency which permits the use of Federal property for purposes of disposal of solid waste shall insure compliance with such guidelines and the purposes of this chapter in the disposal of such waste.

(4) The President or the Committee on House Administration of the House of Representatives and the Committee on Rules and Administration of the Senate with regard to any unit of the legislative branch of the Federal Government shall prescribe regulations to carry out this subsection.

(b) LICENSES AND PERMITS

Each Executive agency which issues any license or permit for disposal of solid waste shall, prior to the issuance of such license or permit, consult with the Administrator to insure compliance with guidelines recommended under section 6907 of this title and the purposes of this chapter. . . .

Subchapter VII — Miscellaneous Provisions

§6972. Citizen Suits

(a) IN GENERAL

Except as provided in subsection (b) or (c) of this section, any person may commence a civil action on his own behalf —

(1)(A) against any person (including (a) the United States, and (b) any other governmental instrumentality or agency, to the extent permitted by the eleventh amendment to the Constitution) who is alleged to be in violation of any permit, standard, regulation, condition, requirement, prohibition, or order which has become effective pursuant to this chapter; or

(B) against any person, including the United States and any other governmental instrumentality or agency, to the extent permitted by the eleventh amendment to the Constitution, and including any past or present generator, past or present transporter, or past or present owner or operator of a treatment, storage, or disposal facility, who has contributed or who is contributing to the past or present handling, storage, treatment, transportation, or disposal of any solid or hazardous waste which may present an imminent and substantial endangerment to health or the environment; or

(2) against the Administrator where there is alleged a failure of the Administrator to perform any act or duty under this chapter which is not discretionary with the Administrator.

Any action under paragraph (a)(1) of this subsection shall be brought in the district court for the district in which the alleged violation occurred or the alleged endangerment may occur. Any action brought under paragraph (a)(2) of this subsection may be brought in the district court for the district in which the alleged violation occurred or in the District Court of the District of Columbia. The district court shall have jurisdiction, without regard to the amount in controversy or the citizenship of the parties, to enforce the permit, standard, regulation, condition, requirement, prohibition, or order, referred to in paragraph (1)(A), to restrain any person who has contributed or who is contributing to the past or present handling, storage, treatment, transportation, or disposal of any solid or hazardous waste referred to in paragraph (1)(B), to order such person to take such other action as may be necessary, or both, or to order the Administrator to perform the act or duty referred to in paragraph (2), as the case may be, and to apply any appropriate civil penalties under section 6928(a) and (g) of this title.

(b) ACTIONS PROHIBITED

(1) No action may be commenced under subsection (a)(1)(A) of this section —

(A) prior to 60 days after the plaintiff has given notice of the violation to —

(i) the Administrator;
(ii) the State in which the alleged violation occurs; and
(iii) to any alleged violator of such permit, standard, regulation, condition, requirement, prohibition, or order,

except that such action may be brought immediately after such notification in the case of an action under this section respecting a violation of subchapter III of this chapter; or

(B) if the Administrator or State has commenced and is diligently prosecuting a civil or criminal action in a court of the United States or a State to require compliance with such permit, standard, regulation, condition, requirement, prohibition, or order.

In any action under subsection (a)(1)(A) of this section in a court of the United States, any person may intervene as a matter of right.

(2)(A) No action may be commenced under subsection (a)(1)(B) of this section prior to ninety days after the plaintiff has given notice of the endangerment to —

    (i) the Administrator;

    (ii) the State in which the alleged endangerment may occur;

    (iii) any person alleged to have contributed or to be contributing to the past or present handling, storage, treatment, transportation, or disposal of any solid or hazardous waste referred to in subsection (a)(1)(B) of this section,

except that such action may be brought immediately after such notification in the case of an action under this section respecting a violation of subchapter III of this chapter.

(B) No action may be commenced under subsection (a)(1)(B) of this section if the Administrator, in order to restrain or abate acts or conditions which may have contributed or are contributing to the activities which may present the alleged endangerment —

    (i) has commenced and is diligently prosecuting an action under section 6973 of this title or under section 106 of the Comprehensive Environmental Response, Compensation and Liability Act of 1980 [42 U.S.C. 9606],[1]

    (ii) is actually engaging in a removal action under section 104 of the Comprehensive Environmental Response, Compensation and Liability Act of 1980 [42 U.S.C. 9604];

    (iii) has incurred costs to initiate a Remedial Investigation and Feasibility Study under section 104 of the Comprehensive Environmental Response, Compensation and Liability Act of 1980 [42 U.S.C. 9604] and is diligently proceeding with a remedial action under that Act [42 U.S.C. 9601 et seq.]; or

    (iv) has obtained a court order (including a consent decree) or issued an administrative order under section 106 of the Comprehensive Environmental Response, Compensation and Liability Act of 980[2] [42 U.S.C. 9606] or section 6973 of this title pursuant to which a responsible party is diligently conducting a removal action, Remedial Investigation and Feasibility Study (RIFS), or proceeding with a remedial action.

In the case of an administrative order referred to in clause (iv), actions under subsection (a)(1)(B) of this section are prohibited only as to the scope and duration of the administrative order referred to in clause (iv).

---

1. So in original. The comma probably should be a semicolon.
2. So in original. Probably should be "1980."

(C) No action may be commenced under subsection (a)(1)(B) of this section if the State, in order to restrain or abate acts or conditions which may have contributed or are contributing to the activities which may present the alleged endangerment —

(i) has commenced and is diligently prosecuting an action under subsection (a)(1)(B) of this section;

(ii) is actually engaging in a removal action under section 104 of the Comprehensive Environmental Response, Compensation and Liability Act of 1980 [42 U.S.C. 9604]; or

(iii) has incurred costs to initiate a Remedial Investigation and Feasibility Study under section 104 of the Comprehensive Environmental Response, Compensation and Liability Act of 1980 [42 U.S.C. 9604] and is diligently proceeding with a remedial action under that Act [42 U.S.C. 9601 et seq.].

(D) No action may be commenced under subsection (a)(1)(B) of this section by any person (other than a State or local government) with respect to the siting of a hazardous waste treatment, storage, or a disposal facility, nor to restrain or enjoin the issuance of a permit for such facility.

(E) In any action under subsection (a)(1)(B) of this section in a court of the United States, any person may intervene as a matter of right when the applicant claims an interest relating to the subject of the action and he is so situated that the disposition of the action may, as a practical matter, impair or impede his ability to protect that interest, unless the Administrator or the State shows that the applicant's interest is adequately represented by existing parties.

(F) Whenever any action is brought under subsection (a)(1)(B) of this section in a court of the United States, the plaintiff shall serve a copy of the complaint on the Attorney General of the United States, and with the Administrator.

(c) NOTICE

No action may be commenced under paragraph (a)(2) of this section prior to sixty days after the plaintiff has given notice to the Administrator that he will commence such action, except that such action may be brought immediately after such notification in the case of an action under this section respecting a violation of subchapter III of this chapter. Notice under this subsection shall be given in such manner as the Administrator shall prescribe by regulation. Any action respecting a violation under this chapter may be brought under this section only in the judicial district in which such alleged violation occurs.

(d) INTERVENTION

In any action under this section the Administrator, if not a party, may intervene as a matter of right.

(e) COSTS

The court, in issuing any final order in any action brought pursuant to this section or section 6976 of this title, may award costs of litigation (including reasonable attorney and expert witness fees) to the prevailing or substantially prevailing party, whenever the court determines such an award is appropriate. The court may, if a temporary restraining order or preliminary injunction is sought, require the filing of a bond or equivalent security in accordance with the Federal Rules of Civil Procedure.

(f) OTHER RIGHTS PRESERVED

Nothing in this section shall restrict any right which any person (or class of persons) may have under any statute or common law to seek enforcement of any standard or requirement relating to the management of solid waste or hazardous waste, or to seek any other relief (including relief against the Administrator or a State agency).

(g) TRANSPORTERS

A transporter shall not be deemed to have contributed or to be contributing to the handling, storage, treatment, or disposal, referred to in subsection (a)(1)(B) of this section taking place after such solid waste or hazardous waste has left the possession or control of such transporter, if the transportation of such waste was under a sole contractual arrangement arising from a published tariff and acceptance for carriage by common carrier by rail and such transporter has exercised due care in the past or present handling, storage, treatment, transportation and disposal of such waste.

§6973. IMMINENT HAZARD

(a) AUTHORITY OF ADMINISTRATOR

Notwithstanding any other provision of this chapter, upon receipt of evidence that the past or present handling, storage, treatment, transportation or disposal of any solid waste or hazardous waste may present an imminent and substantial endangerment to health or the environment, the Administrator may bring suit on behalf of the United States in the appropriate district court against any person (including any past or present generator, past or present transporter, or past or present owner or operator of a treatment, storage, or disposal facility) who has contributed or who is contributing to such handling, storage, treatment, transportation or disposal to restrain such person from such handling, storage, treatment, transportation, or disposal, to order such person to take such other action as may be necessary, or both. A transporter shall not be deemed to have contributed or to be contributing to such handling, storage, treatment, or disposal taking place after such solid waste or hazardous waste has left the possession or control of such transporter if the transportation of such waste was under a sole contractural[3] arrangement arising from a published tariff and acceptance for carriage by common carrier by rail and such transporter has exercised due care in the past or present handling, storage, treatment, transportation and disposal of such waste. The Administrator shall provide notice to the affected State of any such suit. The Administrator may also, after notice to the affected State, take other action under this section including, but not limited to, issuing such orders as may be necessary to protect public health and the environment.

(b) VIOLATIONS

Any person who willfully violates, or fails or refuses to comply with, any order of the Administrator under subsection (a) of this section may, in an action brought in the appropriate United States district court to enforce such order, be fined not more than $5,000 for each day in which such violation occurs or such failure to comply continues.

(c) IMMEDIATE NOTICE

Upon receipt of information that there is hazardous waste at any site which has presented an imminent and substantial endangerment to human health or the environment, the Administrator shall provide immediate notice to the appropriate local government agencies. In addition, the Administrator shall require notice of such endangerment to be promptly posted at the site where the waste is located.

(d) PUBLIC PARTICIPATION IN SETTLEMENTS

Whenever the United States or the Administrator proposes to covenant not to sue or to forbear from suit or to settle any claim arising under this section, notice, and opportunity for a public meeting in the affected area, and a reasonable opportunity to comment on the proposed settlement prior to its final entry shall be afforded to the public. The decision of the United States or the Administrator to enter into or not to enter into such Consent Decree, covenant or agreement shall not constitute a final agency action subject to judicial review under this chapter or chapter 7 of title 5.

§6974. PETITION FOR REGULATIONS; PUBLIC PARTICIPATION

(a) PETITION

Any person may petition the Administrator for the promulgation, amendment, or repeal of any regulation under this chapter. Within a reasonable time following receipt of such petition, the Administrator shall take action with respect to such petition and shall publish notice of such action in the Federal Register, together with the reasons therefor.

3. So in original. Probably should be "contractual."

(b) PUBLIC PARTICIPATION

(1) Public participation in the development, revision, implementation, and enforcement of any regulation, guideline, information, or program under this chapter shall be provided for, encouraged, and assisted by the Administrator and the States. The Administrator, in cooperation with the States, shall develop and publish minimum guidelines for public participation in such processes.

(2) Before the issuing of a permit to any person with any respect to any facility for the treatment, storage, or disposal of hazardous wastes under section 6925 of this title, the Administrator shall —

(A) cause to be published in major local newspapers of general circulation and broadcast over local radio stations notice of the agency's intention to issue such permit, and

(B) transmit in writing notice of the agency's intention to issue such permit to each unit of local government having jurisdiction over the area in which such facility is proposed to be located and to each State agency having any authority under State law with respect to the construction or operation of such facility.

If within 45 days the Administrator receives written notice of opposition to the agency's intention to issue such permit and a request for a hearing, or if the Administrator determines on his own initiative, he shall hold an informal public hearing (including an opportunity for presentation of written and oral views) on whether he should issue a permit for the proposed facility. Whenever possible the Administrator shall schedule such hearing at a location convenient to the nearest population center to such proposed facility and give notice in the aforementioned manner of the date, time, and subject matter of such hearing. No State program which provides for the issuance of permits referred to in this paragraph may be authorized by the Administrator under section 6926 of this title unless such program provides for the notice and hearing required by the paragraph.

§6975. SEPARABILITY OF PROVISIONS

If any provision of this chapter, or the application of any provision of this chapter to any person or circumstance, is held invalid, the application of such provision to other persons or circumstances, and the remainder of this chapter, shall not be affected thereby.

§6976. JUDICIAL REVIEW

(a) REVIEW OF FINAL REGULATIONS AND CERTAIN PETITIONS

Any judicial review of final regulations promulgated pursuant to this chapter and the Administrator's denial of any petition for the promulgation, amendment, or repeal of any regulation under this chapter shall be in accordance with sections 701 through 706 of title 5, except that —

(1) a petition for review of action of the Administrator in promulgating any regulation, or requirement under this chapter or denying any petition for the promulgation, amendment or repeal of any regulation under this chapter may be filed only in the United States Court of Appeals for the District of Columbia, and such petition shall be filed within ninety days from the date of such promulgation or denial, or after such date if such petition for review is based solely on grounds arising after such ninetieth day; action of the Administrator with respect to which review could have been obtained under this subsection shall not be subject to judicial review in civil or criminal proceedings for enforcement; and

(2) in any judicial proceeding brought under this section in which review is sought of a determination under this chapter required to be made on the record after notice and opportunity for hearing, if a party seeking review under this chapter applies to the court for leave to adduce additional evidence, and shows to the satisfaction of the court that the information is material and that there were reasonable grounds for the failure to adduce such evidence in the proceeding before the Administrator, the court may order such additional evidence (and evidence in rebuttal thereof) to be taken before the Administrator, and to be adduced upon the hearing in such manner and upon such terms and conditions as the court may deem proper; the Administrator may modify his findings as to the facts, or make new findings, by reason of the additional evidence so taken, and he shall file with the court such modified or new findings and his recommendation, if any, for the modification or setting aside of his original order, with the return of such additional evidence.

(b) REVIEW OF CERTAIN ACTIONS UNDER SECTIONS 6925 AND 6926 OF THIS TITLE

Review of the Administrator's action (1) in issuing, denying, modifying, or revoking any permit under section 6925 of this title (or in modifying or revoking any permit which is deemed to have been issued under section 6935(d)(1)[4] of this title), or (2) in granting, denying, or withdrawing authorization or interim authorization under section 6926 of this title, may be had by any interested person in the Circuit Court of Appeals of the United States for the Federal judicial district in which such person resides or transacts such business upon application by such person. Any such application shall be made within ninety days from the date of such issuance, denial, modification, revocation, grant, or withdrawal, or after such date only if such application is based solely on grounds which arose after such ninetieth day. Action of the Administrator with respect to which review could have been obtained under this subsection shall not be subject to judicial review in civil or criminal proceedings for enforcement. Such review shall be in accordance with sections 701 through 706 of title 5. . . .

4. See References in Text note below.

Subchapter IX — Regulation of Underground Storage Tanks

§6991. DEFINITIONS AND EXEMPTIONS

For the purposes of this subchapter —

(1) The term "underground storage tank" means any one or combination of tanks (including underground pipes connected thereto) which is used to contain an accumulation of regulated substances, and the volume of which (including the volume of the underground pipes connected thereto) is 10 per centum or more beneath the surface of the ground. Such term does not include any —

(A) farm or residential tank of 1,100 gallons or less capacity used for storing motor fuel for noncommercial purposes,

(B) tank used for storing heating oil for consumptive use on the premises where stored,

(C) septic tank,

(D) pipeline facility (including gathering lines) regulated under —

(i) the Natural Gas Pipeline Safety Act of 1968 [49 App. U.S.C. 1671 et seq.],

(ii) the Hazardous Liquid Pipeline Safety Act of 1979 [49 App. U.S.C. 2001 et seq.], or

(iii) which is an intrastate pipeline facility regulated under State laws comparable to the provisions of law referred to in clause (i) or (ii) of this subparagraph,

(E) surface impoundment, pit, pond, or lagoon,

(F) storm water or waste water collection system,

(G) flow-through process tank,

(H) liquid trap or associated gathering lines directly related to oil or gas production and gathering operations, or

(I) storage tank situated in an underground area (such as a basement, cellar, mineworking, drift, shaft, or tunnel) if the storage tank is situated upon or above the surface of the floor.

The term "underground storage tank" shall not include any pipes connected to any tank which is described in subparagraphs (A) through (I).

(2) The term "regulated substance" means —

(A) any substance defined in section 9601(14) of this title (but not including any substance regulated as a hazardous waste under subchapter III of this chapter), and

(B) petroleum.

(3) The term "owner" means —

(A) in the case of an underground storage tank in use on November 8, 1984, or brought into use after that date, any person who owns an underground storage tank used for the storage, use, or dispensing of regulated sustances,[1] and

---

1. So in original. Probably should be "substances,".

(B) in the case of any underground storage tank in use before November 8, 1984, but no longer in use on November 8, 1984, any person who owned such tank immediately before the discontinuation of its use.

(4) The term "operator" means any person in control of, or having responsibility for, the daily operation of the underground storage tank.

(5) The term "release" means any spilling, leaking, emitting, discharging, escaping, leaching, or disposing from an underground storage tank into ground water, surface water or subsurface soils.

(6) The term "person" has the same meaning as provided in section 6903(15) of this title, except that such term includes a consortium, a joint venture, and a commercial entity, and the United States Government.

(7) The term "nonoperational storage tank" means any underground storage tank in which regulated substances will not be deposited or from which regulated substances will not be dispensed after November 8, 1984.

(8) The term "petroleum" means petroleum, including crude oil or any fraction thereof which is liquid at standard conditions of temperature and pressure (60 degrees Fahrenheit and 14.7 pounds per square inch absolute).

§6991a. NOTIFICATION

(a) UNDERGROUND STORAGE TANKS

(1) Within 18 months after November 8, 1984, each owner of an underground storage tank shall notify the State or local agency or department designated pursuant to subsection (b)(1) of this section of the existence of such tank, specifying the age, size, type, location, and uses of such tank.

(2)(A) For each underground storage tank taken out of operation after January 1, 1974, the owner of such tank shall, within eighteen months after November 8, 1984, notify the State or local agency, or department designated pursuant to subsection (b)(1) of this section of the existence of such tanks (unless the owner knows the tank subsequently was removed from the ground). The owner of a tank taken out of operation on or before January 1, 1974, shall not be required to notify the State or local agency under this subsection.

(B) Notice under subparagraph (A) shall specify, to the extent known to the owner —

(i) the date the tank was taken out of operation,

(ii) the age of the tank on the date taken out of operation,

(iii) the size, type and location of the tank, and

(iv) the type and quantity of substances left stored in such tank on the date taken out of operation.

(3) Any owner which brings into use an underground storage tank after the initial notification period specified under paragraph (1), shall notify the designated State or local agency or department within thirty days of the existence of such tank, specifying the age, size, type, location and uses of such tank.

Resource Conservation and Recovery Act §6991b

(4) Paragraphs (1) through (3) of this subsection shall not apply to tanks for which notice was given pursuant to section 9603(c) of this title.

(5) Beginning thirty days after the Administrator prescribes the form of notice pursuant to subsection (b)(2) of this section and for eighteen months thereafter, any person who deposits regulated substances in an underground storage tank shall reasonably notify the owner or operator of such tank of the owner's notification requirements pursuant to this subsection.

(6) Beginning thirty days after the Administrator issues new tank performance standards pursuant to section 6991b(c) of this title, any person who sells a tank intended to be used as an underground storage tank shall notify the purchaser of such tank of the owner's notification requirements pursuant to this subsection.

(b) AGENCY DESIGNATION

(1) Within one hundred and eighty days after November 8, 1984, the Governors of each State shall designate the appropriate State agency or department or local agencies or departments to receive the notifications under subsection (a)(1), (2), or (3) of this section.

(2) Within twelve months after November 8, 1984, the Administrator, in consultation with State and local officials designated pursuant to subsection (b)(1) of this section, and after notice and opportunity for public comment, shall prescribe the form of the notice and the information to be included in the notifications under subsection (a)(1), (2), or (3) of this section. In prescribing the form of such notice, the Administrator shall take into account the effect on small businesses and other owners and operators.

(c) STATE INVENTORIES

Each State shall make 2 separate inventories of all underground storage tanks in such State containing regulated substances. One inventory shall be made with respect to petroleum and one with respect to other regulated substances. In making such inventories, the State shall utilize and aggregate the data in the notification forms submitted pursuant to subsections (a) and (b) of this section. Each State shall submit such aggregated data to the Administrator not later than 270 days after October 17, 1986.

§6991b. RELEASE DETECTION, PREVENTION, AND CORRECTION REGULATIONS

(a) REGULATIONS

The Administrator, after notice and opportunity for public comment, and at least three months before the effective dates specified in subsection (f) of this section, shall promulgate release detection, prevention, and correction regulations applicable to all owners and operators of underground storage tanks, as may be necessary to protect human health and the environment.

(b) DISTINCTIONS IN REGULATIONS

In promulgating regulations under this section, the Administrator may distinguish between types, classes, and ages of underground storage tanks. In making such distinctions, the Administrator may take into consideration factors, including, but not limited to: location of the tanks, soil and climate conditions, uses of the tanks, history of maintenance, age of the tanks, current industry recommended practices, national consensus codes, hydrogeology, water table, size of the tanks, quantity of regulated substances periodically deposited in or dispensed from the tank, the technical capability of the owners and operators, and the compatibility of the regulated substance and the materials of which the tank is fabricated.

(c) REQUIREMENTS

The regulations promulgated pursuant to this section shall include, but need not be limited to, the following requirements respecting all underground storage tanks —

(1) requirements for maintaining a leak detection system, an inventory control system together with tank testing, or a comparable system or method designed to identify releases in a manner consistent with the protection of human health and the environment;

(2) requirements for maintaining records of any monitoring or leak detection system or inventory control system or tank testing or comparable system;

(3) requirements for reporting of releases and corrective action taken in response to a release from an underground storage tank;

(4) requirements for taking corrective action in response to a release from an underground storage tank;

(5) requirements for the closure of tanks to prevent future releases of regulated substances into the environment; and

(6) requirements for maintaining evidence of financial responsibility for taking corrective action and compensating third parties for bodily injury and property damage caused by sudden and nonsudden accidental releases arising from operating an underground storage tank.

(d) FINANCIAL RESPONSIBILITY

(1) Financial responsibility required by this subsection may be established in accordance with regulations promulgated by the Administrator by any one, or any combination, of the following: insurance, guarantee, surety bond, letter of credit, qualification as a self-insurer or any other method satisfactory to the Administrator. In promulgating requirements under this subsection, the Administrator is authorized to specify policy or other contractual terms, conditions, or defenses which are necessary or are unacceptable in establishing such evidence of financial responsibility in order to effectuate the purposes of this subchapter.

(2) In any case where the owner or operator is in bankruptcy, reorganization, or arrangement pursuant to the Federal Bankruptcy Code or where with

reasonable diligence jurisdiction in any State court of the Federal courts cannot be obtained over an owner or operator likely to be solvent at the time of judgment, any claim arising from conduct for which evidence of financial responsibility must be provided under this subsection may be asserted directly against the guarantor providing such evidence of financial responsibility. In the case of any action pursuant to this paragraph such guarantor shall be entitled to invoke all rights and defenses which would have been available to the owner or operator if any action had been brought against the owner or operator by the claimant and which would have been available to the guarantor if an action had been brought against the guarantor by the owner or operator.

(3) The total liability of any guarantor shall be limited to the aggregate amount which the guarantor has provided as evidence of financial responsibility to the owner or operator under this section. Nothing in this subsection shall be construed to limit any other State or Federal statutory, contractual or common law liability of a guarantor to its owner or operator including, but not limited to, the liability of such guarantor for bad faith either in negotiating or in failing to negotiate the settlement of any claim. Nothing in this subsection shall be construed to diminish the liability of any person under section 9607 or 9611 of this title or other applicable law.

(4) For the purpose of this subsection, the term "guarantor" means any person, other than the owner or operator, who provides evidence of financial responsibility for an owner or operator under this subsection.

(5)(A) The Administrator, in promulgating financial responsibility regulations under this section, may establish an amount of coverage for particular classes or categories of underground storage tanks containing petroleum which shall satisfy such regulations and which shall not be less than $1,000,000 for each occurrence with an appropriate aggregate requirement.

(B) The Administrator may set amounts lower than the amounts required by subparagraph (A) of this paragraph for underground storage tanks containing petroleum which are at facilities not engaged in petroleum production, refining, or marketing and which are not used to handle substantial quantities of petroleum.

(C) In establishing classes and categories for purposes of this paragraph, the Administrator may consider the following factors:

(i) The size, type, location, storage, and handling capacity of underground storage tanks in the class or category and the volume of petroleum handled by such tanks.

(ii) The likelihood of release and the potential extent of damage from any release from underground storage tanks in the class or category.

(iii) The economic impact of the limits on the owners and operators of each such class or category, particularly relating to the small business segment of the petroleum marketing industry.

(iv) The availability of methods of financial responsibility in amounts greater than the amount established by this paragraph.

(v) Such other factors as the Administrator deems pertinent.

(D) The Administrator may suspend enforcement of the financial responsibility requirements for a particular class or category of underground storage tanks or in a particular State, if the Administrator makes a determination that methods of financial responsibility satisfying the requirements of this subsection are not generally available for underground storage tanks in that class or category, and —

    (i) steps are being taken to form a risk retention group for such class of tanks; or

    (ii) such State is taking steps to establish a fund pursuant to section 6991c(c)(1) of this title to be submitted as evidence of financial responsibility.

A suspension by the Administrator pursuant to this paragraph shall extend for a period not to exceed 180 days. A determination to suspend may be made with respect to the same class or category or for the same State at the end of such period, but only if substantial progress has been made in establishing a risk retention group, or the owners or operators in the class or category demonstrate, and the Administrator finds, that the formation of such a group is not possible and that the State is unable or unwilling to establish such a fund pursuant to clause (ii).

(e) **NEW TANK PERFORMANCE STANDARDS**

The Administrator shall, not later than three months prior to the effective date specified in subsection (f) of this section, issue performance standards for underground storage tanks brought into use on or after the effective date of such standards. The performance standards for new underground storage tanks shall include, but need not be limited to, design, construction, installation, release detection, and compatibility standards.

(f) **EFFECTIVE DATES**

(1) Regulations issued pursuant to subsection[2] (c) and (d) of this section, and standards issued pursuant to subsection (e) of this section, for underground storage tanks containing regulated substances defined in section 6991(2)(B) of this title (petroleum, including crude oil or any fraction thereof which is liquid at standard conditions of temperature and pressure) shall be effective not later than thirty months after November 8, 1984.

(2) Standards issued pursuant to subsection (e) of this section (entitled "New Tank Performance Standards") for underground storage tanks containing regulated substances defined in section 6991(2)(A) of this title shall be effective not later than thirty-six months after November 8, 1984.

(3) Regulations issued pursuant to subsection (c) of this section (entitled "Requirements") and standards issued pursuant to subsection (d) of this section (entitled "Financial Responsibility") for underground storage tanks containing regulated substances defined in section 6991(2)(A) of this title shall be effective not later than forty-eight months after November 8, 1984.

    2. So in original. Probably should be "subsections."

Resource Conservation and Recovery Act §6991b

(g) INTERIM PROHIBITION

(1) Until the effective date of the standards promulgated by the Administrator under subsection (e) of this section and after one hundred and eighty days after November 8, 1984, no person may install an underground storage tank for the purpose of storing regulated substances unless such tank (whether of single or double wall construction) —

(A) will prevent releases due to corrosion or structural failure for the operational life of the tank;

(B) is cathodically protected against corrosion, constructed of noncorrosive material, steel clad with a noncorrosive material, or designed in a manner to prevent the release or threatened release of any stored substance; and

(C) the material used in the construction or lining of the tank is compatible with the substance to be stored.

(2) Notwithstanding paragraph (1), if soil tests conducted in accordance with ASTM Standard G57-78, or another standard approved by the Administrator, show that soil resistivity in an installation location is 12,000 ohm/cm or more (unless a more stringent standard is prescribed by the Administrator by rule), a storage tank without corrosion protection may be installed in that location during the period referred to in paragraph (1).

(h) EPA RESPONSE PROGRAM FOR PETROLEUM

(1) BEFORE REGULATIONS

Before the effective date of regulations under subsection (c) of this section, the Administrator (or a State pursuant to paragraph (7)) is authorized to —

(A) require the owner or operator of an underground storage tank to undertake corrective action with respect to any release of petroleum when the Administrator (or the State) determines that such corrective action will be done properly and promptly by the owner or operator of the underground storage tank from which the release occurs; or

(B) undertake corrective action with respect to any release of petroleum into the environment from an underground storage tank if such action is necessary, in the judgment of the Administrator (or the State), to protect human health and the environment.

The corrective action undertaken or required under this paragraph shall be such as may be necessary to protect human health and the environment. The Administrator shall use funds in the Leaking Underground Storage Tank Trust Fund for payment of costs incurred for corrective action under subparagraph (B), enforcement action under subparagraph (A), and cost recovery under paragraph (6) of this subsection. Subject to the priority requirements of paragraph (3), the Administrator (or the State) shall give priority in undertaking such actions under subparagraph (B) to cases where the Administrator (or the State) cannot identify a solvent owner or operator of the tank who will undertake action properly.

(2) **AFTER REGULATIONS**

Following the effective date of regulations under subsection (c) of this section, all actions or orders of the Administrator (or a State pursuant to paragraph (7)) described in paragraph (1) of this subsection shall be in conformity with such regulations. Following such effective date, the Administrator (or the State) may undertake corrective action with respect to any release of petroleum into the environment from an underground storage tank only if such action is necessary, in the judgment of the Administrator (or the State), to protect human health and the environment and one or more of the following situations exists:

(A) No person can be found, within 90 days or such shorter period as may be necessary to protect human health and the environment, who is —

(i) an owner or operator of the tank concerned,
(ii) subject to such corrective action regulations, and
(iii) capable of carrying out such corrective action properly.

(B) A situation exists which requires prompt action by the Administrator (or the State) under this paragraph to protect human health and the environment.

(C) Corrective action costs at a facility exceed the amount of coverage required by the Administrator pursuant to the provisions of subsections (c) and (d)(5) of this section and, considering the class or category of underground storage tank from which the release occurred, expenditures from the Leaking Underground Storage Tank Trust Fund are necessary to assure an effective corrective action.

(D) The owner or operator of the tank has failed or refused to comply with an order of the Administrator under this subsection or section 6991e of this title or with the order of a State under this subsection to comply with the corrective action regulations.

(3) **PRIORITY OF CORRECTIVE ACTIONS**

The Administrator (or a State pursuant to paragraph (7)) shall give priority in undertaking corrective actions under this subsection, and in issuing orders requiring owners or operators to undertake such actions, to releases of petroleum from underground storage tanks which pose the greatest threat to human health and the environment.

(4) **CORRECTIVE ACTION ORDERS**

The Administrator is authorized to issue orders to the owner or operator of an underground storage tank to carry out subparagraph (A) of paragraph (1) or to carry out regulations issued under subsection (c)(4) of this section. A State acting pursuant to paragraph (7) of this subsection is authorized to carry out subparagraph (A) of paragraph (1) only until the State's program is approved by the Administrator under section 6991c of this title. Such orders shall be issued and enforced in the same manner and subject to the same requirements as orders under section 6991e of this title.

(5) ALLOWABLE CORRECTIVE ACTIONS

The corrective actions undertaken by the Administrator (or a State pursuant to paragraph (7)) under paragraph (1) or (2) may include temporary or permanent relocation of residents and alternative household water supplies. In connection with the performance of any corrective action under paragraph (1) or (2), the Administrator may undertake an exposure assessment as defined in paragraph (10) of this subsection or provide for such an assessment in a cooperative agreement with a State pursuant to paragraph (7) of this subsection. The costs of any such assessment may be treated as corrective action for purposes of paragraph (6), relating to cost recovery.

(6) RECOVERY OF COSTS

(A) IN GENERAL

Whenever costs have been incurred by the Administrator, or by a State pursuant to paragraph (7), for undertaking corrective action or enforcement action with respect to the release of petroleum from an underground storage tank, the owner or operator of such tank shall be liable to the Administrator or the State for such costs. The liability under this paragraph shall be construed to be the standard of liability which obtains under section 1321 of title 33.

(B) RECOVERY

In determining the equities for seeking the recovery of costs under subparagraph (A), the Administrator (or a State pursuant to paragraph (7) of this subsection) may consider the amount of financial responsibility required to be maintained under subsections (c) and (d)(5) of this section and the factors considered in establishing such amount under subsection (d)(5) of this section.

(C) EFFECT ON LIABILITY

(i) NO TRANSFERS OF LIABILITY

No indemnification, hold harmless, or similar agreement or conveyance shall be effective to transfer from the owner or operator of any underground storage tank or from any person who may be liable for a release or threat of release under this subsection, to any other person the liability imposed under this subsection. Nothing in this subsection shall bar any agreement to insure, hold harmless, or indemnify a party to such agreement for any liability under this section.

(ii) NO BAR TO CAUSE OF ACTION

Nothing in this subsection, including the provisions of clause (i) of this subparagraph, shall bar a cause of action that an owner or operator or any other person subject to liability under this section, or a guarantor, has or would have, by reason of subrogation or otherwise against any person.

(D) FACILITY

For purposes of this paragraph, the term "facility" means, with respect to any owner or operator, all underground storage tanks used for the storage of petroleum which are owned or operated by such owner or operator and located on a single parcel of property (or on any contiguous or adjacent property).

(7) STATE AUTHORITIES

(A) GENERAL

A State may exercise the authorities in paragraphs (1) and (2) of this subsection, subject to the terms and conditions of paragraphs (3), (5), (9), (10), and (11), and including the authorities of paragraphs (4), (6), and (8) of this subsection if —

(i) the Administrator determines that the State has the capabilities to carry out effective corrective actions and enforcement activities; and

(ii) the Administrator enters into a cooperative agreement with the State setting out the actions to be undertaken by the State.

The Administrator may provide funds from the Leaking Underground Storage Tank Trust Fund for the reasonable costs of the State's actions under the cooperative agreement.

(B) COST SHARE

Following the effective date of the regulations under subsection (c) of this section, the State shall pay 10 per centum of the cost of corrective actions undertaken either by the Administrator or by the State under a cooperative agreement, except that the Administrator may take corrective action at a facility where immediate action is necessary to respond to an imminent and substantial endangerment to human health or the environment if the State fails to pay the cost share.

(8) EMERGENCY PROCUREMENT POWERS

Notwithstanding any other provision of law, the Administrator may authorize the use of such emergency procurement powers as he deems necessary.

(9) DEFINITION OF OWNER

As used in this subsection, the term "owner" does not include any person who, without participating in the management of an underground storage tank and otherwise not engaged in petroleum production, refining, and marketing, holds indicia of ownership primarily to protect the owner's security interest in the tank.

(10) DEFINITION OF EXPOSURE ASSESSMENT

As used in this subsection, the term "exposure assessment" means an assessment to determine the extent of exposure of, or potential for exposure of, individuals to petroleum from a release from an underground storage tank based on such factors as the nature and extent of contamination and the existence of or potential for pathways of human exposure (including ground or surface water contamination, air emissions, and food chain contamination), the size of the community within the likely pathways of exposure, and the comparison of expected human exposure levels to the short-term and long-term health effects associated with identified contaminants and any available recommended exposure or tolerance limits for such contaminants. Such assessment shall not delay corrective action to abate immediate hazards or reduce exposure.

(11) FACILITIES WITHOUT FINANCIAL RESPONSIBILITY

At any facility where the owner or operator has failed to maintain evidence of financial responsibility in amounts at least equal to the amounts established by subsection (d)(5)(A) of this section (or a lesser amount if such amount is applicable to such facility as a result of subsection (d)(5)(B) of this section) for whatever reason the Administrator shall expend no monies from the Leaking Underground Storage Tank Trust Fund to clean up releases at such facility pursuant to the provisions of paragraph (1) or (2) of this subsection. At such facilities the Administrator shall use the authorities provided in subparagraph (A) of paragraph (1) and paragraph (4) of this subsection and section 6991e of this title to order corrective action to clean up such releases. States acting pursuant to paragraph (7) of this subsection shall use the authorities provided in subparagraph (A) of paragraph (1) and paragraph (4) of this subsection to order corrective action to clean up such releases. Notwithstanding the provisions of this paragraph, the Administrator may use monies from the fund to take the corrective actions authorized by paragraph (5) of this subsection to protect human health at such facilities and shall seek full recovery of the costs of all such actions pursuant to the provisions of paragraph (6)(A) of this subsection and without consideration of the factors in paragraph (6)(B) of this subsection. Nothing in this paragraph shall prevent the Administrator (or a State pursuant to paragraph (7) of this subsection) from taking corrective action at a facility where there is no solvent owner or operator or

§6991b   Resource Conservation and Recovery Act

where immediate action is necessary to respond to an imminent and substantial endangerment of human health or the environment.

§6991c. APPROVAL OF STATE PROGRAMS

(a) ELEMENTS OF STATE PROGRAM

Beginning 30 months after November 8, 1984, any State may, submit an underground storage tank release detection, prevention, and correction program for review and approval by the Administrator. The program may cover tanks used to store regulated substances referred to in[3] 6991(2)(A) or (B) or both of this title. A State program may be approved by the Administrator under this section only if the State demonstrates that the State program includes the following requirements and standards and provides for adequate enforcement of compliance with such requirements and standards —

(1) requirements for maintaining a leak detection system, an inventory control system together with tank testing, or a comparable system or method designed to identify releases in a manner consistent with the protection of human health and the environment;

(2) requirements for maintaining records of any monitoring or leak detection system or inventory control system or tank testing system;

(3) requirements for reporting of any releases and corrective action taken in response to a release from an underground storage tank;

(4) requirements for taking corrective action in response to a release from an underground storage tank;

(5) requirements for the closure of tanks to prevent future releases of regulated substances into the environment;

(6) requirements for maintaining evidence of financial responsibility for taking corrective action and compensating third parties for bodily injury and property damage caused by sudden and nonsudden accidental releases arising from operating an underground storage tank;

(7) standards of performance for new underground storage tanks; and

(8) requirements —

(A) for notifying the appropriate State agency or department (or local agency or department) designated according to section 6991a(b)(1) of this title of the existence of any operational or non-operational underground storage tank; and

(B) for providing the information required on the form issued pursuant to section 6991a(b)(2) of this title.

(b) FEDERAL STANDARDS

(1) A State program submitted under this section may be approved only if the requirements under paragraphs (1) through (7) of subsection (a) of this section

---

3. So in original. Probably should be followed by "section."

are no less stringent than the corresponding requirements standards promulgated by the Administrator pursuant to section 6991b(a) of this title.

(2)(A) A State program may be approved without regard to whether or not the requirements referred to in paragraphs (1), (2), (3), and (5) of subsection (a) of this section are less stringent than the corresponding standards under section 6991b(a) of this title during the one-year period commencing on the date of promulgation of regulations under section 6991b(a) of this title if State regulatory action but no State legislative action is required in order to adopt a State program.

(B) If such State legislative action is required, the State program may be approved without regard to whether or not the requirements referred to in paragraphs (1), (2), (3), and (5) of subsection (a) of this section are less stringent than the corresponding standards under section 6991b(a) of this title during the two-year period commencing on the date of promulgation of regulations under section 6991b(a) of this title (and during an additional one-year period after such legislative action if regulations are required to be promulgated by the State pursuant to such legislative action).

(c) **FINANCIAL RESPONSIBILITY**

(1) Corrective action and compensation programs administered by State or local agencies or departments may be submitted for approval under subsection (a)(6) of this section as evidence of financial responsibility.

(2) Financial responsibility required by this subsection may be established in accordance with regulations promulgated by the Administrator by any one, or any combination, of the following: insurance, guarantee, surety bond, letter of credit, qualification as a self-insurer or any other method satisfactory to the Administrator. In promulgating requirements under this subsection, the Administrator is authorized to specify policy or other contractual terms including the amount of coverage required for various classes and categories of underground storage tanks pursuant to section 6991b(d)(5) of this title, conditions, or defenses which are necessary or are unacceptable in establishing such evidence of financial responsibility in order to effectuate the purposes of this subchapter.

(3) In any case where the owner or operator is in bankruptcy, reorganization, or arrangement pursuant to the Federal Bankruptcy Code or where with reasonable diligence jurisdiction in any State court of the Federal courts cannot be obtained over an owner or operator likely to be solvent at the time of judgment, any claim arising from conduct for which evidence of financial responsibility must be provided under this subsection may be asserted directly against the guarantor providing such evidence of financial responsibility. In the case of any action pursuant to this paragraph such guarantor shall be entitled to invoke all rights and defenses which would have been available to the owner or operator if any action had been brought against the owner or operator by the claimant and which would have been available to the guarantor if an action had been brought against the guarantor by the owner or operator.

(4) The total liability of any guarantor shall be limited to the aggregate

amount which the guarantor has provided as evidence of financial responsibility to the owner or operator under this section. Nothing in this subsection shall be construed to limit any other State or Federal statutory, contractual or common law liability of a guarantor to its owner or operator including, but not limited to, the liability of such guarantor for bad faith either in negotiating or in failing to negotiate the settlement of any claim. Nothing in this subsection shall be construed to diminish the liability of any person under section 9607 or 9611 of this title or other applicable law.

(5) For the purpose of this subsection, the term "guarantor" means any person, other than the owner or operator, who provides evidence of financial responsibility for an owner or operator under this subsection.

(d) EPA DETERMINATION

(1) Within one hundred and eighty days of the date of receipt of a proposed State program, the Administrator shall, after notice and opportunity for public comment, make a determination whether the State's program complies with the provisions of this section and provides for adequate enforcement of compliance with the requirements and standards adopted pursuant to this section.

(2) If the Administrator determines that a State program complies with the provisions of this section and provides for adequate enforcement of compliance with the requirements and standards adopted pursuant to this section, he shall approve the State program in lieu of the Federal program and the State shall have primary enforcement responsibility with respect to requirements of its program.

(e) WITHDRAWAL OF AUTHORIZATION

Whenever the Administrator determines after public hearing that a State is not administering and enforcing a program authorized under this subchapter in accordance with the provisions of this section, he shall so notify the State. If appropriate action is not taken within a reasonable time, not to exceed one hundred and twenty days after such notification, the Administrator shall withdraw approval of such program and reestablish the Federal program pursuant to this subchapter.

§6991d. INSPECTIONS, MONITORING, TESTING, AND CORRECTIVE ACTION

(a) FURNISHING INFORMATION

For the purposes of developing or assisting in the development of any regulation, conducting any study[4] taking any corrective action, or enforcing the provisions of this subchapter, any owner or operator of an underground storage tank (or any tank subject to study under section 6991h of this title that is used for storing regulated substances) shall, upon request of any officer, employee or

---

4. So in original. Probably should be followed by a comma.

representative of the Environmental Protection Agency, duly designated by the Administrator, or upon request of any duly designated officer, employee, or representative of a State acting pursuant to subsection (h)(7) of section 6991b of this title or with an approved program, furnish information relating to such tanks, their associated equipment, their contents, conduct monitoring or testing, permit such officer at all reasonable times to have access to, and to copy all records relating to such tanks and permit such officer to have access for corrective action. For the purposes of developing or assisting in the development of any regulation, conducting any study, taking corrective action, or enforcing the provisions of this subchapter, such officers, employees, or representatives are authorized —

(1) to enter at reasonable times any establishment or other place where an underground storage tank is located;

(2) to inspect and obtain samples from any person of any regulated substances contained in such tank;

(3) to conduct monitoring or testing of the tanks, associated equipment, contents, or surrounding soils, air, surface water or ground water; and

(4) to take corrective action.

Each such inspection shall be commenced and completed with reasonable promptness.

(b) CONFIDENTIALITY

(1) Any records, reports, or information obtained from any persons under this section shall be available to the public, except that upon a showing satisfactory to the Administrator (or the State, as the case may be) by any person that records, reports, or information, or a particular part thereof, to which the Administrator (or the State, as the case may be) or any officer, employee, or representative thereof has access under this section if made public, would divulge information entitled to protection under section 1905 of title 18, such information or particular portion thereof shall be considered confidential in accordance with the purposes of that section, except that such record, report, document, or information may be disclosed to other officers, employees, or authorized representatives of the United States concerned with carrying out this chapter, or when relevent[5] in any proceeding under this chapter.

(2) Any person not subject to the provisions of section 1905 of title 18 who knowingly and willfully divulges or discloses any information entitled to protection under this subsection shall, upon conviction, be subject to a fine of not more than $5,000 or to imprisonment not to exceed one year, or both.

(3) In submitting data under this subchapter, a person required to provide such data may —

(A) designate the data which such person believes is entitled to protection under this subsection, and

(B) submit such designated data separately from other data submitted under this subchapter.

---

5. So in original. Probably should be "relevant."

A designation under this paragraph shall be made in writing and in such manner as the Administrator may prescribe.

(4) Notwithstanding any limitation contained in this section or any other provision of law, all information reported to, or otherwise obtained, by the Administrator (or any representative of the Administrator) under this chapter shall be made available, upon written request of any duly authorized committee of the Congress, to such committee (including records, reports, or information obtained by representatives of the Environmental Protection Agency).

§6991e. FEDERAL ENFORCEMENT

(a) COMPLIANCE ORDERS

(1) Except as provided in paragraph (2), whenever on the basis of any information, the Administrator determines that any person is in violation of any requirement of this subchapter, the Administrator may issue an order requiring compliance within a reasonable specified time period or the Administrator may commence a civil action in the United States district court in which the violation occurred for appropriate relief, including a temporary or permanent injunction.

(2) In the case of a violation of any requirement of this subchapter where such violation occurs in a State with a program approved under section 6991c of this title, the Administrator shall give notice to the State in which such violation has occurred prior to issuing an order or commencing a civil action under this section.

(3) If a violator fails to comply with an order under this subsection within the time specified in the order, he shall be liable for a civil penalty of not more than $25,000 for each day of continued noncompliance.

(b) PROCEDURE

Any order issued under this section shall become final unless, no later than thirty days after the order is served, the person or persons named therein request a public hearing. Upon such request the Administrator shall promptly conduct a public hearing. In connection with any proceeding under this section the Administrator may issue subpoenas for the attendance and testimony of witnesses and the production of relevant papers, books, and documents, and may promulgate rules for discovery procedures.

(c) CONTENTS OF ORDER

Any order issued under this section shall state with reasonable specificity the nature of the violation, specify a reasonable time for compliance, and assess a penalty, if any, which the Administrator determines is reasonable taking into account the seriousness of the violation and any good faith efforts to comply with the applicable requirements.

(d) CIVIL PENALTIES

(1) Any owner who knowingly fails to notify or submits false information pursuant to section 6991a(a) of this title shall be subject to a civil penalty not to exceed $10,000 for each tank for which notification is not given or false information is submitted.

(2) Any owner or operator of an underground storage tank who fails to comply with —

(A) any requirement or standard promulgated by the Administrator under section 6991b of this title;

(B) any requirement or standard of a State program approved pursuant to section 6991c of this title; or

(C) the provisions of section 6991b(g) of this title (entitled "Interim Prohibition")

shall be subject to a civil penalty not to exceed $10,000 for each tank for each day of violation.

§6991f. FEDERAL FACILITIES

(a) APPLICATION OF SUBCHAPTER

Each department, agency, and instrumentality of the executive, legislative, and judicial branches of the Federal Government having jurisdiction over any underground storage tank shall be subject to and comply with all Federal, State, interstate, and local requirements, applicable to such tank, both substantive and procedural, in the same manner, and to the same extent, as any other person is subject to such requirements, including payment of reasonable service charges. Neither the United States, nor any agent, employee, or officer thereof, shall be immune or exempt from any process or sanction of any State or Federal court with respect to the enforcement of any such injunctive relief.

(b) PRESIDENTIAL EXEMPTION

The President may exempt any underground storage tanks of any department, agency, or instrumentality in the executive branch from compliance with such a requirement if he determines it to be in the paramount interest of the United States to do so. No such exemption shall be granted due to lack of appropriation unless the President shall have specifically requested such appropriation as a part of the budgetary process and the Congress shall have failed to make available such requested appropriations. Any exemption shall be for a period not in excess of one year, but additional exemptions may be granted for periods not to exceed one year upon the President's making a new determination. The President shall report each January to the Congress all exemptions from the requirements of this section granted during the preceding calendar year, together with his reason for granting each such exemption.

§6991g. STATE AUTHORITY

Nothing in this subchapter shall preclude or deny any right of any State or political subdivision thereof to adopt or enforce any regulation, requirement, or standard of performance respecting underground storage tanks that is more stringent than a regulation, requirement, or standard of performance in effect under this subchapter or to impose any additional liability with respect to the release of regulated substances within such State or political subdivision.

§6991h. STUDY OF UNDERGROUND STORAGE TANKS

(a) PETROLEUM TANKS

Not later than twelve months after November 8, 1984, the Administrator shall complete a study of underground storage tanks used for the storage of regulated substances defined in section 6991(2)(B) of this title.

(b) OTHER TANKS

Not later than thirty-six months after November 8, 1984, the Administrator shall complete a study of all other underground storage tanks.

(c) ELEMENTS OF STUDIES

The studies under subsections (a) and (b) of this section shall include an assessment of the ages, types (including methods of manufacture, coatings, protection systems, the compatibility of the construction materials and the installation methods) and locations (including the climate of the locations) of such tanks; soil conditions, water tables, and the hydrogeology of tank locations; the relationship between the foregoing factors and the likelihood of releases from underground storage tanks; the effectiveness and costs of inventory systems, tank testing, and leak detection systems; and such other factors as the Administrator deems appropriate.

(d) FARM AND HEATING OIL TANKS

Not later than thirty-six months after November 8, 1984, the Administrator shall conduct a study regarding the tanks referred to in section 6991(1)(A) and (B) of this title. Such study shall include estimates of the number and location of such tanks and an analysis of the extent to which there may be releases or threatened releases from such tanks into the environment.

(e) REPORTS

Upon completion of the studies authorized by this section, the Administrator shall submit reports to the President and to the Congress containing the results of the studies and recommendations respecting whether or not such tanks should be subject to the preceding provisions of this subchapter.

(f) REIMBURSEMENT

(1) If any owner or operator (excepting an agency, department, or instrumentality of the United States Government, a State or a political subdivision thereof) shall incur costs, including the loss of business opportunity, due to the closure or interruption of operation of an underground storage tank solely for the purpose of conducting studies authorized by this section, the Administrator shall provide such person fair and equitable reimbursement for such costs.

(2) All claims for reimbursement shall be filed with the Administrator not later than ninety days after the closure or interruption which gives rise to the claim.

(3) Reimbursements made under this section shall be from funds appropriated by the Congress pursuant to the authorization contained in section 6916(g)[6] of this title.

(4) For purposes of judicial review, a determination by the Administrator under this subsection shall be considered final agency action.

§6991i. AUTHORIZATION OF APPROPRIATIONS

For authorization of appropriations to carry out this subchapter, see section 6916(g)[6] of this title. . . .

Subchapter X — Demonstration Medical Waste Tracking Program

§6992c. INSPECTIONS

(a) REQUIREMENTS FOR ACCESS

For purposes of developing or assisting in the development of any regulation or report under this subchapter or enforcing any provision of this subchapter, any person who generates, stores, treats, transports, disposes of, or otherwise handles or has handled medical waste shall, upon request of any officer, employee, or representative of the Environmental Protection Agency duly designated by the Administrator, furnish information relating to such waste, including any tracking forms required to be maintained under section 6992b of this title, conduct monitoring or testing, and permit such person at all reasonable times to have access to, and to copy, all records relating to such waste. For such purposes, such officers, employees, or representatives are authorized to —

   (1) enter at reasonable times any establishment or other place where medical wastes are or have been generated, stored, treated, disposed of, or transported from;

   (2) conduct monitoring or testing; and

---

6. See References in Text note below.

(3) inspect and obtain samples from any person of any such wastes and samples of any containers or labeling for such wastes.

(b) PROCEDURES

Each inspection under this section shall be commenced and completed with reasonable promptness. If the officer, employee, or representative obtains any samples, prior to leaving the premises he shall give to the owner, operator, or agent in charge a receipt describing the sample obtained and, if requested, a portion of each such sample equal in volume or weight to the portion retained if giving such an equal portion is feasible. If any analysis is made of such samples, a copy of the results of such analysis shall be furnished promptly to the owner, operator, or agent in charge of the premises concerned.

(c) AVAILABILITY TO PUBLIC

The provisions of section 6927(b) of this title shall apply to records, reports, and information obtained under this section in the same manner and to the same extent as such provisions apply to records, reports, and information obtained under section 6927 of this title.

§6992d. ENFORCEMENT

(a) COMPLIANCE ORDERS

(1) VIOLATIONS

Whenever on the basis of any information the Administrator determines that any person has violated, or is in violation of, any requirement or prohibition in effect under this subchapter (including any requirement or prohibition in effect under regulations under this subchapter) (A) the Administrator may issue an order (i) assessing a civil penalty for any past or current violation, (ii) requiring compliance immediately or within a specified time period, or (iii) both, or (B) the Administrator may commence a civil action in the United States district court in the district in which the violation occurred for appropriate relief, including a temporary or permanent injunction. Any order issued pursuant to this subsection shall state with reasonable specificity the nature of the violation.

(2) ORDERS ASSESSING PENALTIES

Any penalty assessed in an order under this subsection shall not exceed $25,000 per day of noncompliance for each violation of a requirement or prohibition in effect under this subchapter. In assessing such a penalty, the Administrator shall take into account the seriousness of the violation and any good faith efforts to comply with applicable requirements.

Resource Conservation and Recovery Act §6992d

(3) PUBLIC HEARING

Any order issued under this subsection shall become final unless, not later than 30 days after issuance of the order, the persons named therein request a public hearing. Upon such request, the Administrator shall promptly conduct a public hearing. In connection with any proceeding under this section, the Administrator may issue subpoenas for the production of relevant papers, books, and documents, and may promulgate rules for discovery procedures.

(4) VIOLATION OF COMPLIANCE ORDERS

In the case of an order under this subsection requiring compliance with any requirement of or regulation under this subchapter, if a violator fails to take corrective action within the time specified in an order, the Administrator may assess a civil penalty of not more than $25,000 for each day of continued noncompliance with the order.

(b) CRIMINAL PENALTIES

Any person who —
(1) knowingly violates the requirements of or regulations under this subchapter;
(2) knowingly omits material information or makes any false material statement or representation in any label, record, report, or other document filed, maintained, or used for purposes of compliance with this subchapter or regulations thereunder; or
(3) knowingly generates, stores, treats, transports, disposes of, or otherwise handles any medical waste (whether such activity took place before or takes place after November 1, 1988) and who knowingly destroys, alters, conceals, or fails to file any record, report, or other document required to be maintained or filed for purposes of compliance with this subchapter or regulations thereunder shall, upon conviction, be subject to a fine of not more than $50,000 for each day of violation, or imprisonment not to exceed 2 years (5 years in the case of a violation of paragraph (1)). If the conviction is for a violation committed after a first conviction of such person under this paragraph, the maximum punishment under the respective paragraph shall be doubled with respect to both fine and imprisonment.

(c) KNOWING ENDANGERMENT

Any person who knowingly violates any provision of subsection (b) of this section who knows at that time that he thereby places another person in imminent danger of death or serious bodily injury, shall upon conviction be subject to a fine of not more than $250,000 or imprisonment for not more than 15 years, or both. A defendant that is an organization shall, upon conviction under this subsection, be subject to a fine of not more than $1,000,000. The terms of this paragraph shall be interpreted in accordance with the rules provided under section 6928(f) of this title.

(d) CIVIL PENALTIES

Any person who violates any requirement of or regulation under this subchapter shall be liable to the United States for a civil penalty in an amount not to exceed $25,000 for each such violation. Each day of such violation shall, for purposes of this section, constitute a separate violation.

(e) CIVIL PENALTY POLICY

Civil penalties assessed by the United States or by the States under this subchapter shall be assessed in accordance with the Administrator's "RCRA Civil Penalty Policy," as such policy may be amended from time to time.

§6992e. FEDERAL FACILITIES

(a) IN GENERAL

Each department, agency, and instrumentality of the executive, legislative, and judicial branches of the Federal Government in a demonstration State (1) having jurisdiction over any solid waste management facility or disposal site at which medical waste is disposed of or otherwise handled, or (2) engaged in any activity resulting, or which may result, in the disposal, management, or handling of medical waste shall be subject to, and comply with, all Federal, State, interstate, and local requirements, both substantive and procedural (including any requirement for permits or reporting or any provisions for injunctive relief and such sanctions as may be imposed by a court to enforce such relief), respecting control and abatement of medical waste disposal and management in the same manner, and to the same extent, as any person is subject to such requirements, including the payment of reasonable service charges. The Federal, State, interstate, and local substantive and procedural requirements referred to in this subsection include, but are not limited to, all administrative orders, civil, criminal, and administrative penalties, and other sanctions, including injunctive relief, fines, and imprisonment. Neither the United States, nor any agent, employee, or officer thereof, shall be immune or exempt from any process or sanction of any State or Federal court with respect to the enforcement of any such order, penalty, or other sanction. For purposes of enforcing any such substantive or procedural requirement (including, but not limited to, any injunctive relief, administrative order, or civil, criminal, administrative penalty, or other sanction), against any such department, agency, or instrumentality, the United States hereby expressly waives any immunity otherwise applicable to the United States. The President may exempt any department, agency, or instrumentality in the executive branch from compliance with such a requirement if he determines it to be in the paramount interest of the United States to do so. No such exemption shall be granted due to lack of appropriation unless the President shall have specifically requested such appropriation as a part of the budgetary process and the Congress shall have failed to make available such requested appropriation. Any exemption shall be for a period not in excess of one year, but additional exemptions may be granted for periods not to exceed one year upon the President's making a new determination. The President shall report each January to the Congress all exemptions from the requirements of this section granted during the preceding calendar year, together with his reason for granting each such exemption.

(b) "PERSON" DEFINED

For purposes of this chapter, the term "person" shall be treated as including each department, agency, and instrumentality of the United States.

§6992f. RELATIONSHIP TO STATE LAW

(a) STATE INSPECTIONS AND ENFORCEMENT

A State may conduct inspections under 6992c[1] of this title and take enforcement actions under section 6992d of this title against any person, including any person who has imported medical waste into a State in violation of the requirements of, or regulations under, this subchapter, to the same extent as the Administrator. At the time a State initiates an enforcement action under section 6992d of this title against any person, the State shall notify the Administrator in writing.

(b) RETENTION OF STATE AUTHORITY

Nothing in this subchapter shall —
(1) preempt any State or local law; or
(2) except as provided in subsection (c) of this section, otherwise affect any State or local law or the authority of any State or local government to adopt or enforce any State or local law.

(c) STATE FORMS

Any State or local law which requires submission of a tracking form from any person subject to this subchapter shall require that the form be identical in content and format to the form required under section 6992b of this title, except that a State may require the submission of other tracking information which is supplemental to the information required on the form required under section 6992b of this title through additional sheets or such other means as the State deems appropriate.

---

1. So in original. Probably should be preceded by "section."

§6992g. REPORT TO CONGRESS

(a) **FINAL REPORT**

Not later than 3 months after the expiration of the demonstration program, the Administrator shall report to Congress on the following topics:

(1) The types, number, and size of generators of medical waste (including small quantity generators) in the United States, the types and amounts of medical waste generated, and the on-site and off-site methods currently used to handle, store, transport, treat, and dispose of the medical waste, including the extent to which such waste is disposed of in sewer systems.

(2) The present or potential threat to human health and the environment posed by medical waste or the incineration thereof.

(3) The present and potential costs (A) to local economies, persons, and the environment from the improper handling, storage, transportation, treatment or disposal of medical waste and (B) to generators, transporters, and treatment, storage, and disposal facilities from regulations establishing requirements for tracking,, handling, storage, transportation, treatment, and disposal of medical waste.

(4)(A) The success of the demonstration program established under this subchapter in tracking medical waste,

(B) changes in incineration and storage practices attributable to the demonstration program, and

(C) other available and potentially available methods for tracking medical waste and their advantages and disadvantages, including the advantages and disadvantages of extending tracking requirements to (i) rural areas and (ii) small quantity generators.

(5) Available and potentially available methods for handling, storing, transporting, and disposing of medical waste and their advantages and disadvantages.

(6) Available and potentially available methods for treating medical waste, including the methods of incineration, sterilization, chemical treatment, and grinding, and their advantages, including their ability to render medical waste noninfectious or less infectious, and unrecognizable and otherwise protect human health and the environment, and disadvantages.

(7) Factors affecting the effectiveness of the treatment methods identified in subsection (a)(5) of this section, including quality control and quality assurance procedures, maintenance procedures, and operator training.

(8) Existing State and local controls on the handling, storage, transportation, treatment, and disposal of medical waste, including the enforcement and regulatory supervision thereof.

(9) The appropriateness of using any existing State requirements or the requirements contained in subchapter III of this chapter as nationwide requirements to monitor and control medical waste.

(10) The appropriateness of the penalties provided in section 6992e of this title for insuring compliance with the requirements of this subchapter,

including a review of the level of penalties imposed under this subchapter.

(11)(A) The effect of excluding households and small quantity generators from any regulations governing the handling, storage, transportation, treatment, and disposal of medical waste, and

(B) potential guidelines for the handling, storage, treatment, and disposal of medical waste by households and small quantity generators.

(12) Available and potentially available methods for the reuse or reduction of the volume of medical waste generated.

(b) INTERIM REPORTS

The Administrator shall submit two interim reports to Congress on the topics listed in subsection (a) of this section. The interim reports shall contain the information on the topics available to the Administrator at the time of submission. One interim report shall be due 9 months after November 1, 1988 and one shall be due 12 months after the effective date of regulations under this subchapter.

(c) CONSULTATION

In preparing the reports under this section, the Administrator shall consult with appropriate State and local agencies.

§6992h. HEALTH IMPACTS REPORT

Within 24 months after November 1, 1988, the Administrator of the Agency for Toxic Substances and Disease Registry shall prepare for Congress a report on the health effects of medical waste, including each of the following —

(1) A description of the potential for infection or injury from the segregation, handling, storage, treatment, or disposal of medical wastes.

(2) An estimate of the number of people injured or infected annually by sharps, and the nature and seriousness of those injuries or infections.

(3) An estimate of the number of people infected annually by other means related to waste segregation, handling, storage, treatment, or disposal, and the nature and seriousness of those infections.

(4) For diseases possibly spread by medical waste, including Acquired Immune Deficiency Syndrome and hepatitis B, an estimate of what percentage of the total number of cases nationally may be traceable to medical wastes.

§6992i. GENERAL PROVISIONS

(a) CONSULTATION

(1) In promulgating regulations under this subchapter, the Administrator shall consult with the affected States and may consult with other interested parties.

(2) The Administrator shall also consult with the International Joint Commission to determine how to monitor the disposal of medical waste emanating from Canada.

(b) **PUBLIC COMMENT**

In the case of the regulations required by this subchapter to be promulgated within 9 months after November 1, 1988, the Administrator may promulgate such regulations in interim final form without prior opportunity for public comment, but the Administrator shall provide an opportunity for public comment on the interim final rule. The promulgation of such regulations shall not be subject to the Paperwork Reduction Act of 1980.

(c) **RELATIONSHIP TO SUBCHAPTER III**

Nothing in this subchapter shall affect the authority of the Administrator to regulate medical waste, including medical waste listed under section 6992a of this title, under subchapter III of this chapter.

National Environmental Policy Act of 1969 (NEPA)
42 U.S.C. §§4331-4344

Chapter 55 — National Environmental Policy

SUBCHAPTER I — POLICIES AND GOALS

Sec.
4331. Congressional declaration of national environmental policy.
   (a) Creation and maintenance of conditions under which man and nature can exist in productive harmony.
   (b) Continuing responsibility of Federal Government to use all practicable means to improve and coordinate Federal plans, functions, programs, and resources.
   (c) Responsibility of each person to contribute to preservation and enhancement of environment.
4332. Cooperation of agencies; reports; availability of information; recommendations; international and national coordination of efforts.
4334. Other statutory obligations of agencies.
4335. Efforts supplemental to existing authorizations.

SUBCHAPTER II — COUNCIL ON ENVIRONMENTAL QUALITY

4341. Reports to Congress; recommendations for legislation.
4342. Establishment; membership; Chairman; appointments.
4343. Employment of personnel, experts and consultants.
4344. Duties and functions.

Subchapter I — Policies and Goals

§4331. CONGRESSIONAL DECLARATION OF NATIONAL ENVIRONMENTAL POLICY

CREATION AND MAINTENANCE OF CONDITIONS UNDER WHICH MAN AND NATURE CAN EXIST IN PRODUCTIVE HARMONY.

(a) The Congress, recognizing the profound impact of man's activity on the interrelations of all components of the natural environment, particularly the profound influences of population growth, high-density urbanization, industrial expansion, resource exploitation, and new and expanding technological advances and recognizing further the critical importance of restoring and maintaining environmental quality to the overall welfare and development of man,

§4331

declares that it is the continuing policy of the Federal Government, in cooperation with State and local governments, and other concerned public and private organizations, to use all practicable means and measures, including financial and technical assistance, in a manner calculated to foster and promote the general welfare, to create and maintain conditions under which man and nature can exist in productive harmony, and fulfill the social, economic, and other requirements of present and future generations of Americans.

CONTINUING RESPONSIBILITY OF FEDERAL GOVERNMENT TO USE ALL PRACTICABLE MEANS TO IMPROVE AND COORDINATE FEDERAL PLANS, FUNCTIONS, PROGRAMS, AND RESOURCES.

(b) In order to carry out the policy set forth in this chapter, it is the continuing responsibility of the Federal Government to use all practicable means, consistent with other essential considerations of national policy, to improve and coordinate Federal plans, functions, programs, and resources to the end that the Nation may —

(1) fulfill the responsibilities of each generation as trustee of the environment for succeeding generations;

(2) assure for all Americans safe, healthful, productive, and esthetically and culturally pleasing surroundings;

(3) attain the widest range of beneficial uses of the environment without degradation, risk to health or safety, or other undesirable and unintended consequences;

(4) preserve important historic, cultural, and natural aspects of our national heritage, and maintain, wherever possible, an environment which supports diversity and variety of individual choice;

(5) achieve a balance between population and resource use which will permit high standards of living and a wide sharing of life's amenities; and

(6) enhance the quality of renewable resources and approach the maximum attainable recycling of depletable resources.

RESPONSIBILITY OF EACH PERSON TO CONTRIBUTE TO PRESERVATION AND ENHANCEMENT OF ENVIRONMENT.

(c) The Congress recognizes that each person should enjoy a healthful environment and that each person has a responsibility to contribute to the preservation and enhancement of the environment.

§4332. COOPERATION OF AGENCIES; REPORTS; AVAILABILITY OF INFORMATION; RECOMMENDATIONS; INTERNATIONAL AND NATIONAL COORDINATION OF EFFORTS

The Congress authorizes and directs that, to the fullest extent possible: (1) the policies, regulations, and public laws of the United States shall be interpreted

National Environmental Policy Act §4332

and administered in accordance with the policies set forth in this chapter, and (2) all agencies of the Federal Government shall —

(A) utilize a systematic, interdisciplinary approach which will insure the integrated use of the natural and social sciences and the environmental design arts in planning and in decisionmaking which may have an impact on man's environment;

(B) identify and develop methods and procedures, in consultation with the Council on Environmental Quality established by subchapter II of this chapter, which will insure that presently unquantified environmental amenities and values may be given appropriate consideration in decisionmaking along with economic and technical considerations;

(C) include in every recommendation or report on proposals for legislation and other major Federal actions significantly affecting the quality of the human environment, a detailed statement by the responsible official on —

(i) the environmental impact of the proposed action,

(ii) any adverse environmental effects which cannot be avoided should the proposal be implemented,

(iii) alternatives to the proposed action,

(iv) the relationship between local short-term uses of man's environment and the maintenance and enhancement of long-term productivity, and

(v) any irreversible and irretrievable commitments of resources which would be involved in the proposed action should it be implemented.

Prior to making any detailed statement, the responsible Federal official shall consult with and obtain the comments of any Federal agency which has jurisdiction by law or special expertise with respect to any environmental impact involved. Copies of such statement and the comments and views of the appropriate Federal, State, and local agencies, which are authorized to develop and enforce environmental standards, shall be made available to the President, the Council on Environmental Quality and to the public as provided by section 552 of Title 5, and shall accompany the proposal through the existing agency review processes;

(D) Any detailed statement required under subparagraph (C) after January 1, 1970, for any major Federal action funded under a program of grants to States shall not be deemed to be legally insufficient solely by reason of having been prepared by a State agency or official, if:

(i) the State agency or official has statewide jurisdiction and has the responsibility for such action,

(ii) the responsible Federal official furnishes guidance and participates in such preparation,

(iii) the responsible Federal official independently evaluates such statement prior to its approval and adoption, and

(iv) after January 1, 1976, the responsible Federal official provides early notification to, and solicits the views of, any other State or any Federal land management entity of any action or any alternative thereto which may have significant impacts upon such State or affected Federal land management entity and, if there is any disagreement on such impacts, prepares a written assessment of such impacts and views for incorporation into such detailed statement.

The procedures in this subparagraph shall not relieve the Federal official of his responsibilities for the scope, objectivity, and content of the entire statement or of any other responsibility under this chapter; and further, this subparagraph does not affect the legal sufficiency of statements prepared by State agencies with less than statewide jurisdiction.

(E) study, develop, and describe appropriate alternatives to recommended courses of action in any proposal which involves unresolved conflicts concerning alternative uses of available resources;

(F) recognize the worldwide and long-range character of environmental problems and, where consistent with the foreign policy of the United States, lend appropriate support to initiatives, resolutions, and programs designed to maximize international cooperation in anticipating and preventing a decline in the quality of mankind's world environment;

(G) make available to States, counties, municipalities, institutions, and individuals, advice and information useful in restoring, maintaining, and enhancing the quality of the environment;

(H) initiate and utilize ecological information in the planning and development of resource-oriented projects; and

(I) assist the Council on Environmental Quality established by subchapter II of this chapter.

§4334. OTHER STATUTORY OBLIGATIONS OF AGENCIES

Nothing in section 4332 or 4333 of this title shall in any way affect the specific statutory obligations of any Federal agency (1) to comply with criteria or standards of environmental quality, (2) to coordinate or consult with any other Federal or State agency, or (3) to act, or refrain from acting contingent upon the recommendations or certification of any other Federal or State agency.

§4335. EFFORTS SUPPLEMENTAL TO EXISTING AUTHORIZATIONS

The policies and goals set forth in this chapter are supplementary to those set forth in existing authorizations of Federal agencies.

National Environmental Policy Act §4343

Subchapter II — Council on Environmental Quality

§4341. Reports to Congress; Recommendations for Legislation

The President shall transmit to the Congress annually beginning July 1, 1970, an Environmental Quality Report (hereinafter referred to as the "report") which shall set forth (1) the status and condition of the major natural, manmade, or altered environmental classes of the Nation, including, but not limited to, the air, the aquatic, including marine, estuarine, and fresh water, and the terrestrial environment, including, but not limited to, the forest, dryland, wetland, range, urban, suburban, and rural environment; (2) current and foreseeable trends in the quality, management and utilization of such environments and the effects of those trends on the social, economic, and other requirements of the Nation; (3) the adequacy of available natural resources for fulfilling human and economic requirements of the Nation in the light of expected population pressures; (4) a review of the programs and activities (including regulatory activities) of the Federal Government, the State and local governments, and nongovernmental entities or individuals, with particular reference to their effect on the environment and on the conservation, development and utilization of natural resources; and (5) a program for remedying the deficiencies of existing programs and activities, together with recommendations for legislation.

§4342. Establishment; Membership; Chairman; Appointments

There is created in the Executive Office of the President a Council on Environmental Quality (hereinafter referred to as the "Council"). The Council shall be composed of three members who shall be appointed by the President to serve at his pleasure, by and with the advice and consent of the Senate. The President shall designate one of the members of the Council to serve as Chairman. Each member shall be a person who, as a result of his training, experience, and attainments, is exceptionally well qualified to analyze and interpret environmental trends and information of all kinds; to appraise programs and activities of the Federal Government in the light of the policy set forth in subchapter I of this chapter; to be conscious of and responsive to the scientific, economic, social, esthetic, and cultural needs and interests of the Nation; and to formulate and recommend national policies to promote the improvement of the quality of the environment.

§4343. Employment of Personnel, Experts, and Consultants

(a) The Council may employ such officers and employees as may be necessary to carry out its functions under this chapter. In addition, the Council may employ and fix the compensation of such experts and consultants as may be necessary for the carrying out of its functions under this chapter, in accordance with section 3109 of Title 5 (but without regard to the last sentence thereof).

(b) Notwithstanding section 665(b) of Title 31, the Council may accept and employ voluntary and uncompensated services in furtherance of the purposes of the Council.

§4344. DUTIES AND FUNCTIONS

It shall be the duty and function of the Council —
(1) to assist and advise the President in the preparation of the Environmental Quality Report required by section 4341 of this title;
(2) to gather timely and authoritative information concerning the conditions and trends in the quality of the environment both current and prospective, to analyze and interpret such information for the purpose of determining whether such conditions and trends are interfering, or are likely to interfere, with the achievement of the policy set forth in subchapter I of this chapter, and to compile and submit to the President studies relating to such conditions and trends;
(3) to review and appraise the various programs and activities of the Federal Government in the light of the policy set forth in subchapter I of this chapter for the purpose of determining the extent to which such programs and activities are contributing to the achievement of such policy, and to make recommendations to the President with respect thereto;
(4) to develop and recommend to the President national policies to foster and promote the improvement of environmental quality to meet the conservation, social, economic, health, and other requirements and goals of the Nation;
(5) to conduct investigations, studies, surveys, research, and analyses relating to ecological systems and environmental quality;
(6) to document and define changes in the natural environment, including the plant and animal systems, and to accumulate necessary data and other information for a continuing analysis of these changes or trends and an interpretation of their underlying causes;
(7) to report at least once each year to the President on the state and condition of the environment; and
(8) to make and furnish such studies, reports thereon, and recommendations with respect to matters of policy and legislation as the President may request.

Part II

SUPPLEMENTARY CASES AND NOTES

II

AN INTRODUCTION TO THE ADMINISTRATIVE LAW OF ENVIRONMENT PROTECTION

A. ACCESS TO THE COURTS: STANDING AND RELATED PRECLUSION DOCTRINES

Page 107.   Before the Note, Add the Following:

LUJAN v. NATIONAL WILDLIFE FEDERATION
— U.S. — , 110 S. Ct. 3177 (1990)

Justice SCALIA delivered the opinion of the Court.

In this case we must decide whether respondent, the National Wildlife Federation (hereinafter respondent), is a proper party to challenge actions of the Federal Government relating to certain public lands.

I

Respondent filed this action in 1985 in the United States District Court for the District of Columbia against petitioners the United States Department of the Interior, the Secretary of the Interior, and the Director of the Bureau of Land Management (BLM), an agency within the Department. In its amended complaint, respondent alleged that petitioners had violated the Federal Land Policy and Management Act of 1976 (FLPMA), 90 Stat. 2744, 43 U.S.C. §1701 et seq. (1982 ed.), the National Environmental Policy Act of 1969 (NEPA), 83 Stat. 852, 42 U.S.C. §4321 et seq., and §10(e) of the Administrative Procedure Act (APA), 5 U.S.C. §706, in the course of administering what the complaint called the "land withdrawal review program" of the BLM. Some background information concerning that program is necessary to an understanding of this dispute.

In various enactments, Congress empowered United States citizens to acquire title to, and rights in, vast portions of federally owned land. See, e.g., Rev. Stat. §2319, 30 U.S.C. §22 et seq. (Mining Law of 1872); 41 Stat. 437, as amended, 30 U.S.C. §181 et seq. (Mineral Lands Leasing Act of 1920). Congress also provided means, however, for the Executive to remove public lands from the operation of these statutes. The Pickett Act, 36 Stat. 847, 43 U.S.C. §141 (1970 ed.), repealed, 90 Stat. 2792 (1976), authorized the President "at any time in his discretion, temporarily [to] withdraw from settlement, location, sale, or entry any of the public lands of the United States, . . . and reserve the same for waterpower sites, irrigation, classification of lands, or other public purposes. . . ." Acting under this and under the Taylor Grazing Act of 1934, ch. 865, 48 Stat. 1269, as amended, 43 U.S.C. §315f, which gave the Secretary of the Interior authority to "classify" public lands as suitable for either disposal or federal retention and management, President Franklin Roosevelt withdrew all unreserved public land from disposal until such time as they were classified. Exec. Order No. 6910, Nov. 26, 1934; Exec. Order No. 6964, Feb. 5, 1935. In 1936, Congress amended §7 of the Taylor Grazing Act to authorize the Secretary of the Interior "to examine and classify any lands" withdrawn by these orders and by other authority as "more valuable or suitable" for other uses "and to open such lands to entry, selection, or location for disposal in accordance with such classification under applicable public-land laws." 49 Stat. 1976, 43 U.S.C. §315f. The amendment also directed that "[s]uch lands shall not be subject to disposition, settlement, or occupation until after the same have been classified and opened to entry." Ibid. The 1964 Classification and Multiple Use Act, 78 Stat. 986-988, 43 U.S.C. §§1411-1418 (1970 ed.) (expired 1970), gave the Secretary further authority to classify lands for the purpose of either disposal or retention by the Federal Government.

Management of the public lands under these various laws became chaotic. The Public Land Law Review Commission, established by Congress in 1964 to study the matter, 78 Stat. 982, determined in 1970 that "virtually all" of the country's public domain, see Public Land Law Review Commission, One Third of the Nation's Land 52 (1970) — about one-third of the land within the United States, see id., at 19 — had been withdrawn or classified for retention; that it was difficult to determine "the extent of existing Executive withdrawals and the degree to which withdrawals overlap each other," id., at 52; and that there were inadequate records to show the purposes of withdrawals and the permissible public uses. Ibid. Accordingly, it recommended that "Congress should provide for a careful review of (1) all Executive withdrawals and reservations, and (2) BLM retention and disposal classifications under the Classification and Multiple Use Act of 1964." Ibid.

In 1976, Congress passed the FLPMA, which repealed many of the miscellaneous laws governing disposal of public land, 43 U.S.C. §1701 et seq. (1982 ed.), and established a policy in favor of retaining public lands for multiple use management. It directed the Secretary to "prepare and maintain on a continuing basis an inventory of all public lands and their resource and other values," 43 U.S.C. §1711(a) (1982 ed.), required land use planning for public

II. Introduction to Administrative Law　　　　　　　　　　　　　Page 107

lands, and established criteria to be used for that purpose, §1712. It provided that existing classifications of public lands were subject to review in the land use planning process, and that the Secretary could "modify or terminate any such classification consistent with such land use plans." §1712(d). It also authorized the Secretary to "make, modify, extend or revoke" withdrawals. §1714(a). Finally it directed the Secretary, within 15 years, to review withdrawals in existence in 1976 in 11 western States, §1714(l)(1), and to "determine whether, and for how long, the continuation of the existing withdrawal of the lands would be, in his judgment, consistent with the statutory objectives of the programs for which the lands were dedicated and of the other relevant programs," §1714(l)(2). The activities undertaken by the BLM to comply with these various provisions constitute what respondent's amended complaint styles the BLM's "land withdrawal review program," which is the subject of the current litigation.

Pursuant to the directives of the FLPMA, the petitioners engage in a number of different types of administrative action with respect to the various tracts of public land within the United States. First, the BLM conducts the review and recommends the determinations required by 43 U.S.C. §1714(l) with respect to withdrawals in 11 western States. The law requires the Secretary to "report his recommendations to the President, together with statements of concurrence or nonconcurrence submitted by the heads of the departments or agencies which administer the lands"; the President must in turn submit this report to the Congress, together with his recommendation "for action by the Secretary, or for legislation." 43 U.S.C. §1714(l)(2) (1982 ed.). The Secretary has submitted a number of reports to the President in accordance with this provision.

Second, the Secretary revokes some withdrawals under §204(a) of the Act, which the Office of the Solicitor has interpreted to give the Secretary the power to process proposals for revocation of withdrawals made during the "ordinary course of business." U.S. Dept. of the Interior, Memorandum from the Office of the Solicitor, Oct. 30, 1980. These revocations are initiated in one of three manners: An agency or department holding a portion of withdrawn land that it no longer needs may file a notice of intention to relinquish the lands with the BLM. Any member of the public may file a petition requesting revocation. And in the case of lands held by the BLM, the BLM itself may initiate the revocation proposal. App. 56-57. Withdrawal revocations may be made for several reasons. Some are effected in order to permit sale of the land; some for record-clearing purposes, where the withdrawal designation has been superseded by congressional action or overlaps with another withdrawal designation; some in order to restore the land to multiple use management pursuant to §102(a)(7) of the FLPMA, 43 U.S.C §1701(a)(7) (1982 ed.). App. 142-145.

Third, the Secretary engages in the ongoing process of classifying public lands, either for multiple-use management, 43 CFR Part 2420 (1988), for disposal, 43 CFR Part 2430 (1988), or for other uses. Classification decisions may be initiated by petition, 43 CFR Part 2450 (1988), or by the BLM itself, 43 CFR Part 2460 (1988). Regulations promulgated by the Secretary prescribe the procedures to be followed in the case of each type of classification determination.

II

In its complaint, respondent averred generally that the reclassification of some withdrawn lands and the return of others to the public domain would open the lands up to mining activities, thereby destroying their natural beauty. Respondent alleged that petitioners, in the course of administering the Nation's public lands, had violated the FLPMA by failing to "develop, maintain, and, when appropriate, revise land use plans which provide by tracts or areas for the use of the public lands," 43 U.S.C. §1712(a) (1982 ed.); failing to submit recommendations as to withdrawals in the 11 western States to the President, §1714(*l*); failing to consider multiple uses for the disputed lands, §1732(a), focusing inordinately on such uses as mineral exploitation and development; and failing to provide public notice of decisions, §§1701(a)(5), 1712(c)(9), 1712(f), and 1739(e). Respondent also claimed that petitioners had violated NEPA, which requires federal agencies to "include in every recommendation or report on . . . major Federal actions significantly affecting the quality of the human environment, a detailed statement by the responsible official on . . . the environmental impact of the proposed action." 42 U.S.C. §4332(2)(C). Finally, respondent alleged that all of the above actions were "arbitrary, capricious, an abuse of discretion, or otherwise not in accordance with law," and should therefore be set aside pursuant to §10(e) of the APA, 5 U.S.C. §706. Appended to the amended complaint was a schedule of specific land status determinations, which the complaint stated had been "taken by defendants since January 1, 1981"; each was identified by a listing in the Federal Register.

In December 1985, the District Court granted respondent's motion for a preliminary injunction prohibiting petitioners from "[m]odifying, terminating or altering any withdrawal, classification, or other designation governing the protection of lands in the public domain that was in effect on January 1, 1981," and from "[t]aking any action inconsistent" with any such withdrawal, classification, or designation. App. to Pet. for Cert. 185a. In a subsequent order, the court denied petitioners' motion under Rule 12(b) of the Federal Rules of Civil Procedure to dismiss the complaint for failure to demonstrate standing to challenge petitioners' actions under the APA, 5 U.S.C. §702. App. to Pet. for Cert. 183a. The Court of Appeals affirmed both orders. National Wildlife Federation v. Burford, 835 F.2d 305 (1987). As to the motion to dismiss, the Court of Appeals found sufficient to survive the motion the general allegation in the amended complaint that respondent's members used environmental resources that would be damaged by petitioners' actions. See at 835 F.2d, at 312. It held that this allegation, fairly read along with the balance of the complaint, both identified particular land-status actions that respondent sought to challenge — since at least some of the actions complained of were listed in the complaint's appendix of Federal Register references — and asserted harm to respondent's members attributable to those particular actions. 835 F.2d, at 313. To support the latter point, the Court of Appeals pointed to the affidavits of two of respondent's members, Peggy Kay Peterson and Richard Erman, which claimed use of land "in

616

II. Introduction to Administrative Law   Page 107

the vicinity" of the land covered by two of the listed actions. Thus, the Court of Appeals concluded, there was "concrete indication that [respondent's] members use specific lands covered by the agency's Program and will be adversely affected by the agency's actions," and the complaint was "sufficiently specific for purposes of a motion to dismiss." Ibid. On petitions for rehearing, the Court of Appeals stood by its denial of the motion to dismiss and directed the parties and the District Court "to proceed with this litigation with dispatch.", National Wildlife Federation v. Burford, 844 F.2d 889, 890 (1988).

Back before the District Court, petitioners again claimed, this time by means of a motion for summary judgment under Rule 56 of the Federal Rules of Civil Procedure (which motion had been outstanding during the proceedings before the Court of Appeals), that respondent had no standing to seek judicial review of petitioners' actions under the APA. After argument on this motion, and in purported response to the court's postargument request for additional briefing, respondent submitted four additional member affidavits pertaining to the issue of standing. The District Court rejected them as untimely, vacated the injunction and granted the Rule 56 motion to dismiss. It noted that neither its earlier decision nor the Court of Appeals' affirmance controlled the question, since both pertained to a motion under Rule 12(b). It found the Peterson and Erman affidavits insufficient to withstand the Rule 56 motion, even as to judicial review of the particular classification decisions to which they pertained. And even if they had been adequate for that limited purpose, the court said, they could not support respondent's attempted APA challenge to "each of the 1250 or so individual classification terminations and withdrawal revocations" effected under the land withdrawal review program. National Wildlife Federation v. Burford, 699 F. Supp. 327, 332 (DC 1988).

This time the Court of Appeals reversed. National Wildlife Federation v. Burford, 278 U.S. App. D.C. 320, 878 F.2d 422 (1989). It both found the Peterson and Erman affidavits sufficient in themselves, and held that it was an abuse of discretion not to consider the four additional affidavits as well. The Court of Appeals also concluded that standing to challenge individual classification and withdrawal decisions conferred standing to challenge all such decisions under the land withdrawal review program. We granted certiorari. 493 U.S. — (1990).

III

A

We first address respondent's claim that the Peterson and Erman affidavits alone suffice to establish respondent's right to judicial review of petitioners' actions. Respondent does not contend that either the FLPMA or NEPA provides a private right of action for violations of its provisions. Rather, respondent claims a right to judicial review under §10(a) of the APA, which provides:

617

Page 107   II. Introduction to Administrative Law

> A person suffering legal wrong because of agency action, or adversely affected or aggrieved by agency action within the meaning of a relevant statute, is entitled to judicial review thereof.

5 U.S.C. §702. This provision contains two separate requirements. First, the person claiming a right to sue must identify some "agency action" that affects him in the specified fashion; it is judicial review "thereof" to which he is entitled. The meaning of "agency action" for purposes of §702 is set forth in 5 U.S.C. §551(13), see 5 U.S.C. §701(b)(2) ("For the purpose of this chapter . . . 'agency action' ha[s] the meanin[g] given . . . by section 551 of this title"), which defines the term as "the whole or a part of an agency rule, order, license, sanction, relief, or the equivalent or denial thereof, or failure to act," 5 U.S.C. §551(13). When, as here, review is sought not pursuant to specific authorization in the substantive statute, but only under the general review provisions of the APA, the "agency action" in question must be "final agency action." See 5 U.S.C. §704 ("Agency action made reviewable by statute and *final* agency action for which there is no other adequate remedy in a court are subject to judicial review" (emphasis added).)

Second, the party seeking review under §702 must show that he has "suffer[ed] legal wrong" because of the challenged agency action, or is "adversely affected or aggrieved" by that action "within the meaning of a relevant statute." Respondent does not assert that it has suffered "legal wrong," so we need only discuss the meaning of "adversely affected or aggrieved . . . within the meaning of a relevant statute." As an original matter, it might be thought that one cannot be "adversely affected or aggrieved *within the meaning*" of a statute unless the statute in question uses those terms (or terms like them) — as some pre-APA statutes in fact did when conferring rights of judicial review. See, e.g., Federal Communications Act of 1934, §402(b)(2), 48 Stat. 1093, as amended, 47 U.S.C. §402(b)(6) (1982 ed.). We have long since rejected that interpretation, however, which would have made the judicial review provision of the APA no more than a restatement of pre-existing law. Rather, we have said that to be "adversely affected or aggrieved . . . within the meaning" of a statute, the plaintiff must establish that the injury he complains of (*his* aggrievement, or the adverse effect *upon him*) falls within the "zone of interests" sought to be protected by the statutory provision whose violation forms the legal basis for his complaint. See Clarke v. Securities Industry Assn., 479 U.S. 388, 396-397 (1987). Thus, for example, the failure of an agency to comply with a statutory provision requiring "on the record" hearings would assuredly have an adverse effect upon the company that has the contract to record and transcribe the agency's proceedings; but since the provision was obviously enacted to protect the interests of the parties of the proceedings and not those of the reporters, that company would not be "adversely affected within the meaning" of the statute.

618

B

Because this case comes to us on petitioners' motion for summary judgment, we must assess the record under the standard set forth in Rule 56 of the Federal Rules of Civil Procedure. . . .

. . . Rule 56 does not require the moving party to *negate* the elements of the nonmoving party's case; to the contrary, "regardless of whether the moving party accompanies its summary judgment motion with affidavits, the motion may, and should, be granted so long as whatever is before the District Court demonstrates that the standard for the entry of summary judgment, as set forth in Rule 56(c), is satisfied."

C

We turn, then, to whether the specific facts alleged in the two affidavits considered by the District Court raised a genuine issue of fact as to whether an "agency action" taken by petitioners caused respondent to be "adversely affected or aggrieved . . . within the meaning of a relevant statute." We assume, since it has been uncontested, that the allegedly affected interests set forth in the affidavits — "recreational use and aesthetic enjoyment" — are sufficiently related to the purposes of respondent association that respondent meets the requirements of §702 if any of its members do. Hunt v. Washington State Apple Advertising Comm'n, 432 U.S. 333 (1977).

As for the "agency action" requirement, we think that each of the affidavits can be read, as the Court of Appeals believed, to complain of a particular "agency action" as that term is defined in §551. The parties agree that the Peterson affidavit, judging from the geographic area it describes, must refer to that one of the BLM orders listed in the appendix to the complaint that appears at 49 Fed. Reg. 19904-19905 (1984), an order captioned W-6228 and dated April 30, 1984, terminating the withdrawal classification of some 4500 acres of land in that area. See, e.g., Brief for Petitioners 8-10. The parties also appear to agree, on the basis of similar deduction, that the Erman affidavit refers to the BLM order listed in the appendix that appears at 47 Fed. Reg. 7232-7233 (1982), an order captioned Public Land Order 6156 and dated February 18, 1982.

We also think that whatever "adverse effect" or "aggrievement" is established by the affidavits was "within the meaning of the relevant statute" — i.e., met the "zone of interests" test. The relevant statute, of course, is the statute whose violation is the gravamen of the complaint — both the FLPMA and NEPA. We have no doubt that "recreational use and aesthetic enjoyment" are among the *sorts* of interest those statutes were specifically designed to protect. The only issue, then, is whether the facts alleged in the affidavits showed that those interests *of Peterson and Erman* were actually affected.

The Peterson affidavit averred:

> My recreational use and aesthetic enjoyment of federal lands, particularly those in the vicinity of South Pass–Green Mountain, Wyoming have been and continue to

619

be adversely affected in fact by the unlawful actions of the Bureau and the Department. In particular, the South Pass–Green Mountain area of Wyoming has been opened to the staking of mining claims and oil and gas leasing, an action which threatens the aesthetic beauty and wildlife habitat potential of these lands.

App. to Pet. for Cert. 191a. Erman's affidavit was substantially the same as Peterson's, with respect to all except the area involved; he claimed use of land "in the vicinity of Grand Canyon National Park, the Arizona Strip (Kanab Plateau), and the Kaibab National Forest." Id., at 187a.

The District Court found the Peterson affidavit inadequate for the following reasons:

> Peterson . . . claims that she uses federal lands *in the vicinity* of the South Pass–Green Mountain area of Wyoming for recreational purposes and for aesthetic enjoyment and that her recreational and aesthetic enjoyment has been and continues to be adversely affected as a result of the decision of BLM to open it to the staking of mining claims and oil and gas leasing. . . . This decision [W-6228] opened up to mining approximately 4500 acres within a two million acre area, the balance of which, with the exception of 2000 acres, has always been open to mineral leasing and mining. . . . There is no showing that Peterson's recreational use and enjoyment extends to the particular 4500 acres covered by the decision to terminate classification to the remainder of the two million acres affected by the termination. All she claims is that she uses lands "in the vicinity." The affidavit on its face contains only a bare allegation of injury, and fails to show specific facts supporting the affiant's allegation.

699 F. Supp., at 331 (emphasis in original).

The District Court found the Erman affidavit "similarly flawed."

> The magnitude of Erman's claimed injury stretches the imagination. . . . [T]he Arizona Strip consists of all lands in Arizona north and west of the Colorado River on approximately 5.5 million acres, an area one-eighth the size of the State of Arizona. Furthermore, virtually the entire Strip is and for many years has been open to uranium and other metalliferous mining. The revocation of withdrawal [in Public Land Order 6156] concerned only non-metalliferous mining in the western one-third of the Arizona Strip, an area possessing no potential for non-metalliferous mining.

Id., at 332.

The Court of Appeals disagreed with the District Court's assessment as to the Peterson affidavit (and thus found it unnecessary to consider the Erman affidavit) for the following reason:

> If Peterson was not referring to lands in this 4500-acre affected area, her allegation of impairment to her use and enjoyment would be meaningless, or perjurious. . . . [T]he trial court overlooks the fact that unless Peterson's language is read to refer to the lands affected by the Program, the affidavit is, at best, a meaningless document.
>
> At a minimum, Peterson's affidavit is ambiguous regarding whether the adversely affected lands are the ones she uses. When presented with ambiguity on a

620

II. Introduction to Administrative Law   Page 107

> motion for summary judgment, a District Court must resolve any factual issues of controversy in favor of the nonmoving party. . . . This means that the District Court was obliged to resolve any factual ambiguity in favor of NWF, and would have had to assume, for the purposes of summary judgment, that Peterson used the 4500 affected acres.

878 F.2d, at 431.

That is not the law. In ruling upon a Rule 56 motion, "a District Court must resolve any factual issues of controversy in favor of the non-moving party" only in the sense that, where the facts specifically averred by that party contradict facts specifically averred by the movant, the motion must be denied. That is a world apart from "assuming" that general averments embrace the "specific facts" needed to sustain the complaint. As set forth above, Rule 56(e) provides that judgment "shall be entered" against the nonmoving party unless affidavits or other evidence "set forth specific facts showing that there is a genuine issue for trial." The object of this provision is not to replace conclusory allegations of the complaint or answer with conclusory allegations of an affidavit. Cf. Anderson v. Liberty Lobby, Inc., 477 U.S. 242, 249 (1986) ("[T]he plaintiff could not rest on his allegations of a conspiracy to get to a jury without 'any significant probative evidence tending to support the complaint'"), quoting First National Bank of Arizona v. Cities Service Co., 391 U.S. 253, 290 2d (1968). Rather, the purpose of Rule 56 is to enable a party who believes there is no genuine dispute as to a specific fact essential to the other side's case to demand at least one sworn averment of that fact before the lengthy process of litigation continues.

At the margins there is some room for debate as to how "specific" must be the "specific facts" that Rule 56(e) requires in a particular case. But where the fact in question is the one put in issue by the §702 challenge here — whether one of respondent's members has been, or is threatened to be, "adversely affected or aggrieved" by Government action — Rule 56(e) is assuredly not satisfied by averments which state only that one of respondent's members uses unspecified portions of an immense tract of territory, on some portions of which mining activity has occurred or probably will occur by virtue of the governmental action. It will not do to "presume" the missing facts because without them the affidavits would not establish the injury that they generally allege. That converts the operation of Rule 56 to a circular promenade: plaintiff's complaint makes general allegation of injury; defendant contests through Rule 56 existence of specific facts to support injury; plaintiff responds with affidavit containing general allegation of injury, which must be deemed to constitute averment of requisite specific facts since otherwise allegation of injury would be unsupported (which is precisely what defendant claims it is).

Respondent places great reliance, as did the Court of Appeals, upon our decision in United States v. Students Challenging Regulatory Agency Procedures (SCRAP), 412 U.S. 669 (1973). The SCRAP opinion, whose expansive expression of what would suffice for §702 review under its particular facts has never since been emulated by this Court, is of no relevance here, since it involved not a Rule 56 motion for summary judgment but a Rule 12(b) motion to dismiss on

621

the pleadings. The latter, unlike the former, presumes that general allegations embrace those specific facts that are necessary to support the claim. Conley v. Gibson, 355 U.S. 41 2 (1957).

IV

We turn next to the Court of Appeals' alternative holding that the four additional member affidavits proffered by respondent in response to the District Court's briefing order established its right to §702 review of agency action.

A

It is impossible that the affidavits would suffice, as the Court of Appeals held, to enable respondent to challenge the entirety of petitioners' so-called "land withdrawal review program." That is not an "agency action" within the meaning of §702, much less a "final agency action" within the meaning of §704. The term "land withdrawal review program" (which as far as we know is not derived from any authoritative text) does not refer to a single BLM order or regulation, or even to a completed universe of particular BLM orders and regulations. It is simply the name by which petitioners have occasionally referred to the continuing (and thus constantly changing) operations of the BLM in reviewing withdrawal revocation applications and the classifications of public lands and developing land use plans as required by the FLPMA. It is no more an identifiable "agency action" — much less a "final agency action" — than a "weapons procurement program" of the Department of Defense or a "drug interdiction program" of the Drug Enforcement Administration. As the District Court explained, the "land withdrawal review program" extends to, currently at least, "1250 or so individual classification terminations and withdrawal revocations." 699 F. Supp., at 332.

Respondent alleges that violation of the law is rampant within this program — failure to revise land use plans in proper fashion, failure to submit certain recommendations to Congress, failure to consider multiple use, inordinate focus upon mineral exploitation, failure to provide required public notice, failure to provide adequate environmental impact statements. Perhaps so. But respondent cannot seek *wholesale* improvement of this program by court decree, rather than in the offices of the Department or the halls of Congress, where programmatic improvements are normally made. Under the terms of the APA, respondent must direct its attack against some particular "agency action" that causes it harm. Some statutes permit broad regulations to serve as the "agency action," and thus to be the object of judicial review directly, even before the concrete effects normally required for APA review are felt. Absent such a provision, however, a regulation is not ordinarily considered the type of agency action "ripe" for judicial review under the APA until the scope of the controversy has been reduced to more manageable proportions, and its factual components fleshed out, by some concrete action applying the regulation to the claimant's situation in a fashion that harms or threatens to harm him. (The major exception, of course, is a substantive rule which as a practical matter requires the plaintiff to adjust his conduct immediately. Such agency action is "ripe" for review at once, whether or not explicit statutory review apart from the APA is provided. See Abbott Laboratories v. Gardner, 387 U.S. 136, 152-154 (1967); Gardner v. Toilet Goods Assn., Inc., 387 U.S. 167, 171-173, (1967). Cf. Toilet Goods Assn., Inc. v. Gardner, 387 U.S. 158, 164-166, (1967).)

In the present case, the individual actions of the BLM identified in the six affidavits can be regarded as rules of general applicability (a "rule" is defined in the APA as agency action of "general or particular applicability *and future effect*," 5 U.S.C. §551(4) (emphasis added)) announcing, with respect to vast expanses of territory that they cover, the agency's intent to grant requisite permission for certain activities, to decline to interfere with other activities, and to take other particular action if requested. It may well be, then, that even those individual actions will not be ripe for challenge until some further agency action or inaction more immediately harming the plaintiff occurs. But it is at least entirely certain that the flaws in the entire "program" — consisting principally of the many individual actions referenced in the complaint, and presumably actions yet to be taken as well — cannot be laid before the courts for wholesale correction under the APA, simply because one of them that is ripe for review adversely affects one of respondent's members.

The case-by-case approach that this requires is understandably frustrating to an organization such as respondent, which has as its objective across-the-board protection of our Nation's wildlife and the streams and forests that support it. But this is the traditional, and remains the normal, mode of operation of the courts. Except where Congress explicitly provides for our correction of the administrative process at a higher level of generality, we intervene in the administration of the laws only when, and to the extent that, a specific "final agency action" has an actual or immediately threatened effect. *Toilet Goods Assn.*, 387 U.S., at 164-166. Such an intervention may ultimately have the effect of requiring a regulation, a series of regulations, or even a whole "program" to be revised by the agency in order to avoid the unlawful result that the court discerns. But it is assuredly not as swift or as immediately far-reaching a corrective process as those interested in systemic improvement would desire. Until confided to us, however, more sweeping actions are for the other Branches.

B

The Court of Appeals' reliance upon the supplemental affidavits was wrong for a second reason: the District Court did not abuse its discretion in declining to admit them. Petitions filed their motion for summary judgment in September 1986; respondent filed an opposition but did not submit any new evidentiary materials at that time. On June 27, 1988, after the case had made its way for the first time through the Court of Appeals, the District Court announced that it would hold a hearing on July 22 on "the outstanding motions for summary judgment," which included petitioners' motion challenging respondent's §702 standing. The hearing was held and, as noted earlier, the District Court issued an order directing respondent to file "a supplemental memorandum regarding the issue of its standing to proceed." Record, Doc. No. 274. Although that plainly did not call for the submission of new evidentiary materials, it was in purported response to this order, on August 22, 1988, that respondent submitted (along with the requested legal memorandum) the additional affidavits. The only explanation for the submission (if it can be called an explanation) was contained in a footnote to the memorandum, which simply stated that "NWF now has submitted declarations on behalf of other members of NWF who have been injured by the challenged actions of federal defendants." Record, Doc. No. 278, p.18, n.21. In its November 4, 1988 ruling granting petitioners' motion, the District Court rejected the additional affidavits as "untimely and in violation of [the court's briefing] Order." 699 F. Supp., at 328, n. 3.

Respondent's evidentiary submission was indeed untimely, both under Rule 56, which requires affidavits in opposition to a summary judgment motion to be served "prior to the day of the hearing," Fed. R. Civ. P. 56(c), and under Rule 6(d), which states more generally that "[w]hen a motion is supported by affidavit, . . . opposing affidavits may be served not later than 1 day before the hearing, unless the court permits them to be served at some other time." Rule 6(b) sets out the proper approach in the case of late filings:

> When by these rules or by a notice given thereunder or by order of court an act is required or allowed to be done at or within a specified time, the court for cause shown may at any time in its discretion (1) with or without motion or notice order the period enlarged if request therefor is made before the expiration of the period originally prescribed or as extended by a previous order, or (2) upon motion made after the expiration of the specified period permit the act to be done where the failure to act was the result of excusable neglect. . . .

This provision not only specifically confers the "discretion" relevant to the present issue, but also provides the mechanism by which that discretion is to be invoked and exercised. First, any extension of a time limitation must be "for cause shown." Second, although extensions before expiration of the time period may be "with or without motion or notice," any *post*-deadline extension must be "upon motion made," and is permissible only where the failure to meet the deadline "was the result of excusable neglect." Thus, in order to receive the affidavits here, the District Court would have had to regard the very filing of the late document as the "motion made" to file it; it would have had to interpret "cause shown" to mean merely "cause," since respondent made no "showing" of cause at all; and finally, it would have had to find as a substantive matter that there was indeed "cause" for the late filing, and that the failure to file on time "was the result of excusable neglect."

This last substantive obstacle is the greatest of all. The Court of Appeals presumably thought it was overcome because "the papers on which the trial court relied were two years old by the time it requested supplemental memoranda" and because "there was no indication prior to the trial court's request that [respondent] should have doubted the adequacy of the affidavits it had already submitted." 878 F.2d, at 433. We do not understand the relevance of the first point; the passage of so long a time as two years suggests, if anything, that respondent had more than the usual amount of time to prepare its response to the motion, and was more than moderately remiss in waiting until after the last moment. As to the suggestion of unfair surprise: a litigant is never justified in assuming that the court has made up its mind until the court expresses itself to that effect, and a litigant's failure to buttress its position because of confidence in the strength of that position is always indulged at the litigant's own risk. In any case, whatever erroneous expectations respondent may have had were surely dispelled by the District Court's order in June 1988 announcing that the hearing on petitioners' motion would be held one month later. At least when that order issued, respondent was on notice that its right to sue was at issue, and that (absent proper motion) the time for filing any additional evidentiary materials was, at the latest, the day before the hearing.

Perhaps it is true that the District Court could have overcome all the obstacles we have described — apparent lack of a motion, of a showing, and of excusable neglect — to admit the affidavits at issue here. But the proposition that it was *compelled* to receive them — that it was an abuse of discretion to *reject* them — cannot be accepted.

V

Respondent's final argument is that we should remand this case for the Court of Appeals to decide whether respondent may seek §702 review of petitioners' actions in its own right, rather than derivatively through its members. Specifically, it points to allegations in the amended complaint that petitioners unlawfully failed to publish regulations, to invite public participation, and to prepare an environmental impact statement with respect to the "land withdrawal review program" as a whole. In order to show that it is a "person . . . adversely affected or aggrieved" by these failures, it submitted to the District Court a brief affidavit (two pages in the record) by one of its vice-presidents, Lynn A. Greenwalt, who stated that respondent's mission is to "inform its members and the general public about conservation issues," and to advocate improvements in laws and administrative practices "pertaining to the protection and enhancement of federal lands," Pet. App. 193a-194a; and that its ability to perform this mission has been impaired by the petitioners' failure "to provide adequate information and opportunities for public participation with respect to the Land Withdrawal Review Program." Id., at 194a. The District Court found this affidavit insufficient to establish respondent's right to seek judicial review, since it was "conclusory and completely devoid of specific facts." 699 F. Supp., at 330. The Court of Appeals, having reversed the District Court on the grounds discussed above, did not address the issue.

We agree with the District Court's disposition. Even assuming that the

625

affidavit set forth "specific facts." Fed. R. Civ. P. 56(e), adequate to show injury to respondent through the deprivation of information; and even assuming that providing information to organizations such as respondent was one of the objectives of the statutes allegedly violated, so that respondent is "aggrieved within the meaning" of those statutes; nonetheless, the Greenwalt affidavit fails to identify any particular "agency action" that was the source of these injuries. The only sentences addressed to that point are as follows:

> "NWF's ability to meet these obligations to its members has been significantly impaired by the failure of the Bureau of Land Management and the Department of the Interior to provide adequate information and opportunities for public participation with respect to the Land Withdrawal Review Program. These interests of NWF have been injured by the actions of the Bureau and the Department and would be irreparably harmed by the continued failure to provide meaningful opportunities for public input and access to information regarding the Land Withdrawal Review Program."

App. to Pet. for Cert. 194a. As is evident, this is even more deficient than the Peterson and Erman affidavits, which contained geographical descriptions whereby at least an action as general as a particular classification decision could be identified as the source of the grievance. As we discussed earlier, the "Land Withdrawal Review Program" is not an identifiable action or event. With regard to alleged deficiencies in providing information and permitting public participation, as with regard to the other illegalities alleged in the complaint, respondent cannot demand a general judicial review of the BLM's day-to-day operations. The Greenwalt affidavit, like the others, does not set forth the specific facts necessary to survive a Rule 56 motion.

For the foregoing reasons, the judgment of the Court of Appeals is reversed.

It is so ordered.

Justice BLACKMUN, with whom Justice BRENNAN, Justice MARSHALL, and Justice STEVENS join, dissenting.

In my view, the affidavits of Peggy Kay Peterson and Richard Loren Erman, in conjunction with other record evidence before the District Court on the motions for summary judgment, were sufficient to establish the standing of the National Wildlife Federation (Federation or NWF) to bring this suit. I also conclude that the District Court abused its discretion by refusing to consider supplemental affidavits filed after the hearing on the parties' cross-motions for summary judgment. I therefore would affirm the judgment of the Court of Appeals.

I

The Federation's asserted injury in this case rested upon its claim that the Government actions challenged here would lead to increased mining on public lands; that the mining would result in damage to the environment; and that the recreational opportunities of NWF's members would consequently be diminished. Abundant record evidence supported the Federation's assertion that on lands newly opened for mining, mining in fact would occur. Similarly, the record furnishes ample support for NWF's contention that mining activities can be expected to cause severe environmental damage to the affected lands. The District Court held, however, that the Federation had not adequately identified particular members who were harmed by the consequences of the Government's actions. Although two of NWF's members expressly averred that their recreational activities had been impaired, the District Court concluded that these affiants had not identified with sufficient precision the particular sites on which their injuries occurred. The majority, like the District Court, holds that the averments of Peterson and Erman were insufficiently specific to withstand a motion for summary judgment. Although these affidavits were not models of precision, I believe that they were adequate at least to create a genuine issue of fact as to the organization's injury. . . .

III

PROTECTING THE AIR RESOURCE

C. THE CLEAN AIR ACT TODAY

Page 171. After the first paragraph, add the following:

NOTE ON THE CLEAN AIR ACT AMENDMENTS OF 1990

Congress amended the Clean Air Act late in 1990. Notes prepared for this supplement explain the changes the amendments made and how they affect the program required by the Act prior to 1990. When you review the 1990 amendments, you should keep several points in mind. One is that while Congress added some new programs and revised others, the structure of the Act remains unchanged. Legislative provisions for the National Ambient Air Quality Standards, interstate pollution, emission standards for stationary sources, the prevention of significant deterioration and visibility programs are unchanged or modified slightly. The major changes are a revision of the non-attainment area program, new tailpipe emission standards for motor vehicles, a revision of the air toxics program, a new program for acid rain, and a new comprehensive permit program.

Another point is that Congress legislated in extensive detail, working a marked change in an Act that previously had been comparatively brief. Participants close to the amendment process indicate that the detail in the amendments may reflect congressional impatience with EPA foot-dragging and Office of Management and Budget interference in EPA policies. Congress may also have decided to legislate in detail so that legislative requirements would be clear. Some of this detail is best taught through text. Excerpts from the Clean Air Act in this supplement that provide necessary statutory materials for understanding the major issues the 1990 amendments present.

A final point is that throughout the 1990 amendments Congress provided for a phased implementation of the new statutory provisions over the next decade. In large part this decision was a compromise that traded more stringent standards against a time delay that gives industry more time to comply. Phased implementation means that the provisions of the pre-1990 act will still be in effect during this transition period. Later supplements will elaborate on the programs and revisions enacted by the 1990 amendments as EPA begins to publish implementation rules and develop an implementation program.

For an explanation of the 1990 amendments see, especially, J. Quarles & W. Lewis, The NEW Clean Air Act: A Guide to the Clean Air Program As Amended in 1990 (1990), published by the Washington, D.C., law firm of Morgan, Lewis & Bockius. See also The Clean Air Act Amendments of 1990 — A Detailed Analysis, The Hazardous Waste Consultant, Jan.-Feb., 1991, at 4.1. For a discussion of the political history of the amendments, see Edelson, A Win For Clean Air, Envtl. Forum, Jan.-Feb., 1991, at 10. The Conference Agreement to the amendments also contains a good summary.

E. EMISSIONS STANDARDS IN THE CLEAN AIR ACT

1. Motor Vehicle Emissions Standards

a. From the Goals of 1970 to Contemporary Realities

Page 210. After the carryover paragraph, add the following:

NOTE ON THE 1990 AMENDMENTS TO THE MOBILE SOURCE EMISSIONS STANDARDS

The new program. New and more stringent tailpipe emissions standards for cars and very light trucks are required in two phases. In Tier I, the hydrocarbon standard is 30 percent lower than the present standard, and the nitrogen oxides standard is 60 percent lower. Forty percent of automobiles must meet the new standards by the 1994 model year, 80 percent by 1995, and full compliance must be achieved by 1996. EPA is to establish twice as stringent Tier II standards if they are found to be necessary, technologically feasible, and cost-effective; these standards become effective between 2003 and 2006. See §202(g)-(i). The warranty for most vehicle components is shortened to two years or 24,000 miles, but the emissions control system warranty is extended to eight years or 80,000 miles.

The amendments retain §177, which allows other states to set more stringent standards based on but not different from the stricter California standards. Within one year of the amendments, EPA is also to adopt regulations requiring the installation in automobile fuel systems of equipment to trap evaporative emissions.

The amendments also establish clean fuel and clean-fueled vehicle programs for the worst non-attainment areas. These programs include a California

III. Protecting the Air Resource   Page 235

pilot program requiring the production of significant numbers of clean-fueled vehicles by 1999, a similar program for fleet vehicles in the most serious non-attainment areas, and a program phasing in reformulated gasoline as the only fuel to be sold in nine cities with the highest ozone levels.

Standards reviewed in the Thomas *case.* The criteria for emission standards applicable for heavy duty vehicles, which are reviewed in the *Thomas* case, are not materially changed. The 1990 amendments allow EPA to revise standards adopted under the pre-1990 act. §202(a)(3)(B). This section also requires a minimum nitrogen oxides standard of 4.0/gbh by 1994. Section 219 of the amended act provides for a 50 percent reduction by 1994 of the particulate standard for urban buses unless the reduction is not technologically achievable. For the final rule adopting the standards reviewed in the *Thomas* case, see 50 Fed. Reg. 10606 (1985).

2. *Performance Standards for New Stationary Sources*

Page 228.   Add the following to the discussion of NSPS for coal-fired electrical generating facilities:

The 1990 amendments deleted the percentage reduction requirement.

F. STATE IMPLEMENTATION PLANS

Page 235.   At the end of the first full paragraph, add the following:

NOTE ON THE 1990 AMENDMENTS TO STATE
IMPLEMENTATION PLAN AND PERMIT REQUIREMENTS

The SIPs. The 1990 amendments revised the provisions for state implementation plans. The amendments primarily redistribute some of the requirements previously contained in §110. The amendments do not make major substantive changes, except for implementation plan requirements in non-attainment areas, discussed later in this supplement. The 1990 amendments complete the process, begun in 1977, of making the severity of the controls required by the Act depend on the severity of the air quality problem in the Air Quality Control Region.

The statutory requirements for SIPs are still contained in §110(a)(2). They are revised, and some new requirements are added, but they are not substantially different from what they were pre-1990. The other changes are that provisions governing EPA review and approval are in a new §110(k), and that timetables for compliance are moved to Subpart D on non-attainment plans and the com-

631

pliance schedule is extended. Do these changes affect, in any way, the decision in the *Union Electric* case?

The new comprehensive permit program. Title V of the 1990 amendments adopts a new comprehensive permit program modeled on the permit program in the Clean Water Act. Permits are now required for most significant sources of air pollution. Under the pre-1990 act, permits were required only for new and modified sources, while existing sources were governed at the federal level only by general requirements in SIPs, the new source performance standards, or toxics standards.

States are to adopt permit programs under regulations adopted by EPA. §502(b). Each permit must contain the emissions limitations applicable to the source, a compliance schedule, and any other conditions or requirements. §504. EPA has a veto power similar to the veto power authorized under the Clean Water Act. §504(b).

One important provision in the permit program is the permit shield. A source that complies with its permit will not be in violation of any provision in the act that is directly addressed in the permit, either through incorporation or a finding it is not applicable. §504(f). Congress deleted a proposal that would have allowed states to bypass the cumbersome SIP revision process and instead allow source-specific variations for SIP requirements in the permit process. States may be able to achieve this flexibility by revising their SIPs to delete source-specific emissions limitations. For the rules on when a modification in source operations requires a permit, see §502(b)(10).

G. NON-ATTAINMENT: THE SPECIAL PROBLEMS OF DIRTY AIR AREAS

2. Non-Attainment Area Plans and Sanctions

Page 257. After Note 4, add the following:

NOTE ON REVISED REQUIREMENTS FOR
NON-ATTAINMENT AREAS IN THE CLEAN AIR ACT
AMENDMENTS OF 1990

Non-attainment areas and plans. The 1990 amendments not only retain the statutory requirements for non-attainment areas but strengthen and enhance them. In 1991 all states are to submit, and EPA is to promulgate, the designation of areas as attainment, non-attainment, or unclassifiable. Non-attainment areas are divided into five categories depending on the severity of their pollution problems: Marginal, Moderate, Serious, Severe, and Extreme. Ozone is the serious non-attainment problem, about 100 areas are non-attainment for this pollution,

III. Protecting the Air Resource

but only Los Angeles is classified as Extreme. Eight areas are expected to be classified as Severe and 16 as Serious.

Deadlines for ozone attainment are established in a sliding scale based on the severity of the ozone problem. §181(a). The deadline, from November 15, 1990, ranges from three years for Marginal areas to 20 years for Extreme areas. In addition, all ozone SIPs (except in Marginal areas) must meet an aggressive schedule of percentage reduction of 15 percent during the first six years and three percent after this period. This is a strengthening of the "reasonable" annual progress requirement for non-attainment areas that was added in 1977.

The amendments also extend controls on stationary sources. Reasonably Available Control Technology (RACT) for existing sources is extended to nitrogen oxides and will be applied to smaller sources in the more seriously polluted areas. The amendments direct EPA to accelerate the promulgation of Control Technique Guidelines (CTGs) that provide guidance on RACT for existing sources.

Section 182 contains detailed plan requirement provisions for each ozone non-attainment area category. The amendments also mandate plan requirements for areas that are non-attainment for other pollutants. For the ozone non-attainment areas, plans must contain a wide variety of controls with more demanding controls required for the more severe ozone pollution areas. For the most serious polluted areas, these controls include vapor recovery systems, enhanced monitoring, and enhanced vehicle inspection and maintenance. Severe and Extreme area plans must also include measures to offset growth from vehicle miles travelled, and Extreme areas must include traffic control measures. The amendments also require clean fuel programs for the more serious ozone pollution areas. See the discussion of mobile sources, this supplement, *supra*.

Sanctions are still available under §179 for failure to meet non-attainment plan requirements, but the construction ban sanction is deleted except where it was in effect prior to the 1990 amendments.

New sources and emissions trading. The amendments make no change in the LAER technology requirements for new sources but reduce the threshold for new sources to below 100 tons in the more serious ozone non-attainment areas. The amendments also change the rules for emissions trading, which is discussed in the casebook beginning at p. 261. Emissions trading is generally allowed only in the same non-attainment area, and the amendments enact offset ratios of more than 1:1 that are based on the severity of the ozone pollution problem. Ratios range from 1.1:1 in Marginal areas to 1.5:1 in Extreme areas.

Transportation planning. Motor vehicle use in cities has doubled since the Clean Air Act was adopted in 1970, is continuing at an annual growth rate of 3.5 to 6 percent in most cities, and is expected to erase the gains achieved by future tailpipe emissions controls. The amendments strengthen §176, which requires regional transportation plans and improvement programs to conform with implementation plans. A new §176(c)(2)(A) requires transportation plans and improvements to be consistent with mobile source emission reduction targets required for non-attainment plans. This provision will require a substantial reduction in vehicle miles travelled (VMT) and in some areas a radical shift in vehicle use from single-occupant vehicles. Another provision in the conformity section provides that regional transportation plans may not "delay timely attainment of any standard or any required interim emission reductions or other milestones in any areas." §176(c)(1)(B)(iii).

Section 108(f)(1) requires EPA to develop guidance on the emissions reduction possibilities of transportation control measures. Provisions governing ozone and carbon monoxide non-attainment plans require states to consider and implement measures specified by §108 when necessary to achieve attainment. EPA interpretation of a similar provision in the 1977 amendments required states to adopt all reasonably available control measures if they were necessary to assure attainment. 44 Fed. Reg. 20375 (1979).

I. SPECIAL ISSUES IN THE CLEAN AIR ACT

2. The Acid Rain Controversy

Page 317. After Note 3, add the following:

NOTE ON THE NEW ACID RAIN PROGRAM IN THE
CLEAN AIR ACT AMENDMENTS OF 1990

Title IV of the 1990 amendments adds a complex new program to reduce acid deposition that applies to coal-fired electric utilities. The program is based on a system of sulfur dioxide emissions allowances that utilities can bank or sell to other emitters in an emissions trading program. An allowance is equal to one ton of sulfur dioxide emissions, and the allowances are intended to limit sulfur dioxide emissions to 8.9 tons annually by 2000.

The acid rain program extends the emissions trading concept to a new area of pollution control. See Recent Development, The Clean Air Act Amendments of 1990 and the Use of Market Forces to Control Sulfur Dioxide Emissions, 28 Harv. J. Legis. 235 (1991).

Phase I of the acid rain program imposes controls on 111 "big dirty" plants; the legislation specifies the allowances allocated to each plant. Allowances in this phase are intended to reduce emissions to the emissions level generated between 1985 and 1987 by burning the average amount of fuel at an emissions rate of 2.5lbs./ mmBtu. Each plant is required to reduce emissions to that level unless it acquires additional allowances.

Phase II begins in 2000. It reduces allowances for Phase I plans and extends the acid rain control program to all remaining plants. Phase II reduction requires an 8.9 million ton cap on sulfur dioxide emissions to be achieved by an annual distribution by EPA of 8.9 million pollution allowances. The amendments also require a two-million ton reduction in nitrogen oxide emissions, to

III. Protecting the Air Resource   Page 329

be achieved through emissions standards adopted by EPA based on emissions rates that can be achieved with low-NOx burners.

A proposed cost-sharing plan intended to help avoid rate increases by midwest utilities was not adopted. See Edelson, *supra* this supplement, at 12, 13.

3. Enforcement

Page 329. At the end of the Chapter, add the following:

NOTE ON CHANGES IN ENFORCEMENT PROVISIONS IN THE 1990 AMENDMENTS TO THE CLEAN AIR ACT

The 1990 amendments strengthen the enforcement provisions in the Act. EPA may now impose administrative penalties directly and need not bring in the Department of Justice to initiate a court proceeding. §113(d). Private citizens may now seek civil penalties in citizen suits. §304(a). The knowing violation of almost every requirement is converted into a felony crime, and sanctions include fines and imprisonment. §113(d).

IV

PROTECTING THE WATER RESOURCE

B. BACKGROUND OF WATER POLLUTION REGULATION

2. *The Twentieth Century Evolution of Federal Water Pollution Control Policy*

c. The Clean Water Act: An Overview

A NOTE ON THE OIL POLLUTION ACT OF 1990

In response to the Exxon Valdez and other spectacular oil spills, Congress enacted the Oil Pollution Act of 1990. Pub. L. No. 101-380, 104 Stat. 484 (1990). The Act retains prior federal legislation, but liability is now governed by the Act. The Act applies to spills in navigable waters, the United States exclusive economic zone, or along the shoreline. Responsible parties must pay the removal costs incurred by federal, state, and tribal governments under the Clean Water Act, §1001(31), and are responsible for natural resources damages, which are defined as the cost of damage assessment and the cost restoring, rehabilitating, replacing as well as diminished values during replacement. §1006(d). Damages equal to the loss of profits or the impairment of earning capacity may be recovered for injuries to real and personal property and natural resources. See Rodriguez and Jaffe, The Oil Pollution Act of 1990, 15 Tulane Maritime L.J. 1, 14-16 (1990). §1002(b)(2)(E). Vessel liability limits are increased to the greater of $1,200 pre gross ton or $10 million, §1003(b), and the Act includes a phased double hull requirement to prevent future spills.

C. FEDERAL JURISDICTION

2. *Point and Non-Point Sources*

Page 387. After the first paragraph, add the following:

A new non-point source program: Late in 1990, Congress unexpectedly added a new Coastal Non-point Pollution Control Program to the National Coastal Zone Management Act. Pub. L. 101-508, §6217 (1990). The new non-point program will be implemented through changes to state coastal management programs authorized by the Act and to state programs adopted under §319 of the Clean Water Act. The purpose of the program is to require "management measures" for non-point source pollution control to restore coastal waters. "Management measures" are defined as "economically achievable measures . . . [that include] the best available non-point pollution control practices, technologies, processes, siting criteria, operating methods, or other alternatives."

EPA and the federal coastal zone agency are to publish guidance on the coastal non-point program within 18 months of its enactment, and the states have 30 months from the issuance of the guidance to comply with its requirements. In addition to management measures, state programs are to include other implementation measures such as the identification of "critical coastal areas" within which new and expanded land uses will be subject to management measures.

Funding of this program is in doubt as of April 1991.

D. WATER QUALITY STANDARDS: THEORY AND CURRENT FUNCTION

Page 407. Before Section E, add the following:

OKLAHOMA v. EPA
908 F.2d 595 (10th Cir. 1990), *petition for cert. granted,* — U.S. — 59 U.S. Law Week 3688 (1991)

BRORBY, Circuit Judge.
In these consolidated appeals, appellants challenge certain actions of the U.S. Environmental Protection Agency (EPA) in issuing a discharge permit pursuant to the National Pollutant Discharge Elimination System (NPDES) of the Clean Water Act, 33 U.S.C. §1342. We review EPA's action pursuant to our authority under 33 U.S.C. §1369(b)(1) and reverse.

IV. Protecting the Water Resource　　　　　　　　　　　　　　Page 407

Overview

The city of Fayetteville, Arkansas, applied to EPA for an NPDES permit for a new municipal wastewater treatment plant. Fayetteville proposed to discharge treated wastewater via a split flow into the White River in Arkansas and into Mud Creek, a tributary of the Illinois River, an Arkansas-Oklahoma interstate stream. The State of Oklahoma and a nonprofit group, Save The Illinois River (STIR), requested denial of the permit. The State of Arkansas and the Oklahoma parties requested an evidentiary hearing on EPA's issuance of the permit. A hearing request was granted in part and denied in part by an Administrative Law Judge (ALJ), and the partial denial was upheld by the EPA Administrator acting through his Chief Judicial Officer (CJO). After the evidentiary hearing, the ALJ determined that the permit would not have an undue impact on water quality or violate Oklahoma's water quality standards (WQS). This initial decision was appealed by both Arkansas and Oklahoma. On appeal, the ALJ's decision was affirmed in part and reversed in part and remanded for a determination whether the record showed by a preponderance of the evidence that the permitted discharge would not cause an actual, detectable violation of WQS. On remand the ALJ reviewed the record and made detailed findings. He concluded that the permit could issue as written, finding that it would not result in any measurable violations of Oklahoma's WQS. The ALJ's decision on remand was appealed to the CJO who upheld it in a decision dated December 22, 1988. These petitions for review followed.

Appellants the State of Oklahoma, Oklahoma Scenic Rivers Commission, Oklahoma Pollution Control Coordinating Board, and STIR (the "Oklahoma parties," or Oklahoma) set forth ten issues in their joint brief-in-chief. Essentially they contend that EPA erred in concluding that the permit would not violate Oklahoma's WQS; that EPA did not properly consider the Wild and Scenic Rivers Act, 16 U.S.C. §§1271-1287 (WSRA), as it applies to the upstream portions of the Illinois River; and that EPA erred in denying review of certain issues and in refusing to reopen the evidentiary hearing. The State of Arkansas, Arkansas Department of Pollution Control Ecology, City of Fayetteville, and Beaver Water District (the "Arkansas parties," or Arkansas) challenge EPA's authority to require an Arkansas discharger to comply with Oklahoma water quality standards. . . .

EPA issued Fayetteville's NPDES permit because at the time this proceeding commenced Arkansas had not yet been delegated permitting authority pursuant to §1342(b). The permit was issued on November 5, 1985, and finally approved on December 22, 1988, following the administrative appeals described above. The treatment plant has been in operation since December 1988.

The permit (NPDES Permit No. AR0020010) specifies that half of the city's treated wastewater will be discharged to the White River in Arkansas (this portion of the discharge is not in contention here), and half will be discharged to the Illinois River basin. Specifically, this latter effluent will be discharged to an unnamed stream in northwestern Arkansas, which flows approximately two

639

miles before joining Mud Creek. Mud Creek flows three miles from that point to its confluence with Clear Creek, thirteen miles upstream from the Illinois River in Arkansas. Twenty-two miles downstream from Clear Creek — and thirty-nine miles from the Fayetteville plant — the Illinois River crosses the state line into northeastern Oklahoma and almost immediately flows into Lake Frances. A segment of the Illinois River (including Lake Frances) from the Oklahoma-Arkansas state line to Tenkiller Ferry Reservoir has been designated an Oklahoma state scenic river and was proposed for study as a potential addition to the National Wild and Scenic Rivers System when the WSRA was enacted in 1970. 16 U.S.C. §1276(40). To date, this segment, which is approximately sixty miles long, has not been designated a component of the national system. See 16 U.S.C. §1273.

The Fayetteville permit sets limits on the amounts of certain pollutants that may be discharged and establishes maximum or minimum effluent concentrations of those pollutants and other chemical parameters. Permit, EPA Supp. Addendum at 12-30. The permit prohibits the discharge of any incompletely treated effluent to Mud Creek. Id. at 27. It also includes, *inter alia*, a provision for modifying the permit to incorporate more stringent limitations if an ongoing study of the Illinois River demonstrates such limitations are needed to ensure compliance with water quality standards. Id.

Analysis

I. STANDARD OF REVIEW

Review of the EPA rulings on appeal here is governed by the Administrative Procedure Act, 5 U.S.C. §§701-706. We must uphold the agency's actions, findings, and conclusions unless they are outside the agency's statutory authority, are not supported by substantial evidence, or are arbitrary, capricious, an abuse of discretion, or otherwise not in accordance with law. 5 U.S.C. §706(2)(A), (C), and (E). We may not substitute our judgment for that of the agency. . . .

Determining the extent of EPA's authority under the Clean Water Act is a question of law that we review de novo. "Our first inquiry is whether 'Congress has directly spoken to the precise question at issue. If the intent of Congress is clear that is the end of the matter; for the court, as well as the agency, must give effect to the unambiguously expressed intent of Congress'" Martin Exploration Management Co. v. FERC, 813 F.2d 1059, 1065 (10th Cir. 1987) (quoting Chevron, U.S.A., Inc. v. NRDC, 467 U.S. 837, 842-43, (1984), *rev'd on other grounds*, 486 U.S. 204 (1988). However, where the statute is ambiguous, EPA's construction, as that of the agency charged with administering the statute, is entitled to substantial deference. Chevron, U.S.A., Inc. v. NRDC, 467 U.S. 837, 844 (1984). If EPA's interpretation of the Clean Water Act is reasonable, we should not disturb it unless it "is contrary to the policies Congress sought to implement in enacting the statute." 813 F.2d at 1065; see also 467 U.S. at 845. . . .

III. STATEMENT OF ISSUES

Arkansas poses the fundamental question in this case: Does the Clean Water Act require a point source of pollution to comply with the water quality standards of all affected downstream states? Oklahoma assumes such a requirement in that it challenges EPA's determination that the Fayetteville permit would not result in violation of Oklahoma's water quality standards and argues accordingly that no discharge to Oklahoma's Illinois River system should be allowed.

Oklahoma formulates the issues on appeal as "[w]hether the Chief Judicial Officer erred in denying review" of various ALJ rulings and whether the CJO and ALJ "erred in [refusing] to reopen the evidentiary hearing." Despite this formulation, it seems clear that the Oklahoma parties' chief concerns relate to the substantive issues underlying these procedural questions. The substantive issues are: (1) the adequacy of the treatment technology employed by the Fayetteville plant and the possible superiority of land application methods; (2) the propriety of considering evidence concerning future reductions in the discharges of other Arkansas cities; (3) the propriety of relying on "protective language" in the permit authorizing more stringent discharge limitations if shown to be necessary by an ongoing study of the Illinois River; (4) the correctness of EPA's interpretation and application of Oklahoma's beneficial use limitation, nutrient standard, and anti-degradation policy; (5) the relevance of new information concerning overflows at the old treatment plant; and (6) whether Fayetteville met its burden of proof in showing that a permit should be issued for its treatment plant. Our review of the record convinces us that we need not resolve many of the issues raised by the Oklahoma parties. In the following pages we address first the statutory interpretation question posited by Arkansas and then a significant issue not raised by any party — the significance of evidence of existing degradation of Illinois River water quality.

A. CONSTRUCTION OF THE CLEAN WATER ACT

1. *The Opposing Views*

The full ramifications of Arkansas's formulation of the Clean Water Act issue are exposed once it is realized that an upstream state has the ability (if not the legal right) largely to control the quality of certain of the waters of a downstream state. It can accomplish this simply by setting and enforcing its own water quality standards and releasing water of that quality to the downstream state. If the upstream state's water quality standards are lower than those considered desirable by the downstream state, so will be the actual quality of the interstate waters in the downstream state. In other words, the lowest common denominator will prevail. The ultimate question posed to this court is whose water quality standards take precedence under the Clean Water Act — the upstream state's, the downstream state's, the federal government's, or nobody's. We conclude that no state "imposes" its standards on another state, but rather that the Clean Water

641

Act mandates compliance with federal law, including the federally approved water quality standards of affected states.

Specifically, Arkansas alleges an affected downstream state "may advise and make recommendations, but nowhere in the Clean Water Act did Congress authorize affected states such as Oklahoma to impose their water quality standards upon a discharger in another state." Arkansas's Brief at 39. We treat this, the principal issue of this case, as whether the Clean Water Act requires that any discharge permitted under 33 U.S.C. §1342 comply with all applicable water quality standards, including the EPA-approved regulations of any affected downstream state.[5] This is an issue of first impression in the circuit courts.[6]

5. We reformulate the issue to reflect more accurately the facts and legal context of this case. Section 303 of the CWA, 33 U.S.C. §1313, requires periodic review by states of their WQS and provides for EPA approval of any modified WQS as long as such standard "meets the requirements" of the CWA. §1313(c)(3). Once approved, "such standard shall thereafter be the water quality standard for the applicable waters of that State." Id. EPA is required to promulgate revised WQS for any state that fails to adopt WQS consistent with CWA requirements and in any case where EPA determines that a revised or new standard is necessary to meet the requirements of the Act. §1313(c)(4).

The Fayetteville plant has been required by EPA to observe *federal* law, i.e., Oklahoma's EPA-approved water quality standards. See Order on Petitions for Review, R., A-28, at 11 n.13. Thus, it is misleading to say "Oklahoma . . . impose[d *its*] water quality standards" on Arkansas, or that Oklahoma has the "right to block" a permit issued by Arkansas. See, e.g., Arkansas's Brief at 33, 36, 38-40. The 1982 Oklahoma water quality standards, which EPA judged applicable to the Fayetteville plant, had been approved by EPA. Whether Fayetteville might also be subject to observing Oklahoma state standards that have *not* received EPA approval is not an issue in this case, and we do not address it. Accordingly, throughout this opinion we use "applicable water quality standards" to mean EPA-*approved* water quality standards that govern the affected waters, and "Oklahoma water quality standards" to mean Oklahoma's EPA-*approved* water quality regulations.

6. This statement requires a brief explanation of a recent Fourth Circuit case. In Champion Int'l Corp. v. EPA, 648 F. Supp. 1390 (W.D.N.C. 1986), *motion for withdrawal of mandate denied*, 652 F. Supp. 1398 (W.D.N.C. 1987), the district court upheld EPA's assumption of permitting authority under 33 U.S.C. §1342(d)(4) after EPA objected when North Carolina proposed to permit a discharge in North Carolina without regard for Tennessee water quality standards. The court held that a discharge permit must ensure compliance with the requirements of the CWA, and that EPA reasonably could have concluded that the North Carolina permit, in disregarding the Tennessee water quality standard for color, would not ensure such compliance. 648 F. Supp. at 1394-99. Upon reconsideration in light of an intervening Supreme Court case, however, the district court offered the following limiting statement: "Nothing in the regulatory framework surrounding the CWA would automatically require that a source state comply with the water quality standards of every downstream state." 652 F. Supp. at 1400.

Subsequently, the district court's judgment was vacated by the Fourth Circuit with instructions to dismiss for lack of subject matter jurisdiction. Champion Int'l Corp. v. EPA, 850 F.2d 182 (4th Cir. 1988). The circuit court prefaced and postscripted its decision by expressing its general agreement with "much of the district court's opinion." 850 F.2d at 183, 190. It also stated that "EPA's act in assuming the permit issuing authority was consistent with statute and regulation, and the objections it made to the North Carolina permit do not seem to be out of bounds." Id. at 187. However, the appellate court ultimately concluded:

> The actions of EPA . . . at this stage of the NPDES proceeding are not now subject to judicial review. EPA has neither granted nor denied a permit, so such action is not yet reviewable under [33 U.S.C.] §1369(b)(1). The nature of EPA's objections are well within the contemplation of those it is entitled to make under applicable regulations. 40 C.F.R. §123.44(c). Whatever may be the result should EPA make an objection completely without its delegated authority, so as to subject that action to present judicial review under Leedom v. Kyne, [358 U.S. 184, 79 S. Ct. 180, 3 L. Ed. 2d 210 (1958)], we have no occasion to consider, for such objections have not been made here.

IV. Protecting the Water Resource

EPA's Chief Judicial Officer, in his first order in this case dated June 28, 1988, stated the law and applied it as follows:

> The CWA requires an NPDES permit to impose any effluent limitations necessary to comply with applicable state water quality standards. . . . The meaning of [33 U.S.C. §1311(b)(1)(C)] is plain and straightforward. It requires unequivocal compliance with applicable water quality standards, and does not make any exceptions for cost or technological feasibility. . . .
>
> . . . In this case, the permit should be upheld if the record shows by a preponderance of the evidence that the authorized discharge would not cause an actual *detectable* violation of Oklahoma's water quality standards.

Order on Petitions for Review, R., A-28, at 11-13. The CJO explained that in an interstate dispute the "only applicable water quality standards are those that have been approved by EPA under the CWA." Order on Petitions for Review at 11 n. 13 (citing Illinois v. City of Milwaukee, 731 F.2d 403, 413-14 (7th Cir. 1984), *cert. denied*, 469 U.S. (1985)). In noninterstate disputes, however, "the source state may impose more stringent non-EPA-approved water quality standards in NPDES permits under 33 U.S.C.A. §1370." Order on Petitions for Review at 12 n.13.

On remand, the ALJ expressed similar views:

> It is clear that an out-of-state source must meet the W.Q.S. of another downriver state. See §401(a)(2) of the CWA [33 U.S.C. §1341(a)(2)]; 40 C.F.R. §§122.4(D) and 122.44(d)(4); International Paper Co. v. Ouellette, 479 U.S. 481 (1987). Therefore the Fayetteville discharge must meet Oklahoma's W.Q.S. as they exist at the border of the two states. . . .
>
> . . . To accept [the Arkansas parties' argument that the beneficial use limitations do not apply to Fayetteville] would violate the principals [sic] set out above since it is premised on the notion that such standards only apply to sources located in the State of Oklahoma. There is no factual issue among the parties that the Illinois River at the border of the two states is a Class (A) River and therefore the standards applicable to pollution crossing that border must comply with Oklahoma's W.Q.S. as they exist at that point. Any other interpretation would allow a

---

850 F.2d at 190. The court stated that the district court "properly retained jurisdiction of the case in order to ascertain whether or not EPA acted within its delegated authority," and agreed with the district court's decision that EPA was so acting. But it held that, once the district court made that determination, it should have dismissed for want of subject matter jurisdiction and not reached the merits. Id. *Champion's* holding is limited to the narrow determination that EPA had not acted "clearly beyond the boundaries of its authority." Id. at 186. Indeed, the court added: "Even if EPA may ultimately be shown to be incorrect in its objections to North Carolina's permit (and we do not intimate that they are), its acts are not so clearly outside its authority to subject them to immediate judicial review. . . ." Id. at 187. Thus, *Champion* does not decide the merits of the question we face, i.e., whether the CWA requires that an NPDES permit ensure compliance with an affected downstream state's water quality standards.

One other case deserves brief mention here. In *Montgomery Envtl. Coalition*, the D.C. Circuit stated: "A state whose water quality will be affected by the issuance of a permit for discharge in another state may block that permit until conditions are imposed insuring compliance with applicable water quality requirements of the objecting state." 646 F.2d at 594 n.21. But in the next breath the court acknowledged this was not an issue in *Montgomery*; thus, the language is dictum.

source to locate its discharge just across the line in Arkansas and freely violate Oklahoma standards. Such a result is contrary to the [Clean Water Act], regulations and Court decisions.

Decision on Remand, R., A-33, at 4-5. The ALJ's interpretations of Oklahoma's WQS, including the Beneficial Use Limitations, were ultimately affirmed by the CJO. The CJO also reiterated the mandate of his first order — that "'the permit should be upheld if . . . the authorized discharges would not cause . . . [a] violation of Oklahoma's water quality standards,'" — and accepted the ALJ's conclusion that no violation would occur. Second Order on Petitions for Review, R., A-37, at 7-8.

The Arkansas parties contend we need look no farther than the Clean Water Act to decide this issue because "Congress has clearly manifested its intent [in the CWA] that affected states cannot impose their water quality standards upon dischargers in other states." Arkansas Brief at 42; see id. at 33-40. Alternatively, if we decide congressional intent is ambiguous, they urge us to reject EPA's interpretation as unreasonable. Id. at 42. EPA also claims the CWA is "clear that the terms of an NPDES permit must include compliance with state water quality standards — regardless of the source of a discharge." EPA Brief at 15-16. Therefore, EPA maintains, resort to the legislative history — which EPA contends corroborates EPA's interpretation — is unnecessary. Id. at 20 (citing United States v. Oregon, 366 U.S. 643, 648 (1961)). In the event we conclude congressional intent is ambiguous, EPA alternatively defends the reasonableness of its interpretation of the CWA and argues, that, under *Chevron*, 467 U.S. at 844-45, it must therefore be upheld. EPA Brief at 13, 15.

We do not find the Clean Water Act, on its face, quite as clear a manifestation of congressional intent on this issue as any of the parties suggests. Significantly, however, EPA's interpretation is not one the agency adopted only, or in the first instance, in the context of this permit proceeding. Rather, EPA's position herein is consistent with its CWA-implementing regulations. For example, 40 C.F.R. §122.4(d) expressly provides: "No permit may be issued: . . . (d) When the imposition of conditions cannot ensure compliance with the applicable water quality requirements of *all affected States*." (Emphasis added.) Concomitantly, EPA's rules require permits to include, where applicable, "any requirements . . . necessary to . . . [c]onform to applicable water quality requirements . . . when the discharge affects a state other than the certifying State [i.e., the state in which the discharge will be located]." §122.44(d)(4). See also 40 C.F.R. §131.10(b) (state "shall ensure that its water quality standards provide for the attainment and maintenance of the water quality standards of downstream waters"). We accord deference to the consistent interpretation of a statute by the agency entrusted with its administration. See 33 U.S.C. §1251(d); Federal Election Comm'n v. Democratic Senatorial Campaign Comm., 454 U.S. 27, 37 (1981); cf. E.I. DuPont De Nemours & Co. v. Train, 430 U.S. 112, 135 n.25 (1977) (EPA interpretation entitled to deference, even if not contemporaneous with enactment of CWA, in light of technical nature of statute, agency's expertise, and ambiguous statutory language). After considering the Act as a whole and its legislative history, we conclude EPA's interpretation is reasonable and consistent with Congress's purposes in enacting the CWA.

2. The Parties' Statutory Arguments

In defending its construction of the CWA the EPA relies principally on §301(b)(1)(C) of the Act, 33 U.S.C. § 1311(b)(1)(C), which provides:

> In order to carry out the objective of this chapter [i.e., to "restore and maintain the chemical, physical, and biological integrity of the Nation's waters," 33 U.S.C. §1251] there shall be achieved . . . not later than July 1, 1977, *any more stringent limitation, including those necessary to meet water quality standards*, . . . established pursuant to *any* State law or regulations (under authority preserved by section 1370 of this title) . . . or required to implement *any* applicable water quality standard established pursuant to this chapter.

(Emphasis added.) Section 402(a)(2) and (b)(1)(A) of the CWA, 33 U.S.C. §1342(a)(2), (b)(1)(A), in turn mandates that any NPDES permit issued under the Act contain terms adequate to insure compliance with §301 above. See EPA Brief at 16.

EPA rejects Arkansas's argument that these sections are "mere timing provisions." Id. (citing Arkansas Brief at 34-35). On the contrary, EPA argues, these sections establish fundamental requirements of the Act. Moreover, EPA contends that Congress, by making no distinction between the water quality standards of source and affected states in these requirements, "indicated the uniform applicability of such standards." EPA Brief at 16-17.[7]

Arkansas counters that §1311 does not explain whether the "more stringent limitations" must be achieved by dischargers in other states, but that section 510, 33 U.S.C. §1370 limits the "reach" of any stricter standards to discharges originating within the state imposing those standards. Arkansas Brief at 35. This argument relies largely on language in §1370 preserving "any right or jurisdiction of the States with respect to the waters . . . of such States." The argument suffers from at least three flaws, however.

First, §1370 is a savings clause that merely preserves the preexisting right of the states "to set more restrictive standards than those imposed by [the CWA]."

---

7. Under the 1972 CWA amendments, water quality standards are considered "supplementary control measures" — "supplementary" in the sense that they are in addition to point source effluent limitations, the control measure upon which the 1972 CWA Amendments primarily rely to achieve the Act's objective of eliminating pollutant discharges into navigable waters by 1985. *State Water Resources Control Bd.*, 426 U.S. at 203-05 & n.12 ("[w]ater quality standards are retained as a supplementary basis for effluent limitations . . . so that numerous point sources, despite individual compliance with effluent limitations, may be further regulated to prevent water quality from falling below acceptable levels"). See 33 U.S.C. §§1251(a)(1), 1311(b)(1)(A); see also S. Rep. No. 414, *reprinted in* 1972 U.S.Code Cong. & Admin. News 3668, 3675 ("Under this Act the basis of pollution prevention and elimination will be . . . effluent limitations. Water quality will be a measure of program effectiveness and performance, not a means of elimination and enforcement."). That WQS are "supplementary" in the scheme of the Clean Water Act is, however, irrelevant to the question of their applicability across state lines.

S. Rep. No. 414, *reprinted in* 1972 U.S. Code Cong. & Admin. News 3668, 3751. See also International Paper Co. v. Ouellette, 479 U.S. 481, 493 (1987) (§1370 savings clause "preserves the authority of a State," but "does not preclude pre-emption" of state law); Milwaukee v. Illinois, 451 U.S. 304, 327-28, 68 (1981). Accordingly, there is no basis for believing that Congress intended §1370 to limit or define the scope of one of the CWA's crucial provisions. The cases Arkansas cites to the contrary are unavailing for that purpose. See Arkansas Brief at 35-36 n.28.

Second, the "waters . . . of such States" language, which Arkansas deems significant, occurs in and applies only to the second of two principal provisions of §1370. That provision (subparagraph (2)) refers broadly to "any right or jurisdiction of the States." In contrast, the first provision (subparagraph (1)) specifically addresses the rights of states and their subdivisions to regulate pollution. Subparagraph (1) says nothing about the boundaries within which such rights may be exercised. Thus, "waters . . . of such states" cannot be construed as a limitation on the rights to regulate pollution preserved in the first part of this section.

Third, thoughtful consideration of the language of §1311(b)(1)(C) —

> there *shall be achieved* . . . any more stringent limitation, including those *necessary to meet* water quality standards . . . established pursuant to any State law or regulations . . . or *required to implement* any applicable water quality standard established pursuant to this chapter

(emphasis added) — exposes the irrationality of Arkansas's argument. In order to ensure that the EPA-approved water quality standards in all states are "met" or "implemented," it *is* "necessary" to require dischargers to meet the applicable requirements of other affected states as well as those of the source state. There could be no assurance of achieving a state's more stringent WQS if an upstream, out-of-state discharger were not required to comply with those standards.

EPA concludes and we agree that Arkansas's construction of the Act would make achieving downstream water quality standards "impossible in many circumstances or . . . possible . . . only by imposing a disproportionate burden on dischargers located in the downstream state." EPA Brief at 21. Moreover, rewarding sources for locating in states with less stringent water quality requirements (by relieving them from complying with more stringent downstream WQS) would also result in "pollution shopping," contrary to Congress's intent in passing the 1972 CWA amendments.

Arkansas counters that EPA's construction of the Act would have "chaotic" consequences because any downstream state could impose its requirements on proposed sources in any upstream state. Arkansas Brief at 46-47. Thus, Arkansas hypothesizes, a permit authorizing a discharge to the Mississippi River in Minnesota would be subject to challenge based on the water quality standards of each of the nine downstream states. Id. at 46 (citing *Ouellette*, 479 U.S. at 496 n.17. Arkansas's purported concern is that this would undercut the CWA's "orderly regulatory scheme," making it "'virtually impossible to predict the standard

IV. Protecting the Water Resource

for a lawful discharge into an interstate body of water.'" Arkansas Brief at 47 (quoting Illinois v. Milwaukee, 731 F.2d at 414)).

We find little practical merit in Arkansas's argument. The ability, as well as the authority, to require compliance with the WQS of downstream states is necessarily limited by the ability to measure a source's impact on the water quality of the receiving waters. At some point downstream, the impact on water quality of a particular pollution source becomes so attenuated as to be undetectable. Assuming the quality of the receiving waters currently meets or exceeds standards, there can be no violation of standards if the impact of the proposed source on the water quality could not be measured. Nor is it "impossible to predict the standard[s]" applicable to a new discharge, as Arkansas claims. First, EPA approval of state WQS determines the potentially applicable rules. Furthermore, the permitting system established in the 1972 and 1977 amendments to the CWA clearly provides for consultation with and input by states that may be affected. Finally, computer modeling (such as that performed for the Fayetteville plant) can predict the extent of a new source's potential impact, thus demonstrating which states' WQS must be met.

3. Illinois v. Milwaukee and Ouellette

Arkansas cites International Paper Co. v. Ouellette and Illinois v. Milwaukee in support of its statutory construction argument, but that reliance is misplaced. In each of those cases an affected state was seeking to enjoin an ongoing discharge in another state by resort to its own state law nuisance remedies. 479 U.S. at 483; 731 F.2d at 404. In contrast, this case is a permitting, rather than an enforcement, action wherein Oklahoma seeks to ensure compliance with federal law, i.e., its EPA-approved WQS. . . .

. . . Plainly, *Ouellette* was concerned not with the CWA's provisions for incorporating a downstream's water quality criteria in the permitting process, but with preventing a downstream state from circumventing or superseding that process by imposing on an already-permitted source additional requirements based on its own state law. So viewed, *Ouellette* is entirely consistent with EPA's interpretation of the applicability of Oklahoma's WQS. Cf. *Champion*, 652 F. Supp. at 1400 (concluding that nothing in *Ouellette* required a modification of the decision at 648 F. Supp. 1390 that a North Carolina discharge permit must require compliance with an applicable Tennessee WQS).

4. The Statutory and Regulatory Framework

The erroneous interpretation of *Ouellette*, which Arkansas advocates, runs aground when the Clean Water Act is considered as a whole. The Act contains several mechanisms for ensuring that minimum water quality and pollution criteria will apply to all navigable waters of the United States; for example, prohibiting the discharge of pollutants except pursuant to a permit, 33 U.S.C. §§1311, 1342; requiring EPA to establish effluent limitations for point source discharges,

§§1311-1312; providing for EPA's approval of water quality standards, §1313, and state permit programs, §1342(b); and establishing minimum procedural requirements for state permit programs, §1314(i). As discussed above, however, states are not precluded from imposing pollution limitations more stringent than those promulgated by EPA. 33 U.S.C. §1370; 40 C.F.R. §122.1(f); Milwaukee v. Illinois, 451 U.S. at 327-28, 101 S. Ct. at 1797-98. Moreover, the CWA requires the application of best available control technology or best practicable treatment to discharges of pollutants, 33 U.S.C. §1311, and the Act's legislative history reveals that Congress intended the CWA to be "technology-forcing." S. Rep. No. 414, *reprinted in* 1972 U.S. Code Cong. & Admin. News 3668, 3709 (Act contains a "mandate to press technology and economics" to achieve practicable and attainable levels of effluent reduction; thus, "increasingly tougher controls on industry" will be required); see also Natural Resources Defense Council, Inc. v. EPA, 822 F.2d 104, 123-24 (D.C. Cir. 1987). Any standard or limitation adopted by a state and approved by EPA becomes the "water quality standard for the applicable waters of that State," and thus is federally enforceable. 33 U.S.C. §1313(c)(3). See also §§1319, 1342; S. Rep. 414, *reprinted in* 1972 U.S. Code Cong. & Admin. News 3668, 3672; Order on Petitions for Review, R., A-28, at 11-12 n.13.

a. *33 U.S.C. §1341.* EPA finds support for its action here in certain of the foregoing sections. In addition, we consider 33 U.S.C. §1341 particularly persuasive. It provides that no NPDES permit may be granted until a "certification" is obtained from the state in which the discharge originates (or from EPA where no state agency possesses such authority, §1341(a)(1); 40 C.F.R. §121.21(b)), stating that the discharge will comply with, among other things, §1311 water quality requirements. Section 1341(a)(2) provides:

> Whenever such a discharge may affect, as determined by the [EPA] Administrator, the quality of the waters of any other State, the Administrator . . . shall so notify such other State. . . . If . . . such other State determines that such discharge will affect the quality of its waters so as to violate any water quality requirement in such State, and . . . notifies the Administrator . . . and requests a public hearing . . . , the licensing or permitting agency shall hold such a hearing. . . . [The licensing or permitting] agency, based upon the recommendations of such State, . . . shall condition such license or permit in such manner as may be necessary to insure compliance with applicable water quality requirements. If the imposition of conditions cannot insure such compliance such agency shall not issue such license or permit.

"'[T]he purpose of the [§1341(a)(2)] notice requirement is to enable a state whose water qualities may be affected by the proposed federal activity an opportunity to insure that its standards *will be complied with*.'" EPA Brief at 17-18 (emphasis added) (quoting Lake Erie Alliance for the Protection of the Coastal Corridor v. U.S. Army Corps of Eng'rs, 526 F. Supp. 1063, 1075 (W.D. Pa. 1981), *aff'd without opinion*, 707 F.2d 1392 (3d Cir.), *cert. denied*, 464 U.S. 915 (1983)). EPA's regulations reaffirm this view, see 40 C.F.R. §§121.1-.30, as does the

IV. Protecting the Water Resource

limited case law, see, e.g., United States v. Commonwealth of Puerto Rico, 721 F.2d 832, 833-34 (1st Cir. 1983) (certification is a "condition precedent to the EPA's issuance of a NPDES permit"; "state decision denying certification, or one imposing conditions or restrictions, is not reviewable administratively by the EPA" and is "exempt from review in federal court").

Arkansas disputes that "applicable water quality requirements" in §1341(a)(2) refers to the WQS of the affected state. Based on its plain language, however, we agree with EPA that the purpose of this provision must be to enable affected states to ensure that their water quality will not be jeopardized by a discharge in another state. Only a strained interpretation of the statute could produce the result Arkansas seeks — that "applicable water quality requirements" refers to the WQS of only the source state. Moreover, there would be no reason for §(a)(2) to refer to the effect on the quality of the affected state's waters in terms of "violat[ing] any water quality requirement in such State" if the affected state's water quality requirements were irrelevant in the permitting process. Given that this subsection of the statute deals expressly with effects on states other than the source state, it is much more likely that "applicable" refers simply to those federally approved water quality requirements of affected states that would be violated if the permit were not appropriately conditioned. We reject Arkansas's argument to the contrary.

The legislative history of the certification statute sheds additional light on this matter. In 1977 Congress amended the statute

> to add section 303 [33 U.S.C. §1313, "water quality standards and implementation plans"] to the list of the act's provisions for which a State must certify compliance. . . . This means that a federally licensed or permitted activity, including a discharge permit under section 402, must be certified to comply with State water quality standards adopted under section 303.

S. Rep. No. 370, at 72, *reprinted in* 1977 U.S. Code Cong. & Admin. News 4326, 4397; H. Conf. Rep. No. 830, at 96, *reprinted in* 1977 U.S. Code Cong. & Admin. News 4424, 4471. According to the committees, the amendment was not meant to change the law but to follow and clarify the original congressional intent that "State water quality standards would be imposed through Section 301, and thus certification by the State would include consideration of water quality standards." 1977 U.S. Code Cong. & Admin. News at 4397. The conference committee added that "[s]ection 303 is always included by reference where section 301 is listed." H. Conf. Rep. No. 830, at 96, *reprinted in* 1977 U.S. Code Cong. & Admin. News 4424, 4471. The Senate committee offered this further explanation of the amendment:

> [A]ll States have approved water quality standards. Thus, it is reasonable to require that Federal permits and licenses should take into account State water quality plans, standards and requirements adopted under section 303 to assure maintenance of water quality in the respective States.

Id. at 4398. Neither the statute as amended nor the committee reports concerning the bills distinguish between source and affected states. Thus, EPA's view that sources subject to NPDES permits must comply with all approved state water quality standards is a reasonable interpretation in light of this history.

    b. *33 U.S.C. §1342.* Also germane to EPA's construction of the CWA is the fact that, in those states authorized to issue NPDES permits, the EPA Administrator retains authority to veto any proposed permit if he objects to its issuance. 33 U.S.C. §1342(d)(2) EPA may object on the basis of either of two grounds: (1) that a permitting state failed to accept recommendations from another state whose waters may be affected by permit issuance; or (2) that the permit is "'outside [i.e., inconsistent with] the guidelines and requirements' of the Act." EPA Brief at 18-19 (quoting 33 U.S.C. §1342(d)(2)). The statute mandates that "[n]o permit shall issue" if EPA objects for either reason. §1342(d)(2). If the source state does not revise the proposed permit to satisfy EPA's objection, EPA may issue a discharge permit, §1342(d)(4), but it may not issue a permit less stringent than that required by any state's effluent limitations and water quality criteria. H.R. Conf. Rep. No. 830, 95th Cong., 1st Sess. 97, *reprinted in* 1977 U.S. Code Cong. & Admin. News 4424, 4472. Given that a permit program administered by EPA is subject to the same requirements as apply to an approved state program, §1342(a)(3), no reasonable argument would justify invalidating a state-issued permit that fails to account for the WQS of another state, yet allowing EPA to issue a permit objectionable on the same ground.[19] . . .

---

    19. Section 1342(d)(3), the paragraph immediately following the veto provision, states: "The [EPA] Administrator may, as to any permit application, waive paragraph (2) of this subsection." The discretionary language of this paragraph initially gave us pause, especially in light of the mandatory tone of paragraph (2) ("No permit shall issue" if the Administrator objects). After careful study of the statute and the legislative history, however, we believe the legislative history reveals that EPA's discretion arises only with respect to its authority to choose to review or not review a permit application of which it is notified by a permit-issuing state pursuant to §1342(d)(1). *See Mianus River Preservation Comm. v. Administrator, EPA,* 541 F.2d 899, 907-09 (2d Cir. 1976) (discussing legislative history of §402 of the CWA). Such discretion is consistent with congressional intent to allow EPA-approved, qualified states to administer their own permit programs. An implicit component of this discretion, once exercised, is EPA's authority to determine the impact of a proposed discharge and whether that impact is acceptable under the CWA.
    Once EPA chooses to review a permit application and proposed permit under this section, we do not believe it has "discretion" to overlook any violation of the CWA revealed by its review. *Cf.* §1342(c)(3) (if EPA determines a state permit program is not being administered in accordance with §1342, it "*shall* withdraw approval of such program" (emphasis added)); §1313(c)(4) (EPA "*shall* promulgate" new or revised WQS where necessary to meet CWA requirements or where state has promulgated inadequate standard); *contra Mianus River,* 541 F.2d at 909 & n. 24. Interpreting §1342(d)(3) otherwise (i.e., as making *all* of the provisions of §1342(d)(2) discretionary) is inconsistent with the spirit and framework of the CWA and with the express prohibition against discharging any pollutant except in compliance with the Act. 33 U.S.C. §1311(a).

IV. Protecting the Water Resource

B. SIGNIFICANCE OF EXISTING VIOLATIONS OF ILLINOIS RIVER WATER QUALITY STANDARDS

There is substantial evidence in the record of ongoing violations of Illinois River water quality standards, yet neither of the EPA judicial officers nor any of the parties addresses whether, or how, this is relevant to Fayetteville's application to discharge to the Illinois River. We believe this situation poses an issue of critical importance — whether a new discharge may be permitted when the applicable water quality standards are already being violated. Guided by the Supreme Court's pronouncement that an agency decision is arbitrary and capricious if the agency "entirely failed to consider an important aspect of the problem [or] offered an explanation for its decision that runs counter to the evidence before the agency," *Motor Vehicle Mfrs.*, 463 U.S. at 43, we conclude EPA's decision to issue the Fayetteville permit was arbitrary and capricious. The agency's decision is also flawed by misinterpretation and misapplication of two important Oklahoma water quality regulations and by arbitrary disregard for certain expert testimony. For these reasons, discussed more fully below, we hold that the Clean Water Act prohibits granting an NPDES permit under the circumstances of this case (i.e., where applicable water quality standards have already been violated) and reverse EPA's decision to permit Fayetteville to discharge any part of its effluent to the Illinois River Basin.

1. Law Applicable to Oklahoma Scenic Rivers

The Upper Illinois River, including Lake Frances, from the Arkansas state line down to the 650-foot elevation level of Tenkiller Ferry Reservoir, is designated an Oklahoma state scenic river. Okla. Stat. tit. 82, §1452(b)(1) (1990). As such, certain water quality standards apply to these waters. See Oklahoma Water Quality Standards (OWQS) §4 & App. A (1982). Water quality standards consist of two parts: a designated use or uses for the identified waters and water quality criteria for such waters based on those uses. 40 C.F.R. §130.2(c); Okla. Stat. tit. 82 §904(f); OWQS §4. Of greatest interest for purposes of this discussion are the Illinois River's "fish and wildlife propagation" (primary warmwater fishery), "aesthetics," and "smallmouth bass" designated "beneficial uses." Within the latter two use categories, the following water quality criteria are particularly significant: turbidity (OWQS §4.10(b)), nutrients (OWQS §4.10(c)), and dissolved oxygen (OWQS §4.11(a)). The occurrence of phosphorus and nitrogen in Fayetteville's effluent necessitates the consideration of these criteria.

As a preliminary matter, Oklahoma contends and we agree that EPA's judicial officers erred in concluding that Oklahoma's nutrients standard, §4.10(c), applies only to lakes, not to streams. Decision on Remand, R., A-33, at 6; Second Order on Petitions for Review, R., A-37, at 8. Section 4.10(c) provides: "The total phosphorus concentration and the nitrogen/phosphorus concentration ratio shall not be increased to levels which result in man-induced eutrophication problems." The source of the agency's confusion is the definition of "eutrophication (natural)" (included in Appendix C of the OWQS), which refers only to lakes. An Oklahoma witness at the administrative hearing explained that the definitions in the appendix are "scientific definitions," provided merely for clarification purposes, and that "the state does apply the eutrophication principle . . . to rivers." Tr. at 578. Apparently no one scrutinized the OWQS carefully enough to discover that the regulations themselves define the scope of the nutrient standard's application. Section 4, "Standards for Water Quality," unequivocally states: "Narrative standards '[including] Section . . . 4.10(c) . . .' shall be maintained at all times and *apply to all perennial and intermittent streams.*" (Emphasis added.) In addition, the preface to Appendix A of the OWQS states that §4.10(c) applies even to those stream segments not listed in the appendix (i.e., stream segments for which beneficial uses have not been designated). Accordingly, we reject EPA's ruling that the nutrients standard applies only to Lake Frances and Tenkiller Reservoir and hold that it applies to the entire reach of the Illinois River in Oklahoma.

In addition to the nutrients standard, Oklahoma's "Anti-Degradation Policy," OWQS §3, and "Beneficial Use Limitations," id. §5, also protect the Upper Illinois River. The Oklahoma parties assert that EPA also misinterpreted and misapplied these regulations. Their argument is rather unfocused, but they basically claim that "any increase in any 'wastes' . . . which *may pollute or tend to pollute*" the waters of a scenic river violates these rules. Oklahoma Brief at 32 (emphasis in original); see generally id. at 30-38.

The Beneficial Use Limitations regulation provides that scenic rivers "are protected by prohibition of any new point source discharge of wastes . . . except under conditions described in Section 3 [the Anti-Degradation Policy]." OWQS §5. The relevant provision of §3 states: "No degradation shall be allowed in high quality waters . . . includ[ing] water bodies . . . designated 'Scenic Rivers.'" The Oklahoma courts apparently have not interpreted these provisions. Nevertheless, we believe the plain language of the regulations manifests a clear intent to allow no degradation of the water quality of scenic rivers. More specifically, the regulations disallow any additional discharge of pollution (either a new point source or an increase from an existing source) to a scenic river if its water quality *has been degraded* or if the new source *would degrade* it.

Closer examination of the language and structure of the Anti-Degradation Policy, guided by the minimum requirements for such policies set forth in EPA's regulation, confirms our plain language construction. The Oklahoma regulation allows "no degradation" of water quality in designated scenic rivers. "Limited degradation" is permitted limited *only* in other "high quality waters" where the existing water quality "exceeds those levels necessary to support propagation of fish, shellfish, wildlife, and recreation." OWQS §3, para. 2. Even if the Upper Illinois were not a scenic river, it would not be eligible for the limited degradation exception because its waters in their present condition do not qualify as such "high quality waters." See *infra* part B.2. Clearly, then, the Oklahoma Anti-Degradation Policy prohibits any further degradation of the Illinois scenic river.

We conclude the requirements of the Beneficial Use Limitations/Anti-Degradation Policy are violated when the water quality of a scenic river under-

IV. Protecting the Water Resource   Page 407

goes any human-caused, detectable change. By "detectable change" we mean any detectable change in a water quality parameter such as turbidity or phosphorus (with the perhaps unnecessary qualification that an *improvement* in water quality is excepted). We do *not* mean a detectable change that violates a numeric criterion for that parameter (e.g., 25 NTUs for turbidity), which criterion would otherwise apply if the Beneficial Use Limitations were not applicable (i.e., if the receiving waters were not designated as a scenic river or otherwise as "(a)" in Appendix A). The Beneficial Use Limitations/Anti-Degradation Policy are designed to provide *additional* protection beyond that conferred by the numeric limits of other water quality standards. Interpreting these regulations as merely prohibiting violations of otherwise applicable WQS would render them a nullity because, as we have seen, WQS may not be contravened in any waters, regardless of whether these additional regulations apply.

The ALJ, on remand, did not explicitly address the Anti-Degradation Policy but did construe the Beneficial Use Limitations. The 1985 version of the Beneficial Use Limitations, which the ALJ deemed applicable, provides: "'All streams and bodies of water designated as (a) . . . are protected by prohibition of any new point source discharge which increases pollutant loading or increased load from an existing point source.'" Decision on Remand, R., A-33, at 4. Construing this regulation in light of the OWQS definition of "pollution," he concluded: "[T]he Oklahoma parties must show by substantial evidence that the City's discharge will create a nuisance or render the Illinois River in Oklahoma harmful, detremental [sic] or injurious to any beneficial use of the river." Decision on Remand, R., A-33, at 5. The CJO upheld this interpretation with minimal discussion. Second Order on Petitions for Review, R., A-37, at 8. He excused the ALJ's failure to discuss the Anti-Degradation Policy by explaining that the ALJ "implicitly addressed the policy in his detailed analysis of the discharge's potential impact on all relevant water quality parameters." Id. at 9; see id. at 10 (if ALJ erred in this regard, it was "harmless error"). The CJO reasoned that "if the Fayetteville discharge will not cause a detectible change in any of the relevant water quality parameters [as the ALJ found], it logically follows that there will not be a 'quality degradation.'" Id. at 9-10.

We have considerable difficulty with the agency's treatment of these crucial Oklahoma regulations. First, and most importantly, the ALJ's interpretation defies the plain language of the Beneficial Use Limitations and the Anti-Degradation Policy that it references. Secondly, the CJO ruled that the ALJ erred in applying the 1985, rather than the 1982, OWQS. Second Order on Petitions for Review, R., A-37, at 5-6. The CJO deemed this error harmless, but we disagree. The 1985 version of the Beneficial Use Limitations, which the ALJ improperly applied, states: "All streams . . . designated as (a) in Appendix A are protected by prohibition of any new point source *discharge which increases pollutant loading*. . . ." OWQS §7.11 (1985) (emphasis added), *quoted in* Decision on Remand, R., A-33, at 4. Finding no definition of "pollutant loading" in the 1985 rule, the ALJ consulted the statutory definition of "pollution," Okla. Stat. tit. 82 §926.1.1., to construct his interpretation of the regulation. The applicable 1982 rule, however, prohibits simply "any new point source *discharge of wastes*" (em-

653

phasis added). Oklahoma law defines "wastes" as "industrial waste and all other liquid, gaseous or solid substances which may pollute or tend to pollute any waters of the state." §926.1.2. We do not know whether Oklahoma intended to significantly change the import of the Beneficial Use Limitation by this minor language revision, but we cannot approve a construction of the regulation based on the definition of a term ("pollution") not even contained in the applicable rule.

Finally, the agency's construction of the Beneficial Use Limitation is further flawed by the ALJ's imposition of the burden on Oklahoma to prove that the discharge would "create a nuisance" or "render the Illinois River . . . harmful . . . or injurious to any beneficial use." Decision on Remand at 5. Granted, the opponent of a permit has the "burden of going forward to present an affirmative case at the conclusion of the Agency case on the challenged requirement." 40 C.F.R. §124.85(a)(3)(ii). However, the "Agency has the burden of going forward to present an affirmative case in support of any challenged condition of a final permit," id. §(a)(2), and more importantly, the "permit applicant always bears the burden of persuading the Agency that a permit . . . should be issued and not denied," id. §(a)(1). By requiring Oklahoma to "show by substantial evidence that the City's discharge will create a nuisance," the ALJ improperly transformed Fayetteville's burden of showing the permit should be issued into a burden on Oklahoma to show that it should be denied.

As for the Anti-Degradation Policy, the CJO concluded there could be no violation of the policy if there would be no detectable change in water quality. However, it is not clear whether the CJO interpreted the policy as *requiring* that there be no detectable change in water quality, or whether he was merely reporting the legal significance of the facts found by the ALJ. Although the CJO determined in his first order that the applicable legal standard is "whether [Fayetteville's] discharges under the permit will result in a detectable violation of the applicable water quality standards," Order on Petitions for Review, R. A-28, at 2, 12-13, his subsequent affirmation of the ALJ's erroneous construction of the Beneficial Use Limitations casts doubt on whether he intended the "no detectable change" test to apply to violations of the Beneficial Use Limitations/Anti-Degradation Policy as well. Because of this ambiguity and the errors in interpreting the Beneficial Use Limitations, we agree with the Oklahoma parties that the agency incorrectly construed and applied both Oklahoma regulations.

2. *Existing Degradation of Illinois Scenic River*

Under other circumstances, the errors described above might necessitate remanding to the agency with instructions to apply Oklahoma law as we have construed it. However, given the facts in this record, even proper interpretation and application of Oklahoma water quality standards cannot save this permit. The record contains substantial evidence from which the ALJ could have found that the water quality of the Illinois scenic river has been degraded and that water quality standards were being violated prior to the onset of Fayetteville's discharge to the river (see subpart a. below). We believe that, where a proposed source would discharge effluents that would contribute to conditions currently constituting a violation of applicable water quality standards, such proposed source may not be permitted. The ALJ and the CJO erred in failing to consider whether or how the river's existing degraded condition is relevant to the decision whether to permit a new source discharge.

Three factual subissues are essential to our determination that the Fayetteville discharge to the Illinois River may not be permitted: (1) whether the Illinois scenic river is already degraded (i.e., whether its quality has deteriorated since the river's designation in 1970); (2) whether Fayetteville's effluent will reach the scenic river; and (3) whether and how the components of Fayetteville's discharge would contribute to conditions in the Illinois River. Although it is difficult to summarize a record that consists of five boxes and four years of briefs, orders, transcripts, prepared testimony, correspondence, technical reports and miscellaneous other documents, in the following few pages we attempt to capsulize the evidence relevant to these three issues:

a. Evidence of existing degradation. First, we address the subject of the degradation of the Illinois scenic river's historically pristine water quality. Our review of the record before the ALJ revealed ample evidence from which the ALJ could have concluded that the river's condition has deteriorated since its designation as a scenic river and that water quality standards are being violated. . . .

At this juncture we note that the absence of any evidence in the record that enforcement efforts have been undertaken to remedy the pollution problems in the Illinois River does not undermine our conclusion that water quality violations have occurred and no doubt continue to occur. Enforcement actions are not necessary to document water quality degradation; it is only necessary that there be reliable evidence that water quality criteria have been exceeded. See 33 U.S.C. §1319(a)(1) ("Whenever, *on the basis of any information available* to him, the Administrator finds that any person is in violation of any condition . . . in a permit . . . he shall [commence enforcement proceedings]" (emphasis added)). Such evidence may be found in the dischargers' own monitoring reports, see 40 C.F.R. §122.41(j); the states' obligatory 305(b) or 205(j) (33 U.S.C. §1285(j)) reports; or other studies or surveys conducted according to accepted methods.

Similarly, a history of lax enforcement with respect to existing sources does not justify allowing a new source of pollution. Water quality standards prescribe the desired condition of surface waters to be met at all applicable times; they do not serve merely as a yardstick for enforcement efforts when enforcement personnel may be available to ascertain compliance.

Clearly then, the record before the ALJ contains substantial evidence from which it can be concluded that water quality in the Upper Illinois River is degraded and that Oklahoma water quality standards for nutrients, dissolved oxygen, and/or aesthetics have been and probably continue to be violated. The decisions of EPA's judicial officers ignore the bulk of this evidence. To our consternation, however, the ALJ believed some of the relevant testimony chronicled above, yet remained oblivious to its ramifications. In his Decision on Remand, for example, the ALJ stated that "dissolved oxygen violations in Oklahoma *are occurring* without [Fayetteville's] discharge." R., A-33, at 19 (emphasis added). It also appears he accepted the testimony that nutrients, turbidity, and solids standards were being violated, although he disputed the conclusion that Fayetteville "would increase the spatial and temporal . . . frequencies" of those violations. Id. at 14-15 (citing Dr. Walker's and Dr. Gakstatter's testimony). Significantly, no witness refuted the testimony concerning the river's currently degraded condition, nor did the ALJ discredit (or even comment on) any of that testimony. He simply failed to recognize the significance of this testimony with respect to the permitting decision at hand.

b. Downstream transport of pollution from Fayetteville. Next, we address the question of the downstream migration of Fayetteville's effluent. Our review of the transcript revealed that no person involved in the administrative hearing seriously disputed that pollution from Fayetteville would reach the state line; instead, the parties debated how much would reach Oklahoma and what effect, if any, it would have. Indeed, in his final opinion, the ALJ recites evidence that twenty to twenty-five percent of the nutrients (specifically, phosphorus) in Fayetteville's effluent would be "bio-available" at the Oklahoma state line. Decision on Remand, R., A-33, at 8. . . .

We conclude from the foregoing three-part review of the record that there is substantial evidence that degraded water quality conditions currently exist in the Illinois River in Oklahoma and that these conditions have been caused at least in part by pollutants that are constituents of Fayetteville's effluent. There is also substantial evidence that Fayetteville's effluent will be transported downstream to Oklahoma; thus, the plant can be expected to contribute to the ongoing deterioration of the scenic river and possibly Tenkiller Reservoir as well. It is our inescapable conclusion, given this evidence and the requisites of federal-Oklahoma state water pollution control laws, that the Fayetteville discharge to the Illinois River may not be permitted.

IV. DISCUSSION AND CONCLUSIONS

As explained in part I. of this opinion (Standard of Review), we normally give considerable deference to an agency's interpretation of its obligations and authority under a statute it administers. Here, EPA's view that no discharge to a navigable water may be permitted unless it will comply with the federally approved standards of all affected downstream states is consistent with the statutory language and EPA's implementing regulations, supported by the legislative history, and reasonable on its face; therefore, it is entitled to substantial deference. See *Chevron*, 467 U.S. at 844-45. As we discussed in part III.A. *supra*, we adopt the agency's view on this question of statutory interpretation as our first holding in this case.

The balance of the agency's actions, however, do not warrant similar respect. In part III.B. we have identified several errors or deficiencies in EPA's interpretation of the applicable Oklahoma regulations, in the agency's factual findings, and in its application of the law to the relevant facts. We believe the most serious of these errors is the failure to attribute any significance to the existing WQS violations. In this section we discuss the errors on which we found our conclusion that the Fayetteville permit decision must be set aside as "arbitrary, capricious, . . . or otherwise not in accordance with law." 5 U.S.C. §706(2)(A).

As a preliminary matter, EPA undermined our usual deference to its special expertise by the failure of its presiding officer to consider an important scientific principle, the oxygen-reducing effects of algae respiration and decay, and by his incomplete understanding of phosphorus assimilation. "EPA's failure to base its position on scientific or policy considerations . . . [is] cause for reduced deference." National Wildlife Fed'n v. Gorsuch, 693 F.2d 156, 169 (D.C. Cir. 1982). Similarly, a lack of thoroughness on the part of the agency warrants reduced deference. Id. at 166 ("'thoroughness . . . of an agency's reasoning' bears on the proper degree of deference" (quoting Federal Election Comm'n v. Democratic Senatorial Campaign Comm., 454 U.S. 27, 37 (1981)). In light of other errors in the agency's reasoning, however, we need not decide whether these flaws alone constitute reversible error.

EPA also misinterpreted and misapplied the Oklahoma nutrients standard and the Beneficial Use Limitations/Anti-Degradation Policy. In these respects the permit decision is flawed as a matter of law and must be set aside. 5 U.S.C. §706(2)(A).

Furthermore, the agency's judicial officers believed expert testimony that nutrients in Fayetteville's discharge would be transported downstream to Oklahoma, but they inexplicably rejected or discounted testimony concerning the probable eutrophying effects of these nutrients. This error may have resulted in part from the officers' faulty understanding of eutrophication processes and/or their erroneous interpretation of the nutrients standard. In any event, the net result is that the agency's decision to permit the Fayetteville discharge to the Illinois River "runs counter to the evidence before the agency" and lacks a "satisfactory explanation . . . including a 'rational connection between the facts found and the choice made.'" *Motor Vehicle Mfrs. Ass'n*, 463 U.S. at 43 (citation omitted). As such, it is arbitrary and capricious and must be set aside. Id.

Finally, we hold that EPA's decision is arbitrary and capricious on one significant, additional ground. We believe that EPA, in failing to consider the significance of the evidence of ongoing WQS violations, has not only rendered a decision that "runs counter to the evidence," but has "entirely failed to consider an important aspect of the problem." Id. We consider this the principal flaw in the agency's decision-making rationale.

It cannot be doubted that ongoing violations of federally approved water quality standards constitute "an important aspect" of the decision whether to permit an additional source of pollution on a waterway. Adherence to EPA's treatment of the facts and law of this case would fatally undermine the federal water pollution control strategy engineered by the Clean Water Act and enhanced by Oklahoma law. As we have seen, the "first principle of the [CWA] is . . . that it is unlawful to pollute at all. . . . The foremost national goal enunciated by Congress is the complete elimination of the discharge of pollutants." Natural Resources Defense Council v. EPA, 822 F.2d 104, 123 (D.C. Cir. 1987) (referring to 33 U.S.C. §1251(a)(1); see also §1251(a)(6)).[51]

The CWA further declares that it is the "primary responsibilit[y] . . . of States to prevent, reduce and eliminate pollution." §1251(b). In at least one court's opinion, the "language of the Act indicates that striving for the utter abolition of pollution is an acceptable approach for states to take." *Union Oil Co.*, 813 F.2d at 1487 n.6. Oklahoma dutifully heeds the Act's mandate. Its water pollution control policies and requirements call for: "protect[ing], maintain[ing] and improv[ing] the quality" of the waters of the state, Okla. Stat. tit. 82 §926.2; employing the permitting system "to prevent, control or abate pollution," id. §926.3.10; classifying state waters "for the purpose of progressively improving the[ir] quality" and "upgrading them from time to time by reclassifying them," id. §926.6.A.; and allowing "no degradation" of the state's scenic rivers, OWQS §3. Common sense dictates that a pollution control strategy designed to prevent, abate, and eliminate pollution would be subverted by allowing a new source of pollution on a currently polluted watercourse.

This judgment is corroborated by the Supreme Court's pronouncements concerning the legislative purposes behind the CWA. After painstaking review of the Act's legislative history, the Court declared that "Congress' intent . . . was clearly to establish an all-encompassing program of water pollution regulation," and that the "'major purpose' of the [CWA] Amendments was 'to establish a *comprehensive* long-range policy for the elimination of water pollution.'" Milwaukee v. Illinois, 451 U.S. at 318 (citation omitted; emphasis in original); see also *Ouellette*, 479 U.S. at 489. The Court explained that before it was amended in 1972 and 1977 the Clean Water Act relied solely on water quality standards to control and reduce pollution. But that system "proved ineffective. The problems stemmed from the character of the standards themselves, which focused on the *tolerable effects rather than the preventable causes* of water pollution. . . ." State Water Resources Control Bd., 426 U.S. at 202 (emphasis added). The Court described the effect of the amendments:

---

51. There is extensive legislative history on the goals and policy section, §101, of the CWA, 33 U.S.C. §1251(a). See *National Wildlife Fed'n*, 693 F.2d at 179-81, for one overview of that history. The D.C. Circuit stated:

> [T]he sponsors of the Act successfully insisted on a zero-discharge-of-pollutants goal despite strong objection from both within and without. . . . Senator Muskie, the Senate sponsor and principal force behind the bill, stated, in the post-conference debate on the bill: "These [goals] are not merely the pious declarations that Congress so often makes in passing its laws; on the contrary, this is literally a life or death proposition for the nation."

693 F.2d at 179 (quoting 118 Cong. Rec. 33,693 (1972)).

IV. Protecting the Water Resource

> [The 1972] Amendments introduced two major changes. . . . First, the Amendments are aimed at achieving maximum "effluent limitations" on "point sources," as well as achieving acceptable water quality standards. . . .
>
> Second, the Amendments establish the National Pollutant Discharge Elimination System (NPDES) as a means of achieving and enforcing the effluent limitations. . . .
>
> Water quality standards are retained [in the amended Act] as a supplementary basis for effluent limitations . . . *so that numerous point sources, despite individual compliance with effluent limitations, may be further regulated to prevent water quality from falling below acceptable levels.* . . .

Id. at 204-05 & n.12 (emphasis added).

Water quality standards could still be said to "focus on the tolerable effects of water pollution," but the focus of the NPDES program clearly is the "preventable causes" of pollution. As the passage quoted above reveals, even licensed polluters in compliance with their permit limitations may be further regulated if necessary to ensure that water quality standards are achieved and maintained. This authority to regulate, along with the absence of any right to pollute, necessarily subsumes the authority to deny a requested permit. These powers are essential to the ability to prevent pollution and thereby accomplish the Act's ultimate goal of eliminating pollutant discharges to water.

EPA and the Arkansas parties urge that the Fayetteville discharge should be permitted because its individual impact on Illinois River water quality will not be detectable. While this may prove true (and we pass no judgment thereon), we reject the argument because of its unavoidable result. If we were to accept this logic, once water quality standards in a stream were violated, additional new discharges might be permitted indefinitely so long as each one would have an unmeasurable individual impact. The absurdity of such a policy is manifest.

Congress cannot reasonably be presumed to have intended to exclude from the CWA's "all-encompassing program," 451 U.S. at 318, a permitting decision arising in circumstances such as those of this case. It is even more unfathomable that Congress fashioned a "*comprehensive . . . policy for the elimination* of water pollution," id. which sanctions continued pollution once minimum water quality standards have been transgressed. More likely, Congress simply never contemplated that EPA or a state would consider it permissible to authorize further pollution under such circumstances. We will not ascribe to the Act either the gaping loophole or the irrational purpose necessary to uphold EPA's action in this case.

We agree there must be an initial, detectable change in the water quality of a particular body of water for that water to qualify as "degraded." However, in circumstances such as those extant here, we reject any notion that, once water quality standards have been violated (i.e., the quality of the receiving waters has been degraded), the incremental impact of a proposed additional discharge must itself be detectable. Nor is it necessary to demonstrate that the proposed discharge would necessarily increase the frequency of violations. Contra Decision on Remand, R., A-33, at 19 ("no credible evidence to suggest that the frequency of

659

[dissolved oxygen] violations would increase due solely to [Fayetteville's] discharge"). Rather, if a body of water is experiencing WQS violations and a proposed new source would discharge the same pollutants to which those standards apply, that source may not be permitted if its effluent will reach the degraded waters. Here, Fayetteville's effluent contains phosphorus and nitrogen, each of which impacts several Illinois River water quality criteria — nutrients, turbidity, dissolved oxygen, aesthetics. Violations of at least two of these criteria are already occurring. See *supra* part III.B.2.a. Fayetteville's effluent will be carried downstream to the scenic river. At worst, it will increase the frequency and severity of ongoing violations; at best, it will thwart efforts to bring the river back into compliance with the applicable standards. These factors are sufficient to deny the permit. . . .

In conclusion, we hold that the Clean Water Act requires point sources to comply with the federally approved water quality standards of affected downstream states. We further hold that where water quality standards violations are already occurring in the receiving waters, no additional point source discharge to those waters may be permitted if it would contribute to the conditions that produced the violations. Accordingly, we reverse EPA's decision authorizing Fayetteville's municipal treatment plant to discharge a portion of its effluent to the Illinois River Basin pursuant to the terms of Permit No. AR0020010. . . .

V

CONTROLLING TOXIC AND HAZARDOUS SUBSTANCES

D. HAZARDOUS SUBSTANCES IN THE AIR AND WATER

1. Emissions Standards for Hazardous Air Pollutants

Page 567. After Note 4, add the following:

NOTE ON THE NEW PROGRAM FOR AIR TOXICS IN THE CLEAN AIR ACT AMENDMENTS OF 1990

Air toxics program. The Clean Air Act amendments of 1990 thoroughly revise §112 to establish a new program for the control of air toxics. Congress responded to EPA's failure over the years to identify toxic substances that produce adverse health effects by enacting a new §112(b)(1) that lists 118 substances EPA is required to regulate. EPA is authorized to add or delete substances from the list. §112(b)(2).

In another major departure from the old program, EPA is no longer required to establish controls for each substance. EPA will now identify categories of industrial facilities that emit substantial amounts of air toxics. All "major sources" in each category are regulated. A "major source" is defined as a source that emits 10 tons a year of one air toxic or 25 tons a year of a combination of air toxics. §112(a)(1).

Air toxics standards will be imposed on categories of sources in two phases. The first phase requires EPA to adopt technology standards that will achieve the maximum available control technology (MACT). A standard may include a prohibition on a toxic pollutant. §112(d)(2). This section also spells out the measures EPA can adopt to implement the MACT standard.

The second phase contemplates the possible adoption of residual risk standards. EPA is to report to Congress by 1996 on any remaining risks from air toxics. If Congress does not act on the report, EPA is to adopt residual risk standards within eight years after MACT standards were adopted for a category of sources. Section 112(f)(2) contains the criteria for setting residual risk standards. Does it codify the vinyl chloride decision, casebook p. 557? The amendments also contain requirements for the control of area sources of air toxics.

Accidental releases. Section 112(r) establishes an independent new program for the prevention of "accidental releases" by "regulated substances." EPA is required to use the extremely hazardous substance list under Title III of SARA to prepare a list of 100 regulated substances. By 1993, EPA is to adopt regulations and guidance to prevent, detect, and respond to accidental releases of these substances. The requirements for these regulations are in §112(r)(7)(B).

E. PREVENTING THE ENTRY OF TOXIC SUBSTANCES INTO THE STREAM OF COMMERCE

2. Toxic Chemicals and Other Substances

b. Federal Toxic Substances Control Act

Page 593. After carryover paragraph, add the following:

NOTE ON THE PROGRAM FOR
CHLOROFLUOROCARBONS IN THE 1990 AMENDMENTS
TO THE CLEAN AIR ACT

The 1990 amendments, in legislation that goes beyond the Montreal protocol, enacted a program for the production phaseout of CFCs and several other chemicals. EPA is required to list regulated substances in two classes. Class I, at a minimum, includes specified CFCs, halons, methyl chloroform, and carbon tetrachloride. All of these substances are banned by the year 2000 except methyl chloride, which is banned by 2002. The principal substance in Class II is hydrochlorofluorocarbons (HCFCs), whose production is phased out by 2030.

EPA regulations, to be adopted by 1992, must require reductions in the use and emission of Class I and Class II substances and must also maximize recapture and recycling. Consumer product restrictions are required, including a ban on nonessential CFC-containing consumer products.

F. PREVENTING HARM FROM HAZARDOUS WASTES

2. Dangerous Existing Sites: Of Deep Pockets, Orphans, and Superfunds

b. Potentially Responsible Parties: Liability, Site Nexus, and Cost Recovery

Page 634. Before the Notes and Questions section, add the following:

LOUISIANA-PACIFIC CORP. v. ASARCO, INC.
909 F.2d 1260 (9th Cir. 1990)

Before WRIGHT, POOLE and BRUNETTI, Circuit Judges.
Eugene A. Wright, Circuit Judge:

This appeal arises out of consolidated actions brought by Louisiana-Pacific Corporation and the Port of Tacoma against Asarco, Inc., under the Comprehensive Environmental Response, Compensation and Liability Act of 1980 (CERCLA), as amended by the Superfund Amendments and Reauthorization Act of 1986, 42 U.S.C. §§9607, 9613, for recovery of costs incurred in cleaning up the release of hazardous waste. Asarco brought a third-party claim against L-Bar Products, Inc. seeking contribution or indemnity based on L-Bar's status as a corporate successor to Industrial Mineral Products (IMP) which marketed the waste for Asarco. Asarco challenges the district court's grant of summary judgment in favor of L-Bar. We affirm.

Background

For almost 80 years, Asarco had a copper smelter at Ruston, Washington. As part of its operations, it produced a by-product called "slag," a hard rock-like substance. IMP sold the slag to several businesses, including Louisiana-Pacific, from the early 1970s until March 1985 when the copper smelter ceased operations. About nine months after IMP stopped selling the slag, it sold substantially all its assets to L-Bar.

One major use of the slag was as ballast to stabilize the ground at log sort yards in the Tacoma area. Government agencies now assert that the slag reacted with the acidic wood-waste in the log sort yards, causing heavy metals from the slag to leach into the groundwater and soil. It appears that the log yards may require substantial environmental clean up.

Louisiana-Pacific and the Port of Tacoma sued Asarco under CERCLA, claiming that it was liable for the costs of cleaning up and abating the release of the hazardous substances. Asarco brought third-party claims against L-Bar and others for contribution or indemnity in the event that Louisiana-Pacific and the Port of Tacoma succeed in their action against it. It sued L-Bar as successor in interest to IMP.

L-Bar moved for summary judgment, claiming that it was not the successor to IMP and could not be liable under CERCLA for IMP's actions. Judge Bryan applied Washington law to successor liability, reasoning that there was not a significant difference between federal and Washington law. See Louisiana-Pacific Corp. v. Asarco, Inc., 29 Env't Rep. Cas. (BNA) 1450, 1452 (W.D. Wash. 1989). He granted L-Bar's motion for summary judgment and denied Asarco's motion for reconsideration.

Analysis

I. STANDARD OF REVEIW

We review de novo a district court's grant of summary judgment. Kruso v. International Tel. & Tel. Corp., 872 F.2d 1416, 1421 (9th Cir. 1989). We must determine, viewing the evidence in the light most favorable to the nonmoving party, if there are genuine issues of material fact and if the district court applied the law correctly. Tzung v. State Farm Fire & Casualty Co., 873 F.2d 1338, 1339-40 (9th Cir. 1989).

II. SUCCESSOR LIABILITY UNDER CERCLA

Preliminarily, we must decide whether there is successor liability under CERCLA. Although Congress failed to address specifically the issue of corporate successor liability in CERCLA, we find Third Circuit authority persuasive on this issue and hold that Congress did intend successor liability. See Smith Land & Improvement Corp. v. Celotex Corp., 851 F.2d 86, 91-92 (3rd Cir. 1988), *cert. denied*, — U.S. — (1989) (citing Oner II, Inc. v. United States Environmental Protection Agency, 597 F.2d 184 (9th Cir. 1979)); see also In re Acushnet River & New Bedford Harbor Proceedings, 712 F. Supp. 1010, 1013 (D. Mass. 1989). But see Anspec Co. v. Johnson Controls, Inc., 30 Env't Rep. Cas. (BNA) 1672, 1674-75 (E.D. Mich. 1989) (successor liability does not exist under CERCLA).

We also agree with the Third Circuit that the issue of successor liability under CERCLA is governed by federal law.[1] *Smith Land*, 851 F.2d at 91 ("The

---

1. This case is distinguishable from Levins Metal Corp. v. Parr-Richmond Terminal Co., 817 F.2d 1448 (9th Cir. 1987), where the court applied California state law in determining successor liability under CERCLA. There, the court explained that when the issue deals with the "capacity to be sued" rather than the "imposition of liability," state law applies. In the case at hand, L-Bar does not contest its "capacity to be sued," but instead contends that it "cannot be liable" under CERCLA. Therefore, federal common law applies.

meager legislative history available indicates that Congress expected the courts to develop a federal common law to supplement the statute.") (citations omitted); see also United States v. Chem-Dyne Corp., 572 F. Supp. 802, 808-09 (S.D. Ohio 1983) (analyzing legislative history of CERCLA and determining that federal common law applies).

Because Congress has not addressed the issue of successor liability under CERCLA, we must look to other circuits and the states for guidance in fashioning the federal law. When examining successor liability under CERCLA in the context of a merger or consolidation, the Third Circuit said:

> We believe it in line with the thrust of the legislation to permit — if not require — successor liability under traditional concepts. . . .
>
> In resolving the successor liability issues here, the district court must consider national uniformity; . . . The general doctrine of successor liability in operation in most states should guide the court's decision rather than the excessively narrow statutes which might apply in only a few states.

Smith Land, 851 F.2d at 92. We believe its analysis is equally applicable to successor liability in the context of an asset sale, and hold that the traditional rules of successor liability in operation in most states should govern.[2] See *Acushnet*, 712 F. Supp. at 1014 (adopting the traditional rules of successor liability in the context of an asset purchase on the basis of *Smith Land*).

III. TRADITIONAL RULES OF SUCCESSOR LIABILITY

Under traditional rules of successor liability, asset purchasers are not liable as successors unless one of the following four exceptions applies:

(1) The purchasing corporation expressly or impliedly agrees to assume the liability;
(2) The transaction amounts to a "de-facto" consolidation or merger;
(3) The purchasing corporation is merely a continuation of the selling corporation; or
(4) The transaction was fraudulently entered into in order to escape liability.

---

2. Because of the need for national uniformity in the successor liability area and because of the possibility that CERCLA's purposes could be frustrated by state law, we believe that this case is distinguishable from Mardan v. C.G.C. Music Ltd., 804 F.2d 1454, 1458-60 (9th Cir. 1986) (incorporating state law to govern the validity of contractual releases of CERCLA liability). A state law which unduly limits successor liability could cut off the EPA's ability to seek reimbursement from responsible parties for cleaning up a hazardous waste site under 42 U.S.C. §§9604 and 9607. This would result in great expense to the taxpayer, which is contrary to CERCLA's purposes. Cf. *Smith Land*, 851 F.2d at 92 ("the district court must consider national uniformity; otherwise, CERCLA aims may be evaded easily by a responsible party's choice to arrange a merger or consolidation under the laws of particular states which unduly restrict successor liability").

See, e.g., Martin v. Abbott Laboratories, 102 Wash. 2d 581, 609, 689 P.2d 368, 384 (1984);[3] *Gee v. Tenneco, Inc.*, 615 F.2d 857, 863 (9th Cir. 1980) (applying California law); 15 W. Fletcher, Cyclopedia of the Law of Private Corporations §7122 (rev. perm. ed. 1983).

Asarco argues that it has established genuine issues of material fact under both the implied assumption of liability and defacto merger exceptions. It also argues that it has established material facts under an expanded version of the mere continuation exception, known as the continuing business enterprise exception. We disagree.

A. IMPLIED LIABILITY EXCEPTION

Asarco argues for the first time on appeal that L-Bar may have impliedly assumed IMP's liability. As a general rule, we will not consider issues on appeal that were not raised in the district court. See Bolker v. Commissioner, 760 F.2d 1039, 1042 (9th Cir. 1985). Although the rule permits discretion, we see no reason to depart from it in this case. The question of implied assumption of liability is a fact specific question, rather than a purely legal issue, and additional facts would have to be developed.[4] See Abex Corp. v. Ski's Enter., Inc., 748 F.2d 513, 516 (9th Cir. 1984) (rule is waived when the question is a purely legal one that is central to the case and important to the public).

B. DE FACTO MERGER EXCEPTION

Asarco also argues that there are genuine issues of fact as to whether the asset purchase was a de facto merger. Courts have recognized de facto mergers when:

(1) there is a continuation of the enterprise of the seller in terms of continuity of management, personnel, physical location, assets, and operations;

---

3. Washington and a few other states recognize a fifth exception known as the product-line exception. See, e.g., Ray v. Alad Corp., 19 Cal. 3d 22, 560 P.2d 3, 136 Cal. Rptr. 574 (1977); *Martin*, 102 Wash. 2d at 615, 689 P.2d at 388. Because Asarco has not argued this exception on appeal, we need not decide whether to adopt it under CERCLA. See United States v. Valentine, 783 F.2d 1413, 1417 n.5 (9th Cir. 1986) ("This claim was not raised on appeal and consequently we do not address it.").

4. Citing Jordan v. Clark, 847 F.2d 1368, 1374 n.6 (9th Cir. 1988), *cert. denied*, 488 U.S. 1006 (1989), Asarco argues that waiver of the rule is appropriate because the district court fully developed the record, even though implied liability was not framed as an additional theory. In *Jordan*, the parties argued over the relevant issue without framing it as a separate theory of recovery so no additional facts were necessary. Id. Here, the parties did not argue the issue of implied liability, and L-Bar would have brought forth more facts had it been raised as an issue below.

We have recognized two other exceptions to the general rule: (1) when review is necessary to prevent miscarriage of justice or to preserve the integrity of the judicial process, and (2) when a new issue arises during a pending appeal because of a change in the law. *See Bolker*, 760 F.2d at 1042. Neither exception applies here.

(2) there is a continuity of shareholders;
(3) the seller ceases operations, liquidates, and dissolves as soon as legally and practically possible; and
(4) the purchasing corporation assumes the obligations of the seller necessary for uninterrupted continuation of business operations.

See, e.g., Philadelphia Elec. Co. v. Hercules, Inc., 762 F.2d 303, 310 (3rd Cir.), *cert. denied*, 474 U.S. 980 (1985); Bud Antle, Inc. v. Eastern Foods, Inc., 758 F.2d 1451, 1457-58 (11th Cir. 1985).

Asarco argues that continuity of shareholders is not necessary for finding a de facto merger. Its argument has no merit because courts have consistently required continuity of shareholders, accomplished by paying for the acquired corporation with shares of stock. See, e.g., Arnold Graphics Indus. v. Independent Agent Center, Inc., 775 F.2d 38, 42 (2d Cir. 1985) ("'[t]o find that a *de facto* merger has occurred there must be . . . continuity of stockholders'") (emphasis in original) (quoting Ladjevardian v. Laidlaw-Coggeshall, Inc., 431 F. Supp. 834, 838 (S.D.N.Y. 1977)); Dayton v. Peck, Stow & Wilcox Co., 739 F.2d 690, 693 (1st Cir. 1984) (continuity of shareholders is "[o]ne of the key requirements" of the doctrine).

Here, there was no continuity of shareholders. The consideration paid by L-Bar for IMP was a combination of cash, a promissory note and payment of some debts. No stock in L-Bar or Reserve Industries Corporation, L-Bar's parent corporation, was exchanged as part of the sale. Although a few IMP shareholders now own stock in Reserve, that was bought on the open market, and no former IMP shareholder holds more than 2½% of Reserve stock. Because there is no genuine issue of material fact as to continuity of shareholders, the district court did not err in finding that the asset purchase was not a de facto merger.

C. CONTINUING BUSINESS ENTERPRISE EXCEPTION

Citing our decision in Oner II, Inc. v. United States Environmental Protection Agency, 597 F.2d 184 (9th Cir. 1979), Asarco argues that in keeping with the purposes of CERCLA, we should adopt a more expansive version of the mere continuation exception, known as the continuing business enterprise exception. See, e.g., Cyr v. B. Offen & Co., 501 F.2d 1145, 1152-54 (1st Cir. 1974); Turner v. Bituminous Casualty Co., 397 Mich. 406, 244 N.W.2d 873, 881-83 (1976). Even were we to adopt the exception, it is inapplicable here.[7]

---

7. When applying this exception, courts look at several factors including:
   1. continuity of employees, supervisory personnel and physical location;
   2. production of the same product;
   3. retention of the same name;
   4. continuity of general business operations;
   5. purchaser holding itself out as a continuation of the seller.

Mozingo v. Correct Mfg. Corp., 752 F.2d 168, 175 (5th Cir. 1985).

In *Oner II*, 597 F.2d at 186-87, we addressed the question of successor liability of an asset purchaser under the Federal Insecticide, Fungicide and Rodenticide Act (FIFRA), 7 U.S.C. §§136-136w. There, the EPA had issued a complaint and recommended a fine against Del Chemical Corporation for violations of FIFRA. *Oner II*, 597 F.2d at 185. Three months later, Oner II was formed to purchase Del's assets and to continue distributing the same pesticides for which the EPA had recommended the fine. When the EPA amended its complaint to name Oner II, Oner II objected to the EPA's decision to extend liability to it. Id. at 185-86. We affirmed the EPA's authority to extend liability to successor corporations under FIFRA, noting that:

> Oner II had notice of the outstanding debt to the EPA since Saylor served as president of both Del and Oner II. Oner II was formed to continue distributing pesticides, and in Saylor's case maintained the same personnel in a responsible position. Oner II was engaged in the business of distributing pesticides and was thus subject to sanctions by the agency, and we think the sanctions were properly imposed upon it by reason of its having succeeded to operations found to have been conducted in violation of the Act.
>
> In view of the enunciated purposes of the Act, the potential injury to the public for violations of the Act and the circumstances surrounding the transfer of assets, the imposition of liability on Oner II was justified.

Id. at 186-87.

Two key facts distinguish the circumstances surrounding the transfer of assets in this case from Oner II. First, L-Bar did not have actual notice of IMP's potential CERCLA liability. At the time of the asset sale, IMP had not been identified as a potentially responsible party by any state or federal agency and no one had asserted or threatened a claim against IMP for clean up costs. Second, and perhaps more importantly, L-Bar did not continue IMP's slag business. In fact, IMP had ceased its slag business nine months before L-Bar purchased its assets. Because we find this case distinguishable from *Oner II*, we need not decide whether to adopt the continuing business enterprise exception under CERCLA.

Asarco has failed to establish that under traditional concepts of successor liability there is a genuine issue of material fact as to L-Bar's liability as successor to IMP.

IV. SANCTIONS

L-Bar has requested sanctions under Fed. R. Civ. P. 11, asserting that Asarco has misrepresented facts on appeal. Rule 11 permits, however,

> [A]n award only of those expenses directly caused by the filing, logically, those at the trial level. . . . On appeal, the litigant's conduct is governed by Federal Rule of Appellate Procedure 38, which provides: "If a court of appeals shall determine that an appeal is frivolous, it may award just damages and single or double costs to the appellee."

Cooter v. Hartmarx Corp., — U.S. —, —, 110 S. Ct. 2447, 2451 (1990). We deny sanctions because Rule 11 does not apply here and this appeal was not frivolous under Rule 38.

Conclusion

The district court did not err in granting summary judgment to L-Bar because Asarco has failed to establish a genuine issue of material fact as to L-Bar's successor liability under CERCLA.

Affirmed.

VI

THE ENVIRONMENT AND THE COMMON LAW

A. COMMON LAW DAMAGES FOR ENVIRONMENT HARM

2. Causation: Multiple Defendants and Alternative, Concert of Action, Enterprise, and Market Share Liability

Page 738. After Note 2, add the following:

In re PAOLI RAILROAD YARD PCB LITIGATION
916 F.2d 829 (3d Cir. 1990)

Before BECKER, MANSMANN and NYGAARD, Circuit Judges.

Opinion of the Court

BECKER, Circuit Judge.

    This is a toxic tort case brought by some thirty-eight persons who have either worked in or lived adjacent to the Paoli railyard, an electric railcar maintenance facility at the western terminus of the noted Paoli Local, which serves the Philadelphia Main Line. The plaintiffs' primary claim is that they have contracted a variety of illnesses as the result of exposure to polychlorinated biphenyls, better known as PCBs. PCBs are toxic substances which, as the result of decades of PCB use in the Paoli railcar transformers, can be found in extremely high concentration at the railyard and in the ambient air and soil. The defendants are Monsanto Corporation, the nation's leading manufacturer of PCBs (marketed under the trade name "Aroclor"); General Electric Company, manufacturer of the transformers; Amtrak, owner of the railyard site since 1976; Conrail, which operated the facility between 1976 and 1983; the Southeastern Pennsylvania Transit Authority (SEPTA), which has operated the facility since 1983; and the City of Philadelphia, which owns some of the railroad cars at the facility. . . .

III. THE SUMMARY JUDGMENT RECORD

A. THE PLAINTIFFS' SUBMISSIONS

Plaintiffs set out to prove that their personal injuries were proximately caused by their exposure to the PCBs that defendants permitted to contaminate the area surrounding the Paoli Railyard. Their case depends upon expert testimony pertaining to exposure and causation. The attorneys for different plaintiffs employed different expert witnesses, and it is therefore convenient, in discussing the record before us, to categorize plaintiffs according to which counsel represents them. . . .

Dr. Herbert Allen received his doctorate in environmental chemistry from the University of Michigan in 1974. He is currently employed as a professor of chemistry at Drexel University, where he serves as the director of Drexel's Environmental Studies Institute. Allen has published numerous scholarly articles. His primary role was to testify to the Kohn/Klehr plaintiffs' exposure to the Paoli Railyard's elevated PCB levels.

Initially, Allen noted the "extremely high levels" of PCBs in soil samples taken from the neighborhood adjacent to the yard. He explained that runoff from the railyard caused contamination in the soil in Central Avenue, with the highest concentrations of PCBs being found in residential yards adjacent to the railyard. Central Avenue samples contained concentrations as high as 577 mg/kg, while some residential yard concentrations were as high as 1000 mg/kg. Dr. Allen opined that the high concentrations of PCBs found deep in the soil indicated a discharge of extremely high amounts of PCBs. He also noted specifically that certain "heat-producing" operations, such as the welding and cutting of contaminated equipment and the burning of contaminated railroad ties, which employees testified had occurred at the yard, could have converted PCBs into other toxins such as PCDD's (dioxins) and PCDF's (furans). This testimony is particularly significant in view of the conclusion of certain of plaintiffs' proffered studies that exposure to PCDFs can cause numerous adverse health effects. . . .

Relying on his knowledge of the scientific literature, his own testing, the testimony of employees, and a scientific formula which he had devised, Dr. Allen calculated the amount of PCBs in plaintiffs' bodies based on the amount of PCBs in the soil. Among other things, he relied on the affidavit of an employee named Kraljevich who stated that the use of heat-producing tools caused PCBs to "hang in the air like a fog," and that leaking transformers caused foul PCB odors to permeate the air. Allen then concluded that neighborhood residents had been exposed to elevated PCB concentrations since approximately 1940. Although unable to quantify the extent of plaintiffs' exposure, Allen opined that the residential plaintiffs may have been exposed to air containing more than 10 g/m3 of PCBs, while railyard employees may have suffered even greater exposure.

Deborah A. Barsotti, Ph.D., offered expert opinions on both exposure and causation for the Kohn/Klehr plaintiffs. Dr. Barsotti, a toxicologist, received her doctorate in pathology from the University of Wisconsin Medical School in 1980, and is qualified to interpret human clinical tests. She has published a number of articles on the toxicity of PCBs, and her work has been cited in the Congressional Record and in legislative debates on the Toxic Substances Control Act. She is currently employed as the Chief of the Research Analysis Branch of the Agency for Toxic Substance and Disease Registry (ATSDR) of the United States Government.

Barsotti based her opinions regarding exposure on her review of the relevant scientific literature and on her own gas chromatography testing. She explained that PCBs may be absorbed into the body by oral ingestion, through the skin, or by inhalation, and that PCBs are transported through the body in blood, and eventually redistributed to fat and organs containing fat. She concluded that the plaintiffs had in fact ingested PCBs. A major part of Dr. Barsotti's exposure testimony consisted of her attempt to show, through gas chromatography tracing, that the PCBs to which plaintiffs were exposed came specifically from the Paoli Railyard. She did this by comparing chromatographic tracings of plaintiffs' blood to similar tracings from soil at Paoli. She then attempted to match certain "early emerging peaks," (in plaintiffs' blood tests which she testified related) to particular PCB isomers.

Barsotti used the results of these tests, along with medical and clinical records from the plaintiffs, to buttress her testimony regarding causation. In determining causation, she also personally inspected the railyard, and reviewed, *inter alia*, the Kraljevich affidavit, published reports and studies, and soil samples taken from the yard. She concluded that plaintiffs' exposure to PCBs at Paoli was a substantial factor in causing their particular injuries, including elevations in triglyceride, cholesterol, and liver enzyme levels. . . .

B. THE DEFENDANTS' SUBMISSIONS

Defendants' view of the case, as encapsulated in their joint motion for summary judgment, is that plaintiffs "failed to submit competent evidence creating a genuine issue of material fact concerning either of two essential elements on which plaintiffs bore the burden of proof: abnormal exposure, and causation." Appellees' Br. at 36. In support of this assertion, defendants adopted a two-pronged approach. First, they vigorously attacked plaintiffs' expert testimony and sought to have it excluded under Fed. R. Evid. 702, 703, and 403. Second, defendants submitted studies and expert testimony of their own on both exposure and causation issues. Because the case was resolved at the summary judgment stage, where credibility determinations are inappropriate, the latter evidence is significant only insofar as it relates, within the contours of our Rule 703 jurisprudence, to whether certain of plaintiffs' expert opinions should have been excluded because they were not based on facts or data reasonably relied on by experts in the field.

On the question of exposure, defendants attack the opinions of both Dr. Allen and Dr. Barsotti. Defendants submit that Dr. Allen's testimony should not be considered because his data and methodology were unreliable. They assert that Dr. Allen ignored the actual measured body samples of PCB exposure, and instead attempted to calculate exposure levels from levels of PCBs in the soil by using a formula "of his own devising." Dr. Allen's opinion is unhelpful, defendants say, because he was unable to provide "an exact calculation of the PCB dose received by the inhabitants." Further, defendants submitted the affidavit of a physical chemist and chemical hazard control specialist, Neil Jurinski, Ph.D., who expressed the view that Dr. Allen's soil-to-air migration hypotheses were "pure speculation unsupported by the data available or by scientific principles," and that they "were not arrived at by using accepted scientific methods." . . .

IV. THE DISTRICT COURT'S OPINION

The district court's opinion is devoted primarily to a discussion of the opinions of plaintiffs' experts. The court seems to have envisioned plaintiffs' experts as relying on three primary sources for their testimony: (1) animal studies purporting to show the deleterious health effects of PCBs; (2) studies employing data from the Yusho and Yu Cheng studies; and (3) their own opinions and research. With one or two exceptions explained below, the court analyzed this evidence pursuant to Fed. R. Evid. 703, which provides that facts or data not otherwise admissible in evidence may nevertheless serve as the basis for an expert opinion if the information is "of a type reasonably relied upon by experts in the particular field in forming opinions or inferences upon the subject." The court appears to have excluded the bulk of the expert opinion under Rule 703.

With regard to the animal studies, the court's analysis was bifurcated, discussing first whether it could look beyond an expert's assertion that his opinion is reasonably relied upon by experts in the field, and second whether animal studies are a proper basis for an opinion about causation. The court answered the first question readily, concluding that an expert's opinion on the reasonableness of his or her own data could not be dispositive or Rule 703's limitation would be meaningless. In reaching this conclusion, the court distinguished this court's opinion in In re Japanese Electronic Products Antitrust Litigation, 723 F.2d 238 (3d Cir. 1983), *rev'd on other grounds sub nom.*, Matsushita Elec. Ind. Co., Ltd. v. Zenith Radio Corp., 475 U.S. 574 (1986), which held, *inter alia*, that a court may not ignore an expert's uncontradicted testimony that his opinions are "of a type reasonably relied upon by experts in the field." Id. at 276. The court reasoned that, unlike *Japanese Electronics*, in the present case "we have very convincing evidence on the record that says that these studies are irrelevant." Apparently relying on that evidence, the court proceeded to exclude the animal studies. However, the court neither detailed the "very convincing evidence" indicating that the studies are "irrelevant," nor explained why the relevancy of the studies pertains to their reliability under Rule 703. The opinion is similarly silent as to precisely which expert opinions it meant to exclude in this manner.

The court's consideration of the Yusho and Yu Cheng studies as possible bases for expert opinions as to causation is similarly abbreviated. The court's holding is found in the following two sentences:

> It does seem clear that the consensus conclusion from the scientific literature is that the diseases that occurred in the victims of these incidents were caused by the ingestion of highly toxic PCDF's with their food and is not evidence of the effects of PCBs. Therefore, for the same reasons as addressed above regarding animal studies, I will exclude from evidence any expert opinion based on studies of the Yusho or Yu Cheng incidents.

Again, the court did not state which of the expert opinions were tainted by reliance on these studies or which opinions offered in rebuttal suggested a "consensus conclusion" indicating unreliability. . . .

. . . Not surprisingly, given the consequent lack of evidence, the court found that the plaintiffs have not met their burden on any of these issues. It therefore granted summary judgment for defendants.

V. MEDICAL MONITORING

Because it bears on the question of what evidence is admissible, we turn first to the viability of certain plaintiffs' "medical surveillance," or "medical monitoring," claims, by which plaintiffs sought to recover the costs of periodic medical examinations that they contend are medically necessary to protect against the exacerbation of latent diseases brought about by exposure to PCBs. Neither the Pennsylvania Supreme Court nor the Pennsylvania Superior Court has decided whether a demonstrated need for medical monitoring creates a valid cause of action.[20] Therefore, sitting in diversity, we must predict whether the Pennsylvania Supreme Court would recognize a claim for medical monitoring under the substantive law of Pennsylvania and, if so, what its elements are. See Erie R.R. Co. v. Tompkins, 304 U.S. 64 (1938).

Medical monitoring is one of a growing number of non-traditional torts that have developed in the common law to compensate plaintiffs who have been exposed to various toxic substances.[21] Often, the diseases or injuries caused by

---

20. The one Pennsylvania trial court to have considered this type of claim allowed it to proceed. See Habitants Against Landfill Toxicants v. City of York. No. 84-S-3820 (Pa. York Co. May 20, 1985), 15 Envtl. L. Rep. 20,937 (allowing an action seeking relief in the form of a medical surveillance trust fund). For the reasons expressed below in note 22, we believe that Peterman v. Techalloy Co., Inc., 29 Pa. D.&C.3d 104 (Mont. Co. 1982), a Pennsylvania trial court decision, which denied relief, is distinguishable because plaintiffs in that case requested relief in the form of a trust fund for future medical expenses, including, presumably, medical treatment, not just medical surveillance.

21. See generally Note, The Inapplicability of Traditional Tort Analysis to Environmental

this exposure are latent. This latency leads to problems when the claims are analyzed under traditional common law tort doctrine because, traditionally, injury needed to be manifest before it could be compensable. Thus, plaintiffs have encountered barriers to recovery which "arise from the failure of toxic torts to conform with the common law conception of an injury." Note, Medical Surveillance Damages, *supra* note 21, at 852.

Nonetheless, in an effort to accommodate a society with an increasing awareness of the danger and potential injury caused by the widespread use of toxic substances, courts have begun to recognize claims like medical monitoring, which can allow plaintiffs some relief even absent present manifestations of physical injury. More specifically, in the toxic tort context, courts have allowed plaintiffs to recover for emotional distress suffered because of the fear of contracting a toxic exposure disease, see, e.g., Sterling v. Velsicol Chemical Corp., 855 F.2d 1188, 1206 (6th Cir. 1988) (applying Tennessee law), the increased risk of future harm, see generally Note, Decreasing the Risks Inherent in Claims for Increased Risk of Future Disease, 43 U. Miami L. Rev. 1081 (1989), and the reasonable costs of medical monitoring or surveillance, see, e.g., Ayers v. Township of Jackson, 106 N.J. 557, 525 A.2d 287 (1987); Burns v. Jaquays Mining Corp., 156 Ariz. 375, 752 P.2d 28 (Ct. App. 1988); Merry v. Westinghouse Electric Corp., 684 F. Supp. 847 (M.D. Pa. 1988); Villari v. Terminix International, Inc., 663 F. Supp. 727 (E.D. Pa. 1987).[23]

It is easy to confuse the distinctions between these various non-traditional torts. However, the torts just mentioned involve fundamentally different kinds of injury and compensation. Thus, an action for medical monitoring seeks to recover only the quantifiable costs of periodic medical examinations necessary to detect the onset of physical harm, whereas an enhanced risk claim seeks compensation for the anticipated harm itself, proportionately reduced to reflect the chance that it will not occur. We think that this distinction is particularly important because the Pennsylvania Supreme Court has expressed some reluctance to recognize claims for enhanced risk of harm. In Martin v. Johns-Manville Corp., 508 Pa. 154, 494 A.2d 1088 (1985), the Court made clear that a plaintiff in an enhanced risk suit must prove that future consequences of an injury are reasonably probable, not just possible. Id. at 165 n.5, 494 A.2d at 1094 n.5.

Martin does not lead us to believe that Pennsylvania would not recognize a claim for medical monitoring, however. First, the injury that the Court was worried about finding with reasonable probability in *Martin* is different from the injury involved here. The injury in an enhanced risk claim is the anticipated

---

Risks: The Example of Toxic Waste Pollution Victim Compensation, 35 Stan. L. Rev. 575, 576-78 (1983) (collecting cases); Note, Medical Surveillance Damages: A Solution to the Inadequate Compensation of Toxic Tort Victims, 63 Ind. L. J. 849 (1988) (same).

23. In addition, several courts have modified the traditional rules discussed above to better serve in the toxic tort context. See, e.g., *Ayers*, 106 N.J. at 584, 525 A.2d at 300 (stating that "neither the statute of limitations nor the single controversy rule should bar timely causes of action in toxic-tort cases instituted after discovery of a disease or injury related to tortious conduct, although there has been prior litigation between the parties of different claims based on the same tortious conduct").

harm itself. The injury in a medical monitoring claim is the cost of the medical care that will, one hopes, detect that injury.[24] The former is inherently speculative because courts are forced to anticipate the probability of future injury.

. . . The latter is much less speculative because the issue for the jury is the less conjectural question of whether the plaintiff needs medical surveillance. Second, the Pennsylvania Supreme Court's concerns about the degree of certainty required can easily be accommodated by requiring that a jury be able reasonably to determine that medical monitoring is probably, not just possibly, necessary.

Defining injury in this way is not novel. In Friends for All Children, Inc. v. Lockheed Aircraft Corp., 746 F.2d 816 (D.C. Cir. 1984), the court, in recognizing a claim for medical monitoring damages for children exposed to the depressurization of an airplane cabin, noted that "[i]t is difficult to dispute that an individual has an interest in avoiding expensive diagnostic examinations just as he or she has an interest in avoiding physical injury." Id. at 826. See also Laxton v. Orkin Exterminating Co., 639 S.W.2d 431 (Tenn. 1982) (ingestion of contaminated water requiring testing held to be injury in itself, even though ingestion found to be harmless).

Similarly, in Askey v. Occidental Chemical Corp., 102 A.D.2d 130, 477 N.Y.S.2d 242 (1984), the court analyzed the issue as follows:

> Damages for the prospective consequences of a tortious injury are recoverable only if the prospective consequences may with reasonable probability be expected to flow from the past harm. Consequences which are contingent, speculative, or merely possible are not properly considered in ascertaining damages. If a plaintiff seeks future medical expenses as an element of consequential damage, he must establish with a degree of reasonable medical certainty through expert testimony that such expenses will be incurred.
>
> In light of the foregoing, it would appear that under the proof offered here persons exposed to toxic chemicals emanating from the landfill have an increased risk of invisible genetic damage and a present cause of action for their injury, and may recover all "reasonably anticipated" consequential damages. The future expense of medical monitoring could be a recoverable consequential damage provided that plaintiffs can establish with a reasonable degree of medical certainty that such expenditures are "reasonably anticipated" to be incurred by reason of their exposure.

Id. at 136-37, 477 N.Y.S.2d at 247 (citations omitted). Thus, the appropriate inquiry is not whether it is reasonably probable that plaintiffs will suffer harm in the future, but rather whether medical monitoring is, to a reasonable degree of medical certainty, necessary in order to diagnose properly the warning signs of disease.[25]

---

24. Once the injury is detected, the plaintiff may or may not have a cause of action against the same defendant for the injury itself. See generally Note, Claim Preclusion in Modern Latent Disease Cases: A Proposal for Allowing Second Suits, 103 Harv. L. Rev. 1989 (1990). Because that situation is not before us, we do not reach it.

25. Our research has yielded only two cases in which courts have purported to disallow

Federal district courts, sitting in diversity, have addressed the medical monitoring issue under Pennsylvania law. In Villari v. Terminix International, Inc., 663 F. Supp. 727 (E.D. Pa. 1987), the court allowed plaintiffs, who had presented sufficient medical evidence of present physical injuries resulting from exposure to an allegedly carcinogenic pesticide, to recover the costs of future medical surveillance. Id. at 735. The court required a showing of present physical injury and expressly refused to follow *Ayers*, which it characterized as holding that "the cost of future medical monitoring is a proper element of damages whenever medical testimony establishes the need for future monitoring." Id. at 735 n.5. However, because the plaintiffs in *Villari* had demonstrated sufficient physical injury, the question whether the cause of action could be sustained without it was not squarely raised.

Villari's putative physical injury requirement was rejected in *Merry v. Westinghouse Electric Corp.*, 684 F. Supp. 847 (M.D. Pa. 1988). In *Merry*, property owners whose wells had been contaminated by toxic substances sought recovery for, inter alia, the cost of medical surveillance. In denying defendant's motion for summary judgment, the court agreed with *Villari* that "a plaintiff need not exhibit symptoms of a disease before medical surveillance is sought," id. at 849, but disagreed to the extent that *Villari* required "*physical* injury before a claim for future medical monitoring can be maintained." Id. (emphasis in original). Consequently, *Merry* suggested that a medical monitoring action could be premised upon proof of exposure to hazardous substances resulting in the potential for injury and the need for early detection and treatment. Id. at 850.

We agree with *Merry*, and predict that the Supreme Court of Pennsylvania would follow the weight of authority and recognize a cause of action for medical monitoring established by proving that:

1. Plaintiff was significantly exposed to a proven hazardous substance through the negligent action of the defendant.

---

recovery based on a medical monitoring theory. Both cases are distinguishable. In Rheingold v. E.R. Squibb & Sons, No. 74 Civ. 3420 (S.D.N.Y. Oct. 8, 1975), the court rejected a class action claim for what might more accurately be called "medical management" damages. Plaintiffs, who had used DES during pregnancy, sought to establish a fund to finance the periodic examinations of plaintiffs' affected female offspring, as well as, inter alia, the medical *treatment* of "such girls as develop or show any propensity toward development of [vaginal cancer or other related conditions]." Id. at 7. This remedy is far broader than a mere claim for medical monitoring as we have defined it. Moreover, to the extent that the *Rheingold* court interpreted New York law as requiring actual injury as a prerequisite to recovery, such reasoning is seriously called into question by subsequent New York state appellate court decisions to the contrary, see Askey, 102 A.D.2d at 130, 477 N.Y.S.2d at 242.

In Morrissy v. Eli Lilly & Co., 76 Ill. App. 3d 753, 32 Ill. Dec. 30, 394 N.E.2d 1369 (1979), the plaintiffs explicitly characterized their claims as requesting, inter alia, that defendants "establish and maintain a fund of money reasonably calculated to compensate all class members for such medical expenses which have been and will continue to be incurred due to the physiological damage done by DES," id. at 757, 32 Ill. Dec. at 34, 394 N.E.2d at 1373. The court held that "[t]he nexus thus suggested between exposure to DES in utero and the possibility of developing cancer or other injurious conditions in the future is an insufficient basis upon which to recognize a present injury." Id. at 761, 32 Ill. Dec. at 37, 394 N.E.2d at 1376. However, as in *Rheingold*, the plaintiffs' request in *Morrissy* was for treatment as well as monitoring. Thus, it is inapposite to the case at bar.

2. As a proximate result of exposure, plaintiff suffers a significantly increased risk of contracting a serious latent disease.
3. That increased risk makes periodic diagnostic medical examinations reasonably necessary.
4. Monitoring and testing procedures exist which make the early detection and treatment of the disease possible and beneficial.

These factors would, of course, be proven by competent expert testimony, see *Ayers*, 106 N.J. at 606, 525 A.2d at 312.

The policy reasons for recognizing this tort are obvious. Medical monitoring claims acknowledge that, in a toxic age, significant harm can be done to an individual by a tortfeasor, notwithstanding latent manifestation of that harm. Moreover, as we have explained, recognizing this tort does not require courts to speculate about the probability of future injury. It merely requires courts to ascertain the probability that the far less costly remedy of medical supervision is appropriate. Allowing plaintiffs to recover the cost of this care deters irresponsible discharge of toxic chemicals by defendants and encourages plaintiffs to detect and treat their injuries as soon as possible. These are conventional goals of the tort system as it has long existed in Pennsylvania.

Having established the applicable standard, we discuss below, in Part VII, whether summary judgment was properly granted for the defendants on the medical monitoring claim. . . .

In sum, we hold that in order to exclude evidence under Rule 403 at the pretrial stage, a court must have a record complete enough on the point at issue to be considered a virtual surrogate for a trial record.

VII. Was Summary Judgment Properly Granted?

Because the district court excluded the bulk of plaintiffs' proffered evidence on causation, it had no difficulty concluding that plaintiffs had failed to produce sufficient evidence to survive summary judgment under the standards announced in the Supreme Court's noted trilogy, Celotex Corp. v. Catrett, 477 U.S. 317 (1986); Anderson v. Liberty Lobby, Inc., 477 U.S. 242 (1986); and Matsushita Electric Industrial Co. v. Zenith Radio Corp., 475 U.S. 574 (1986). As we have explained, the district court erred in its exclusion of this evidence. However, defendants argue that even if we were to admit all of the evidence excluded by the district court, summary judgment would nonetheless be appropriate because plaintiffs are unable to create a genuine issue of material fact as to the required elements of the *prima facie* case on causation. Consequently, we must presume the admissibility of all of plaintiffs' proffered evidence, and determine sufficiency under the prevailing standards for summary judgment.

Under *Celotex*, a court must enter summary judgment when the nonmoving party "after adequate time for discovery . . . fails to make a showing sufficient to establish the existence of an element essential to that party's case, and on which that party will bear the burden of proof at trial." 477 U.S. at 322. A party cannot survive summary judgment simply by presenting conclusory allegations or denials; the existence of specific material evidentiary facts must be shown. *Liberty Lobby*, 477 U.S. at 256. Moreover, the *Liberty Lobby* Court points out that

> there is no issue for trial unless there is sufficient evidence favoring the nonmoving party for a jury to return a verdict for that party. If the evidence is merely colorable or is not significantly probative summary judgment may be granted.

Id. at 249-50 (citations omitted). Consequently, the court must ask whether, on the summary judgment record, reasonable jurors could find facts that demonstrated, by a preponderance of the evidence, that the nonmoving party is entitled to a verdict.

As noted above, the district court defined the *prima facie* case as consisting of four elements:

1. that defendants released PCBs into the environment;
2. that plaintiffs somehow ingested these PCBs into their bodies;
3. that plaintiffs have an injury;
4. that PCBs are the cause of that injury.

The first element (release of PCBs) was not disputed, but the district court found against the plaintiffs on the other three elements. We, however, believe that the evidence described in Part IIA, if admissible, creates a genuine issue of material fact on all three contested elements.

With regard to exposure, prong two of the district court's *prima facie* case, defendants assert that plaintiffs have not adduced sufficient evidence indicating that they have been exposed to PCBs to a greater extent than anyone else. More specifically, defendants maintain that plaintiffs' exposure does not exceed the normal "background" level of PCB exposure in the United States. However, whether plaintiffs have proffered sufficient evidence to show that their exposure level exceeds the normal background level depends on what that normal background level is. There is conflicting evidence on this point. Defendants' evidence suggests that PCB levels in the general United States population range up to 40 parts per billion (ppb) as measured in the bloodstream, while plaintiffs' evidence suggests that the level is "well below 3 ppb," and that a 5 ppb level falls within the 90th percentile in the United States. . . . This conflict creates a genuine issue of material fact sufficient to withstand summary judgment on the exposure question, because if a jury could reasonably believe plaintiffs' background level statistics, then there is ample evidence from which to conclude that the plaintiffs, who lived adjacent to the railyard, had a higher PCB level than usual due to their exposure to defendants' PCBs.

There are also genuine issues of material fact with regard to the third element of the *prima facie* case, i.e., injury. Although most of the plaintiffs presented evidence of physical injury, defendants point out that several plaintiffs failed to allege or submit any evidence demonstrating physical injury. This appears to be an accurate observation, but regardless of whether all plaintiffs alleged demonstrable physical injury, they all clearly alleged monetary injury. The medical monitoring claim is a claim for monetary damages. Plaintiffs are asking for money because, allegedly, their exposure to PCBs requires them to bear the costs associated with increased medical surveillance. This is an economic injury, which, according to the plaintiffs, is attributable to the defendants.

The court dismissed the medical monitoring claim as follows:

> Dr. Calesnick provides a two page affidavit which states that he has experience in treating persons exposed to PCB's, that he has performed physical examinations on some of the plaintiffs and concludes: "To a reasonable degree of medical certainty, these plaintiffs have been exposed to PCBs, there is a potential for them to sustain injuries from PCB exposure, if they have not already sustained these injuries, and there is a need for early detection and treatment of these PCB induced injuries for plaintiffs." This seems to be strikingly similar to the opinion offered in Martin v. Johns Manville Corp., [508 Pa. 154, 494 A.2d 1088 (1985),] and ruled inadmissible by the Pennsylvania Supreme Court. Because that was an asbestos case, and it has been epidemiologically proven that asbestos exposure can cause cancer, that doctor might have had more of a basis for his opinion.
>
> [Dr. Calesnick] is unwilling to say that any particular disease the plaintiffs have is caused by PCBs, just that they should be regularly checked because of the possibility of future harm. The plaintiffs call this a "medical monitoring claim." However, the claim is barred because the testimony of Dr. Calesnick and the other plaintiffs' experts who testify regarding the risk of future injury is insufficient to support it under Pennsylvania law.

This language strongly suggests that the court, rather than measuring sufficiency of plaintiffs' evidence regarding a medical monitoring claim, evaluated plaintiffs' evidence as if it were offered to prove an action for enhanced risk of future harm, and "barred" the action, following its interpretation of *Martin*, as a matter of law. As we have explained, *supra* Part V, medical monitoring and enhanced risk claims are distinct causes of action. The question on the medical monitoring claim is whether the jury could reasonably believe Dr. Calesnick's assertion that there is a reasonable "need" for medical surveillance. Because the district court appears to have applied the standards for enhanced risk claims in an action for medical monitoring, we find error, and we will therefore reverse the grant of summary judgment on this point.

On the fourth prong of the *prima facie* case, causation, defendants submit that plaintiffs have not offered any admissible toxicological or epidemiological evidence showing a correlation between PCBs and adverse health effects in humans. Appellants' Br. at 97. However, if we assume all proffered evidence is admissible, this is not so. Both Drs. Barsotti and Nicholson testified to a positive correlation between PCB exposure and human illness. Drs. Barsotti, Nicholson, Zahalsky, Shubin, and DiGregorio gave testimony, with reference to scientific studies, from which a jury could infer that there is a causal relationship between PCB exposure and the various illnesses contracted by plaintiffs. See DeLuca v. Merrell Dow Pharmaceuticals, Inc., 911 F.2d 941 (3d Cir. 1990). The principles of *DeLuca* respecting statistical significance are also, of course, applicable to any studies relied on. The defendants' experts offer evidence to the contrary, but that makes the issue suitable for a jury, not dismissible.

Defendants also argue that plaintiffs cannot possibly meet their burden on causation because no qualified expert submitted the differential diagnoses required to prove causation. Although defendants make this argument in terms of causation, we believe it is really an evidentiary contention, and it is a contention that we have dealt with *supra* in Part VIC1 [omitted]. Admittedly, plaintiffs did not submit differential diagnoses performed by medical doctors, but they did submit differential diagnoses from non-medical doctors. We do not believe that the diagnoses are invalid simply because they were performed by non-physician experts.

As our discussion, *supra* Part VIC1, makes clear, our Rule 702 expert qualification jurisprudence rejects rigid formalism. The decision to qualify someone as an expert rests not on the specific academic degree held, but on the presence of sufficient knowledge, skill, experience, training, or education. It would make little sense to exalt the opinion of a medical doctor with no experience in toxic exposure over the opinion of, for example, an eminently qualified toxicologist with a Ph.D. and years of experience and training. As Judge Pollak noted in denying a defendant's motion to exclude medical testimony by a non-medical doctor:

> [w]hile it is true that an expert must demonstrate special competence to present expert testimony there is no *per se* rule that non-physicians are unqualified to testify about the medical condition of individuals exposed to chemicals.

Villari v. Terminix International, Inc., 692 F. Supp. 568, 573 (E.D. Pa. 1986) (citation omitted). Therefore, we must consider the diagnoses of plaintiffs' experts. In light of that evidence, we are left with a genuine issue of material fact on the issue of causation.

In sum, if we consider all of the evidence improperly excluded by the district court, plaintiffs have submitted sufficient evidence to survive summary judgment on each element of the *prima facie* case. A jury could believe plaintiffs' evidence regarding normal PCB background levels and from there could conclude that these plaintiffs were exposed to a larger than average dose of PCBs. Plaintiffs' evidence regarding the likelihood of latent disease could lead a reasonable jury to conclude that plaintiffs needed to be monitored by medical experts. Finally, if the opinions of plaintiffs' experts are admissible, a jury could conclude that the defendants' PCBs caused plaintiffs' injuries. Hence, the grant of summary judgment must be reversed. Needless to say, if, after further proceedings consistent with this opinion, the district court were to exclude enough of plaintiffs' expert's evidence on causation (or other critical issues) such that no genuine issue of material fact remained, it would be free to grant summary judgment for the defendants. . . .

VII. Conclusion

For all of the foregoing reasons, the summary judgment will be reversed, and the case remanded to the district court for further proceedings consistent with this opinion.